THE MODERN EGYPTIANS.

SKETCH IN A GUEST-CHAMBER

An Account of the Manners and Customs of

THE MODERN EGYPTIANS

BY

EDWARD WILLIAM LANE

FIFTH (STANDARD) EDITION

EDITED BY

EDWARD STANLEY POOLE

WITH A NEW INTRODUCTION BY

JON MANCHIP WHITE

AUTHOR OF

Ancient Egypt, Everyday Life in Ancient Egypt,

ETC.

DOVER PUBLICATIONS INC.

NEW YORK

Published in Canada by General Publishing Company, Ltd., 30 Lesmill Road, Don Mills, Toronto, Ontario.
Published in the United Kingdom by Constable and Company, Ltd., 10 Orange Street, London WC 2.

This Dover edition, first published in 1973, is an unabridged republication of the fifth edition of the work as published by John Murray, London, in 1860 (first edition, 1836). The errata of the original have been corrected in the text in the present edition. A new Introduction has been written specially for this edition by Jon Manchip White.

International Standard Book Number: 0-486-22935-1
Library of Congress Catalog Card Number: 72-93077

Manufactured in the United States of America
Dover Publications, Inc.
180 Varick Street
New York, N. Y. 10014

INTRODUCTION
TO THE DOVER EDITION

An Account of the Manners and Customs of the Modern Egyptians appeared in 1836, and was an early-Victorian best-seller. It has always been considered one of the most thorough, as well as one of the most entertaining, studies of its kind ever attempted. It offered the Victorians, as it offers us, a unique picture of a segment of Islamic society, captured at a point in time when it was soon to pass away and be succeeded by a newer and different way of life. It holds up for our inspection the warp and woof of the rich tapestry of Islam before the fabric was rent by the corruptions and self-corruptions that came with Western influence. As James Aldridge has written in his excellent and exhaustive study, *Cairo* (1969): "Europeans considered it a revelation. And so it was, because Lane's was the most truthful and detailed account in English of how Egyptians lived and behaved. It was one of the books that inspired several subsequent generations of Europeans to dress up in Arab clothes (as Lane did) and play the role of Arab (as Lane did) and even embrace Islam (as Lane pretended to do)."

Nothing in Edward Lane's birth and background would have led one to anticipate the romantic travels of the first part of his life. He was born in 1801, of solid English provincial stock. His ancestors had been for four generations mayors of his native Hereford, most rural and beautiful of English country towns. His father was a solid country clergyman. After a sound education at West Country grammar schools, he was sent to Cambridge to train for his father's profession, although he already showed a talent for mathematics that amounted almost to genius. There must already, however, have been some dark and restless strain in his nature, for he suddenly abandoned the university and went to London to join his artist-brother Richard as apprentice to a famous engraver.

Like many of the Englishmen who went to Egypt during the last century-and-a-half to study its civilization, ancient or modern, he was an accomplished artist. His great-uncle on his mother's side was Thomas Gainsborough. His brother, his senior by a year, was in fact destined to become a considerable artist, a noted engraver and lithographer, and an associate of the Royal Academy. Like Gainsborough, Richard Lane was a man of great charm and address; he was taken up in court circles while still a young man, and remained in them thereafter, enjoying a fashionable and comfortable career.

Edward might very well have followed his brother's easy existence if he had not quickly developed an incipient consumption, which demanded a speedy removal to a drier and sunnier climate. Even in his teens he had shown an interest in the East, and in 1825 he set sail for Alexandria, drawn to Egypt by the half-promise of a consulship there. The two-month voyage was eventful; the crew mutinied, and the ship sailed through a tremendous hurricane and was saved, typically, by the purely theoretical knowledge of navigation which this insatiable young polymath happened to have picked up from some textbook or other.

Needless to say, Lane spoke and wrote Arabic fluently within a few weeks of landing in Egypt. His grandnephew, the distinguished Arabist Stanley Lane-Poole, tells us that during the first six months of Lane's residence in Cairo he lived for some time in abandoned tombs—which are certainly very cool and commodious if one does not mind the associations—after which he set out on the first of two long and arduous journeys up the Nile to Upper Egypt. The earlier journey took him to the Second Cataract, the next to Wadi Halfa, and on both he was able to spend some months at Thebes, describing and sketching the ancient monuments.

He returned to England in the autumn of 1828, bringing with him a lengthy *Description of Egypt* furnished with over a hundred sepia drawings. He could not find a publisher, but that splendid Victorian organization, the Society for the Diffusion of Useful Knowledge, decided on the recommendation of Lord Brougham to publish the sections relating to modern Egypt. As Lane-Poole says, "It was characteristic of Lane's thoroughness that he refused to print the chapters as they stood, and insisted upon revisiting Egypt for the sole purpose of revising and expanding what most men would have considered an adequate account." It was to this second visit to Egypt, which began in December 1833 and lasted eighteen months, that the present book owes its final form. Lane adopted Muslim dress, took the name of Mansur Effendi, and consorted almost exclusively with Muslims in the manner described in the book. He returned to England in August 1835 and his *Modern Egyptians* was issued at the end of the following year.

He was only thirty-five, and at one stroke had established himself as one of the leading authorities on Islam. He was to live another forty years, devoting himself with his usual heroic tenacity to enlarging his reputation and deepening his knowledge of his chosen field. Nevertheless, in retrospect, and in view of the almost Byronic character of his twenties and thirties, the remainder of his life seems rather melancholy. The private pleasures of scholarship are, of course, intense; but an obsessional strain now began to assert itself in his nature. He spent the next seven years living quietly in England, marrying a Greek lady in 1840 and devoting himself to his translation of the *Arabian Nights* and a volume of selections from the Koran. The translation of the *Arabian Nights*, though it enjoyed public esteem, is too stiff in style and too heavily bowdlerized to appeal to us today, and although the copious notes remain interesting it cannot take the place of other renderings, such as the enjoyable Olde Englysshe version of Burton or the incomparable one made by Powys Mathers from the French of Mardrus. The selections from the Koran have long been superseded.

He had now conceived the idea of compiling an exhaustive thesaurus of Arabic words, a kind of super-dictionary. It was to prove a colossal and somewhat demented undertaking. He returned to Egypt to pursue his new project in 1842, but now the humorous, carefree Edward Lane of the 1820s and 1830s had disappeared. No longer did he wander the teeming streets of Cairo in Arab dress, notebook in hand, mingling with the crowds that used formerly to delight him, visiting the *souks* and *wekalehs* he loved, reveling in the sights and sounds and even the smells of the great city. "His work," writes Lane-Poole, "kept him almost confined to his study. He denied himself to every one, except on Friday, the Muslim sabbath, and devoted all his energies to the composition of the lexicon. Twelve to fourteen hours a day were his ordinary allowance for study; for six months together he never crossed the threshold of his house, and in all the seven years of his residence he only left Cairo once, for a three days' visit to the pyramids."

He had become inured to this inhuman regimen when he finally left Egypt in 1849. He settled at Worthing, most placid of English seaside resorts, "and for more than a quarter of a century devoted all his efforts to completing his task. He worked from morning till night, sparing little time for meals or exercise, and none to recreation, and rigidly denying himself to all but a very few chosen friends. On Sunday, however, he closed his Arabic books, but only to take up Hebrew and study the Old Testament." He remained chained to his desk, "performing his usual toil in his unchanging delicate handwriting," until his death in 1876.

"In spite of his retired life and his devotion to study," says his grandnephew, "his conversation and manner possessed unusual charm and grace." It is this unusual charm and grace which delight us in the present book, and he could not have survived and flourished as he did in Saracenic Cairo without such attractive and anodyne qualities. He was obviously a young man with a cool head, a strong stomach and a serviceable sense of humor. However, it must not be supposed that he was the only pioneer, or even the earliest, among Europeans who lived and worked in the Egypt of those times. As early as 1743 Richard Pococke had published his impressions of Egypt in his *Description of the East*, and the German Carsten Niebuhr wrote a thoughtful account of Cairo in the 1760s. Other eighteenth-century travelers who wrote about Cairo included W. G. Browne and Count Constantin de Volney, whose *Voyage en Egypte et en Syrie* (1787) might have sown in the mind of Napoleon, with his early dreams of imitating Alexander the Great, the idea of conquering a weak Egypt as a stepping-stone to India.

Napoleon entered Cairo, after defeating the Mamelukes at the battle of the Pyramids, on July 25, 1798. He left the city over a full year later, on August 24, 1799, having in the interim suffered a humiliating defeat at Acre at the hands of Sir Sidney Smith. He had brought with him to Egypt a corps of a hundred scholars and scientists who established the Institut d'Egypte, and who laid the foundations of all subsequent historical, natural and sociological studies in Egypt. When he abandoned the Army of Egypt to its fate, and returned to France to become First Consul, and when his able deputy Marshal Kléber had been stabbed by an Azharite fanatic, the way was open for the British; they defeated General Menou at Alexandria, and Sir John Hutchinson occupied Cairo at the end of March, 1801.

Officially, the British restored the Turks, who were the nominal rulers of the country, and remained the Western protectors of Egypt until 1807, when they were driven out by Mohammed Ali. However, the European presence in the country was now well established. Giovanni Belzoni, the circus strong man turned maverick archaeologist, began his disastrous activities in 1815, and soon Salt, Burckhardt and Howard-Vyse were battering, boring and blowing their way into tombs and pyramids, while Robert Hay, John Phillip, Owen Carter and other artists were busying themselves more constructively with pencil and sketchpad. By the 1830s the American contingent was beginning to arrive, and included the great John L. Stephens, the virtual discoverer of the Mayan civilization, and a redoubtable battalion of transatlantic ladies on their way to or from the Holy Land.

This is not at all to detract from Lane's achievement, merely to set it in perspective and to demonstrate how it was part of the growing European interest in the East. He was certainly one of the early founders of the European community in Cairo, which rose from a few score in the 1820s to between 25,000 and 30,000 by 1870. Once aroused, that interest never waned. While the military power of Egypt remained weak, there was no need for France or Britain to dominate the country directly; it was easier to control it behind the scenes by means of financial manipulation, first by means of management of the cotton industry, introduced into Egypt in 1818, and of the Suez Canal, begun in 1854. But Egypt, as Napoleon knew, was the key to the Franco-British empires in the East, and to lose Egypt and the Canal, as the British realized after the Indian Mutiny of 1857, was to lose India, Ceylon and the Eastern dependencies, and to imperil the link with Australia and New Zealand. The screw was tightened. In 1875 the Egyptian Khedive was forced to sell his Canal shares to Britain for the derisory sum of £4 million; in 1876 the British and French assumed direct economic rule in Egypt; and in 1882 the British invaded the country and ruled it through High Commissioners until 1922. It remained a British fief until after World War II, by which time India had gained its independence, the African colonies were about to be let go, and the Suez Canal itself was seen to be a wasting asset.

The Egypt of the 1820s and 1830s about which Lane wrote had, then, endured its first bout of European interference and was living uneasily in the expectation of another. As we noted earlier, Lane was witnessing the last flare-up of the relatively unalloyed Islamic way of life. It was, in any case, no novelty for the Egyptians to live in subjection to foreign and un-Egyptian rulers: they had been doing so without intermission for over two thousand years. In 526 B.C. the Persians invaded Egypt and became its rulers, to be followed in 332 B.C. by the Greeks, in 30 B.C. by the Romans, and in 323 A.D. by the Eastern Romans or Byzantines. The Arab conquest of 640 A.D. only substituted Islam for Christianity, making Egypt finally turn away from the Mediterranean towards the Levant; it did not mean liberation for the people of Egypt from the yoke of foreign oppressors. From 640 until 1952, another thirteen centuries, Egypt was governed by dynasties that were alien to it. They poured into Egypt in flamboyant succession: the Ommeyads, the Abbassids, the Tulunids, the Fatimids, the Ayubites, the Mamelukes, and finally the Turks.

This is the Egypt and the Cairo which Lane is describing: an Egypt Islamicized since 640, but still retaining its own essential character and traditions. The Egyptians, of course, were not and are not Arabs, any more than the Syrians, the Iraqis, the Lebanese, the Libyans, the Tunisians, the Algerians and the Moroccans are Arabs. "The Arab world" is in many ways a peculiarly misleading and deceptive phrase. The only true Arabs are the Central Arabians of the Arabian Peninsula, the homeland of the Prophet; all that the various and varied countries of the so-called Arab world actually have in common is their Muslim faith and the Arabic language. Ethnically, and in their attitudes and traditions, they are very different from each other: there is scarcely any useful way of comparing, say, a Syrian with a Saudi Arabian. Thus the life of Cairo continued on its own individual and uninterrupted course as emperors and caliphs cut each other's throats and dynasties rose and fell; while in Upper Egypt the *fellahin* followed the immemorial ways they had hewn to since the days of the pyramid-builders.

It may be worth devoting a few sentences to the story of Cairo, with which Lane's book is principally concerned. In Lane's time Egypt *was* Cairo: there were no other cities worth speaking of; even Alexandria had declined to a miserable fishing-village of 5000 people. The Egyptians, in fact, call both their capital and their country *Misr*, in the way that Mexicans speak interchangeably of Mexico and Mexico City as *México*. In both cases the capital is synonymous with the whole country. The pull and influence of Cairo, indeed, is greater today than ever: in 1836 Lane estimated its population at about 240,000; by 1882 it had risen to 400,000; and in 1966 it was estimated at 4,000,000.

By the time Lane took up his residence there, in his convenient tomb, there had already been eight distinct Cairos, all built on the same soil, or nearly the same soil, or touching or overlapping one another; traces of all of them can be discerned by the enterprising visitor today. That is what makes Cairo unique and gives it its eternal fascination: that this radiant patch of ground beside the Nile, at the exact spot where Upper Egypt joins Lower Egypt, where East meets West, where the Mediterranean meets the Orient, where Europe meets Africa, has been a great and flourishing capital for five thousand years. Imperious and capricious rulers have put their mark on it, while the Cairenes themselves have continued their bright and chattering existence. First came Heliopolis, a dependency of Memphis, and one of the most revered intellectual centers of Ancient Egypt; then came the sturdy old Roman fortress quaintly called Babylon; and then the first, sprawling, prosperous Islamic township of Fustat (from the Latin *fossatum*, a camp). Fustat, which resembled a haphazard Arab tribal encampment, was founded in 640 by the Arab general Amr Ibn el 'As, one of those irresistible captains who swept out of Arabia to bring a huge slice of the Middle East under Muslim rule less than ten years after the Prophet's death in 632. After the decline of the Ommeyads, in 750 the Abbassids established a new capital in northern Fustat called Al-Askar, and in 870 the Tulunids established their own, Al-Kataiya, on the same soil.

The next city was a regular and imposing structure. We know the exact day on which it was started. On August 5, 969, the Fatimid general Gawhar marked out with his own hands the site of the city that came to be called Al-Kahira (from which we get the word Cairo), because the planet Mars (Al-Kahira) was in the ascendant at the moment when the first bricks were being laid. At the same time Gawhar began to build the mosque of Al-Azhar, which in 996 became a theological school and thereafter the most important university in the Islamic world. In 1176 Saladin, the new conqueror, began his own citadel, during the course of which he made modifications of his own, and additions and alterations were made to this amazing site thereafter in the colorful and interminable succession of Islamic feuds, assassinations, civil wars and usurpations. Today the mosques erected by these men of war, many of them bad and mad, are serene oases in the clamorous city. One has one's own favorite, whether it be the splendid, austere mosque of Amr himself, the magnificent yet simple mosque of Ibn Tulun, or the great, gloomy mosque of the caliph Hakim, the crazy Fatimid who began to rule at eleven, declared himself God, and in his twenty-year reign killed the men of Cairo for eating honey or playing chess, killed the women of Cairo for leaving their houses, killed all the dogs of Cairo, and perpetrated ceaseless and horrible cruelties that made poor degenerate Farouk look like a naughty schoolboy.

The Turkish khedives, under whose rule Lane lived in Egypt, were as thoroughly detested by the native Egyptians as most of their other foreign rulers. During the whole of Lane's time in the country it was ruled by Mohammed Ali, to whom Lane makes frequent references in his text and to whom his attitude betrays an almost comical ambivalence. The best he seems able to say about him is that he was brutal and greedy but perhaps not quite as brutal and greedy as his brother Turks; not much of a recommendation. It might be useful to review the career of this genial ruffian, whom Lane could hardly criticize too severely if he wished to remain both *persona grata* and healthy in his adoptive country.

The lion of the Levant, as he liked to be called, was the son of a Turkish farmer. He was born in 1769 in Kavalla, a town in Rumelia. He arrived in Egypt in 1798 as second-in-command of a rabble of Turkish irregulars called *bashi-bazouks*, who had been raised to help combat Napoleon. Fighting side by side with the Mamelukes, the part-Mongol, part-Circassian warlords who were the current overlords of Egypt, these irregulars were defeated at the battle of the Pyramids, but fought with the British the following year at the victory of Aboukir Bay. At Aboukir, Mohammed Ali was almost drowned, and was hauled out of the water by a British sailor. The Mamelukes, less a dynasty than a military caste, had been shaken by the defeat at the Pyramids, where 7000 of them had been killed, 3000 had fled to Upper Egypt, and another 1500 to Syria. Now, in the aftermath of French rule, with the British halfheartedly occupying Cairo, both the British and the sheikhs of Cairo needed a man to govern and to keep the peace. They chose Mohammed Ali. Soon he had prevailed on the Sultan of Turkey to name him Pasha, and set about the extirpation of the Mamelukes. In 1805 he crushed a Mameluke attempt to capture Cairo, decapitating his prisoners, skinning and stuffing their heads with straw while their comrades looked on, and sending a number of heads to the Sultan in Constantinople. In 1807, when the British attempted to intervene, he threw 500 British soldiers in jail, cut off the heads of 500 more and stuck them up on pikes; gratitude was not his strong point. Then, in 1811, he struck the final blow: he lured 470 Mameluke chieftains into the Citadel for a banquet, locked the gates on them, and shot them to death from the top of the walls.

Thus encouraged, he decided to attack Turkey itself and seize control of the Ottoman Empire. With armies excellently trained by Colonel François Février, who became a Muslim under the name of Suleiman Pasha, in 1831 he turned on Sultan Mahmud II and invaded

Syria and Asia Minor. It took the combined threats and persuasions of Britain, France and Russia, who did not want Turkey destroyed, to prevent him from reaching Constantinople. In 1839 he resolved to try again, and sent his armies into Anatolia, where they defeated the Turks at the battle of Nezib. Again he was only prevented from seizing Constantinople by the intervention of the Great Powers. However, as a consolation prize he was named Viceroy of Egypt and assured of the hereditary possession of his throne. Even so, his realm came to include the Sudan, the Sinai and large parts of Arabia. One can understand what he meant when he closed one eye when a clerk was reading Machiavelli's *The Prince* to him (he was illiterate) and remarked, "I think I could teach him something."

Like Porfirio Díaz in Mexico, Mohammed Ali sold Egypt to foreign investors in return for a share of the loot. His Turkish overseers beat taxes out of the peasants with the *khurbash* or rhinoceros-whip. He established a personal monopoly on all types of produce and manufacture, and plundered the country unmercifully. When he went mad in 1848, after 43 years of rule, his successors continued where he left off. Poor Egypt. Let us draw a veil over the careers of his descendants, Abbas, Said, Ismail, Tewfik. Fuad, who ruled as king between 1922 and 1936, after World War I had dissolved the connection with Turkey, was in some respects more enlightened, but still inordinately rapacious. As Hugh MacLeave says of him in his entertaining *The Last Pharaoh* (1969), "He died the most powerful and the richest man in Egypt. And the most hated."

Fuad's son, Farouk, brought the dynasty of Mohammed Ali to an appropriate and ugly end. James Aldridge relates how "Farouk signed his abdication document with a shaking hand, illegibly, even making a spelling mistake in the Arabic version of his own name, because he still could not write the language of the country his family had ruled for more than a hundred years."

And so, in 1952, the Egyptians ruled in their own capital and their own country for the first time since 526 B.C. Who can blame them if they have dismantled the grosser monuments of Turkish rule, even though they retain respect for the old Lion of the Levant himself and his son Ibrahim, the great general? Suleiman Pasha Street has become Talaat Harb Street, Fuad I Street has become July 26th Street, Ismailia Square is Liberation Square. Cairo sparkles less than it did in the days of the old Franco-British ascendancy, it is less opulent and sophisticated; but it has an encouraging air of purpose and pride.

What differences and similarities would Lane notice if he returned to Egypt today? He would find that the secretive, claustrophobic Cairo with its atmosphere of blood and torture has totally departed; most of the stink and much of the poverty has been eliminated; above all, as a result of the enlightened teaching of Mohammed Abdu, rector of Al-Azhar University seventy years ago, and the reforms of the 1952 revolution, women are no longer veiled and separated but are almost totally emancipated and everywhere work side by side with men. Yet everywhere he would still encounter the same cheerful, irrepressible, ebullient spirit of the *baladi* Cairene, the Cairene "of the village," gay and grinning and irreverent in his *gallabya*. The dancing-girls still dance, though their considerable tummies are discreetly veiled as a sop to revolutionary morality; the *Khawals* can still be seen, though *Khawal* is an obscene word and it is more polite to call them *Abu'lgheit*. The food, the music, the amusements, the superstitions, the gestures, the love of scandal and sweet cakes are still the same. Readers with a love and nostalgia for Cairo may like to read Stanley Lane-Poole's beautifully written, beautifully illustrated books on the city, *Cairo* (1892) and *The Story of Cairo* (1922); while Desmond Stewart's graceful monograph (1965) is informative about contemporary matters.

Lane would notice less change in the countryside. The Egyptian peasant still lives the life he has led for almost three millennia; he still carries out many of those fascinating rituals and festivals described by Lane, some of which are recognizable survivals from pharaonic times. But even here a sense of progress is in the air. The Aswan Dam has altered the habits of the mighty Nile; soon the power of its turbines will bring light and power to every town and village along its banks. These are beneficent developments; no one will grudge the hard-working, long-suffering Egyptian some softening of his lot.

And yet there will be times, for the twentieth- and twenty-first-century traveler, when he will look back with a sense of regret at some of the aspects of the strange and complex style of an Egypt that has largely vanished, and which Lane has so faithfully and vividly recorded.

JON MANCHIP WHITE

CONTENTS.

ILLUSTRATIONS.

EDITOR'S PREFACE.

THE present edition of the "Modern Egyptians" is printed in the same manner as the companion-volumes of the "Thousand and One Nights," from the text of Mr. Lane's last edition, with the additions and alterations which he has, from time to time, made in a copy of the work.[1]

The duty of correcting the press I undertook because important studies rendered it impossible for the Author to do so: and my endeavour has been to produce, by careful collation, a faithful text of a book which I feel it is not in my power to improve. In superintending a new edition of the "Thousand and One Nights" I was conscious how little might be added of use or relevance. What was then difficult I found in the "Modern Egyptians" to be impossible, and determined to insert nothing in the text, even as a foot-note. The notes I wished to make are therefore confined to an Appendix, and even in that form I have doubted the propriety of printing them. But though not necessary to the completeness of an account of manners and customs, they touch on subjects relative to the Muslim inhabitants of Egypt, and may therefore be found of interest. What I have said in them, I have endeavoured to say as briefly as may be, relying on facts rather than opinions, in the hope of supplying materials for more elaborate treatises.

Of the "Modern Egyptians," as the work of an Uncle and Master, it would be difficult for me to speak, were its merits less known and recognized than they are. At once the most remarkable description of a people ever written, and one that cannot now be rewritten, it will always live in the literature of England. With a thorough

1 These have been, in some portions, considerable, and such as render this the Standard Edition of the work.

knowledge of the people and of their language, singular power of description, and minute accuracy, Mr. Lane wrote his account of the "Modern Egyptians," when they could, for the last time, be described. Twenty-five years of steam-communication with Egypt have more altered its inhabitants than had the preceding five centuries. They then retained the habits and manners of their remote ancestors: they now are yearly straying from old paths into the new ways of European civilization. Scholars will ever regard it as most fortunate that Mr. Lane seized his opportunity, and described so remarkable a people while yet they were unchanged.

A residence of seven years in Egypt, principally in Cairo, while it enabled me to become familiar with the people, did not afford me any new fact that might be added to this work: and a distinguished English as well as Biblical scholar, the Author of "Sinai and Palestine," not long ago remarked to me, "'The Modern Egyptians' is the most provoking book I ever read: whenever I thought I had discovered, in Cairo, something that must surely have been omitted, I invariably found my new fact already recorded." I may add that a well-known German Orientalist has lately visited Cairo with the express intention of correcting Mr. Lane's descriptions, and confessed that his search after mistakes was altogether vain.

I have not thought it expedient to add to the chapter on Late Innovations in Egypt. That chapter brought down the history of its inhabitants to the best time of the rule of Moḥammad 'Alee, and closed the record of an exclusively Eastern nation. To continue it would be only to chronicle the gradual disuse of their national and characteristic customs, and the adoption of Western habits that must mark a new era in their history as a nation.

The woodcuts in this edition are the same as those of the former editions, printed from the same blocks, with the exception of the Frontispiece, which, though it is from a sketch of Mr. Lane's, was not, like the rest, drawn by him on the wood.

London, November, 1860.

AUTHOR'S PREFACE.

Cairo, 1835.

During a former visit to this country, undertaken chiefly for the purpose of studying the Arabic language in its most famous school, I devoted much of my attention to the manners and customs of the Arab inhabitants; and in an intercourse of two years and a half with this people, soon found that all the information which I had previously been able to obtain respecting them was insufficient to be of much use to the student of Arabic literature, or to satisfy the curiosity of the general reader. Hence I was induced to cover some quires of paper with notes on the most remarkable of their usages, partly for my own benefit, and partly in the hope that I might have it in my power to make some of my countrymen better acquainted with the domiciliated classes of one of the most interesting nations of the world, by drawing a detailed picture of the inhabitants of the largest Arab city. The period of my first visit to this country did not, however, suffice for the accomplishment of this object, and for the prosecution of my other studies; and I relinquished the idea of publishing the notes which I had made on the modern inhabitants: but, five years after my return to England, those notes were shown to some members of the Committee of the Society for the Diffusion of Useful Knowledge, at whose suggestion, the Committee, interested with the subjects of them, and with the novelty of some of their contents, engaged me to complete and print them. Encouraged by their approbation, and relying upon their judgment, I immediately determined to follow their advice, and, by the earliest opportunity, again departed to Egypt. After another residence of more than a year in the metropolis of this country, and half a year in Upper Egypt, I have now accomplished, as well as I am able, the task proposed to me.[1]

It may be said, that the English reader already possesses an excellent and ample description of Arab manners and customs in Dr. Russell's account of the people of Aleppo. I will not forfeit my own claim to the reputation of an honest writer by attempting to detract from the just merits of that valuable and interesting work; but must assert that it is, upon the whole, rather an account of *Turkish* than of *Arab* manners; and that neither the original Author, nor his brother, to whom we are indebted for the enlarged and much improved edition, was sufficiently acquainted with the Arabic language to scrutinize some of the most interesting subjects of inquiry which the plan of the work required them to treat: nor would their well-known station in Aleppo, or perhaps their national feelings, allow them to assume those disguises which were necessary to enable them to become familiar with many of the most remarkable religious ceremonies, opinions, and superstitions of the people whom they have described. Deficiencies in their remarks on these subjects are the only faults of any importance that I can discover in their excellent and learned work.[2]

---

[1] It gives me great pleasure to find, that, while I have been attempting to preserve memorials of the manners and customs of the most polished modern Arab people, one of my learned friends (M. Fulgence Fresnel) has been occupied, with eminent success, in rescuing from oblivion many interesting notices of the history of the *early* Arabs, and that another (Mr. [now, Sir Gardner] Wilkinson) has been preparing to impart to us an account of the private life, manners, &c., of the Ancient Egyptians. [The very high and just commendation which the works of these two authors (published since the above was written) have obtained from eminent critics renders it needless for me to add my humble testimony to their merits.]

[2] Among the memoirs in "the great French work" on Egypt, is one entitled "Essai sur les mœurs des habitans modernes de l'Égypte;" but its author appears to me to have fallen into an error of considerable magnitude, in applying to the Egyptians, in general, observations which were, in truth, for the most part descriptive of the manners and customs of their naturalized rulers, the Memlooks. It is probable that the Egyptians in some degree imitated, when they were able to do so, the habits and customs of this class: I may, however, venture to affirm, that the essay here alluded to does not convey a true notion of their *present* moral and social state. Its author, moreover, shews himself to have been often extremely careless both in his observations and inquiries: this is particularly evident in his singular misstatement of the correspondence of French and Moḥammedan hours, and in the first two pages (in the 8vo. edition) of the section on public fêtes. He has given many just philosophical observations; but these occupy too large a proportion of a memoir scarcely exceeding one-third of the extent of the present work. To shew that these remarks are not made in an invidious spirit, I most willingly express my high admiration of other parts of "the great work" (especially the contributions of M. Jomard), relating to subjects which have alike employed my mind and pen, and upon which I shall probably publish my observations.—Burckhardt's "Arabic Proverbs," and their illustrations, convey many notions of remarkable customs and traits of character of the modern Egyptians; but are very far from composing a complete exposition, or, in every case, a true one; for national proverbs are bad tests of the morality of a people.—There is one work, however, which presents most admirable pictures of the manners and customs of the Arabs, and particularly of those of the Egyptians; it is "The Thousand and One Nights; or, Arabian Nights' Entertainments:" if the English reader had possessed a close translation of it with sufficient illustrative notes, I might almost have spared myself the labour of the present undertaking.—[This

I have been differently circumstanced. Previously to my first visit to this country, I acquired some knowledge of the language and literature of the Arabs; and in a year after my first arrival here, I was able to converse with the people among whom I was residing, with tolerable ease. I have associated, almost exclusively, with Muslims, of various ranks in society: I have lived as they live, conforming with their general habits; and, in order to make them familiar and unreserved towards me on every subject, have always avowed my agreement with them in opinion whenever my conscience would allow me, and in most other cases refrained from the expression of my dissent, as well as from every action which might give them disgust; abstaining from eating food forbidden by their religion, and drinking wine, &c.; and even from habits merely disagreeable to them; such as the use of knives and forks at meals. Having made myself acquainted with all their common religious ceremonies, I have been able to escape exciting, in strangers, any suspicion of my being a person who had no right to intrude among them, whenever it was necessary for me to witness any Muslim rite or festival. While, from the dress which I have found most convenient to wear, I am generally mistaken, in public, for a Turk, my acquaintances, of course, know me to be an Englishman; but I constrain them to treat me as a Muslim, by my freely acknowledging the hand of Providence in the introduction and diffusion of the religion of El-Islám, and, when interrogated, avowing my belief in the Messiah, in accordance with the *words* of the Ḳur-án, as the Word of God infused into the womb of the Virgin Mary, and a Spirit proceeding from Him. Thus, I believe, I have acquired their good opinion, and much of their confidence; though not to such an extent as to prevent my having to contend with many difficulties. The Muslims are very averse from giving information on subjects connected with their religion or superstitions to persons whom they suspect of differing from them in sentiments; but very ready to talk on such subjects with those whom they think acquainted with them. Hence I have generally obtained some slight knowledge of matters difficult for me thoroughly to learn from one of the most lax, and of the least instructed, of my friends; so as to be able to draw into con-

---

remark, respecting "The Thousand and One Nights," was, I believe, the cause of my being employed, since the publication of the first edition of the present work, to translate those admirable tales, and to illustrate them by explanatory notes.]

versation, upon the desired topics, persons of better information; and by this mode I have invariably succeeded in overcoming their scruples. I have had two professors of Arabic and of Muslim religion and law as my regular, salaried tutors; and, by submitting to them questions on any matters respecting which I was in doubt, have authenticated or corrected, and added to, the information derived from conversation with my other friends. Occasionally, also, I have applied to higher authorities; having the happiness to number among my friends in this city some persons of the highest attainments in Eastern learning.

Perhaps the reader may not be displeased if I here attempt to acquaint him more particularly with one of my Muslim friends, the first of those above alluded to; and to shew, at the same time, the light in which he, like others of his country, regards me in my present situation. The sheykh Aḥmad (or seyyid Ahmad, for he is one of the numerous class of "shereefs," or descendants of the Prophet,) is somewhat more than forty years of age, by his own confession; but appears more near to fifty. He is as remarkable in physiognomy as in character. His stature is under the middle size: his beard reddish, and now becoming grey. For many years he has been nearly blind: one of his eyes is almost entirely closed; and both are ornamented on particular occasions (at least on the two grand annual festivals) with a border of the black pigment called "koḥl," which is seldom used but by women. He boasts his descent not only from the Prophet, but also from a very celebrated saint, Esh-Shaạráwee;[1] and his complexion, which is very fair, supports his assertion that his ancestors, for several generations, lived in the north-western parts of Africa. He obtains his subsistence from a slender patrimony, and by exercising the trade of a bookseller. Partly to profit in this occupation, and partly for the sake of society, or at least to enjoy some tobacco and coffee, he is a visiter in my house almost every evening.

For several years before he adopted the trade of a bookseller, which was that of his father, he pursued no other occupation than that of performing in the religious ceremonies called "zikrs;" which consist in the repetition of the name and attributes &c. of God, by a number of persons, in chorus; and in such performances he is still often em-

[1] Thus commonly pronounced, for Esh-Shaạránee.

ployed. He was then a member of the order of the Saạdeeyeh darweeshes, who are particularly famous for devouring live serpents; and he is said to have been one of the serpent-eaters: but he did not confine himself to food so easily digested. One night, during a meeting of a party of darweeshes of his order, at which their Sheykh was present, my friend became affected with religious frenzy, seized a tall glass shade which surrounded a candle placed on the floor, and ate a large portion of it. The Sheykh and the other darweeshes, looking at him with astonishment, upbraided him with having broken the institutes of his order; since the eating of glass was not among the miracles which they were allowed to perform; and they immediately expelled him. He then entered the order of the Aḥmedeeyeh; and as they, likewise, never ate glass, he determined not to do so again. However, soon after, at a meeting of some brethren of this order, when several Saạdeeyeh also were present, he again was seized with frenzy, and, jumping up to a chandelier, caught hold of one of the small glass lamps attached to it, and devoured about half of it, swallowing also the oil and water which it contained. He was conducted before his Sheykh, to be tried for this offence; but on his taking an oath never to eat glass again, he was neither punished nor expelled the order. Notwithstanding this oath, he soon again gratified his propensity to eat a glass lamp; and a brother-darweesh, who was present, attempted to do the same; but a large fragment stuck between the tongue and palate of this rash person; and my friend had great trouble to extract it. He was again tried by his Sheykh; and, being reproached for having broken his oath and vow of repentance, he coolly answered, "I repent again: repentance is good: for He whose name be exalted hath said, in the Excellent Book, 'Verily God loveth the repentant.'" The Sheykh, in anger, exclaimed, "Dost thou dare to act in this manner, and then come and cite the Ḳur-án before me?"—and with this reproof, he ordered that he should be imprisoned ten days; after which, he made him again swear to abstain from eating glass; and on this condition he was allowed to remain a member of the Aḥmedeeyeh. This second oath he professes not to have broken.—The person whose office it was to prosecute him related to me these facts; and my friend reluctantly confessed them to be true.

When I was first acquainted with the sheykh Aḥmad, he had long been content with one wife; but now he has indulged himself with a second,[1] who continues to live in her parents' house: yet he has taken care to assure me that he is not rich enough to refuse my yearly present of a dress. On my visiting him for the second time during my present residence in this place, his mother came to the door of the room in which I was sitting with him, to complain to me of his conduct in taking this new wife. Putting her hand within the door, to give greater effect to her words by proper action (or perhaps to shew how beautifully the palm, and the tips of the fingers, glowed with the fresh red dye of the "ḥennà"), but concealing the rest of her person, she commenced a most energetic appeal to my sympathy.—"O Efendee!" she exclaimed, "I throw myself upon thy mercy! I kiss thy feet! I have no hope but in God and thee!" "What words are these, my mistress?" said I: "what misfortune hath befallen thee? and what can I do for thee? Tell me."—"This son of mine," she continued, "this my son Ahmad, is a worthless fellow; he has a wife here, a good creature, with whom he has lived happily, with God's blessing, for sixteen years; and now he has neglected her and me, and given himself up to a second wife, a young, impudent wench: he lavishes his money upon this monkey, and others like her, and upon her father and mother and uncles and brother and brother's children, and I know not whom besides, and abridges us, that is, myself and his first wife, of the comforts to which we were before accustomed. By the Prophet! and by thy dear head! I speak truth. I kiss thy feet, and beg thee to insist upon his divorcing his new wife." The poor man looked a little foolish while his mother was thus addressing me from behind the door; and as soon as she was gone, promised to do what she desired. "But," said he, "it is a difficult case. I was in the habit of sleeping occasionally in the house of the brother of the girl whom I have lately taken as my wife: he is a clerk in the employ of 'Abbás Báshà; and, rather more than a year ago, 'Abbás Báshà sent for me, and said, 'I hear that you are often sleeping in the house of my clerk Moḥammad. Why do you act so? Do you not know that it is very improper, when there are women in the house?' I said, 'I am going to marry his sister.' 'Then why have you not married her already?' asked the Báshà. 'She is only nine years of age.' 'Is the marriage contract made?'—'No.' 'Why not?'—'I

[1] He professes to have had more than thirty wives in the course of his life; but, in saying so, I believe he greatly exaggerates.

cannot afford, at present, to give the dowry.' 'What is the dowry to be?'—'Ninety piasters.' 'Here, then,' said the Báshà, 'take the money, and let the contract be concluded immediately.' So you see I was obliged to marry the girl; and I am afraid that the Báshà will be angry if I divorce her: but I will act in such a manner that her brother shall insist upon the divorce; and then, please God, I shall live in peace again."—This is a good example of the comfort of having two wives.

A short time since, upon his offering me a copy of the Ḳur-án, for sale, he thought it necessary to make some excuse for doing so. He remarked that by my conforming with many of the ceremonies of the Muslims, I tacitly professed myself to be one of them; and that it was incumbent upon him to regard me in the most favourable light, which he was the more willing to do because he knew that I should incur the displeasure of my King by making an open profession of the faith of El-Islám, and therefore could not do it.[1] "You give me," said he, "the salutation of 'Peace be on you!' and it would be impious in me, being directly forbidden by my religion, to pronounce you an unbeliever; for God, whose name be exalted, hath said, 'Say not unto him who greeteth thee with peace, Thou art not a believer:'[2] therefore," he added, "it is no sin in me to put into your hands the noble Ḳur-án: but there are some of your countrymen who will take it in unclean hands, and even sit upon it! I beg God's forgiveness for talking of such a thing: far be it from you to do so: you, praise be to God, know and observe the command, 'None shall touch it but they who are purified.'"[3] He once sold a copy of the Ḳur-án, on my application, to a countryman of mine, who, being disturbed, just as the bargain was concluded, by some person entering the room, hastily put the sacred book upon the seat, and under a part of his dress, to conceal it. The bookseller was much scandalized by this action; thinking that my friend was sitting upon the book, and that he was doing so to shew his contempt of it: he declares his belief that he has been heavily punished by God for this unlawful sale.—There was only one thing that I had much difficulty in persuading him to do during my

---

1 It is a common belief among the Egyptians, that every European traveller who visits their country is an emissary from his King; and it is difficult to convince them that this is not the case: so strange to them is the idea of a man's incurring great trouble and expense for the purpose of acquiring the knowledge of foreign countries and nations.

2 Ḳur-án, ch. iv. v. 96.

3 Ḳur-án, ch. lvi. v. 78.

former visit to this country; which was, to go with me, at a particular period, into the mosque of the Ḥasaneyn, the reputed burial-place of the head of El-Ḥoseyn, and the most sacred of the mosques in the Egyptian metropolis. On my passing with him before one of the entrances of this building, one afternoon during the fast of Ramaḍán, when it was crowded with Turks, and many of the principal people of the city were among the congregation, I thought it a good opportunity to see it to the greatest advantage, and asked my companion to go in with me. He positively refused, in the fear of my being discovered to be an Englishman, which might so rouse the fanatic anger of some of the Turks there, as to expose me to some act of violence. I therefore entered alone. He remained at the door, following me with his eye only (or his only eye), and wondering at my audacity; but as soon as he saw me acquit myself in the usual manner, by walking round the bronze screen which surrounds the monument over the spot where the head of the martyr is said to be buried, and then putting myself into the regular postures of prayer, he came in, and said his prayers by my side.

After relating these anecdotes, I should mention that the characters of my other acquaintances here are not marked by similar eccentricities. My attentions to my visiters have been generally confined to the common usages of Eastern hospitality; supplying them with pipes and coffee, and welcoming them to a share of my dinner or supper. Many of their communications I have written in Arabic, at their dictation, and since translated, and inserted in the following pages. What I have principally aimed at, in this work, is correctness; and I do not scruple to assert that I am not conscious of having endeavoured to render interesting any matter that I have related by the slightest sacrifice of truth.

P. S. With regard to the engravings which accompany this work, I should mention that they are from drawings which I have made, not to embellish the pages, but merely to explain the text.

ADVERTISEMENT TO THE THIRD EDITION.

SINCE the publication of the first edition of the present work, the studies in which I have been engaged have enabled me to improve it by various corrections and additions; and the success which it has obtained (a success very far beyond my expectations) has excited me to use my utmost endeavours to rectify its errors and supply its defects.

In reading the Ḳur-án, with an Arabic commentary, I have found that Sale's version, though deserving of high commendation for its general accuracy, is incorrect in many important passages; and hence I have been induced to revise with especial care my abstract of the principal Muslim laws: for as Sale had excellent commentaries to consult, and I, when I composed that abstract, had none, I placed great reliance on his translation. My plan, in the execution of that portion of my work, was to make use of Sale's translation as the basis, and to add what appeared necessary from the Sunneh and other sources, chiefly at the dictation of a professor of law, who was my tutor: but I have found that my foundation was in several points faulty.

I am indebted to a gentleman who possesses a thorough knowledge of the spirit of Muslim institutions[1] for the suggestion of some improvements in the same and other portions of this work; and observations made by several intelligent critics have lessened the labour of revision and emendation.

I have also profited, on this occasion, by a paper containing a number of corrections and additions written in Egypt, which I had mislaid and forgotten: but none of these are of much importance.

[1] David Urquhart, Esq., author of "The Spirit of the East," &c.

The mode in which Arabic words were transcribed in the previous editions I thought better calculated than any other to enable an English reader, unacquainted with the Arabic language, to pronounce those words with tolerable accuracy; but it was liable to serious objections, and was disagreeable, in some respects, to most Oriental scholars, and to myself. I have therefore now employed, in its stead, as I did in my translation of "The Thousand and One Nights," a system congenial with our language, and of the most simple kind; and to this system I adhere in every case, for the sake of uniformity, as well as *truth.*[1] It requires little explanation: the general reader may be directed to pronounce

"a" as in our word "beggar:"[2]	"i" as in "bid:"
"á" as in "father:"[3]	"o" as in "obey" (short):
"e" as in "bed:"	"ó" as in "bone:"
"é" as in "there:"	"oo" as in "boot:"
"ee" as in "bee:"	"ow" as in "down:"
"ei" as in our word "eye:"	"u" as in "bull:"
"ey" as in "they:"	"y" as in "you."

An *apostrophe,* when immediately preceding or following a vowel, I employ to denote the place of a letter which has no equivalent in our alphabet: it has a guttural sound, like that which is heard in the bleating of sheep.

The vowel "a" with a *dot* beneath (ạ) represents the same sound when it is more forcibly pronounced.

Each of the *consonants* distinguished by a *dot* beneath has a peculiarly hard sound. The distinction of these letters is of great importance to Arabic scholars, and to travellers in Egypt.[4]

The usual sign of a *diæresis* I sometimes employ to shew that a final "e" is not mute, but pronounced as that letter, when unaccented, in the beginning or middle of a word.

---

[1] Here I must mention, that I have written "Báshà" instead of "Páshá" in conformity with the pronounciation of the Egyptians.

[2] Strictly speaking, it has a sound between that of "a" in "bad" and that of "u" in "bud;" sometimes approximating more to the former, and sometimes to the latter.

[3] Its sound, however, often approximates to that of "a" in "ball."

[4] "Dh" is pronounced as "th" in "that:"—"g," generally as in "give;" but in some parts of Egypt as in "gem," or nearly so:—"gh" represents a guttural sound, like that produced in gargling:—"ḥ" is a very strong aspirate:—"ḳ" has properly a guttural sound (most of the people of Cairo, and those of some provinces, cannot pronounce it, and substitute for it an *hiatus;* while in Upper Egypt the sound of "g" in "give" is used in its stead)—"kh" represents a guttural sound like that which is produced in expelling saliva from the throat, and approaching nearer to the sound of "ḥ" than to that of "k:"—"sh" is pronounced as in "shall:" and "th" as in "thin."

Having avoided as much as possible marking the *accentuation* in Arabic words, I must request the reader to bear in mind, not only that a single vowel, when not marked with an accent, is always short; but that a double vowel or diphthong, at the end of a word, when not so marked, is not accented ("Welee," for instance, being pronounced "Wĕ'lee," or "Wel'ee"): also, that the accents do not always denote the principal or only emphasis ("Sháweesh" being pronounced "Shá-wee'sh"); and that "dh," "gh," "kh," "sh," and "th," when not divided by a hyphen, represent, each, a single Arabic letter.

As some readers may observe that many Arabic words are written differently in this work and in my translation of "The Thousand and One Nights," it is necessary to add, that in the present case I write such words agreeably with the general pronunciation of the educated classes in Cairo. For the same reason I often use the same European character to express two Arabic letters which in Egypt are pronounced alike.

E. W. L.

May, 1842.

THE

MODERN EGYPTIANS.

INTRODUCTION.

COUNTRY AND CLIMATE—METROPOLIS—HOUSES—POPULATION.

It is generally observed that many of the most remarkable peculiarities in the manners, customs, and character of a nation are attributable to the physical peculiarities of the country. Such causes, in an especial manner, affect the moral and social state of the modern Egyptians, and therefore here require some preliminary notice; but it will not as yet be necessary to explain their particular influences: these will be evinced in many subsequent parts of the present work.

The Nile, in its course through the narrow and winding valley of Upper Egypt, which is confined on each side by mountainous and sandy deserts, as well as through the plain of Lower Egypt, is everywhere bordered, except in a very few places, by cultivated fields of its own formation. These cultivated tracts are not perfectly level, being somewhat lower towards the deserts than in the neighbourhood of the river. They are interspersed with palm-groves and villages, and intersected by numerous canals. The copious summer rains that prevail in Abyssinia and the neighbouring countries begin to shew their effects in Egypt, by the rising of the Nile, about the period of the summer solstice. By the autumnal equinox the river attains its greatest height, which is always sufficient to fill the canals by which the fields are irrigated, and, generally, to inundate large portions of the cultivable land: it then gradually falls until the period when it again begins to rise. Being impregnated, particularly during its rise, with rich soil washed down from the mountainous countries whence it flows, a copious deposit is annually spread, either by the natural inundation or by artificial irrigation, over the fields which border it; while its bed, from the same cause, rises in an equal degree. The Egyptians depend entirely upon their river for the fertilization of the soil, rain being a very rare phenomenon in their country, except in the neighbourhood of the Mediterranean; and as the seasons are perfectly regular, the peasant may make his arrangements with the utmost precision respecting the labour he will have to perform. Sometimes his labour is light; but when it consists in raising water for irrigation, it is excessively severe.

The climate of Egypt, during the greater part of the year, is remarkably salubrious. The exhalations from the soil after the period of the inundation render the latter part of the autumn less healthy than the summer and winter; and cause ophthalmia and dysentery, and some other diseases, to be more prevalent then than at other seasons; and during a period of somewhat more or less than fifty days (called "el-khamáseen"[1]), commencing in April and lasting throughout May, hot southerly winds occasionally prevail for about three days together. These winds, though they seldom cause the thermometer of Fahrenheit to rise above 95° in Lower Egypt, or in Upper Egypt 105°,[2] are dreadfully oppressive, even to the natives. When the plague visits Egypt, it is generally in the spring; and this disease is most severe in the period of the khamáseen. Egypt is also subject, particularly during the spring and summer, to the hot wind called the "samoom," which is still more oppressive than the khamáseen winds, but of much shorter duration, seldom lasting longer than a quarter of an hour or twenty minutes. It generally proceeds from the south-east or south-south-east, and carries with it clouds of dust and sand. The general height of the thermometer in the middle of winter in Lower Egypt, in the afternoon, and in the shade, is from 50° to 60°: in the hottest season it is from 90° to 100°; and about ten degrees higher in the southern parts of Upper Egypt. But though the summer heat is so great, it is seldom very oppressive; being generally accompanied by a refreshing northerly breeze, and the air being extremely dry. There is, however, one great source of discomfort arising from this dryness, namely, an excessive quantity of dust: and there

---

1 Respecting this term, see a note to the first paragraph of Chapter XXVI.

2 This is the temperature in the shade. At Thebes, I have observed the thermometer to rise above 110° during a khamáseen wind in the shade.

are other plagues which very much detract from the comfort which the natives of Egypt, and visiters to their country, otherwise derive from its genial climate. In spring, summer, and autumn, flies are so abundant as to be extremely annoying during the daytime, and musquitoes are troublesome at night (unless a curtain be made use of to keep them away), and often even in the day; and almost every house that contains much woodwork (as most of the better houses do) swarms with bugs during the warm weather. Lice are not always to be avoided in any season, but they are easily got rid of; and in the cooler seasons fleas are excessively numerous.

The climate of Upper Egypt is more healthy, though hotter, than that of Lower Egypt. The plague seldom ascends far above Cairo, the metropolis; and is most common in the marshy parts of the country near the Mediterranean. During the last ten years before my second visit to Egypt, the country having been better drained, and quarantine regulations adopted to prevent or guard against the introduction of this disease from other countries, very few plague-cases occurred, except in the parts above mentioned, and in those parts the pestilence was not severe.[1] Ophthalmia is also more common in Lower Egypt than in the southern parts. It generally arises from checked perspiration; but is aggravated by the dust and many other causes. When remedies are promptly employed, this disease is seldom alarming in its progress; but vast numbers of the natives of Egypt, not knowing how to treat it, or obstinately resigning themselves to fate, are deprived of the sight of one or both of their eyes.

When questioned respecting the salubrity of Egypt, I have often been asked whether many aged persons are seen among the inhabitants: few, certainly, attain a great age in this country; but how few do, in our own land, without more than once suffering from an illness that would prove fatal without medical aid, which is obtained by a very small number in Egypt! The heat of the summer months is sufficiently oppressive to occasion considerable lassitude, while, at the same time, it excites the Egyptian to intemperance in sensual enjoy-

[1] This remark was written before the terrible plague of the year 1835, which was certainly introduced from Turkey, and extended throughout the whole of Egypt, though its ravages were not great in the southern parts. It destroyed not less than eighty thousand persons in Cairo, that is, one-third of the population; and far more, I believe, than two hundred thousand in all Egypt. According to a report made by the government, the victims of this plague in Cairo were about *forty* thousand; but I was informed, on high authority, that the government made it a rule to report only half the number of deaths in this case.

ments; and the exuberant fertility of the soil engenders indolence, little nourishment sufficing for the natives, and the sufficiency being procurable without much exertion.

The modern Egyptian metropolis, to the inhabitants of which most of the contents of the following pages relate, is now called "Maṣr,"[1] more properly, "Miṣr;" but was formerly named "El-Ḳáhireh;" whence Europeans have formed the name of *Cairo*. It is situate at the entrance of the valley of Upper Egypt, midway between the Nile and the eastern mountain range of the Muḳaṭṭam. Between it and the river there intervenes a tract of land, for the most part cultivated, which, in the northern parts (where the port of Booláḳ is situate), is more than a mile in width, and, at the southern part, less than half a mile wide. The metropolis occupies a space equal to about three square miles; and its population, during my second visit (since which it has much increased in consequence of the reduction of the army and from other causes) I calculated to amount to about two hundred and forty thousand. It is surrounded by a wall, the gates of which are shut at night, and is commanded by a large citadel, situate at an angle of the town, near a point of the mountain. The streets are unpaved; and most of them are narrow and irregular: they might more properly be called lanes.

By a stranger who merely passed through the streets, Cairo would be regarded as a very close and crowded city; but that this is not the case is evident to a person who overlooks the town from the top of a lofty house, or from the menaret of a mosque. The great thoroughfare-streets have generally a row of shops along each side.[2] Above the shops are apartments which do not communicate with them, and which are seldom occupied by the persons who rent the shops. To the right and left of the great thoroughfares are by-streets and quarters. Most of the by-streets are thoroughfares, and have a large wooden gate at each end, closed at night, and kept by a porter within, who opens to any persons requiring to be admitted. The quarters mostly consist of several narrow lanes, having but one general entrance, with a gate, which is also closed at night; but several have a by-street passing through them.[3]

Of the private houses of the metropolis it is particularly necessary

---

[1] This is the name by which the modern Egyptians call their country, as well as its metropolis.

[2] Views of shops in Cairo will be found in a subsequent Chapter.

[3] A great thoroughfare-street is called "sháre'"; a by-street, "darb"; a lane, "'aṭfeh"; and a quarter, "ḥárah."

Private Houses in Cairo.

that I should give a description. The preceding engraving will serve to give a general notion of their exterior. The foundation-walls, to the height of the first floor, are cased externally, and often internally, with the soft calcareous stone of the neighbouring mountain. The surface of the stone, when newly cut, is of a light-yellowish hue: but its colour soon darkens. The alternate courses of the front are sometimes coloured red and white,[1] particularly in large houses; as is the case with most mosques.[2] The superstructure, the front of which generally projects about two feet, and is supported by corbels or piers, is of brick, and often plastered. The bricks are burnt, and of a dull red colour. The mortar is generally composed of mud in the proportion of one-half, with a fourth part of lime, and the remaining part of the ashes of straw and rubbish. Hence the unplastered walls of brick are of a dirty colour, as if the bricks were unburnt. The roof is flat, and covered with a coat of plaster. It is generally without a parapet.

The most usual architectural style of the entrance of a private house in Cairo is shewn by the sketch in the opposite page. The door is often ornamented in the manner there represented: the compartment in which is the inscription, and the other similarly-shaped compartments, are painted red, bordered with white; the rest of the surface of the door is painted green. The inscription, "He (*i. e.* God) is the Great Creator, the Everlasting" (the object of which will be explained when I treat of the superstitions of the Egyptians), is seen on many doors; but is far from being general: it is usually painted in black or white characters. Few doors but those of large houses are painted. They generally have an iron knocker and a wooden lock; and there is usually a mounting-stone by the side.

The ground-floor apartments next the street have small wooden grated windows, placed sufficiently high to render it impossible for a person passing by in the street, even on horseback, to see through them. The windows of the upper apartments generally project a foot and a half, or more, and are mostly made of turned wooden lattice-work, which is so close that it shuts out much of the light and sun,

---

1 With red ochre and limewash.

2 This mode of decorating the houses became more general than it had been previously in consequence of an order of the government, whereby the inhabitants were required thus to honour the arrival of Ibráheem Báshà from Syria. Several years later, the people of Cairo were ordered to whitewash the superstructures of their houses; and thus the picturesque aspect of the city was much injured; the contrast between the white walls and the dark wood of the old windows producing a disagreeable effect.

The street in the view which I have given is wider than usual. The projecting windows on opposite sides of a street often nearly meet each other; almost entirely excluding the sun, and thus producing an agreeable coolness in the summer months. On account of their facilitating the spreading of fires, their construction has of late years been prohibited.

Door of a Private House in Cairo.

and screens the inmates of the house from the view of persons without, while at the same time it admits the air. They are generally of unpainted wood; but some few are partially painted red and green, and some are entirely painted. A window of this kind is called a

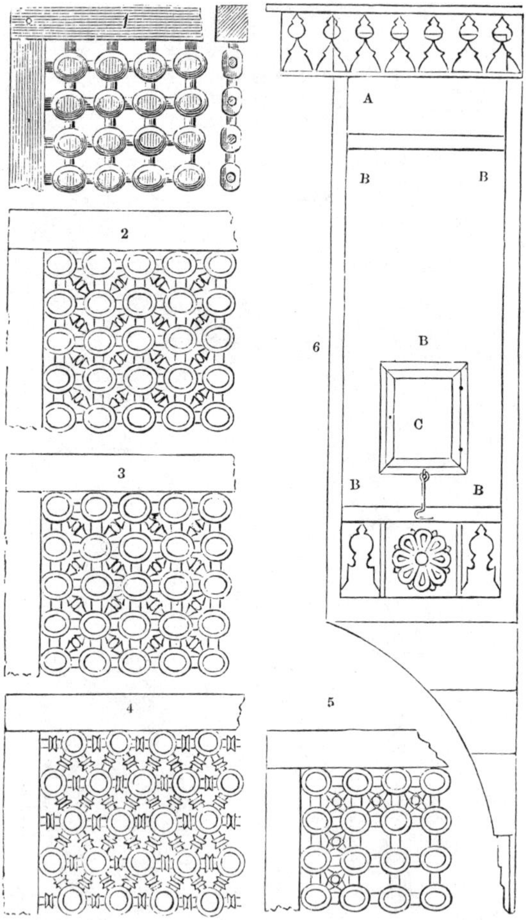

Specimens of Lattice-work.—*From the centre of one row of beads to that of the next (in these specimens) is between an inch and a quarter and an inch and three-quarters.*

"róshan," or, more commonly, a "meshrebeeyeh," which latter word has another application that will be presently mentioned. Several windows of different descriptions are represented in some of the illustrations of this work; and sketches of the most common patterns of the lattice-work, on a larger scale, are given in the opposite page.[1] Sometimes a window of the kind above described has a little meshrebeeyeh, which somewhat resembles a róshan in miniature, projecting from the front or from each side. In this, in order to be exposed to a current of air, are placed porous earthen bottles, which are used for cooling water by evaporation. Hence the name of "meshrebeeyeh," which signifies "a place for drink," or "—for drinking." The projecting window has a flat one of lattice-work, or of grating of wood, or of coloured glass, immediately above it. This upper window, if of lattice-work, is often of a more fanciful construction than the others; exhibiting a representation of a basin with a ewer above it, or the figure of a lion, or the name of "Allah," or the words "God is my hope," &c. Some projecting windows are wholly constructed of boards, and a few of these lean forward, from the bottom upwards, at an angle of about 20°, being open at the top for the admission of light. Some of the more common form have frames of glass in the sides. In the better houses, also, the windows of lattice-work are now generally furnished with frames of glass in the inside, which in the winter are wholly closed; for a penetrating cold is felt in Egypt when the thermometer of Fahrenheit is below 60°.[2] The windows of inferior houses are mostly of a different kind, being even with the exterior surface of the wall: the upper part is of wooden lattice-work,[3] or grating; and the lower, closed by hanging shutters; but many of these have a little meshrebeeyeh for the water-bottles projecting from the lower part.

The houses in general are two or three stories high; and almost every house that is sufficiently large encloses an open, unpaved court, called a "ḥósh," which is entered by a passage that is constructed with one or two turnings, for the purpose of preventing passengers in the street from seeing into it. In this passage, just within the door, there is a long stone seat, called "maṣṭabah,"[4] built against the back or side wall, for the door-keeper and other servants. In the court is a well of

---

[1] No. 1 is a view and section of a portion of the most simple kind. This and the other four kinds are here represented on a scale of about one-seventh of the real size. No. 6 shews the general proportions of the side of a projecting window. The portion A is, in most instances, of lattice-work similar to No. 1, and comprises about twelve rows of beads in the width; the portion B is commonly either of the same kind, or like No. 2 or No. 3; and the small lattice C, which is attached by hinges, is generally similar to No. 4.

[2] Windows with European sashes of glass, each with a sash of close trellis-work outside the lower half, have lately become common in new houses, in many parts of Cairo. They are mostly in houses built in the Turkish style, more or less approaching to European fashions; not well adapted to a hot climate, though comfortable in winter.

[3] Commonly similar to No. 1 or No. 5.

[4] Pronounced "maṣṭab'ah."

Court of a Private House in Cairo.

slightly-brackish water, which filters through the soil from the Nile; and on its most shaded side are, commonly, two water-jars, which are daily replenished with water of the Nile, brought from the river in skins.[1] The principal apartments look into the court: and their exterior walls (those which are of brick) are plastered and whitewashed. There are several doors which are entered from the court. One of these is called "báb el-ḥareem" (the door of the ḥareem): it is the entrance of the stairs which lead to the apartments appropriated exclusively to the women, and their master and his children.[2]

In general, there is, on the ground-floor, an apartment called a "manḍarah,"[3] in which male visiters are received. This has a wide, wooden, grated window, or two windows of this kind, next the court. A small part of the floor, extending from the door to the opposite side of the room, is about four or five inches lower than the rest; this part is called the "durḳá'ah."[4] In a handsome house, the durḳá'ah of the manḍar'ah is paved with white and black marble, and little pieces of fine red tile, inlaid in complicated and tasteful patterns, and has in the centre a fountain (called "fasḳeeyeh") which plays into a small, shallow pool, lined with coloured marbles, &c., like the surrounding pavement. I give, as a specimen, the pattern of the pavement of a durḳá'ah, such as I have above described, and a sketch of the fountain. The water that falls from the fountain is drained off from the pool by a pipe. There is generally, fronting the door, at the end of the durḳá'ah, a shelf of marble or of common stone, about four feet high, called a "ṣuffeh," supported by two or more arches, or by a single arch, under which are placed utensils in ordinary use; such as perfuming vessels, and the basin and ewer which are used for washing before and after meals, and for the ablution preparatory to prayer: water-bottles, coffee-cups, &c., are placed upon the ṣuffeh. In handsome houses, the arches of the ṣuffeh are faced with marble and tile, like the pool of the fountain; see the two sketches in page 13: and sometimes the wall over it, to the height of about four feet or more, is also cased with similar materials; partly with large upright slabs, and partly with small pieces, like the durḳá'ah. The estrade, or

---

[1] Some large houses have two courts: the inner for the ḥareem; and in the latter, or both of these, there is usually a little enclosure of arched wood-work, in which trees and flowers are raised. The most common kind of tree in the court of a house is the grape-vine or the mulberry; but with one or both of these we often find the banana, the palm, and other trees.

[2] In the view which I have given of the court of a house, the door of the ḥareem is that which faces the spectator.

[3] Pronounced "manḍar'ah."

[4] Apparently a corruption of the Persian "dargáh."—The frontispiece to this work will serve to illustrate the description of the manḍarah.

raised part of the floor of the room, is called "leewán."[1] Every person slips off his shoes on the durḳá'ah before he steps upon the leewán.[2]

Pavement of a "Durḳá'ah."—*The width of this is about eight feet.*

The latter is generally paved with common stone, and covered with a mat in summer, and a carpet over the mat in winter; and has a

[1] The "leewán" is not to be confounded with the "deewán," which is afterwards mentioned. It is also, sometimes, called "eewán," which more properly signifies "an open-fronted porch or portico," and "a palace," &c. "Leewán" and "eewán" are both of Persian origin: but the former is commonly said to be a corruption of "el-eewán."

[2] One of the chief reasons of the custom here mentioned is, to avoid defiling a mat or carpet upon which prayer is usually made. This, as many authors have observed, illustrates passages of the Scriptures,—Exodus iii. 5, and Joshua v. 15.

mattress and cushions placed against each of its three walls, composing what is called a "deewán," or divan. The mattress, which is about three feet, or somewhat less, in width, and three or four inches thick, is generally placed on the ground; and the cushions, which

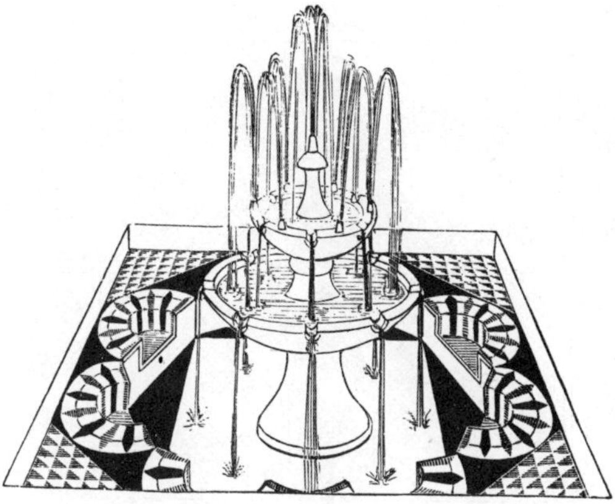

Fountain.

Ṣuffeh.

are usually of a length equal to the width of the mattress, and of a height equal to half that measure, lean against the wall. Both mattresses and cushions are stuffed with cotton, and are covered with printed calico, cloth, or some more expensive stuff. Sometimes the mattress is supported by a frame made of palm-sticks, called "sereer;" and sometimes it lies upon a platform of stone, about half a foot high, called "sidilleh" or "sidillè," a word of Persian origin, and also applied to a recess, of which the floor is similarly elevated, and nearly equal in width and depth, with a mattress and cushions laid against one, or two, or each, of its three sides. Some rooms have one, and some have two or more, of such recesses, generally used as sitting-places in cool weather, and therefore without windows. The walls of the room are plastered and whitewashed. There are generally, in the walls, two or three shallow cupboards, the doors of which are composed

Specimens of Panel-work.—*These are represented on a scale of one inch to twenty-four or thirty.*

of very small panels on account of the heat and dryness of the climate, which cause wood to warp and shrink as if it were placed in an oven; for which reason the doors of the apartments, also, are constructed in the same manner. We observe great variety and much ingenuity displayed in the different modes in which these small panels are formed and disposed. I insert a few select specimens. The ceiling

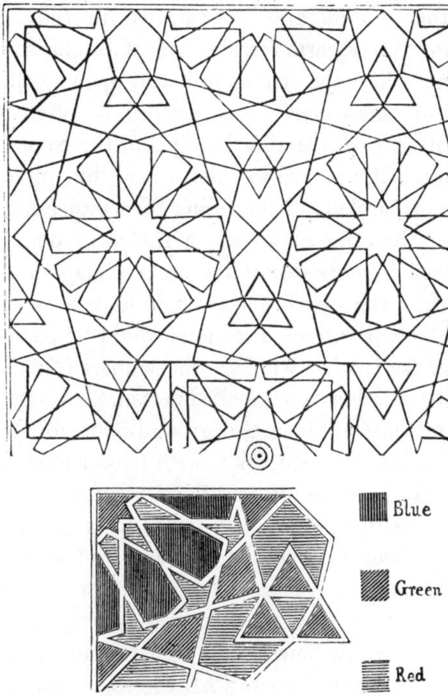

Ceiling of a Durḳá'ah.—*About eight feet wide.*

Ceiling of a projecting window.—*The dimensions of this are about eight feet by three.*

over the leewán is of wood, with carved beams, generally about a foot apart, partially painted, and sometimes gilt. But that part of the ceiling which is over the durḳá'ah, in a handsome house, is usually more richly decorated: here, instead of beams, numerous thin strips of wood are nailed upon the planks, forming patterns curiously complicated, yet perfectly regular, and having a highly ornamental effect. I give a sketch of the half of a ceiling thus decorated, but not in the most complicated style. The strips are painted yellow, or gilt; and the spaces within, painted green, red, and blue.[1] In the example which I insert, the colours are as indicated in the sketch of a portion of the same on a larger scale, except in the square in the centre of the ceiling, where the strips are black, upon a yellow ground. From the centre of this square, a chandelier is often suspended. There are many patterns of a similar kind; and the colours generally occupy similar places with regard to each other; but in some houses these ceilings are not painted. The ceiling of a projecting window is often ornamented in the same manner. A sketch of one is inserted. Good taste is evinced by only decorating in this manner parts which are not always before the eyes; for to look long at so many lines intersecting each other in various directions would be painful.

In some houses (as in that which is the subject of the engraving in page 10) there is another room, called a "maḳ'ad," generally elevated about eight or ten feet above the ground-floor, for the same use as the manḍarah, having an open front, with two or more arches, and a low railing; and also, on the ground-floor, a square recess, called a "takhtabósh," with an open front, and generally a pillar to support the wall above: its floor is a paved leewán; and there is a long wooden sofa (called "dikkeh") placed along one, or two, or each, of its three walls. The court, during the summer, is frequently sprinkled with water, which renders the surrounding apartments agreeably cool, or at least those on the ground-floor. All the rooms are furnished in the same manner as that first described.

Among the upper apartments, or those of the ḥareem, there is generally one called a "ḳá'ah," which is particularly lofty. It has two leewáns, one on each hand of a person entering: one of these is generally larger than the other, and is the more honourable part. A portion of the roof of this saloon, the part which is over the durḳá'ah that divides the two leewáns, is more elevated than the rest, and has, in the centre, a small lantern, called "memraḳ," the sides of which are composed of lattice-work, like the windows before described, and support a cupola. The durḳá'ah is commonly without a fountain; but is often paved in a similar manner to that of the manḍarah: which the ḳá'ah also resembles in having a handsome ṣuffeh, and

---

1 See Jeremiah xxii. 14.

A Ḳá'ah.

cupboards of curious panel-work. There is, besides, in this and some other apartments, a narrow shelf of wood, extending along two or each of the three walls which bound the leewán, about seven feet or more from the floor, just above the cupboards; but interrupted in some parts, at least in those parts where the windows are placed: upon this are arranged several vessels of china, not so much for general use as for ornament.[1] All the apartments are lofty, generally fourteen feet or more in height; but the ḳá'ah is the largest and most lofty room, and in a large house it is a noble saloon.

In several of the upper rooms, in the houses of the wealthy, there are, besides the windows of lattice-work, others, of coloured glass, representing bunches of flowers, peacocks, and other gay and gaudy objects, or merely fanciful patterns, which have a pleasing effect. These coloured glass windows, which are termed "ḳamareeyehs,"[2] are mostly from a foot and a half to two feet and a half in height, and from one to two feet in width; and are generally placed along the upper part of the projecting lattice-window, in a row; or above that kind of window, disposed in a group, so as to form a large square; or elsewhere in the upper parts of the walls, usually singly, or in pairs, side by side. They are composed of small pieces of glass, of various colours, set in rims of fine plaster, and enclosed in a frame of wood. On the plastered walls of some apartments are rude paintings of the temple of Mekkeh, or of the tomb of the Prophet, or of flowers and other objects, executed by native Muslim artists, who have not the least notion of the rules of perspective, and who consequently deface what they thus attempt to decorate. In most cases, these daubs have been executed to gratify the bad taste of Turks; and they are seldom seen in houses of good Arabian architecture. Sometimes the walls are beautifully ornamented with Arabic inscriptions, of maxims, &c., which are more usually written on paper, in an embellished style, and enclosed in glazed frames. No chambers are furnished as bed-rooms. The bed, in the day-time, is rolled up, and placed on one side, or in an adjoining closet, called "khazneh," which, in the winter,

[1] In the larger houses, and some others, there is also, adjoining the principal saloon of the ḥareem, an elevated closet, designed as an orchestra, for female singers, to conceal them from the view of the men of the family, as well as from that of the male guests if any of these (the women having retired) be present. A description of this will be found in the chapter on music.

[2] This word is derived from "ḳamar" (the "moon"). Baron Hammer-Purgstall thinks (see the Vienna "Jahrbücher der Literatur," lxxxi. bd., pp. 71 & 72) that it has its origin from "Chumaruje" [or, as he is called by the Arabs in general, Khumáraweyh], the second prince of the dynasty of the Benee-Ṭooloon, who governed in Egypt in the end of the ninth century of the Christian era, and that it proves the art of staining glass to have been in a flourishing state in Cairo at that period.

is a sleeping-place: in summer, many people sleep upon the house-top. A mat, or carpet, spread upon the raised part of the stone floor, and a deewán, constitute the complete furniture of a room. For meals, a round tray is brought in, and placed upon a low stool, and the company sit round it on the ground. There is no fire-place:[1] the room is warmed, when necessary, by burning charcoal in a chafing-dish. Many houses have, at the top, a sloping shed, mainly of boards, or of timbers and reeds, the latter plastered and whitewashed within and without, called a "malkaf,"[2] directed towards the north, and open in that direction, and generally on the west side also, to convey to a "fes-ḥah" or "fesaḥah" (an open apartment) below, the cool breezes which generally blow from those quarters. There is commonly a fes-ḥah before the entrance of one or more of the principal apartments; and in it the family often sit and sleep in the hot season.

Every door is furnished with a wooden lock, called a "ḍabbeh," the mechanism of which is shewn by a sketch here inserted. No. 1 in this sketch is a front view of the lock, with the bolt drawn back; Nos. 2, 3, and 4, are back views of the separate parts, and the key.

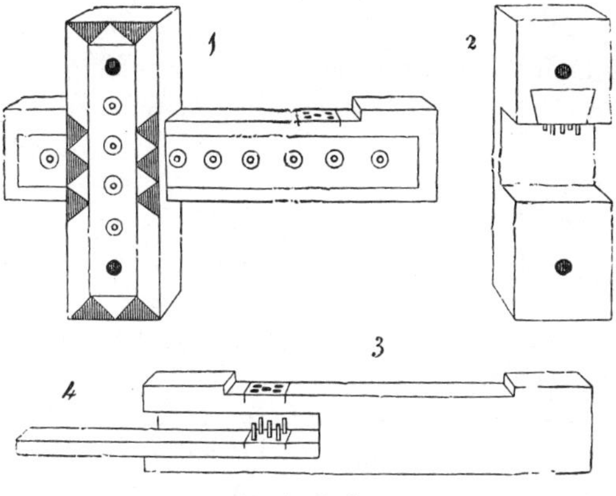

Wooden Lock.

A number of small iron pins (four, five, or more,) drop into corresponding holes in the sliding bolt, as soon as the latter is pushed into the

[1] Except in the kitchen, in which are several small receptacles for fire, constructed on a kind of bench of brick. Hence, and for several other reasons (among which may be mentioned the sober and early habits of the people, the general absence of draperies in the apartments, and the construction of the floors, which are of wood overlaid with stone), the destruction of a house by fire seldom happens in Cairo; but when such an accident does occur, an extensive conflagration is the usual result; for a great quantity of wood, mostly deal, and of course excessively dry, is employed in the construction of the houses.

[2] See again the engraving in p. 10.

hole or staple of the door-post. The key, also, has small pins, made to correspond with the holes, into which they are introduced to open the lock: the former pins being thus pushed up, the bolt may be drawn back. The wooden lock of a street-door is commonly about fourteen inches long:[1] those of the doors of apartments, cupboards, &c., are about seven, or eight, or nine inches. The locks of the gates of quarters, public buildings, &c., are of the same kind, and mostly two feet, or even more, in length. It is not difficult to pick this kind of lock.

In the plan of almost every house there is an utter want of regularity. The apartments are generally of different heights, so that a person has to ascend or descend one, two, or more steps, to pass from one chamber to another adjoining it. The principal aim of the architect is to render the house as private as possible; particularly that part of it which is inhabited by the women; and not to make any window in such a situation as to overlook the apartments of another house. Another object of the architect, in building a house for a person of wealth or rank, is to make a secret door ("báb sirr"[2]), from which the tenant may make his escape in case of danger from an arrest, or an attempt at assassination, or by which to give access and egress to a paramour; and it is also common to make a hiding-place for treasure (called "makhbà") in some part of the house. In the ḥareem of a large house there is generally a bath, which is heated in the same manner as the public baths.

Another style of building, after the fashion of Turkey, lately very generally adopted for houses of the more wealthy, has been mentioned before (page 9, note 2). These houses do not differ much from those already described, except in the windows, and these are generally placed almost close together.

When shops occupy the lower part of the buildings in a street (as is generally the case in the great thoroughfares of the metropolis, and in some of the by-streets), the superstructure is usually divided into distinct lodgings, and is termed "rabạ." These lodgings are separate from each other, as well as from the shops below, and let to families who cannot afford the rent of a whole house. Each lodging in a rabạ comprises one or two sitting and sleeping rooms, and generally a kitchen and latrina. It seldom has a separate entrance from

---

1 This is the measure of the sliding bolt.
2 This term is also applied, sometimes, to the door of the ḥareem.

the street; one entrance and one staircase usually admitting to a range of several lodgings. The apartments are similar to those of the private houses first described. They are never let ready-furnished; and it is very seldom that a person who has not a wife nor a female slave is allowed to reside in them, or in any private house: such a person (unless he have parents or other near relations to dwell with) is usually obliged to take up his abode in a "wekáleh," which is a building chiefly designed for the reception of merchants and their goods.[1]

Very few large or handsome houses are to be seen in Egypt, except in the metropolis and some other towns. The dwellings of the lower orders, particularly those of the peasants, are of a very mean description: they are mostly built of unbaked bricks, cemented together with mud. Some of them are mere hovels. The greater number, however, comprise two or more apartments; though few are two stories high. In one of these apartments, in the houses of the peasants in Lower Egypt, there is generally an oven ("furn"), at the end furthest from the entrance, and occupying the whole width of the chamber. It resembles a wide bench or seat, and is about breast-high: it is constructed of brick and mud; the roof arched within, and flat on the top. The inhabitants of the house, who seldom have any night-covering during the winter, sleep upon the top of the oven, having previously lighted a fire within it; or the husband and wife only enjoy this luxury, and the children sleep upon the floor. The chambers have small apertures high up in the walls, for the admission of light and air, sometimes furnished with a grating of wood. The roofs are formed of palm-branches and palm-leaves, or of millet-stalks, &c.; laid upon rafters of the trunk of the palm, and covered with a plaster of mud and chopped straw. The furniture consists of a mat or two to sleep upon, a few earthen vessels, and a hand-mill to grind the corn. In many villages, large pigeon-houses, of a square form, but with the walls slightly inclining inwards (like many of the ancient Egyptian buildings), or of the form of a sugar-loaf, are constructed upon the roofs of the huts, with crude brick, pottery, and mud.[2] Most of the villages of Egypt are situate upon eminences of rubbish, which rise a few feet above the reach of the inundation, and are surrounded by palm-trees, or have a few of these trees in their vicinity.

---

1 Franks, however, are now exempted from this restriction.

2 The earthen pots used in the construction of these pigeon-houses are of an oval form, with a wide mouth, which is placed outwards, and a small hole at the other end. Each pair of pigeons occupies a separate pot.

The rubbish which they occupy chiefly consists of the materials of former huts, or of an ancient town, and seems to increase in about the same degree as the level of the alluvial plains and the bed of the river.

In a country where neither births nor deaths are registered, it is next to impossible to ascertain, with precision, the amount of the population. A few years before this work was written, a calculation was made, founded on the number of houses in Egypt, and the supposition that the inhabitants of each house in the metropolis amounted to eight persons, and in the provinces to four. This computation approximates, I believe, very nearly to the truth; but personal observation and inquiry incline me to think that the houses of such towns as Alexandria, Booláḳ, and Maṣr el-'Ateeḳah contain each, on the average, at least five persons: Rasheed (or Rosetta) is half deserted; but as to the crowded town of Dimyáṭ[1] (or Damietta), we must reckon as many as six persons to each house, or our estimate will fall far short of what is generally believed to be the number of its inhabitants. The addition of one or two persons to each house in the above-mentioned towns will, however, make little difference in the computation of the whole population of Egypt, which was found, by this mode of reckoning, to amount to rather more than 2,500,000; but it afterwards became reduced. Of 2,500,000 souls, I supposed about 1,200,000 to be males; and one-third of this number (400,000) to be men fit for military service: from this latter number Moḥammad 'Alee had taken, at the least, 200,000 (that is, one-half of the most serviceable portion of the male population,) to form and recruit his armies of regular troops, and for the service of his navy. The further loss caused by withdrawing so many men from their wives, or preventing their marrying, during ten years, must have far exceeded 300,000: consequently, I reckoned the whole population as less than two millions. The numbers of the principal classes of the population I found to be nearly as follow:—[2]

Muslim Egyptians (felláḥeen, or peasants, and townspeople)	1,750,000
Christian Egyptians (Copts)	150,000
'Osmánlees, or Turks	10,000
Syrians	5,000
Greeks	5,000
Armenians	2,000
Jews	5,000

[1] Vulgarly called "Dumyáṭ."

[2] The numbers given in a recent Government census will be found in an Appendix to this work.

Of the remainder (namely, Arabians, Western Arabs, Nubians, Negro slaves, Memlooks [or white male slaves], female white slaves, Franks, &c.), supposed to amount to about 70,000, the respective numbers are very uncertain and variable. The Arabs of the neighbouring deserts ought not to be included among the population of Egypt.[1]

Cairo, I have said, contained about 240,000 inhabitants when this work was written.[2] We should be greatly deceived if we judged of the population of this city from the crowds that we meet in the principal thoroughfare-streets and markets: in most of the by-streets and quarters very few passengers are seen. Nor should we judge from the extent of the city and suburbs; for there are within the walls many vacant places, some of which, during the season of the inundation, are lakes.[3] The gardens, several burial-grounds, the courts of houses, and the mosques, also occupy a considerable space. Of the inhabitants of the metropolis, I computed about 190,000 to be Egyptian Muslims; about 10,000, Copts; 3,000 or 4,000, Jews; and the rest, strangers from various countries.[4]

The population of Egypt in the times of the Pharaohs was probably about six or seven millions.[5] The produce of the soil in the present age would suffice, if none were exported, for the maintenance of a population amounting to 4,000,000; and if all the soil which is capable of cultivation were sown, the produce would be sufficient for the maintenance of 8,000,000. But this would be the utmost number that Egypt could maintain in years of plentiful inundation: I therefore compute the ancient population, at the time when agriculture was in a very flourishing state, to have amounted to what I first stated; and must suppose it to have been scarcely more than half as numerous in the times of the Ptolemies, and at later periods, when a great quantity of corn was annually exported.[6] This calculation agrees

1 The Muslim Egyptians, Copts, Syrians, and Jews of Egypt, with few exceptions, speak no language but the Arabic, which is also the language generally used by the foreigners settled in this country. The Nubians, among themselves, speak their own dialects.

2 The population of Cairo had increased to this amount, from about 200,000, within three or four years. Since the computation here stated was made, the plague of 1835 destroyed not fewer than one-third of its inhabitants, as before mentioned; but this deficiency was rapidly supplied from the villages.

3 The largest of these lakes, which was (as its place is still) called Birket El-Ezbekeeyeh, was filled up and planted with trees a few years after the present work was written.

4 About one-third of the population of the metropolis consists of adult males. Of this number I reckoned about 30,000 to be merchants, petty shopkeepers, and artisans; 20,000, domestic servants; 15,000, common labourers, porters, &c.: the remainder chiefly consisting of military and civil servants of the government.

5 I place but little reliance on the accounts of ancient authors on this subject.

6 It has been suggested to me, that, if corn was exported, something of equal value was imported; and that the exportation of corn, or anything else, would give a stimulus to industry and to population: but I do not know what could be imported that would fill up the measure of the food necessary to sustain a population much greater than that which would consume the corn retained.

with what Diodorus Siculus says (in lib. i. cap. 31); namely, that Egypt contained, in the times of the ancient kings, 7,000,000 inhabitants, and in his own time not less than 3,000,000.

In considering the policy of Moḥammad 'Alee, I could not but lament the difference of the state of Egypt under his rule from what it might be; possessing a population of scarcely more than one quarter of the number that it might be rendered capable of supporting! How great a change might have been effected in it by a truly enlightened government; by a prince who (instead of impoverishing the peasantry by depriving them of their lands, by his monopolies of the most valuable productions of the soil, and by employing the best portion of the population to prosecute his ambitious schemes of foreign conquest, and another large portion in the vain attempt to rival European manufactures,) would have given his people a greater interest in the cultivation of the fields, and made Egypt what nature designed it to be, almost exclusively an agricultural country! Its produce of cotton alone would more than suffice to procure all the articles of foreign manufacture, and all the natural productions of foreign countries, that the wants of its inhabitants demand.[1]

---

[1] During the year 1835 more than 100,000 bales of cotton (each bale weighing a hundred-weight and three-quarters) were shipped at Alexandria. The price paid for this quantity by the merchants exceeded 700,000*l.* The quantity exported in the year next preceding was 34,000 bales, which is considerably less than usual.

CHAPTER I.

PERSONAL CHARACTERISTICS, AND DRESS, OF THE MUSLIM EGYPTIANS.

Muslims, in a great degree of Arabian origin, have, for many centuries, mainly composed the population of Egypt: they have changed its language, laws, and general manners; and its metropolis they have made the principal seat of Arabian learning and arts. To the description of this people, and especially of the middle and higher classes in the Egyptian capital, will be devoted the chief portion of the present work. In every point of view, Maṣr (or Cairo) must be regarded as the first Arab city of our age; and the manners and customs of its inhabitants are particularly interesting, as they are a combination of those which prevail most generally in the towns of Arabia, Syria, and the whole of Northern Africa, and in a great degree in Turkey. There is no other place in which we can obtain so complete a knowledge of the most civilized classes of the Arabs.

From statements made in the introduction to this work, it appears that Muslim Egyptians (or Arab-Egyptians) compose nearly four-fifths of the population of the metropolis, and just seven-eighths of that of all Egypt.

The Muslim Egyptians are a mixed race, in a great measure descended from various Arab tribes and families which have settled in Egypt at different periods, mostly soon after the conquest of this country by 'Amr, its first Arab governor. These Arab immigrants were chiefly tribes of the desert; but their abandonment of the life of wanderers for that of agriculturists or citizens, and the frequent intermarriages of themselves and their descendants with Copts who became proselytes to the faith of El-Islám, have resulted in the production of a race bearing, in general, much resemblance to the ancient Egyptians; whose type was predominantly Caucasian, but inclining in various degrees towards that of the Negro. In many individuals among them we find this resemblance to be strikingly exact, though more frequently in Copts and in Nubians; and in the Muslim Egyptians (as well as in the Copts) it is generally most observable in Middle and Upper Egypt. Yet they are to be regarded as not less genuine Arabs than many of the townspeople of Arabia itself; among whom has long and very generally prevailed a custom of keeping Galla and Abyssinian female slaves, either instead of marrying their own countrywomen, or (as is commonly the case with the opulent) in addition to their Arab wives: so that they now bear almost as much resemblance to the Gallas and Abyssinians as to the Bedawees, or Arabs of the Desert. Such, at least, is the case in the towns of the south-western side of Arabia: in the southern parts of that country, the townspeople are much intermixed with Indian and Malayan races, as well as with Africans. In the Egyptians in general, and in the Arabians also though in a less degree, an admixture of aboriginal African blood is plainly discernible. The term "'Arab,"[1] it should here be remarked, is now used, wherever the Arabic language is spoken, only to designate the Bedawees, collectively: in speaking of a tribe, or of a small number of those people, the word "'Orban" is also used; and a single individual is called "Bedawee."[2] In the metropolis and other towns of Egypt, the distinction of tribes is almost wholly lost; but it is preserved among the peasants, who have retained many Bedawee customs, of which I shall have to speak. In various parts of the country, there are families, or small tribes, descended from Arab settlers who have generally disdained marrying women of less pure race than themselves; and these are hardly, if at all, to be distinguished in their persons from the tribes in the Arabian deserts. The native Muslim inhabitants of Cairo commonly call themselves "El-Maṣreeyeen," "Owlád-Maṣr" (or "Ahl-Maṣr"), and "Owlád-el-Beled," which signify People of Maṣr, Children of Maṣr, and Children of the Town: the singular forms of these appellations are "Maṣree," "Ibn-Maṣr," and "Ibn-el-Beled."[3] Of these three terms, the last is most common in the town itself. The country people are called "El-Felláḥeen" (or the agriculturists), in the singular "Felláḥ."[4] The Turks often

---

[1] This term was formerly used to designate the Arabian *townspeople* and *villagers*, while the Arabs who dwelt in the *Desert* were called "Aạráb," or "Aạrábees." The Arabs dwelling in houses now term themselves "Owlád-el-'Arab," or Sons of the Arabs.

[2] Feminine, "Bedaweeyeh."

[3] In the feminine, "Maṣreeyeh," "Bint-Maṣr," and "Bint-el-Beled."

[4] Feminine, "Felláḥah."

apply this term to the Egyptians in general in an abusive sense, as meaning the "boors," or "the clowns;" and improperly stigmatize them with the appellation of "Ahl-Far'oon,"[1] or "the People of Pharaoh;" the latter, when they dare to do so, retorting by calling the former "Ahl-Nemrood," or "the People of Nimrod."

In general, the Muslim Egyptians attain the height of about five feet eight, or five feet nine inches. Most of the children under nine or ten years of age have spare limbs and a distended abdomen; but, as they grow up, their forms rapidly improve: in mature age, most of them are remarkably well-proportioned; the men, muscular and robust; the women, very beautifully formed, and plump; and neither sex is too fat. I have never seen corpulent persons among them, except a few in the metropolis and other towns, rendered so by a life of inactivity. In Cairo, and throughout the northern provinces, where immigrants from more temperate climates have been most numerous, those who have not been much exposed to the sun have a yellowish, but very clear complexion, and soft skin; the rest are of a considerably darker and coarser complexion. The people of Middle Egypt are of a more tawny colour; and those of the more southern provinces are of a deep bronze or brown complexion, darkest towards Nubia, where the climate is hottest, and where Egyptians gradually give place to Nubians. In general, the countenance of the Muslim Egyptian (I here speak of the *men*) is of a fine oval form: the forehead, of moderate size, seldom high, but generally prominent: the eyes are deep sunk, or appear to be so in consequence of a common habit of depressing the eyebrows for the sake of shade; and are black and brilliant; but not without some resemblance to those of Ethiopian races: the nose is straight, but rather thick: the mouth well formed: the lips are rather full than otherwise: the teeth particularly beautiful; and so, if we may judge from the generality of the mummies, were those of the ancient Egyptians:[2] the beard is commonly black and curly, but scanty. I have seen very few individuals among them with gray eyes; and these may be reasonably regarded as the offspring or descendants of Egyptian women by Europeans or by other foreigners. The Felláheen, from constant exposure to the sun, have a habit of half-shutting their eyes: this is also characteristic of the Bedawees.

---

[1] Thus commonly pronounced for "Fir'own."

[2] Tooth-ache is, however, a very common disorder in Egypt, as it was in ancient times: this, at least, was probably the case, as Herodotus (lib. ii. cap. 84) mentions dentists among the classes of Egyptian physicians. It is, of course, most prevalent among the higher orders.

Great numbers of the Egyptians are blind in one or both of the eyes. They generally shave portions of the beard above and below the lower jaw, and likewise a small portion under the lower lip, leaving, however, after the example of the Prophet, the hairs that grow in the middle under the mouth; or, instead of shaving these parts, they pluck out the hair. Very few shave the rest of the beard,[1] and none the mustache. The former they suffer to grow to the length of about a hand's breadth below the chin (such, at least, is the general rule, and such was the custom of the Prophet); and (in imitation of the Prophet) the mustache they do not allow to become so long as to hide completely the skin beneath, or to extend in the least over the upper lip and thus incommode them in eating and drinking. The practice of dyeing the beard is not common; for a gray beard is much respected. The Egyptians shave all the rest of the hair, or leave only a small tuft (called "shoosheh") upon the crown of the head.[2] This last custom (which is almost universal among them) is said to have originated in the fear that if the Muslim should fall into the hands of an infidel, and be slain, the latter might cut off the head of his victim, and, finding no hair by which to hold it, put his impure hand into the mouth, in order to carry it; for the beard might not be sufficiently long: but it was probably adopted from the Turks; for it is generally neglected by the Bedawees; and the custom of shaving the head is of late origin among the Arabs in general, and practised for the sake of cleanliness.[3] With the like view of avoiding impurity, the Egyptians observe other customs, which need not here be described.[4] Many men of the lower orders, and some others, make blue marks upon their arms, and sometimes upon the hands and chest, as do the women, in speaking of whom this operation will be described.

The dress of the men of the middle and higher classes consists of the following articles.[5] First, a pair of full drawers[6] of linen or

---

1 A few of the servants, generally the grooms, and some others, shave their beards, but none shaves his mustache. The respect which Orientals in general pay to the beard has often been remarked. They swear by it, and say that a man disgraces it by an evil action. The punishment recorded in 2 Samuel, x. 4, has frequently been practised in modern times, but not so often as the shaving of the whole of the beard.

2 The Muslims hold it to be inconsistent with the honour that is due to everything that has appertained to the human body to leave upon the ground the shavings or clippings of hair, the parings of nails, &c.; which, therefore, they generally bury in the earth, or otherwise conceal; the women commonly stuffing them into crevices in the walls of rooms.

3 Persons of literary and religious professions generally disapprove of the shoosheh.

4 They are mentioned in the "Mishcát-ul-Masábíh," vol. ii. p. 359, and are observed by both sexes.

5 The fashion of their dress remains almost the same during the lapse of centuries.

6 In Arabic, "libás."

Men of the Middle and Higher Classes.

cotton, tied round the body by a running string or band,[1] the ends of which are embroidered with coloured silks, though concealed by the outer dress. The drawers descend a little below the knees, or to the ankles; but many of the Arabs will not wear long drawers, because prohibited by the Prophet. Next is worn a shirt,[2] with very full sleeves, reaching to the wrist: it is made of linen, of a loose, open texture, or of cotton stuff, or of muslin, or silk, or of a mixture of silk and cotton, in stripes, but all white.[3] Over this, in winter, or in cool weather, most persons wear a "ṣudeyree,"[4] which is a short vest of cloth, or of striped coloured silk and cotton, without sleeves.[5] Over the shirt and the ṣudeyree, or the former alone, is worn a long vest of striped silk and cotton[6] (called "ḳafṭán," or more commonly "ḳufṭán"), descending to the ankles, with long sleeves extending a few inches beyond the fingers' ends, but divided from a point a little above the wrist, or about the middle of the fore-arm; so that the hand is generally exposed, though it may be concealed by the sleeve when necessary; for it is customary to cover the hands in the presence of a person of high rank. Round this vest is wound the girdle,[7] which is a coloured shawl, or a long piece of white figured muslin. The ordinary outer robe is a long cloth coat, of any colour, called by the Turks "jubbeh," but by the Egyptians "gibbeh," the sleeves of which reach not quite to the wrist.[8] Some persons also wear a "beneesh," or "benish;" which is a robe of cloth, with long sleeves, like those of the ḳufṭán, but more ample:[9] it is, properly, a robe of ceremony, and should be worn over the other cloth coat; but many persons wear it *instead* of the gibbeh. Another robe, called "farageeyeh," nearly resembles the beneesh: it has very long sleeves; but these are not slit; and it is chiefly worn by men of the learned professions. In cold or cool weather, a kind of black woollen cloak, called "'abáyeh," is commonly worn.[10] Sometimes this is drawn over the head. In winter also many persons wrap a muslin or other shawl (such as they use for a turban) about the head and shoulders.

---

[1] Called "dikkeh," or "tikkeh."

[2] "Ḳameeṣ."

[3] The Prophet forbade men to wear silk clothing, but allowed women to do so. The prohibition is, however, attended to by very few modern Muslims, except the Wahhábees.

[4] More properly, "ṣudeyreh."

[5] In this, as in all the other under-clothing of the Egyptians, the back is of the same material as the front.

[6] The stripes are seldom plain: they are generally figured or flowered.

[7] "Ḥezám."

[8] See the foremost figure in the preceding engraving.

[9] See the figure to the left in the same engraving.

[10] See engraving, p. 33, in which is represented a striped 'abáyeh. This garment is also called "'abáäh," and "'abà."

The head-dress consists, first, of a small, close-fitting, cotton cap,[1] which is often changed; next, a "ṭarboosh," which is a red cloth cap, also fitting close to the head, with a tassel of dark-blue silk at the crown; lastly, a long piece of white muslin, generally figured, or a Kashmeer shawl, which is wound round the ṭarboosh. Thus is formed the turban.[2] The Kashmeer shawl is seldom worn except in cool weather. Some persons wear two or three ṭarbooshes, one over another. A "shereef" (or descendant of the Prophet) wears a green turban, or is privileged to do so; but no other person; and it is not common for any but a shereef to wear a bright green dress. Stockings are not in use; but some few persons, in cold weather, wear woollen or cotton socks. The shoes[3] are of thick red morocco, pointed and turning up at the toes. Some persons also wear inner shoes[4] of soft yellow morocco, and with soles of the same: the outer shoes are taken off on stepping upon a carpet or mat; but not the inner: for this reason, the former are often worn turned down at the heel.

On the little finger of the right hand is worn a seal-ring,[5] which is generally of silver, with a carnelion, or other stone, upon which is engraved the wearer's name: the name is usually accompanied by the words "his servant" (signifying "the servant, or worshipper, of God"), and often by other words expressive of the person's trust in God, &c.[6] The Prophet disapproved of gold; therefore few Muslims wear gold rings: but the women have various ornaments (rings, bracelets, &c.,) of that precious metal. The seal-ring is used for signing letters and other writings; and its impression is considered more valid than the sign-manual.[7] A little ink is dabbed upon it with one of the fingers, and it is pressed upon the paper; the person who uses it having first touched his tongue with another finger, and moistened the place in the paper which is to be stamped. Almost every person who can afford it has a seal-ring, even though he be a servant. The regular scribes, literary men, and many others, wear a silver, brass, or copper "dawáyeh," which is an inkhorn, or a case with receptacles for ink and pens, stuck in the girdle.[8] Some have, in the place of this, or in addition to it, a case-knife, or a dagger.

---

1 Called "ṭáḳeeyeh," or "'araḳeeyeh."

2 "'Emámeh," vulg. "'Immeh."

3 "Markoob."

4 "Mezz," or, more properly, "mezd;" from the Turkish "mest."

5 "Khátim."—It is *allowable* to wear it on a finger of the *left* hand.

6 See St. John's Gospel, iii. 33; and Exodus, xxxix. 30.

7 Therefore, giving the ring to another person is the utmost mark of confidence.—See Genesis, xli. 42.

8 This is a very ancient custom.—See Ezekiel, ix. 2, 3, 11.—The dawáyeh is represented in a cut in Chapter IX. of this work.

The Egyptian generally takes his pipe with him wherever he goes (unless it be to the mosque), or has a servant to carry it, though it is not a common custom to smoke while riding or walking. The tobacco-purse he crams into his bosom, the ḳufṭán being large, and lapping over in front. A handkerchief, embroidered with coloured silks and gold, and neatly folded, is also placed in the bosom.

Many persons of the middle orders, who wish to avoid being thought rich, conceal such a dress as I have described by a long black gown of cotton, similar to the gown worn by most persons of the lower classes.

The costume of the men of the lower orders is very simple. These, if not of the very poorest class, wear a pair of drawers, and a long and full shirt or gown of blue linen or cotton, or of brown woollen stuff (the former called "'eree," and the latter "zaạbooṭ"), open from the neck nearly to the waist, and having wide sleeves.[1] Over this, some wear a white or red woollen girdle; for which servants often substitute a broad red belt,[2] of woollen stuff or of leather, generally containing a receptacle for money. Their turban is generally composed of a white, red, or yellow woollen shawl, or of a piece of coarse cotton or muslin, wound round a ṭarboosh, under which is a white or brown felt cap;[3] but many are so poor as to have no other cap than the latter—no turban, nor even drawers, nor shoes, but only the blue or brown shirt, or merely a few rags; while many, on the other hand, wear a ṣudeyree under the blue shirt; and some, particularly servants in the houses of great men, wear a white shirt, a ṣudeyree, and a ḳufṭán or gibbeh, or both, and the blue shirt over all. The full sleeves of this shirt are sometimes drawn up, by means of a cord,[4] which passes round each shoulder and crosses behind, where it is tied in a knot. This custom is adopted by servants (particularly grooms), who have cords of crimson or dark-blue silk for this purpose. In cold weather, many persons of the lower classes wear an 'abáyeh, like that before described, but coarser, and sometimes (instead of being black) having broad stripes, brown and white, or blue and white, but the latter rarely. Another kind of cloak, more full than the 'abáyeh, of black or deep-blue woollen stuff, is also very commonly worn: it is called "diffeeyeh."[5] The shoes are of red or yellow morocco, or of sheep-

[1] The zaạbooṭ is mostly worn in the winter.
[2] Called "kamar."
[3] Called "libdeh."
[4] Called "shimár."
[5] A kind of blue and white plaid (called "miláyeh") is also worn by some men, but more commonly by women, in the account of whose dress it will be further described: the men throw it over the shoulders, or wrap it about the body.

Men of the Lower Classes.

skin. Those of the groom are of dark-red morocco: those of the door-keeper and the water-carrier of a private house, generally yellow.

Several different forms of turbans are represented in some of the engravings which illustrate this work. The Muslims are distinguished by the colours of their turbans from the Copts and the Jews, who (as well as other subjects of the Turkish Sulṭán who are not Muslims) wear black, blue, gray, or light-brown turbans, and generally dull-coloured dresses. The distinction of sects, families, dynasties, &c., among the Muslim Arabs, by the colour of the turban and other articles of dress, is of very early origin. When the Imám Ibráheem Ibn-Moḥammad, asserting his pretensions to the dignity of Khaleefeh,[1] was put to death by the Umawee Khaleefeh Marwán, many persons of the family of El-'Abbás assumed black clothing, in testimony of their sorrow for his fate; and hence the black dress and turban (which latter is now characteristic, almost solely, of Christian and Jewish tributaries to the 'Osmánlee, or Turkish, Sulṭán,) became the distinguishing costume of the 'Abbásee Khaleefehs, and of their officers. When an officer under this dynasty was disgraced, he was made to wear a white dress. White was adopted by the false prophet El-Muḳanna', to distinguish his party from the 'Abbásees; and the Fawáṭim of Egypt (or Khaleefehs of the race of Fáṭimeh), as rivals of the 'Abbásees, wore a white costume. El-Melik el-Ashraf Shaạbán, a Sulṭán of Egypt (who reigned from the year of the Flight 764 to 778, or A.D. 1362 to 1376), was the first who ordered the "shereefs" to distinguish themselves by the green turban and dress. Some darweeshes of the sect of the Rifá'ees, and a few, but very few, other Muslims, wear a turban of black woollen stuff, or of a very deep olive-coloured (almost black) muslin; but that of the Copts, Jews, &c., is generally of black or blue muslin, or linen. There are not many different *forms* of turbans now worn in Egypt: that worn by most of the servants is peculiarly formal, consisting of several spiral twists, one above another like the threads of a screw. The kind common among the middle and higher classes of the tradesmen and other citizens of the metropolis and large towns is also very formal, but less so than that just before alluded to. The Turkish turban worn in Egypt is of a more elegant fashion. The Syrian is distinguished by its width. The 'Ulamà, and men of religion and letters in general, used to wear, as some do still, one particularly wide and formal, called a "muḳleh."

---

[1] Commonly written by English authors "Caliph," or "Khalif."

The turban is much respected. In the houses of the more wealthy classes, there is usually a chair[1] on which it is placed at night. This is often sent with the furniture of a bride; as it is common for a lady to have one upon which to place her head-dress. It is never used for any other purpose. As an instance of the respect paid to the turban,

The Muḳleh.

one of my friends mentioned to me that an 'álim[2] being thrown off his donkey in a street of this city, his muḳleh fell off, and rolled along for several yards: whereupon the passengers ran after it, crying, "Lift up the crown of El-Islám!" while the poor 'álim, whom no one came to assist, called out in anger, "Lift up the *sheykh*[3] of El-Islám!"

The general form and features of the *women* must now be described. From the age of about fourteen to that of eighteen or twenty, they are generally models of beauty in body and limbs;[4] and in countenance most of them are pleasing, and many exceedingly lovely: but soon after they have attained their perfect growth, they rapidly decline; the bosom early loses all its beauty, acquiring, from the relaxing nature of the climate, an excessive length and flatness in its forms, even while the face retains its full charms; and though, in most other respects, time does not commonly so soon nor so much deform them, at the age of forty it renders many, who in earlier years possessed considerable attractions, absolutely ugly. In the Egyptian females, the forms of womanhood begin to develop themselves about the ninth or tenth year: at the age of fifteen or sixteen they generally attain their highest degree of perfection. With regard to their complexions, the same remarks apply to them as to the men, with only this differ-

1 Called "kursee el-'emámeh."

2 This appellation (of which "'ulamà" is the plural) signifies a man of science or learning.

3 "Sheykh" here signifies *master*, or *doctor*.

4 The dress of many of the females in the villages is such as displays much of the person; and a man often comes unexpectedly in close view of a group of maidens bathing in the Nile.

ence, that their faces, being generally veiled when they go abroad, are not quite so much tanned as those of the men. They are characterized, like the men, by a fine oval countenance; though, in some instances, it is rather broad. The eyes, with very few exceptions, are black, large, and of a long almond-form, with long and beautiful lashes, and an exquisitely soft, bewitching expression: eyes more beautiful can hardly be conceived: their charming effect is much heightened by the concealment of the other features (however pleasing the latter may be), and is rendered still more striking by a practice universal among the females of the higher and middle classes, and very common among those of the lower orders, which is that of blackening the edge of the eyelids, both above and below the eye, with a black powder called "koḥl." This is a collyrium commonly composed of the smoke-black

An Eye ornamented with Koḥl.

which is produced by burning a kind of "libán," an aromatic resin, a species of frankincense, used, I am told, in preference to the better kind of frankincense, as being cheaper, and equally good for this purpose. Koḥl is also prepared of the smoke-black produced by burning the shells of almonds. These two kinds, though believed to be beneficial to the eyes, are used merely for ornament; but there are several kinds used for their real or supposed medical properties; particularly the powder of several kinds of lead ore;[1] to which are often added sarcocolla,[2] long pepper,[3] sugar-candy, fine dust of a Venetian sequin, and sometimes powdered pearls. Antimony, it is said, was formerly used for painting the edges of the eyelids. The koḥl is applied with a small probe, of wood, ivory, or silver, tapering towards the end, but blunt: this is moistened, sometimes with rose-water, then dipped in the powder, and drawn along the edges of the eyelids: it is called "mirwed;" and the glass vessel in which the koḥl is kept, "muk-ḥulah."[4] The custom of thus ornamenting the eyes prevailed among both sexes in Egypt in very ancient times: this is shewn by the sculptures and paintings in the temples and tombs of this country; and koḥl-vessels, with the probes, and even with remains of the black

---

1 "Koḥl el-ḥagar."
2 "'Anzaroot."
3 "'Erḳ ed-dahab."
4 Pronounced "muk-ḥul'ah."

powder, have often been found in the ancient tombs. But in many

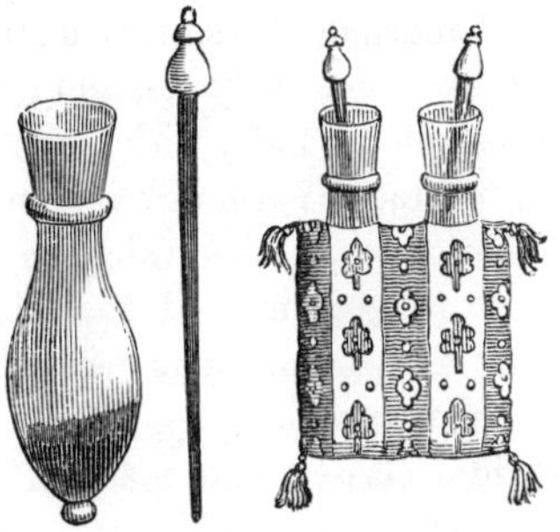

Muk-ḥulahs and Mirweds.
These are represented on scales of one-third, and a quarter, of the real size.

Ancient Vessel and Probe for Koḥl.

cases, the ancient mode of ornamenting with the koḥl was a little different from the modern, as shewn by the subjoined sketch: I have,

An Eye and Eyebrow ornamented with Koḥl, as represented in ancient Paintings.

however, seen this ancient mode practised in the present day in the neighbourhood of Cairo; though I only remember to have noticed it in two instances. The same custom existed among the ancient Greek ladies, and among the Jewish women in early times.[1] The eyes of the Egyptian women are generally the most beautiful of their features. Countenances altogether handsome are far less common among this race than handsome figures; but I have seen among them faces distinguished by a style of beauty possessing such sweetness of expression that they have struck me as exhibiting the perfection of female loveliness, and impressed me at the time with the idea that their equals could not be found in any other country. Few, however, of the Egyptian women suffer themselves to be seen unveiled by men who are not their near relations; and those who do so are generally such as are conscious of possessing some degree of beauty, which they like to exhibit, though usually pretending the display to be uninten-

[1] See 2 Kings, ix. 30 (where, in our common version, we find the words, "painted her face" for "painted her eyes"), and Ezekiel, xxiii. 40.—Scissors are often used to reduce the width of the eyebrows, and to give them a more arched form.

tional. The stranger, therefore, cannot form a correct general opinion from the specimens that he sees of these women: but with such eyes as many of them have, the face must be handsome if its other features are but moderately well formed. The nose is generally straight; and the lips are mostly rather fuller than those of the men, without in the least degree partaking of the Negro character: though in many instances, an approach to the Ethiopian type is observable in the mouth as well as in the other features. The hair is of that deep, glossy black, which best suits all but fair complexions: in some instances it is rather coarse, and crisp, but never woolly.

The females of the higher and middle classes, and many of the

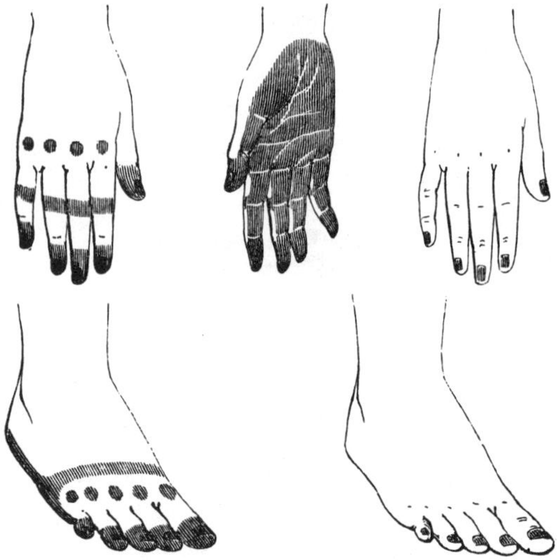

Hands and Feet stained with Ḥennà.

poorer women, stain certain parts of their hands and feet (which are, with very few exceptions, beautifully formed,) with the leaves of the ḥennà-tree,[1] which impart a yellowish red, or deep-orange colour. Many thus dye only the nails of the fingers and toes; others extend the dye as high as the first joint of each finger and toe; some also make a stripe along the next row of joints; and there are several other fanciful modes of applying the ḥennà; but the most common practice is to dye the tips of the fingers and toes as high as the first joint, and the whole of the inside of the hand and the sole of the foot;[2] adding,

[1] *Lawsonia inermis;* also called "Egyptian privet."

[2] The application of this dye to the palms of the hands and the soles of the feet is said to have an agreeable effect upon the skin; particularly to prevent its being too tender and sensitive.

though not always, the stripe above mentioned along the middle joints of the fingers, and a similar stripe a little above the toes. The ḥennà is prepared for this use merely by being powdered, and mixed with a little water, so as to form a paste. Some of this paste being spread in the palm of the hand, and on other parts of it which are to be dyed, and the fingers being doubled, and their extremities inserted into the paste in the palm, the whole hand is tightly bound with linen, and remains thus during a whole night. In a similar manner it is applied to the feet. The colour does not disappear until after many days: it is generally renewed after about a fortnight or three weeks. This custom prevails not only in Egypt, but in several other countries of the East, which are supplied with ḥennà from the banks of the Nile. To the nails, the ḥennà imparts a more bright, clear, and permanent colour than to the skin. When this dye alone is applied to the nails, or to a larger portion of the fingers and toes, it may, with some reason, be regarded as an embellishment; for it makes the general complexion of the hand and foot appear more delicate; but many ladies stain their hands in a manner much less agreeable to our taste: by applying, immediately after the removal of the paste of ḥennà, another paste composed of quicklime, common smoke-black, and linseed-oil, they convert the tint of the ḥennà to a black, or to a blackish-olive hue. Ladies in Egypt are often seen with their nails stained with this colour, or with their fingers of the same dark hue from the extremity to the first joint, red from the first to the second joint, and of the former colour from the second to the third joint; with the palm also stained in a similar manner, having a broad, dark stripe across the middle, and the rest left red; the thumb dark from the extremity to the first joint, and red from the first to the second joint. Some, after a more simple fashion, blacken the ends of the fingers and the whole of the inside of the hand.

Among the females of the lower orders, in the country-towns and villages of Egypt, and among the same classes in the metropolis, but in a less degree, prevails a custom somewhat similar to that above described: it consists in making indelible marks of a blue or greenish hue upon the face and other parts, or, at least, upon the front of the chin, and upon the back of the right hand, and often also upon the left hand, the right arm, or both arms, the feet, the middle of the bosom, and the forehead: the most common of these marks made upon the chin and hands are represented in the next page. The operation is performed with several needles (generally seven) tied together: with these the skin is pricked in the desired pattern: some smoke-black (of wood or oil), mixed with milk from the breast of a woman, is then rubbed in; and about a week after, before the skin has healed, a paste of the pounded fresh leaves of white beet or clover is applied, and gives a blue or greenish colour to the marks: or, to produce the

A tattooed Girl.

Specimens of tattooing on the Chin.

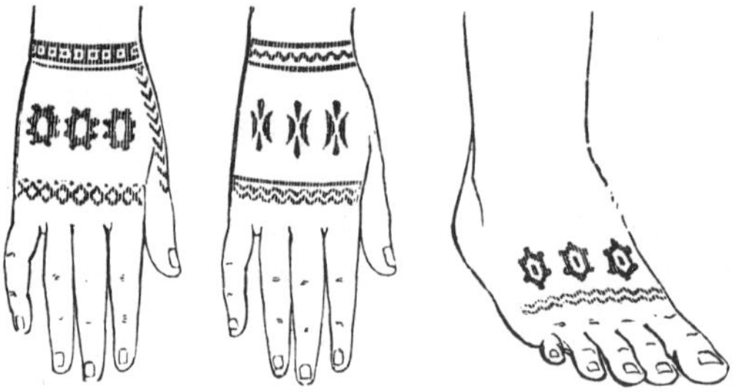

Tattooed Hands and Foot.

same effect, in a more simple manner, some indigo is rubbed into the punctures, instead of the smoke-black, &c. It is generally performed at the age of about five or six years, and by gipsy-women. The term applied to it is "daḳḳ." Most of the females of the higher parts of Upper Egypt (who are of a very dark complexion), for the purpose of making their teeth to glisten, tattoo their lips instead of the parts above mentioned; thus converting their natural colour to a dull, bluish hue, which, to the eye of a stranger, is extremely displeasing.[1]

Another characteristic of the Egyptian women that should be here mentioned, is their upright carriage and gait. This is most remarkable in the female peasantry, owing, doubtless, in a great measure, to their habit of bearing a heavy earthen water-vessel, and other burdens, upon the head.

The dress of the women of the middle and higher orders is handsome and elegant. Their shirt is very full, like that of the men, but shorter, not reaching to the knees: it is also, generally, of the same kind of material as the men's shirt, or of coloured crape, sometimes black. A pair of very wide trousers (called "shintiyán"), of a coloured, striped stuff of silk and cotton, or of printed, or worked, or plain white, muslin, is tied round the hips, under the shirt,[2] with a dikkeh: its lower extremities are drawn up and tied just below the knee with running strings; but it is sufficiently long to hang down to the feet, or almost to the ground, when attached in this manner. Over the shirt and shintiyán is worn a long vest (called "yelek"), of the same material as the latter: it nearly resembles the ḳufṭán of the men; but is more tight to the body and arms: the sleeves also are longer; and it is made to button down the front, from the bosom to a little below the girdle, instead of lapping over: it is open, likewise, on each side, from the height of the hip, downwards. In general, the yelek is cut in such a manner as to leave half of the bosom uncovered, except by the shirt; but many ladies have it made more ample at that part: and, according to the most approved fashion, it should be of a sufficient length to reach to the ground, or should exceed that length by two or three inches, or more. A short vest

1 The depilatory most commonly used by the Egyptian women is a kind of resin, called libán shámee, applied in a melted state: but this, they pretend, is not always necessary: by applying the blood of a bat to the skin of a newly-born female infant, on the parts where they wish no hair to grow, they assert that they accomplish this desire. A female upon whom this application has been made is termed "muwaṭwaṭah;" from "waṭwáṭ," a bat. Some women pluck out the hair after merely rubbing the part with the ashes of charcoal.

2 Turkish ladies (I am told) generally tie it *over* the shirt.

A Lady in the Dress worn in private.

(called "'anteree"[1]), reaching only a little below the waist, and exactly resembling a yelek of which the lower part has been cut off, is sometimes worn instead of the latter. A square shawl, or an embroidered kerchief, doubled diagonally, is put loosely round the waist as a girdle; the two corners that are folded together hanging down behind: or, sometimes, the lady's girdle is folded after the ordinary Turkish fashion, like that of the men, but more loosely. Over the yelek is worn a gibbeh of cloth, or velvet, or silk, usually embroidered with gold or with coloured silk: it differs in form from the gibbeh of the men chiefly in being not so wide; particularly in the fore part; and is of the same length as the yelek. Instead of this, a jacket (called "salṭah"), generally of cloth or velvet, and embroidered in the same manner as the gibbeh, is often worn. The head-dress consists of a ṭáḳeeyeh and ṭarboosh, with a square kerchief (called "faroodeeyeh") of printed or painted muslin, or one of crape, wound tightly round, composing what is called a "rabṭah." Two or more such kerchiefs were commonly used, a short time since, and are still sometimes, to form the ladies' turban, but always wound in a high, flat shape, very different from that of the turban of the men. A kind of crown, called "ḳurṣ," and other ornaments, are attached to the ladies' head-dress: descriptions and engravings of these and other ornaments of the women of Egypt will be found in the Appendix to this work. A long piece of white muslin embroidered at each end with coloured silks and gold, or of coloured crape ornamented with gold thread, &c., and spangles, rests upon the head, and hangs down behind, nearly or quite to the ground: this is called "ṭarḥah"—it is the head-veil: the face-veil I shall presently describe. The hair, except over the forehead and temples, is divided into numerous braids or plaits, generally from eleven to twenty-five in number, but always of an *uneven* number: these hang down the back. To each braid of hair are usually added three black silk cords, with little ornaments of gold, &c., attached to them. For a description of these, which are called "ṣafà," I refer to the Appendix. Over the forehead, the hair is cut rather short; but two full locks[2] hang down on each side of the face: these are often curled in ringlets, and sometimes plaited.[3] Few of the ladies of Egypt wear stockings or socks, but many of them wear "mezz" (or inner shoes), of yellow or red morocco, sometimes em-

1 Pronounced "'anter'ee."

2 Called "maḳáṣeeṣ;" singular "maḳṣooṣ."

3 Egyptian women swear by the side-lock (as men do by the beard), generally holding it when they utter the oath, "Wa-ḥayát maḳṣooṣee!"

A Lady adorned with the Ḳurṣ and Ṣafà, &c.—(*The Hand is partially stained with Ḥennà.*)

broidered with gold: over these, whenever they step off the matted or carpeted part of the floor, they put on "báboog" (or slippers) of yellow morocco, with high, pointed toes; or use high wooden clogs or pattens,[1] generally from four to nine inches in height, and usually ornamented with mother-of-pearl, or silver, &c. These are always used in the bath by men and women, but not by many ladies at home: some ladies wear them merely to keep their skirts from trailing on the ground: others, to make themselves appear tall.—Such is the dress which is worn by the Egyptian ladies in the house.

The riding or walking attire is called "tezyeereh." Whenever a lady leaves the house, she wears, in addition to what has been above described, first a large, loose gown (called "tób," or "sebleh"), the sleeves of which are nearly equal in width to the whole length of the gown:[2] it is of silk; generally of a pink, or rose, or violet colour. Next is put on the "burḳo'," or face-veil, which is a long strip of white muslin, concealing the whole of the face except the eyes, and reaching nearly to the feet. It is suspended at the top by a narrow band, which passes up the forehead, and which is sewed, as are also the two upper corners of the veil, to a band that is tied round the head. The lady then covers herself with a "ḥabarah," which, for a married lady, is composed of two breadths of glossy, black silk, each ell-wide, and three yards long: these are sewed together, at or near the selvages (according to the height of the person); the seam running horizontally, with respect to the manner in which it is worn: a piece of narrow black riband is sewed inside the upper part, about six inches from the edge, to tie round the head. This covering is generally worn by the Egyptian ladies in the manner shewn by the sketch in the next page; but some of them imitate the Turkish ladies of Egypt in holding the front part so as to conceal all but that portion of the veil that is above the hands. The unmarried ladies wear a ḥabarah of white silk, or a shawl. Some females of the middle classes, who cannot afford to purchase a ḥabarah, wear instead of it an "eezár," or "izár;" which is a piece of white calico, of the same form and size as the former, and is worn in the same manner. On the feet are worn short boots or socks (called "khuff"), of yellow morocco, and over these the "báboog."

This dress, though chiefly designed for females of the higher classes,

---

[1] Called "ḳabḳáb," or, more commonly, "ḳubḳáb."

[2] This is similar in form to the tób of women of the lower orders, represented in the engraving in page 48.

Ladies attired for Riding or Walking.

who are seldom seen in public on foot, is worn by many women who cannot often afford so far to imitate their superiors as to hire an ass to carry them. It is extremely inconvenient as a walking attire. Viewing it as a disguise for whatever is attractive or graceful in the person and adornments of the wearer, we should not find fault with it for being itself deficient in grace: we must remark, however, that, in one respect, it fails in accomplishing its main purpose; displaying the eyes, which are almost always beautiful; making them to appear still more so by concealing the other features, which are seldom of equal beauty; and often causing the stranger to imagine a defective face perfectly charming. The veil is of very remote antiquity;[1] but, from the sculptures and paintings of the ancient Egyptians, it seems not to have been worn by the females of that nation. In the present day, even the female servants generally draw a portion of the head-veil before the face in the presence of the men of the family whom they serve, so as to leave only one eye visible.

The dress of a large proportion of those women of the lower orders who are not of the poorest class consists of a pair of trousers or drawers (similar in form to the shintiyán of the ladies, but generally of plain white cotton or linen), a blue linen or cotton shirt (not quite so full as that of the men), reaching to the feet, a burḳo' of a kind of coarse black crape,[2] and a dark blue ṭarḥah of muslin or linen. Some wear, over the long shirt, or instead of the latter, a linen tób, of the same form as that of the ladies:[3] and within the long shirt, some wear a short white shirt; and some, a sudeyree also, or an 'anteree. The sleeves of the tób are often turned up over the head; either to prevent their being incommodious, or to supply the place of a ṭarḥah.[4] In addition to these articles of dress, many women who are not of the very poor classes wear, as a covering, a kind of plaid, similar in form to the ḥabarah, composed of two pieces of cotton, woven in small chequers of blue and white, or cross stripes, with a mixture of red at each end. It is called "miláyeh:"[5] in general it is worn in the same manner as the ḥabarah; but sometimes like the ṭarḥah.[6] The upper part of the black burḳo' is often ornamented with false pearls,

---

1 See Genesis, xxiv. 65; and Isaiah, iii. 23. See also 1 Corinthians, xi. 10, and a marginal note on that verse.

2 Some of those who are descended from the Prophet wear a green burḳo'.

3 See the figure to the left in page 48.

4 See the figure to the right in page 48.

5 For "muláäh."

6 There is a superior kind of miláyeh, of silk, and of various colours; but this is now seldom worn. The two pieces which compose the miláyeh are sewed together, like those which compose the ḥabarah."

Women and Children of the Lower Classes.

A Woman clad in the Miláyeh, &c.

small gold coins, and other little flat ornaments of the same metal (called "barḳ"); sometimes with a coral bead, and a gold coin

Ornamented black Veils.—*Only one of these (that to the right) is represented in its whole length.*

beneath; also with some coins of base silver; and more commonly with a pair of chain tassels, of brass or silver (called "'oyoon"), attached

The 'Aṣbeh.

to the corners. A square black silk kerchief (called "'aṣbeh"), with a border of red and yellow, is bound round the head, doubled

A Woman of the Southern Province of Upper Egypt.—(*Sketched at Thebes.*)

diagonally, and tied with a single knot behind; or, instead of this, the ṭarboosh and faroodeeyeh are worn, though by very few women of the lower classes. The best kind of shoes worn by the females of the lower orders are of red morocco, turned up, but generally round, at the toes. The burḳo' and shoes are most common in Cairo, and are also worn by many of the women throughout Lower Egypt; but in Upper Egypt, the burḳo is very seldom seen, and shoes are scarcely less uncommon. To supply the place of the former, when necessary, a portion of the ṭarḥah is drawn before the face, so as to conceal nearly all the countenance except one eye. Many of the women of the lower orders, even in the metropolis, never conceal their faces. Throughout the greater part of Egypt the most common dress of the women merely consists of the blue shirt, or tób, and ṭarḥah. In the southern parts of Upper Egypt, chiefly above Akhmeem,[1] most of the women envelop themselves in a large piece of dark-brown woollen stuff (called a "ḥulaleeyeh"), wrapping it round the body, and attaching the upper parts together over each shoulder;[2] and a piece of the same they use as a ṭarḥah. This dull dress, though picturesque, is almost as disguising as the blue tinge which, as I have before mentioned, the women in these parts of Egypt impart to their lips. Most of the women of the lower orders wear a variety of trumpery ornaments, such as ear-rings, necklaces, bracelets, &c., and sometimes a nose-ring. Descriptions and engravings of some of these ornaments will be found in the Appendix.

The women of Egypt deem it more incumbent upon them to cover the upper and back part of the head than the face; and more requisite to conceal the face than most other parts of the person. I have often seen, in this country, women but half covered with miserable rags; and several times, females in the prime of womanhood, and others in more advanced age, with nothing on the body but a narrow strip of rag bound round the hips.

---

1 Said to be more properly called Ikhmeem.

2 The reader will recognise, in this picturesque garment, an article of ancient Greek and Roman female attire.

CHAPTER II.

INFANCY AND EARLY EDUCATION.

In the rearing and general treatment of their children, the Muslims are chiefly guided by the directions of their Prophet, and other religious institutors. One of the first duties required to be performed on the birth of a child is to pronounce the adán (or call to prayer) in the infant's right ear; and this should be done by a male. Some persons also pronounce the iḳámeh (which is nearly the same as the adán) in the left ear.[1] The object of each of these ceremonies is to preserve the infant from the influence of the "ginn," or genii. Another custom, observed with the same view, is to say, "In the name of the Prophet and of his cousin[2] 'Alee!"

It was a custom very common in Egypt, as in other Muslim countries, to consult an astrologer previously to giving a name to a child, and to be guided by his choice; but very few persons now conform with this old usage: the father makes choice of a name for his son, and confers it without any ceremony: a daughter is generally named by her mother. Boys are often named after the Prophet (Moḥammad, Aḥmad, or Muṣṭafà[3]), or some of the members of his family ('Alee, Ḥasan, Ḥoseyn, &c.), or his eminent companions ('Omar, 'Osmán, 'Amr, &c.), or some of the prophets and patriarchs of early times (as Ibráheem, Is-ḥáḳ, Isma'eel, Yaạḳoob, Moosà, Dáood,[4] Suleymán, &c.), or receive a name signifying "Servant of God," "Servant of the Compassionate," "Servant of the Powerful," &c. ('Abd-Allah, 'Abd-Er-Raḥmán, 'Abd-El-Ḳádir). Girls are mostly named after the wives or the favourite daughter of the Arabian Prophet, or after others of his family (as Khadeegeh, 'Áïsheh, Ám'neh, Fáṭ'meh, Zeyneb), or are distinguished by a name implying that they are "beloved," "blessed,"

---

1 For the words of the adán and the iḳámeh, see the pages referred to after these two words in the Index.

2 Literally, "the son of his paternal uncle."

3 This name is pronounced "Muṣṭafà," or, more commonly, "Muṣṭafè."

4 Thus commonly pronounced, for "Dáwood."

"precious," &c. (Maḥboobeh, Mebrookeh, Nefeeseh), or the name of a flower, or of some other pleasing object.[1]

As the proper name does not necessarily or generally descend from parent to child, persons are usually distinguished by one or more surnames of the following kinds:—a surname of relationship;[2] as "Aboo-'Alee"[3] (Father of 'Alee), "Ibn-Aḥmad" (Son of Aḥmad), &c.:—a surname of honour, or a nickname;[4] as "Noor-ed-Deen" (The Light of the Religion), "Eṭ-Ṭaweel" (The Tall), &c.:—an appellation relating to country, birth-place, origin, family, sect, trade or occupation, &c.;[5] as "Er-Rasheedee" (of the town of Rasheed), "Eṣ-Ṣabbágh" (The Dyer), "Et-Tágir" (The Merchant). The second kind of surname, and that relating to country &c., are often inherited; thus becoming family-names. Each kind of surname is now generally placed *after* the proper name.

The dress of the children of the middle and higher orders is similar to that of the parents, but generally slovenly. The children of the poor are either clad in a shirt and a cotton skull-cap or a ṭarboosh, or (as is mostly the case in the villages) are left quite naked until the age of six or seven years or more, unless a bit of rag can be easily obtained to serve them as a partial covering. Those little girls who have only a piece of ragged stuff not large enough to cover both the head and body, generally prefer wearing it upon the head, and sometimes have the coquetry to draw a part of it before the face, as a veil, while the whole body is exposed. Little ladies, four or five years of age, mostly wear the white face-veil, like their mothers. When a boy is two or three years old, or often earlier, his head is shaven; a tuft of hair only being left on the crown, and another over the forehead:[6]

---

1 In Cairo, it is the fashion to change the first five female names here mentioned, and the last, into Khaddoogeh, 'Eiyoosheh, Ammooneh, Faṭṭoomeh, Zennoobeh, and Neffooseh; and some other names are changed to the same "measure" as these; which measure implies, in these cases, a superior degree of dignity. (The name of the celebrated traveller Ibn-Baṭṭooṭah is erroneously written by European authors Ibn-Batootah, or Ibn-Batútah).

2 This is termed "kunyeh."

3 On an improper use of this kind of surname, see a note towards the close of Chapter iv. in this work.

4 Termed "laḳab."

5 Termed "nisbeh," or "ism mensoób;" or an appellation resembling an "ism mensoob."

6 It is customary among the peasants throughout a great part of Egypt, on the first occasion of shaving a child's head, to slay a victim, generally a goat, at the tomb of some saint in or near their village, and to make a feast with the meat, of which their friends, and any other persons who please, partake. This is most common in Upper Egypt, and among the tribes not very long established on the banks of the Nile. Their Pagan ancestors in Arabia observed this custom, and usually gave, as alms to the poor, the weight of the hair in silver or gold. (This custom may perhaps throw some light on the statement in 2 Sam. xiv. 26, respecting Absalom's weighing the hair of his head "when he polled it.") The victim is called "'aḳeeḳah," and is offered as a ransom for the child from hell. The custom of shaving one part of a child's head and leaving another was forbidden by the Prophet.

the heads of female infants are seldom shaven. The young children, of both sexes, are usually carried, by their mothers and nurses, not in the arms, but on the shoulder, seated astride,[1] and sometimes, for a short distance, on the hip.

In the treatment of their children, the women of the wealthier classes are remarkable for their excessive indulgence; and the poor, for the little attention they bestow, beyond supplying the absolute wants of nature. The mother is prohibited, by the Muslim law, from weaning her child before the expiration of two years from the period of its birth, unless with the consent of her husband, which, I am told, is generally given after the first year or eighteen months. In the houses of the wealthy, the child, whether boy or girl, remains almost constantly confined in the ḥareem (or the women's apartments), or, at least, in the house: sometimes the boy continues thus an effeminate prisoner until a master, hired to instruct him daily, has taught him to read and write. But it is important to observe, that an affectionate respect for parents and elders inculcated in the ḥareem fits the boy for an abrupt introduction into the world, as will presently be shewn. When the ladies go out to pay a visit, or to take an airing, mounted on asses, the children generally go with them, each carried by a female slave or servant, or seated between her knees upon the fore part of the saddle; the female attendants, as well as the ladies, being usually borne by asses, and it being the custom of all the women to sit astride. But it is seldom that the children of the rich enjoy this slight diversion; their health suffers from confinement and pampering, and they are often rendered capricious, proud, and selfish. The women of the middle classes are scarcely less indulgent mothers. The estimation in which the wife is held by her husband, and even by her acquaintance, depends, in a great degree, upon her fruitfulness, and upon the preservation of her children; for by men and women, rich and poor, barrenness is still considered, in the East, a curse and a reproach; and it is regarded as disgraceful in a man to divorce, without some cogent reason, a wife who has borne him a child, especially while her child is living. If, therefore, a woman desire her husband's love, or the respect of others, her giving birth to a child is a source of great joy to herself and him, and her own interest alone is a sufficient motive for maternal tenderness. Very little expense is required, in Egypt, for the maintenance of a numerous offspring.[2]

[1] See Isaiah, xlix. 22.

[2] It is mentioned by Diodorus Siculus (lib. i. cap. 20), that the ancient Egyptians clothed and reared their children at a very trifling expense.

However much the children are caressed and fondled, in general they feel and manifest a most profound and praiseworthy respect for their parents. Disobedience to parents is considered by the Muslims as one of the greatest of sins, and classed, in point of heinousness, with six other sins, which are idolatry, murder, falsely accusing modest women of adultery, wasting the property of orphans, taking usury, and desertion in an expedition against infidels. An undutiful child is very seldom heard of among the Egyptians or the Arabs in general. Among the middle and higher classes, the child usually greets the father in the morning by kissing his hand, and then stands before him in an humble attitude, with the left hand covered by the right, to receive any order, or to await his permission to depart; but after the respectful kiss, is often taken on the lap; and nearly the same respect is shewn towards the mother. Other members of the family, according to age, relationship, and station, are also similarly regarded by the young; and hence arise that ease and propriety with which a child, emerging from the ḥareem, conducts himself in every society, and that loyalty which is often improperly regarded as the result of Eastern despotism.[1] Sons scarcely ever sit, or eat, or smoke, in the presence of the father, unless bidden to do so; and they often even wait upon him, and upon his guests, at meals and on other occasions: they do not cease to act thus when they have become men.—I once partook of breakfast with an Egyptian merchant, before the door of his house, in the month of Ramaḍán (and therefore a little after sunset); and though every person who passed by, however poor, was invited to partake of the meal, we were waited upon by two of my host's sons; the elder about forty years of age. As they had been fasting during the whole of the day, and had as yet only taken a draught of water, I begged the father to allow them to sit down and eat with us: he immediately told them that they might do so; but they declined.—The mothers generally enjoy, in a greater degree than the fathers, the affection of their children; though they do not receive from them equal outward marks of respect. I have often known servants to hoard their wages for their mothers, though seldom for their fathers.

With the exception of those of the wealthier classes, the young children in Egypt, though objects of so much solicitude, are generally

[1] 'The structure of Eastern government is but the enlargement of the paternal roof." (Urquhart's Spirit of the East, vol. ii. p. 249.)

very dirty, and shabbily clad. The stranger here is disgusted by the sight of them, and at once condemns the modern Egyptians as a very filthy people, without requiring any other reason for forming such an opinion of them; but it is often the case that those children who are most petted and beloved are the dirtiest, and worst clad. It is not uncommon to see, in the city in which I am writing, a lady shuffling along in her ample tób and ḥabarah of new and rich and glistening silks, and one who scents the whole street with the odour of musk or civet as she passes along, with all that appears of her person scrupulously clean and delicate, her eyes neatly bordered with koḥl applied in the most careful manner, and the tip of a finger or two shewing the fresh dye of the ḥennà, and by her side a little boy or girl, her own child, with a face besmeared with dirt, and with clothes appearing as though they had been worn for months without being washed. Few things surprised me so much as sights of this kind on my arrival in this country. I naturally inquired the cause of what struck me as so strange and inconsistent, and was informed that the affectionate mothers thus neglected the appearance of their children, and purposely left them unwashed, and clothed them so shabbily, particularly when they had to take them out in public, *from fear of the evil eye,* which is excessively dreaded, and especially in the case of children, since they are generally esteemed the greatest of blessings, and therefore most likely to be coveted. It is partly for the same reason that many of them confine their boys so long in the ḥareem. Some mothers even dress their young sons as girls, because the latter are less obnoxious to envy.

The children of the poor have a yet more neglected appearance: besides being very scantily clad, or quite naked, they are, in general, excessively dirty: their eyes are frequently extremely filthy: it is common to see half-a-dozen or more flies in each eye, unheeded and unmolested. The parents consider it extremely injurious to wash, or even touch, the eyes, when they discharge that acrid humour which attracts the flies: they even affirm that the loss of sight would result from frequently touching or washing them when thus affected; though washing is really one of the best means of alleviating the complaint.

At the age of about five or six years, or sometimes later, the boy is circumcised.[1] Previously to the performance of this rite in the metropolis and other towns of Egypt, the parents of the youth, if not

1 Among the peasants, not unfrequently at the age of twelve, thirteen, or fourteen years.

in indigent circumstances, generally cause him to be paraded through several streets in the neighbourhood of their dwelling. They mostly avail themselves of the occurrence of a bridal procession, to lessen the expenses of the parade: and, in this case, the boy and his attend-

Parade previous to Circumcision.

ants lead the procession. He generally wears a red Kashmeer turban; but, in other respects, is dressed as a girl, with a yelek and salṭah, and with a ḳurṣ, ṣafà, and other female ornaments, to attract the eye, and so divert it from his person.[1] These articles of dress are of the richest

[1] For a description of the ornaments here mentioned, see the Appendix: the ḳurṣ and ṣafà are also represented in a preceding engraving, page 44.

description that can be procured: they are usually borrowed from some lady, and much too large to fit the boy. A horse, handsomely caparisoned, is also borrowed to convey him; and in his hand is placed a folded embroidered handkerchief, which he constantly holds before his mouth in his right hand, to hide part of his face, and thus protect himself from the evil eye. He is preceded by a servant of the barber, who is the operator, and by three or more musicians, whose instruments are commonly a hautboy and drums. The foremost person in the procession is generally the barber's servant, bearing his "ḥeml," which is a case of wood, of a semi-cylindrical form, with four short legs; its front (the flat surface) covered with pieces of looking-glass and embossed brass; and its back, with a curtain. This is merely the barber's sign: the servant carries it in the manner represented in the engraving here inserted. The musicians follow next (or some of them precede the "ḥeml"), and then follows the boy; his horse led by a groom. Behind him walk several of his female relations and friends. Two boys are often paraded together, and sometimes borne by one horse. Of the bridal processions, with which that above described is so often united, an account will be found in the proper place. A description, also, of some further customs observed on the occasion of a circumcision, and particularly of a more genteel but less general mode of celebrating that event, will be given in another chapter, relating to various private festivities.[1]

The parents seldom devote much of their time or attention to the intellectual education of their children; generally contenting themselves with instilling into their young minds a few principles of religion, and then submitting them, if they can afford to do so, to the instruction of a schoolmaster. As early as possible, the child is taught to say, "I testify that there is no deity but God; and I testify that Moḥammad is God's Apostle." He receives also lessons of religious pride, and learns to hate the Christians, and all other sects but his own, as thoroughly as does the Muslim in advanced age. Most of the children of the higher and middle classes, and some of those of the lower orders, are taught by the schoolmaster to read, and to recite and chant[2] the whole or certain portions of the Ḳur-án

---

[1] A custom mentioned by Strabo (p. 824), as prevailing among the Egyptians in his time, is still universally practised in every part of Egypt, both by the Muslims and Copts, except in Alexandria and perhaps a few other places on the shore of the Mediterranean: it is also common, if not equally prevalent, in Arabia. Reland, who imperfectly describes this custom (De Religione Mohammedica, p. 75, ed. 1717), remarks its being mentioned likewise by Galen.

[2] See the Chapter on music.

by memory.[1] They afterwards learn the most common rules of arithmetic.

Schools are very numerous, not only in the metropolis, but in every large town; and there is one, at least, in every considerable village. Almost every mosque, "sebeel" (or public fountain), and "ḥóḍ" (or drinking-place for cattle) in the metropolis has a "kuttáb" (or school) attached to it, in which children are instructed for a very trifling expense; the "sheykh" or "fiḳee"[2] (the master of the school) receiving from the parent of each pupil half a piaster (about five farthings of our money), or something more or less, every Thursday.[3] The master of a school attached to a mosque or other public building in Cairo also generally receives yearly a ṭarboosh, a piece of white muslin for a turban, a piece of linen, and a pair of shoes; and each boy receives, at the same time, a linen skull-cap, four or five cubits[4] of cotton cloth, and perhaps half a piece (ten or twelve cubits) of linen, and a pair of shoes, and, in some cases, half a piaster or a

A Schoolboy learning the Alphabet.

piaster. These presents are supplied by funds bequeathed to the school, and are given in the month of Ramaḍán. The boys attend only during the hours of instruction, and then return to their homes.

[1] It has been said that I have represented the Egyptian boys as being very generally perfect in *understanding* the Ḳur-án. If the reader can find in this work any expression implying so monstrous an untruth, I shall be obliged if he will erase it. I have stated, in Chapter ix., that the exposition of the Ḳur-án is a branch of *collegiate* education.

[2] This term is a corruption of "faḳeeh," which latter appellation is generally given in Egypt only to a person versed in religion and law; a man who merely recites the Ḳur-án, &c., professionally, or who teaches others to do so, being commonly called a "fiḳee."

[3] Friday, being the sabbath of the Muslims, is a holiday to the school-boys and fiḳee.

[4] The cubit employed in measuring Egyptian cloths is equal to twenty-two inches and two-thirds.

The lessons are generally written upon tablets of wood, painted white; and when one lesson is learnt, the tablet is washed and another is written. They also practise writing upon the same tablet. The schoolmaster and his pupils sit upon the ground, and each boy has his tablet in his hands, or a copy of the Ḳur-án, or of one of its thirty sections, on a little kind of desk of palm-sticks. All the boys, in learning to read, recite or chant their lessons aloud, at the same time rocking their heads or bodies incessantly backwards and forwards; which practice is observed by almost all persons in reciting the Ḳur-án; being thought to assist the memory. The noise may be imagined.[1]

The boys first learn the letters of the alphabet; next, the vowel-points and other syllabical signs; and then, the numerical value of each letter of the alphabet.[2] Previously to this third stage of the pupil's progress, it is customary for the master to ornament the tablet with black and red ink, and green paint, and to write upon it the letters of the alphabet in the order of their respective numerical values, and convey it to the father, who returns it with a piaster or two placed upon it. The like is also done at several subsequent stages of the boy's progress, as when he begins to learn the Ḳur-án, and six or seven times as he proceeds in learning the sacred book; each time the next lesson being written on the tablet. When he has become acquainted with the numerical values of the letters, the master writes for him some simple words, as the names of men; then, the ninety-nine names or epithets of God: next, the Fát'ḥah (or opening chapter of the Ḳur-án) is written upon his tablet, and he reads it repeatedly until he has perfectly committed it to memory. He then proceeds to learn the other chapters of the Ḳur-án: after the first chapter he learns the last; then the last but one; next the last but two, and so on, in inverted order, ending with the second; as the chapters in general successively decrease in length from the second to the last inclusively. It is seldom that the master of a school teaches writing; and few boys learn to write unless destined for some employment which absolutely requires that they should do so; in which latter case they are generally taught the art of writing, and likewise arithmetic, by a "ḳabbánee," who is a person employed to weigh goods in a market or bázár, with the steelyard. Those who are to

---

1 The usual punishment is beating on the soles of the feet with a palm-stick.

2 The Arabic letters are often used as numerals. When thus used, they are arranged in the order of the Hebrew alphabet.

devote themselves to religion, or to any of the learned professions, mostly pursue a regular course of study in the great mosque El-Azhar.

The schoolmasters in Egypt are mostly persons of very little learning: few of them are acquainted with any writings except the Ḳur-án, and certain prayers, which, as well as the contents of the sacred volume, they are hired to recite on particular occasions. I was lately told of a man who could neither read nor write succeeding to the office of a schoolmaster in my neighbourhood. Being able to recite the whole of the Ḳur-án, he could hear the boys repeat their lessons: to write them, he employed the "'areef" (or head-boy and monitor in the school), pretending that his eyes were weak. A few days after he had taken upon himself this office, a poor woman brought a letter for him to read to her from her son, who had gone on pilgrimage. The fiḳee pretended to read it, but said nothing; and the woman, inferring from his silence that the letter contained bad news, said to him, "Shall I shriek?" He answered, "Yes." "Shall I tear my clothes?" she asked; he replied, "Yes." So the poor woman returned to her house, and with her assembled friends performed the lamentation and other ceremonies usual on the occasion of a death. Not many days after this, her son arrived, and she asked him what he could mean by causing a letter to be written stating that he was dead? He explained the contents of the letter, and she went to the schoolmaster and begged him to inform her why he had told her to shriek and to tear her clothes, since the letter was to inform her that her son was well, and he was now arrived at home. Not at all abashed, he said, "God knows futurity. How could I know that your son would arrive in safety? It was better that you should think him dead than be led to expect to see him and perhaps be disappointed." Some persons who were sitting with him praised his wisdom, exclaiming, "Truly, our new fiḳee is a man of unusual judgment!" and, for a little while, he found that he had raised his reputation by this blunder.[1]

Some parents employ a sheykh or fiḳee to teach their boys at home. The father usually teaches his son to perform the "wuḍoó,"

[1] I have since found an anecdote almost exactly similar to the above in the Cairo edition of the 'Thousand and One Nights;' it is one of the anecdotes appended to Chapter xviii. of my translation of that work: therefore either my informant's account is not strictly true, or the man alluded to by him was, in the main, an imitator: the latter is not improbable, as I have been credibly informed of several similar imitations, and of one which I know to be a fact.

and other ablutions, and to say his prayers, and instructs him in other religious and moral duties to the best of his ability. The Prophet directed his followers to order their children to say their prayers when seven years of age, and to beat them if they failed to do so when ten years old; and at the latter age to make them sleep in separate beds: in Egypt, however, very few persons pray before they have attained to manhood.

The female children are very seldom taught to read or write; and not many of them, even among the higher orders, learn to say their prayers. Some of the rich engage a "sheykhah" (or learned woman) to visit the ḥareem daily; to teach their daughters and female slaves to say their prayers, and to recite a few chapters of the Ḳur-án; and sometimes to instruct them in reading and writing; but these are very rare accomplishments for females even of the highest class in Egypt.[1] There are many schools in which girls are taught plain needlework, embroidery, &c. In families in easy circumstances a "m'allimeh,"[2] or female teacher of such kinds of work, is often engaged to attend the girls at their own home.

---

1 The young daughters of persons of the middle classes are sometimes instructed with the boys in a public school; but they are usually veiled, and hold no intercourse with the boys. I have often seen a well-dressed girl reading the Ḳur-án in a boys' school.

2 Thus pronounced, for "mo'allimeh."

CHAPTER III.

RELIGION AND LAWS.

As the most important branch of their education, and the main foundation of their manners and customs, the religion and laws of the people who are the subject of these pages must be well understood, not only in their general principles, but in many minor points, before we can proceed to consider their social condition and habits in the state of manhood.

A difference of opinion among Muslims, respecting some points of religion and law, has given rise to four parties, or persuasions, which consider each other orthodox as to fundamental matters, and call themselves "Sunnees," or followers of the Traditions, while they designate all other Muslims by the term "Shiya'ees," or "Shee'ahs;" and collectively, the "Shee'ah;" signifying, according to their acceptation, "Heretics." The Sunnees alone are the class which we have to consider. The four parties, or persuasions, into which they are divided are the "Ḥanafees," "Sháfe'ees," "Málikees,"[1] and "Ḥambelees;"[2] so called from the names of the respective doctors whose tenets they have adopted. The Turks are of the first persuasion, which is the most reasonable: the inhabitants of Cairo, a small proportion excepted (who are Ḥanafees), are either Sháfe'ees or Málikees; and it is generally said that they are mostly of the former of these persuasions, as are also the people of Arabia: those of the Sharḳeeyeh, on the east of the Delta, Sháfe'ees: those of the Gharbeeyeh, or Delta, Sháfe'ees, with a few Málikees: those of the Boḥeyreh, on the west of the Delta, Málikees: the inhabitants of the Ṣa'eed, or the valley of Upper Egypt, are likewise, with few exceptions, Málikees: so too are the Nubians, and the Western Arabs. To the fourth persuasion, very few persons in the present day belong.—All these persuasions agree in deriving their code of religion

---

[1] Commonly pronounced "Mál'kee."

[2] Pronounced "Ḥambel'ee."

and law from four sources; namely, the Ḳur-án, the Traditions of the Prophet, the concordance of his early disciples, and analogy.

The religion which Moḥammad taught is generally called by the Arabs "El-Islám." "Eemán" and "Deen" are the particular terms applied, respectively, to faith and practical religion.

The grand principles of the faith are expressed in two articles; the first of which is this—

"*There is no deity but God.*"

God, who created all things in heaven and in earth, who preserveth all things, and decreeth all things, who is without beginning, and without end, omnipotent, omniscient, and omnipresent, is *one.* His unity is thus declared in a short chapter of the Ḳur-án:[1] "Say, He is God; one [God]. God is the Eternal. He begetteth not, nor is He begotten; and there is none equal unto Him." He hath no partner, nor any offspring, in the creed of the Muslim. Though our Lord Jesus Christ (whose name should not be mentioned without adding "on whom be peace") is believed to have been born of a pure virgin, by the miraculous operation of God,[2] without any natural father, and to be the Messiah, and "the Word of God, which He transmitted unto Mary, and a Spirit [proceeding] from Him,"[3] yet He is not called the Son of God; and no higher titles are given to Him than those of a Prophet and an Apostle: He is even considered as of inferior dignity to Moḥammad, inasmuch as the Gospel is held to be superseded by the Ḳur-án. The Muslim believes that Seyyidnà 'Eesà[4] (or "our Lord Jesus"), after He had fulfilled the object of his mission, was taken up unto God from the Jews, who sought to slay Him; and that another person, on whom God had stamped the likeness of Christ, was crucified in his stead.[5] He also believes that Christ is to come again upon the earth, to establish the Muslim religion, and perfect peace and security, after having killed Antichrist, and to be a sign of the approach of the last day.

---

[1] Ch. 112.—In quoting passages in the Ḳur-án, I have sometimes followed Sale's translation; to the general fidelity of which I willingly add my testimony. I should, however, mention that some of his explanatory notes are unauthorized and erroneous: as, for instance, with respect to the laws of inheritance; on which subject his version of the text also is faulty. When necessary, I have distinguished the verses by numbers. In doing this I had originally adopted the divisions made by Marracci, but have since made the numbers to agree with those in the late edition of the Arabic text by Fluegel, which, from its superior accuracy, is likely to supersede the former editions.

[2] Ḳur-án, ch. iii. vv. 40—42.

[3] Ḳur-án, ch. iv. v. 169.

[4] The title of "Seyyidnà" (our Lord) is given by the Muslims to prophets and other venerated persons.

[5] Ḳur-án, ch. iv. v. 156.

The other grand article of the faith, which cannot be believed without the former, is this—

"*Moḥammad is God's Apostle.*"

Moḥammad is believed, by his followers, to have been the last and greatest of Prophets and Apostles.[1] Six of these, namely, Adam, Noah, Abraham, Moses, Jesus, and Moḥammad, are believed each to have received a revealed law, or system of religion and morality. That, however, which was revealed to Adam was abrogated by the next; and each succeeding law, or code of laws, abrogated the preceding; though all are believed to have been the same in every essential point: therefore, those who professed the Jewish religion from the time of Moses to that of Jesus were true believers; and those who professed the Christian religion (uncorrupted, as the Muslims say, by the tenet that Christ was the *son* of God,) until the time of Moḥammad are held, in like manner, to have been true believers. But the copies of the Pentateuch, the Psalms of David (which the Muslims also hold to be of divine origin), and the Gospels now existing, are believed to have been so much altered as to contain very little of the true word of God. The Ḳur-án is commonly believed to have suffered no essential alteration whatever.

It is further necessary that the Muslim should believe in the existence of angels, and of good and evil genii; the evil genii being devils, whose chief is Iblees:[2] also, in the immortality of the soul, the general resurrection and judgment, in future rewards and punishments in Paradise[3] and Hell,[4] in the balance in which good and evil works shall be weighed, and in the bridge "Eṣ-Ṣiráṭ" (which extends over the midst of Hell, finer than a hair, and sharper than the edge of a sword), over which all must pass, and from which the wicked shall fall into Hell. He believes, also, that they who have acknowledged the faith of El-Islám and yet acted wickedly will not remain in Hell for ever; but that all of other religions must: that there are, however, degrees of punishments, as well as of rewards; the former consisting in severe torture by excessive heat and cold; and the latter, partly in the indulgence of the appetites by most

---

[1] The Muslim seldom mentions the name of the Prophet without adding, "Ṣalla-lláhu 'aleyhi wa-sellem:" *i. e.*, "God bless and save him!"

[2] In the first edition of this work, I here mentioned *the* Devil as distinct from the genii; but I have since found that the majority of the most esteemed Arab authors are of the contrary opinion. Theirs is also the *general* opinion of the *modern* Arabs.—The angelic nature is considered as inferior to the human (because the angels were commanded to prostrate themselves before Adam), and still more so is the nature of genii.

[3] "El-Genneh," or "the garden."

[4] "Gahennem."

delicious meats and drinks, and in the pleasures afforded by the company of the girls of Paradise, whose eyes will be very large and entirely black,[1] and whose stature will be proportioned to that of the men, which will be the height of a tall palm-tree, or about sixty feet. Such, the Muslims generally believe, was the height of Adam and Eve. It is said that the souls of martyrs reside, until the judgment, in the crops of green birds, which eat of the fruits of Paradise and drink of its rivers.[2] Women are not to be excluded from Paradise, according to the faith of El-Islám; though it has been asserted, by many Christians, that the Muslims believe women to have no souls. In several places in the Ḳur-án, Paradise is promised to all true believers, whether males or females. It is the doctrine of the Ḳur-án that no person will be admitted into Paradise by his own merits; but that admission will be granted to the believers merely by the mercy of God, on account of their faith; yet that the felicity of each person will be proportioned to his good works. The very meanest in Paradise is promised "eighty thousand servants" (beautiful youths, called "weleeds"[3]), "seventy-two wives of the girls of Paradise" ("ḥooreeyehs"[4]), "besides the wives he had in this world," if he desire to have the latter (and the good will doubtless desire the good), "and a tent erected for him of pearls, jacinths, and emeralds, of a very large extent;" "and will be waited on by three hundred attendants while he eats, and served in dishes of gold, whereof three hundred shall be set before him at once, each containing a different kind of food, the last morsel of which will be as grateful as the first." Wine also, "though forbidden in this life, will yet be freely allowed to be drunk in the next, and without danger, since the wine of Paradise will not inebriate."[5] We are further told, that all superfluities from the bodies of the inhabitants of Paradise will be carried off by perspiration, which will diffuse an odour like that of musk; and that they will be clothed in the richest silks, chiefly of green. They are also promised perpetual youth, and children as many as they may desire. These pleasures, together with the songs of the angel Isráfeel, and many other gratifications of the senses, will charm

---

[1] Like those of the gazelle: this meaning of their common appellation (which is mentioned afterwards) is, however, disputed.

[2] The title of martyr is given to the unpaid soldier killed in a war for the defence of the faith, to a person who has innocently met with his death from the hand of another, to a victim of the plague (if he has not fled from the disease) or of dysentery, to a person who has been drowned, and to one who has been killed by the fall of any building.

[3] Or "wildán."

[4] Or "el-ḥoor el-'een," or "el-ḥoor el-'oyoon."

[5] See Sale's Preliminary Discourse to his Translation of the Ḳur-án, sect. iv.

even the meanest inhabitant of Paradise. But all these enjoyments will be lightly esteemed by those more blessed persons who are to be admitted to the highest of all honours, that spiritual pleasure of beholding, morning and evening, the face of God.[1]—The Muslim must also believe in the examination of the dead in the sepulchre, by two angels, called Munkar and Nekeer,[2] of terrible aspect, who will cause the body (to which the soul shall, for the time, be reunited,) to sit upright in the grave,[3] and will question the deceased respecting his faith. The wicked they will severely torture; but the good they will not hurt. Lastly, he should believe in God's absolute decree of every event, both good and evil. This doctrine has given rise to as much controversy among the Muslims as among Christians; but the former, generally, believe in predestination as, in some respects, conditional.

The most important duties enjoined in the *ritual and moral laws* are *prayer*, *alms-giving*, *fasting*, and *pilgrimage*.

The religious *purifications*, which are of two kinds,—first, the ordinary ablution preparatory to *prayer*, and secondly, the washing of the whole body, together with the performance of the former ablution, —are of primary importance: for prayer, which is a duty so important that it is called "the Key of Paradise," will not be accepted from a person in a state of uncleanness. It is therefore also necessary to avoid impurity by clipping the nails, and other similar practices.[4]

There are partial washings, or purifications, which all Muslims perform on certain occasions, even if they neglect their prayers, and which are considered as religious acts.[5] The ablution called "el-wuḍoó," which is preparatory to prayer, I shall now describe. The purifications just before alluded to are a part of the wuḍoó: the other washings are not, of necessity, to be performed immediately after, but only when the person is about to say his prayers; and these are performed in the mosque or in the house, in public or in private. There is in every mosque a tank (called "meyḍaäh") or a "ḥanafeeyeh," which is a raised reservoir, with spouts round it, from which the

---

[1] A Muslim of some learning professed to me that he considered the description of Paradise given in the Ḳur-án to be, in a great measure, figurative: "like those," said he, "in the book of the Revelation of St. John;" and he assured me that many learned Muslims were of the same opinion.

[2] Vulgarly called "Nákir" and "Nekeer."

[3] The corpse is always deposited in a vault, and not placed in a coffin, but merely wrapped in winding-sheets or clothes.

[4] Alluded to in the first chapter.

[5] For an account of these private ablutions, and the occasions which require their performance, the reader may consult Reland, De Rel. Moh. pp. 80—83, ed. 1717.

water falls. In some mosques there are both these. The Muslims of the Ḥanafee sect (of which are the Turks) perform the ablution at the latter (which has received its name from that cause); for they must do it with running water, or from a tank or pool at least ten cubits in breadth, and the same in depth; and I believe that there is only one meyḍaäh in Cairo of that depth, which is in the great mosque El-Azhar. A small ḥanafeeyeh of tinned copper, placed on a low shelf, and a large basin, or a small ewer and basin of the same metal, are generally used in the house for the performance of the wuḍoó.

Vessels for Ablution.—*The upper vessel* (*or* ḥanafeeyeh) *is generally about a foot and a half in height.*

The person, having tucked up his sleeves a little higher than his elbows, says, in a low voice, or inaudibly, "I purpose performing the wuḍoó, for prayer."[1] He then washes his hands three times; saying, in the same manner as before, "In the name of God, the Compassionate, the Merciful. Praise be to God, who hath sent down water for purification, and made El-Islám to be a light and a conductor, and a guide to thy gardens, the gardens of delight, and to thy mansion, the mansion of peace." Then he rinses his mouth three

[1] All persons do not use exactly the same words on this occasion, nor during the performance of the wuḍoó; and most persons use no words during the performance.

times, throwing the water into it with his right hand;[1] and in doing this he says, "O God, assist me in the reading of thy book, and in commemorating Thee, and in thanking Thee, and in worshipping Thee well." Next, with his right hand, he throws water up his nostrils (snuffing it up at the same time), and then blows it out, compressing his nostrils with the thumb and finger of the *left* hand; and this also is done three times. While doing it, he says, "O God, make me to smell the odours of Paradise, and bless me with its delights; and make me not to smell the smell of the fires [of Hell]." He then washes his face three times, throwing up the water with both hands, and saying, "O God, whiten my face with thy light, on the day when Thou shalt whiten the faces of thy favourites; and do not blacken my face, on the day when Thou shalt blacken the faces of thine enemies."[2] His right hand and arm, as high as the elbow, he next washes three times, and as many times causes some water to run along his arm, from the palm of the hand to the elbow, saying, as he does this, "O God, give me my book in my right hand;[3] and reckon with me with an easy reckoning." In the same manner he washes the left hand and arm, saying, "O God, do not give me my book in my left hand, nor behind my back; and do not reckon with me with a difficult reckoning; nor make me to be one of the people of the fire." He next draws his wetted right hand over the upper part of his head, raising his turban or cap with his left: this he does but once; and he accompanies the action with this supplication, "O God, cover me with thy mercy, and pour down thy blessing upon me; and shade me under the shadow of thy canopy, on the day when there shall be no shade but its shade." If he has a beard, he then combs it with the wetted fingers of his right hand; holding his hand with the palm forwards, and passing the fingers through his beard from the throat upwards. He then puts the tips of his forefingers into his ears, and twists them round, passing his thumbs at the same time round the back of the ears, from the bottom upwards; and saying, "O God, make me to be of those who hear what is said, and obey what is best;" or, "O God, make me to hear good." Next he wipes

[1] He should also use a tooth-stick (miswák) to clean his teeth; but few do so.

[2] It is believed that the good man will rise to judgment with his face white; and the bad, with his face black. Hence a man's face is said to be white or black according as he is in good or bad repute; and "may God blacken thy face!" is a common imprecation.

[3] To every man is appropriated a book, in which all the actions of his life are written. The just man, it is said, will receive his book in his right hand; but the wicked, in his left, which will be tied behind his back; his right hand being tied up to his neck.

his neck with the back of the fingers of both hands, making the ends of his fingers meet behind his neck, and then drawing them forward; and in doing so, he says, "O God, free my neck from the fire; and keep me from the chains, and the collars, and the fetters." Lastly, he washes his feet, as high as the ankles, and passes his fingers between the toes: he washes the right foot first, saying, at the same time, "O God, make firm my feet upon the Ṣirâṭ, on the day when feet shall slip upon it:" on washing the left foot, he says, "O God, make my labour to be approved, and my sin forgiven, and my works accepted, merchandise that shall not perish, by thy pardon, O Mighty, O very Forgiving; by thy mercy, O most Merciful of those who shew mercy." After having thus completed the ablution, he says, looking towards heaven, "Thy perfection, O God, [I extol] with thy praise: I testify that there is no deity but Thou alone: Thou hast no companion: I implore thy forgiveness, and turn to Thee with repentance." Then, looking towards the earth, he adds, "I testify that there is no deity but God: and I testify that Moḥammad is his servant and his apostle." Having uttered these words, he should recite, once, twice, or three times, the "Soorat el-Ḳadr," or 97th chapter of the Ḳur-án.

The wuḍoó is generally performed in less than two minutes; most persons hurrying through the act, as well as omitting almost all the prayers, &c., which should accompany and follow the actions. It is not required before each of the five daily prayers, when the person is *conscious* of having avoided every kind of impurity since the last performance of this ablution. When water cannot be easily procured, or would be injurious to the health of the individual, he may perform the ablution with dust or sand. This ceremony is called "tayemmum." The person, in this case, strikes the palms of his hands upon any dry dust or sand (it will suffice to do so upon his cloth robe, as it must contain some dust), and, with both hands, wipes his face: then, having struck his hands again upon the dust, he wipes his right hand and arm as high as the elbow; and then, the left hand and arm, in the same manner. This completes the ceremony. The washing of the whole body is often performed merely for the sake of cleanliness; but not as a religious act, except on particular occasions, as on the morning of Friday, and on the two grand festivals, &c.,[1] when it is called "ghusl."

---

[1] Here, again, I must beg to refer the reader (if he desire such information) to Reland's account of the ghusl, and the occasions which require its performance.—De Rel. Moh. pp. 66—77, ed. 1717.

Cleanliness is required not only in the worshipper, but also in the ground, mat, carpet, robe, or whatever else it be, upon which he prays. Persons of the lower orders often pray upon the bare ground, which is considered clean if it be dry; and they seldom wipe off immediately the dust which adheres to the nose and forehead in prostration; for it is regarded as ornamental to the believer's face: but when a person has a cloak or any other garment that he can take off without exposing his person in an unbecoming manner, he spreads it upon the ground to serve as a prayer-carpet. The rich use a prayer-carpet (called "seggádeh") about the size of a wide hearth-rug, having a niche represented upon it, the point of which is turned towards Mekkeh.[1] It is reckoned sinful to pass near before a person engaged in prayer. When so engaged, the Muslim should station himself a few feet before a wall or the like, or should place before him a "sutrah," which may be a staff stuck upright or (if the ground is hard) laid horizontally, or a whip, or his saddle, or his shoes; in order that no living being, nor any image, may be the object next before him.[2] If he has nothing to place as a "sutrah," he should draw a line on the ground before him.

Prayer is called "ṣalah;" thus commonly pronounced for "ṣaláh." Five times in the course of every day is its performance required of the Muslim: but there are comparatively few persons in Egypt who do not sometimes, or often, neglect this duty; and there are many who scarcely ever pray. Certain portions of the ordinary prayers are called "farḍ," which are appointed by the Ḳur-án; and others, "sunneh," which are appointed by the Prophet, without allegation of a divine order.

The first time of prayer commences at the "maghrib," or sunset,[3] or rather, about four minutes later; the second, at the "'eshè," or nightfall, when the evening has closed, and it is quite dark;[4] the

---

[1] Seggádehs, of the kind here described, are now sold in London, under the name of "Persian carpets" or "Persian rugs."

[2] This was probably a custom of the Jews in Arabia, and borrowed from them by Moḥammad; and it may explain a difficulty which has much perplexed the commentators of the Bible, in Gen. xlvii. 31. I think that the pointing of the Hebrew text is there manifestly wrong, as many critics have supposed; and that the true meaning will now be seen to be, "Israel worshipped," or "bowed himself," "before," or "toward," "the head of the staff;" agreeably with the rendering of the Septuagint, and with Hebr. xi. 21. The Hebrew and Greek prepositions which are rendered "upon" in both these instances in the authorized English version signify also "before," and "to," or "towards:" and the Hebrew preposition in question, preceded by the same verb that precedes it in the instance in Gen. xlvii. 31, is rendered "unto" in Lev. xxvi. 1, a strikingly apposite passage.

[3] I have called this the first, because the Moḥammadan day commences from sunset; but the morning-prayer is often termed the first; the prayer of noon, the second; and so on.

[4] The 'eshè of the Sháfe'ees, Málikees, and Ḥambelees, is when the red gleam ("esh-shafaḳ el-aḥmar") after sunset has disappeared; and that of the Ḥanafees, when both the red and the white gleam have disappeared.

third, at the "ṣubḥ" or "fegr;" *i. e.*, daybreak;[1] the fourth, at the "ḍuhr," or noon, or, rather, a little later, when the sun has begun to decline; the fifth, at the "'aṣr," or afternoon; *i. e.*, about mid-time between noon and nightfall.[2] Each period of prayer ends when the next commences, except that of daybreak, which ends at sunrise. The Prophet would not have his followers commence their prayers at sunrise, nor exactly at noon or sunset, because, he said, infidels worshipped the sun at such times.

Should the time of prayer arrive when they are eating, or about to eat, they are not to rise to prayer till they have finished their meal. The prayers should be said as nearly as possible at the commencement of the periods above mentioned: they may be said after, but not before. The several times of prayer are announced by the "muëddin" of each mosque. Having ascended to the gallery of the "mád'neh," or menaret, he chants the "adán," or call to prayer, which is as follows: "God is most Great" (this is said four times). "I testify that there is no deity but God" (twice). "I testify that Moḥammad is God's Apostle" (twice). "Come to prayer" (twice). "Come to security" (twice).[3] "God is most Great" (twice). "There is no deity but God."—Most of the muëddins of Cairo have harmonious and sonorous voices, which they strain to the utmost pitch: yet there is a simple and solemn melody in their chants which is very striking, particularly in the stillness of night.[4] *Blind* men are generally preferred for the office of muëddins, that the ḥareems and terraces of surrounding houses may not be overlooked from the mád'nehs.

Two other calls to prayers are made during the night, to rouse those persons who desire to perform supererogatory acts of devotion.[5] A little after midnight, the muëddins of the great royal mosques in Cairo (*i. e.*, of each of the great mosques founded by a Sulṭán, which is called "Gámë' Sulṭánee"), and of some other large mosques, ascend the mád'nehs, and chant the following call, which, being one of the two night-calls not at the regular periods of obligatory prayers, is called the "Oolà," a term signifying merely the "First." Having

---

1 Generally on the first faint appearance of light in the east. The Ḥanafees mostly perform the morning-prayer a little later, when the yellow gleam ("el-iṣfirár") appears: this they deem the most proper time; but they may pray earlier.

2 The 'aṣr, according to the Sháfe'ees, Málikees, and Ḥambelees, is when the shade of an object, cast by the sun, is equal to the length of that object, added to the length of the shade which the same object casts at noon; and, according to the Ḥanafees, when the shadow is equal to *twice* the length of the object, added to the length of its mid-day shadow.

3 Here is added, in the morning-call, "Prayer is better than sleep" (twice).

4 A common air, to which the adán is chanted in Cairo, will be given in the chapter on Egyptian music.

5 They are few who do so.

commenced by chanting the common adán, with those words which are introduced in the call to morning-prayer ("Prayer is better than sleep"), he adds, "There is no deity but God" (three times) "alone: He hath no companion: to Him belongeth the dominion; and to Him belongeth praise. He giveth life, and causeth death; and He is living, and shall never die. In his hand is blessing [or good]; and He is Almighty.—There is no deity but God" (three times), "and we will not worship any beside Him, 'serving Him with sincerity of religion,'[1] 'though the infidels be averse'[2] [thereto]. This is no deity but God. Moḥammad is the most noble of the creation in the sight of God. Moḥammad is the best prophet that hath been sent, and a lord by whom his companions became lords; comely; liberal of gifts; perfect; pleasant to the taste; sweet; soft to the throat [or to be drunk]. Pardon, O Lord, thy servant and thy poor dependant, the endower of this place, and him who watcheth it with goodness and beneficence, and its neighbours, and those who frequent it at the times of prayers and good acts, O thou Bountiful:—O Lord"[3] (three times). "Thou art He who ceaseth not to be distinguished by mercy: Thou art liberal of thy clemency towards the rebellious; and protectest him; and concealest what is foul; and makest manifest every virtuous action; and Thou bestowest thy beneficence upon the servant, and comfortest him, O thou Bountiful:—O Lord" (three times). "My sins, when I think upon them, [I see to be] many; but the mercy of my Lord is more abundant than are my sins: I am not solicitous on account of good that I have done; but for the mercy of God I am most solicitous. Extolled be the Everlasting. He hath no companion in his great dominion. His perfection [I extol]: exalted be his name: [I extol] the perfection of God."

About an hour before daybreak, the muëddins of most mosques chant the second call, named the "Ebed," and so called from the occurrence of that word near the commencement.[4] This call is as follows: "[I extol] the perfection of God, the Existing for ever and ever" (three times): "the perfection of God, the Desired, the Existing, the Single, the Supreme: the perfection of God, the One, the Sole: the perfection of Him who taketh to Himself, in his great dominion, neither female companion, nor male partner, nor any like unto Him, nor any that is disobedient, nor any deputy, nor any equal,

---

1 Ḳur-án, ch. xcviii. v. 4.

2 Idem, ch. ix. v. 32, and ch. lxi. v. 8.

3 This thrice-uttered exclamation ("Yá Rabb!") is made in a very loud tone.

4 The word "ebed" is here used adverbially, signifying "for ever."

nor any offspring. His perfection [be extolled] : and exalted be his name. He is a Deity who knew what hath been before it was, and called into existence what hath been; and He is now existing as He was [at the first]. His perfection [be extolled] : and exalted be his name. He is a Deity unto whom there is none like existing. There is none like unto God, the Bountiful, existing. There is none like unto God, the Clement, existing. There is none like unto God, the Great, existing. And there is no deity but Thou, O our Lord, to be worshipped and to be praised and to be desired and to be glorified. [I extol] the perfection of Him who created all creatures, and numbered them, and distributed their sustenance, and decreed the terms of the lives of his servants: and our Lord, the Bountiful, the Clement, the Great, forgetteth not one of them. [I extol] the perfection of Him who, of his power and greatness, caused the pure water to flow from the solid stone, the mass of rock: the perfection of Him who spake with our lord Moosà [or Moses] upon the mountain;[1] whereupon the mountain was reduced to dust,[2] through dread of God, whose name be exalted, the One, the Sole. There is no deity but God. He is a just Judge. [I extol] the perfection of the First. Blessing and peace be on thee, O comely of countenance: O Apostle of God. Blessing and peace be on thee, O first of the creatures of God, and seal of the apostles of God. Blessing and peace be on thee, O thou Prophet: on thee and on thy Family, and all thy Companions. God is most Great. God is most Great:" &c., to the end of the call to morning-prayer. "O God, bless and save and still beatify the beatified Prophet, our lord Moḥammad. And may God, whose name be blessed and exalted, be well pleased with thee, O our lord El-Ḥasan, and with thee, O our lord El-Ḥoseyn, and with thee, O Aboo-Farrág,[3] O Sheykh of the Arabs, and with all the favourites [the "welees"] of God. Amen."

The prayers which are performed daily at the five periods before mentioned are said to be of so many "rek'ahs," or inclinations of the head.[4]

---

[1] These words, "The perfection of Him who spake," &c. ("subḥána men kellema," &c.), are pronounced in a very high and loud tone.

[2] See Ḳur-án, ch. vii. v. 139.

[3] "Aboo-Farrág" is a surname of a famous saint, the seyyid Aḥmad El-Bedawee, buried at Ṭanṭà in the Delta: it implies that he obtains relief to those who visit his tomb, and implore his intercession.

[4] The morning-prayers, two rek'ahs sunneh and two farḍ; the noon, four sunneh and four farḍ; the afternoon, the same; the evening, three farḍ and two sunneh; and the night-prayers (or 'eshè), four sunneh and four farḍ, and two sunneh again. After these are yet to be performed three rek'ahs "witr;" *i. e.*, single or separate prayers: these may be performed immediately after the 'eshè prayers, or at any time in the night; but are more meritorious if *late* in the night.

The worshipper, standing with his face towards the Ḳibleh (that is, towards Mekkeh), and his feet not quite close together, says, inaudibly, that he has purposed to recite the prayers of so many rek'ahs (sunneh or farḍ) the morning-prayers (or the noon, &c.,) of the present day (or night); and then, raising his open hands on each side of his face, and touching the lobes of his ears with the ends of his thumbs, he says, "God is most Great" ("Alláhu Akbar"). This ejaculation is

Postures of Prayer.

called the "tekbeer." He then proceeds to recite the prayers of the prescribed number of rek'ahs,[1] thus:—

Still standing, and placing his hands before him, a little below his girdle, the left within the right, he recites (with his eyes directed towards the spot where his head will touch the ground in prostration) the Fát'ḥah, or opening chapter of the Ḳur-án,[2] and after it three or more other verses, or one of the short chapters, of the Ḳur-án; very

[1] There are some little differences in the attitudes of the four great sects during prayer. I describe those of the Ḥanafees.—The two cuts here inserted comprise the postures of two rek'ahs; the first rek'ah ending with No. 8.

[2] Some persons previously utter certain supererogatory ejaculations, expressive of the praise and glory of God; and add, "I seek refuge with God from Satan the accursed;" which petition is often offered up before reciting any part of the

commonly the 112th chapter; but without repeating the "besmeleh" (in the name of God, &c.,) before the second recitation. He then says, "God is most Great:" and makes, at the same time, an inclination of his head and body, placing his hands upon his knees, and separating his fingers a little. In this posture he says, "[I extol] the perfection of my Lord the Great" (three times), adding, "May

Postures of Prayer—*continued.*

God hear him who praiseth Him. Our Lord, praise be unto Thee." Then, raising his head and body, he repeats, "God is most Great." He next drops gently upon his knees, and, saying again, "God is most Great," places his hands upon the ground, a little before his knees, and puts his nose and forehead also to the ground (the former first), between his two hands. During this prostration he says, "[I extol] the perfection of my Lord the Most High" (three times). He raises his head and body (but his knees remain upon the ground),

Ḳur-án on other occasions, as commanded by the Ḳur-án itself (ch. xvi. v. 100). The Ḳur-án is usually recited, in the farḍ prayers, in a voice slightly audible, except at noon and the 'aṣr, when it is recited inaudibly. By Imáms, when praying at the head of others, and sometimes by persons praying alone, it is chanted. In the sunneh prayers it is recited inaudibly.

sinks backwards upon his heels, and places his hands upon his thighs, saying, at the same time, "God is most Great:" and this he repeats as he bends his head a second time to the ground. During this second prostration he repeats the same words as in the first; and in raising his head again, he utters the tekbeer as before. Thus are completed the prayers of one rek'ah. In all the changes of posture, the toes of the right foot must not be moved from the spot where they were first placed, and the left foot should be moved as little as possible.

Having finished the prayers of one rek'ah, the worshipper rises upon his feet (but without moving his toes from the spot where they were, particularly those of the right foot), and repeats the same; only he should recite some other chapter, or portion, after the Fát'ḥah, than that which he repeated before, as, for instance, the 108th chapter.[1]

After every *second* rek'ah (and after the *last*, though there be an odd number, as in the evening farḍ), he does not immediately raise his knees from the ground, but bends his left foot under him, and sits upon it, and places his hands upon his thighs, with the fingers a little apart. In this posture, he says, "Praises are to God, and prayers, and good works. Peace be on thee, O Prophet, and the mercy of God, and his blessings. Peace be on us, and on [all] the righteous worshippers of God." Then raising the first finger of the right hand[2] (but not the hand itself), he adds, "I testify that there is no deity but God; and I testify that Moḥammad is his servant and his apostle."

After the *last* rek'ah of each of the prayers (that is, after the sunneh prayers and the farḍ alike), after saying, "Praises are to God," &c., the worshipper, looking upon his right shoulder, says, "Peace be on you, and the mercy of God." Then looking upon the left, he repeats the same. These salutations are considered by some as addressed only to the guardian angels who watch over the believer, and note all his actions;[3] but others say that they are addressed both to angels and men (*i. e.*, believers only), who may be present; no person, however, returns them. Before the salutations in the *last*

---

[1] In the third and fourth farḍ rek'ahs, the recitation of a second portion of the Ḳur-án after the Fát'ḥah should be omitted; and before farḍ prayers of four rek'ahs, the "iḳámeh" (which consists of the words of the adán, with the addition of "the time of prayer is come," pronounced twice after "come to security,") should be repeated; but most persons neglect doing this, and many do not observe the former rule.

[2] The doctors of El-Islám differ respecting the proper position of the fingers of the right hand on this occasion: some hold that all the fingers but the first are to be doubled, as represented in the second sketch of the postures of prayer.

[3] Some say that every believer is attended by two angels; others say, five; others, sixty, or a hundred and sixty.

prayer, the worshipper may offer up any short petition (in Scriptural language rather than his own); while he does so looking at the palms of his two hands, which he holds like an open book before him, and then draws over his face, from the forehead downwards.

Having finished both the sunneh and farḍ prayers, the worshipper, if he would acquit himself completely, or rather, perform supererogatory acts, remains sitting (but may then sit more at his ease), and recites the "Áyet el-Kursee," or Throne-Verse, which is the 256th of the 2nd chapter of the Ḳur-án;[1] and adds, "O High: O Great: thy perfection [I extol]." He then repeats, "The perfection of God" (thirty-three times). "The perfection of God the Great, with his praise for ever" (once). "Praise be to God" (thirty-three times). "Extolled be his dignity: there is no deity but He" (once). "God is most Great" (thirty-three times). "God is most Great in greatness, and praise be to God in abundance" (once). He counts these repetitions with a string of beads called "sebḥah" (more properly "subḥah"). The beads are ninety-nine, and have a mark between each thirty-three. They are of aloes, or other odoriferous or precious wood, or of coral, or of certain fruit-stones, or seeds, &c.

Any wandering of the eyes, or of the mind, a coughing, or the like, answering a question, or any action not prescribed to be performed, must be strictly avoided (unless it be *between* the sunneh prayers and the farḍ, or be difficult to avoid; for it is held allowable to make three slight irregular motions, or deviations from correct deportment); otherwise the worshipper must begin again, and repeat his prayers with due reverence. It is considered extremely sinful to interrupt a man when engaged in his devotions. The time usually occupied in repeating the prayers of four rek'ahs, without the supererogatory additions, is less than four, or even three, minutes. The Muslim says the five daily prayers in his house or shop or in the mosque, according as may be most convenient to him: it is seldom that a person goes from his house to the mosque to pray, except to join the congregation on Friday. Men of the lower orders oftener pray in the mosques than those who have a comfortable home, and a mat or carpet upon which to pray.

The same prayers are said by the congregation in the mosque on

---

1 Beginning with the words "God: there is no deity but He;" and ending with, "He is the High, the Great."

the noon of Friday; but there are additional rites performed by the Imám and other ministers on this occasion. The chief reasons for fixing upon Friday as the Sabbath of the Muslims were, it is said, because Adam was created on that day, and died on the same day of the week, and because the general resurrection was prophesied to happen on that day; whence, particularly, Friday was named the day of "El-Gum'ah" (or the assembly). The Muslim does not abstain from worldly business on Friday, except during the time of prayer, according to the precept of the Ḳur-án, ch. lxii. vv. 9 and 10.

Interior of a Mosque.

To form a proper conception of the ceremonials of the Friday-prayers, it is necessary to have some idea of the interior of a mosque. A mosque in which a congregation assembles to perform the Friday-prayers is called "gámè'." The mosques of Cairo are so numerous, that none of them is inconveniently crowded on the Friday; and some of them are so large as to occupy spaces three or four hundred feet square. They are mostly built of stone, the alternate courses of which are generally coloured externally red and white. Most commonly a large mosque consists of porticoes surrounding a square open court, in the centre of which is a tank or a fountain for ablution. One side of the building faces the direction of Mekkeh, and the portico on this side, being the principal place of prayer, is more spacious than those on the three other sides of the court: it generally has two or more rows of columns, forming so many aisles, parallel with the exterior wall. In some cases, this portico, like the other three, is open to the court; in other cases, it is separated from the court by partitions of wood, connecting the front row of columns. In the centre of its exterior wall is the "meḥráb" (or niche) which marks the direction of Mekkeh; and to the right of this is the "mimbar" (or pulpit). Opposite the meḥráb, in the fore part of the portico, or in its central part, there is generally a platform (called "dikkeh"), surrounded by a parapet, and supported by small columns; and by it, or before it, are one or two seats, having a kind of desk to bear a volume of the Ḳur-án, from which a chapter is read to the congregation. The walls are generally quite plain, being simply white-washed; but in some mosques the lower part of the wall of the place of prayer is lined with coloured marbles, and the other part ornamented with various devices executed in stucco, but mostly with texts of the Ḳur-án (which form long friezes, having a pleasing effect),[1] and never with the representation of anything that has life. The pavement is covered with matting, and the rich and poor pray side by side; the man of rank or wealth enjoying no peculiar distinction or comfort, unless (which is sometimes the case) he have a prayer-carpet brought by his servant, and spread for him.[2]

The Prophet did not forbid *women* to attend public prayers in a mosque, but pronounced it better for them to pray in private: in

---

1 The "Throne-Verse" (see p. 79) is one of the most common.

2 Adjoining each mosque are several "latrinæ," in each of which is a receptacle with water, for ablution.

Cairo, however, neither females nor young boys are allowed to pray with the congregation in the mosque, or even to be present in the mosque at any time of prayer: formerly women were permitted (and perhaps are still in some countries), but were obliged to place themselves apart from the men, and behind the latter; because, as Sale has remarked, the Muslims are of opinion that the presence of females inspires a different kind of devotion from that which is requisite in a place dedicated to the worship of God. Very few women in Egypt even pray at home.

Over each of the mosques of Cairo presides a "Náẓir" (or warden), who is the trustee of the funds which arise from lands, houses, &c., bequeathed to the mosque by the founder and others, and who appoints the religious ministers and the inferior servants. Two "Imáms" are employed to officiate in each of the larger mosques: one of them, called the "Khaṭeeb," preaches and prays before the congregation on the Friday: the other is an "Imám Rátib," or ordinary Imám, who recites the five prayers of every day in the mosque, at the head of those persons who may be there at the exact times of those prayers: but in most of the smaller mosques both these offices are performed by one Imám. There are also to each mosque one or more "muëddins" (to chant the call to prayer), and "bowwábs" (or door-keepers), according as there are one or more mád'nehs (or menarets) and entrances; and several other servants are employed to sweep the mosque, spread the mats, light the lamps, and attend to the sáḳiyeh (or water-wheel), by which the tank or fountain, and other receptacles for water, necessary to the performance of ablutions, are supplied. The Imáms, and those persons who perform the lower offices, are all paid from the funds of the mosque, and not by any contributions exacted from the people.

The condition of the Imáms is very different, in most respects, from that of Christian priests. They have no authority above other persons, and do not enjoy any respect but what their reputed piety or learning may obtain for them: nor are they a distinct order of men set apart for religious offices, like our clergy, and composing an indissoluble fraternity; for a man who has acted as the Imám of a mosque may be displaced by the warden of that mosque, and, with his employment and salary, loses the *title* of Imám, and has no better chance of being again chosen for a religious minister than any other person competent to perform the office. The Imáms obtain their livelihood chiefly by other means than the service of the mosque, as their salaries are very small: that of a Khaṭeeb being generally about a piaster ($2\frac{2}{5}d.$ of our money) per month; and that of an ordinary Imám, about five piasters. Some of them engage in trade; several of them are "'aṭṭárs" (or druggists and perfumers), and many of them are schoolmasters: those who have no regular occupations of these kinds often recite the Ḳur-án for hire in private houses. They are mostly chosen from among the poor students of the great mosque El-Azhar.

The large mosques are open from day-break till a little after the 'eshè, or till nearly two hours after sunset. The others are closed between the hours of morning and noon prayers; and most mosques are also closed in rainy weather (except at the times of prayer), lest persons who have no shoes should enter, and dirt the pavement and matting. Such persons always enter by the door nearest the tank or fountain (if there be more than one door), that they may wash before they pass into the place of prayer; and generally this door alone is left open in dirty weather. The great mosque El-Azhar remains open all night, with the exception of the principal place of prayer, which is called the "maḳṣoorah," being partitioned off from the rest of the building. In many of the larger mosques, particularly in the afternoon, persons are seen lounging, chatting together, eating, sleeping, and sometimes spinning or sewing, or engaged in some other simple craft; but, notwithstanding such practices, which are contrary to precepts of their prophet, the Muslims very highly respect their mosques. There are several mosques in Cairo (as the Azhar, Ḥasaneyn, &c.), *before* which no Frank, nor any other Christian, nor a Jew, were allowed to pass, till of late years, since the French invasion.

On the Friday, half an hour before the "ḍuhr" (or noon), the muëddins of the mosques ascend to the galleries of the mád'nehs, and chant the "Selám," which is a salutation to the Prophet, not always expressed in the same words, but generally in words to the following effect:—"Blessing and peace be on thee, O thou of great dignity: O Apostle of God. Blessing and peace be on thee, to whom the Truth said, I am God. Blessing and peace be on thee, thou first of the creatures of God, and seal of the Apostles of God. From me be [invoked] peace on thee, on thee and on thy Family and all thy Companions."—Persons then begin to assemble in the mosques.

The utmost solemnity and decorum are observed in the public

worship of the Muslims. Their looks and behaviour in the mosque are not those of enthusiastic devotion, but of calm and modest piety. Never are they guilty of a designedly irregular word or action during their prayers. The pride and fanaticism which they exhibit in common life, in intercourse with persons of their own, or of a different faith, seem to be dropped on their entering the mosque, and they appear wholly absorbed in the adoration of their Creator; humble and downcast, yet without affected humility, or a forced expression of countenance.

The Muslim takes off his shoes at the door of the mosque, carries them in his left hand, sole to sole, and puts his right foot first over the threshold. If he have not previously performed the preparatory ablution, he repairs at once to the tank or fountain to acquit himself of that duty. Before he commences his prayers, he places his shoes (and his sword and pistols, if he have such arms,) upon the matting, a little before the spot where his head will touch the ground in prostration: his shoes are put one upon the other, sole to sole.

The people who assemble to perform the noon-prayers of Friday arrange themselves in rows parallel to that side of the mosque in which is the niche, and facing that side. Many do not go until the adán of noon, or just before. When a person goes at, or a little after, the Selám, as soon as he has taken his place in one of the ranks, he performs two rek'ahs, and then remains sitting, on his knees or cross-legged, while a reader, having seated himself on the reading-chair immediately after the Selám, is occupied in reciting (usually without book) the Soorat el-Kahf (the 18th chapter of the Ḳur-án), or a part of it; for, generally, he has not finished it before the adán of noon, when he stops. All the congregation, as soon as they hear the adán (which is the same as on other days), sit on their knees and feet. When the adán is finished, they stand up, and perform, each separately, two[1] rek'ahs, "sunnet el-gum'ah" (or the sunneh ordinance for Friday), which they conclude, like the ordinary prayers, with the two salutations. A servant of the mosque, called a "Muraḳḳee," then opens the folding-doors at the foot of the pulpit-stairs, takes from behind them a straight, wooden sword, and, standing a little to the right of the door-way, with his right side towards the ḳibleh, holds this sword in his right hand, resting the point on the ground. In

[1] If of the sect of the Sháfe'ees, to which most of the people of Cairo belong; but if of that of the Ḥanafees, *four* rek'ahs.

this position he says, "Verily God and his angels bless the Prophet. O ye who believe, bless him, and greet him with a salutation."[1] Then, one or more persons, called "Muballighs," stationed on the dikkeh, chant the following, or similar words.[2] "O God, bless and save and beatify the most noble of the Arabs and 'Agam [or foreigners], the Imám of Mekkeh and El-Medeeneh and the Temple, to whom the spider shewed favour, and wove its web in the cave; and whom the ḍabb[3] saluted; and before whom the moon was cloven in twain; our lord Moḥammad, and his Family and Companions." The Muraḳḳee then recites the adán (which the Mueddins have already chanted): after every few words he pauses, and the Muballighs, on the dikkeh, repeat the same words in a sonorous chant.[4] Before the adán is finished, the Khaṭeeb, or Imám, comes to the foot of the pulpit, takes the wooden sword from the Muraḳḳee's hand, ascends the pulpit, and sits on the top step or platform. The pulpit of a large mosque, on this day, is decorated with two flags, with the profession of the faith, or the names of God and Moḥammad, worked upon them: these are fixed at the top of the stairs, slanting forward. The Muraḳḳee and Muballighs having finished the adán, the former repeats a tradition of the Prophet, saying, "The Prophet (upon whom be blessing and peace) hath said, 'If thou say unto thy companion while the Imám is preaching on Friday, Be thou silent, thou speakest rashly.' Be ye silent: ye shall be rewarded: God shall recompense you." He then sits down. The Khaṭeeb now rises, and, holding the wooden sword[5] in the same manner as the Muraḳḳee did, delivers an exhortation, called "khuṭbet el-waạẓ." As the reader may be curious to see a translation of a Muslim sermon, I insert one. The following is a sermon preached on the first Friday of the Arab year.[6] The original, as usual, is in rhyming prose.

"Praise be to God, the Renewer of years, and the Multiplier of favours, and the Creator of months and days, according to the most perfect wisdom and most admirable regulation; who hath dignified

---

1 Ḳur-án, ch. xxxiii. v. 56.

2 There are some trifling differences in the forms of salutations on the Prophet in the Friday-prayers in different mosques: I describe what is most common.

3 A kind of lizard, the *lacerta Libyca.*

4 In the great mosque El-Azhar, there are several Muballighs in different places, to make the adán heard to the whole congregation.

5 To commemorate the acquisition of Egypt by the sword. It is never used by the Khaṭeeb but in a country or town that has been so acquired by the Muslims from unbelievers.

6 During my first visit to Egypt, I went to the great mosque El-Azhar, to witness the performance of the Friday-prayers by the largest congregation in Cairo. I was pleased with the preaching of the Khaṭeeb of the mosque, Gád-El-Mowlà, and afterwards procured his sermon-book ("deewán khuṭab"), containing sermons for every Friday in the year, and for the two "'eeds," or grand festivals. I translate the first sermon.

the months of the Arabs above all other months, and pronounced that among the more excellent of them is El-Moḥarram the Sacred, and commenced with it the year, as He hath closed it with Zu-l-Ḥeggeh. How propitious is the beginning, and how good is the end! [1] [I extol] his perfection, exempting Him from the association of any other deity with Him. He hath well considered what He hath formed, and established what He hath contrived, and He alone hath the power to create and to annihilate. I praise Him, extolling his perfection, and exalting his name, for the knowledge and inspiration which He hath graciously vouchsafed; and I testify that there is no deity but God alone; He hath no companion; He is the most holy King; the [God of] peace: and I testify that our lord and our Prophet and our friend Moḥammad is his servant and his apostle and his elect and his friend, the guide of the way, and the lamp of the dark. O God, bless and save and beatify this noble Prophet, and chief and excellent apostle, the merciful-hearted, our lord Moḥammad, and his family, and his companions, and his wives, and his posterity, and the people of his house, the noble persons, and grant them ample salvation.—O servants of God, your lives have been gradually curtailed, and year after year hath passed away, and ye are sleeping on the bed of indolence and on the pillow of iniquity. Ye pass by the tombs of your predecessors, and fear not the assault of destiny and destruction, as if others departed from the world and ye must of necessity remain in it. Ye rejoice at the arrival of new years, as if they brought an increase to the term of life, and swim in the seas of desires, and enlarge your hopes, and in every way exceed other people [in presumption], and ye are sluggish in doing good. O how great a calamity is this! God teacheth by an allegory. Know ye not that in the curtailment of time by indolence and sleep there is very great trouble? Know ye not that in the cutting short of lives by the termination of years is a very great warning? Know ye not that the night and day divide the lives of numerous souls? Know ye not that health and capacity are two blessings coveted by many men? But the truth hath become manifest to him who hath eyes. Ye are now between two years: one year hath passed away, and come to an end, with its evils; and ye have entered upon another year, in which, if it please God, mankind

[1] The year begins and ends with a sacred month. The sacred months are four; the first, seventh, eleventh, and twelfth. During these, war was forbidden to be waged against such as acknowledged them to be sacred; but was afterwards allowed. The first month is also held to be excellent on account of the day of 'Áshoorà (respecting which see chapter xxiv. of this work); and the last, on account of the pilgrimage.

shall be relieved. Is any of you determining upon diligence [in doing good] in the year to come? or repenting of his failings in the times that are passed? The happy is he who maketh amends for the time passed in the time to come; and the miserable is he whose days pass away and he is careless of his time. This new year hath arrived, and the sacred month of God hath come with blessings to you, the first of the months of the year, and of the four sacred months, as hath been said, and the most worthy of preference and honour and reverence. Its fast is the most excellent of fasts after that which is obligatory,[1] and the doing of good in it is among the most excellent of the objects of desire. Whosoever desireth to reap advantage from it, let him fast the ninth and tenth days, looking for aid.[2] Abstain not from this fast through indolence, and esteeming it a hardship; but comply with it in the best manner, and honour it with the best of honours, and improve your time by the worship of God morning and evening. Turn unto God with repentance, before the assault of death: He is the God who accepteth repentance of his servants, and pardoneth sins.—*The Tradition.*[3]—The Apostle of God (God bless and save him) hath said, 'The most excellent prayer, after the prescribed,[4] is the prayer that is said in the last third of the night; and the most excellent fast, after Ramaḍán, is that of the month of God, El-Moḥarram.'"

The Khaṭeeb, having concluded his exhortation, says to the congregation, "Supplicate God." He then sits down, and prays privately; and each member of the congregation at the same time offers up some private petition, as after the ordinary prayers, holding his hands before him (looking at the palms), and then drawing them down his face. This done, the Muballighs say, "Ámeen. Ámeen! (Amen. Amen.) O Lord of the beings of the whole world."—The Khaṭeeb now rises again, and recites another Khuṭbeh, called "khuṭbet en-naạt," of which the following is a translation:—[5]

"Praise be to God, abundant praise, as He hath commanded. I testify that there is no deity but God alone: He hath no companion: affirming his supremacy, and condemning him who denieth and disbelieveth: and I testify that our lord and our prophet Moḥammad is his servant and his apostle, the lord of mankind, the intercessor, the

---

1 That of the month of Ramaḍán.

2 See an account of the customs observed in honour of the day of 'Áshoorà, chap. xxiv.

3 The Khaṭeeb always closes his exhortation with one or two traditions of the Prophet.

4 The five daily prayers ordained by the Ḳur-án.

5 This is always the same, or nearly so.

accepted intercessor, on the day of assembling: God bless him and his family as long as the eye seeth and the ear heareth. O people, reverence God by doing what He hath commanded, and abstain from that which He hath forbidden and prohibited. The happy is he who obeyeth, and the miserable is he who opposeth and sinneth. Know that the present world is a transitory abode, and that the world to come is a lasting abode. Make provision, therefore, in your transitory state for your lasting state, and prepare for your reckoning and standing before your Lord: for know that ye shall to-morrow be placed before God, and reckoned with according to your deeds; and before the Lord of Might ye shall be present, 'and those who have acted unjustly shall know with what an overthrowal they shall be overthrown.'[1] Know that God, whose perfection I extol, and whose name be exalted, hath said (and ceaseth not to say wisely, and to command judiciously, warning you, and teaching, and honouring the dignity of your Prophet, extolling and magnifying him), 'Verily, God and his angels bless the Prophet: O ye who believe, bless him, and greet him with a salutation.'[2] O God, bless Moḥammad and the family of Moḥammad, as Thou blessedst Ibráheem[3] and the family of Ibráheem; and beatify Moḥammad and the family of Moḥammad, as Thou hast beatified Ibráheem and the family of Ibráheem among all creatures—for Thou art praiseworthy and glorious. O God, do Thou also be well pleased with the four Khaleefehs, the orthodox lords, of high dignity and illustrious honour, Aboo-Bekr Eṣ-Ṣiddeeḳ, and 'Omar, and 'Osmán, and 'Alee; and be Thou well pleased, O God, with the six who remained of the ten noble and just persons who swore allegiance to thy Prophet Moḥammad (God bless him and save him) under the tree (for Thou art the Lord of piety, and the Lord of pardon); those persons of excellence and clemency, and rectitude and prosperity, Ṭalḥah, and Ez-Zubeyr, and Saạd, and Sa'eed, and 'Abd-Er-Raḥmán Ibn-'Owf, and Aboo-'Obeydeh 'Ámir Ibn-El-Garráḥ; and with all the Companions of the Apostle of God (God bless and save him); and be Thou well pleased, O God, with the two martyred descendants, the two bright moons, 'the two lords of the youths of the people of Paradise in Paradise,' the two sweet-smelling flowers of the Prophet of this nation, Aboo-Moḥammad El-Ḥasan, and Aboo-'Abd-Allah El-Ḥoseyn: and be Thou well pleased, O God, with their mother, the daughter of the Apostle of God (God

---

[1] Ḳur-án, ch. xxvi. last verse. [2] Idem, ch. xxxiii. v. 56. [3] The patriarch Abraham.

bless and save him), Fáṭimeh Ez-Zahrà, and with their grandmother Khadeegeh El-Kubrà, and with 'Aisheh, the mother of the faithful, and with the rest of the pure wives, and with the generation which succeeded the Companions, and the generation which succeeded that, with beneficence to the day of judgment. O God, pardon the believing men and the believing women, and the Muslim men and the Muslim women, those who are living, and the dead; for Thou art a hearer near, an answerer of prayers, O Lord of the beings of the whole world. O God, aid El-Islám, and strengthen its pillars, and make infidelity to tremble, and destroy its might, by the preservation of thy servant, and the son of thy servant, the submissive to the might of thy majesty and glory, whom God hath aided, by the care of the Adored King, our master the Sulṭán, son of the Sulṭán, the Sulṭán Maḥmood[1] Khán: may God assist him, and prolong [his reign]. O God, assist him, and assist his armies, O thou Lord of the religion, and of the world present, and the world to come. O Lord of the beings of the whole world. O God, assist the forces of the Muslims, and the armies of the Unitarians. O God, frustrate the infidels and polytheists, thine enemies, the enemies of the religion. O God, invert their banners, and ruin their habitations, and give them and their wealth as booty to the Muslims.[2] O God, unloose the captivity of the captives, and annul the debts of the debtors; and make this town to be safe and secure, and blessed with wealth and plenty, and all the towns of the Muslims, O Lord of the beings of the whole world. And decree safety and health to us and to all travellers, and pilgrims, and warriors, and wanderers, upon thy earth, and upon thy sea, such as are Muslims, O Lord of the beings of the whole world. 'O Lord, we have acted unjustly towards our own souls, and if Thou do not forgive us and be merciful unto us, we shall surely be of those who perish.'[3] I beg of God, the Great, that He may forgive me and you, and all the people of Moḥammad, the servants of God. 'Verily God commandeth justice, and the doing of good, and giving [what is due] to kindred; and forbiddeth wickedness, and iniquity, and oppression: He admonisheth you that ye may reflect.'[4] Remember God; He

---

1 The reigning Sulṭán at the time when the above was written. The Turkish Sulṭán is prayed for as the Khaleefeh, or Vicar of Moḥammad. Formerly, the 'Abbásee or Fáṭimee Khaleefehs were thus mentioned in the congregational prayers of Friday.

2 This sentence, beginning "O God, frustrate," was not inserted in one copy of this prayer, which I obtained from an Imám. Another Imám, at whose dictation I wrote the copy here translated, told me that this sentence and some others were often omitted.

3 Ḳur-án, ch. vii. v. 22.

4 Idem, ch. xvi. v. 92.

will remember you: and thank Him; He will increase to you [your blessings]. Praise be to God, the Lord of the beings of the whole world!"

During the rise of the Nile, a good inundation is also prayed for in this Khuṭbeh. The Khaṭeeb, or Imám, having ended it, descends from the pulpit, and the Muballighs chant the "iḳámeh" (described in a foot-note to page 78): the Imám, stationed before the niche, then recites the "farḍ" prayers of Friday, which consist of two rek'ahs, and are similar to the ordinary prayers. The people do the same, but silently, and keeping time exactly with the Imám in the various postures. Those who are of the Málikee sect then leave the mosque; and so also do many persons of the other sects: but some of the Sháfe'ees and Ḥanafees (there are scarcely any Ḥambelees in Cairo) remain, and recite the *ordinary* farḍ prayers of noon; forming a number of separate groups, in each of which one acts as Imám. The rich, on going out of the mosque, often give alms to the poor outside the door.

There are other prayers to be performed on particular occasions—on the two grand annual festivals, on the nights of Ramaḍán (the month of abstinence), on the occasion of an eclipse of the sun or moon, for rain, previously to the commencement of battle, in pilgrimage, and at funerals.

I have spoken thus fully of Muslim worship because my countrymen in general have very imperfect and erroneous notions on this subject; many of them even imagining that the Muslims ordinarily pray to their *Prophet* as well as to God. Invocations to the Prophet, for his *intercession*, are, indeed, frequently made, particularly at his tomb, where pious visiters generally say, "We ask thy intercession, O Apostle of God." The Muslims also even implore the intercession of their numerous saints.

The duty next in importance to prayer is that of giving *alms*. Certain alms are prescribed by law, and are called "zekah" (thus commonly pronounced for "zekáh"): others, called "ṣadaḳah," are voluntary. (These two terms, however, are properly synonymous.) The former, or obligatory alms, were, in the earlier ages of El-Islám, collected, by officers appointed by the sovereign, for pious uses, such as building mosques, &c.; but now it is left to the Muslim's conscience to give them, and to apply them in what manner he thinks fit; that is, to bestow them upon whatever needy persons he may choose. They are to be given once in every year; of cattle and sheep, generally in the proportion of one in forty, two in a hundred and twenty; of camels, for every five, a ewe; or for twenty-five, a pregnant camel; and likewise of money, and, among the Ḥanafees, of merchandize, &c. He who has money to the amount of two hundred dirhems (or drams) of silver, or twenty mitḳáls (*i. e.* thirty drams) of gold, or, among the Ḥanafees, the value of the above in gold or silver ornaments, utensils, &c., must annually give the fortieth part ("rubạ el-'oshr"), or the value of that part.

Fasting is the next duty. The Muslim is commanded to fast during the whole month of Ramaḍán[1] every day, from the first appearance of daybreak, or rather from the hour when a person can distinguish plainly the white thread from the black thread,[2] meaning the white streak and the black streak seen in the eastern horizon at the first appearance of daybreak (in Egypt about two hours before sunrise), until sunset. He must abstain from eating, drinking, smoking, smelling perfumes, and every unnecessary indulgence or pleasure of a worldly nature; even from intentionally swallowing his spittle. When Ramaḍán falls in summer,[3] the fast is very severe; the abstinence from drinking being most painfully felt. Persons who are sick, or on a journey, and soldiers in time of war, are not obliged to observe the fast during Ramaḍán; but if they do not keep it in this month they should fast an equal number of days at a future time. Fasting is also to be dispensed with in the cases of a nurse and a pregnant woman. The Prophet even disapproved of any person's keeping the fast of Ramaḍán if not perfectly able; and desired no man to fast so much as to injure his health, or disqualify himself for necessary labour. The modern Muslims seem to regard the fast of Ramaḍán as of more importance than any other religious act, for many of them keep this fast who neglect their daily prayers; and even those who break the fast, with very few exceptions, pretend to keep it. Many Muslims of the wealthy classes eat and drink in secret during Ramaḍán; but the greater number strictly keep the fast, which is fatal to numerous persons in a weak state of health. There are some other days on which it is considered meritorious to fast, but not absolutely necessary. On the two grand festivals, namely, that following Ramaḍán, and that which succeeds the pilgrimage, it is *unlawful* to do so, being expressly forbidden by the Prophet.

---

1 Because the Prophet received the first revelation in that month.

2 Ḳur-án, ch. ii. v. 183.

3 The year being lunar, each month retrogrades through all the seasons in the course of about thirty-three years and a half.

The last of the four most important duties, that of *pilgrimage*, remains to be noticed. It is incumbent on every Muslim to perform, once in his life, the pilgrimage to Mekkeh and Mount 'Arafát, unless poverty or ill health prevent him; or, if a Ḥanafee, he may send a deputy, whose expenses he must pay.[1] Many, however, neglect the duty of pilgrimage who cannot plead a lawful excuse; and they are not reproached for so doing. It is not merely by the visit to Mekkeh, and the performance of the ceremonies of compassing the Kaạbeh seven times and kissing the "black stone" in each round, and other rites in the Holy City, that the Muslim acquires the title of "el-ḥágg"[2] (or the pilgrim): the final object of the pilgrimage is Mount 'Arafát, six hours' journey distant from Mekkeh. During his performance of the required ceremonies in Mekkeh, and also during his journey to 'Arafát, and until his completion of the pilgrimage, the Muslim wears a peculiar dress, called "eḥrám" (vulgarly ḥerám), generally consisting of two simple pieces of cotton, or linen, or woollen cloth, without seam or ornament, one of which is wrapped round the loins, and the other thrown over the shoulders: the instep and heel of each foot, and the head, must be bare; but umbrellas are now used by many of the pilgrims. It is necessary that the pilgrim be present on the occasion of a Khuṭbeh which is recited on Mount 'Arafát in the afternoon of the 9th of the month of Zu-l-Ḥeggeh. In the ensuing evening, after sunset, the pilgrims commence their return to Mekkeh. Halting the following day in the valley of Minè (or, as it is more commonly called, Munà), they complete the ceremonies of the pilgrimage by a sacrifice (of one or more rams, he-goats, cows, or she-camels, part of the flesh of which they eat, and part give to the poor), and by shaving the head and clipping the nails. Every one, after this, resumes his usual dress, or puts on a new one, if provided with such. The sacrifice is called "el-fidà" (or the ransom), as it is performed in commemoration of the ransom of Isma'eel (or Ishmael) by the sacrifice of the ram, when he was himself about to be offered up by his father; for it is the general opinion of the Muslims that it was this son, not Isaac, who was to be sacrificed by his father.

There are other ordinances, more or less connected with those which have been already explained.

---

1 A Málikee is held bound to perform the pilgrimage if strong enough to bear the journey on foot, and able to earn his food on the way.

2 On the pronunciation of this word, see a note to the second paragraph of Chapter V.

The two festivals called "el-'Eed eṣ-Ṣugheiyir,"[1] or the Minor Festival, and "el-'Eed el-Kebeer," or the Great Festival, the occasions of which have been mentioned above, are observed with public prayer and general rejoicing. The first of these lasts three days; and the second, three or four days. The festivities with which they are celebrated will be described in a subsequent chapter. On the first day of the latter festival (it being the day on which the pilgrims perform their sacrifice) every Muslim should slay a victim, if he can afford to purchase one. The wealthy person slays several sheep, or a sheep or two, and a buffalo, and distributes the greater portion of the meat to the poor. The slaughter may be performed by a deputy.

War against enemies of El-Islám, who have been the first aggressors, is enjoined as a sacred duty; and he who loses his life in fulfilling this duty, if unpaid, is promised the rewards of a martyr. It has been said, even by some of their leading doctors, that the Muslims are commanded to put to death all idolaters who refuse to embrace El-Islám, except women and children, whom they are to make slaves:[2] but the precepts on which this assertion is founded relate to the pagan Arabs, who had violated their oaths and long persevered in their hostility to Moḥammad and his followers. According to the decisions of the most reasonable doctors, the laws respecting other idolaters, as well as Christians and Jews, who have drawn upon themselves the hostility of the Muslims, are different: of such enemies, if reduced by force of arms, refusing to capitulate or to surrender themselves, the men may be put to death or be made slaves; and the women and children also, under the same circumstances, may be made slaves: but life and liberty are to be granted to those enemies who surrender themselves by capitulation or otherwise, on the condition of their embracing El-Islám or paying a poll-tax, unless they have acted perfidiously towards the Muslims, as did the Jewish tribe of Ḳureyḍhah, who, being in league with Moḥammad, went over to his enemies and aided them against him: for which conduct, when they surrendered, the men were slain, and the women and children were made slaves.—The Muslims, it may here be added, are forbidden to contract intimate friendship with unbelievers.

---

[1] More properly "Ṣagheer." This is what many travellers have incorrectly called "the Great Festival."

[2] Misled by the decision of those doctors, and an opinion prevalent in Europe, I represented the laws of "holy war" as more severe than I find them to be according to the letter and spirit of the Ḳur-án, when carefully examined, and according to the Ḥanafee code. I am indebted to Mr. Urquhart for suggesting to me the necessity of revising my former statement on this subject; and must express my conviction that no precept is to be found in the Ḳur-án which, taken with the context, can justify unprovoked war.

There are certain prohibitory laws in the Ḳur-án which must be mentioned here, as remarkably affecting the moral and social condition of its disciples.

Wine, and all inebriating liquors, are forbidden, as being the cause of "more evil than profit."[1] Many of the Muslims, however, in the present day, drink wine, brandy, &c., in secret; and some, thinking it no sin to indulge thus in moderation, scruple not to do so openly; but among the Egyptians there are few who transgress in this flagrant manner. "Boozeh," or "booẓah," which is an intoxicating liquor made with barley-bread, crumbled, mixed with water, strained, and left to ferment, is commonly drunk by the boatmen of the Nile, and by other persons of the lower orders.[2] Opium, and other drugs which produce a similar effect, are considered unlawful, though not mentioned in the Ḳur-án; and persons who are addicted to the use of these drugs are regarded as immoral characters; but in Egypt, such persons are not very numerous. Some Muslims have pronounced tobacco, and even coffee, unlawful.

The eating of swine's flesh is strictly forbidden. The unwholesome effects of that meat in a hot climate would be a sufficient reason for the prohibition; but the pig is held in abhorrence by the Muslim chiefly on account of its extremely filthy habits.[3] Most animals prohibited for food by the Mosaic law are alike forbidden to the Muslim. The camel is an exception. The Muslim is "forbidden [to eat] that which dieth of itself, and blood, and swine's flesh, and that on which the name of any beside God hath been invoked; and that which hath been strangled, or killed by a blow, or by a fall, or by the horns [of another beast]; and that which hath been [partly] eaten by a wild beast, except what he shall [himself] kill; and that which hath been sacrificed unto idols."[4] An animal that is killed for the food of man must be slaughtered in a particular manner: the person who is about to perform the operation must say, "In the name of God: God is most great:" and then cut its throat, at the part next the head, taking care to divide the windpipe, gullet, and carotid arteries; unless

---

[1] Ḳur-án, ch. ii. v. 216. A kind of wine, formerly called "nebeedh" (a name now given to prohibited kinds), may be lawfully drunk. This is generally an infusion of dry grapes, or dry dates. The Muslims used to keep it until it had slightly fermented; and the Prophet himself was accustomed to drink it, but not when it was more than two days old. The nebeedh of raisins is now called "zebeeb."

[2] A similar beverage, thus prepared from barley, was used by the ancient Egyptians. (Herodotus, lib. ii. cap. 77.) The modern inhabitants of Egypt also prepare boozeh from wheat and from millet in the same manner, but less commonly.

[3] Swine were universally deemed impure by the ancient Egyptians. (Herodotus, lib. ii. cap. 47.)

[4] Ḳur-án, ch. v. v. 4.

it be a camel, in which case he should *stab* the throat at the part next the breast. It is forbidden to utter, in slaughtering an animal, the phrase which is so often made use of on other occasions, "In the name of God, the Compassionate, the Merciful," because the mention of the most benevolent epithets of the Deity on such an occasion would seem like a mockery of the sufferings which it is about to endure. Some persons in Egypt, but mostly women, when about to kill an animal for food, say, "In the name of God: God is most great: God give thee patience to endure the affliction which He hath allotted thee." [1] If the sentiment which first dictated this prayer were always felt, it would present a beautiful trait in the character of the people who use it. In cases of necessity, when in danger of starving, the Muslim is allowed to eat any food which is unlawful under other circumstances. The mode of slaughter above described is, of course, only required to be practised in the cases of domestic animals. Most kinds of fish are lawful food:[2] so too are many birds; the tame kinds of which must be killed in the same manner as cattle; but the wild may be shot. The hare, rabbit, gazelle, &c., are lawful food; and may either be shot (as birds may be), or killed by a dog, provided the name of God was uttered at the time of discharging the arrow, &c., or slipping the dog, and he (the dog) has not eaten any part of the prey. This animal, however, is considered very unclean: the Sháfe'ees hold themselves to be polluted by the touch of its nose, if it be wet; and if any part of their clothes be so touched, they must wash that part with seven waters, and once with clean earth: some others are only careful not to let the animal lick, or defile in a worse manner, their persons or their dress, &c. When game has been struck down by any weapon, but not killed, its throat must be immediately cut: otherwise it is unlawful food.

Gambling and usury are prohibited,[3] and all games of chance; and likewise the making of images or pictures of anything that has life.[4]

---

1 The Arabic words of this prayer, "God give thee patience," &c., are, "Allah yeṣabbirak (for yuṣabbirak) 'alà má belák."

2 In some respects the Muslim code does not appear to be so strictly founded upon exigencies of a sanitary nature as the Mosaic. See Leviticus, xi. 9—12. In Egypt, fish which have not scales are generally found to be unwholesome food. One of the few reasonable laws of El-Ḥákim was that which forbade the selling or catching such kinds of fish. See De Sacy, Chrestomathie Arabe, 2nd ed., vol. i. p. 98.

3 It is unlawful to give or receive interest, however small, for a loan, or on account of credit; and to exchange any article for another article of the same species, but differing in quantity. These and several other commercial transactions of a similar kind are severely condemned; but they are not very uncommon among modern Muslims, some of whom take exorbitant interest.

4 Many of the Muslims hold that only sculptures which cast a shadow, representing living creatures, are unlawful; but the Prophet certainly condemned pictures also.

The Prophet declared that every representation of this kind would be placed before its author on the day of judgment, and that he would be commanded to put life into it; which not being able to do, he would be cast, for a time, into hell.

The principal *civil* and *criminal laws* remain to be stated. Their origin we discover partly in customs of the Pagan Arabs; but mostly in the Bible and the Jewish traditions.

The civil and criminal laws are chiefly and immediately derived from the Ḳur-án;[1] but, in many important cases, this highest authority affords no precept. In most of these cases the Traditions of the Prophet direct the decisions of the judge.[2] There are, however, some important cases, and many of an inferior kind, respecting which both the Ḳur-án and the Traditions are silent or indecisive. These are determined by the explanations and amplifications derived either from the concordance of the principal early disciples, or from analogy, by the four great Imáms, or founders of the four orthodox persuasions of El-Islám; generally on the authority of the Imám of that persuasion to which the ruling power belongs, which persuasion, in Egypt, and throughout the Turkish Empire, is that of the Ḥanafees: or, if none of the decisions of the Imám relate to a case in dispute (which not unfrequently happens), judgment is given in accordance with a sentence of some other eminent doctor, founded upon analogy.—In general, only the principal laws, as laid down in the Ḳur-án and the Traditions, will be here stated.

The laws relating to *marriage* and the licence of *polygamy*, the facility of *divorce* allowed by the Ḳur-án, and the permission of *concubinage*, are essentially the natural and necessary consequences of the main principle of the constitution of Muslim society—the restriction of the intercourse between the sexes before marriage. Few men would marry if he who was disappointed in a wife whom he had never seen before were not allowed to take another; and in the case of a man's doing this, his own happiness, or that of the former wife, or the happiness of both these parties, may require his either retaining this wife or divorcing her. But I hope that my reader will admit a much stronger reason for these laws, regarding them as designed for the *Muslims*. As Moses allowed God's chosen people, for the hardness of their hearts, to put away their wives, and forbade neither polygamy

[1] A law given in the Ḳur-án is called "farḍ."

[2] A law derived from the Traditions is called "sunneh."

nor concubinage, he who believes that Moses was divinely inspired, to enact the best laws for his people, must hold the permission of these practices to be less injurious to morality than their prohibition, among a people similar to the ancient Jews. Their permission, though certainly productive of injurious effects upon morality and domestic happiness, prevents a profligacy that would be worse than that which prevails to so great a degree in European countries, where parties are united in marriage after an intimate mutual acquaintance. As to the licence of polygamy, which seems to be unfavourable to the accomplishment of the main object for which marriage was instituted, as well as to the exercise and improvement of the nobler powers of the mind, we should remark, that it was not introduced, but limited, by the legislator of the Muslims. It is true that he assumed to himself the privilege of having a greater number of wives than he allowed to others; but, in doing so, he may have been actuated by the want of male offspring, rather than impelled by voluptuousness.

The law respecting marriage and concubinage is perfectly explicit as to the number of wives whom a Muslim may have at the same time; but it is not so with regard to the number of concubine-slaves whom he may have. It is written, "Take in marriage, of the women who please you, two, three, or four; but if ye fear that ye cannot act equitably [to so many, take] one; or, [take] those whom your right hands have acquired,"[1] that is, your slaves. Therefore many of the wealthy Muslims marry two, three, or four wives, and keep besides several concubine-slaves; and many of the most revered characters, even Companions of the Prophet, are recorded to have done the same. The conduct of the latter clearly shews that the number of concubine-slaves whom a man may have is not limited by the law in the opinion of the orthodox.[2]

It is held lawful for a Muslim to marry a Christian or a Jewish woman, if induced to do so by excessive love of her, or if he cannot obtain a wife of his own faith; but in this case the offspring must follow the father's faith,[3] and the wife does not inherit when the father dies. A Muslimeh, however, is not allowed in any circumstances,

---

1 Ḳur-án, ch. iv. v. 3.

2 Some Muslim moralists argue, that, as four wives are a sufficient number for one man, so also are four concubine-slaves, or four women consisting of these two classes together; but, notwithstanding what Sale and some other learned men have asserted on this subject, the Muslim law certainly does not limit the number of concubine-slaves whom a man may have, whether in addition to, or without, a wife or wives.

3 In like manner, when a Christian man marries a Jewess, the Muslim law requires the offspring to profess "the better faith," namely, the Christian, if unwilling to embrace El-Islám.

but when force is employed, to marry a man who is not of her own faith. A man is forbidden, by the Ḳur-án[1] and the Sunneh, to marry his mother, or other ascendant; his daughter, or other descendant; his sister, or half-sister; the sister of his father or mother, or other ascendant; his niece, or any of her descendants; his foster-mother,[2] or a woman related to him by milk in any of the degrees which would preclude his marriage with her if she were similarly related to him by consanguinity; the mother of his wife, even if he have not consummated his marriage with this wife; the daughter of his wife if he have consummated his marriage with the latter, and she be still his wife; his father's wife, and his son's wife; and to have at the same time two wives who are sisters, or aunt and niece: he is forbidden also to marry his unemancipated slave, or another man's slave, if he have already a free wife. It is lawful for the Muslim to see the faces of these women whom he is forbidden to marry, but of no others, except his own wives and female slaves. The marriage of a man and woman, or of a man and a girl who has arrived at puberty, is lawfully effected by their declaring (which the latter generally does by a "wekeel," or deputy,) their consent to marry each other, in the presence of two witnesses (if witnesses can be procured), and by the payment, or part-payment, of a dowry. But the consent of a girl under the age of puberty is not required; her father, or, if he be dead, her nearest adult male relation, or any person appointed as her guardian by will or by the Ḳáḍee, acting for her as he pleases.[3] The giving of a dowry is indispensable, and the least sum that is allowed by law is ten "dirhems" (or drachms of silver), which is equal to about five shillings of our money. A man may legally marry a woman without mentioning a dowry; but after the consummation of the marriage she can, in this case, compel him to pay the sum of ten dirhems.[4]

A man may divorce his wife twice, and each time take her back without any ceremony, except in a case to be mentioned below; but if he divorce her the third time, or put her away by a triple divorce conveyed in one sentence, he cannot receive her again until she has

---

1 Ch. iv. vv. 26 and 27.

2 By the Ḥanafee code, a man may not marry a woman from whose breast he has received a single drop of milk; but Esh-Sháfe'ee does not prohibit the marriage unless he has been suckled by her five times in the course of the first two years.

3 A boy may be thus married; but he may divorce his wife.

4 Whatever property the wife receives from her husband, parents, or any other person, is entirely at her own disposal, and not subject to any claim of her husband or his creditors.

been married and divorced by another husband, who must have consummated his marriage with her.[1] When a man divorces his wife (which he does by merely saying, "Thou art divorced," or "I divorce thee"), he pays her a portion of her dowry (generally one-third), which he had kept back from the first, to be paid on this occasion or at his death; and she takes away with her the furniture, &c., which she brought at her marriage. He may thus put her away from mere dislike,[2] and without assigning any reason; but a woman cannot separate herself from her husband against his will, unless it be for some considerable fault on his part, as cruel treatment, or neglect; and even then, application to the Ḳáḍee's court is generally necessary to compel the man to divorce her; and she forfeits the above-mentioned remnant of the dowry.

The first and second divorce, if made without any mutual agreement for a compensation from the woman, or a pecuniary sacrifice on her part, is termed "ṭaláḳ reg'ee" (a divorce which admits of return); because the husband may take back his wife, without her consent, during the period of her "'eddeh" (which will be presently explained), but not after, unless with her consent, and by a new contract. If he divorce her the first or second time for a compensation, she perhaps requesting, "Divorce me for what thou owest me," or "— hast of mine" (that is, of the dowry, furniture, &c.), or for an additional sum, he cannot take her again but by her own consent, and by a new contract. This is a "ṭaláḳ báïn" (or separating divorce), and is termed "the lesser separation," to distinguish it from the third divorce, which is called "the greater separation." The "'eddeh" is the period during which a divorced woman, or a widow, must wait before marrying again; in either case, if pregnant, until delivery: otherwise, the former must wait three lunar periods, or three months; and the latter, four months and ten days. A woman who is divorced when in a state of pregnancy, though she may make a new contract of marriage immediately after her delivery, must wait forty days longer before she can complete her marriage by receiving her husband. The man who divorces his wife must maintain her in his own house, or in that of her parents, or elsewhere, during the period of her 'eddeh; but must cease to live with her as her husband from the commencement of that period. A divorced woman who has a son under two years of age may retain him until he has attained that age,

---

[1] Ḳur-án, ch. ii. vv. 229, 230.

[2] As the law of Moses also allows. See Deut. xxiv. 1.

and may be compelled to do so by the law of the Sháfe'ees; and, by the law of the Málikees, until he has arrived at puberty; but the Ḥanafee law limits the period during which the boy should remain under her care to seven years: her daughter she should retain until nine years of age, or the period of puberty. If a man divorce his wife before the consummation of marriage, he must pay her half the sum which he has promised to give her as a dowry; or, if he have promised no dowry, he must pay her the half of the smallest dowry allowed by law, which has been above mentioned; and she may marry again immediately.

When a wife refuses to obey the lawful commands of her husband, he may, and generally does, take her, or two witnesses[1] against her, to the Ḳáḍee's court, to prefer a complaint against her; and, if the case be proved, a certificate is written declaring the woman "náshizeh," or rebellious against her husband. This process is termed "writing a woman náshizeh." It exempts her husband from obligation to lodge, clothe, and maintain her. He is not obliged to divorce her; and, by refusing to do this, he may prevent her marrying another man as long as he lives; but, if she promise to be obedient afterwards, he must take her back, and maintain her, or divorce her. It is more common, however, for a wife whose husband refuses to divorce her, if she have parents or other relations able and willing to support her comfortably, to make a complaint at the Ḳáḍee's court, stating her husband's conduct to be of such a nature towards her that she will not live with him, and thus cause herself to be registered "náshizeh," and separated from him. In this case, the husband generally persists, from mere spite, in refusing to divorce her.

As concubines are *slaves*, some account of slaves in general may here be appropriately inserted, with a statement of the principal laws respecting concubines and their offspring, &c.—The slave is either a person taken captive in war, or carried off by force from a foreign hostile country, and being at the time of capture an infidel; or the offspring of a female slave by another slave, or by any man who is not her owner, or by her owner if he do not acknowledge himself to be the father; but a person cannot be the slave of a relation who is within the prohibited degrees of marriage. The power of the owner is such that he may even kill his slave with impunity for any offence; and he incurs but a slight punishment (as imprisonment for a period

[1] The witnesses must always be Muslims in accusations against a person of the same faith.

at the discretion of the judge) if he do so wantonly. He may give or sell his slaves, except in some cases which will be mentioned; and may marry them to whom he will, but not separate them when married. A slave, however, according to most of the doctors, cannot have more than two wives at the same time. As a slave enjoys less advantages than a free person, the law, in some cases, ordains that his punishment for an offence shall be half of that to which the free is liable for the same offence, or even less than half: if it be a fine, or pecuniary compensation, it must be paid by the owner, to the amount, if necessary, of the value of the slave, or the slave must be given in compensation. An unemancipated slave, at the death of the owner, becomes the property of the heirs of the latter; and when an emancipated slave dies, leaving no male descendant or collateral relation, the former owner is the heir; or, if he be dead, his heirs inherit the slave's property. But an unemancipated slave can acquire no property without the permission of the owner. Complete and immediate emancipation is sometimes granted to a slave gratuitously, or for a future pecuniary compensation. It is conferred by means of a written document, or by a verbal declaration in the presence of two witnesses, or by presenting the slave with the certificate of sale obtained from the former owner. Future emancipation is sometimes covenanted to be granted on the fulfilment of certain conditions; and more frequently, to be conferred on the occasion of the owner's death. In the latter case, the owner cannot sell the slave to whom he has made this promise; and as he cannot alienate by will more than one-third of the whole property that he leaves, the law ordains that, if the value of the said slave exceed that portion, the slave must obtain, and pay to the owner's heirs, the additional sum.—A Muslim may take as his concubine any of his female slaves who is a Muslimeh, or a Christian, or a Jewess, if he have not married her to another man; but he may not have as his concubines, at the same time, two or more who are sisters, or who are related to each other in any of the degrees which would prevent their both being his wives at the same time if they were free. A Christian is not by the law allowed, nor is a Jew, to have a Muslimeh slave as his concubine.[1] The master must wait a certain period (generally from a month to three months) after his acquisition of a female slave, before he can take her as his concubine. When a female slave becomes a mother by her master, the child

[1] Yet many Christians and Jews in Egypt infringe the law in this respect with impunity.

which she bears to him is free, if he acknowledge it to be his own; but if not (which I believe is seldom the case), it is his slave. In the former case the mother cannot afterwards be sold nor given away by her master (though she must continue to serve him and be his concubine as long as he desires); and she is entitled to emancipation at his death. Her bearing a child to him is called the cause of her emancipation or liberty; but it does not oblige him to emancipate her as long as he lives, though it is commendable if he do so, and make her his wife, provided he have not already four wives, or if he marry her to another man, should it be her wish. A free person cannot become the husband or wife of his, or her, own slave, without first emancipating that slave; and the marriage of a free person with the slave of another is dissolved if the former become the owner of the latter, and cannot be renewed but by emancipation and a regular legal contract.

The most remarkable general principles of the laws of *inheritance* are the denial of any privileges to primogeniture,[1] and in most cases awarding to a female a share equal to half that of a male of the same degree of relationship to the deceased.[2] A person may bequeath one-third of his or her property; but not a larger portion, unless he or she has no legal heir; nor any portion to a legal heir, except wife or husband, without the consent of all the other heirs. The children of a person deceased inherit the whole of that person's property, or what remains after the deduction of certain shares to be mentioned below, and after payment of the legacies and debts, &c.; and the share of a male is double the share of a female. If the children of the deceased be only females, two or more in number, they inherit together, by the law of the Ḳur-án, two-thirds; and if there be but one child, and that a female, she inherits by the same law half. [But the remaining third, or half, is also assigned to the said daughters or daughter, by a law of the Sunneh (which applies also to other cases), if there be no other legal heir.] If the deceased have

---

1 In this the Muslim law differs from the Mosaic, which assigns a double portion to the first-born son. See Deut. xxi. 17.

2 In my summary of the principal laws relating to inheritance, in the first two editions of this work, there were some errors, occasioned by my relying too much upon Sale's version of the Ḳur-án; for I doubted not his accuracy, as he had several commentaries to consult, and I had none; wherefore, in my inquiries respecting these laws, I sought only to add to, not to correct, the information conveyed by his version. I have here given a corrected statement, derived from the Ḳur-án and the Commentary of the Geláleyn, supplying some words of necessary explanation (which are enclosed in brackets) partly on the authority of a sheykh who was my tutor, and partly from the valuable work of D'Ohsson, "Tableau Général de l'Empire Othoman," Code Civil, livre iv.

left no immediate descendant, the sons and daughters of his son or sons inherit as immediate descendants [and so on]. If the deceased have left a child or a son's child [and so on], each of the parents of the deceased inherits one-sixth. If the father be dead, his share falls to *his* father. [If the mother be dead, her share falls to *her* mother.] If the deceased have left no child or son's child [and so on], the mother has one-third of the property, or of what remains after deducting the share of the wife or wives or husband, and the residue is for the father; unless the deceased has left two or more brothers or sisters, in which case the mother inherits one-sixth, and the father the residue; the said brothers or sisters receiving nothing;[1] [if the deceased have left a father or any ascendant in the male line.] A man inherits half of what remains of his wife's property after the payment of her legacies, &c., if she have left no child or son's child, [and so on;] and one-fourth if she have left a child or son's child, [and so on.] One-fourth is the share of the wife, or of the wives conjointly, if the deceased husband have left no child or son's child, [and so on;] and one-eighth if he have left any such descendant.[2] If the deceased have not left a father, [nor any ascendant in the male line,] nor a child, [nor a son's child, and so on,] the law ordains as follows:—1. A sole brother, or sister, only by the mother's side, inherits one-sixth; and if there be two or more brothers or sisters only by the mother's side, or one or more of such relations of each sex, they inherit collectively one-third, which is equally divided, without distinction of male and female.—2. If the deceased have left a sole sister by his father and mother, [and no such brother,] she inherits half; and a man inherits the whole property of such a sister, [or what remains after the payment of her legacies, &c.,] if she have left no child; but if she have left a male child, [or son's child, and so on,] he (the brother) inherits nothing; and if she have left a female child, the said brother inherits what remains after deducting

1 According to Sale's translation of the 12th verse of chap. iv., and a note thereon, if the deceased have no child, and his parents be his heirs, then his mother shall have the third part, and his father the other two-thirds: but if he have brethren, his mother shall have a sixth part:—and by his translation of the last verse of the same chapter, stating that the brothers of a man who has died *without issue* have a claim to inheritance, it is implied that the brothers, *if the father be living*, must have a share; consequently, that they would have, in the case above mentioned, a sixth part: for he has not stated that this portion which is deducted from the mother's share goes to the father, nor that the father's share is diminished.—Why the mother's share is diminished and the father's increased, in the case to which this note relates, I do not see: the reason might be easily inferred, were it not that the surviving brothers or sisters of the deceased may be his brothers or sisters by the mother's side only.

2 This is exclusive of what may remain due to her of her dowry, of which one-third is usually held in reserve by the husband, to be paid to her if he divorce her or when he dies.

that child's share [and after the payment of the legacies, &c.]. If the deceased have left two or more sisters by his father and mother, [and no such brother,] they inherit together two-thirds. If the deceased have left one or more brothers, and one or more sisters, by his father and mother, they inherit the whole, [or what remains after the payment of the legacies, &c.,] and the share of a male is double the share of a female.—3. Brothers and sisters by the father's side only, [when there is no brother or sister by the father and mother,] inherit as brothers and sisters by the father and mother.[1] No distinction is made between the child of a wife and that borne by a slave to her master (if the master acknowledge the child to be his own): both inherit equally. So also do the child of a wife and the adopted child. A bastard inherits only from his mother, and *vice versâ*. When there is no legal heir, or legatee, the property falls to the government-treasury, which is called "beyt el-mál." The laws respecting certain remote degrees of kindred, &c., I have not thought it necessary to state.[2] The property of the deceased is nominally divided into "ḳeeráṭs" (or twenty-fourth parts); and the share of each son, or other heir, is said to be so many ḳeeráṭs.

The law is remarkably lenient towards *debtors*. "If there be any [debtor]," says the Ḳur-án,[3] "under a difficulty [of paying his debt], let [his creditor] wait till it be easy [for him to do it]; but if ye remit it as alms, it will be better for you." The Muslim is commanded (in the chapter from which the above extract is taken), when he contracts a debt, to cause a statement of it to be written, and attested by two men, or a man and two women, of his own faith. The debtor is imprisoned for non-payment of his debt; but if he establish his insolvency, he is liberated. He may be compelled to work for the discharge of his debt, if able.

The Ḳur-án ordains that *murder* shall be punished with death; or rather, that the free shall die for the free, the slave for the slave, and a woman for a woman; or that the perpetrator of the crime shall pay to the heirs of the person whom he has killed, if they allow it, a fine, which is to be divided according to the laws of inheritance.[4] It also ordains that *unintentional homicide* shall be expiated by freeing a believer from slavery, and paying, to the family of the person killed, a fine, unless they remit it.[5] But these laws are amplified and ex-

---

[1] The portions of the Ḳur-án upon which the above laws are founded are verses 12—15, and the last verse, of ch. iv.

[2] The reader may see them in D'Ohsson's work before mentioned.

[3] Ch. ii. v. 280.

[4] Ch. ii. v. 173.

[5] Ch. iv. v. 94.

plained by the same book and by the Imáms.—A fine is not to be accepted for murder unless the crime has been attended by some palliating circumstance. This fine, which is the price of blood, is a hundred camels; or a thousand deenárs (about 500*l.*) from him who possesses gold; or from him who possesses silver, twelve thousand dirhems [1] (about 300*l.*) This is for killing a free man: for a woman, half the sum: for a slave, his or her value; but that must fall short of the price of blood for the free. A person unable to free a believer must fast two months, as in Ramaḍán. The accomplices of a murderer are liable to the punishment of death. By the Sunneh also, a man is obnoxious to capital punishment for the murder of a woman; and by the Ḥanafee law, for the murder of another man's slave. But he is exempted from this punishment who kills his own child or other descendant, or his own slave, or his son's slave, or a slave of whom he is part-owner: so also are his accomplices; and according to Esh-Sháfe'ee, a Muslim, though a slave, is not to be put to death for killing an infidel, though the latter be free. In the present day, however, murder is generally punished with death; the government seldom allowing a composition in money to be made. A man who kills another in self-defence, or to defend his property from a robber, is exempt from all punishment. The price of blood is a debt incumbent on the family, tribe, or association, of which the homicide is a member. It is also incumbent on the inhabitants of an enclosed quarter, or the proprietor or proprietors of a field, in which the body of a person killed by an unknown hand is found; unless the person has been found killed in his own house. A woman, convicted of a capital crime, is generally put to death by drowning in the Nile.

The Bedawees have made the law of the avenging of blood terribly severe and unjust, transgressing the limits assigned by the Ḳur-án: for, with them, any single person descended from the homicide, or from the homicide's father, grandfather, great-grandfather, or great-grandfather's father, may be killed by any of such relations of the person murdered, or killed in fight; but, among most tribes, the fine is generally accepted instead of the blood. Cases of blood-revenge are very common among the peasantry of Egypt, who, as I have before remarked, retain many customs of their Bedawee ancestors. The relations of a person who has been killed, in an Egyptian village,

[1] Or, according to some, ten thousand dirhems.

generally retaliate with their own hands rather than apply to the government, and often do so with disgusting cruelty, and even mangle and insult the corpse of their victim. The relations of a homicide usually flee from their own to another village, for protection. Even when retaliation has been made, animosity frequently continues between the two parties for many years; and often a case of blood-revenge involves the inhabitants of two or more villages in hostilities, which are renewed, at intervals, during the period of several generations.

Retaliation for unintentional *wounds* and *mutilations* is allowed, like as for murder; "eye for eye," &c.;[1] but a fine may be accepted instead, which the law allows also for unintentional injuries. The fine for a member that is single (as the nose) is the whole price of blood, as for homicide; for a member of which there are two, and not more (as a hand), half the price of blood; for one of which there are ten (a finger or toe), a tenth of the price of blood: but the fine of a man for maiming or wounding a woman is half of that for the same injury to a man; and that of a free person for injuring a slave varies according to the value of the slave. The fine for depriving a man of any of his five senses, or dangerously wounding him, or grievously disfiguring him for life, is the whole price of blood.

Theft, whether committed by a man or by a woman, according to the Ḳur-án,[2] is to be punished by cutting off the offender's right hand for the first offence; but a Sunneh law ordains that this punishment shall not be inflicted if the value of the stolen property is less than a quarter of a deenár;[3] and it is also held necessary, to render the thief obnoxious to this punishment, that the property stolen should have been deposited in a place to which he had not ordinary or easy access: whence it follows, that a man who steals in the house of a near relation is not subject to this punishment; nor is a slave who robs the house of his master. For the second offence, the left foot is to be cut off; for the third, according to the Sháfe'ee law, the left hand; for the fourth, the right foot; and for further offences of the same kind, the culprit is to be flogged or beaten; or, by the Ḥanafee code, for the third and subsequent offences, the criminal is to be punished by a long imprisonment. A man may steal a free-born infant without offending against the law, because it

---

[1] Ḳur-án, ch. v. v. 49.

[2] Ch. v. v. 42.

[3] The deenár is a mitḳál (or nearly 72 English grains) of gold. Sale, copying a false translation by Marracci, and neglecting to examine the Arabic text quoted by the latter, has stated the sum in question to be four deenárs.

is not property; but not a slave: and the hand is not to be cut off for stealing any article of food that is quickly perishable; because it may have been taken to supply the immediate demands of hunger. There are also some other cases in which the thief is exempt from the punishments above mentioned. In Egypt, of late years, these punishments have not been inflicted. Beating and hard labour have been substituted for the first, second, or third offence, and frequently death for the fourth. Most petty offences are usually punished by beating with the "kurbág" (a thong or whip of hippopotamus' hide, hammered into a round form,) or with a stick, generally on the soles of the feet.[1]

Adultery is most severely visited; but to establish a charge of this crime against a wife, four eye-witnesses are necessary.[2] If convicted thus, she is to be put to death by stoning.[3] I need scarcely say, that cases of this kind have very seldom occurred, from the difficulty of obtaining such testimony.[4] Further laws on this subject, and still more favourable to the women, are given in the Ḳur-án,[5] in the following words:—"But [as to] those who accuse women of reputation, [of fornication or adultery,] and produce not four witnesses [of the fact], scourge them with eighty stripes, and receive not their testimony for ever; for such are infamous prevaricators: except those who shall afterwards repent; for God is gracious and merciful. They who shall accuse their wives, [of adultery,] and shall have no witnesses [thereof] besides themselves, the testimony [which shall be required] of one of them [shall be] that he swear four times by God that he speaketh the truth, and the fifth [time that he imprecate] the curse of God on him if he be a liar; and it shall avert the punishment [of the wife] if she swear four times by God that he is a liar, and if the fifth [time she imprecate] the wrath of God on her if he speak the truth." The commentators and lawyers have agreed that, in these circumstances, the marriage must be dissolved. In the chapter from which the above quotation is made, it is ordained (in verse 2) that unmarried persons convicted of

---

1 The feet are confined by a chain or rope attached at each end to a staff, which is turned round to tighten it. This is called a "falaḳah." Two persons (one on each side) strike alternately.

2 Ḳur-án, ch. iv. v. 19.

3 This is a "Sunneh" law. The law is the same in the case of the adulterer, if married; but it is never enforced. See Leviticus, xx. 10, and St. John, viii. 4, 5.

4 It is worthy of remark, that the circumstance which occasioned the promulgation of this extraordinary law was an accusation of adultery preferred against the Prophet's favourite wife, 'Áïsheh: she was thus absolved from punishment, and her reputation was cleared by additional "revelations."

5 Ch. xxiv. vv. 4—9.

fornication shall be punished by scourging, with a hundred stripes; and a Sunneh law renders them obnoxious to the further punishment of banishment for a whole year.[1] Of the punishment of women convicted of incontinence in Cairo, I shall speak in the next chapter; as it is an arbitrary act of the government, not founded on the laws of the Ḳur-án, or the Traditions.[2]

Drunkenness was punished, by the Prophet, by flogging; and is still in Cairo, though not often: the "ḥadd," or number of stripes, for this offence, is eighty in the case of a free man, and forty in that of a slave.

Apostacy from the faith of El-Islám is considered a most heinous sin, and must be punished with death, unless the apostate will recant on being thrice warned. I once saw a woman paraded through the streets of Cairo, and afterwards taken down to the Nile to be drowned, for having apostatized from the faith of Moḥammad, and having married a Christian. Unfortunately, she had tattooed a blue cross on her arm, which led to her detection by one of her former friends in a bath. She was mounted upon a high-saddled ass, such as ladies in Egypt usually ride, and very respectably dressed, attended by soldiers, and surrounded by a rabble, who, instead of commiserating, uttered loud imprecations against her. The Ḳáḍee, who passed sentence upon her, exhorted her, in vain, to return to her former faith. Her own father was her accuser! She was taken in a boat into the midst of the river, stripped nearly naked, strangled, and then thrown into the stream.[3] The Europeans residing in Cairo regretted that the Báshà (Moḥammad 'Alee) was then at Alexandria, as they might have prevailed upon him to pardon her. Once before they interceded with him for a woman who had been condemned for apostacy. The Báshà ordered that she should be brought before him: he exhorted her to recant; but finding her resolute, reproved her for her *folly*, and sent her home, commanding that no injury should be done to her.

Still more severe is the law with respect to *blasphemy*. The person who utters blasphemy against God, or Moḥammad, or Christ,

[1] An unmarried person convicted of adultery is likewise obnoxious only to this punishment. The two laws mentioned in Leviticus, xx. 13 and 15, have been introduced into the Muslim code; but, in the present day, they are never executed.

[2] In the villages of Egypt, a woman found, or suspected, to have been guilty of this crime, if she be not a common prostitute, often experiences a different fate, which will be described in the account of the domestic life and customs of the lower orders.

[3] The conduct of the lower orders in Cairo on this occasion speaks sadly against their character. A *song* was composed on the victim of this terrible law, and became very popular in the metropolis.

or Moses, or any Prophet, is to be put to death without delay, even though he profess himself repentant; repentance for such a sin being deemed impossible. Apostacy or infidelity is occasioned by misjudgment; but blasphemy is the result of utter depravity.

A few words may here be added respecting the sect of the "Wahhábees," also called "Wahabees," which was founded, less than a century ago, by Moḥammad Ibn-'Abd-El-Wahháb, a pious and learned sheykh of the province of Nejd, in central Arabia. About the middle of the last century, he had the good fortune to convert to his creed a powerful chief of Ed-Dir'eeyeh, the capital of Nejd. This chief, Moḥammad Ibn-So'ood, became the sovereign of the new sect, their religious and political head, and under him and his successors the Wahhábee doctrines were spread throughout the greater part of Arabia. He was next succeeded by his son, 'Abd-El-'Azeez; next, by So'ood, the son of the latter, and the greatest of the Wahhábee leaders; and, lastly, by 'Abd-Allah, the son of this So'ood, who, after an arduous warfare with the armies of Moḥammad 'Alee, surrendered himself (it is said, on receiving promise of safe-conduct and life,) to his victorious enemies, was sent to Egypt, thence to Constantinople, and there beheaded. The wars which Moḥammad 'Alee carried on against the Wahhábees had for their chief object the destruction of the political power of the new sect: their religious tenets are still professed by many of the Arabs, and allowed to be orthodox by the most learned of the 'Ulamà of Egypt. The Wahhábees are merely reformers, who believe all the fundamental points of El-Islám, and all the accessory doctrines of the Ḳur-án and the Traditions of the Prophet: in short, their tenets are those of the primitive Muslims. They disapprove of gorgeous sepulchres, and domes erected over tombs: such they invariably destroy when in their power. They also condemn, as idolaters, those who pay peculiar veneration to deceased saints; and even declare all other Muslims to be heretics, for the extravagant respect which they pay to the Prophet. They forbid the wearing of silk, and gold ornaments, and all costly apparel; and also the practice of smoking tobacco. For the want of this last luxury, they console themselves in some degree by an immoderate use of coffee.[1] There are many learned men among them, and they have collected many valuable books (chiefly historical) from various parts of Arabia, and from Egypt.

[1] Among many other erroneous statements respecting the Wahhábees, it has been asserted that they prohibit the drinking of coffee.

CHAPTER IV.

GOVERNMENT.[1]

Egypt has, of late years, experienced great political changes, and nearly ceased to be a province of the Turkish Empire. Its present Báshà (Moḥammad 'Alee), having exterminated the Ghuzz, or Memlooks, who shared the government with his predecessors, has rendered himself almost an independent prince. He, however, professes allegiance to the Sulṭán, and remits the tribute, according to former custom, to Constantinople: he is, moreover, under an obligation to respect the fundamental laws of the Ḳur-án and the Traditions; but he exercises a dominion otherwise unlimited.[2] He may cause any one of his subjects to be put to death without the formality of a trial, or without assigning any cause: a simple horizontal motion of his hand is sufficient to imply the sentence of decapitation. But I must not be understood to insinuate that he is prone to shed blood without any reason: severity is a characteristic of this prince, rather than wanton cruelty; and boundless ambition has prompted him to almost every action by which he has attracted either praise or censure.[3]

In the Citadel of the Metropolis is a court of judicature, called

---

[1] As the political reforms effected by Moḥammad 'Alee will always be extremely interesting, and as the changes made in his institutions by his successors have been inconsiderable, and generally the contrary of improvements, I retain here, without any essential alteration, an account of the government of Egypt written in the years 1834 and 1835, during the best period of his rule.

[2] Though his territory was greatly lessened since the above was written, his power in Egypt remained nearly the same.

[3] The government of Egypt, from the period of the conquest of this country by the Arabs, has been nearly the same as it is at present in its influence on the manners and customs and character of the inhabitants; and I therefore do not deem a historical retrospect necessary to the illustration of this work. It should, however, be mentioned, that the people of Egypt are not now allowed to indulge in that excessive fanatical rudeness with which they formerly treated Christians and Jews; and hence European travellers have one great cause for gratitude to Moḥammad 'Alee. Restraint may, at first, increase, but will probably, in the course of time, materially diminish, the feeling of fanatical intolerance.—This prediction has not yet been fulfilled: on the contrary, European innovations in the dress and domestic manners and customs of the grandees, and of persons in the employ of the government, have enormously increased the fanaticism of those who belong to the religious and learned professions, and, generally speaking, of the bulk of the population.

"ed-Deewán el-Khideewee,"[1] where, in the Báshà's absence, presides his "Kikhyà,"[2] or deputy, Ḥabeeb Efendee. In cases which do not fall within the province of the Ḳáḍee, or which are sufficiently clear to be decided without referring them to the court of that officer, or to another council, the president of the Deewán el-Khideewee passes judgment. Numerous guard-houses have been established throughout the metropolis, at each of which is stationed a body of Niẓám, or regular troops. The guard is called "Ḳulluḳ,"[3] or, more commonly, at present, "Ḳarà-ḳól."[4] Persons accused of thefts, assaults, &c., in Cairo, are given in charge to a soldier of the guard, who takes them to the chief guard-house, in the Mooskee, a street in that part of the town in which most of the Franks reside. The charges being here stated, and committed to writing, he conducts them to the "Ẓábiṭ," or chief magistrate of the police of the metropolis. The Ẓábiṭ, having heard the case, sends the accused for trial to the Deewán el-Khideewee.[5] When a person denies the offence with which he is charged, and there is not sufficient evidence to convict him, but some ground of suspicion, he is generally bastinaded, in order to induce him to confess; and then, if not before, when the crime is not of a nature that renders him obnoxious to a very heavy punishment, he, if guilty, admits it. A thief, after this discipline, generally confesses, "The devil seduced me, and I took it." The punishment of the convicts is regulated by a system of arbitrary, but lenient and wise, policy: it usually consists in their being compelled to labour, for a scanty sustenance, in some of the public works; such as the removal of rubbish, digging canals, &c.; and sometimes the army is recruited with able-bodied young men convicted of petty offences. In employing malefactors in labours for the improvement of the country, Moḥammad 'Alee merits the praises bestowed upon Sabacon, the Ethiopian conqueror and king of Egypt, who is said to have introduced this policy. The Báshà is, however, very severe in punishing thefts, &c., committed against himself:—death is the usual penalty in such cases.

There are several inferior councils for conducting the affairs of

1 "Khideewee" is a relative adjective formed from the Turkish "Khideev," which signifies "a prince."

2 Thus pronounced in Egypt, but more properly "Kyáḥyà," or "Ketkhud'à."

3 From the Turkish "Ḳool-luḳ."

4 Vulgarly, "Karakón."

5 A very arbitrary power is often exercised in this and similar courts, and the proceedings are conducted with little decorum. Many Turkish officers, even of the highest rank, make use of language far too disgusting for me to mention, towards persons brought before them for judgment, and towards those who appeal to them for justice.

different departments of the administration. The principal of these are the following:—1. The "Meglis el-Meshwarah"[1] (the Council of Deliberation); also called "Meglis el-Meshwarah el-Melekeeyeh" (the Council of Deliberation on the Affairs of the State), to distinguish it from other councils. The members of this and of the other similar councils are chosen by the Báshà, for their talents or other qualifications; and consequently his will and interest sway them in all their decisions. They are his instruments, and compose a committee for presiding over the general government of the country, and the commercial and agricultural affairs of the Báshà. Petitions, &c., addressed to the Báshà, or to his Deewán, relating to private interests or the affairs of the government, are generally submitted to their consideration and judgment, unless they more properly come under the cognizance of other councils hereafter to be mentioned. 2. The "Meglis el-Gihádeeyeh" (the Council of the Army); also called "Meglis el-Meshwarah el-'Askereeyeh" (the Council of Deliberation on Military Affairs). The province of this court is sufficiently shewn by its name. 3. The Council of the "Tarskháneh," or Navy. 4. The "Deewán et-Tuggár" (or Court of the Merchants). This court, the members of which are merchants of various countries and religions, presided over by the "Sháh-Bandar" (or chief of the merchants of Cairo), was instituted in consequence of the laws of the Ḳur-án and the Sunneh being found not sufficiently explicit in some cases arising out of modern commercial transactions.

The "Ḳáḍee" (or chief judge) of Cairo presides in Egypt only a year, at the expiration of which term, a new Ḳáḍee having arrived from Constantinople, the former returns. It was customary for this officer to proceed from Cairo, with the great caravan of pilgrims, to Mekkeh, perform the ceremonies of the pilgrimage, and remain one year as Ḳáḍee of the holy city, and one year at El-Medeeneh.[2] He purchases his place privately of the government, which pays no particular regard to his qualifications; though he must be a man of some knowledge, an 'Osmánlee (that is, a Turk), and of the sect of the Ḥanafees. His tribunal is called the "Maḥkemeh"[3] (or Place of Judgment). Few Ḳáḍees are very well acquainted with the Arabic language; nor is it necessary for them to have such knowledge. In Cairo, the Ḳáḍee has little or nothing to do but to confirm the

---

[1] Pronounced "Meshwar'ah."

[2] He used to arrive in Cairo in the beginning of Ramaḍán; but the beginning of the first month, Moḥarram, has of late been fixed upon, instead of the former period.

[3] Pronounced "Maḥkem'eh."

sentence of his "Náïb" (or deputy), who hears and decides the more ordinary cases, and whom he chooses from among the 'Ulamà of Istambool, or the decision of the "Muftee" (or chief doctor of the law) of his own sect, who constantly resides in Cairo, and gives judgment in all cases of difficulty. But in general, the Náïb is, at the best, but little conversant with the popular dialect of Egypt; therefore, in Cairo, where the chief proportion of the litigants at the Maḥkemeh are Arabs, the judge must place the utmost confidence in the "Básh-Turgumán" (or Chief Interpreter), whose place is permanent, and who is consequently well acquainted with all the customs of the court, particularly with the system of bribery; and this knowledge he is generally very ready to communicate to every new Ḳáḍee and Náïb. A man may be grossly ignorant of the law in many important particulars, and yet hold the office of Ḳáḍee of Cairo: several instances of this kind have occurred; bút the Náïb must be a lawyer of learning and experience.

When a person has a suit to prefer at the Maḥkemeh against another individual or party, he goes thither, and applies to the "Básh-Rusul" (or chief of the bailiffs or sergeants who execute arrests) for a "Rasool" to arrest the accused. The Rasool receives a piaster or two,[1] and generally gives half of this fee privately to his chief. The plaintiff and defendant then present themselves in the great hall of the Maḥkemeh; which is a large saloon, facing a spacious court, and having an open front, formed by a row of columns and arches. Here are seated several officers called "Sháhids," whose business is to hear and write the statements of the cases to be submitted to judgment, and who are under the authority of the "Básh-Kátib" (or Chief Secretary). The plaintiff, addressing any one of the Sháhids whom he finds unoccupied, states his case, and the Sháhid commits it to writing, and receives a fee of a piaster or more; after which, if the case be of a trifling nature, and the defendant acknowledge the justice of the suit, he (the Sháhid) passes sentence; but otherwise he conducts the two parties before the Náïb, who holds his court in an inner apartment. The Náïb, having heard the case, desires the plaintiff to procure a "fetwà" (or judicial decision) from the Muftee of the sect of the Ḥanafees, who receives a fee, seldom less than ten piasters, and often more than a hundred or two hundred. This is the course pursued in all cases but those of a very trifling

[1] The Egyptian piaster, when this was written, was equivalent to the fifth part of a shilling, or $2\frac{2}{5}d$.

nature, which are settled with less trouble, by the Náïb alone, and those of great importance or intricacy. A case of the latter kind is tried in the private apartment of the Ḳáḍee, before the Ḳáḍee himself, the Náïb, and the Muftee of the Ḥanafees, who is summoned to hear it, and to give his decision; and sometimes, in cases of very great difficulty or moment, several of the 'Ulamà of Cairo are, in like manner, summoned. The Muftee hears the case, and writes his sentence; and the Ḳáḍee confirms his judgment, and stamps the paper with his seal, which is all that he has to do in any case. The accused may clear himself by his oath, when the plaintiff has not witnesses to produce: placing his right hand on a copy of the Ḳur-án, which is held out to him, he says, "By God, the Great," three times; adding, "By what is contained in this of the word of God." The witnesses must be men of good repute, or asserted to be such, and not interested in the cause: in every case, at least two witnesses are requisite[1] (or one man and two women); and each of these must be attested to be a person of probity by two others. An infidel cannot lawfully bear witness against a Muslim in a case involving capital or other heavy punishment; and evidence in favour of a son or grandson, or of a father or grandfather, is not received; nor is the testimony of slaves; neither can a master testify in favour of his slave.

The fees, until lately, used to be paid by the successful party; but now they are paid by the other party. The Ḳáḍee's fees for decisions in cases respecting the sale of property are two per cent. on the amount of the property: in cases of legacies, four per cent., except when the heir is an orphan not of age, who pays only two per cent. For decisions respecting property in houses or land, when the cost of the property in question is known, his fees are two per cent.; but when the cost is not known, one year's rent. These are the legitimate fees; but more than the due amount is often exacted. In cases which do not concern property, the Ḳáḍee's Náïb fixes the amount of the fees. There are also other fees than those of the Ḳáḍee to be paid after the decision of the case: for instance, if the Ḳáḍee's fees be two or three hundred piasters, a fee of about two piasters must be paid to the Básh-Turgumán; about the same to the Básh-Rusul; and one piaster to the Rasool, or to each Rasool employed.

The rank of a plaintiff or defendant, or a bribe from either, often

[1] This law is borrowed from the Pentateuch. See Deut. xix. 15.—A man may refuse to give his testimony.

influences the decision of the judge. In general the Náïb and Muftee take bribes, and the Ḳáḍee receives from his Náïb. On some occasions, particularly in long litigations, bribes are given by each party, and the decision is awarded in favour of him who pays highest. This frequently happens in difficult law-suits; and even in cases respecting which the law is perfectly clear, strict justice is not always administered; bribes and false testimony being employed by one of the parties. The shocking extent to which the practices of bribery and suborning false witnesses are carried in Muslim courts of law, and among them in the tribunal of the Ḳáḍee of Cairo, may be scarcely credited on the bare assertion of the fact: some strong proof, resting on indubitable authority, may be demanded; and here I shall give such proof, in a summary of a case which was tried not long since, and which was related to me by the Secretary and Imám of the Sheykh El-Mahdee, who was then supreme Muftee of Cairo (being the chief Muftee of the Ḥanafees), and to whom this case was referred after judgment in the Ḳáḍee's court.

A Turkish merchant, residing at Cairo, died, leaving property to the amount of six thousand purses,[1] and no relation to inherit but one daughter. The seyyid Moḥammad El-Maḥrooḳee, the Sháh-Bandar (chief of the merchants of Cairo), hearing of this event, suborned a common fellááḥ, who was the bowwáb (or door-keeper) of a respected sheykh, and whose parents (both of them Arabs) were known to many persons, to assert himself a son of a brother of the deceased. The case was brought before the Ḳáḍee, and, as it was one of considerable importance, several of the principal 'Ulamà of the city were summoned to decide it. They were all bribed or influenced by El-Maḥrooḳee, as will presently be shewn; false witnesses were brought forward to swear to the truth of the bowwáb's pretensions, and others to give testimony to the good character of these witnesses. Three thousand purses were adjudged to the daughter of the deceased, and the other half of the property to the bowwáb. El-Maḥrooḳee received the share of the latter, deducting only three hundred piasters, which he presented to the bowwáb. The chief Muftee, El-Mahdee, was absent from Cairo when the case was tried. On his return to the metropolis, a few days after, the daughter of the deceased merchant repaired to his house, stated her case to him, and earnestly solicited redress. The Muftee, though convinced of the

[1] A purse is the sum of five hundred piasters, and was then equivalent to nearly seven pounds sterling, but is now equal to only five pounds.

injustice which she had suffered, and not doubting the truth of what she related respecting the part which El-Maḥrooḳee had taken in this affair, told her that he feared it was impossible for him to annul the judgment, unless there were some informality in the proceedings of the court, but that he would look at the record of the case in the register of the Maḥkemeh. Having done this, he betook himself to the Báshà, with whom he was in great favour for his knowledge and inflexible integrity, and complained to him that the tribunal of the Ḳáḍee was disgraced by the administration of the most flagrant injustice; that false witness was admitted by the 'Ulamà, however evident and glaring it might be; and that a judgment which they had given in a late case, during his absence, was the general talk and wonder of the town. The Báshà summoned the Ḳáḍee and all the 'Ulamà who had tried this case, to meet the Muftee in the Citadel; and when they had assembled there, addressed them, as from himself, with the Muftee's complaint. The Ḳáḍee, appearing, like the 'Ulamà, highly indignant at this charge, demanded to know upon what it was grounded. The Báshà replied that it was a general charge, but particularly grounded on the case in which the court had admitted the claim of a bowwáb to a relationship and inheritance which they could not believe to be his right. The Ḳáḍee here urged that he had passed sentence in accordance with the unanimous decision of the 'Ulamà then present. "Let the record of the case be read," said the Báshà. The journal being sent for, this was done; and when the secretary had finished reading the minutes, the Ḳáḍee, in a loud tone of proud authority, said, "And I judged so." The Muftee, in a louder and more authoritative tone, exclaimed, "And thy judgment is false!" All eyes were fixed in astonishment, now at the Muftee, now at the Báshà, now at the other 'Ulamà. The Ḳáḍee and the 'Ulamà rolled their heads and stroked their beards. The former exclaimed, tapping his breast, "I, the Ḳáḍee of Miṣr, pass a false sentence!" "And we," said the 'Ulamà, "we, Sheykh Mahdee! we, 'Ulamà el-Islám, give a false decision!" "O Sheykh Mahdee," said El-Maḥrooḳee (who, from his commercial transactions with the Báshà, could generally obtain a place in his councils), "respect the 'Ulamà as they respect thee." "O Maḥrooḳee," exclaimed the Muftee, "art thou concerned in this affair? Declare what part thou hast in it, or else hold thy peace: go, speak in the assemblies of the merchants, but presume not again to open thy mouth in the council of the 'Ulamà!" El-Maḥrooḳee immediately left the palace, for he saw how the affair would terminate, and had to make his arrangements accordingly. The Muftee was now desired, by the other 'Ulamà, to adduce a proof of the invalidity of their decision. Drawing from his bosom a small book on the laws of inheritance, he read from it, "To establish a claim to relationship and inheritance, the names of the father and mother of the claimant, and those of his father's father and mother, and of his mother's father and mother, must be ascertained." The names of the father and mother of the pretended father of the bowwáb the false witnesses had not been prepared to give; and this deficiency in the testimony (which the 'Ulamà, in trying the case, purposely overlooked,) now caused the sentence to be annulled. The bowwáb was brought before the council, and, denying the imposition of which he had been made the principal instrument, was, by order of the Báshà, very severely bastinaded; but the only confession that could be drawn from him by the torture which he endured was, that he had received nothing more of the three thousand purses than three hundred piasters. Meanwhile, El-Maḥrooḳee had repaired to the bowwáb's master: he told the latter what had happened at the Citadel, and what he had foreseen would be the result, put into his hand three thousand purses, and begged him immediately to go to the council, give this sum of money, and say that it had been placed in his hands in trust by his servant. This was done, and the money was paid to the daughter of the deceased.

In another case, when the Ḳáḍee and the council of the 'Ulamà were influenced in their decision by a Báshà (not Moḥammad 'Alee), and passed a sentence contrary to law, they were thwarted in the same manner by El-Mahdee. This Muftee was a rare example of integrity. It is said that he never took a fee for a fetwà. He died shortly after my first visit to this country.—I could mention several other glaring cases of bribery in the court of the Ḳáḍee of Cairo; but the above is sufficient.

There are five minor Maḥkemehs in Cairo; and likewise one at its principal port, Booláḳ; and one at its southern port, Maṣr el-'Ateeḳah. A Sháhid from the great Maḥkemeh presides at each of them, as deputy of the chief Ḳáḍee, who confirms their acts. The matters submitted to these minor tribunals are chiefly respecting the sales of property, and legacies, marriages, and divorces; for the Ḳáḍee marries female orphans under age who have no relations of age to act as their guardians; and wives often have recourse to law to compel their husbands to divorce them. In every country-town there is also a Ḳáḍee, generally a native of the place, and never a Turk, who decides all cases, sometimes from his own knowledge of the law, but commonly on the authority of a Muftee. One Ḳáḍee generally serves for two or three or more villages.

Each of the four orthodox sects of the Muslims (the Ḥanafees, Sháfe'ees, Málikees, and Ḥambelees,) has its "Sheykh," or religious chief, who is chosen from among the most learned of the body, and resides in the metropolis. The Sheykh of the great mosque El-Azhar (who is always of the sect of the Sháfe'ees, and sometimes Sheykh of that sect), together with the other Sheykhs above mentioned, and the Ḳáḍee, the Naḳeeb el-Ashráf (the chief of the Shereefs, or descendants of the Prophet), and several other persons, constitute the council of the 'Ulamà[1] (or learned men), by whom the Turkish Báshàs and Memlook chiefs have often been kept in awe, and by whom their tyranny has frequently been restricted: but now this learned body has lost almost all its influence over the government. Petty disputes are often, by mutual consent of the parties at variance, submitted to the judgment of one of the four Sheykhs first mentioned, as they are the chief Muftees of their respective sects; and the utmost deference is always paid to them. Difficult and delicate causes, which concern the laws of the Ḳur-án or the Traditions, are also frequently referred by the Báshà to these Sheykhs; but their opinion is not always followed by him: for instance, after consulting them respecting the legality of dissecting human bodies, for the sake of acquiring anatomical knowledge, and receiving their declaration that it was repugnant to the laws of the religion, he, nevertheless, has caused it to be practised by Muslim students of anatomy.

The police of the metropolis is more under the direction of the military than of the civil power. A few years ago it was under the authority of the "Wálee" and the "Ẓábiṭ;" but since my first visit to this country the office of the former has been abolished. He was charged with the apprehension of thieves and other criminals; and under his jurisdiction were the public women, of whom he kept a list, and from each of whom he exacted a tax. He also took cognizance of the conduct of the women in general; and when he found a female to have been guilty of a single act of incontinence, he added her name to the list of the public women, and demanded from her the tax, unless

[1] In the singular "'Álim." This title is more particularly given to a professor of jurisprudence. European writers generally use the plural form of this appellation for the singular.

she preferred, or could afford, to escape that ignominy, by giving to him, or to his officers, a considerable bribe. This course was always pursued, and is still, by a person who farms the tax of the public women,[1] in the case of unmarried females, and generally in the case of the married also; but the latter are sometimes privately put to death, if they cannot, by bribery or some other artifice, save themselves. Such proceedings are, however, in two points, contrary to the law, which ordains that a person who accuses a woman of adultery or fornication, without producing four witnesses of the crime, shall be scourged with eighty stripes, and decrees other punishments than those of degradation and tribute against women convicted of such offences.

The office of the Ẓábiṭ has before been mentioned. He is now the chief of the police. His officers, who have no distinguishing mark to render them known as such, are interspersed through the metropolis: they often visit the coffee-shops, and observe the conduct, and listen to the conversation, of the citizens. Many of them are pardoned thieves. They accompany the military guards in their nightly rounds through the streets of the metropolis. Here, none but the blind are allowed to go out at night later than about an hour and a half after sunset, without a lantern or a light of some kind. Few persons are seen in the streets later than two or three hours after sunset. At the fifth or sixth hour, one might pass through the whole length of the metropolis and scarcely meet more than a dozen or twenty persons, except the watchmen and guards, and the porters at the gates of the by-streets and quarters. The sentinel, or guard, calls out to the approaching passenger, in Turkish, "Who is that?"[2] and is answered, in Arabic, "A citizen."[3] The private watchman, in the same case, exclaims, "Attest the unity of God,"[4] or merely, "Attest the unity."[5] The reply given to this is, "There is no deity but God,"[6] which Christians, as well as Muslims, object not to say; the former understanding these words in a different sense from the latter. It is supposed that a thief, or a person bound on any unlawful undertaking, would not dare to utter these words. Some persons loudly exclaim, in reply to the summons of the watchman, "There is no deity but God: Moḥammad is God's Apostle." The private watch-

1 Since this was written, the public women throughout Egypt have been compelled to relinquish their licentious profession.

2 "Keemen dur ó," for "keem dur ó."

3 "Ibn-beled." If blind, he answers "Aạmà."

4 "Waḥḥed Alláh."

5 "Waḥḥed;" or, to more than one person, "Waḥḥedoo."

6 "Lá iláha illa-lláh."

men are employed to guard, by night, the sooḳs (or market-streets) and other districts of the town. They carry a nebboot (or long staff), but no lantern.

The Ẓábiṭ, or Ághà of the police, used frequently to go about the metropolis by night, often accompanied only by the executioner and the "sheạlegee,"[1] or bearer of a kind of torch called "sheạleh," which is still in use.[2] This torch burns, soon after it is lighted, without a flame, except when it is waved through the air, when it suddenly blazes forth: it therefore answers the same purpose as our dark lantern. The burning end is sometimes concealed in a small pot or jar, or covered with something else, when not required to give light; but it is said that thieves often smell it in time to escape meeting the bearer. When a person without a light is met by the police at night, he seldom attempts resistance or flight; the punishment to which he is liable is beating. The chief of the police had an arbitrary power to put any criminal or offender to death without trial, and when not obnoxious, by law, to capital punishment; and so also had many inferior officers, as will be seen in subsequent pages of this work: but within the last two or three years, instances of the exercise of such power have been very rare, and I believe they would not now be permitted. The officers of the Ẓábiṭ perform their nightly rounds with the military guards merely as being better acquainted than the latter with the haunts and practices of thieves and other bad characters; and the Ẓábiṭ himself scarcely ever exercises any penal authority beyond that of beating or flogging.

Very curious measures, such as we read of in some of the tales of 'the Thousand and One Nights,' were often adopted by the police magistrates of Cairo, to discover an offender, before the late innovations. I may mention an instance. The authenticity of the following case, and of several others of a similar nature, is well known. I shall relate it in the manner in which I have heard it told.—A poor man applied one day to the Ághà of the police, and said, "Sir, there came to me, to-day, a woman, and she said to me, 'Take this "ḳurṣ,"[3] and let it remain in your possession for a time, and lend me five hundred piasters:' and I took it from

---

1 Pronounced "sheạleg'ee."

2 Baron Hammer-Purgstall is mistaken in substituting "meschaaledschi" for "sheạlegee." The officer who bears the latter appellation does not carry a mesh'al, but a twisted torch. The mesh'al is described and figured in Chapter VI. of this work.

3 An ornament worn on the crown of the head-dress by women, described in the Appendix to this work.

her, Sir, and gave her the five hundred piasters, and she went away :
and when she was gone away, I said to myself, ' Let me look at this
ḳurṣ :' and I looked at it, and, behold, it was yellow brass : and I
slapped my face, and said, ' I will go to the Ághà, and relate my
story to him : perhaps he will investigate the affair, and clear it up ;'
for there is none that can help me in this matter but thou." The
Ághà said to him, " Hear what I tell thee, man. Take whatever is
in thy shop; leave nothing; and lock it up; and to-morrow
morning go early, and, when thou hast opened the shop, cry out,
' Alas for my property !' then take in thy hands two clods, and beat
thyself with them, and cry, ' Alas for the property of others !' and
whoever says to thee, ' What is the matter with thee ?' do thou
answer, ' The property of others is lost : a pledge that I had, belonging to a woman, is lost ; if it were my own, I should not thus lament
it :' and this will clear up the affair." The man promised to do as
he was desired. He removed everything from his shop, and early the
next morning he went and opened it, and began to cry out, " Alas
for the property of others !" and he took two clods, and beat himself
with them, and went about every district of the city, crying, " Alas
for the property of others ! a pledge that I had, belonging to a
woman, is lost ; if it were my own, I should not thus lament it."
The woman who had given him the ḳurṣ in pledge heard of this, and
discovered that it was the man whom she had cheated ; so she said to
herself, " Go and bring an action against him." She went to his
shop, riding on an ass, to give herself consequence, and said to him,
" Man, give me my property that is in thy possession." He
answered, " It is lost." " Thy tongue be cut out !" she cried :
" dost thou lose my property ? By Allah ! I will go to the Ághà,
and inform him of it." " Go," said he ; and she went, and told her
case. The Ághà sent for the man ; and, when he had come, said to
his accuser, " What is thy property in his possession ?" She
answered, " A ḳurṣ of red Venetian gold." " Woman," said the
Ághà, " I have a gold ḳurṣ here : I should like to shew it thee."
She said, " Shew it me, Sir, for I shall know my ḳurṣ." The Ághà
then untied a handkerchief, and, taking out of it the ḳurṣ which she
had given in pledge, said, " Look." She looked at it and knew it,
and hung down her head. The Ághà said, " Raise thy head, and
say where are the five hundred piasters of this man." She answered,
" Sir, they are in my house." The executioner was sent with her to
her house, but without his sword ; and the woman, having gone into

the house, brought out a purse containing the money, and went back with him. The money was given to the man from whom it had been obtained, and the executioner was then ordered to take the woman to the Rumeyleh (a large open place below the Citadel), and there to behead her; which he did.

The markets of Cairo, and the weights and measures, are under the inspection of an officer called the "Moḥtesib."[1] He occasionally rides about the town, preceded by an officer who carries a large pair of scales, and followed by the executioners and numerous other servants. Passing by shops, or through the markets, he orders each shopkeeper, one after another, or sometimes only one here and there, to produce his scales, weights, and measures, and tries whether they be correct. He also inquires the prices of provisions at the shops where such articles are sold. Often, too, he stops a servant, or other passenger, in the street, whom he may chance to meet carrying any article of food that he has just bought, and asks him for what sum, or at what weight, he purchased it. When he finds that a shopkeeper has incorrect scales, weights, or measures, or that he has sold a thing deficient in weight, or above the regular market price, he punishes him on the spot. The general punishment is beating or flogging. Once I saw a man tormented in a different way, for selling bread deficient in weight. A hole was bored through his nose, and a cake of bread, about a span wide, and a finger's breadth in thickness, was suspended to it by a piece of string. He was stripped naked, with the exception of having a piece of linen about his loins, and tied, with his arms bound behind him, to the bars of a window of a mosque called the Ashrafeeyeh, in the main street of the metropolis, his feet resting upon the sill. He remained thus about three hours, exposed to the gaze of the multitude which thronged the street, and to the scorching rays of the sun.

A person who was appointed Moḥtesib shortly after my first visit to this country (Muṣṭafà Káshif, a Kurd,) exercised his power in a most brutal manner, clipping men's ears (that is, cutting off the lobe, or ear-lap), not only for the most trifling transgression, but often for no offence whatever. He once met an old man, driving along several asses laden with water-melons, and, pointing to one of the largest of these fruits, asked its price. The old man put his finger and thumb to his ear-lap, and said, "Cut it, Sir." He was asked again and

---

[1] Pronounced "Moḥtes'ib."

again, and gave the same answer. The Moḥtesib, angry, but unable to refrain from laughing, said, "Fellow, are you mad or deaf?" "No," replied the old man, "I am neither mad nor deaf; but I know that, if I were to say the price of the melon is ten faḍḍahs, you would say, 'Clip his ear;' and if I said *five* faḍḍahs, or *one* faḍḍah, you would say, 'Clip his ear;' therefore clip it at once, and let me pass on." His humour saved him.—Clipping ears was the usual punishment inflicted by this Moḥtesib; but sometimes he tortured in a different manner. A butcher, who had sold some meat wanting two ounces of its due weight, he punished by cutting off two ounces of flesh from his back. A seller of "kunáfeh" (a kind of paste resembling vermicelli) having made his customers pay a trifle more than was just, he caused him to be stripped, and seated upon the round copper tray on which the kunáfeh was baked, and kept so until he was dreadfully burnt. He generally punished dishonest butchers by putting a hook through the nose, and hanging a piece of meat to it. Meeting, one day, a man carrying a large crate full of earthern water-bottles from Semennood, which he offered for sale as made at Ḳinè, he caused his attendants to break each bottle separately against the vender's head. Muṣṭafà Káshif also exercised his tyranny in other cases than those which properly fell under his jurisdiction. He once took a fancy to send one of his horses to a bath, and desired the keeper of a bath in his neighbourhood to prepare for receiving it, and to wash it well, and make its coat very smooth. The bath-keeper, annoyed at so extraordinary a command, ventured to suggest that, as the pavements of the bath were of marble, the horse might slip, and fall; and also, that it might take cold on going out; and that it would, therefore, be better for him to convey to the stable the contents of the cistern of the bath in buckets, and there to perform the operation. Muṣṭafà Káshif said, "I see how it is; you do not like that my horse should go into your bath." He desired some of his servants to throw him down, and beat him with staves till he should tell them to stop. They did so; and beat the poor man till he died.

A few years ago there used to be carried before the Moḥtesib, when going his rounds to examine the weights and measures, &c., a pair of scales larger than that used at present. Its beam, it is said, was a hollow tube, containing some quicksilver; by means of which the bearer, knowing those persons who had bribed his master, and those who had not, easily made either scale preponderate.

As the Moḥtesib is the overseer of the public markets, so there are officers who have a similar charge in superintending each branch of the Báshà's trade and manufactures; and some of these persons have been known to perpetrate most abominable acts of tyranny and cruelty. One of this class, who was named 'Alee Bey, "Náẓir el-Ḳumásh" (or Overseer of the Linen), when he found a person in possession of a private loom, or selling the produce of such a loom, generally bound him up in a piece of his linen, soaked in oil and tar; then suspended him, thus enveloped, to a branch of a tree, and set light to the wrapper. After having destroyed a number of men in this horrible manner, he was himself, among many others, burnt to death, by the explosion of a powder-magazine on the northern slope of the Citadel of Cairo, in 1824, the year before my first arrival in Egypt. A friend of mine, who spoke to me of the atrocities of this monster, added, "When his corpse was taken to be buried, the Sheykh El-'Aroosee (who was Sheykh of the great mosque El-Azhar) recited the funeral prayers over it, in the mosque of the Ḥasaneyn; and I acted as 'muballigh' (to repeat the words of the Imám): when the Sheykh uttered the words, 'Give your testimony respecting him,' and when I had repeated them, no one of all the persons present, and they were many, presumed to give the answer, 'He was of the virtuous:' all were silent. To make the circumstance more glaring, I said again, 'Give your testimony respecting him:' but not an answer was heard; and the Sheykh, in confusion, said, but in a very low voice, 'May God have mercy upon him.' Now we may certainly say of this cursed man," continued my friend, "that he is gone to hell: yet his wife is constantly having 'khatmehs' (recitations of the Ḳur-án) performed in her house for him; and lights two wax candles for his sake, every evening, at the niche of the mosque of the Ḥasaneyn."

Every quarter in the metropolis has its sheykh, called "Sheykh el-Ḥárah," whose influence is exerted to maintain order, to settle any trifling disputes among the inhabitants, and to expel those who disturb the peace of their neighbours. The whole of the metropolis is also divided into eight districts, over each of which is a sheykh, called "Sheykh et-Tumn."

The members of various trades and manufactures in the metropolis and other large towns have also their respective sheykhs, to whom all disputes respecting matters connected with those trades or crafts are submitted for arbitration; and whose sanction is required for the admission of new members.

The servants in the metropolis are likewise under the authority of particular sheykhs. Any person in want of a servant may procure one by applying to one of these officers, who, for a small fee (two or three piasters), becomes responsible for the conduct of the man whom he recommends. Should a servant so engaged rob his master, the latter gives information to the sheykh, who, whether he can recover the stolen property or not, must indemnify the master.

Even the common thieves used, not many years since, to respect a superior, who was called their sheykh. He was often required to search for stolen goods, and to bring offenders to justice; which he generally accomplished. It is very remarkable that the same strange system prevailed among the ancient Egyptians.[1]

The Coptic Patriarch, who is the head of his church, judges petty causes among his people in the metropolis; and the inferior clergy do the same in other places; but an appeal may be made to the Ḳáḍee. A Muslim aggrieved by a Copt may demand justice from the Patriarch or the Ḳáḍee: a Copt who seeks redress from a Muslim must apply to the Ḳáḍee. The Jews are similarly circumstanced. The Franks, or Europeans in general, are not answerable to any other authority than that of their respective consuls, except when they are aggressors against a Muslim: they are then surrendered to the Turkish authorities, who, on the other hand, must be appealed to by the Frank who is aggrieved by a Muslim.

The inhabitants of the country towns and villages are under the government of Turkish officers and of their own countrymen. The whole of Egypt is divided into several large provinces, each of which is governed by an 'Osmánlee (*i. e.* a Turk); and these provinces are subdivided into districts, which are governed by native officers, with the titles of "Ma-moor" and "Náẓir." Every village, as well as town, has also its sheykh, called "Sheykh el-Beled;" who is one of the native Muslim inhabitants. All the officers above mentioned, except the last, were formerly Turks; and there were other Turkish governors of small districts, who were called "Káshifs," and "Ḳáïm-maḳáms:" the change was made very shortly before my second visit to this country; and the Fellá‌ḥeen complain that their condition is worse than it was before: but it is generally from the tyranny of their great Turkish governors that they suffer most severely.

---

1 See Diodorus Siculus, lib. i. cap. 80.

The following case will convey some idea of the condition of Egyptian peasants in some provinces. A Turk,[1] infamous for many barbarous acts, presiding at the town of Ṭanṭà,[2] in the Delta, went one night to the government granary of that town, and, finding two peasants sleeping there, asked them who they were, and what was their business in that place. One of them said that he had brought 130 ardebbs of corn from a village of the district; and the other, that he had brought 60 ardebbs from the land belonging to the town. "You rascal!" said the governor to the latter; "this man brings 130 ardebbs from the lands of a small village; and you bring but 60 from the lands of the town." "This man," answered the peasant of Ṭanṭà, "brings corn but once a week; and I am now bringing it every day." "Be silent!" said the governor; and, pointing to a neighbouring tree, he ordered one of the servants of the granary to hang the peasant to one of its branches. The order was obeyed, and the governor returned to his house. The next morning he went again to the granary, and saw a man bringing in a large quantity of corn. He asked who he was, and what quantity he had brought; and was answered, by the hangman of the preceding night, "This is the man, Sir, whom I hanged by your orders, last night; and he has brought 160 ardebbs." "What!" exclaimed the governor: "has he risen from the dead?" He was answered, "No, Sir; I hanged him so that his toes touched the ground; and when you were gone, I untied the rope: you did not order me to *kill* him." The Turk muttered, "Aha! hanging and killing are different things: Arabic is copious: next time I will say kill. Take care of Aboo-Dá-ood."[3] This is his nickname.

Another occurrence may here be aptly related, as a further illustration of the nature of the government to which the people of Egypt are subjected. A felláḥ, who was appointed Náẓir (or governor) of the district of El-Manoofeeyeh (the southernmost district of the Delta), a short time before my second visit to Egypt, in collecting the taxes at a village, demanded of a poor peasant the sum of sixty riyáls (ninety faḍḍahs each, making a sum total of a hundred and thirty-five piasters, which was then equivalent to about thirty shillings).

---

1 Suleymán Ághà, the Silaḥdár: he has died since this was written.

2 Thus commonly pronounced in the present day; formerly, "Ṭandetè."

3 Aboo-Dá-ood, Aboo-'Alee, &c., are patronymics, used by the Egyptian peasants in generâl, not as signifying "Father of Dá-ood," "Father of 'Alee," &c., but "whose father is (or was) Dá-ood," "—— 'Alee," &c.

The poor man urged that he possessed nothing but a cow, which barely afforded sustenance to himself and his family. Instead of pursuing the method usually followed when a fellá̤h declares himself unable to pay the tax demanded of him, which is to give him a severe bastinading, the Ná̤zir, in this case, sent the Sheykh el-Beled to bring the poor peasant's cow, and desired some of the fellá̤heen to buy it. They saying that they had not sufficient money, he sent for a butcher, and desired him to kill the cow; which was done: he then told him to divide it into sixty pieces. The butcher asked for his pay; and was given the head of the cow. Sixty fellá̤heen were then called together; and each of them was compelled to purchase, for a riyál, a piece of the cow. The owner of the cow went, weeping and complaining, to the Ná̤zir's superior, the late Mo̤hammad Bey, Deftardár. "O my master," said he, "I am oppressed and in misery: I had no property but one cow, a milch cow: I and my family lived upon her milk; and she ploughed for me, and threshed my corn; and my whole subsistence was derived from her: the Ná̤zir has taken her, and killed her, and cut her up into sixty pieces, and sold the pieces to my neighbours; to each a piece, for one riyál; so that he obtained but sixty riyáls for the whole, while the value of the cow was a hundred and twenty riyáls, or more. I am oppressed and in misery, and a stranger in the place, for I came from another village; but the Ná̤zir had no pity on me. I and my family are become beggars, and have nothing left. Have mercy upon me, and give me justice: I implore it by thy ̤hareem." The Deftardár, having caused the Ná̤zir to be brought before him, asked him, "Where is the cow of this fellá̤h?" "I have sold it," said the Ná̤zir. "For how much?" "For sixty riyáls." "Why did you kill it and sell it?" "He owed sixty riyáls for land: so I took his cow, and killed it, and sold it for the amount." "Where is the butcher that killed it?" "In Manoof." The butcher was sent for, and brought. The Deftardár said to him, "Why did you kill this man's cow?" "The Ná̤zir desired me," he answered, "and I could not oppose him: if I had attempted to do so, he would have beaten me, and destroyed my house: I killed it; and the Ná̤zir gave me the head as my reward." "Man," said the Deftardár, "do you know the persons who bought the meat?" The butcher replied that he did. The Deftardár then desired his secretary to write the names of the sixty men, and an order to the Sheykh of their village to bring them to Manoof, where this complaint was made. The Ná̤zir and butcher were placed in confinement till the next morning; when the Sheykh of the village came, with the sixty fellâḥeen. The two prisoners were then brought again before the Deftardár, who said to the Sheykh and the sixty peasants, "Was the value of this man's cow sixty riyáls?" "O our master," they answered, "her value was greater." The Deftardár sent for the Ḳáḍee of Manoof, and said to him, "O Ḳáḍee, here is a man oppressed by this Náẓir, who has taken his cow, and killed it; and sold its flesh for sixty riyáls. What is thy judgment?" The Ḳáḍee replied, "He is a cruel tyrant, who oppresses every one under his authority. Is not a cow worth a hundred and twenty riyáls, or more? and he has sold this one for sixty riyáls: this is tyranny towards the owner." The Deftardár then said to some of his soldiers, "Take the Náẓir, and strip him, and bind him." This done, he said to the butcher, "Butcher, dost thou not fear God? Thou hast killed the cow unjustly." The butcher again urged that he was obliged to obey the Náẓir. "Then," said the Deftardár, "if I order thee to do a thing wilt thou do it?" "I will do it," answered the butcher. "Slaughter the Náẓir," said the Deftardár. Immediately, several of the soldiers present seized the Náẓir, and threw him down; and the butcher cut his throat, in the regular orthodox manner of killing animals for food. "Now, cut him up," said the Deftardár, "into sixty pieces." This was done: the people concerned in the affair, and many others, looking on; but none daring to speak. The sixty peasants who had bought the meat of the cow were then called forward, one after another, and each was made to take a piece of the flesh of the Náẓir, and to pay for it two riyáls; so that a hundred and twenty riyáls were obtained from them. They were then dismissed; but the butcher remained. The Ḳáḍee was asked what should be the reward of the butcher; and answered that he should be paid as he had been paid by the Náẓir. The Deftardár therefore ordered that the head of the Náẓir should be given to him; and the butcher went away with his worse than valueless burden, thanking God that he had not been more unfortunate, and scarcely believing himself to have so easily escaped until he arrived at his village. The money paid for the flesh of the Náẓir was given to the owner of the cow.

Most of the governors of provinces and districts carry their oppression far beyond the limits to which they are authorized to proceed by the Báshà; and even the Sheykh of a village, in executing the commands of his superiors, abuses his lawful power: bribes, and the ties of relationship and marriage, influence him and them, and by lessening the oppression of some, who are more able to bear it, greatly increase that of others. But the office of a Sheykh of a village is far from being a sinecure: at the period when the taxes are demanded of him, he frequently receives a more severe bastinading than any of his inferiors; for when the population of a village does not yield the sum required, their Sheykh is often beaten for their default: and not always does he produce his own proportion until he has been well thrashed. All the felláḥeen are proud of the stripes they receive for withholding their contributions; and are often heard to boast of the number of blows which were inflicted upon them before they would give up their money. Ammianus Marcellinus gives precisely the same character to the Egyptians of his time.[1]

The revenue of the Báshà of Egypt is generally said to amount to about three millions of pounds sterling.[2] Nearly half arises from the direct taxes on land, and from indirect exactions from the felláḥeen: the remainder, principally from the custom-taxes, the tax on palm-trees, a kind of income-tax, and the sale of various productions of the land; by which sale, the government, in most instances, obtains a profit of more than fifty per cent.

The present Báshà has increased his revenue to this amount by most oppressive measures. He has dispossessed of their lands almost all the private proprietors throughout Egypt, allotting to each, as a partial compensation, a pension for life, proportioned to the extent and quality of the land which belonged to him. The farmer has, therefore, nothing to leave to his children but his hut, and perhaps a few cattle and some small savings.

The direct taxes on land are proportioned to the natural advantages of the soil. Their average amount is about 8*s*. per feddán, which is nearly equal to an English acre.[3] But the cultivator can never calculate exactly the full amount of what the government will require of him: he suffers from indirect exactions of quantities (differing in different years, but always levied per feddán,) of butter, honey, wax, wool, baskets of palm-leaves, ropes of the fibres of the palm-tree, and other commodities: he is also obliged to pay the hire of the camels which convey his grain to the government "shooneh"

---

1 Lib. xxii. The more easily the peasant pays, the more is he made to pay.

2 Some estimate it at *five* millions; others, at little more than *two* millions.

3 The feddán has lately been reduced: it was equal to about an English acre and one-tenth a few years ago; and somewhat more at an earlier period.

(or granary), and to defray various other expenses. A portion of the produce of his land is taken by the government,[1] and sometimes the whole produce, at a fixed and fair price, which, however, in many parts of Egypt, is retained to make up for the debts of the insolvent peasants.[2] The fellâḥ, to supply the bare necessaries of life, is often obliged to steal, and convey secretly to his hut, as much as he can of the produce of his land. He may either himself supply the seed for his land, or obtain it as a loan from the government: but in the latter case he seldom obtains a sufficient quantity; a considerable portion being generally stolen by the persons through whose hands it passes before he receives it. To relate all the oppressions which the peasantry of Egypt endure from the dishonesty of the Ma-moors and inferior officers would require too much space in the present work. It would be scarcely possible for them to suffer more, and live. It may be hardly necessary, therefore, to add, that few of them engage, with assiduity, in the labours of agriculture, unless compelled to do so by their superiors.

The Báshà has not only taken possession of the lands of the private proprietors, but he has also thrown into his treasury a considerable proportion of the incomes of religious and charitable institutions, deeming their accumulated wealth superfluous. He first imposed a tax (of nearly half the amount of the regular land-tax) upon all land which had become a "waḳf" (or legacy unalienable by law) to any mosque, fountain, public school, &c.; and afterwards took absolute possession of such lands, granting certain annuities in lieu of them, for keeping in repair the respective buildings, and for the maintenance of those persons attached to them, as Náẓirs (or wardens), religious ministers, inferior servants, students, and other pensioners. He has thus rendered himself extremely odious to most persons of the religious and learned professions, and especially to the Náẓirs of the mosques, who too generally enriched themselves from the funds intrusted to their care, which were, in most cases, superabundant. The *household* property of the mosques and other public institutions (the waḳfs of numerous individuals of various ranks) the Báshà has hitherto left inviolate.

The tax upon the palm-trees has been calculated to amount to

---

[1] Of some productions, as cotton, flax, &c., the government always takes the whole.

[2] Even the debts of the peasantry of one village are often imposed upon the inhabitants of another who have paid all that is justly due from them.

about a hundred thousand pounds sterling. The trees are rated according to their qualities; generally at a piaster and a half each.

The income-tax, which is called "firdeh," is generally a twelfth or more of a man's annual income or salary, when that can be ascertained. The maximum, however, is fixed at five hundred piasters. In the large towns it is levied upon individuals; in the villages, upon houses. The income-tax of all the inhabitants of the metropolis amounts to eight thousand purses, or about forty thousand pounds sterling.

The inhabitants of the metropolis and of other large towns pay a heavy tax on grain, &c. The tax on each kind of grain is eighteen piasters per ardebb (or about five bushels); which sum is equal to the price of wheat in the country after a good harvest.

CHAPTER V.

DOMESTIC LIFE.

HAVING sufficiently considered the foundations of the moral and social state of the Muslims of Egypt, we may now take a view of their domestic life and ordinary habits; and, first, let us confine our attention to the higher and middle orders.

A master of a family, or any person who has arrived at manhood, and is not in a menial situation, or of very low condition, is commonly honoured with the appellation of "the sheykh," prefixed to his name. The word "sheykh" literally signifies "an elder," or "an aged person;" but it is often used as synonymous with our appellation of "Mister;" though more particularly applied to a learned man, or a reputed saint. A "shereef," or descendant of the Prophet, is called "the seyd," or "the seyyid" (master, or lord), whatever be his station. Many shereefs are employed in the lowest offices: there are servants, dustmen, and beggars, of the honoured race of Moḥammad; but all of them are entitled to the distinctive appellation above mentioned, and privileged to wear the green turban:[1] many of them, however, not only among those of humble station, but also among the wealthy, and particularly the learned, assume neither of these prerogatives; preferring the title of "sheykh," and the white turban. A man who has performed the pilgrimage is generally called "the ḥágg;"[2] and a woman who has alike distinguished herself, "the ḥággeh:" yet there are many pilgrims who, like those shereefs just before alluded to, prefer the title of "sheykh." The general appellation of a lady is "the sitt," which signifies "the mistress," or "the lady."

---

[1] Men and women of this race often contract marriages with persons who are not members of the same; and as the title of shereef is inherited from either of the parents, the number of persons who enjoy this distinction has become very considerable.

[2] This word is thus pronounced by the inhabitants of Cairo and the greater part of Egypt; but in most other countries where Arabic is spoken, "ḥájj." The Turks and Persians use, instead of it, the synonymous Arabic word "ḥájjee." The former of these two terms also means "pilgrims," as a collective noun.

Before I describe the ordinary habits of the master of a family, I must mention the various classes of persons of whom the family may consist. The ḥareem, or the females of the house, have distinct apartments allotted to them; and into these apartments (which, as well as the persons to whom they are appropriated, are called "the ḥareem,") no males are allowed to enter, except the master of the family, and certain other near relations, and children. The ḥareem may consist, first, of a wife, or wives (to the number of four); secondly, of female slaves, some of whom, namely, white and (as they are commonly called) Abyssinian (but more properly Galla) slaves, are generally concubines, and others (the black slaves) kept merely for servile offices, as cooking, waiting upon the ladies, &c.; thirdly, of female free servants, who are, in no case, concubines, or not legitimately so. The male dependants may consist of white and of black slaves, and free servants; but are mostly of the last-mentioned class. Very few of the Egyptians avail themselves of the licence, which their religion allows them, of having four wives; and still smaller is the number of those who have two or more wives, and concubines besides. Even most of those men who have but one wife are content, for the sake of domestic peace, if for no other reason, to remain without a concubine-slave: but some prefer the possession of an Abyssinian slave to the more expensive maintenance of a wife; and keep a black slave-girl, or an Egyptian female servant, to wait upon her, to clean and keep in order the apartments of the ḥareem, and to cook. It is seldom that two or more wives are kept in the same house: if they are, they generally have distinct apartments. Of male servants, the master of a family keeps, if he can afford to do so, one or more to wait upon him and his male guests; another, who is called a "saḳḳà," or water-carrier, but who is particularly a servant of the ḥareem, and attends the ladies only when they go out;[1] a "bowwáb," or door-keeper, who constantly sits at the door of the house; and a "sáïs," or groom, for the horse, mule, or ass. Few of the Egyptians have "memlooks," or male white slaves; most of these being in the possession of rich 'Osmánlees (or Turks); and scarcely any but Turks of high rank keep eunuchs: but a wealthy Egyptian merchant is proud of having a black slave to ride or walk behind him, and to carry his pipe.

The Egyptian is a very early riser, as he retires to sleep at an early

---

[1] Unless there be a eunuch. The saḳḳà is generally the chief of the servants.

hour: it is his duty to be up and dressed before daybreak, when he should say the morning-prayers. In general, while the master of a family is performing the religious ablution, and saying his prayers, his wife or slave is preparing for him a cup of coffee, and filling his pipe, to present to him as soon as he has acquitted himself of his religious duties.

Many of the Egyptians take nothing before noon but the cup of coffee and the pipe: others take a light meal at an early hour. The meal of breakfast ("el-faṭoor") generally consists of bread, with eggs, butter, cheese, clouted cream, or curdled milk, &c.; or of a "faṭeereh," which is a kind of pastry, saturated with butter, made very thin, and folded over and over like a napkin: it is eaten alone, or with a little honey poured over it, or sugar. A very common dish for breakfast is "fool mudemmes," or beans, similar to our horse-beans, slowly boiled, during a whole night, in an earthen vessel, buried, all but the neck, in the hot ashes of an oven or a bath, and having the mouth closely stopped: they are eaten with linseed-oil, or butter, and generally with a little lime-juice: thus prepared, they are sold in the morning in the sooḳs (or markets) of Cairo and other towns. A meal is often made (by those who cannot afford luxuries) of bread and a mixture called "duḳḳah," which is commonly composed of salt and pepper, with "zaạtar" (or wild marjoram) or mint or cumin-seed, and with one, or more, or all, of the following ingredients: namely, coriander-seed, cinnamon, sesame, and "ḥommuṣ" (or chick-peas): each mouthful of bread is dipped in this mixture. The bread is always made in the form of a round flat cake, generally about a span in width, and a finger's breadth, or less, in thickness.

The pipe and the cup of coffee are enjoyed by almost all persons who can afford such luxuries, very early in the morning, and oftentimes during the day. There are many men who are scarcely ever seen without a pipe either in their hand or carried behind them by a servant. The smoker keeps his tobacco for daily use in a purse or bag made of shawl-stuff, or silk, or velvet, which is often accompanied with a small pouch containing a flint and steel, and some agaric tinder, and is usually crammed into his bosom.

The pipe (which is called by many names, as "shibuk,"[1] "'ood," &c.,) is generally between four and five feet long: some pipes are

[1] From the Turkish "chibooḳ."

shorter, and some are of greater length. The most common kind used in Egypt is made of a kind of wood called "garmashaḳ."[1] The

Pipes.

greater part of the stick (from the mouthpiece to about three-quarters of its length) is covered with silk, which is confined at each extremity by gold thread, often intertwined with coloured silks, or by

[1] Pronounced "garmash'aḳ." I believe it is maple.

a tube of gilt silver; and at the lower extremity of the covering is a tassel of silk. The covering was originally designed to be moistened with water, in order to cool the pipe, and, consequently, the smoke, by evaporation: but this is only done when the pipe is old, or not handsome. Cherry-stick pipes, which are never covered, are also used by many persons, particularly in the winter. In summer, the smoke is not so cool from the cherry-stick pipe as from the kind before mentioned. The bowl[1] is of baked earth, coloured red or brown.[2] The mouthpiece[3] is composed of two or more pieces of opaque, light-coloured amber, interjoined by ornaments of enamelled gold, agate, jasper, carnelion, or some other precious substance. It is the most costly part of the pipe: some mouthpieces are adorned with diamonds: the price of one of the kind most generally used by persons of the middle orders is from about one to three pounds sterling. A wooden tube passes through it. This is often changed, as it soon becomes foul from the oil of the tobacco. The pipe also requires to be cleaned very often, which is done with tow, by means of a long wire. Many poor men in Cairo gain their livelihood by going about to clean pipes.

The tobacco smoked by persons of the higher orders, and some others, in Egypt, is of a very mild and delicious flavour. It is mostly from the neighbourhood of El-Ládiḳeeyeh, in Syria. The best kind is the "mountain tobacco,"[4] grown on the hills about that town. A stronger kind, which takes its name from the town of Ṣoor,[5] sometimes mixed with the former, is used by most persons of the middle orders. In smoking, the people of Egypt and of other countries of the East draw in their breath freely; so that much of the smoke descends into the lungs; and the terms which they use to express "smoking tobacco" signify "*drinking* smoke," or "*drinking* tobacco:" for the same word signifies both "smoke" and "tobacco." Few of them spit while smoking: I have very seldom seen any do so.

Some of the Egyptians use the Persian pipe, in which the smoke passes through water. The pipe of this kind most commonly used by persons of the higher classes is called "nárgeeleh," because the vessel that contains the water is a cocoa-nut, of which "nárgeeleh"

---

1 "Ḥagar."

2 To preserve the matting or carpet from injury, a small brass tray is often placed beneath the bowl; and a small tray of wood is made use of to receive the ashes of the tobacco.

3 "Fum," or "tarkeebeh."

4 "Dukhkhán gebelee."

5 "Dukhkhán Ṣooree."

is an Arabic name. Another kind, which has a glass vase, is called "sheesheh."[1] Each has a very long, flexible tube. A particular kind of tobacco, called "tumbák," from Persia, is used in the water-pipe: it is first washed several times, and put into the pipe-bowl while damp; and two or three pieces of live charcoal are placed on the top. Its flavour is mild, and very agreeable; but the strong inhalation necessary in this mode of smoking is injurious to persons of delicate lungs.[2] In using the Persian pipe, the person as freely draws the smoke into his lungs as he would inhale pure air. The great prevalence of liver-complaints in Arabia is attributed to the general use of the nárgeeleh; and many persons in Egypt suffer severely from the same cause. A kind of pipe commonly called "gózeh," which is similar to the nárgeeleh, except that it has a short cane tube, instead of the snake (or flexible one), and no stand, is used by men of the lowest class, for smoking both the tumbák and the intoxicating "ḥasheesh," or hemp.

The coffee ("ḳahweh"[3]) is made very strong, and without sugar or milk. The coffee-cup (which is called "fingán") is small;

Coffee-service.

generally holding not quite an ounce and a half of liquid. It is of porcelain, or Dutch-ware, and, being without a handle, is placed within another cup (called "ẓarf"), of silver or brass, according to the circumstances of the owner, and, both in shape and size, nearly

[1] A Persian word, signifying "glass."

[2] It is, however, often recommended in the case of a cough. One of my friends, the most celebrated of the poets of Cairo, who is much troubled by asthma, uses the nárgeeleh almost incessantly from morning till night.

[3] This is the name of the *beverage*: the *berries* (whether whole or pounded) are called "bunn."

resembling our egg-cup.[1] In preparing the coffee, the water is first made to boil: the coffee (freshly roasted, and pounded,) is then put in, and stirred; after which the pot is again placed on the fire, once or twice, until the coffee begins to simmer; when it is taken off, and its contents are poured out into the cups while the surface is yet creamy. The Egyptians are excessively fond of pure and strong coffee, thus prepared; and very seldom add sugar to it (though some do so when they are unwell), and never milk or cream; but a little cardamom-seed[2] is often added to it. It is a common custom, also, to fumigate the cup with the smoke of mastic; and the wealthy sometimes impregnate the coffee with the delicious fragrance of ambergris.[3] The most general mode of doing this is, to put about a carat-weight of ambergris in a coffee-pot, and melt it over a fire; then make the coffee in another pot, in the manner before described, and, when it has settled a little, pour it into the pot which contains the ambergris. Some persons make use of the ambergris, for the same purpose, in a different way; sticking a piece of it, of the weight of about two carats, in the bottom of the cup, and then pouring in the coffee: a piece of the weight above mentioned will serve for two or three weeks. This mode is often adopted by persons who like always to have the coffee which they themselves drink flavoured with this perfume, and do not give all their visiters the same luxury. The coffee-pot is sometimes brought in a vessel of silver or brass (called "'áz'ḳee"[4]) containing burning charcoal. This vessel is suspended by three chains. In presenting the coffee, the servant holds the foot of the ẓarf with his thumb and first finger. In receiving the fingán and ẓarf, he makes use of both hands, placing the left beneath and the right above at the same instant.

In cold weather, a brasier, or chafing-dish (called "manḳal," and vulgarly "manḳad"), of tinned copper, full of burning charcoal, is placed on the floor; and sometimes perfume is burnt in it. The

---

1 In a full service there are ten fingáns and ẓarfs of uniform kinds, and often another fingán and ẓarf of a superior kind for the master of the house, or for a distinguished guest. In the cut next preceding, the coffee-pot ("bekreg," or "bakrag,") and the ẓarfs and tray are of silver, and are represented on a scale of one-eighth of the real size. Below this set are a similar ẓarf and fingán, on a scale of one-fourth, and a brass ẓarf, with the fingán placed in it. Some ẓarfs are of plain or gilt silver filigree; and a few opulent persons have them of gold, and sometimes set with diamonds, rubies, and other gems. Many Muslims, however, religiously disallow all utensils of gold and of silver.

2 "Ḥabb-hán."

3 "'Ambar."

4 Baron Hammer-Purgstall considers this word a corruption, and writes "chasseki" in its stead: "'áz'ḳee" (for "'áziḳee") is, however, the term used by the Egyptians.

Egyptians take great delight in perfumes;[1] and often fumigate their apartments. The substance most commonly used for this purpose is

'Áz'ḳee and Manḳals.[2]

frankincense of an inferior quality, called "bakhoor el-barr." Benzoin[3] and aloes-wood[4] are also used for the same purpose.

If he can conveniently afford to keep a horse, mule, or ass, or to hire an ass, the Egyptian is seldom seen walking far beyond the threshold of his own house; but very few of the people of Cairo, or of the other towns, venture to expose themselves to the suspicion of possessing superfluous wealth, and, consequently, to greater exactions of the government than they would otherwise suffer, by keeping horses.[5] The modern saddle of the horse is generally padded, and covered with cloth or velvet, embroidered, or otherwise ornamented; and the head-stall and breast-leather are adorned with silk-tassels, and coins, or other ornaments, of silver. Wealthy merchants, and the great 'Ulamà, usually ride mules. The saddle of the mule is, generally, nearly the same as that of the ass, of which a sketch is inserted: when the rider is one of the 'Ulamà, it is covered with a "seggádeh" (or prayer-carpet): so, too, sometimes, is the ladies' saddle; from which, however, the former differs considerably, as will be shewn hereafter. Asses are most generally used for riding through the narrow and crowded streets of Cairo; and there are

---

1 They sometimes perfume the beard and mustaches with civet.

2 One of the latter (that to the right) is an earthen vessel. Each of the above utensils is represented on a scale of about one-eighth of the real size.

3 "Gáwee."

4 "'Ood."

5 Whether walking or riding, a person of the higher classes is usually attended by a servant bearing his pipe.

many for hire: their usual pace is an easy amble. Egypt has long been famed for its excellent asses, which are, in general, larger than those of our country, and very superior to the latter in every respect. The usual price of one of a good breed and well trained is about three or four pounds sterling; but some are of higher price than an ordinary horse. The ass is furnished with a stuffed saddle; the fore part of which is covered with red leather, and the seat, most commonly, with

An Ass equipped in the usual manner for riding.[1]

a kind of soft woollen lace, similar to our coach-lace, of red, yellow, and other colours. The stirrup-leathers are, in every case, very short. The horseman is preceded by a groom, or by two grooms, to clear the way; the groom, or each groom, generally carrying a long staff, called "nebboot," which he holds perpendicularly, grasping it near the lower extremity: and, for the same purpose, a servant generally runs beside or behind the ass, or sometimes before; calling out to the passengers to move out of the way to the right or left, or to take care of their backs, faces, sides, feet, or heels.[2] The rider, however, must

[1] Nearly the whole of its coat is closely shorn.

[2] Such ejaculations as "ó'à!" (take care!), "yemeenak! shimálak!" (to thy right! to thy left!), "ḍahrak!" (thy back!), "wishshak!" (thy face!), "gembak!" (thy side!), "riglak!" (thy foot!), "kaạbak!" (thy heel!), and, to a Turk, "ṣáḳin!" (take care!), are the most common cries. The following appellations are also often added:--"yá efendee!" (to a Turk), "yá sheykh!" (to an old or a middle-aged Muslim native), "yá ṣabee!" (to a young man), "yá weled!" or "yá ibnee!" (to a boy), "yá shereef!" (to a green-turbaned descendant of the Prophet), "yá m'allim!" (to a native Christian, or a Jew), "yá khawágeh!" (to a Frank), "yá sitt!" (to a lady, or a female of the middle orders), and "yá bint!" that is, "daughter,'

be vigilant, and not trust merely to his servant, or he may be thrown down by the wide load of a camel; which accident, indeed, is sometimes unavoidable in the more narrow and crowded streets. His pipe is generally carried by the servant; and filled and lighted when he dismounts at a house or shop.

If he have no regular business to employ him, the Egyptian spends the greater part of the day in riding, paying visits, or making purchases; or in smoking and sipping coffee and chatting with a friend at home; or he passes an hour or more in the morning enjoying the luxuries of a public bath. At noon, he has again to say prayers, if he fulfil the duties imposed on him by his religion: but, as I have remarked on a former occasion, there are comparatively few persons among the Egyptians who do not sometimes neglect these duties; and there are many who scarcely ever pray. Directly after midday (if he has not taken a late breakfast), he eats a light dinner; then takes a pipe and a cup of coffee, and, in hot weather, usually indulges himself with a nap. Often he retires to recline in the ḥareem; where a wife or female slave watches over his repose, or rubs the soles of his feet with her hands. On such occasions, and at other times when he wishes to enjoy privacy, every person who comes to pay him a visit is told, by the servant, that he is in the ḥareem; and no friend expects him to be called thence, unless on very urgent business. From the time of the afternoon-prayers, until sunset (the next time of prayer), he generally enjoys, again, his pipe and a cup of coffee in the society of some one or more of his friends at home or abroad. Shortly after sunset he sups.

I must now describe the meals of dinner ("el-ghadà") and supper ("el-'ashà"), and the manner and etiquette of eating. The same remarks will apply to both these repasts; except that supper is always the principal meal. It is the general custom to cook in the afternoon; and what remains of the supper is eaten the next day for dinner, if there are no guests in the house. The master of a family generally dines and sups with his wife or wives and children; but there are many men, particularly of the higher classes, who are too proud to do this, or too much engaged in society to be able to do so, unless on some few occasions; and there are men even of the lowest class who

or "girl" (to a poor female). A woman of the lower class, however old she be, the servant must call "girl," or "daughter," or probably she will not move an inch out of the way. A little girl, or young woman, is often called "'arooseh," or "bride;" and "ḥággeh," or "female pilgrim," is an appellation often given to women in the streets.

scarcely ever eat with their wives or children. When a person is paying a visit to a friend, and the hour of dinner or supper arrives, it is incumbent on the master of the house to order the meal to be brought; and the same is generally considered necessary if the visiter be a stranger.

Every person, before he sits down to the table, or rather to the tray, washes his hands,[1] and sometimes his mouth also, with soap and water; or, at least, has some water poured upon his right hand. A servant brings to him a basin and ewer (called "ṭisht" and "ibreeḳ"), of tinned copper, or of brass.[2] The former of these has a

Ṭisht and Ibreeḳ.[3]

cover pierced with holes, with a raised receptacle for the soap in the middle; and the water, being poured upon the hands, passes through this cover into the space below; so that when the basin is brought to a second person, the water with which the former one has washed is not seen. A napkin ("fooṭah") is given to each person.

A round tray (called "ṣeeneeyeh," and "ṣáneeyeh,") of tinned copper, or sometimes of brass, generally between two and three feet in diameter, serves as a table; being placed upon a stool ("kursee") about fifteen inches high, made of wood, and often covered with mother-of-pearl, tortoise-shell, bone, &c. These two pieces of furniture compose the "sufrah." Round cakes of bread, such as have been before described, sometimes cut in halves across the middle, are placed round the tray, with several limes, cut in two, to be squeezed

---

1 See Mark, vii. 3.

2 In the houses of some of the opulent, these utensils are of silver. I have also seen some of gilt copper.

3 The width of the former is fourteen inches; and the height of the latter, the same.

Washing before or after a Meal.

Kursee and Seeneeyeh.

over any of the dishes that may require the acid; and a spoon of box-wood, or of ebony, or tortoise-shell, is put for each person. The bread often serves as a plate. Several dishes of tinned copper, or of china, containing different kinds of viands, vegetables, &c., are then placed upon the tray, according to the common fashion of the country; or only one dish is put on at a time, after the Turkish mode.

The persons who are to partake of the repast sit upon the floor around the tray; each with his napkin upon his knees: or, if the tray be placed near the edge of a low deewán, which is often done, some of the persons may sit on the deewán, and the others on the floor: but if the party be numerous, the tray is placed in the middle of the room, and they sit round it with one knee on the ground, and the other (the right) raised; this being the most approved posture at meals in every case: and in this manner, as many as twelve persons may sit round a tray three feet wide. Each person bares his right arm to the elbow, or tucks up the hanging end of his sleeve. Before he begins to eat, he says, "Bi-smi-llah" (In the name of God).

A Party at Dinner or Supper.[2]

This is generally said in a low, but audible voice; and by the master of the house first. It is considered both as a grace and as an invitation to any person to partake of the meal; and when any one is addressed with "Bi-smi-llah," or "Tafaḍḍal" (which latter signifies, in this case, "Do me the favour to partake of the repast"), he must

[1] Or "Bi-smi-lláhi-r-raḥmáni-r-raḥeem" (In the name of God, the Compassionate, the Merciful).

[2] One of the servants is holding a water-bottle the other, a fly-whisk made of palm-leaves.

reply, if he do not accept the invitation, "Heneeän" (or "May it be productive of enjoyment"), or use some similar expression: else it will be feared that an evil eye has been cast upon the food; and they say that, "in the food that is coveted" (or upon which an envious eye has fallen) "there is no blessing." But the manner in which the Egyptian often presses a stranger to eat with him shews that feelings of hospitality most forcibly dictate the "Bi-smi-llah." The master of the house first begins to eat; the guests or others immediately follow his example. Neither knives nor forks are used: the thumb and two fingers of the right hand serve instead of those instruments; but the spoons are used for soup or rice or other things that cannot be easily taken without; and both hands may be used in particular cases, as will be presently explained. When there are several dishes upon the tray, each person takes of any that he likes, or of every one in succession: when only one dish is placed upon the tray at a time, each takes from it a few mouthfuls, and it is quickly removed, to give place to another.[1] To pick out a delicate morsel, and hand it to a friend, is esteemed polite. The manner of eating with the fingers, as practised in Egypt and other Eastern countries, is more delicate than may be imagined by Europeans who have not witnessed it, nor heard it correctly described. Each person breaks off a small piece of bread, dips it in the dish, and then conveys it to his mouth, together with a small portion of the meat or other contents of the dish.[2] The piece of bread is generally doubled together, so as to enclose the morsel of meat, &c.; and only the thumb and first and second fingers are commonly used. When a person takes a piece of meat too large for a single mouthful, he usually places it upon his bread.

The food is dressed in such a manner that it may be easily eaten in the mode above described. It generally consists, for the most part, of "yakhnee," or stewed meat, with chopped onions, or with a quantity of "bámiyehs,"[3] or other vegetables; "ḳáwurmeh," or a richer stew, with onions; "waraḳ maḥshee," or vine-leaves, or bits of lettuce-leaf or cabbage-leaf, with a mixture of rice and minced-meat

---

[1] Our Saviour and his disciples thus ate from one dish. See Matt. xxvi. 23.

[2] Or he merely sops his morsel of bread in the dish. See Ruth, ii. 14; and John, xiii. 26.

[3] The bámiyeh is the esculent "hibiscus:" the part which is eaten is a polygonal pod, generally between one and three inches in length, and of the thickness of a small finger: it is full of seeds and nutritive mucilage, and has a very pleasant flavour. A little lime-juice is usually dropped on the plate of bámiyehs when they are cooked alone, and also when they have a little fried minced-meat sprinkled upon them, as is often done.

(delicately seasoned with salt, pepper, and onions, and often with garlic, parsley, &c.,) wrapped up in them, and boiled; cucumbers ("khiyár"), or black, white, or red "bádingáns,"[1] or a kind of gourd (called "ḳaraḳ kooseh") of the size and shape of a small cucumber, which are all "maḥshee" (or stuffed) with the same composition as the leaves above mentioned; and "kebáb," or small morsels of mutton or lamb, roasted on skewers. Many dishes consist wholly, or for the most part, of vegetables; such as cabbage, purslain, spinach, bámiyehs, beans, lupins, chick-peas, gourd cut into small pieces, colocasia, lentils, &c. Fish, dressed with oil, is also a common dish. Most of the meats are cooked with clarified butter, on account of the deficiency of fat; and are made very rich: the butter, in the hot season, is perfectly liquid. When a fowl is placed whole on the tray, both hands are generally required to separate the joints; or two persons, each using the right hand alone, perform this operation together; but some will do it very cleverly without assistance, and with a single hand. Many of the Arabs will not allow the left hand to touch food in any case,[2] except when the right is maimed. A boned fowl, stuffed with raisins, pistachio-nuts, crumbled bread, and parsley, is not an uncommon dish; and even a whole lamb, stuffed with pistachio-nuts, &c., is sometimes served up; but the meat is easily separated with one hand. Sweets are often mixed with stewed meat, &c.; as, for instance, "'annáb" (or jujubes), peaches, apricots, &c., and sugar, with yakhnee. Various kinds of sweets are also served up, and often in no particular order with respect to other meats. A favourite sweet dish is "kunáfeh," which is made of wheat-flour, and resembles vermicelli, but is finer; it is fried with a little clarified butter, and sweetened with sugar or honey. A dish of water-melon ("baṭṭeekh"[3]), if in season, generally forms part of the meal. This is cut up about a quarter of an hour before, and left to cool in the external air, or in a current of air, by the evaporation of the juice on the surfaces of the slices; but it is always watched during this time, lest a serpent should come to it, and poison it by its breath or bite; for this reptile is said to be extremely fond of the water-melon, and to smell it at a great distance. Water-melons are very abundant in Egypt, and mostly very delicious and wholesome. A dish of boiled rice (called "ruzz mufelfel," the "piláv" of the Turks), mixed with a little butter, and seasoned with salt and pepper,

---

[1] The black and white bádingán are the fruits of two kinds of egg-plant: the red is the tomata.

[2] Because used for unclean purposes.

[3] So commonly pronounced, for "biṭṭeekh."

is generally that from which the last morsels are taken; but, in the houses of the wealthy, this is often followed by a bowl of "khusháf,"[1] a sweet drink, commonly consisting of water with raisins boiled in it, and then sugar: when cool, a little rose-water is dropped into it.[2] The water-melon frequently supplies the place of this.[3]

The Egyptians eat very moderately, though quickly. Each person, as soon as he has finished, says, "El-ḥamdu li-lláh" (Praise be to God),[4] and gets up, without waiting till the others have done:[5] he then washes his hands and mouth with soap and water; the basin and ewer being held by a servant, as before.

The only beverage at meals is water of the Nile, or, sometimes, at the tables of the rich, sherbet, which will presently be described. The Arabs drink little or no water *during* a meal, but generally take

Water-bottles (Dóraḳs), with covers of different kinds.—*The bottles in the foremost row are one-sixth of the real size.*

---

[1] So called from the Persian "khósh áb," or "sweet water."

[2] It is drunk with ladles of tortoise-shell or cocoa-nut.

[3] The principal and best fruits of Egypt are dates, grapes, oranges and citrons of various kinds, common figs, sycamore-figs, prickly-pears, pomegranates, bananas, and a great variety of melons. Peaches and apricots are plentiful, but not of good flavour. Pears are rare; mostly brought from Mount Sinai or Syria. From this enumeration it appears that there are not many good fruits in Egypt.

[4] Or "El-ḥamdu li-lláhi rabbi-l-'álameen" (Praise be to God, the Lord of the beings of the whole world).

[5] It is deemed highly improper to rise during a meal, even from respect to a superior who may approach. It has been mentioned before, that the Prophet forbade his followers to rise while eating, or when about to eat, even if the time of prayer arrived.

a large draught immediately *after*. The water of the Nile is remarkably good; but that of all the wells in Cairo and in other parts of Egypt is slightly brackish. In general, water is drunk either from an earthen bottle or from a brass cup.[1] The water-bottles are of two kinds; one called "dórak̦," and the other, "k̦ulleh:" the former has

Water-bottles (K̦ullehs).

a narrow, and the latter a wide, mouth. They are made of a greyish, porous earth, which cools the water deliciously, by evaporation; and they are, therefore, generally placed in a current of air. The interior is often blackened with the smoke of some resinous wood, and then perfumed with the smoke of "k̦afal"[2]-wood and mastic; the latter used last. A small earthen vessel (called "mibkharah"[3]) is employed in performing these operations, to contain the burning charcoal, which is required to ignite the wood, and the mastic; and the water-bottle is held inverted over it. A strip of rag is tied round the

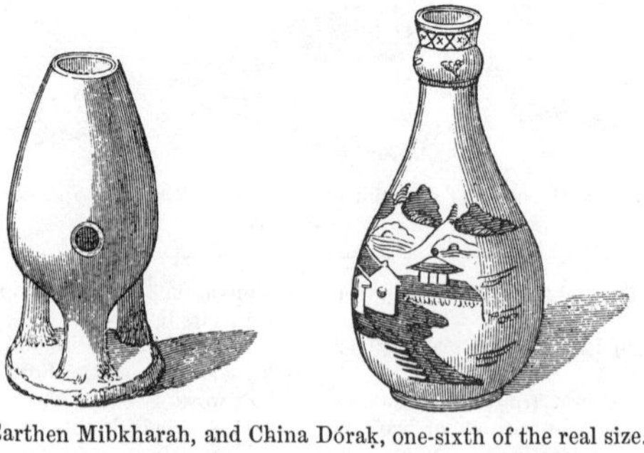

Earthen Mibkharah, and China Dórak̦, one-sixth of the real size.

[1] The ancient Egyptians used drinking-cups of brass. (Herodotus, lib. ii. cap. 37.)

[2] "Amyris kafal" of Forskal. An Arabian tree.

[3] Pronounced "mibkhar'ah."

neck of the dórak, at the distance of about an inch from the mouth, to prevent the smoke-black from extending too far upon the exterior of the bottle. Many persons also put a little orange-flower water[1] into the bottles. This gives a very agreeable flavour to their contents. The bottles have stoppers of silver, brass, tin, or wood; or covers of woven palm-leaves; and are generally placed in a tray of tinned copper, which receives the water that exudes from them. In cold weather, china bottles are used in many houses instead of those above described, which then render the water too cold.[2] The two most common forms of drinking-cups are here represented. Some of

Brass Drinking-cups, one-fifth of the real size.

them have texts of the Ḳur-án, &c., engraved in the interior, or the names of "the Seven Sleepers:" but inscriptions of the former kind I have seldom seen. Every person, before and after drinking, repeats the same ejaculations as before and after eating; and this he does each time that he drinks during a meal: each friend present then says to him, "May it be productive of enjoyment;"[3] to which the reply is, "God cause thee to have enjoyment."[4]

Though we read, in some of the delightful tales of 'The Thousand and One Nights,' of removing "the table of viands"[5] and bringing "the table of wine,"[6] this prohibited beverage is not often introduced in general society, either during or after the meal, or at other times, by the Muslims of Egypt in the present day. Many of them, however, habitually indulge in drinking wine with select parties of their acquaintance. The servants of a man who is addicted to this habit know such of his friends as may be admitted, if they happen to call when he is engaged in this unlawful pleasure; and to all others they say that he is not at home, or that he is in the ḥareem. Drinking

1 "Móyet zahr," or "móyet zahr náring."

2 Baron Hammer-Purgstall has remarked, that two other vessels should have been mentioned here (in the first edition of this work), more especially because their names have been adopted in European languages: they are the "garrah" or "jarrah," a water-jar or pitcher, and the "demigán" or "demiján," a large bottle, "la dame-jeanne."

3 "Henceän."

4 "Allah yehenneek" (for "yuhenneek").

5 "Sufrat eṭ-ṭa'ám."

6 "Sufrat el-mudám."

wine is indulged in by such persons before and after supper, and during that meal; but it is most approved *before* supper, as they say that it quickens the appetite. The "table of wine" is usually thus prepared, according to a penitent Muslim wine-bibber, who is one of my friends (I cannot speak on this subject from my own experience; for, as I never drink wine, I have never been invited to join a Muslim wine-party):—a round japanned tray, or a glass dish, is placed on the stool before mentioned: on this are generally arranged two cut-glass jugs, one containing wine,[1] and the other, rosoglio;[2] and sometimes two or more bottles besides: several small glasses are placed with these; and glass saucers of dried and fresh fruits, and, perhaps, pickles: lastly, two candles, and often a bunch of flowers stuck in a candlestick, are put upon the tray.

The Egyptians have various kinds of sherbets, or sweet drinks. The most common kind[3] is merely sugar and water, but very sweet: lemonade[4] is another: a third kind, the most esteemed,[5] is prepared from a hard conserve of violets, made by pounding violet-flowers, and then boiling them with sugar: this violet-sherbet is of a green colour: a fourth kind[6] is prepared from mulberries: a fifth,[7] from sorrel. There is also a kind of sherbet sold in the streets,[8] which is made with raisins, as its name implies: another kind, which is a strong infusion of licorice-root, and called by the name of that root;[9] and a third kind, which is prepared from the fruit of the locust-tree, and called, in like manner, by the name of the fruit.[10] The sherbet is

Sherbet-cups.

served in covered glass cups, generally called "ḳullehs," containing about three-quarters of a pint; some of which (the more common

1 "Nebeed" (more properly, "nebeedh:" see page 94), or "mudám."

2 "'Amber'ee."

3 Called simply "sharbát," or "sharbát sukkar," or only "sukkar."

4 "Leymoonáteh," or "sharáb el-leymoon."

5 "Sharáb el-benefseg."

6 "Sharáb et-toot."

7 "Sharáb el-ḥommeyḍ."

8 Called "zebeeb." This name is also given to an intoxicating conserve.

9 "'Erḳ soos."

10 "Kharroob."

kind) are ornamented with gilt flowers, &c. The sherbet-cups are placed on a round tray, and covered with a round piece of embroidered silk, or cloth of gold. On the right arm of the person who presents the sherbet is hung a large oblong napkin with a wide embroidered border of gold and coloured silks at each end. This is ostensibly offered for the purpose of wiping the lips after drinking the sherbet; but it is really not so much for use as for display: the lips are seldom or scarcely touched with it.

The interval between supper and the "'eshè," or time of the prayers of nightfall, is generally passed in smoking a pipe, and sipping a cup of coffee. The enjoyment of the pipe may be interrupted by prayer, but is continued afterwards; and sometimes draughts or chess, or some other game, or at least conversation, contributes to make the time glide away more agreeably. The members of an Egyptian family in easy circumstances may pass their time very pleasantly; but they do so in a quiet way. The men often pay evening visits to their friends, at, or after, supper-time. They commonly use, on these and similar occasions, a folding lantern ("fánoos"), made of waxed cloth strained over rings of wire, and a top and bottom of tinned copper. This kind of lantern is here represented, together with the common lamp ("ḳandeel"), and its

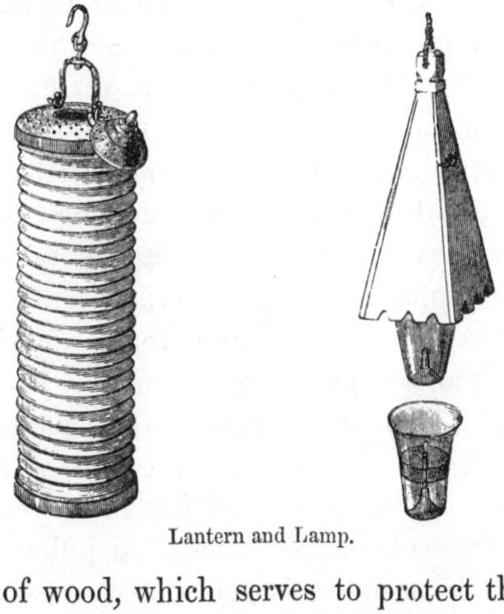

Lantern and Lamp.

usual receptacle of wood, which serves to protect the flame from the wind. The lamp is a small vessel of glass, having a little tube in the bottom, in which is stuck a wick formed of cotton twisted round a piece of straw. Some water is poured in first, and then the oil. A lamp of this kind is often hung over the entrance of a house. By night, the interiors of the houses present a more dull appearance than in the day: the light of one or two candles (placed on the floor or on a stool, and sometimes surrounded by a large glass shade, or enclosed in a glass lantern, on account of the windows' being merely of lattice-work,) is generally thought sufficient for a large and lofty saloon. Few of the Egyptians sit up later, in summer, than three or four o'clock, which is three or four hours after sunset; for their reckoning of time is from sunset at every season of the year: in winter they often sit up five or six hours.

Thus the day is usually spent by men of moderate wealth who have no regular business to attend to, or none that requires their own active superintendence. But it is the habit of the *tradesman* to repair, soon after breakfast, to his shop or warehouse, and to remain there until near sunset.[1] He has leisure to smoke as much as he likes; and his customers often smoke with him. To some of these he offers his own pipe (unless they have theirs with them), and a cup of coffee, which is obtained from the nearest coffee-shop. A great portion of the day he sometimes passes in agreeable chat with customers, or with the tradesmen of the next or opposite shops. He generally says his prayers without moving from his shop. Shortly after the noon-prayers, or sometimes earlier or later, he eats a light meal, such as a plate of kebáb and a cake of bread (which a boy or maid daily brings from his house, or procures in the market), or some bread and cheese or pickles, &c., which are carried about the streets for sale: and if a customer be present, he is always invited, and often pressed, to partake of this meal. A large earthen bottle of water is kept in the shop, and replenished, whenever necessary, by a passing "saḳḳà," or water-carrier. In the evening, the tradesman returns to his house, eats his supper, and, soon after, retires to bed.

It is the general custom in Egypt for the husband and wife to sleep in the same bed, except among the wealthy classes, who mostly prefer separate beds. The bed is usually thus prepared in the houses of persons of moderate wealth:—a mattress,[2] stuffed with cotton, about six feet long, and three or four feet in width, is placed upon a low frame, generally made of palm-sticks:[3] a pillow is placed for the head, and a sheet spread over this and the mattress: the only covering in summer is generally a thin blanket;[4] and in winter, a thick

[1] A description of the shops, and a further account of the tradesmen of Cairo, will be given in another chapter, on Industry.

[2] "Ṭarráḥah."

[3] "Sereer."

[4] "Ḥerám."

quilt,[1] stuffed with cotton. If there be no frame, the mattress is placed upon the floor; or two mattresses are laid together, one upon the other, with the sheet, pillow, &c.; and often, a cushion of the deewán is placed on each side. A musquito-curtain[2] is suspended over the bed by means of four strings, which are attached to nails in the wall. The dress is seldom changed on going to bed; and in winter, many people sleep with all their ordinary clothes on, except the gibbeh, or cloth coat; but in summer, they sleep almost, or entirely, unclad. In winter, the bed is prepared in a small closet (called "khazneh"): in summer, in a large room. All the bed-clothes are rolled up, in the day-time, and placed on one side, or in the closet above-mentioned. During the hottest weather, many people sleep upon the house-top, or in a "fes-ḥah" (or "fesaḥah"), which is an uncovered apartment; but ophthalmia and other diseases often result from their thus exposing themselves to the external air at night. The most common kind of frame for the bed, made of palm-sticks, harbours bugs, which are very abundant in Egypt in the summer, as fleas are in the winter. These and other plagues to which the people of Egypt are exposed by night and day have been before mentioned.[3] With regard to the most disgusting of them, the lice, it may here be added, that, though they are not always to be avoided even by the most scrupulous cleanliness, a person who changes his linen after two or three days' wear is very seldom annoyed by these vermin; and when he is, they are easily removed, not attaching themselves to the skin: they are generally found in the linen. A house may be kept almost clear of fleas by frequent washing and sweeping; and the flies may be kept out by placing nets at the doors and windows, even though the meshes be large enough to admit them: but it is impossible to purify an Egyptian house from bugs, if it contain much wood-work, which is generally the case.

The male servants[4] lead a very easy life, with the exception of the "sáïs," or groom, who, whenever his master takes a ride, runs before or beside him; and this he will do in the hottest weather for hours together, without appearing fatigued. Almost every wealthy person in Cairo has a "bowwáb," or door-keeper, always at the door of his house, and several other male servants. Most of these are natives of Egypt; but many Nubians are also employed as servants in Cairo

---

1 "Leḥáf."

2 "Námooseeyeh." It is composed of muslin, or linen of an open texture, or crape, and forms a close canopy of the width and length of the bed.

3 In the Introduction to this work.

4 "Khaddámeen," singular "khaddám."

and other Egyptian towns. The latter are mostly bowwábs, and are generally esteemed more honest than the Egyptian servants. The wages of the male servants are very small, usually from a dollar to two dollars (or from four to eight shillings) per month: but they receive many presents.[1] On the "'eed" (or festival) after Ramaḍán, the master generally gives, to each of his servants, part or the whole of a new suit of clothes, consisting of an "'eree" (a blue shirt, which is their outer dress), a "ṭarboosh," and a turban. Other articles of dress which they require during the year (except, sometimes, shoes,) the servants are obliged to provide for themselves. Besides what their master gives them, they also receive small presents of money from his visiters, and from the tradespeople with whom he deals; particularly whenever he has made any considerable purchase. They sleep in the clothes which they wear during the day, each upon a small mat; and in winter they cover themselves with a cloak[2] or blanket. In some respects, they are often familiar in their manners to their master, even laughing and joking with him: in others, they are very submissive; paying him the utmost honour, and bearing corporal chastisement from his hand with child-like patience.

The male black slave[3] is treated with more consideration than the free servant; and leads a life well suited to his lazy disposition. If discontented with his situation, he can legally compel his master to sell him. Many of the slaves in Egypt wear the Turkish military dress. They are generally the greatest fanatics in the East; and more accustomed than any other class to insult the Christians and every people who are not of the faith which they have themselves adopted without knowing more of its doctrines than Arab children who have been but a week at school. Of the female slaves, some account will be given in the next chapter.

An acquaintance with the modern inhabitants of Egypt leads us often to compare their domestic habits with those of Europeans in the middle ages; and, perhaps, in this comparison, the points of resemblance which we observe, with regard to the men, are more striking than the contrasts; but the reverse will be found to be the case when we consider the state of the females.

---

1 The wages required from European travellers are much higher than those obtained from natives; and larger and more frequent presents are expected from the former. These presents, when judiciously bestowed, are generally productive of excellent effects; but they too often serve to encourage roguery.

2 See Exodus, xxii. 26, 27.

3 Called "'abd."

CHAPTER VI.

DOMESTIC LIFE—*continued.*

QUITTING the lower apartments, where we have been long detained, I must enter upon a more presumptuous office than I have yet undertaken, which is that of a guide to the "ḥareem:"[1] but first I must give some account of marriage, and the marriage-ceremonies.

To abstain from marrying when a man has attained a sufficient age, and when there is no just impediment, is esteemed, by the Egyptians, improper, and even disreputable. For being myself guilty of this fault (to use no harsher term), I suffered much inconvenience and discomfort during my first and second visits to this country, and endured many reproaches. During the former of those visits, having occasion to remove from a house which I had occupied for some months in a great thoroughfare-street in Cairo, I engaged another house, in a neighbouring quarter: the lease was written, and some money paid in advance; but a day or two after, the agent of the owner came to inform me that the inhabitants of the quarter, who were mostly "shereefs" (or descendants of the Prophet), objected to my living among them, because I was not married. He added, however, that they would gladly admit me if I would even purchase a female slave, which would exempt me from the opprobrium cast upon me by the want of a wife. I replied that, being merely a sojourner in Egypt, I did not like to take either a wife or female slave, whom I must soon abandon: the money that I had paid was, therefore, returned to me. In another quarter, I was less unfortunate; such heavy objections on account of my being unmarried were not raised: I was only required to promise that no person wearing a hat should come into the quarter to visit me; yet, after I had established myself in my new residence, the Sheykh (or chief) of the quarter often endeavoured to persuade

---

1 The term "ḥareem" (which, as before mentioned, is applied both to the females of a family and to the apartments which they occupy,) signifies *prohibited, sacred,* &c. The Turks, and many of the Arabs, use the synonymous Arabic term "ḥaram," which the former pronounce "ḥarem."

me to marry. All my arguments against doing so he deemed of no weight. "You tell me," said he, "that in a year or two you mean to leave this country: now, there is a young widow, who, I am told, is handsome, living within a few doors of you, who will be glad to become your wife, even with the express understanding that you shall divorce her when you quit this place; though, of course, you may do so before, if she should not please you." This young damsel had several times contrived to let me catch a glimpse of a pretty face, as I passed the house in which she and her parents lived. What answer could I return? I replied, that I had actually, by accident, seen her face, and that she was the last woman I should wish to marry, in such circumstances; for I was sure that I could never make up my mind to part with her. But I found it rather difficult to silence my officious friend.—It has been mentioned before, in the Introduction, that an unmarried man, or one who has not a female slave, is usually obliged to dwell in a wekáleh, unless he have some near relation with whom to reside; but that Franks are now exempted from this restriction.

The Egyptian females arrive at puberty much earlier than the natives of colder climates. Many marry at the age of twelve or thirteen years; and some remarkably precocious girls are married at the age of *ten:*[1] but such occurrences are not common. Few remain unmarried after sixteen years of age. An Egyptian girl at the age of thirteen, or even earlier, may be a mother. The women of Egypt are generally very prolific; but females of other countries residing here often are childless; and the children of foreigners from comparatively cool countries, born in Egypt, seldom live to a mature age, even when the mother is a native. It was partly on this account that the emancipated Memlooks (or military slaves) usually adopted Memlooks.

It is very common among the Arabs of Egypt and of other countries, but less so in Cairo than in other parts of Egypt, for a man to marry his first cousin. In this case, the husband and wife continue to call each other "cousin;" because the tie of blood is indissoluble, but that of matrimony very precarious. A union of this kind is generally lasting, on account of this tie of blood; and because mutual intercourse may have formed an attachment between the parties in tender age; though, if they be of the higher or middle

---

[1] They are often betrothed two or three or more years earlier.

classes, the young man is seldom allowed to see the face of his female cousin, or even to meet and converse with her, after she has arrived at or near the age of puberty, until she has become his wife.

Marriages in Cairo are generally conducted, in the case of a virgin, in the following manner; but in that of a widow, or a divorced woman, with little ceremony. Most commonly, the mother, or some other near female relation, of the youth or man who is desirous of obtaining a wife, describes to him the personal and other qualifications of the young women with whom she is acquainted, and directs his choice:[1] or he employs a "kháṭ'beh," or "kháṭibeh;" a woman whose regular business it is to assist men in such cases. Sometimes two or more women of this profession are employed. A kháṭ'beh gives her report confidentially, describing one girl as being like a gazelle, pretty and elegant and young; and another, as not pretty, but rich, and so forth. If the man have a mother and other near female relations, two or three of these usually go with a kháṭ'beh to pay visits to several ḥareems, to which she has access in her professional character of a match-maker; for she is employed as much by the women as by the men. She sometimes also exercises the trade of a "delláleh" (or broker) for the sale of ornaments, clothing, &c., which procures her admission into almost every ḥareem. The women who accompany her in search of a wife for their relation are introduced to the different ḥareems merely as ordinary visiters; and as such, if disappointed, they soon take their leave, though the object of their visit is of course understood by the other party: but if they find among the females of a family (and they are sure to see all who are marriageable) a girl or young woman having the necessary personal qualifications, they state the motive of their visit, and ask, if the proposed match be not at once disapproved of, what property, ornaments, &c., the object of their wishes may possess. If the father of the intended bride be dead, she may perhaps possess one or more houses, shops, &c.; and in almost every case, a marriageable girl of the middle or higher ranks has a set of ornaments of gold and jewels. The women-visiters, having asked these and other questions, bring their report to the expectant youth or man. If satisfied with their report, he gives a present to the kháṭ'beh, and sends her again to the

[1] Abraham's sending a messenger to his own country to seek a wife for his son Isaac (see Genesis, xxiv.) was just such a measure as most modern Arabs would adopt in similar circumstances, if easily practicable.

family of his intended wife, to make known to them his wishes. She generally gives an exaggerated description of his personal attractions, wealth, &c. For instance, she will say, of a very ordinary young man, of scarcely any property, and of whose disposition she knows nothing, "My daughter, the youth who wishes to marry you is young, graceful, elegant, beardless, has plenty of money, dresses handsomely, is fond of delicacies, but cannot enjoy his luxuries alone; he wants you as his companion; he will give you everything that money can procure; he is a stayer-at-home, and will spend his whole time with you, caressing and fondling you."

The parents may betroth their daughter to whom they please, and marry her to him without her consent, if she be not arrived at the age of puberty; but after she has attained that age, she may choose a husband for herself, and appoint any man to arrange and effect her marriage. In the former case, however, the khâṭ'beh and the relations of a girl sought in marriage usually endeavour to obtain her consent to the proposed union. Very often, a father objects to giving a daughter in marriage to a man who is not of the same profession or trade as himself; and to marrying a younger daughter before an elder.[1] The bridegroom can scarcely ever obtain even a surreptitious glance at the features of his bride, until he finds her in his absolute possession, unless she belong to the lower classes of society; in which case, it is easy enough for him to see her face.

When a female is about to marry, she should have a "wekeel" (or deputy) to settle the compact, and conclude the contract, for her, with her proposed husband. If she be under the age of puberty, this is absolutely necessary; and in this case, her father, if living, or (if he be dead) her nearest adult male relation, or a guardian appointed by will, or by the Ḳáḍee, performs the office of wekeel: but if she be of age, she appoints her own wekeel, or may even make the contract herself; though this is seldom done.

After a youth or man has made choice of a female to demand in marriage, on the report of his female relations, or that of the khâṭ'beh, and, by proxy, made the preliminary arrangements before described with her and her relations in the ḥareem, he repairs with two or three of his friends to her wekeel. Having obtained the wekeel's consent to the union, if the intended bride be under age, he asks what is the amount of the required "mahr" (or dowry).

[1] See Genesis, xxix. 26.

The giving of a dowry is indispensable, as I have mentioned in a former chapter. It is generally calculated in "riyáls," of ninety faḍḍahs (equivalent to about five pence and two-fifths) each. The riyál is an imaginary money; not a coin. The usual amount of the dowry, if the parties be in possession of a moderately good income, is about a thousand riyáls (or twenty-two pounds ten shillings); or, sometimes, not more than half that sum. The wealthy calculate the dowry in purses, of five hundred piasters (about five pounds sterling) each; and fix its amount at ten purses, or more. It must be borne in mind that we are considering the case of a virgin-bride; the dowry of a widow or a divorced woman is much less. In settling the amount of the dowry, as in other pecuniary transactions, a little haggling frequently takes place: if a thousand riyáls be demanded through the wekeel, the party of the intended bridegroom will probably make an offer of six hundred: the former party then gradually lowering the demand, and the other increasing the offer, they at length agree to fix it at eight hundred. It is generally stipulated that two-thirds of the dowry shall be paid immediately before the marriage-contract is made; and the remaining third held in reserve, to be paid to the wife in case of divorcing her against her own consent, or in case of the husband's death.

This affair being settled, and confirmed by all persons present reciting the opening chapter of the Ḳur-án (the Fát'ḥah), an early day (perhaps the day next following) is appointed for paying the money, and performing the ceremony of the marriage-contract, which is properly called "'aḳd en-nikáḥ."[1] The making this contract is commonly called "ketb el-kitáb" (or the writing of the writ); but it is very seldom the case that any document is written to confirm the marriage, unless the bridegroom is about to travel to another place, and fears that he may have occasion to prove his marriage where witnesses of the contract cannot be procured. Sometimes the marriage-contract is concluded immediately after the arrangement respecting the dowry, but more generally a day or two after. On the day appointed for this ceremony, the bridegroom, again accompanied by two or three of his friends, goes to the house of the bride, usually about noon, taking with him that portion of the dowry which he has promised to pay on this occasion. He and his companions are

---

[1] It is a common belief in Egypt, that, if any one make a marriage-contract in the month of Moḥarram, the marriage will be unhappy, and soon dissolved: wherefore, few persons do so. The most propitious period is the month of Showwál.

received by the bride's wekeel; and two or more friends of the latter are usually present. It is necessary that there be two witnesses (and those must be Muslims) to the marriage-contract, unless in a situation where witnesses cannot be procured. All persons present recite the Fát'ḥah; and the bridegroom then pays the money. After this, the marriage-contract is performed. It is very simple. The bridegroom and the bride's wekeel sit upon the ground, face to face, with one knee upon the ground, and grasp each other's right hand, raising the thumbs, and pressing them against each other. A fiḳee[1] is generally employed to instruct them what they are to say. Having placed a handkerchief over their joined hands, he usually prefaces the words of the contract with a "khuṭbeh," consisting of a few words of exhortation and prayer, with quotations from the Ḳur-án and Traditions, on the excellence and advantages of marriage. He then desires the bride's wekeel to say, "I betroth [or marry] to thee, my daughter [or the female who has appointed me her wekeel], such a one [naming the bride], the virgin[2] [or the adult virgin], for a dowry of such an amount." (The words "for a dowry," &c., are sometimes omitted.) The bride's wekeel having said this, the bridegroom, prompted in the same manner by the fiḳee, says, "I accept from thee her betrothal [or marriage] to myself, and take her under my care, and bind myself to afford her my protection; and ye who are present bear witness of this." The wekeel addresses the bridegroom in the same manner a second and a third time; and each time, the latter replies as before. Both then generally add, "And blessing be on the Apostles, and praise be to God, the Lord of the beings of the whole world: amen:" after which, all present again repeat the Fát'ḥah. It is not always the same form of "khuṭbeh" that is recited on these occasions: any form may be used; and it may be repeated by any person: it is not even necessary; and is often altogether omitted. The contract concluded, the bridegroom sometimes (but seldom unless he be a person of the lower orders) kisses the hands of his friends and others there present; and they are presented with sherbet, and generally remain to dinner. Each of them receives an embroidered handkerchief, provided by the family of the bride; except the fiḳee, who receives a similar handkerchief, with a small gold coin tied up in it, from the bridegroom. Before the persons

1 This appellation is commonly given to a schoolmaster. See a note in page 60.

2 If the bride be not a virgin, a word importing this is substituted; namely, "seyyib," or, more properly, "theyyib."

assembled on this occasion disperse, they settle when the "leylet ed-dukhleh" is to be: this is the night when the bride is brought to the house of the bridegroom, and the latter, for the first time, visits her.

In general, the bridegroom waits for his bride about eight or ten days after the conclusion of the contract. Meanwhile, he sends to her, two or three or more times, some fruit, sweetmeats, &c.; and perhaps makes her a present of a shawl, or some other article of value. The bride's family are at the same time occupied in preparing for her a stock of household furniture (as deewáns, matting, carpets, bedding, kitchen-utensils, &c.,) and dress. The portion of the dowry which has been paid by the bridegroom, and generally a much larger sum (the additional money, which is often more than the dowry itself, being supplied by the bride's family), is expended in purchasing the articles of furniture, dress, and ornaments, for the bride. These articles, which are called "gaház," are the property of the bride; and if she be divorced, she takes them away with her. She cannot, therefore, with truth be said to be *purchased*.[1] The furniture is sent, commonly borne by a train of camels, to the bridegroom's house. Often, among the articles of the gaház is a chair for the turban or head-dress,[2] alluded to in a former page. It is of a large size, but slight make; the bottom and back being generally of cane-work; sometimes with a canopy. It is never used to sit upon. The turban, when placed upon it, is covered with a kerchief of thick silk stuff, usually ornamented with gold thread. There are sometimes sent two of these chairs; one for the turban of the husband, and the other for the head-dress of the wife.

The bridegroom should receive his bride on the eve of Friday, or that of Monday;[3] but the former is generally esteemed the more fortunate period. Let us say, for instance, that the bride is to be conducted to him on the eve of Friday. During two or three or more

---

1 Among the peasants, however, the father, or other lawful guardian of the bride, receives the dowry, and gives nothing in return but the girl, and sometimes a little corn, &c. The bridegroom, in this case, supplies everything; even the dress of the bride.

2 "Kursee el-'emámeh."

3 Burckhardt has erred in stating that *Monday* and Thursday are the days on which the ceremonies *immediately previous* to the marriage-night are performed: he should have said *Sunday* and Thursday. He has also fallen into some other errors in the account which he has given of the marriage-ceremonies of the Egyptians, in the illustrations of his "Arabic Proverbs" (pp. 112—118). To mention this I feel to be a duty to myself; but one which I perform with reluctance, and not without the fear that Burckhardt's just reputation for general accuracy may make my reader think that he is right in these cases, and that I am wrong. I write these words in Cairo, with his book before me, and after sufficient experience and inquiries.

preceding nights, the street or quarter in which the bridegroom lives is illuminated with chandeliers and lanterns, or with lanterns and small lamps, some suspended from cords drawn across from the bridegroom's and several other houses on each side to the houses opposite;

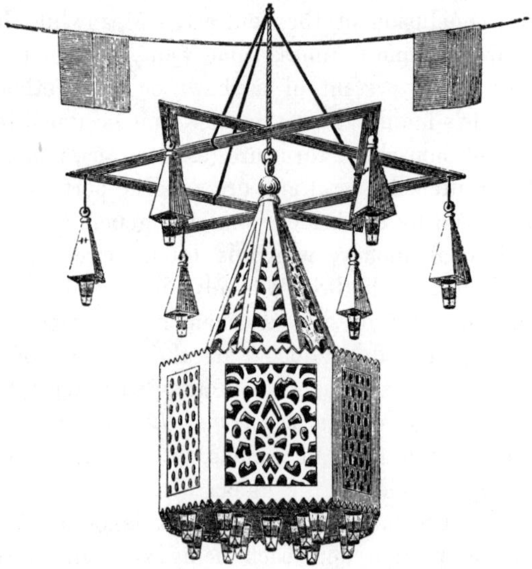

Lantern, &c., suspended on the occasion of a Wedding.

and several small silk flags, each of two colours, generally red and green, are attached to these or other cords.[1] An entertainment is also given on each of these nights, particularly on the *last* night before that on which the wedding is concluded, at the bridegroom's house. On these occasions, it is customary for the persons invited, and for all intimate friends, to send presents to his house, a day or two before the feast which they purpose or expect to attend: they generally send sugar, coffee, rice, wax-candles, or a lamb: the former articles are usually placed upon a tray of copper or wood, and covered with a silk or embroidered kerchief. The guests are entertained on these occasions by musicians and male or female singers, by dancing girls, or by the performance of a "khatmeh" or a "zikr."[2]

---

1 The lantern here represented, which is constructed of wood, and painted green, red, white, and blue, is called "tureiyà" (the Arabic name of the Pleiades), and, together with the frame above, from which six lamps are suspended, and which is termed "khátim Suleymán" (or Solomon's seal), composes what is called a "ḥeml ḳanádeel."

2 These entertainments I do not here particularly describe, as it is my intention to devote the whole of a subsequent chapter to the subject of private festivities. The "khatmeh" is the re-

In the houses of the wealthy, the kháṭ'beh or kháṭ'behs, together with the "dáyeh" (or midwife) of the family, the "belláneh" (or female attendant of the bath), and the nurse of the bride, are each presented, a day or two after the conclusion of the contract, with a piece of gold stuff, a Kashmeer shawl, or a piece of striped silk, such as yeleks and shintiyáns are made of; and, placing these over the left shoulder, and attaching the edges together on the right side, go upon asses, with two or more men before them beating kettle-drums or tabours, to the houses of all the friends of the bride, to invite the females to accompany her to and from the bath, and to partake of an entertainment given on that occasion. At every house where they call, they are treated with a repast, having sent notice the day before of their intended visit. They are called "mu-dinát," or, more properly, "mu-dhinát," vulgarly pronounced "mudnát." I have sometimes seen them walking, and without the drums before them; but making up for the want of these instruments by shrill, quavering cries of joy, called "zagháreeṭ."[1]

The customs which I am now about to describe are observed by those classes that compose the main bulk of the population of Cairo.

On the preceding Wednesday (or on the Saturday if the wedding be to conclude on the eve of Monday), at about the hour of noon, or a little later, the bride goes in state to the bath.[2] The procession to the bath is called "Zeffet el-Ḥammám." It is headed by a party of musicians with a hautboy, or two, and drums of different kinds.[3] Frequently, as I have mentioned in a former chapter, some person avails himself of this opportunity to parade his young son previously to circumcision: the child and his attendants, in this case, follow next after the musicians, in the manner already described. Sometimes, at the head of the bride's party are two men who carry the utensils and linen used in the bath, upon two round trays, each of which is covered with an embroidered or a plain silk kerchief: also, a saḳḳà, who gives water to any of the passengers, if asked; and two other

citation of the whole of the Ḳur-án; and the "zikr," the repetition of the name of God, or of the profession of his unity, &c.: I shall have occasion to speak of both more fully in another chapter, on the periodical public festivals.

[1] These cries of the women, which are heard on various occasions of rejoicing in Egypt and other Eastern countries, are produced by a sharp utterance of the voice, accompanied by a quick, tremulous motion of the tongue.

[2] I have once seen this "zeffeh," or procession, and a second which will be described hereafter, go forth much later, and return an hour after sunset.

[3] The music is generally of a very rude kind; and the airs usually played are those of popular songs; specimens of which will be found in this work.

persons, one of whom bears a "ḳumḳum," or bottle, of plain or gilt silver, or of china, containing rose-water, or orange-flower water, which he occasionally sprinkles on the passengers; and the other, a "mibkharah"[1] (or perfuming-vessel) of silver, with aloes-wood, or

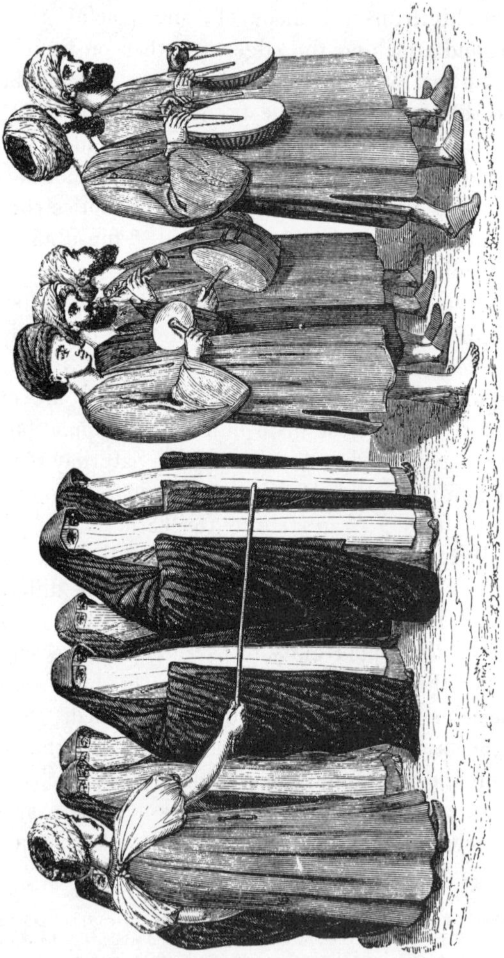

Bridal Procession. (Part I.)

some other odoriferous substance, burning in it: but it is seldom that the procession is thus attended. In general, the first persons among the bride's party are several of her married female relations and friends,

[1] Pronounced "mibkhar'ah."

walking in pairs; and next, a number of young virgins. The former are dressed in the usual manner, covered with the black silk ḥabarah: the latter have white silk ḥabarahs, or shawls. Then follows the bride, walking under a canopy of silk, of some gay colour, as pink,

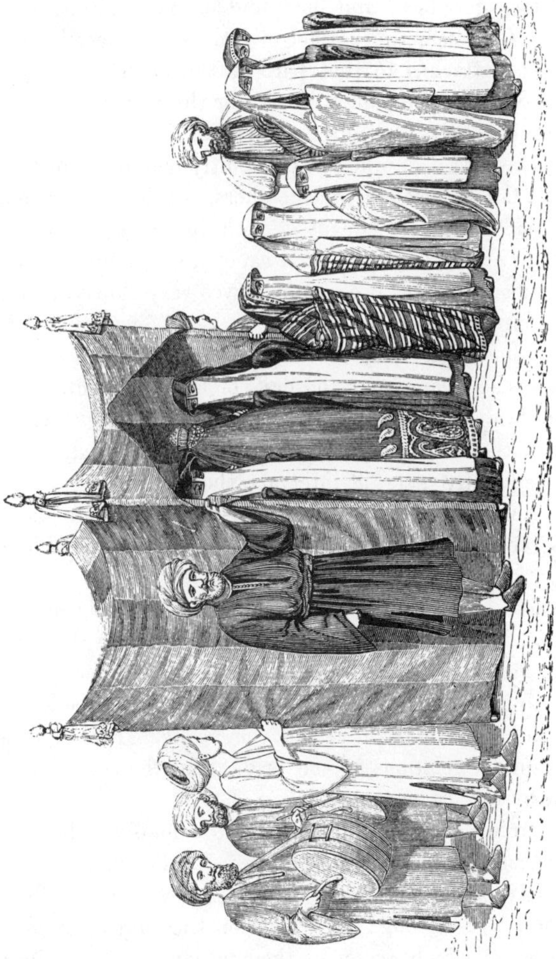

Bridal Procession. (Part II.)

rose-colour, or yellow: or of two colours composing wide stripes, often rose-colour and yellow. It is carried by four men, by means of a pole at each corner, and is open only in front; and at the top of each of the four poles is attached an embroidered handkerchief. The dress of the bride, during this procession, entirely conceals her person.

She is generally covered, from head to foot, with a red Kashmeer shawl; or with a white or yellow shawl, though rarely. Upon her head is placed a small pasteboard cap, or crown. The shawl is placed over this, and conceals from the view of the public the richer articles of her dress, her face, and her jewels, &c., except one or two "ḳuṣṣahs"[1] (and sometimes other ornaments), generally of diamonds and emeralds, attached to that part of the shawl which covers her forehead. She is accompanied by two or three of her female relations within the canopy; and often, when in hot weather, a woman, walking backwards before her, is constantly employed in fanning her, with a large fan of black ostrich-feathers, the lower part of the front of which is usually ornamented with a piece of looking-glass. Sometimes one zeffeh, with a single canopy, serves for two brides, who walk side by side. The procession moves very slowly, and generally pursues a circuitous route, for the sake of greater display. On leaving the house, it turns to the right. It is closed by a second party of musicians, similar to the first, or by two or three drummers.

In the bridal processions of the lower orders, which are often conducted in the same manner as that above described, the women of the party frequently utter, at intervals, those shrill cries of joy called zagháreeṭ, which I have before had occasion to mention; and females of the poorer classes, when merely spectators of a zeffeh, often do the same.

The whole bath is sometimes hired for the bride and her party exclusively. They pass several hours, or seldom less than two, occupied in washing, sporting, and feasting; and frequently "'ál'mehs" (or female singers) are hired to amuse them in the bath: they then return in the same order in which they came. The expense of the zeffeh falls on the relations of the bride; but the feast that follows it is supplied by the bridegroom.

Having returned from the bath to the house of her family, the bride and her companions sup together. If 'ál'mehs have contributed to the festivity in the bath, they, also, return with the bride, to renew their concert. Their songs are always on the subject of love, and of the joyous event which occasions their presence. After the company have been thus entertained, a large quantity of ḥennà having been prepared, mixed into a paste, the bride takes a lump of it in her hand, and receives contributions (called "nuḳooṭ") from her guests: each

[1] For a description of these ornaments, see the Appendix.

of them sticks a coin (usually of gold) in the ḥennà which she holds upon her hand; and when the lump is closely stuck with these coins, she scrapes it off her hand upon the edge of a basin of water. Having collected in this manner from all her guests, some more ḥennà is applied to her hands and feet, which are then bound with pieces of linen; and in this state they remain until the next morning, when they are found to be sufficiently dyed with its deep orange-red tint. Her guests make use of the remainder of the dye for their own hands. This night is called "Leylet el-Ḥennà," or "the Night of the Ḥennà."

It is on this night, and sometimes also during the latter half of the preceding day, that the bridegroom gives his chief entertainment. "Moḥabbaẓeen" (or low farce-players) often perform on this occasion before the house, or, if it be large enough, in the court. The other and more common performances by which the guests are amused have been before mentioned.

On the following day, the bride goes in procession to the house of the bridegroom. The procession before described is called "the zeffeh of the bath" to distinguish it from this, which is the more important, and which is therefore particularly called "Zeffet el-'Arooseh," or "the Zeffeh of the Bride." In some cases, to diminish the expenses of the marriage-ceremonies, the bride is conducted privately to the bath, and only honoured with a zeffeh to the bridegroom's house. This procession is exactly similar to the former. The bride and her party, after breakfasting together, generally set out a little after midday. They proceed in the same order, and at the same slow pace, as in the zeffeh of the bath; and, if the house of the bridegroom is near, they follow a circuitous route, through several principal streets, for the sake of display. The ceremony usually occupies three or more hours.

Sometimes, before bridal processions of this kind, two swordsmen, clad in nothing but their drawers, engage each other in a mock combat; or two peasants cudgel each other with nebboots, or long staves. In the procession of a bride of a wealthy family, any person who has the art of performing some extraordinary feat to amuse the spectators is almost sure of being a welcome assistant, and of receiving a handsome present.[1] When the seyyid 'Omar, the Naḳeeb el-Ashráf

---

[1] One of the most common of the feats witnessed on such an occasion is the performance of a laborious task by a water-carrier, termed a "ḳeiyim," who, for the sake of a present, and this empty title, carries a water-skin filled with sand and water, of greater weight, and for a longer period, than any of his brethren will venture to do; and this he must accomplish without ever

(or chief of the descendants of the Prophet), who was the main instrument of advancing Moḥammad 'Alee to the dignity of Báshà of Egypt, married a daughter, about forty-five years since, there walked before the procession a young man who had made an incision in his abdomen, and drawn out a large portion of his intestines, which he carried before him on a silver tray. After the procession, he restored them to their proper place, and remained in bed many days before he recovered from the effects of this foolish and disgusting act. Another man, on the same occasion, ran a sword through his arm, before the crowding spectators, and then bound, over the wound, without withdrawing the sword, several handkerchiefs, which were soaked with the blood. These facts were described to me by an eye-witness. A spectacle of a more singular and more disgusting nature used to be not uncommon on similar occasions, but is now very seldom witnessed.[1] Sometimes, also, "ḥáwees" (or conjurers and sleight-of-hand performers) exhibit a variety of tricks on these occasions. But the most common of all the performances here mentioned are the mock fights. Similar exhibitions are also sometimes witnessed on the occasion of a circumcision. Grand zeffehs are sometimes accompanied by a number of cars, each bearing a group of persons of some manufacture or trade performing the usual work of their craft; even such as builders, white-washers, &c.; including members of all, or almost all, the arts and manufactures practised in the metropolis. In one car are generally some men making coffee, which they occasionally present to spectators: in another, instrumental musicians: and in another, 'ál'mehs (or female singers). The bride, in zeffehs of this kind, is sometimes conveyed in a close European carriage; but more frequently she and her female relations and friends are mounted on high-saddled asses, and, with musicians and female singers before and behind them, close the procession.

The bride and her party, having arrived at the bridegroom's house, sit down to a repast. Her friends, shortly after, take their departure; leaving with her only her mother and sister, or other near female relations, and one or two other women; usually the belláneh. The ensuing night is called "Leylet ed-Dukhleh," or "the Night of the Entrance."

---

sitting down, except in a crouching position, to rest. In the case of a bridal procession which I lately witnessed, the ḳeiyim began to carry his burden, a skin of sand and water weighing about two hundred pounds, at sunset of the preceding day; bore it the whole night, and the ensuing day, before and during the procession, and continued to do so till sunset.

[1] A correct description of this is given in Burckhardt's "Arabic Proverbs," pp. 115, 116.

The bridegroom sits below. Before sunset, he goes to the bath, and there changes his clothes; or he merely does the latter at home; and, after having supped with a party of his friends, waits till a little before the "'eshè" (or time of the night-prayer), or until the third or fourth hour of the night, when, according to general custom, he should repair to some celebrated mosque, such as that of the Ḥasaneyn, and there say his prayers. If young, he is generally honoured with a zeffeh on this occasion: in this case, he goes to the mosque preceded by musicians with drums and a hautboy or two, and accompanied by a number of friends, and by several men bearing "mesh'als." The mesh'al is a kind of cresset, that is, a staff with a

Mesh'als.

cylindrical frame of iron at the top filled with flaming wood, or having two, three, four, or five of these receptacles for fire. The party usually proceeds to the mosque with a quick pace, and without much order. A second group of musicians, with the same instruments, or with drums only, closes the procession. The bridegroom is generally dressed in a ḳufṭán with red stripes, and a red gibbeh, with a Kashmeer shawl of the same colour for his turban; and walks between two friends similarly dressed. The prayers are commonly performed merely as a matter of ceremony; and it is frequently the case that the bridegroom does not pray at all, or prays without having previously performed the wuḍoó, like memlooks who say their prayers only because they fear their master.[1] The procession returns from the mosque with more order and display, and very slowly; perhaps because it would be considered unbecoming in the bridegroom to hasten home to take possession of his bride. It is headed, as before, by musicians, and two or more bearers of mesh'als. These are generally followed by two men, bearing, by means of a pole resting horizontally upon their shoulders, a hanging frame, to which are attached about sixty or more small lamps, in four circles, one above another; the uppermost of which circles is made to revolve, being turned round occasionally by one of the two bearers. These numerous lamps, and several mesh'als besides those before mentioned, brilliantly illumine the streets through which the procession passes, and produce a remarkably picturesque effect. The bridegroom and his friends and other attendants follow, advancing in the form of an oblong ring, all facing the interior of the ring, and each bearing in his hand one or more wax candles, and sometimes a sprig of ḥennà or some other flower, except the bridegroom and the friend on either side of him. These three form the latter part of the ring, which generally consists of twenty or more persons. At frequent intervals, the party stops for a few minutes; and during each of these pauses, a boy or man, one of the persons who compose the ring, sings a few words of an epithalamium. The sounds of the drums, and the shrill notes of the hautboy (which the bride hears half an hour or more before the procession arrives at the house), cease during these songs. The train is closed, as in the former case (when on its way to the mosque), by a second group of musicians.

In the manner above described, the bridegroom's zeffeh is most commonly conducted; but there is another mode, that is more respectable, called "zeffeh sádátee," which signifies "the gentlemen's zeffeh." In this, the bridegroom is accompanied by his friends in the manner described above, and attended and preceded by men bearing mesh'als, but not by musicians: in the place of these are about six or eight men, who, from their being employed as singers on occasions of this kind, are called "wilád el-läyálee," or "sons of the nights." Thus attended, he goes to the mosque; and while he returns slowly thence to his house, the singers above mentioned chant, or rather

---

[1] Hence this kind of prayer is called "ṣalah memáleekeeyeh," or "the prayer of memlooks."

sing, "muweshshaḥs" (lyric odes) in praise of the Prophet. Having returned to the house, these same persons chant portions of the Ḳur-án, one after another, for the amusement of the guests; then, all together, recite the opening chapter (the Fát'ḥah); after which, one of them sings a "ḳaṣeedeh" (or short poem) in praise of the Prophet: lastly, all of them again sing muweshshaḥs. After having thus performed, they receive "nuḳooṭ" (or contributions of money) from the bridegroom and his friends.

Soon after his return from the mosque, the bridegroom leaves his friends in a lower apartment, enjoying their pipes and coffee and sherbet. The bride's mother and sister, or whatever other female relations were left with her, are above; and the bride herself, and the belláneh, in a separate apartment. If the bridegroom is a youth or young man, it is considered proper that he, as well as the bride, should exhibit some degree of bashfulness: one of his friends, therefore, carries him a part of the way up to the ḥareem. Sometimes, when the parties are persons of wealth, the bride is displayed before the bridegroom in different dresses, to the number of seven: but generally he finds her with the belláneh alone; and on entering the apartment, he gives a present to this attendant, and she at once retires. The bride has a shawl thrown over her head; and the bridegroom must give her a present of money, which is called "the price of the uncovering of the face,"[1] before he attempts to remove this, which she does not allow him to do without some apparent reluctance, if not violent resistance, in order to shew her maiden modesty. On removing the covering, he says, "In the name of God, the Compassionate, the Merciful;" and then greets her with this compliment: "The night be blessed," or "—is blessed:" to which she replies, if timidity do not choke her utterance, "God bless thee." The bridegroom now, in most cases, sees the face of his bride for the first time, and generally finds her nearly what he has been led to expect. Often, but not always, a curious ceremony is then performed. The bridegroom takes off every article of the bride's clothing except her shirt; seats her upon a mattress or bed, the head of which is turned towards the direction of Mekkeh, placing her so that her back is also turned in that direction; and draws forward, and spreads upon the bed, the lower part of the front of her shirt: having done this, he stands at the distance of rather less than three feet before

[1] "Ḥaḳḳ keshf el-wishsh." "Wishsh" is a vulgar corruption of "wegh," or "wejh."

her, and performs the prayers of two rek'ahs; laying his head and hands, in prostration, upon the part of her shirt that is extended before her lap. He remains with her but a few minutes longer:[1] having satisfied his curiosity respecting her personal charms, he calls to the women (who generally collect at the door, where they wait in anxious suspense,) to raise their cries of joy, or zagháreeṭ; and the shrill sounds make known to the persons below and in the neighbourhood, and often, responded to by other women, spread still further the news, that he has acknowledged himself satisfied with his bride: he soon after descends to rejoin his friends, and remains with them an hour, or more, before he returns to his wife. It very seldom happens that the husband, if disappointed in his bride, immediately disgraces and divorces her; in general, he retains her, in this case, a week or more.

Having now described the most usual manner in which the marriages of virgin-brides are conducted in Cairo, I may add a few words on some of the ceremonies observed in other cases of matrimony, both of virgins and of widows or divorced women.

The daughters of the great, generally having baths in their own houses, seldom go to the public bath previously to marriage. A bride of a wealthy family, or of one that affects gentility, and her female relations and friends, if there is not a bath in her house, go to the public bath, which is hired for them exclusively; but many of such persons prefer to go thither, and to the bridegroom's house, without music or canopy, mounted on high-saddled asses: the bride herself generally wearing a Kashmeer shawl, in the manner of a ḥabarah. Sometimes, however, the bridal party is accompanied by a group of female singers ('ál'mehs), likewise mounted on asses, and singing as they pass along.

If the bridegroom or the bride's family have eunuchs, these ride before the bride; and sometimes a man runs at the head of the procession, crying, "Bless ye the Prophet!"[2] This man, on entering the house, throws down upon the threshold some leaves of the white beet ("salḳ"), over which the ladies ride. The object of this act is to propitiate fortune. The same man then exclaims, "Assistance from God, and a speedy victory!"[3]

---

[1] I beg to refer the reader, if he desire further details on this subject, to page 117 of Burckhardt's "Arabic Proverbs." His account might have been more complete; but he seems to have studied to be particularly concise in this case.

[2] "Ṣalloo 'a-n-nebee." "'A-n-nebee" is a vulgar contraction of "'ala-n-nebee."

[3] Ḳur-án, ch lxi. v. 13.

Marriages, among the Egyptians, are sometimes conducted without any pomp or ceremony even in the case of virgins, by mutual consent of the bridegroom and the bride's family, or the bride herself; and widows and divorced women are never honoured with a zeffeh on marrying again. The mere sentence, "I give myself up to thee,"[1] uttered by a female to a man who proposes to become her husband (even without the presence of witnesses, if none can easily be procured), renders her his legal wife, if arrived at puberty; and marriages with widows and divorced women, among the Muslims of Egypt, and other Arabs, are sometimes concluded in this simple manner. The dowry of widows and divorced women is generally one quarter or third or half the amount of that of a virgin.

In Cairo, among persons not of the lowest order, though in very humble life, the marriage-ceremonies are conducted in the same manner as among the middle orders. But when the expenses of such zeffehs as I have described cannot by any means be paid, the bride is paraded in a very simple manner, covered with a shawl (generally red), and surrounded by a group of her female relations and friends, dressed in their best, or in borrowed, clothes, and enlivened by no other sounds of joy than their zagháreeṭ, which they repeat at frequent intervals.

The general mode of zeffeh among the inhabitants of the villages is different from those above described. The bride, usually covered with a shawl, is seated on a camel; and so conveyed to the bridegroom's dwelling. Sometimes four or five women or girls sit with her, on the same camel; one on either side of her, and two or three others behind: the seat being made very wide, and usually covered with carpets or other drapery. She is followed by a group of women singing. In the evening of the wedding, and often during several previous evenings, in a village, the male and female friends of the two parties meet at the bridegroom's house, and pass several hours of the night, in the open air, amusing themselves with songs and a rude kind of dance, accompanied by the sounds of a tambourine or some kind of drum: both sexes sing; but only the women dance. I have introduced here these few words on the marriage-ceremonies of the peasantry to avoid scattering notes on subjects of the same nature. I now revert to the customs of the people of Cairo.

On the morning after the marriage, "khäwals"[2] or "gházeeyehs"

---

[1] "Wahebtu lak nefsee."

[2] A khäwal is also called "gháïsh;" plural, "gheeyásh."

(dancing men or girls) perform in the street before the bridegroom's house, or in the court.[1] On the same morning also, if the bridegroom is a young man, the person who carried him up stairs generally takes him and several friends to an entertainment in the country, where they spend the whole day. This ceremony is called "el-huroobeh," or the flight. Sometimes the bridegroom himself makes the arrangements for it; and pays part of the expenses, if they exceed the amount of the contributions of his friends; for they give nuḳooṭ on this occasion. Musicians and dancing-girls are often hired to attend the entertainment. If the bridegroom is a person of the lower orders, he is conducted back in procession, preceded by three or four musicians with drums and hautboys; his friends and other attendants carrying each a nosegay, as they sometimes do in the zeffeh of the preceding night; and if their return is after sunset, they are accompanied by men bearing mesh'als, lamps, &c.; and the friends of the bridegroom carry lighted wax candles, besides the nosegays.[2] Subsequent festivities occasioned by marriage will be described in a later chapter.

The husband, if he can conveniently so arrange, generally prefers that his mother should reside with him and his wife; that she may protect his wife's honour, and consequently his own also. It is said that the mother-in-law is for this reason called "ḥamah."[3] The women of Egypt are said to be generally prone to criminal intrigues; and I fear that, in this respect, they are not unjustly accused. Sometimes a husband keeps his wife in the house of her mother, and pays the daily expenses of both. This ought to make the mother very careful with regard to expenditure, and strict as to her daughter's conduct, lest the latter should be divorced; but it is said that, in this case, she often acts as her daughter's procuress, and teaches her innumerable tricks, by which to gain the upper hand over her husband, and to drain his purse. The influence of the wife's mother is also scarcely less feared when she only enjoys occasional oppor-

---

[1] This performance is called the bride's "ṣabáḥeeyeh."

[2] Among the peasants of Upper Egypt, the relations and acquaintances of the bridegroom and bride meet together on the day after the marriage; and while a number of the men clap their hands, as an accompaniment to a tambourine, or two, and any other instruments that can be procured, the bride dances before them for a short time. She has a head-veil reaching to her heels, and a printed cotton handkerchief completely covering her face, and wears, externally, the most remarkable of her bridal garments (mentioned by Burckhardt in the place before referred to), which, in some parts of Egypt, is hung over the door of a peasant's house after marriage. Other women, similarly veiled, and dressed in their best, or borrowed, clothes, continue the dance about two hours, or more.

[3] Thus commonly pronounced, for "ḥamáh," a word derived from the verb "ḥamà," "he protected, or guarded."

tunities of seeing her daughter: hence it is held more prudent for a man to marry a female who has neither mother nor any near relations of her own sex; and some wives are even prohibited receiving any female friends but those who are relations of the husband: they are very few, however, upon whom such severe restrictions are imposed.

For a person who has become familiar with male Muslim society in Cairo, without marrying, it is not so difficult as might be imagined by a stranger to obtain, directly and indirectly, correct and ample information respecting the condition and habits of the women. Many husbands of the middle classes, and some of the higher orders, freely talk of the affairs of the ḥareem with one who professes to agree with them in their general moral sentiments, if they have not to converse through the medium of an interpreter.

Though the women have a particular portion of the house allotted to them, the *wives*, in general, are not to be regarded as prisoners; for they are usually at liberty to go out and pay visits, as well as to receive female visiters, almost as often as they please. The slaves, indeed, being subservient to the wives, as well as to their master, or, if subject to the master only, being under an authority almost unlimited, have not that liberty. One of the chief objects of the master in appropriating a distinct suite of apartments to his women is to prevent their being seen by the male domestics and other men without being covered in the manner prescribed by their religion. The following words of the Ḳur-án shew the necessity under which a Muslimeh is placed of concealing whatever is attractive in her person or attire from all men, except certain relations and some other persons. "And speak unto the believing women, that they restrain their eyes, and preserve their modesty, and discover not their ornaments, except what [necessarily] appeareth thereof: and let them throw their veils over their bosoms, and not shew their ornaments, unless to their husbands, or their fathers, or their husbands' fathers, or their sons, or their husbands' sons, or their brothers, or their brothers' sons, or their sisters' sons, or their women, or those [captives] which their right hands shall possess, or unto such men as attend [them] and have no need [of women], or unto children:" "and let them not make a noise with their feet, that their ornaments which they hide may [thereby] be discovered."[1] The last passage alludes to the practice of knocking together the anklets which the

[1] Chapter xxiv. v. 31.

Arab women in the time of the Prophet used to wear; and which are still worn by many women in Egypt.[1]

I must here transcribe two notes of eminent commentators on the Ḳur-án, in illustration of the above extract, and inserted in Sale's translation. This I do, because they would convey an erroneous idea of modern customs with regard to the admission, or non-admission, of certain persons into the ḥareem. The first is on the above words "or their women," which it thus explains:—"That is, such as are of the Mohammadan religion: it being reckoned by some unlawful, or, at least, indecent, for a woman who is a true believer to uncover herself before one who is an infidel; because the latter will hardly refrain from describing her to the men: but others suppose all women in general are here excepted; for, in this particular, doctors differ." In Egypt, and, I believe, in every other Muslim country, it is not now considered improper for any woman, whether independent, or a servant, or a slave, a Christian, a Jewess, a Muslimeh, or a pagan, to enter a Muslim's ḥareem.—The second of the notes above alluded to is on the words "or those captives;" and is as follows:—"Slaves of either sex are included in this exception, and, as some think, domestic servants who are not slaves, as those of a different nation. It is related that Moḥammad once made a present of a man-slave to his daughter Fáṭimeh; and when he brought him to her, she had on a garment which was so scanty, that she was obliged to leave either her head or her feet uncovered: and that the Prophet, seeing her in great confusion on that account, told her, she need be under no concern, for that there was none present but her father and her slave." Among the Arabs of the Desert, this may still be the case; but in Egypt I have never heard of an instance of an adult male slave being allowed to see the ḥareem of a respectable man, whether he belonged to that ḥareem or not; and am assured that it is never permitted. Perhaps the reason why the man-slave of a woman is allowed this privilege by the Ḳur-án is, because she cannot become his lawful wife as long as he continues her slave: but this is a poor reason for granting him access to the ḥareem, in such a state of society. It is remarkable that, in the verse of the Ḳur-án above quoted, uncles are not mentioned as privileged to see their nieces unveiled: some think that they are not admissible, and for this reason, lest they should describe the persons of their nieces to

---

[1] See Isaiah, iii. 16.

their sons; for it is regarded as highly improper for a man to describe the features or person of a female (as to say, that she has large eyes, a straight nose, small mouth, &c.,) to one of his own sex by whom it is unlawful for her to be seen, though it is not considered indecorous to describe her in general terms, as, for instance, to say, "She is a sweet girl, and set off with koḥl and ḥennà."

It may be mentioned here, as a general rule, that a man is allowed to see unveiled only his own wives and female slaves, and those females whom he is prohibited, by law, from marrying, on account of their being within certain degrees of consanguinity or family connection, or having given him suck, or being nearly related to his foster-mother.[1] The high antiquity of the veil has been alluded to in the first chapter of this work. It has also been mentioned, that it is considered more necessary, in Egypt, for a woman to cover the upper and back part of her head than her face; and more requisite for her to conceal her face than most other parts of her person: for instance, a female who cannot be persuaded to unveil her face in the presence of men, will think it but little shame to display the whole of her bosom, or the greater part of her leg. There are, it is true, many women among the lower classes in this country who constantly appear in public with unveiled face; but they are almost constrained to do so by the want of a burḳo' (or face-veil), and the difficulty of adjusting the ṭarḥah (or head-veil), of which scarcely any woman is destitute, so as to supply the place of the former; particularly when both their hands are occupied in holding some burden which they are carrying upon the head. When a respectable woman is, by any chance, seen with her head or face uncovered, by a man who is not entitled to enjoy that privilege, she quickly assumes or adjusts her ṭarḥah, and often exclaims, "O my fright!"[2] or "O my sorrow!"[3] Motives of coquetry, however, frequently induce an Egyptian woman to expose her face before a man when she thinks that she may appear to do so unintentionally, or that she may be supposed not to see him. A man may also occasionally enjoy opportunities of seeing the face of an Egyptian lady when she really thinks herself unobserved; sometimes at an open lattice, and sometimes on a house-top. Many small houses in Cairo have no apartment on the ground-floor for the reception of male visiters, who therefore ascend to an upper

[1] See the chapter on Religion and Laws. Eunuchs are allowed to see the face of any woman; and so are young boys.

[2] "Yá dahwet'ee."

[3] "Yá nedám'tee," for "nedámetee."

room; but as they go upstairs, they exclaim, several times, "Destoor!" ("Permission!"), or "Yá Sátir!" ("O Protector!" that is, "O protecting God!"), or use some similar ejaculation, in order to warn any woman who may happen to be in the way, to retire, or to veil herself; which she does by drawing a part of her ṭarḥah before her face, so as to leave, at most, only one eye visible. To such an absurd pitch do the Muslims carry their feeling of the sacredness of women, that entrance into the *tombs* of some females is denied to men; as, for instance, the tombs of the Prophet's wives and other females of his family, in the burial-ground of El-Medeeneh; into which women are freely admitted: and a man and woman they never bury in the same vault, unless a wall separate the bodies. Yet there are, among the Egyptians, a few persons who are much less particular in this respect: such is one of my Muslim friends here, who generally allows me to see his mother when I call upon him. She is a widow, of about fifty years of age; but, being very fat, and not looking so old, she calls herself forty. She usually comes to the door of the apartment of the ḥareem in which I am received (there being no lower apartment in the house for male visiters), and sits there upon the floor, but will never enter the room. Occasionally, and as if by accident, she shews me the whole of her face, with plenty of koḥl round her eyes; and does not attempt to conceal her diamonds, emeralds, and other ornaments; but rather the reverse. The wife, however, I am never permitted to see; though once I was allowed to talk to her, in the presence of her husband, round the corner of a passage at the top of the stairs.

I believe that, in Egypt, the women are generally under less restraint than in any other country of the Turkish Empire; so that it is not uncommon to see females of the lower orders flirting and jesting with men in public, and men laying their hands upon them very freely. Still it might be imagined that the women of the higher and middle classes feel themselves severely oppressed, and are much discontented with the state of seclusion to which they are subjected: but this is not commonly the case; on the contrary, an Egyptian wife who is attached to her husband is apt to think, if he allow her unusual liberty, that he neglects her, and does not sufficiently love her; and to envy those wives who are kept and watched with greater strictness.

It is not very common for an Egyptian to have more than one wife, or a concubine-slave; though the law allows him *four* wives (as

I have before stated), and, according to common opinion, as many concubine-slaves as he may choose. But, though a man restrict himself to a single wife, he may change as often as he desires; and there are certainly not many persons in Cairo who have not divorced one wife, if they have been long married. The husband may, whenever he pleases, say to his wife, "Thou art divorced:"[1] if it be his wish, whether reasonable or not, she must return to her parents or friends. This liability to an unmerited divorcement is the source of more uneasiness to many wives than all the other troubles to which they are exposed; as they may thereby be reduced to a state of great destitution: but to others, who hope to better their condition, it is, of course, exactly the contrary. I have mentioned, in a former chapter,[2] that a man may divorce his wife twice, and each time receive her again without any ceremony; but that he cannot legally take her again after a third divorce until she has been married and divorced by another man. The consequences of a triple divorce conveyed in one sentence[3] are the same, unless the man and his wife agree to infringe the law, or the former deny his having pronounced the sentence; in which latter case, the woman may have much difficulty to enforce his compliance with the law, if she be inclined to do so.

In illustration of this subject, I may mention a case in which an acquaintance of mine was concerned as a witness of the sentence of divorce. He was sitting in a coffee-shop with two other men, one of whom had just been irritated by something that his wife had said or done. After a short conversation upon this affair, the angry husband sent for his wife, and, as soon as she came, said to her, "Thou art trebly divorced:" then, addressing his two companions, he added, "You, my brothers, are witnesses." Shortly after, however, he repented of this act, and wished to take back his divorced wife; but she refused to return to him, and appealed to the "Sharạ Allah" (or Law of God). The case was tried at the Maḥkemeh. The woman, who was the plaintiff, stated that the defendant was her husband; that he had pronounced against her the sentence of a triple divorce; and that he now wished her to return to him, and live with him as his wife, contrary to the law, and consequently in a state of sin. The defendant denied that he had divorced her. "Have you witnesses?" said the judge to the plaintiff. She answered, "I have here two witnesses." These were the men who were present in the coffee-shop

[1] "Entee ṭáliḳah."
[2] On the Religion and Laws.
[3] "Entee ṭáliḳah bi-t-telátch."

when the sentence of divorce was pronounced. They were desired to give their evidence; and they stated that the defendant divorced his wife, by a triple sentence, in their presence. The defendant averred that she whom he divorced in the coffee-shop was another wife of his. The plaintiff declared that he had no other wife: but the judge observed to her that it was impossible she could know that; and asked the witnesses what was the name of the woman whom the defendant divorced in their presence? They answered that they were ignorant of her name. They were then asked if they could swear that the plaintiff was the woman who was divorced before them? Their reply was, that they could not swear to a woman whom they had never seen unveiled. In these circumstances, the judge thought it right to dismiss the case; and the woman was obliged to return to her husband. She might have demanded that he should produce the woman whom he professed to have divorced in the coffee-shop; but he would easily have found a woman to play the part he required; as it would not have been necessary for her to shew a marriage-certificate; marriages being almost always performed in Egypt without any written contract, and sometimes even without witnesses.

It not unfrequently happens that, when a man who has divorced his wife the third time wishes to take her again (she herself consenting to their reunion, and there being no witnesses to the sentence of divorce), he does so without conforming to the offensive law before mentioned. It is also a common custom for a man in similar circumstances to employ a person to marry the divorced woman on the condition of his resigning her, the day after their union, to him, her former husband, whose wife she again becomes, by a second contract; though this is plainly contrary to the spirit of the law. The wife, however, can withhold her consent, unless she is not of age; in which case, her father, or other lawful guardian, may marry her to whom he pleases. A poor man (generally a very ugly person, and often one who is blind,) is usually chosen to perform this office. He is termed a "mustaḥall," or "mustaḥill," or a "moḥallil." It is often the case that the man thus employed is so pleased with the beauty of the woman to whom he is introduced on these terms, or with her riches, that he refuses to give her up; and the law cannot compel him to divorce her unless he act unjustly towards her as her husband, which of course he takes good care not to do. But a person may employ a mustaḥall without running this risk. It is the custom of many wealthy Turks, and of some of the people of Egypt, to make use of a slave, generally a black, their own property, to officiate in this character. Sometimes, a slave is purchased for this purpose; or if the person who requires him for such a service be acquainted with a slave-dealer, he asks from the latter a present of a slave; signifying that he will give him back again. The uglier the slave, the better. The Turks generally choose one not arrived at puberty; which the tenets of their sect allow. As soon as the woman has accomplished her "'eddeh" (or the period during which she is obliged to wait before she can marry again), the husband who divorced her, having previously obtained her consent to what he is about to do, introduces the slave to her, and asks her if she will be married to him. She replies that she will. She is accordingly wedded to the slave, in the presence of witnesses; and a dowry is given to her, to make the marriage perfectly legal. The slave consummates the marriage; and thus becomes the woman's legitimate husband. Immediately after, or on the following morning, her former husband presents this slave to her as her own property, and the moment that she accepts him, her marriage with him becomes dissolved; for it is unlawful for a woman to be the wife of her own slave: though she may emancipate a slave, and *then* marry him. As soon as her marriage is dissolved by her accepting the gift of the slave, she may give back this slave to her husband: but it seldom happens that the latter will allow a person who has been a mustaḥall for him to remain in his house. The wife, after this proceeding, may, as soon as she has again accomplished her 'eddeh, become reunited to her former husband, after having been separated from him, by the necessity of her fulfilling two 'eddehs, about half a year, or perhaps more.

That the facility of divorce has depraving effects upon both sexes may be easily imagined. There are many men in this country who, in the course of ten years, have married as many as twenty, thirty, or more wives; and women not far advanced in age who have been wives to a dozen or more men successively. I have heard of men who have been in the habit of marrying a new wife almost every month. A person may do this although possessed of very little property: he may choose, from among the females of the lower orders in the streets of Cairo, a handsome young widow or divorced woman who will consent to become his wife for a dowry of about ten shillings; and when he divorces her, he need not give her more than double that sum to maintain her during her ensuing 'eddeh. It is but just, however, to add, that such conduct is generally regarded as very disgraceful; and that few parents in the middle or higher classes will give a daughter in marriage to a man who has divorced many wives.

Polygamy, which is also attended with very injurious effects upon the morals of the husband and the wives, and only to be defended because it serves to prevent a greater immorality than it occasions, is more rare among the higher and middle classes than it is among the lower orders; and it is not very common among the latter. A poor man may indulge himself with two or more wives, each of whom may be able, by some art or occupation, nearly to provide her own subsistence; but most persons of the middle and higher orders are deterred from doing so by the consideration of the expense and discomfort which they would incur. A man having a wife who has the misfortune to be barren, and being too much attached to her to divorce her, is sometimes induced to take a second wife, merely in the hope of obtaining offspring; and from the same motive, he may take a third, and a fourth; but fickle passion is the most evident and common motive both to polygamy and repeated divorces. They are comparatively very few who gratify this passion by the former practice. I believe that not more than one husband among twenty has two wives.

When there are two or more wives belonging to one man, the first (that is, the one first married,) generally enjoys the highest rank; and is called "the great lady."[1] Hence it often happens that, when a man who has already one wife wishes to marry another girl or woman, the father of the latter, or the female herself who is sought in marriage, will not consent to the union unless the first wife be previously divorced. The women, of course, do not approve of a man's marrying more than one wife. Most men of wealth, or of moderate circumstances, and even many men of the lower orders, if they have two or more wives, have, for each, a separate house. The wife has, or can oblige her husband to give her, a particular description of lodging,[2] which is either a separate house, or a suite of apartments (consisting of a room in which to sleep and pass the day, a kitchen, and a latrina,) that are, or may be made, separate and shut out from any other apartments in the same house. A fellow-wife is called "ḍurrah."[3] The quarrels of ḍurrahs are often talked of: for it may be naturally inferred, that, when two wives share the affection and attentions of

---

1 "Es-sitt el-kebeereh."

2 Called "meskin shar'ee."

3 Commonly thus pronounced (or rather "durrah," with a soft *d*,) for "ḍarrah;" originally, perhaps, by way of a pun; as "durrah" is a common name for a *parrot*.

the same man, they are not always on terms of amity with each other; and the same is generally the case with a wife and a concubine-slave living in the same house, and in similar circumstances.[1] If the chief lady be barren, and an inferior (either wife or slave) bear a child to her husband or master, it commonly results that the latter woman becomes a favourite of the man, and that the chief wife or mistress is "despised in her eyes," as Abraham's wife was in the eyes of Hagar on the same account.[2] It therefore not very unfrequently happens that the first wife loses her rank and privileges; another becomes the chief lady, and, being the favourite of her husband, is treated by her rival or rivals, and by all the members and visiters of the ḥareem, with the same degree of outward respect which the first wife previously enjoyed: but sometimes the poisoned cup is employed to remove her. A preference given to a second wife is often the cause of the first's being registered as "náshizeh,"[3] either on her husband's or her own application at the Maḥkemeh. Yet many instances are known of neglected wives behaving with exemplary and unfeigned submission to the husband, in such cases, and with amiable good nature towards the favourite.[4]

Some wives have female slaves who are their own property, generally purchased for them, or presented to them, before marriage. These cannot be the husband's concubines without their mistress's permission, which is sometimes granted (as it was in the case of Hagar, Sarah's bondwoman); but very seldom. Often, the wife will not even allow her female slave or slaves to appear unveiled in the presence of her husband. Should such a slave, without the permission of her mistress, become the concubine of the husband, and bear him a child, the child is a slave, unless, prior to its birth, the mother be sold, or presented, to the father.

The white female slaves are mostly in the possession of wealthy Turks. The concubine-slaves[5] in the houses of Egyptians of the higher and middle classes are, generally, what are termed "Ḥabasheeyehs," that is, Abyssinians, of a deep brown or bronze complexion.

---

1 The law enjoins a husband who has two or more wives, to be strictly impartial to them in every respect; but compliance with its dictates in this matter is rare.

2 See Genesis, xvi. 4.

3 This has been explained in the 3rd chapter, page 100.

4 In general, the most beautiful of a man's wives or slaves is, of course, for a time, his greatest favourite; but in many (if not most) cases, the lasting favourite is not the most handsome. The love of a Muslim, therefore, is not always merely sensual; nor does the relative condition and comfort of his wife, or of each of his wives, invariably depend so much on his caprice, or her own personal charms, as on her general conduct and disposition.

5 A Muslim cannot take as a concubine a slave who is an idolatress.

In their features, as well as their complexions, they appear to be an intermediate race between the negroes and white people: but the difference between them and either of the above-mentioned races is considerable. They themselves, however, think that they differ so little from the white people, that they cannot be persuaded to act as servants, with due obedience, to their master's wives; and the black (or negro) slave-girl feels exactly in the same manner towards the Abyssinian, but is perfectly willing to serve the white ladies. I should here mention, that the slaves who are termed "Abyssinians" are, with few exceptions, not from the country properly called Abyssinia, but from the neighbouring territories of the Gallas. Most of them are handsome. The average price of one of these girls is from ten to fifteen pounds sterling, if moderately handsome; but this is only about half the sum that used to be given for one a few years ago. They are much esteemed by the voluptuaries of Egypt; but are of delicate constitution: many of them die, in this country, of consumption. The price of a white slave-girl is usually from treble to tenfold that of an Abyssinian; and the price of a black girl, about half or two-thirds, or considerably more if well instructed in the art of cookery. The black slaves are generally employed as menials.[1]

Almost all of the slaves become converts to the faith of El-Islám; but, in general, they are little instructed in the rites of their new religion; and still less in its doctrines. Most of the white female slaves who were in Egypt during my first visit to this country were Greeks; vast numbers of that unfortunate people having been made prisoners by the Turkish and Egyptian army under Ibráheem Báshà, and many of them, males and females, including even infants scarcely able to walk, sent to Egypt to be sold. Latterly, from the impoverishment of the higher classes in this country, the demand for white slaves has been small. A few, some of whom undergo a kind of preparatory education (being instructed in music or other accomplishments, at Constantinople), are brought from Circassia and Georgia. The white slaves, being often the only female companions, and sometimes the wives, of the Turkish grandees, and being generally preferred by them before the free ladies of Egypt, hold a higher rank than the latter in common opinion. They are richly dressed, presented with valuable ornaments, indulged, frequently, with almost every luxury

[1] The white female slave is called "Gáriyeh Beyḍà;" the Abyssinian, "Gáriyeh Ḥabasheeyeh;" and the black, "Gáriyeh Sódà."

that can be procured, and, when it is not their lot to wait upon others, may, in some cases, be happy: as lately has been proved, since the termination of the war in Greece, by many females of that country, captives in Egyptian ḥareems, refusing their offered liberty, which all of these cannot be supposed to have done from ignorance of the state of their parents and other relations, or the fear of exposing themselves to poverty; though not a few of them may probably have been induced to remain in bondage by a sense of the religious and moral degradation to which they had been forcibly subjected, and by their having borne children to their masters. But, if some of them are undoubtedly happy, at least for a time, their number is comparatively small: most are fated to wait upon more favoured fellow-prisoners, or upon Turkish ladies, or to receive the unwelcome caresses of a wealthy dotard, or of a man who has impaired his body and mind by excesses of every kind; and, when their master or mistress becomes tired of them, or dies, are sold again (if they have not borne children), or emancipated, and married to some person in humble life, who can afford them but few of the comforts to which they have been accustomed. The female slaves in the houses of persons of the middle classes in Egypt are generally more comfortably circumstanced than those in the ḥareems of the wealthy: if concubines, they are, in most cases, without rivals to disturb their peace; and if menials, their service is light, and they are under less restraint. Often, indeed, if mutual attachment subsist between her and her master, the situation of a concubine-slave is more fortunate than that of a wife: for the latter may be cast off by her husband in a moment of anger, by an irrevocable sentence of divorce, and reduced to a state of poverty; whereas a man very seldom dismisses a female slave without providing for her in such a manner that, if she have not been used to luxuries, she suffers but little, if at all, by the change: this he generally does by emancipating her, giving her a dowry, and marrying her to some person of honest reputation; or by presenting her to a friend. I have already mentioned, that a master cannot sell nor give away a slave who has borne him a child, if he acknowledge it to be his own; and that she is entitled to her freedom on his death. It often happens that such a slave, immediately after the birth of her child, is emancipated, and becomes her master's wife: when she has become free, she can no longer lawfully supply the place of a wife unless he marry her. Many persons consider it disgraceful even to sell a female slave who has been long in their service. Most of the Abyssinian and black slave-girls are abominably corrupted by the Gellábs, or slave-traders, of Upper Egypt and Nubia, by whom they are brought from their native countries: there are very few of the age of eight or nine years who have not suffered brutal violence; and so severely do these children, particularly the Abyssinians, and boys as well as girls, feel the treatment which they endure from the Gellábs, that many instances occur of their drowning themselves during the voyage down the Nile.[1] The female slaves of every class are somewhat dearer than the males of the same age. Those who have not had the small-pox are usually sold for less than the others. Three days' trial is generally allowed to the purchaser; during which time, the girl remains in his, or some friend's, ḥareem; and the women make their report to him. Snoring, grinding the teeth, or talking during sleep, are commonly considered sufficient reasons for returning her to the dealer.—The dresses of the female slaves are similar to those of the Egyptian women.

The female servants, who are Egyptian girls or women, are those to whom the lowest occupations are allotted. They generally veil their faces in the presence of their masters, with the head-veil; drawing a part of this before the face, so that they leave only one eye and one hand at liberty to see and perform what they have to do. When a male visiter is received by the master of a house in an apartment of the ḥareem (the females of the family having been sent into another apartment on the occasion), he is usually, or often, waited upon by a female servant, who is always veiled.

Such are the relative conditions of the various classes in the ḥareem. A short account of their usual habits and employments must be added.

The wives, as well as the female slaves, are not only often debarred from the privilege of eating with the master of the family, but also required to wait upon him when he dines or sups, or even takes his pipe and coffee, in the ḥareem. They frequently serve him as menials; fill and light his pipe, make coffee for him, and prepare his food, or, at least, certain dainty dishes; and, if I might judge from my own experience, I should say that most of them are excellent cooks; for, when a dish has been recommended to me because made by the wife of my host, I have generally found it especially good. The wives of men of the higher and middle classes make a great study of pleasing and fascinating their husbands by unremitted attentions, and by

[1] The Gellábs generally convey their slaves partly over the desert and partly down the river.

various arts. Their coquetry is exhibited, even in their ordinary gait, when they go abroad, by a peculiar twisting of the body.[1] In the presence of the husband, they are usually under more or less restraint; and hence they are better pleased when his visits, during the day, are not very frequent or long: in his absence, they often indulge in noisy merriment.

The diet of the women is similar to that of the men, but more frugal; and their manner of eating is the same. Many of them are allowed to enjoy the luxury of smoking; for this habit is not considered unbecoming in a female, however high her rank; the odour of the finer kinds of the tobacco used in Egypt being very delicate. Their pipes are generally more slender than those of the men, and more ornamented; and the mouth-piece is sometimes partly composed of coral, in the place of amber. They generally make use of perfumes, such as musk, civet, &c.; and often, also, of cosmetics, and particularly of several preparations which they eat or drink with the view of acquiring what they esteem a proper degree of plumpness:[2] one of these preparations is extremely disgusting; being chiefly composed of mashed beetles. Many of them also have a habit of chewing frankincense,[3] and labdanum,[4] which impart a perfume to the breath. The habit of frequent ablutions renders them cleanly in person. They spend but little time in the operations of the toilet; and, after having dressed themselves in the morning, seldom change their clothes during the day. Their hair is generally braided in the bath; and not undone afterwards for several days.

The care of their children is the primary occupation of the ladies of Egypt: they are also charged with the superintendence of domestic affairs; but, in most families, the husband alone attends to the household expenses. Their leisure hours are mostly spent in working with the needle; particularly in embroidering handkerchiefs, head-veils, &c., upon a frame called "menseg," with coloured silks and gold. Many women, even in the houses of the wealthy, replenish their private purses by ornamenting handkerchiefs and other things in this manner, and employing a "delláleh" (or female broker) to take them to the market, or to other ḥareems, for sale. The visit of one ḥareem

---

1 The motion here described they term "ghung."

2 The Egyptians (unlike the Maghrabees, and some other people of Africa and of the East,) do not generally admire very fat women. In his love-songs, the Egyptian commonly describes the object of his affections as of slender figure and small waist.

3 "Libán."

4 "Ládin."

The Menseg.—*This is of walnut-wood, inlaid with mother-of-pearl and tortoise-shell. The more common sort is of beech.*

to another often occupies nearly a whole day. Eating, smoking, drinking coffee and sherbet, gossiping, and displaying their finery, are sufficient amusements to the company. On such occasions, the master of the house is never allowed to enter the ḥareem, unless on some particular and unavoidable business; and in this case, he must give notice of his approach, and let the visiters have sufficient time to veil themselves, or to retire to an adjoining room. Being thus under no fear of his sudden intrusion, and being naturally of a lively and an unreserved disposition, they indulge in easy gaiety, and not unfrequently in youthful frolic. When their usual subjects of conversation are exhausted, sometimes one of the party entertains the rest with the recital of some wonderful or facetious tale. The Egyptian ladies are very seldom instructed either in music or dancing; but they take great delight in the performances of professional musicians and public dancers; and often amuse themselves and their guests, in the absence of better performers and better instruments, by beating the "daráb-bukkeh" (which is a kind of drum) and the "ṭár" (or tambourine[1]); though seldom in houses so situate that many passengers might hear the sounds of festivity. On the occasion of any great rejoicing among

[1] Descriptions and engravings of these instruments will be given in another chapter.

the women (such as takes place on account of the birth of a son, or the celebration of a circumcision, or a wedding, &c.), "'ál'mehs" (professional female singers) are often introduced; but not for the mere amusement of the women, on common occasions, in any respectable family; for this would be considered indecorous. The "ghấzeeyehs" (or public dancing-girls), who exhibit in the streets with unveiled faces, are very seldom admitted into a ḥareem; but on such occasions as those above mentioned, they often perform in front of the house, or in the court; though, by many persons, even this is not deemed strictly proper. The "álátees" (or male musicians) are never hired exclusively for the amusement of the women; but chiefly for that of the men: they always perform in the assembly of the latter: their concert, however, is distinctly heard by the inmates of the ḥareem.[1]

When the women of the higher or middle classes go out to pay a visit, or for any other purpose, they generally ride upon asses. They sit astride, upon a very high and broad saddle, which is covered with a small carpet; and each is attended by a man on one or on each side. Generally, all the women of a ḥareem ride out together; one behind another. Mounted as above described, they present a very singular appearance. Being raised so high above the back of the "ḥomár[2] 'álee" (or the "high ass"—for so the animal which they ride, furnished with the high saddle, is commonly called[3]), they seem very insecurely seated; but I believe this is not really the case: the ass is well girthed, and sure-footed; and proceeds with a slow, ambling pace, and very easy motion. The ladies of the highest rank, as well as those of the middle classes, ride asses thus equipped: they are very seldom seen upon mules or horses. The asses are generally hired. When a lady cannot procure a ḥomár 'álee, she rides one of the asses equipped for the use of the men; but has a "seggádeh" (or prayer-carpet) placed over its saddle; and the inferior members of the ḥareem, and females of the middle orders, often do the same. Ladies never walk abroad, unless they have to go but a very short distance. They have a slow and shuffling gait, owing to the difficulty of retaining the slippers upon their feet; and, in walking, they generally hold the front edges of the ḥabarah in the manner represented in the engraving in page 46. Whether walking or riding,

[1] The performances of the álátees, 'ál'mehs, and ghấzeeyehs, will be described in a later chapter.

[2] Thus commonly pronounced, for "ḥemár."

[3] It is also called "ḥomár mughaṭṭee" (covered ass).

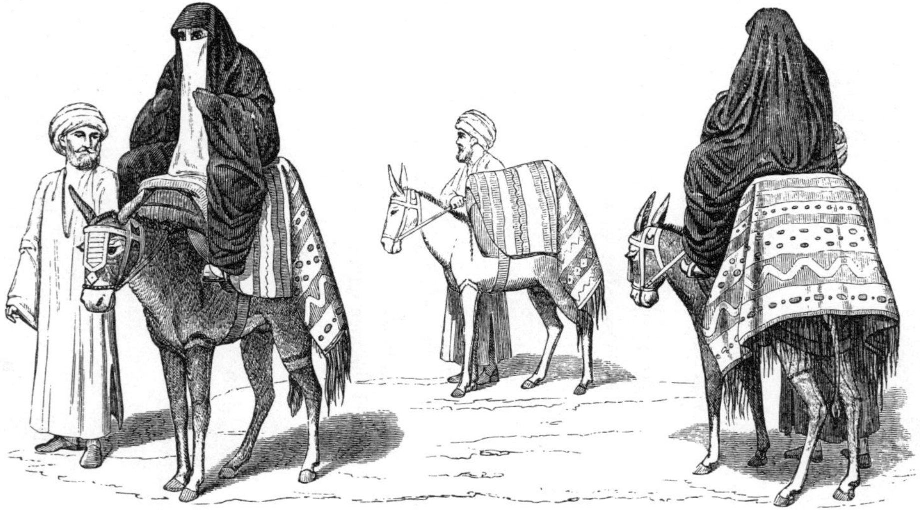

Ladies Riding.

they are regarded with much respect in public: no well-bred man stares at them; but rather directs his eyes another way. They are never seen abroad at night, if not compelled to go out or return at that time by some pressing and extraordinary necessity: it is their usual rule to return from paying a visit before sunset. The ladies of the higher orders never go to a shop, but send for whatever they want; and there are numerous dellálehs who have access to the ḥareems, and bring all kinds of ornaments, articles of female apparel, &c., for sale. Nor do these ladies, in general, visit the public bath, unless invited to accompany thither some of their friends; for most of them have baths in their own houses.[1]

[1] Since the third edition of this work issued from the press, my sister (Mrs. Poole) has resided, with her two sons and my wife and myself, more than seven years in Cairo, and has published, in a series of letters (entitled "The Englishwoman in Egypt"), an account of female society in that city, chiefly from observations made in the ḥareems of Turks, which has been too well received to need my recommendation.

CHAPTER VII.

DOMESTIC LIFE—*continued.*

The domestic life of the *lower orders* will be the subject of the present chapter. In most respects it is so simple, that, in comparison with the life of the middle and higher classes, of which we have just been taking a view, it offers but little to our notice.

The lower orders in Egypt, with the exception of a very small proportion, chiefly residing in the large towns, consist of Fellá‌ḥeen (or Agriculturists). Most of those in the great towns, and a few in the smaller towns and some of the villages, are petty tradesmen or artificers, or obtain their livelihood as servants, or by various labours. In all cases, their earnings are very small; barely sufficient, in general, and sometimes insufficient, to supply them and their families with the cheapest necessaries of life.

Their food chiefly consists of bread (made of millet or of maize), milk, new cheese, eggs, small salted fish,[1] cucumbers and melons and gourds of a great variety of kinds, onions and leeks,[2] beans, chick-peas, lupins, the fruit of the black egg-plant, lentils, &c., dates (both fresh and dried), and pickles. Most of the vegetables they eat in a crude state. When the maize (or Indian corn) is nearly ripe, many ears of it are plucked, and toasted or baked, and eaten thus by the peasants. Rice is too dear to be an article of common food for the fellá‌ḥeen; and flesh-meat they very seldom taste. There is one luxury, however, which most of them enjoy; and that is, smoking the cheap tobacco of their country, merely dried, and broken up. It is of a pale, greenish colour, when dried, and of a mild flavour. Though all the articles of food mentioned above are extremely cheap, there are many poor persons who often have nothing with which to season their coarse bread but the mixture called "duḳḳah," described in a former chapter.[3] It is surprising to observe how simple and poor is the diet

[1] Called "fesee‌kh." [2] See Numbers, xi. 5. [3] Page 134.

of the Egyptian peasantry, and yet how robust and healthy most of them are, and how severe is the labour which they can undergo!

The women of the lower orders seldom pass a life of inactivity. Some of them are even condemned to greater drudgery than the men. Their chief occupations are the preparing of the husband's food, fetching water (which they carry in a large vessel on the head), spinning cotton, linen, or woollen yarn, and making the fuel called "gelleh," which is composed of the dung of cattle, kneaded with chopped straw, and formed into round flat cakes: these they stick upon the walls or roofs of their houses, or upon the ground, to dry in the sun; and then use for heating their ovens, and for other purposes. They are in a state of much greater subjection to their husbands than is the case among the superior classes. Not always is a poor woman allowed to eat with her husband. When she goes out with him, she generally walks behind him; and if there be anything for either of them to carry, it is usually borne by the wife; unless it be merely a pipe or a stick. Some women, in the towns, keep shops, and sell bread, vegetables, &c.; and thus contribute as much as their husbands, or even more than the latter, to the support of their families. When a poor Egyptian is desirous of marrying, the chief object of his consideration is the dowry, which is usually from about twenty "riyáls" (or nine shillings) to four times that amount if consisting only of money, and rather less if (as is the case throughout a great part of Egypt) it comprise certain articles of clothing. If he can afford to give the dowry, he seldom hesitates to marry; for a little additional exertion will enable him to support a wife and two or three children. At the age of five or six years, the children become of use to tend the flocks and herds; and at a more advanced age, until they marry, they assist their fathers in the operations of agriculture. The poor in Egypt have often to depend entirely upon their sons for support in their old age; but many parents are deprived of these aids, and consequently reduced to beggary, or almost to starvation. A short time ago, Moḥammad 'Alee, during his voyage from Alexandria to this city (Cairo), happening to land at a village on the bank of the Nile, a poor man of the place ran up to him, and grasped his sleeve so tightly, that the surrounding attendants could not make him quit his hold: he complained, that, although he had been once in very comfortable circumstances, he had been reduced to utter destitution by having his sons taken from him in his old age as recruits for the army. The Básha (who generally paid attention to personal applications) relieved him; but it was by ordering that the richest man in the village should give him a cow.

A young family, however, is sometimes an insupportable burden to poor parents. Hence, it is not a very rare occurrence, in Egypt, for children to be publicly carried about for sale, by their mothers or by women employed by the fathers: but this very seldom happens except in cases of great distress. When a mother dies, leaving one or more children unweaned, and the father and other surviving relations are so poor as not to be able to procure a nurse, this singular mode of disposing of the child or children is often resorted to; or sometimes an infant is laid at the door of a mosque, generally when the congregation is assembled to perform the noon-prayers of Friday; and in this case it usually happens that some member of the congregation, on coming out of the mosque, and seeing the poor foundling, is moved with pity, and takes it home to rear in his family, not as a slave, but as an adopted child; or, if not, it is taken under the care of some person until an adoptive father or mother be found for it. A short time ago, a woman offered for sale, to the mistress of a family with whom a friend of mine is acquainted in this city, a child a few days old, which she professed to have found at the door of a mosque. The lady said that she would take the child, to rear it for the sake of God, and in the hope that her own child, an only one, might be spared to her as a reward for her charity; and handed, to the woman who brought the infant, ten piasters (then equivalent to a little more than two shillings): but the offered remuneration was rejected. This shews that infants are sometimes made mere objects of traffic; and some persons who purchase them may make them their slaves, and sell them again. I have been informed by a slave-dealer (and his assertion has been confirmed to me by other persons) that young Egyptian girls are sometimes sold as slaves from other countries, either by a parent or by some other relation. The slave-dealer here alluded to said that several such girls had been committed to him for sale, and by their own consent: they were taught to expect rich dresses, and great luxuries; and were instructed to say that they had been brought from their own country when only three or four years of age, and that they consequently were ignorant of their native language, and could speak only Arabic.

It often happens, too, that a fellâḥ, in a state of great poverty, is induced, by the offer of a sum of money, to place his son in a situation far worse than that of ordinary slavery. When a certain number of recruits are required from a village, the Sheykh of the village often adopts the plan that gives him the least trouble to obtain them, which is, to take the sons of those persons who are possessed of most property. In such circumstances, a father, rather than part with his son, generally offers, to one of his poorer fellow-villagers, a sum equivalent to one or two pounds sterling, to procure a son of the latter as a substitute for his own; and usually succeeds; though the love of offspring prevails among the Egyptians as much as filial piety, and most parents have a great horror of parting with their children, particularly if taken for recruits, as is proved by the means to which they have recourse for the prevention of such an occurrence. In the time of my second visit to Egypt, there was seldom to be found, in any of the villages, an able-bodied youth or young man who had not had one or more of his teeth broken out (that he might not be able to bite a cartridge), or a finger cut off, or an eye pulled out or blinded, to prevent his being taken for a recruit. Old women and others made a regular trade of going about from village to village, to perform these operations upon the boys; and the parents themselves were sometimes the operators. But, from what has been said before, it appears that it was not always affection alone that prompted the parents to have recourse to such expedients to prevent their being deprived of their children.

The Felláḥeen of Egypt cannot be justly represented in a very favourable light with regard to their domestic and social condition and manners. In the worst points of view, they resemble their Bedawee ancestors, without possessing many of the virtues of the inhabitants of the desert, unless in an inferior degree; and the customs which they have inherited from their forefathers often have a very baneful effect upon their domestic state. It has before been mentioned that they are descended from various Arab tribes who have settled in Egypt at different periods, intermixed with Copts; and that the distinction of tribes is still preserved by the inhabitants of the villages throughout this country. In the course of years, the descendants of each tribe of settlers have become divided into numerous branches, and these minor tribes have distinct appellations, which have also often been given to the village or villages, or district, which they inhabit. Those who have been longest established in Egypt have retained less of

Bedawee manners, and have more infringed the purity of their race by intermarriages with Copt proselytes to the Muslim faith, or with the descendants of such persons: hence, they are often despised by the tribes more lately settled in this country, who frequently, in contempt, term the former "Felláheen," while they arrogate to themselves the appellation of "Arabs" or "Bedawees." The latter, whenever they please, take the daughters of the former in marriage, but will not give their own daughters in return; and if one of them be killed by a person of the inferior tribe, they kill two, three, or even four, in blood-revenge. The prevalence of the barbarous Bedawee law of blood-revenge among the inhabitants of the villages of Egypt has been mentioned in a former chapter: the homicide, or any person descended from him, or from his great-grandfather's father, is killed by any of such relations of the person whom he has slain; and when the homicide happens to be of one tribe, and the person killed of another, often a petty war breaks forth between these two tribes, and is sometimes continued, or occasionally renewed, during a period of several years. The same is also frequently the result of a trifling injury committed by a member of one tribe upon a person of another. In many instances, the blood-revenge is taken a century or more after the commission of the act which has occasioned it; when the feud, for that time, has lain dormant, and perhaps is remembered by scarcely more than one individual. Two tribes in Lower Egypt, which are called "Saạd" and "Ḥarám," are most notorious for these petty wars and feuds;[1] and hence their names are commonly applied to any two persons or parties at enmity with each other. It is astonishing that, in the present day, such acts (which, if committed in a town or city in Egypt, would be punished by the death of, perhaps, more than one of the persons concerned,) should be allowed. Some other particulars respecting blood-revenge, and its consequences, have been stated in the chapter above alluded to. The avenging of blood is allowed by the Ḳur-án; but moderation and justice are enjoined in its execution; and the petty wars which it so often occasions in the present age are in opposition to a precept of the Prophet, who said, "If two Muslims contend with their swords, the slayer and the slain will be in the fire of Hell]."

The Felláheen of Egypt resemble the Bedawees in other respects.

---

[1] Like the "Ḳeys" and "Yemen" of Syria.

When a Felláḥah is found to have been unfaithful to her husband, in general he or her brother throws her into the Nile, with a stone tied to her neck; or cuts her in pieces, and then throws her remains into the river. In most instances, also, a father or brother punishes in the same manner an unmarried daughter or sister who has been guilty of incontinence. These relations are considered as more disgraced than the husband by the crime of the woman; and are often despised if they do not thus punish her.

CHAPTER VIII.

COMMON USAGES OF SOCIETY.

THE respect in which trade is held by the Muslim greatly tends to enlarge the circle of his acquaintance with persons of different ranks; and freedom of intercourse with his fellow-men is further and very greatly promoted by the law of the separation of the sexes, as it enables him to associate with others, regardless of difference of wealth or station, without the risk of occasioning unequal matrimonial connections. The women, like the men, enjoy extensive intercourse with persons of their own sex.

The Muslims are extremely formal and regular in their social manners; though generally very easy in their demeanour, and free in their conversation. Several of their most common usages are founded upon precepts of their religion, and distinguish them in society from all other people. Among these is their custom of greeting each other with the salutation of "Peace be on you:"[1] to which the proper and general reply is, "On you be peace, and the mercy of God, and his blessings."[2] This salutation is never to be addressed by a Muslim to a person whom he knows to be of another religion;[3] nor *vice versâ.*[4] The giving it, by one Muslim to another, is a duty; but one that may be omitted without sin: the returning it is absolutely obligatory: the former is a "sunneh" ordinance; and the latter, "farḍ." Should a Muslim, however, thus salute, by mistake, a person not of the same faith, the latter should not return it; and the former, on discovering his mistake, generally revokes his salutation: so too he sometimes

[1] "Es-selámu 'aleykum," or "Selámun 'aleykum," or, vulgarly, "Es-selám 'aleykum."

[2] "Aleykumu-s-selámu wa-raḥmatu-lláhi wa-barakátuh," or merely "'Aleykum es-selám" (On you be peace); but the longer salutation is more commonly used, in accordance with an injunction in the Ḳur-án, ch. iv. v. 88.

[3] Very few Muslims in Egypt do so. A European traveller, not disguised by Turkish dress, often fancies that he is greeted with this salutation, when it is really intended for his Muslim attendant.

[4] A Muslim, however, when he receives this salutation from a person of another religion, sometimes replies, "And on you" (Wa-'aleykum).

does if a Muslim refuse to return his salutation; usually saying, "Peace be on *us*, and on [all] the righteous worshippers of God."

The chief rules respecting salutation, as dictated by the Prophet, and generally observed by modern Muslims, are as follow:—The person riding should first salute him who is on foot; and he who passes by, the person or persons who are sitting down or standing still; and a small party, or one of such a party, should give the salutation to a large party; and the young, to the aged.[1] As it is sufficient for one of a party to *give*, so is it also for one only to *return*, the salutation. It is required, too, that a Muslim, when he enters a house, should salute the people of that house; and that he should do the same when he leaves it. He should always salute first, and then talk.—But, to the above rules, there are some exceptions. For instance, in a crowded city, it is not necessary (indeed it is hardly possible) to salute many of those whom one may pass; nor on a road where one meets numerous passengers. Yet it is usual for a wealthy or well-dressed person, or a venerable sheykh, or any person of distinction, to salute another who appears to be a man of rank, wealth, or learning, even in a crowded street. Among polite people, it is customary for him who gives or returns the salutation to place his right hand upon his breast at the same time; or to touch his lips, and then his forehead, or turban, with the same hand. This action is called "teymeeneh." The latter mode of teymeeneh, which is the more respectful, is often performed to a person of superior rank, not only at first, with the selám (or salutation of "Peace be on you"), but also frequently during a conversation, and in the latter case without the selám.

A person of the lower orders, on approaching a superior, particularly if the latter be a Turk, does not always give the selám, but only performs this teymeeneh; and he shews his respect to a man of high rank by bending down his hand to the ground, and then putting it to his lips and forehead, without pronouncing the selám. It is a common custom, also, for a man to kiss the hand of a superior (generally on the back only, but sometimes on the back and front), and then to put it to his forehead, in order to pay him particular respect: but in most cases the latter does not allow this; and only touches the hand that is extended towards his: the other person, then, merely puts his own hand to his lips and forehead. To testify

[1] Herodotus speaks of the respect paid in Egypt to the aged, and of the polite salutations of the Egyptians to each other. (Lib. ii. cap. 80.)

abject submission, in craving pardon for an offence, or interceding for another person, or begging any favour of a superior, not unfrequently the feet are kissed instead of the hand. The son kisses the hand of the father; the wife, that of her husband; and the slave, and often the free servant, that of the master. The slaves and servants of a grandee kiss their lord's sleeve, or the skirt of his clothing.

When particular friends salute each other, they join their right hands, and then each kisses his own hand, or puts it to his lips and forehead, or raises it to his forehead only; or merely places it on his breast, without kissing it: if after a long absence, and on some other occasions, they embrace each other; each falling upon the other's neck, and kissing him on the right side of the face or neck, and then on the left. Another mode of salutation is very commonly practised among the lower orders, when two friends or acquaintances meet after a journey: joining their right hands, each of them compliments the other on his safety, and expresses his wishes for his welfare, by repeating, alternately, many times, the words "selámát" and "ṭeiyibeen."[1] In commencing this ceremony, which is often continued for nearly a minute before they proceed to make any particular inquiries, they join their hands in the same manner as is usually practised by us; and at each alternation of the two expressions above mentioned, they change the position of the hands: in repeating the second word, each of the two persons turns his fingers over the thumb of the other; and in repeating the first word again, the former position is resumed.

In polite society, various other formal salutations and compliments follow the selám. To most of these there are particular replies; or two or more different forms of reply may be used in some cases; but to return any that custom has not prescribed would be considered as a proof of ignorance or vulgarity. When a person asks his friend, "How is your health?"[2] the latter replies, "Praise be to God:"[3] and it is only by the tone of voice in which he makes this answer, that the inquirer can infer whether he be well or ill. When one greets the other with "Ṭeiyibeen," the usual reply is, "God bless thee,"[4] or "God save thee."[5] A friend or an acquaintance, on meeting another whom he has not seen for several days, or for a longer period, generally says, after the selám, "Thou hast made us desolate [by thy

---

[1] Meaning, "I congratulate you on your safety," and "I hope you are well."

[2] "Eysh ḥál'kum."

[3] "El-ḥamdu li-lláh."

[4] "Allah yebárik (for "yubárik") feek."

[5] "Allah yesellimak" (for "yusellimak").

absence from us];"[1] and is usually answered, "May God not make [us] desolate by thy absence."[2]—The ordinary set compliments in use in Egyptian society are so numerous, that a dozen pages of this work would not suffice for the mention of those which may be heard almost every day.

When a person goes to the house of another, to pay a visit, or for any other purpose, he never enters unawares; for this is expressly forbidden by the Ḳur-án:[3] and particularly if he have to ascend to an upper apartment; in which case he should call out for permission, or announce his approach, as he goes upstairs, in the manner which I have had occasion to describe in a former chapter.[4] Should he find no person below, he generally claps his hands, at the door, or in the court; and waits for a servant to come down to him; or for permission to be given him to seat himself in a lower apartment, or to ascend to an upper room. On entering the room in which the master of the house is seated, he gives the selám. The master returns the salutation; and welcomes the visiter with courteousness and affability. To his superiors,[5] and generally to his equals, he rises. Persons more or less above him in rank he proceeds to meet in the court, or between the court and the room, or at the entrance of the room, or in the middle of the room, or a step from the place where he was sitting: but often, to equals, he merely makes a slight motion, as if about to rise; and to most inferiors, he remains undisturbed. To his superiors, and often to his equals, he yields the most honourable place, which is a corner of the deewán: it is that corner which is to the right of a person facing the upper end of the room. This end of the room is called the "ṣadr;" and the whole of the seat which extends along it is more honourable than those which extend along the sides; each of which is called "gemb." Visiters inferior in rank to the master of the house never seat themselves at the upper end, unless invited to do so by him; and when so invited, they often decline the offered honour. His equals sit at their ease, cross-legged, or with one knee raised; and recline against the cushions: his inferiors (first, at least,) often sit upon their heels, or take their place upon the edge of the deewán; or, if very much beneath him in grade, seat themselves upon the mat or carpet. In strict etiquette, the visiter should not, at first, suffer his hands to appear, when entering the room, or when seated; but should

---

1 "Owḥashten'è."
2 "Allah lá yooḥesh minnak."
3 Ch. xxiv. v. 27.
4 Chapter VI. p. 178.
5 That is, to those who are above him either in office, wealth, or religious or literary reputation.

let the sleeves fall over them; and when he has taken his place on the deewán, he should not stretch out his legs, nor even allow his feet to be seen: but these rules are not often attended to, except in the houses of the great. Various formal compliments and salutations are given and returned after the selám; and some of them, particularly the expressions of "ṭeiyibeen" and "eysh ḥál'kum," are repeated several times during the same interview.

Sometimes the visiter's own servant attends him with his pipe: the former takes his tobacco-purse out of his bosom, and gives it to the servant, who folds it up and returns it after having filled the pipe, or after the termination of the visit: otherwise, a servant of the host brings a pipe for the visiter, and one for his master; and next, a cup of coffee is presented to each;[1] for "tobacco without coffee," say the Arabs, "is like meat without salt." On receiving the pipe and the coffee, the visiter salutes the master of the house with the "teymeeneh," which the latter returns; and the same is done on returning the cup to the servant. The master of the house also salutes his guest in the same manner, if the latter be not much beneath him in rank, on receiving and returning his own cup of coffee. Servants often remain in the room during the whole period of a visit, stationed at the lower end, in a respectful attitude, with their hands joined (the left within the right), and held before the girdle. The usual mode of summoning a servant or other attendant who is not present is by clapping the hands, striking the palm of the left hand with the fingers of the right: the windows being of open lattice-work, the sound is heard throughout the house.—The subjects of conversation are generally the news of the day, the state of trade, the prices of provisions, and sometimes religion and science. Facetious stories are often related; and, very frequently, persons in the best society tell tales, and quote proverbs, of the most indecent nature. In good society, people seldom talk of each other's ḥareems; but intimate friends, and many persons who do not strictly observe the rules of good breeding, very often do so, and in a manner not always delicate. Genteel people inquire respecting each other's "houses," to ascertain whether their wives and families are well.—Visits not unfrequently occupy several hours; and sometimes (especially those of ḥareems), nearly a whole day. The pipes are replenished, or replaced by others, as often as is necessary: for, however long a visiter may stay, he generally continues smoking during

[1] The visiter, if a superior, or not much inferior in rank to the master of the house, receives his pipe and coffee before the latter.

the whole time; and sometimes coffee is brought again, or sherbet. The manner in which the coffee and sherbet are served has been before described. A person receives the same compliment after drinking a glass of sherbet as after taking a draught of water;[1] and replies to it in the same manner.

In the houses of the rich, it used to be a common custom to sprinkle the guest, before he rose to take his leave, with rose-water or orange-flower water; and to perfume him with the smoke of some odoriferous substance; but of late years, this practice has become unfrequent. The scent-bottle, which is called "ḳumḳum," is of plain or gilt silver, or fine brass, or china, or glass; and has a cover pierced with a small hole. The perfuming-vessel, or "mibkharah,"[2] is generally of one or the other of the metals above mentioned: the receptacle for the burning charcoal is lined, or half filled, with gypsum-plaster; and its cover is pierced with apertures for the emission of the smoke. The mibkharah is used last: it is presented by a servant to

Ḳumḳum and Mibkharah.—*Each is about eight inches high.*

the visiter or master, who wafts the smoke towards his face, beard, &c., with his right hand. Sometimes it is opened, to emit the smoke more freely. The substance most commonly used in the mibkharah is aloes-wood,[3] or benzoin,[4] or cascarilla-bark.[5] The wood is moistened before it is placed upon the burning coals. Ambergris[6] is also used for the

1 Mentioned in Chapter V., p. 149.
2 Pronounced "mibkhar'ah."
3 "'Ood."
4 "Gáwee."
5 "Ḳishr 'ambar."
6 "'Ambar."

same purpose; but very rarely, and only in the houses of persons of great wealth, as it is extremely costly. As soon as the visiter has been perfumed, he takes his leave; but he should not depart without previously asking permission to do so, and then giving the selám, which is returned to him, and paying other set compliments, to which there are appropriate replies. If he is a person of much higher rank than the master of the house, the latter not only rises, but also accompanies him to the top of the stairs, or to the door of the room, and then commends him to the care of God.

It is usual for a person, after paying a visit of ceremony, and on some other occasions, previously to his leaving the house, to give a small present (two or three piasters, or more, according to circumstances,) to one, or to several, of the servants: and if his horse or mule or ass is waiting for him at the door, or in the court, one of the servants goes with him to adjust his dress when he mounts: this officious person particularly expects a present. When money is thus given to a man's servants, it is considered incumbent upon their master to do exactly the same when he returns the visit.

Friends very often send presents to each other, merely for the sake of complying with common custom. When a person celebrates any private festivity, he generally receives presents from most of his friends; and it is a universal rule that he should repay the donor by a similar gift, or one of the same value, on a similar occasion. It is common for the receiver of a present, on such an event, even to express to the giver his hope that he may have to repay it on the occasion of a like festivity. An acknowledgment accompanied by such an allusion to the acquitment of the obligation imposed by the gift, which would be offensive to a generous European, is, in this country, esteemed polite. The present is generally wrapped in an embroidered handkerchief, which is returned, with a trifling pecuniary gratification, to the bearer. Fruit, laid upon leaves, and sweetmeats and other dainties, placed in a dish or on a tray, and covered with a rich handkerchief or napkin, are common presents. Very frequently, a present is given by a person to a superior with a view of obtaining something more valuable in return. This is often done by a servant to his master, and the gift is seldom refused, but often paid for immediately in money, more than equivalent. It is generally with the expectation above mentioned that an Arab gives a present to a European. The custom of giving money to the servants of a friend, after paying him a visit, is not so common now as it was a few years since; but it is still observed by most persons on the occasion of a visit of ceremony; and particularly on the two "'eeds," or religious festivals, and by the guests at private festivities. Other customs of a similar nature, which are observed at these festivities, will be described in a subsequent chapter.[1] To decline the acceptance of a present generally gives offence; and is considered as reflecting disgrace upon the person who has offered it.

There are many formal usages which are observed in Egypt, not merely on the occasions of ceremonious visits, or in the company of strangers, or at the casual meetings of friends, but also in the ordinary intercourse of familiar acquaintance. When a man happens to sneeze, he says, "Praise be to God."[2] Each person present (servants generally excepted) then says to him, "God have mercy upon you:"[3] to which the former generally replies, "God guide us and guide you:"[4] or he returns the compliment in words of a similar purport. Should he yawn, he puts the back of his left hand to his mouth, and then says, "I seek refuge with God from Satan the accursed:"[5] but he is not complimented on this act, as it is one which should rather be avoided; for it is believed that the devil is in the habit of leaping into a gaping mouth. For a breach of good manners, it is more common to ask the pardon of God than that of the present company, by saying, "I beg pardon of God, the Great."[6] When a man has just been shaved, or been to the bath, when he has just performed the ablution preparatory to prayer, when he has been saying his prayers, or doing any other meritorious act, when he has just risen from sleep, when he has purchased or put on any new article of dress, and on many other occasions, there are particular compliments to be paid to him, and particular replies for him to make.

It is a rule with the Muslims to honour the right hand and foot above the left: to use the right hand for all honourable purposes; and the left for actions which, though necessary, are unclean: to put on and take off the right shoe before the left; and to put the right foot first over the threshold of a door.

The Egyptians are extremely courteous to each other, and have a peculiar grace and dignity in their manner of salutation and their general demeanour, combined with easiness of address, which seem natural to them, being observable even in the peasants. The

---

1 In Chapter XXVII.

2 "El-ḥamdu li-lláh."

3 "Raḥemkum Alláh."

4 "Yahdeenè wa-yahdeekum Alláh."

5 "A'ooz bi-lláh min esh-sheyṭán er-regeem."

6 "Astaghfir Alláh el-'Aẓeem."

middle and higher classes of townspeople pride themselves upon their politeness and elegance of manners, and their wit, and fluency of speech; and with some justice: but they are not less licentious in their conversation than their less accomplished fellow-countrymen. Affability is a general characteristic of the Egyptians of all classes. It is common for strangers, even in a shop, after mutual salutation, to enter into conversation with each other with as much freedom as if they were old acquaintances, and for one who has a pipe to offer it to another who has none; and it is not unusual, nor is it generally considered unpolite, for persons in a first, casual meeting, to ask each other's names, professions or trades, and places of abode. Lasting acquaintances are often formed on such occasions.[1] In the middle and higher ranks of Egyptian society, it is very seldom that a man is heard to say anything offensive to the feelings of another in his company; and the most profligate never venture to utter an expression meant to cast ridicule upon sincere religion: most persons, however, in every class, are otherwise more or less licentious in their conversation, and extremely fond of joking. They are generally very lively and dramatic in their talk; but scarcely ever noisy in their mirth. They seldom indulge in loud laughter; expressing their enjoyment of anything ludicrous by a smile or an exclamation.

---

1 Acquaintances, and even strangers, often address each other as relations, by the terms "Father," "Son," "Paternal uncle," "Son of my paternal uncle," "Brother," "Mother," "Daughter," "Maternal aunt," "Daughter of my maternal aunt," "Sister," &c.

CHAPTER IX.

LANGUAGE, LITERATURE, AND SCIENCE.

THE metropolis of Egypt maintains the comparative reputation by which it has been distinguished for many centuries, of being the best school of Arabic literature, and of Muslim theology and jurisprudence. Learning, indeed, has much declined among the Arabs universally; but least in Cairo: consequently, the fame of the professors of this city still remains unrivalled; and its great collegiate mosque, the Azhar, continues to attract innumerable students from every quarter of the Muslim world.

The Arabic spoken by the middle and higher classes in Cairo is generally inferior, in point of grammatical correctness and pronunciation, to the dialects of the Bedawees of Arabia, and of the inhabitants of the towns in their immediate vicinity; but much to be preferred to those of Syria; and still more, to those of the Western Arabs. The most remarkable peculiarities in the pronunciation of the people of Egypt are the following:—The fifth letter of the alphabet is pronounced by the natives of Cairo, and throughout the greater part of Egypt, as *g* in *give;* while, in most parts of Arabia, and in Syria and other countries, it receives the sound of *j* in *joy:* but it is worthy of remark that, in a part of southern Arabia, where, it is said, Arabic was first spoken, the former sound is given to this letter.[1] In those parts of Egypt where this pronunciation of the fifth letter prevails, the sound of "hemzeh" (which is produced by a sudden emission of the voice after a total suppression) is given to the twenty-first letter, except by the better instructed, who give to this letter its true sound, which I represent by "ḳ." In other parts of Egypt, the pronunciation of the fifth letter is the same as that of *j* in *joy,* or nearly so; and the twenty-first letter is pronounced as *g* in *give.*

[1] It seems probable that the Arabs of Egypt have retained, in this case, a pronunciation which was common, if not almost universal, with their ancestors in Asia.—See De Sacy's Grammaire Arabe, 2nd ed. vol. i. pp. 17 and 18.

By all the Egyptians, in common with most other modern peoples who speak the Arabic language, the third and fourth letters of the alphabet are generally pronounced alike, as our *t;* and the eighth and ninth, as our *d:* the fifteenth and seventeenth are also generally pronounced alike, as a very hard *d;* but sometimes as a hard *z.* Of the peculiarities in the *structure* of the Egyptian dialect of Arabic, the most remarkable are, the annexation of the letter "sheen" in negative phrases, in the same manner as the word "pas" is used in French; as "má yerḍásh" for "má yerḍà," "he will not consent;" "má hoosh ṭeiyib" (vulgarly, "mósh ṭeiyib,') for "má huwa ṭeiyib," "it is not good:" the placing the demonstrative pronoun *after* the word to which it relates; as "el-beyt dé," "this house:" and a frequent unnecessary use of the diminutive form in adjectives; as "ṣugheiyir" for "ṣagheer," "small;" "ḳureiyib" for "ḳareeb," "near."

There is not so much difference between the literary and vulgar dialects of Arabic as some European Orientalists have supposed: the latter may be described as the ancient dialect *simplified,* principally by the omission of final vowels, and by otherwise neglecting to distinguish the different cases of nouns and some of the persons of verbs.[1] Nor is there so great a difference between the dialects of Arabic spoken in different countries as some persons, who have not held intercourse with the inhabitants of such countries, have imagined: they resemble each other more than the dialects of some of the different counties in England. The Arabic language abounds with synonyms; and, of a number of words which are synonymous, one is in common use in one country, and another elsewhere. Thus, the Egyptian calls milk "leben;" the Syrian calls it "ḥaleeb:" the word "leben" is used in Syria to denote a particular preparation of *sour* milk. Again, bread is called in Egypt "'eysh;" and in other Arab countries, "khubz;" and many examples of a similar kind might be adduced.—The pronunciation of Egypt has more softness than that of Syria and most other countries in which Arabic is spoken.

The literature of the Arabs is very comprehensive; but the number of their books is more remarkable than the variety. The

---

[1] The Arabs began to simplify their spoken language in the first century of the Flight, in consequence of their spreading among foreigners, who could not generally acquire the difficult language which their conquerors had hitherto used. For a proof of this, see "Abulfedæ Annales Muslemici, Arab. et Lat." vol. i. pp. 432 and 434. Many other proofs might be mentioned; the fact being notorious. The modern Arabic, by its resemblance to the Biblical Hebrew, confirms the evidences of decay that the latter in itself exhibits.

relative number of the books which treat of religion and jurisprudence may be stated to be about one-fourth: next in number are works on grammar, rhetoric, and various branches of philology: the third in the scale of proportion are those on history (chiefly that of the Arab nation), and on geography: the fourth, poetical compositions. Works on medicine, chymistry, the mathematics, algebra, and various other sciences, &c., are comparatively very few.

There are, in Cairo, many large libraries; most of which are attached to mosques, and consist, for the greater part, of works on theology and jurisprudence, and philology: but these libraries are deplorably neglected, and their contents are rapidly perishing, in a great measure from the dishonesty and carelessness of their keepers and of those who make use of them. Several rich merchants, and others, have also good libraries. The booksellers of Cairo are, I am informed, only eight in number;[1] and their shops are but ill stocked. Whenever a valuable book comes into the possession of one of these persons, he goes round with it to his regular customers; and is almost sure of finding a purchaser. The leaves of the books are seldom sewed together; but they are usually enclosed in a cover bound with leather; and mostly have, also, an outer case[2] of pasteboard and leather. Five sheets, or double leaves, are commonly placed together, one within another; composing what is called a "karrás." The leaves are thus arranged, in small parcels, without being sewed, in order that one book may be of use to a number of persons at the same time; each taking a karrás. The books are laid flat, one upon another; and the name is written upon the front of the outer case, or upon the edge of the leaves. The paper is thick and glazed: it is mostly imported from Venice, and glazed in Egypt. The ink is very thick and gummy. Reeds are used for pens; and they suit the Arabic character much better. The Arab, in writing, places the paper upon his knee, or upon the palm of his left hand, or upon what is called a "misnedeh,"[3] composed of a dozen or more pieces of paper attached together at the four corners, and resembling a thin book, which he rests on his knee. His ink and pens are contained in an inkhorn, called "dawáyeh," mentioned in the first chapter of this work, together with the penknife, and an ivory instrument ("miḳaṭṭah") upon which the pen is laid to be nibbed. He rules his paper by laying under it a piece of paste-

1 These are natives. There are also a few Turkish booksellers.

2 Called ẓarf.

3 Pronounced "misned'eh."

board with strings strained and glued across it (called a "misṭarah"),[1] and slightly pressing it over each string. Scissors are included among the apparatus of a writer: they are used for cutting the paper; a torn edge being considered as unbecoming. In Cairo there are many persons

Books and Apparatus for Writing.[2]

who obtain their livelihood by copying manuscripts. The expense of writing a karrás of twenty pages, quarto-size, with about twenty-five lines to a page, in an ordinary hand, is about three piasters (or a little more than sevenpence of our money); but more if in an elegant hand; and about double the sum if with the vowel points, &c.

In Egypt, and particularly in its metropolis, those youths or men who purpose to devote themselves to religious employments, or to any of the learned professions, mostly pursue a course of study in the great mosque El-Azhar; having previously learned nothing more than to read, and perhaps to write and to recite the Ḳur-án. The Azhar, which is regarded as the principal university[3] of the East, is an extensive building, surrounding a large, square court. On one side of

---

1 Pronounced "misṭar'ah."

2 The latter consist of the reed ("ḳalam"), the "miḳaṭṭah," the penknife ("miḳshaṭ"), the "dawáyeh," the "misṭarah," the "misnedeh" (upon which the five articles before mentioned lie), and the scissors ("miḳaṣṣ,") which, with their sheath, are placed upon the upper book.

3 The Azhar is not called a "university" with strict propriety; but is regarded as such by the Muslims, as whatever they deem worthy of the name of science, or necessary to be known, is taught within its walls. Its name has been translated, by European travellers, "the Mosque of Flowers;" as though it had been called "Gámè' el-Azhár," instead of "El-Gámè' el-Azhar," which is its proper appellation, and signifies "the Splendid Mosque." It is the first with respect to the period of its foundation, as well as in size, of all the mosques within the original limits of the city.—The preceding portion of this note (which was inserted in the first edition of the present work) apparently escaped the notice of Baron Hammer-Purgstall; for he remarked (in the Vienna "Jahrbücher der Literatur," lxxxi. Bd., p. 71) that, instead of "Azhar," I should have written, in this case, "Esher," [or "Ezher"]; the former, he says, signifying "flowers." The name of the mosque in question (synonymous with "neiyir," or "splendid," &c.,) is pronounced by almost all the natives of Egypt, and the Arabs in general, as I have written it, "Azhar," with the accent on the first syllable; and the plural of "zahreh" (a flower), "azhár:" but by the Turks the former word is pronounced "ezher."

this court, the side towards Mekkeh, is the chief place of prayer; a spacious portico: on each of the other three sides are smaller porticoes, divided into a number of apartments, called "riwáḳs," each of which is destined for the use of natives of a particular country, or of a particular province of Egypt. This building is situate within the metropolis. It is not remarkable in point of architecture, and is so surrounded by houses that very little of it is seen externally. The students are called "mugáwireen."[1] Each riwáḳ has a library for the use of its members; and from the books which it contains, and the lectures of the professors, the students acquire their learning. The regular subjects of study are grammatical inflexion and syntax,[2] rhetoric,[3] versification,[4] logic,[5] theology,[6] the exposition of the Ḳur-án,[7] the Traditions of the Prophet,[8] the complete science of jurisprudence, or rather of religious, moral, civil, and criminal law,[9] which is chiefly founded on the Ḳur-án and the Traditions; together with arithmetic,[10] as far as it is useful in matters of law. Lectures are also given on algebra,[11] and on the calculations of the Mohammadan calendar, the times of prayer, &c.[12] The lecturer seats himself on the ground, at the foot of a column; and his hearers, with him, seated also on the ground, form a ring. Different books are read by students of different sects. Most of the students, being natives of Cairo, are of the Sháfe'ee sect; and always the Sheykh, or head of the mosque, is of this sect. None of the students pay for the instruction they receive; being mostly of the poorer classes. Most of those who are strangers, having riwáḳs appropriated to them, receive a daily allowance of food, provided from funds chiefly arising from the rents of houses bequeathed for their maintenance. Those of Cairo and its neighbourhood used to receive a similar allowance; but this they no longer enjoy, except during the month of Ramaḍán: for Moḥammad 'Alee took possession of all the cultivable land which belonged to the mosques, and thus the Azhar lost the greater portion of the property which it possessed: nothing but the expenses of necessary repairs, and the salaries of its principal officers, are provided for by the government. The professors, also, receive no salaries. Unless they inherit property, or have relations to maintain them, they have no regular means of subsistence but

1 In the singular, "mugáwir."
2 "Ṣarf" and "naḥw."
3 "El-ma'ánee wa-l-bayán."
4 "El-'arooḍ."
5 "El-manṭiḳ."
6 "Et-towḥeed."
7 "Et-tefseer."
8 "El-aḥádees."
9 "El-fiḳ-h."
10 "El-ḥesáb."
11 "El-gebr wa-l-muḳábaleh."
12 "El-meeḳát."

teaching in private houses, copying books, &c.; but they sometimes receive presents from the wealthy. Any person who is competent to the task may become a professor by obtaining a licence from the Sheykh of the mosque. The students mostly obtain their livelihood by the same means as the professors; or by reciting the Ḳur-án in private houses, and at the tombs and other places. When sufficiently advanced in their studies, some of them become ḳáḍees, muftees, imáms of mosques, or schoolmasters, in their native villages or towns, or in Cairo: others enter into trade: some remain all their lifetime studying in the Azhar, and aspire to be ranked among the higher 'Ulamà. Since the confiscation of the lands which belonged to the Azhar, the number of that class of students to whom no endowed riwáḳ is appropriated has very much decreased. The number of students, including all classes except the blind, is (as I am informed by one of the professors) about one thousand five hundred.[1]

There is a chapel (called "Záwiyet el-'Omyán," or the Chapel of the Blind), adjacent to the eastern angle of the Azhar, and one of the dependencies of that mosque, where at present about three hundred poor blind men, most of whom are students, are maintained, from funds bequeathed for that purpose. These blind men often conduct themselves in a most rebellious and violent manner: they are notorious for such conduct, and for their fanaticism. A short time ago, a European traveller entering the Azhar, and his presence there being buzzed about, the blind men eagerly inquired, "Where is the infidel?" adding, "We will kill him;" and groping about at the same time to feel and lay hold of him: they were the only persons who seemed desirous of shewing any violence to the intruder. Before the accession of Moḥammad 'Alee Báshà, they often behaved in a very outrageous manner whenever they considered themselves oppressed, or scanted in their allowance of food: they would, on these occasions, take a few guides, go about with staves, seize the turbans of passengers in the streets, and plunder the shops. The most celebrated of the present professors in the Azhar, the sheykh El-Ḳuweysinee,[2] who is himself blind, being appointed, a few years ago, Sheykh of the Záwiyet el-'Omyán, as soon as he entered upon his office, caused every one of the blind men there to be flogged; but they rose against him, bound him, and inflicted upon him a flogging far more severe than that

[1] Many persons say that their number is not less than three thousand: others, not more than one thousand. It varies very much at different times.

[2] Since this was written he became Sheykh of the Azhar. He is now dead.

which they had themselves endured; and obliged him to give up his office.

Learning was in a much more flourishing state in Cairo before the entrance of the French army than it has been in later years. It suffered severely from this invasion; not through direct oppression, but in consequence of the panic which this event occasioned, and the troubles by which it was followed. Before that period, a sheykh who had studied in the Azhar, if he had only two boys, sons of a moderately rich fellá'ḥ, to educate, lived in luxury: his two pupils served him, cleaned his house, prepared his food, and, though they partook of it with him, were his menial attendants at every time but that of eating: they followed him whenever he went out; carried his shoes (and often kissed them when they took them off) on his entering a mosque; and in every case treated him with the honour due to a prince. He was then distinguished by an ample dress, and the large formal turban called a "muḳleh;" and as he passed along the street, whether on foot or mounted on an ass or mule, passengers often pressed towards him to implore a short ejaculatory prayer on their behalf; and he who succeeded in obtaining this wish believed himself especially blessed: if he passed by a Frank riding, the latter was obliged to dismount: if he went to a butcher, to procure some meat (for he found it best to do so, and not to send another), the butcher refused to make any charge; but kissed his hand, and received as an honour and a blessing whatever he chose to give.—The condition of a man of this profession is now so fallen, that it is with difficulty he can obtain a scanty subsistence, unless possessed of extraordinary talent.

The Muslim 'Ulamà are certainly much fettered by their religion in the pursuit of some of the paths of learning; and superstition sometimes decides a point which has been controverted for centuries. There is one singular means of settling a contention on any point of faith, science, or fact, of which I must give an instance. The following anecdote was related to me by the Imám of the late Muftee (the sheykh El-Mahdee): I wrote it in Arabic, at his dictation, and shall here translate his words. The sheykh Moḥammad El-Baháee (a learned man, whom the vulgar regard as a "welee," or especial favourite of heaven,) was attending the lectures of the sheykh El-Emeer el-Kebeer (Sheykh of the sect of the Málikees), when the professor read, from the Gámè' eṣ-Ṣagheer[1] of Es-Suyooṭee, this saying

[1] A celebrated compendious collection of the Traditions of the Prophet.

of the Prophet: "Verily El-Ḥasan and El-Ḥoseyn are the two lords of the youths of the people of Paradise, in Paradise;" and proceeded to remark, in his lecture, after having given a summary of the history of El-Ḥasan and El-Ḥoseyn, that, as to the common opinion of the people of Maṣr (or Cairo) respecting the head of El-Ḥoseyn, holding it to be in the famous Mesh-hed in this city (the mosque of the Ḥasaneyn), it was without foundation; not being established by any credible authority. "I was affected," says Moḥammad El-Baháee, "with excessive grief, by this remark; since I believed what is believed by people of integrity and of intuition, that the noble head was in this Mesh-hed; and I entertained no doubt of it: but I would not oppose the sheykh El-Emeer, on account of his high reputation and extensive knowledge. The lecture terminated, and I went away, weeping; and when night overshaded the earth, I rose upon my feet, praying, and humbly supplicating my Lord, and betaking myself to his most noble apostle (God bless and save him), begging that I might see him in my sleep, and that he would inform me in my sleep of the truth of the matter concerning the place of the noble head. And I dreamed that I was walking on the way to visit the celebrated Mesh-hed El-Ḥoseynee in Maṣr, and that I approached the ḳubbeh,[1] and saw in it a spreading light, which filled it: and I entered its door, and found a shereef standing by the door; and I saluted him, and he returned my salutation, and said to me, 'Salute the Apostle of God (God bless and save him);' and I looked towards the ḳibleh,[2] and saw the Prophet (God bless and save him) sitting upon a throne, and a man standing on his right, and another man standing on his left: and I raised my voice, saying, 'Blessing and peace be on thee, O Apostle of God:' and I repeated this several times, weeping as I did it: and I heard the Apostle of God (God bless and save him) say to me, 'Approach, O my son, O Moḥammad.' Then the first man took me, and conducted me towards the Prophet (God bless and save him), and placed me in his noble presence; and I saluted him, and he returned my salutation, and said to me, 'God recompense thee for thy visit to the head of El-Ḥoseyn my son.' I said, 'O Apostle of God, is the head of El-Ḥoseyn here?' He answered, 'Yes, it is here.' And I became cheerful: grief fled from me; and my heart was strengthened. Then I said, 'O Apostle of God, I will relate to thee

[1] The saloon of the tomb.
[2] That is, towards the niche which marks the direction of Mekkeh.

what my sheykh and my preceptor El-Emeer hath affirmed in his lecture:' and I repeated to him the words of the sheykh: and he (God bless and save him) looked down, and then raised his head, and said, 'The copyists are excused.' I awoke from my sleep joyful and happy: but I found that much remained of the night; and I became impatient of its length; longing for the morn to shine, that I might go to the sheykh, and relate to him the dream, in the hope that he might believe me. When the morn rose, I prayed, and went to the house of the sheykh; but found the door shut. I knocked it violently; and the porter came in alarm, asking, 'Who is that?' but when he knew me, for he had known my abode from the sheykh, he opened the door to me: if it had been another person, he would have beaten him. I entered the court of the house, and began to call out, 'My master! My master!' The sheykh awoke, and asked, 'Who is that?' I answered, 'It is I, thy pupil, Moḥammad El-Baháee.' The sheykh was in wonder at my coming at this time, and exclaimed, 'God's perfection! What is this? What is the news?' thinking that some great event had happened among the people. He then said to me, 'Wait while I pray.' I did not sit down until the sheykh came down to the lower room; when he said to me, 'Come up:' and I went up, and neither saluted him, nor kissed his hand, from the effect of the dream which I had seen; but said, 'The head of El-Ḥoseyn is in this well-known Mesh-hed in Maṣr: there is no doubt of it.' The sheykh said, 'What proof have you of that? If it be a true record, adduce it.' I said, 'From a book, I have none.' The sheykh said, 'Hast thou seen a vision?' I replied, 'Yes;' and I related it to him; and informed him that the Apostle of God (God bless and save him) had told me that the man who was standing by the door was 'Alee the son of Aboo-Ṭálib, and that he who was on the right of the Prophet, by the throne, was Aboo-Bekr, and that he on his left was 'Omar the son of El-Khaṭṭáb; and that they had come to visit the head of the Imám El-Ḥoseyn. The sheykh rose, and took me by the hand, and said, 'Let us go and visit the Mesh-hed El-Ḥoseynee;' and when he entered the ḳubbeh, he said, 'Peace be on thee, O son of the daughter of the Apostle of God. I believe that the noble head is here, by reason of the vision which this person has seen; for the vision of the Prophet is true; since he hath said, 'Whoso seeth me in his sleep seeth me truly; for Satan cannot assume the similitude of my form.' Then the sheykh said to me, 'Thou hast believed, and I have believed: for these lights are not illusive.'"—

The above-quoted tradition of the Prophet has often occasioned other points of dispute to be settled in the same manner, by a dream; and when the dreamer is a person of reputation, no one ventures to contend against him.

The remark made at the commencement of this chapter implies that there are, in the present day, many learned men in the metropolis of Egypt; and there are some also in other towns of this country. One of the most celebrated of the modern 'Ulamà of Cairo is the sheykh Ḥasan El-'Aṭṭár, who is the present Sheykh of the Azhar.[1] In theology and jurisprudence, he is not so deeply versed as some of his contemporaries, particularly the sheykh El-Ḳuweysinee, whom I have before mentioned; but he is eminently accomplished in polite literature.[2] He is the author of an "Inshà," an excellent collection of Arabic letters, on various subjects, which are intended as models of epistolary style. This work has been printed at Booláḳ. In mentioning its author, I fulfil a promise which he condescended to ask of me: supposing that I should publish, in my own country, some account of the people of Cairo, he desired me to state that I was acquainted with him, and to give my opinion of his acquirements.—The sheykh Moḥammad Shiháb is also deservedly celebrated as an accomplished Arabic scholar, and elegant poet. His affability and wit attract to his house, every evening, a few friends, in whose pleasures, on these occasions, I sometimes participate. We are received in a small, but very comfortable room: each of us takes his own pipe; and coffee alone is presented to us: the sheykh's conversation is the most delightful banquet that he can offer us.—There are also several other persons in Cairo who enjoy considerable reputation as philologists and poets.—The sheykh 'Abd-Er-Raḥmán El-Gabartee, another modern author, and a native of Cairo, particularly deserves to be mentioned, as having written a very excellent history of the events which have taken place in Egypt since the commencement of the twelfth century of the Flight.[3] He died in 1825, or 1826, soon after my first arrival in Cairo. His family was of El-Gabart, on the south-east of Abyssinia, bordering on the ocean. The Gabartees (or natives of that country) are Muslims. They have a riwáḳ (or apartment appropriated to such of them as wish to study) in the Azhar; and there is a similar provision for them at Mekkeh, and also at El-Medeeneh.

---

1 Since the above was written, this eminent scholar has died.

2 "'Ilm el-adab."

3 The twelfth century of the Flight commenced on the 16th or 17th of October, A. D. 1688.

The works of the ancient Arab poets were but imperfectly understood (in consequence of many words contained in them having become obsolete) between two and three centuries, only, after the time of Moḥammad: it must not therefore be inferred, from what has been said in the preceding paragraph, that persons able to explain the most difficult passages of the early Arab authors are now to be found in Cairo, or elsewhere. There are, however, many in Egypt who are deeply versed in Arabic grammar, rhetoric, and polite literature; though the sciences mostly pursued in this country are theology and jurisprudence. Few of the 'Ulamà of Egypt are well acquainted with the history of their own nation; much less with that of other people.

The literary acquirements of those who do not belong to the classes who make literature their profession are of a very inferior kind. Many of the wealthy tradespeople are well instructed in the arts of reading and writing; but few of these devote much time to the pursuit of literature. Those who have committed to memory the whole, or considerable portions, of the Ḳur-án, and can recite two or three celebrated "ḳaṣeedehs" (or short poems), or introduce, now and then, an apposite quotation in conversation, are considered accomplished persons. Many of the tradesmen of Cairo can neither read nor write, or can only read; and are obliged to have recourse to a friend to write their accounts, letters, &c.: but these persons generally cast accounts, and make intricate calculations, mentally, with surprising rapidity and correctness.

It is a very prevalent notion among the Christians of Europe, that the Muslims are enemies to almost every branch of knowledge. This is an erroneous idea; but it is true that their studies, in the present age, are confined within very narrow limits. Very few of them study medicine, chymistry (for our first knowledge of which we are indebted to the Arabs), the mathematics, or astronomy. The Egyptian medical and surgical practitioners are mostly barbers, miserably ignorant of the sciences which they profess, and unskilful in their practice; partly in consequence of their being prohibited by their religion from availing themselves of the advantage of dissecting human bodies. But a number of young men, natives of Egypt, are now receiving European instruction in medicine, anatomy, surgery, and other sciences, for the service of the government. Many of the Egyptians, in illness, neglect medical aid; placing their whole reliance on Providence or on charms. Alchymy is more studied in this country than pure chymistry; and astrology, more than astronomy. The astrolabe and quadrant are almost the only astronomical instruments used in Egypt. Telescopes are rarely seen here; and the magnetic needle is seldom employed, except to discover the direction of Mekkeh; for which purpose, convenient little compasses (called "ḳibleeyehs"), shewing the direction of the ḳibleh at various large towns in different countries, are constructed, mostly at Dimyáṭ: many of these have a dial, which shews the time of noon, and also that of the 'aṣr, at different places and different seasons. Those persons in Egypt who profess to have considerable knowledge of astronomy are generally blind to the true principles of the science: to say that the earth revolves round the sun, they consider absolute heresy. Pure astronomy they make chiefly subservient to their computations of the calendar.

The Muslim year consists of twelve lunar months; the names of which are pronounced by the Egyptians in the following manner:—

1. Moḥarram.
2. Ṣafar.
3. Rabeeạ el-Owwal.
4. Rabeeạ et-Tánee.
5. Gumád el-Owwal, or Gumáda-l-Oolà.
6. Gumád et-Tánee, or Gumáda-t-Tániyeh.
7. Regeb.
8. Shaạbán.
9. Ramaḍán.
10. Showwál.
11. Zu-l-Ḳaạdeh, or El-Ḳaạdeh.
12. Zu-l-Ḥeggeh, or El-Ḥeggeh.[1]

[1] It is the general opinion of our chronologers, that the first day of the Muslim era of "the Flight" (in Arabic, "el-Hijrah," or, as it is pronounced by most of the Egyptians, "el-Higreh," more correctly translated "the Emigration,") was Friday, the 16th of July, A. D. 622. But M. Caussin de Perceval (in his "Essai sur l'Histoire des Arabes," &c.,) has shewn that this is a mistake. The first year of the Flight was the two hundred and eleventh year of a period during which the Arabs made use of a defective luni-solar reckoning, making every third year to consist of thirteen lunar months; the others consisting of twelve such months. This mode of reckoning was abolished by Moḥammad in the twelfth month of the tenth year of the Flight, at the time of the pilgrimage; whence it appears that the first year of the Flight commenced, most probably, on Monday, the nineteenth of April, A. D. 622. According to M. Caussin de Perceval, the first ten years of the Flight commenced at the following periods:—

1st.	[Monday]	April 19, 622.
2nd.	[Saturday]	May 7, 623.
3rd.	[Thursday]	April 26, 624.
4th.	[Monday]	April 15, 625.
5th.	[Saturday]	May 3, 626.
6th.	[Thursday]	April 23, 627.
7th.	[Tuesday]	April 12, 628.
8th.	[Monday]	May 1, 629.
9th.	[Friday]	April 20, 630.
10th.	[Tuesday]	April 9, 631.

Thus it appears that the first and fourth and seventh years were of thirteen lunar months each; and the seventh was the last year that was thus augmented; therefore, with the eighth year com-

Each of these months retrogrades through all the different seasons of the solar year in the period of about thirty-three years and a half: consequently, they are only used for fixing the anniversaries of most religious festivals, and for the dates of historical events, letters, &c.; and not in matters relating to astronomy or the seasons. In the latter cases, the Coptic months are still in general use.

With the modern names of the latter I give the corresponding periods of our calendar:—

1.	Toot commences on the	10th or 11th of September.
2.	Bábeh	10th or 11th of October.
3.	Hătoor	9th or 10th of November.
4.	Kiyahk (vulg. Kiyák) .	9th or 10th of December.
5.	Ṭoobeh	8th or 9th of January.
6.	Amsheer	7th or 8th of February.
7.	Barmahát	9th of March.
8.	Barmoodeh	8th of April.
9.	Beshens	8th of May.
10.	Ba-ooneh	7th of June.
11.	Ebeeb	7th of July.
12.	Misrà	6th of August.[1]

The Eiyám en-Nesee (Intercalary days), five or six days, complete the year.

These months, it will be observed, are of thirty days each. Five intercalary days are added at the end of three successive years; and six at the end of the fourth year. The Coptic leap-year immediately precedes ours: therefore the Coptic year begins on the 11th of September only when it is the next after their leap-year; or when our next ensuing year is a leap-year; and consequently, after the following February, the corresponding days of the Coptic and our months will be the same as in other years. The Copts begin their reckoning from the era of Diocletian, A.D. 284.

---

menced the reckoning by common lunar years; and from this point we may use the tables that have often been published for finding the periods of commencement of years of the Flight. But we must not rely upon the exact accuracy of these tables: for the commencement of the month was generally determined by actual observation of the new moon, and therefore differed in different places. The era does not commence from the day on which the Prophet departed from Mekkeh (as supposed by most of our authors who have mentioned this subject), but from the first day of the moon or month of Moḥarram preceding that event. It is said that Moḥammad, after he had remained three days concealed in a cave near Mekkeh, with Aboo-Bekr, began his journey, or "flight," to El-Medeeneh, on the ninth day of the third month (Rabeeạ el-Owwal), sixty-eight days after the commencement of the era.

[1] The Coptic names, of which these are corruptions, are given in "Horæ Ægyptiacæ," by R. S. Poole, pp. 7—9; and their derivation from the names of the ancient Egyptian divinities of the months is shewn in pp. 14, 15, and 18, of that work.

The modern (like the ancient) Egyptians divide the year into three seasons; namely, the winter ("esh-shità"), the summer ("eṣ-ṣeyf"), and the inundation ("en-neel," properly the Nile). Their astronomers also make use of the calendar of the Mansions of the Moon, by which the people of Arabia used to regulate all affairs relating to the seasons.

In Egypt, and other Muslim countries, from sunset to sunset is reckoned as the civil day; the night being classed with the day which *follows* it: thus the night *before* Friday is called the night *of* Friday. Sunset is twelve o'clock: an hour after sunset, one o'clock; two hours, two o'clock; and so on to twelve: after twelve o'clock in the morning, the hours are again named one, two, three, and so on.[1] The Egyptians wind up and (if necessary) set their watches at sunset; or rather, a few minutes after; generally when they hear the call to evening-prayer. Their watches, according to this system of reckoning from sunset, to be always quite correct, should be set every evening, as the days vary in length.

The following Table shews the times of Muslim prayer,[2] with the apparent European time of sunset, in and near the latitude of Cairo, at the commencement of each zodiacal month:—

		Sunset.		'Eshè.	Day-break.	Noon.	'Aṣr.
		Mo. T. h. m.	Eur. T. h. m.	Mo. T. h. m.	Mo. T. h. m.	Mo. T. h. m.	Mo. T. h. m.
June 21		12 0	7 4	1 34	8 6	4 56	8 31
July 22	May 21	12 0	6 53	1 30	8 30	5 7	8 43
Aug. 23	Apr. 20	12 0	6 31	1 22	9 24	5 29	9 4
Sep. 23	Mar. 20	12 0	6 4	1 18	10 24	5 56	9 24
Oct. 23	Feb. 18	12 0	5 37	1 18	11 18	6 23	9 35
Nov. 22	Jan. 20	12 0	5 15	1 22	11 59	6 45	9 41
Dec. 21		12 0	5 4	1 24	12 15	6 56	9 43

A pocket almanac is annually printed at the government-press at Boolák.[3] It comprises the period of a solar year, commencing and terminating with the vernal equinox; and gives, for every day, the

[1] Consequently the time of noon according to Mohammadan reckoning, on any particular day, subtracted from twelve, gives the apparent time of sunset, on that day, according to European reckoning.

[2] The periods of the 'eshè, daybreak, and 'aṣr, are here given according to the reckoning most commonly followed in Egypt. (See the chapter on religion and laws.) "Mo. T." denotes Mohammadan Time: "Eur. T.," European Time.

[3] More than a hundred books had been printed at this press at the time of my second visit to Egypt: most of them for the use of the military, naval, and civil servants of the government. Since that time, the Thousand and One Nights, and the "Khiṭaṭ" of El-Maḳreezee, and several other important works, have been printed in the same press, at the expense of private individuals.

day of the week, and of the Mohammadan, Coptic, Syrian, and European months; together with the sun's place in the zodiac, and the time of sunrise, noon, and the 'aṣr. It is prefaced with a summary of the principal eras and feast-days of the Muslims, Copts, and others; and remarks and notices relating to the seasons. Subjoined to it is a calendar containing physical, agricultural, and other notices for every day in the year; mentioning eclipses, &c.; and comprising much matter suited to the superstitions of the people, together with some remains of the ancient calendar of Egypt. It is the work of Yaḥyà Efendee, originally a Christian priest of Syria; but now a Muslim.[1]

Of geography, the Egyptians in general, and, with very few exceptions, the best instructed among them, have scarcely any knowledge: having no good maps, they are almost wholly ignorant of the relative situations of the several great countries of Europe. Some few of the learned venture to assert that the earth is a globe; but they are opposed by a great majority of the 'Ulamà. The common opinion of all classes of Muslims is, that our earth is an almost plane expanse, surrounded by the ocean,[2] which, they say, is encompassed by a chain of mountains called "Ḳáf." They believe it to be the uppermost of *seven* earths; and in like manner they believe that there are seven heavens, one above another.

Such being the state of science among the modern Egyptians, the reader will not be surprised at finding the present chapter followed by a long account of their superstitions; a knowledge of which is necessary to enable him to understand their character, and to make due allowances for many of its faults. We may hope for, and, indeed, reasonably expect, a very great improvement in the intellectual and moral state of this people, in consequence of the introduction of European sciences, by which Moḥammad 'Alee, in some degree, made amends for his oppressive sway; but it is not probable that this hope will be soon realized to any considerable extent.[3]

---

1 During my last residence in Egypt, the almanac of Yaḥyà Efendee was superseded by one better adapted to astronomical purposes, and very creditable to its author, Maḥmood Efendee.

2 As the Greeks believed in the age of Homer and Hesiod.

3 It has been justly remarked, by Baron Hammer-Purgstall, that the present Chapter of this work is very deficient. I should gladly have made its contents more ample, had I not felt myself obliged to consult the taste of the general reader, upon whose patience I fear I have already trespassed to too great an extent by the insertion of much matter calculated to interest only Orientalists. With respect to recent innovations, I have made but few and brief remarks in this work, in consequence of my having found the lights of European science almost exclusively confined to those servants of the government who have been *compelled* to study under Frank instructors, and European customs adopted by scarcely any persons except a few *Turks*. Some Egyptians who had studied for a few years in France declared to me that they could not instil any of the notions which they had there acquired even into the minds of their most intimate friends.

CHAPTER X.

SUPERSTITIONS.

The Arabs are a very superstitious people; and none of them are more so than those of Egypt. Many of their superstitions form a part of their religion, being sanctioned by the Ḳur-án; and the most prominent of these is the belief in "Ginn," or Genii, in the singular, "Ginnee."

The Ginn are said to be of pre-adamite origin, and, in their general properties, an intermediate class of beings between angels and men, but inferior in dignity to both, created of fire, and capable of assuming the forms and material fabric of men, brutes, and monsters, and of becoming invisible at pleasure. They eat and drink, propagate their species (like, or in conjunction with, human beings), and are subject to death; though they generally live many centuries. Their principal abode is in the chain of mountains called "Ḳáf," which are believed to encompass the whole earth: as mentioned near the close of the preceding chapter. Some are believers in El-Islám: others are infidels: the latter are what are also called "Sheyṭáns," or devils; of whom Iblees (that is, Satan, or *the* devil,) is the chief: for it is the general and best-supported opinion, that he (like the other devils) is a ginnee, as he was created of fire; whereas the *angels* are created of *light*, and are impeccable. Of both the classes of ginn, good and evil, the Arabs stand in great awe; and for the former they entertain a high degree of respect. It is a common custom of this people, on pouring water, &c., on the ground, to exclaim, or mutter, "Destoor;" that is, to ask the permission, or crave the pardon, of any ginnee that may chance to be there: for the ginn are supposed to pervade the solid matter of the earth, as well as the firmament, where, approaching the confines of the lowest heaven, they often listen to the conversation of the angels respecting future things, thus enabling themselves to assist diviners and magicians. They are also believed to inhabit rivers, ruined houses, wells, baths,[1] ovens, and even the *latrina:* hence, persons, when they enter the latter place, and when they let down a bucket into a well, or light a fire, and on other occasions, say, "Permission," or "Permission, ye blessed:"[2]—which words, in the case of entering the latrina, they sometimes preface with a prayer for God's protection against all evil spirits; but in doing this, some persons are careful not to mention the name of God after they have entered (deeming it improper in such a place), and only say, "I seek refuge with *Thee* from the male and female devils." These customs present a commentary on the story in the "Thousand and One Nights," in which a merchant is described as having killed a ginnee by throwing aside the stone of a date which he had just eaten. In the same story, and in others of the same collection, a ginnee is represented as approaching in a whirlwind of sand or dust; and it is the general belief of the Arabs of Egypt, that the "zóba'ah," or whirlwind which raises the sand or dust in the form of a pillar of prodigious height, and which is so often seen sweeping across the fields and deserts of this country, is caused by the flight of one of these beings; or, in other words, that the ginnee "rides in the zóba'ah."[3] A charm is usually uttered by the Egyptians to avert the zóba'ah, when it seems to be approaching them: some of them exclaim, "Iron, thou unlucky!"[4]—as ginn are supposed to have a great dread of that metal: others endeavour to drive away the monster by exclaiming, "God is most great!"[5] What we call a "falling star" (and which the Arabs term "shiháb") is commonly believed to be a dart thrown by God at an evil ginnee; and the Egyptians, when they see it, exclaim, "May God transfix the enemy of the religion!"[6] The evil ginnees are commonly termed "'Efreets;" and one of this class is mentioned in the Ḳur-án in these words, "An 'efreet of the ginn answered" (ch. xxvii. v. 39): which words Sale translates, "A terrible genius answered." They are generally believed to differ from the other ginn in being very powerful, and always malicious; but to

---

1 In the belief that it will prevent the ginn from entering the bath, it is a common custom in Egypt, of Muslims as well as Christians, to draw, or paint, a cross over its entrance.

2 "Destoor," or "Destoor yá mubárakeen."

3 I measured the height of a zóba'ah, with a sextant, at Thebes, in circumstances which insured a very near approximation to perfect accuracy (observing its altitude, from an elevated spot, at the precise moment when it passed through, and violently agitated, a distant group of palm-trees), and found it to be seven hundred and fifty feet. I think that several zóba'ahs which I have seen were of greater height. Others, which I measured at the same place, were between five hundred and seven hundred feet in height.

4 "Ḥadeed yá mashoom."

5 "Alláhu akbar."

6 "Saham Alláh fee 'adoó ed-deen."

be, in other respects, of a similar nature. An evil ginnee of the most powerful class is called a "Márid."

Connected with the history of the ginn are many fables not acknowledged by the Ḳur-án, and therefore not credited by the more sober Muslims, but only by the less instructed. All agree that the ginn were created before mankind; but some distinguish another class of pre-adamite beings of a similar nature. It is commonly believed that the earth was inhabited, before the time of Adam, by a race of beings differing from ourselves in form, and much more powerful; and that forty (or, according to some, seventy-two,) pre-adamite kings, each of whom bore the name of Suleymán (or Solomon), successively governed this people. The last of these Suleymáns was named Gánn Ibn-Gánn; and from him, some think, the ginn (who are also called "gánn")[1] derive their name. Hence, some believe the ginn to be the same with the pre-adamite race here mentioned: but others assert that they (the ginn) were a distinct class of beings, and brought into subjection by the other race.

Ginnees are believed often to assume, or perpetually to wear, the shapes of cats, dogs, and other brute animals. The sheykh Khaleel El-Medábighee, one of the most celebrated of the 'Ulamà of Egypt, and author of several works on various sciences, who died, at a very advanced age, during the period of my first visit to this country, used to relate the following anecdote:—He had, he said, a favourite black cat, which always slept at the foot of his musquito-curtain. Once, at midnight, he heard a knocking at the door of his house; and his cat went, and opened the hanging shutter of his window, and called, "Who is there?" A voice replied, "I am such a one" (mentioning a strange name) "the ginnee: open the door." "The lock," said the sheykh's cat, "has had the name [of God] pronounced upon it."[2] "Then throw me down," said the other, "two cakes of bread." "The bread-basket," answered the cat at the window, "has had the name pronounced upon it." "Well," said the stranger, "at least give me a draught of water." But he was answered that the water-jar had been secured in the same manner; and asked what he was to do, seeing that he was likely to die of hunger and thirst: the sheykh's cat told

---

[1] According to some writers, the Gánn are the least powerful class of Ginn.

[2] It is a custom of many "fuḳahà" (or learned and devout persons), and some others, to say, "In the name of God, the Compassionate, the Merciful," on locking a door, covering bread, laying down their clothes at night, and on other occasions; and this, they believe, protects their property from genii. The thing over which these words have been pronounced is termed "musemmee (for "musemmà") 'aleyh."

him to go to the door of the next house; and went there also himself, and opened the door, and soon after returned. Next morning, the sheykh deviated from a habit which he had constantly observed: he gave, to the cat, half of the faṭeereh upon which he breakfasted, instead of a little morsel, which he was wont to give; and afterwards said, "O my cat, thou knowest that I am a poor man: bring me, then, a little gold:" upon which words, the cat immediately disappeared, and he saw it no more.—Ridiculous as stories of this kind really are, it is impossible, without relating one or more, to convey a just notion of the opinions of the people whom I am attempting to describe.

It is commonly affirmed, that malicious or disturbed ginn very often station themselves on the roofs, or at the windows, of houses in Cairo, and other towns of Egypt, and throw bricks and stones down into the streets and courts. A few days ago, I was told of a case of this kind, which had alarmed the people in the main street of the metropolis for a whole week; many bricks having been thrown down from some of the houses every day during this period, but nobody killed or wounded. I went to the scene of these pretended pranks of the ginn, to witness them, and to make inquiries on the subject; but on my arrival there, I was told that the "regm" (that is, the throwing,) had ceased. I found no one who denied the throwing down of the bricks, or doubted that it was the work of ginn; and the general remark, on mentioning the subject, was, "God preserve us from their evil doings!"

One of my friends observed to me, on this occasion, that he had met with some Englishmen who disbelieved in the existence of ginn; but he concluded that they had never witnessed a public performance, though common in their country, of which he had since heard, called "kumedyeh" (or comedy); by which term he meant to include all theatrical performances. Addressing one of his countrymen, and appealing to me for the confirmation of his words, he then said, "An Algerine, a short time ago, gave me an account of a spectacle of this kind which he had seen in London."—Here his countryman interrupted him, by asking, "Is not England in London? or is London a town in England?"—My friend, with diffidence, and looking to me, answered that London was the metropolis of England; and then resumed the subject of the theatre.—"The house," said he, "in which the spectacle was exhibited cannot be described: it was of a round form, with many benches on the floor, and closets all round, in rows, one above another, in which people of the higher classes sat; and there was a large square aperture, closed with a curtain. When the house was full of people, who paid large sums of money to be admitted, it suddenly became very dark: it was at night; and the house had been lighted up with a great many lamps; but these became almost entirely extinguished, all at the same time, without being touched by anybody. Then, the great curtain was drawn up: they heard the roaring of the sea and wind; and indistinctly perceived, through the gloom, the waves rising and foaming, and lashing the shore. Presently a tremendous peal of thunder was heard; after a flash of lightning had clearly shewn to the spectators the agitated sea: and then there fell a heavy shower of real rain. Soon after, the day broke; the sea became more plainly visible; and two ships were seen in the distance: they approached, and fought each other, firing their cannons; and a variety of other extraordinary scenes were afterwards exhibited. Now it is evident," added my friend, "that such wonders must have been the works of ginn, or at least performed by their assistance."—He could not be convinced of his error by my explanations of these phenomena.

During the month of Ramaḍán, the ginn, it is said, are confined in prison; and hence, on the eve of the festival which follows that month, some of the women of Egypt, with the view of preventing these objects of dread from entering their houses, sprinkle salt upon the floors of the apartments; saying, as they do it, "In the name of God, the Compassionate, the Merciful."

A curious relic of ancient Egyptian superstition must here be mentioned. It is believed that each quarter in Cairo has its peculiar guardian-genius, or Agathodæmon, which has the form of a serpent.

The ancient tombs of Egypt, and the dark recesses of the temples, are commonly believed, by the people of this country, to be inhabited by 'efreets. I found it impossible to persuade one of my servants to enter the Great Pyramid with me, from his having this idea. Many of the Arabs ascribe the erection of the Pyramids, and all the most stupendous remains of antiquity in Egypt, to Gánn Ibn-Gánn, and his servants, the ginn; conceiving it impossible that they could have been raised by human hands.

The term 'efreet is commonly applied rather to an evil ginnee than any other being; but the ghosts of dead persons are also called by this name; and many absurd stories are related of them; and great are the fears which they inspire. There are some persons, however, who hold them in no degree of dread.—I had once a humorous cook, who was somewhat addicted to the intoxicating ḥasheesh: soon after he had entered my service, I heard him, one evening, muttering and exclaiming, on the stairs, as if in surprise at some event; and then politely saying, "But why are you sitting here in the draught?—Do me the favour to come up into the kitchen, and amuse me with your conversation a little." The civil address, not being answered, was repeated and varied several times; till I called out to the man, and asked him to whom he was speaking. "The 'efreet of a Turkish soldier," he replied, "is sitting on the stairs, smoking his pipe, and refuses to move: he came up from the well below: pray step and see him." On my going to the stairs, and telling the servant that I could see nothing, he only remarked that it was because I had a clear conscience. He was told, afterwards, that the house had long been haunted; but asserted that he had not been previously informed of the supposed cause; which was the fact of a Turkish soldier having been murdered there. My cook professed to see this 'efreet frequently after.

The existence of "Ghools" likewise obtains almost universal credence among the modern Egyptians, in common with several other Eastern nations. These beings are generally believed to be a class of evil ginnees, and are said to appear in the forms of various animals, and in many monstrous shapes; to haunt burial-grounds, and other sequestered spots; to feed upon dead bodies; and to kill and devour every human creature who has the misfortune to fall in their way. Hence, the term "ghool" is applied, in general, to any cannibal.

That fancies such as these should exist in the minds of a people so ignorant as those who are the subject of these pages cannot reasonably excite our surprise. But the Egyptians pay a superstitious reverence not to imaginary beings alone: they extend it to certain individuals of their own species; and often to those who are justly the least entitled to such respect.[1] An *idiot* or a *fool* is vulgarly regarded by them as a being whose mind is in heaven, while his grosser part mingles among ordinary mortals; consequently, he is considered an especial favourite of heaven. Whatever enormities a reputed saint may commit (and there are many who are constantly infringing precepts of their religion), such acts do not affect his fame for sanctity: for they are considered as the results of the abstraction

[1] As is the case also in Switzerland.

of his mind from worldly things; his soul, or reasoning faculties, being wholly absorbed in devotion, so that his passions are left without control. Lunatics who are dangerous to society are kept in confinement; but those who are harmless are generally regarded as saints. Most of the reputed saints of Egypt are either lunatics, or idiots, or impostors. Some of them go about perfectly naked, and are so highly venerated, that the women, instead of avoiding them, sometimes suffer these wretches to take any liberty with them in a public street; and, by the lower orders, are not considered as disgraced by such actions, which, however, are of very rare occurrence. Others are seen clad in a cloak or long coat composed of patches of various coloured cloths, which is called a "dilḳ,"[1] adorned with numerous strings of beads, wearing a ragged turban, and bearing a staff with shreds of cloth of various colours attached to the top. Some of them eat straw, or a mixture of chopped straw and broken glass; and attract observation by a variety of absurd actions. During my first visit to this country, I often met, in the streets of Cairo, a deformed man, almost naked, with long matted hair, and riding upon an ass, led by another man. On these occasions, he always stopped his beast directly before me, so as to intercept my way, recited the Fát'ḥah (or opening chapter of the Ḳur-án), and then held out his hand for an alms. The first time that he thus crossed me, I endeavoured to avoid him; but a person passing by remonstrated with me, observing that the man before me was a saint, and that I ought to respect him, and comply with his demand, lest some misfortune should befall me. Men of this class are supported by alms, which they often receive without asking for them. A reputed saint is commonly called "sheykh," "murábiṭ," or "welee." If affected with lunacy or idiotcy, or of weak intellect, he is also, and more properly, termed "megzoob," or "mesloob." "Welee" is an appellation correctly given only to an eminent and a very devout saint; and means "a favourite of heaven;" but it is so commonly applied to real or pretended idiots, that some wit has given it a new interpretation, as equivalent to "beleed," which means "a fool" or "simpleton;" remarking that these two terms are equivalent both in sense and in the numerical value of the letters composing them: for "welee" is written with the letters "wä'w," "lám," and "yé," of which the numerical values are 6, 30, and 10, or, together, 46; and "beleed" is written with "bé," "lám," "yé,"

---

[1] Also (and more properly) pronounced "daliḳ," but commonly pronounced as above.

and "dál," which are 2, 30, 10, and 4, or, added together, 46. A simpleton is often jestingly called a welee.

The Muslims of Egypt, in common with those of other countries, entertain very curious superstitions respecting the persons whom they call welees. I have often endeavoured to obtain information on the most mysterious of these superstitions; and have generally been answered, "You are meddling with the matters of the 'ṭareeḳah,'" or the religious course of the darweeshes; but I have been freely acquainted with general opinions on these subjects, and such are perhaps all that may be required to be stated in a work like the present: I shall, however, also relate what I have been told by learned persons, and by darweeshes, in elucidation of the popular belief.

In the first place, if a person were to express a doubt as to the existence of true welees, he would be branded with infidelity; and the following passage of the Ḳur-án would be adduced to condemn him: "Verily, on the favourites[1] of God no fear shall come, nor shall they grieve."[2] This is considered as sufficient to prove that there is a class of persons distinguished above ordinary human beings. The question then suggests itself, "Who, or of what description, are these persons?" and we are answered, "They are persons wholly devoted to God, and possessed of extraordinary faith; and, according to their degree of faith, endowed with the power of performing miracles."[3]

The most holy of the welees is termed the Ḳuṭb; or, according to some persons, there are two who have this title; and again, according to others, four. The term "ḳuṭb" signifies an *axis;* and hence is applied to a welee who rules over others; they depending upon him, and being subservient to him. For the same reason it is applied to temporal rulers, or any person of high authority. The opinion that there are *four* ḳuṭbs, I am told, is a vulgar error, originating from the frequent mention of "the four ḳuṭbs," by which expression are meant the founders of the four most celebrated orders of darweeshes (the Rifá'eeyeh, Ḳádireeyeh, Aḥmedeeyeh, and Baráhimeh); each of whom is believed to have been the ḳuṭb of his time. I have also generally been told, that the opinion of there being *two* ḳuṭbs is a vulgar error, founded upon two names, "Ḳuṭb el-Ḥaḳeeḳah" (said

---

[1] In the original, "owliyà," plural of "welee."

[2] Ch. x. v. 63.

[3] A miracle performed by a welee is termed "karámeh:" one performed by a prophet, "moạgizeh."

to mean the Ḳuṭb of Truth), and "Ḳuṭb el-Ghós" (or the Ḳuṭb of Invocation for help), which properly belong to but one person. The term "el-Ḳuṭb el-Mutawellee" is applied, by those who believe in but one ḳuṭb, to the one ruling at the present time; and by those who believe in two, to the *acting* ḳuṭb. The ḳuṭb who exercises a superintendence over all other welees (whether or not there be another ḳuṭb, for if there be, he is inferior to the former,) has, under his authority, welees of different ranks, to perform different offices; "Naḳeebs," "Negeebs," "Bedeels,"[1] &c.; who are known only to each other, and perhaps to the rest of the welees, as holding such offices.

The Ḳuṭb, it is said, is often seen, but not known as such; and the same is said of all who hold authority under him. He always has a humble demeanour, and mean dress; and mildly reproves those whom he finds acting impiously; particularly such as have a false reputation for sanctity. Though he is unknown to the world, his favourite stations are well known; yet at these places he is seldom visible. It is asserted that he is almost constantly seated at Mekkeh, on the roof of the Kaạbeh; and, though never seen there, is always heard at midnight to call twice, "O Thou most merciful of those who shew mercy!"[2] which cry is then repeated from the mád'nehs of the temple, by the muëddins: but a respectable pilgrim, whom I questioned upon this matter, confessed to me that he himself had witnessed that this cry was made by a regular minister of the mosque; yet that few pilgrims knew this: he believed, however, that the roof of the Kaạbeh is the chief "markaz" (or station) of the Ḳuṭb. Another favourite station of this revered and unknown person is the gate of Cairo called Báb Zuweyleh, which is at the southern extremity of that part of the metropolis which constituted the old city; though now in the heart of the town; for the capital has greatly increased towards the south, as it has also towards the west. From its being a supposed station of this mysterious being, the Báb Zuweyleh is commonly called "El-Mutawellee."[3] One leaf of its great wooden door (which is never shut), turned back against the eastern side of the interior of the gateway, conceals a small vacant space, which is said to be the place of the Ḳuṭb. Many persons, on passing by it, recite the Fát'ḥah; and some give alms to a beggar who is generally seated there, and who is regarded by the vulgar as one of the servants

---

1 In the plural forms, "Nuḳabà," "Angáb" or "Nugabà," and "Abdál."

2 "Yá arḥama-r-ráḥemeen."

3 For "Báb El-Mutawellee."

of the Ḳuṭb. Numbers of persons afflicted with head-ache drive a nail into the door, to charm away the pain; and many sufferers from the tooth-ache extract a tooth, and insert it in a crevice of the door, or fix it in some other way, to insure their not being attacked again by the same malady. Some curious individuals often try to peep behind the door, in the vain hope of catching a glimpse of the Ḳuṭb, should he happen to be there, and not at the moment invisible. He has also many other stations, but of inferior celebrity, in Cairo; as well as one at the tomb of the seyyid Aḥmad El-Bedawee, at Ṭanṭà; another at El-Maḥalleh (which, as well as Ṭanṭà, is in the Delta); and others in other places. He is believed to transport himself from Mekkeh to Cairo in an instant; and so too from any one place to another. Though he has a number of favourite stations, he does not abide solely at these; but wanders throughout the whole world, among persons of every religion, whose appearance, dress, and language he assumes; and distributes to mankind, chiefly through the agency of the subordinate welees, evils and blessings, the awards of destiny. When a Ḳuṭb dies, he is immediately succeeded in his office by another.

Many of the Muslims say that Elijah, or Elias, whom the vulgar confound with El-Khiḍr,[1] was the Ḳuṭb of his time; and that he invests the successive ḳuṭbs: for they acknowledge that he has never died; asserting him to have drunk of the Fountain of Life. This particular in their superstitious notions respecting the ḳuṭbs, and some other particulars which I have before mentioned, appear to have been suggested by what we are told, in the Bible, of Elijah, of his translation, of his being transported from place to place by the Spirit of God, of his investing Elisha with his miraculous powers and his offices, and of the subjection of the other prophets to him and to his immediate successor.[2] Some welees renounce the pleasures of the world, and the society of mankind; and, in a desert place, give themselves up to meditation upon heaven, and prayer; depending upon divine providence for their support: but their retreat becomes known; and the Arabs daily bring them food. This, again, reminds us of the history of Elijah, if, as is the opinion of some critics, we should read,

---

1 This mysterious person, according to the more approved opinion of the learned, was not a prophet, but a just man, or saint, the Wezeer and counsellor of the first Zu-l-Ḳarneyn, who was a universal conqueror, but an equally doubtful personage, contemporary with the patriarch Ibrâheem, or Abraham. El-Khiḍr is said to have drunk of the Fountain of Life, in consequence of which he lives till the day of judgment, and to appear frequently to Muslims in perplexity. He is generally clad in green garments; whence, according to some, his name.

2 See 1 Kings, xviii. 12, and 2 Kings, ii. 9—16.

instead of "ravens," in the fourth and sixth verses of the seventeenth chapter of the second book of Kings, "Arabs:"—"I have commanded the *Arabs* to feed thee"—"And the *Arabs* brought him bread," &c.

Certain welees are said to be commissioned by the Ḳuṭb to perform offices which, according to the accounts of my informants here, are far from being easy. These are termed "Aṣ-ḥáb ed-Darak," interpreted to me (but I know not on what ground) as meaning "watchmen," or "overseers."[1] In illustration of their employments, the following anecdote was related to me.—A devout tradesman in this city, who was ardently desirous of becoming a welee, applied to a person who was generally believed to belong to this holy class, and implored the latter to assist him to obtain the honour of an interview with the Ḳuṭb. The applicant, after having undergone a strict examination as to his motives, was desired to perform the ordinary ablution (el-wuḍoó) very early the next morning; then to repair to the mosque of El-Mu-eiyad (at an angle of which is the Báb Zuweyleh, or El-Mutawellee, before mentioned), and to lay hold of the first person whom he should see coming out of the great door of this mosque. He did so. The first person who came out was an old, venerable-looking man; but meanly clad; wearing a brown woollen gown (or zaạbooṭ); and this proved to be the Ḳuṭb. The candidate kissed his hand, and entreated to be admitted among the Aṣ-ḥáb ed-Darak. After much hesitation, the prayer was granted: the Ḳuṭb said, "Take charge of the district which consists of the Darb el-Aḥmar[2] and its immediate neighbourhood;" and immediately the person thus addressed found himself to be a welee; and perceived that he was acquainted with things concealed from ordinary mortals: for a welee is said to be acquainted by God with all secrets necessary for him to know.—It is commonly said of a welee, that he knows what is secret,[3] or not discoverable by the senses; which seems plainly contradictory to what we read in several places in the Ḳur-án, that none knoweth what is secret (or hidden from the senses) but God: the Muslims, however, who are seldom at a loss in a discussion, argue that the passages above alluded to, in the Ḳur-án, imply the knowledge of secrets in an

---

[1] This rendering is agreeable with an explanation of "darak" by M. Quatremère (in his "Histoire des Sultans Mamlouks," vol. i. p. 169), elicited from a comparison of a number of passages in which it occurs.

[2] A street leading from the Báb Zuweyleh towards the south-east, and forming a part of a great thoroughfare-street that extends to the citadel.

[3] "Yaạlam el-gheyb."

unrestricted sense; and that God imparts to welees such secrets only as He thinks fit.

The welee above mentioned, as soon as he had entered upon his office, walked through his district; and seeing a man at a shop with a jar full of boiled beans before him, from which he was about to serve his customers as usual, took up a large piece of stone, and, with it, broke the jar. The bean-seller immediately jumped up; seized hold of a palm-stick that lay by his side; and gave the welee a severe beating: but the holy man complained not; nor did he utter a cry: as soon as he was allowed, he walked away. When he was gone, the bean-seller began to try if he could gather up some of the scattered contents of the jar. A portion of the jar remained in its place; and on looking into this, he saw a venomous serpent in it, coiled round, and dead. In horror at what he had done, he exclaimed, "There is no strength nor power but in God! I implore forgiveness of God, the Great. What have I done! This man is a welee; and has prevented my selling what would have poisoned my customers." He looked at every passenger all that day, in the hope of seeing again the saint whom he had thus injured, that he might implore his forgiveness; but he saw him not; for he was too much bruised to be able to walk. On the following day, however, with his limbs still swollen from the blows he had received, the welee limped through his district, and broke a great jar of milk at a shop not far from that of the bean-seller; and its owner treated him as the bean-seller had done the day before; but while he was beating him, some persons ran up, and stopped his hand, informing him that the person whom he was thus punishing was a welee, and relating to him the affair of the serpent that was found in the jar of beans. "Go, and look," said they, "in your jar of milk, and you will find, at the bottom of it, something either poisonous or unclean." He looked; and found, in the remains of the jar, a dead dog.—On the third day, the welee, with the help of a staff, hobbled painfully up the Darb el-Aḥmar, and saw a servant carrying, upon his head, a supper-tray covered with dishes of meat, vegetables, and fruit, for a party who were going to take a repast in the country; whereupon he put his staff between the man's legs, and overthrew him; and the contents of the dishes were scattered in the street. With a mouth full of curses, the servant immediately began to give the saint as severe a thrashing as he himself expected to receive from his disappointed master for this accident: but several persons soon collected around him; and one of these bystanders observed a dog eat part of the contents of one of the dishes, and, a moment after, fall down dead: he therefore instantly seized the hand of the servant, and informed him of this circumstance, which proved that the man whom he had been beating was a welee. Every apology was made to the injured saint, with many prayers for his forgiveness: but he was so disgusted with his new office, that he implored God and the Ḳuṭb to release him from it; and, in answer to his solicitations, his supernatural powers were withdrawn, and he returned to his shop, more contented than before.—This story is received as true by the people of Cairo; and therefore I have inserted it: for, in treating of superstitions, we have more to do with opinions than with facts. I am not sure, indeed, that it is altogether false: the supposed saint might have employed persons to introduce the dead serpent and dog into the vessels which he broke. I am told that many a person has obtained the reputation of being a welee by artifices of the kind just mentioned.

There have been many instances, in Egypt, of welees afflicting themselves by austerities similar to those which are often practised by devotees in India. At the present time there is living, in Cairo, a welee who has placed an iron collar round his neck, and chained himself to a wall of his chamber; and it is said that he has been in this state more than thirty years: but some persons assert that he has often been seen to cover himself over with a blanket, as if to sleep, and that the blanket has been removed immediately after, and nobody found beneath it! Stories of this kind are related and believed by persons who, in many respects, are endowed with good sense; and to laugh, or express discredit, on hearing them, would give great offence. I was lately told that, a certain welee being beheaded, for a crime of which he was not guilty, his head spoke after it was cut off;[1] and, of another decapitated under similar circumstances, that his blood traced upon the ground, in Arabic characters, the following declaration of his innocence—"I am a welee of God; and have died a martyr."

It is a very remarkable trait in the character of the people of Egypt and other countries of the East, that Muslims, Christians, and Jews, adopt each other's superstitions, while they abhor the leading doctrines of each other's faiths. In sickness, the Muslim sometimes employs Christian and Jewish priests to pray for him: the Christians and Jews, in the same predicament, often call in Muslim

---

1 Like that of the Sage Doobán, whose story is told in "The Thousand and One Nights."

saints for the like purpose. Many Christians are in the frequent habit of visiting certain Muslim saints here; kissing their hands; begging their prayers, counsels, or prophecies; and giving them money and other presents.

Though their prophet disclaimed the power of performing miracles, the Muslims attribute to him many; and several miracles are still, they say, constantly or occasionally performed for his sake, as marks of the divine favour and honour. The pilgrims who have visited El-Medeeneh relate that there is seen, every night, a ray or column of faint light rising from the cupola over the grave of the Prophet to a considerable height, apparently to the clouds, or, as some say, to Paradise; but that the observer loses sight of it when he approaches very near the tomb.[1] This is one of the most remarkable of the miracles which are related as being still witnessed. On my asking one of the most grave and sensible of all my Muslim friends here, who had been on a pilgrimage, and visited El-Medeeneh, whether this assertion were true, he averred that it was; that he had seen it every night of his stay in that city; and he remarked that it was a most striking and impressive proof of God's favour and honour for "our lord Moḥammad." I did not presume to question the truth of what he asserted himself to have seen; nor to suggest that the great number of lights kept burning every night in the mosque might produce this effect: but to judge whether this might be the case, I asked my friend to describe to me the construction of the apartment of the tomb, its cupola, &c. He replied, that he did not enter it, nor the Kaạbeh at Mekkeh, partly from his being in a state of excessive nervous excitement (from his veneration for those holy buildings, but particularly for the former, which almost affected him with a kind of hysteric fit), and partly because, being of the sect of the Ḥanafees, he held it improper, after he should have stepped upon such sacred ground, ever again to run the risk of defiling his feet, by walking barefooted: consequently, he would have been obliged always to wear leather socks, or mezz, within his outer shoes; which, he said, he could not afford to do.—The pilgrims also assert, that, in approaching El-Medeeneh, from the distance of three days' journey, or more, they always see a flickering lightning, in the direction of the sacred city, which they believe to proceed from the Prophet's tomb. They say,

---

1 It is also said that similar phenomena, but not so brilliant, distinguish some other tombs at El-Medeeneh and elsewhere.

that, however they turn, they always see this lightning in the direction of El-Medeeneh. There is something strikingly poetical in this and in the former statement.

A superstitious veneration, and honours unauthorized by the Ḳur-án or any of the Traditions, are paid, by all sects of Muslims, except the Wahhábees, to deceased saints, even more than to those who are living; and more particularly by the Muslims of Egypt.[1] Over the graves of most of the more celebrated saints are erected large and handsome mosques: over that of a saint of less note (one who, by a life of sanctity or hypocrisy, has acquired the reputation of being a welee, or devout sheykh,) is constructed a small, square, whitewashed building, crowned with a cupola. There is generally, directly over the vault in which the corpse is deposited, an oblong monument of stone or brick (called "tarkeebeh") or wood (in which case it is called "táboot"); and this is usually covered with silk or linen, with some words from the Ḳur-án worked upon it, and surrounded by a railing or screen, of wood or bronze, called "maḳṣoorah." Most of the sanctuaries of saints in Egypt are tombs; but there are several which only contain some inconsiderable relic of the person to whom they are dedicated; and there are a few which are mere cenotaphs. The most sacred of all these sanctuaries is the mosque of the Ḥasaneyn, in which the head of the martyr El-Ḥoseyn, the son of the Imám 'Alee, and grandson of the Prophet, is said to be buried. Among others but little inferior in sanctity, are the mosques of the seyyideh Zeyneb (daughter of the Imám 'Alee, and grand-daughter of the Prophet), the seyyideh Sekeeneh (daughter of the Imám El-Ḥoseyn), the seyyideh Nefeeseh (great-grand-daughter of the Imám El-Ḥasan), and the Imám Esh-Sháfe'ee, already mentioned as the author of one of the four great Muslim persuasions, that to which most of the people of Cairo belong. The buildings above mentioned, with the exception of the last two, are within the metropolis: the last but one is in a southern suburb of Cairo; and the last, in the great southern cemetery.

---

[1] Several superstitious customs, observed in the performance of many ordinary actions, result from their extravagant respect for their prophet, and their saints in general. For instance, on lighting the lamp in the evening, more particularly at a shop, it is customary to say, "Commemorate Moḥammad, and forget not the excellencies of 'Alee: the Fát'ḥah for the Prophet, and for every welee:" and then, to repeat the Fát'ḥah. It is usual to say, on first seeing the new moon, "O God, bless our lord Moḥammad. God make thee a blessed moon (or month):" and on looking at one's face in a glass, "O God, bless our lord Moḥammad." This ejaculation being used to counteract the influence of the evil eye, it seems as if an Arab feared the effect even of his own admiring look.

The Egyptians occasionally visit these and other sanctuaries of their saints, either merely with the view of paying honour to the deceased, and performing meritorious acts for the sake of these venerated persons, which they believe will call down a blessing on themselves, or for the purpose of urging some special petition, as for the restoration of health, or for the gift of offspring, &c.; in the persuasion that the merits of the deceased will insure a favourable reception of the prayers which they offer up in such consecrated places. The generality of the Muslims regard their deceased saints as intercessors with the Deity; and make votive offerings to them. The visiter, on arriving at the tomb, should greet the deceased with the salutation of peace, and should utter the same salutation on entering the burial-ground; but I believe that few persons observe this latter custom. In the former case, the visiter should front the face of the dead, and consequently turn his back to the ḳibleh. He walks round the maḳṣoorah or the monument from left to right; and recites the Fát'ḥah, inaudibly, or in a very low voice, before its door, or before each of its four sides. Sometimes a longer chapter of the Ḳur-án than the first (or Fát'ḥah) is recited afterwards: and sometimes a "khatmeh" (or recitation of the whole of the Ḳur-án) is performed on such an occasion. These acts of devotion are generally performed for the sake of the saint; though merit is likewise believed to reflect upon the visiter who makes a recitation. He usually says at the close of this, "[Extol] the perfection of thy Lord, the Lord of Might, exempting Him from that which they [that is, the unbelievers,] ascribe to Him" (namely, the having a son, or a partaker of his godhead); and adds, "And peace be on the Apostles; and praise be to God, the Lord of the beings of the whole world. O God, I have transferred the merit of what I have recited from the excellent Ḳur-án to the person to whom this place is dedicated," or—"to the soul of this welee." Without such a declaration, or an intention to the same effect, the merit of the recital belongs solely to the person who performs it. After this recital, the visiter, if it be his desire, offers up any prayer, for temporal or spiritual blessings; generally using some such form as this:—"O God, I conjure Thee by the Prophet, and by him to whom this place is dedicated, to grant me such and such blessings:" or "My burdens be on God and on thee, O thou to whom this place is dedicated." In doing this, some persons face any side of the maḳṣoorah: it is said to be more proper to face the maḳṣoorah and the ḳibleh; but I believe that the same rule should be observed in this case as in the salutation. During the prayer, the hands are held as in the private supplications after the ordinary prayers of every day; and afterwards they are drawn down the face. Many of the visiters kiss the threshold of the building, and the walls, windows, maḳṣoorah, &c. This, however, the more strict disapprove; asserting it to be an imitation of a custom of the Christians. The rich, and persons in easy circumstances, when they visit the tomb of a saint, distribute money or bread to the poor; and often give money to one or more water-carriers to distribute water to the poor and thirsty, for the sake of the saint.[1] There are particular days of the week on which certain tombs are more generally visited: thus, the mosque of the Ḥasaneyn is mostly visited, by men, on Tuesday, and by women, on Saturday: that of the seyyideh Zeyneb, on Wednesday: that of the Imám Esh-Sháfe'ee, on Friday. On these occasions, it is a common custom for the male visiters to take with them sprigs of myrtle: they place some of these on the monument, or on the floor within the maḳṣoorah; and take back the remainder, which they distribute to their friends. The poor sometimes place "khooṣ" (or palm-leaves); as most persons do upon the tombs of their friends and relations. The women of Cairo, instead of the myrtle or palm-leaves, often place roses, flowers of the ḥennà-tree, jasmine, &c.

At almost every village in Egypt is the tomb of some favourite or patron saint, which is generally visited, on a particular day of the week, by many of the inhabitants; chiefly women; some of whom bring thither bread, which they leave there for poor travellers or any other persons. Some also place small pieces of money in these tombs. These gifts are offerings to the sheykh; or given for his sake. Another custom common among the peasants is, to make votive sacrifices at the tombs of their sheykhs. For instance, a man makes a vow ("nedr") that, if he recover from a sickness, or obtain a son, or any other specific object of desire, he will give, to a certain sheykh (deceased), a goat, or a lamb, or a sheep, &c.: if he attain his object, he sacrifices the animal which he has vowed at the tomb of the sheykh, and makes a feast with its meat for any persons who may choose to attend. Having given the animal to the saint, he thus gives to the latter the merit of feeding the poor. Little kids are often vowed as future sacrifices; and have the right ear slit; or are marked

---

[1] See the account of the water-carriers in Chapter XIV.

in some other way. It is not uncommon, too, without any definite view but that of obtaining general blessings, to make these vows: and sometimes, a peasant vows that he will sacrifice, for the sake of a saint, a calf which he possesses, as soon as it is full-grown and fatted: it is let loose, by consent of all his neighbours, to pasture where it will, even in fields of young wheat; and at last, after it has been sacrificed, a public feast is made with its flesh. Many a large bull is thus given away.

Almost every celebrated saint, deceased, is honoured by an anniversary birthday festival, which is called "moolid," or, more properly, "mólid." On the occasions of such festivals, many persons visit the tomb, both as a duty and as a supposed means of obtaining a special blessing; fiḳees are hired to recite the Ḳur-án, for the sake of the saint; faḳeers often perform zikrs; and the people living in the neighbourhood of the tomb hang lamps before their doors, and devote half the night to such pleasures as those of smoking, sipping coffee, and listening to story-tellers at the coffee-shops, or to the recitals of the Ḳur-án, and the zikrs. I have now a cluster of lamps hanging before my door, in honour of the moolid of a sheykh who is buried near the house in which I am living. Even the native Christians often hang up lamps on these occasions. The festivities often continue several days. The most famous moolids celebrated in Cairo, next to that of the Prophet, are those of the Ḥasaneyn and the seyyideh Zeyneb; accounts of which will be found in a subsequent chapter, on the periodical public festivals, &c., of the people of Egypt. Most of the Egyptians not only expect a blessing to follow their visiting the tomb of a celebrated saint, but they also dread that some misfortune will befall them if they neglect this act. Thus, while I am writing these lines, an acquaintance of mine is suffering from an illness which he attributes to his having neglected, for the last two years, to attend the festivals of the seyyid Aḥmad El-Bedawee, at Ṭanṭà; this being the period of one of these festivals. The tomb of this saint attracts almost as many visiters, at the periods of the great annual festivals, from the metropolis, and from various parts of Lower Egypt, as Mekkeh does pilgrims from the whole of the Muslim world. Three moolids are celebrated in honour of him every year; one, about the tenth of the Coptic month of Ṭoobeh (17th or 18th of January); the second, at, or about, the Vernal Equinox;[1]

[1] Called the "Shems el-Kebeereh."

and the third, or great moolid, about a month after the Summer Solstice (or about the middle of the Coptic month of Ebeeb), when the Nile has risen considerably, but the dams of the canals are not yet cut. Each lasts one week and a day; beginning on a Friday, and ending on the afternoon of the next Friday; and, on each night, there is a display of fireworks. One week after each of these, is celebrated the moolid of the seyyid Ibráheem Ed-Dasooḳee, at the town of Dasooḳ, on the east bank of the western branch of the Nile. The seyyid Ibráheem was a very famous saint; next in rank to the seyyid El-Bedawee. These moolids, both of the seyyid El-Bedawee and of the seyyid Ibráheem, are great fairs, as well as religious festivals. At the latter, most of the visiters remain in their boats; and some of the Saạdeeyeh darweeshes of Rasheed exhibit their feats with serpents: some carrying serpents with silver rings in their mouths, to prevent their biting: others partly devouring these reptiles alive. The religious ceremonies at both are merely zikrs,[1] and recitals of the Ḳur-án.—It is customary among the Muslims, as it was among the Jews, to rebuild, whitewash, and decorate, the tombs of their saints, and occasionally to put a new covering over the tarkeebeh or táboot; and many of them do this from the same pharisaic motives which actuated the Jews.[2]

"Darweeshes" are very numerous in Egypt; and some of them who confine themselves to religious exercises, and subsist by alms, are much respected in this country; particularly by the lower orders. Various artifices are employed by persons of this class to obtain the reputation of superior sanctity, and of being endowed with the power of performing miracles. Many of them are regarded as welees.

A direct descendant of Aboo-Bekr, the first Khaleefeh, having the title of "Esh-Sheykh el-Bekree," and regarded as the representative of that prince, holds authority over all orders of darweeshes in Egypt. The present Sheykh el-Bekree, who is also descended from the Prophet, is Naḳeeb el-Ashráf, or chief of the Shereefs. The second Khaleefeh, 'Omar, has likewise his representative, who is the sheykh of the 'Enáneeyeh, or Owlád 'Enán, an order of darweeshes so named from one of their celebrated sheykhs, Ibn-'Enán. 'Osmán has no representative, having left no issue. The representative of 'Alee is called Sheykh es-Sádát,[3] or Sheykh of the Seyyids, or Shereefs; a

---

[1] The "zikr" will be fully described in another chapter, on the periodical public festivals, &c.

[2] See St. Matthew, xxiii. 29.

[3] Often improperly called "esh-Sheykh es-Sádát."

title of less importance than that of Naḳeeb of the Shereefs. Each of these three sheykhs is termed the occupant of the "seggádeh" (or prayer-carpet) of his great ancestor. So too the sheykh of an order of darweeshes is called the occupant of the seggádeh of the founder of the order.[1] The seggádeh is considered as the spiritual throne. There are four great seggádehs of darweeshes in Egypt; which are those of four great orders about to be mentioned.

The most celebrated orders of darweeshes in Egypt are the following.—1. The "Rifá'eeyeh" (in the singular "Rifá'ee"). This order was founded by the seyyid Aḥmad Rifá'ah El-Kebeer. Its banners, and the turbans of its members, are black; or the latter are of a very deep-blue woollen stuff, or muslin of a very dark greenish hue. The Rifá'ee darweeshes are celebrated for the performance of many wonderful feats.[2] The "'Ilwáneeyeh," or "Owlád 'Ilwán," who are a sect of the Rifá'ees, pretend to thrust iron spikes into their eyes and bodies without sustaining any injury; and in appearance they do this, in such a manner as to deceive any person who can believe it possible for a man to do such things in reality. They also break large masses of stone on their chests; eat live coals, glass, &c.; and are said to pass swords completely through their bodies, and packing-needles through both their cheeks, without suffering any pain, or leaving any wound: but such performances are now seldom witnessed. I am told that it was a common practice for a darweesh of this order to hollow out a piece of the trunk of a palm-tree, fill it with rags soaked with oil and tar, then set fire to these contents, and carry the burning mass under his arm, in a religious procession (wearing only drawers); the flames curling over his bare chest, back, and head, and apparently doing him no injury. The "Saạdeeyeh," an order founded by the sheykh Saạd-ed-Deen El-Gibáwee, are another and more celebrated sect of the Rifá'ees. Their banners are green; and their turbans, of the same colour or of the dark hue of the Rifá'ees in general. There are many darweeshes of this order who handle, with impunity, live, venomous serpents, and scorpions; and partly devour them. The serpents, however, they render incapable of doing any injury, by extracting their venomous fangs; and doubtless they also deprive the scorpions of their poison. On certain occasions (as, for instance, on that of the festival of the birth of the Prophet), the Sheykh of the Saạdeeyeh rides, on horseback, over the bodies of a

[1] The title is "ṣáḥeb seggádeh."

[2] In most of their juggling performances, the darweeshes of Egypt are inferior to the most expert of the Indians.

number of his darweeshes, and other persons, who throw themselves on the ground for the purpose; and all assert that they are not injured by the tread of the horse.[1] This ceremony is called the "dóseh." Many Rifá'ee and Saạdee darweeshes obtain their livelihood by going about to charm away serpents from houses. Of the feats of these modern Psylli, an account will be given in another chapter.—2. The "Ḳádireeyeh;" an order founded by the famous seyyid 'Abd-El-Ḳádir El-Geelánee. Their banners and turbans are white. Most of the Ḳádireeyeh of Egypt are fishermen: these, in religious processions, carry, upon poles, nets of various colours (green, yellow, red, white, &c.), as the banners of their order.—3. The "Aḥmedeeyeh," or order of the seyyid Aḥmad El-Bedawee, whom I have lately mentioned. This is a very numerous and highly respected order. Their banners and turbans are red. The "Beiyoomeeyeh" (founded by the seyyid 'Alee El-Beiyoomee), the "Shaạráweeyeh" (founded by the sheykh Esh-Shaạráwee[2]), the "Shinnáweeyeh" (founded by the seyyid 'Alee Esh-Shinnáwee), and many other orders, are sects of the Aḥmedeeyeh. The Shinnáweeyeh train an *ass* to perform a strange part in the ceremonies of the last day of the moolid of their great patron saint, the seyyid Aḥmad El-Bedawee, at Ṭanṭà: the ass, of its own accord, enters the mosque of the seyyid, proceeds to the tomb, and there stands while multitudes crowd around it, and each person who can approach near enough to it plucks off some of its hair, to use as a charm, until the skin of the poor beast is as bare as the palm of a man's hand. There is another sect of the Aḥmedeeyeh, called "Owlád Nooḥ," all young men; who wear "ṭarṭoors" (or high caps), with a tuft of pieces of various-coloured cloth on the top, wooden swords, and numerous strings of beads; and carry a kind of whip (called "firḳilleh"), a thick twist of cords.—4. The "Baráhimeh," or "Burhámeeyeh;" the order of the seyyid Ibráheem Ed-Dasooḳee, whose moolid has been mentioned above. Their banners and turbans are green.—There are many other classes of darweeshes; some of whom are sects of one or other of the above orders. Among the more celebrated of them are the "Ḥefnáweeyeh," the "'Afeefeeyeh," the "Demirdásheeyeh," the "Naḳshibendeeyeh," the "Bekreeyeh," and the "Leyseeyeh."

It is impossible to become acquainted with all the tenets, rules,

---

[1] In the chapters on the periodical public festivals, &c., this and other performances of the darweeshes of Cairo will be described more fully.

[2] Thus commonly pronounced, for Esh-Shaạránee.

and ceremonies of the darweeshes, as many of them, like those of the freemasons, are not to be divulged to the uninitiated. A darweesh with whom I am acquainted thus described to me his taking the "'ahd," or initiatory covenant, which is nearly the same in all the orders. He was admitted by the sheykh of the Demirdásheeyeh. Having first performed the ablution preparatory to prayer (the wuḍoó), he seated himself upon the ground before the sheykh, who was seated in like manner. The sheykh and he (the "mureed," or candidate,) then clasped their right hands together in the manner which I have described as practised in making the marriage-contract: in this attitude, and with their hands covered by the sleeve of the sheykh, the candidate took the covenant; repeating, after the sheykh, the following words, commencing with the form of a common oath of repentance. "I beg forgiveness of God, the Great" (three times); "than whom there is no other deity; the Living, the Everlasting: I turn to Him with repentance, and beg his grace, and forgiveness, and exemption from the fire." The sheykh then said to him, "Dost thou turn to God with repentance?" He replied, "I do turn to God with repentance; and I return unto God; and I am grieved for what I have done [amiss]; and I determine not to relapse:" and then repeated, after the sheykh, "I beg for the favour of God, the Great, and the noble Prophet; and I take as my sheykh, and my guide unto God (whose name be exalted), my master 'Abd-Er-Raḥeem Ed-Demirdáshee El-Khalwetee Er-Rifá'ee En-Nebawee; not to change, nor to separate; and God is our witness: by God, the Great!" (this oath was repeated three times): "there is no deity but God" (this also was repeated three times). The sheykh and the mureed then recited the Fát'ḥah together; and the latter concluded the ceremony by kissing the sheykh's hand.

The religious exercises of the darweeshes chiefly consist in the performance of "zikrs." Sometimes standing in the form of a circular or an oblong ring, or in two rows, facing each other, and sometimes sitting, they exclaim, or chant, "Lá iláha illa-lláh" (There is no deity but God), or "Alláh! Alláh! Alláh!" (God! God! God!), or repeat other invocations, &c., over and over again, until their strength is almost exhausted; accompanying their ejaculations or chants with a motion of the head, or of the whole body, or of the arms. From long habit they are able to continue these exercises for a surprising length of time without intermission. They are often accompanied, at intervals, by one or more players upon a kind of flute called "náy," or a double reed-pipe, called "arghool," and by persons singing religious odes; and some darweeshes use a little drum, called "báz,"[1] or a tambourine, during their zikrs: some, also, perform a peculiar dance; the description of which, as well as of several different zikrs, I reserve for future chapters.

Some of the rites of darweeshes (as forms of prayer, modes of zikr, &c.,) are observed only by particular orders: others, by members of various orders. Among the latter may be mentioned the rites of the "Khalwetees" and "Shάzilees;" two great classes, each of which has its sheykh. The chief difference between these is that each has its particular form of prayer to repeat every morning; and that the former distinguish themselves by occasional seclusion; whence their appellation of "Khalwetees:"[2] the prayer of this class is repeated before day-break, and is called "wird es-saḥar:" that of the Shάzilees, which is called "ḥezb esh-Shάzilee," after day-break. Sometimes, a Khalwetee enters a solitary cell, and remains in it for forty days and nights, fasting from day-break till sunset the whole of this period. Sometimes also a number of the same class confine themselves, each in a separate cell, in the sepulchral mosque of the sheykh Ed-Demirdáshee, on the north of Cairo, and remain there three days and nights, on the occasion of the moolid of that saint, and only eat a little rice, and drink a cup of sherbet, in the evening: they employ themselves in repeating certain forms of prayer, &c. not imparted to the uninitiated; only coming out of their cells to unite in the five daily prayers in the mosque; and never answering any one who speaks to them but by saying, "There is no deity but God." Those who observe the forty days' fast, and seclude themselves during that long period, practise nearly the same rules; and employ their time in repeating the testimony of the faith, imploring forgiveness, praising God, &c.

Almost all the darweeshes of Egypt are tradesmen or artisans or agriculturists; and only occasionally assist in the rites and ceremonies of their respective orders: but there are some who have no other occupations than those of performing zikrs at the festivals of saints and at private entertainments, and of chanting in funeral-processions. These are termed "fuḳarà," or "faḳeers;" which is an appellation given also to the poor in general, but especially to poor devotees.

---

1 For descriptions of the instruments here mentioned, see a subsequent chapter, on the Egyptian music, &c.

2 From "khalweh," a cell, or closet.

Some obtain their livelihood as water-carriers, by supplying the passengers in the streets of Cairo, and the visiters at religious festivals, with water, which they carry in an earthen vessel, or a goat's skin, on the back. A few lead a wandering life, and subsist on alms; which they often demand with great importunacy and effrontery. Some of these distinguish themselves in the same manner as certain reputed saints before mentioned, by the "dilk̦," or coat of patches, and the staff with shreds of cloth of different colours attached to the top: others wear fantastic dresses of various descriptions.

Some Rifá'ee darweeshes (besides those who follow the occupation of charming away serpents from houses) pursue a wandering life; travelling about Egypt, and profiting by a ridiculous superstition which I must here mention. A venerated saint, called See[1] Dá-ood El-'Azab (or Master David the Bachelor), who lived at Tefáhineh, a village in Lower Egypt, had a calf, which always attended him, and brought him water, &c. Since his death, some Rifá'ee darweeshes have been in the habit of rearing a number of calves at his native place, or burial-place, above named; teaching them to walk up stairs, to lie down at command, &c.; and then going about the country, each with his calf, to obtain alms. The calf is called "'Egl El-'Azab" (the Calf of El-'Azab, or—of the Bachelor). I once called into my house one of these darweeshes, with his calf, the only one I have seen: it was a buffalo-calf; and had two bells suspended to it; one attached to a collar round its neck, and the other to a girth round its body. It walked up the stairs very well; but shewed that it had not been very well trained in every respect. The 'Egl El-'Azab is vulgarly believed to bring into the house a blessing from the saint after whom it is called.

There are numerous wandering Turkish and Persian darweeshes in Egypt; and to these, more than to the few Egyptian darweeshes who lead a similar life, must the character for impudence and importunacy be ascribed. Very often, particularly in Ramaḍán, a foreign darweesh goes to the mosque of the Ḥasaneyn, which is that most frequented by the Turks and Persians, at the time of the Friday-prayers; and, when the Khaṭeeb is reciting the first khuṭbeh, passes between the ranks of persons who are sitting upon the floor, and places before each a little slip of paper upon which are written a few words, generally exhorta-

---

1 "See" is a vulgar contraction of "Seedee," which is itself a contraction of "Seyyidee," signifying "My Master," or "Mister."

tive to charity (as "He who giveth alms will be provided for"—"The poor darweesh asketh an alms," &c.); by which proceeding he usually obtains from each, or almost every person, a piece of five or ten faḍḍahs, or more. Many of the Persian darweeshes in Egypt carry an oblong bowl of cocoa-nut or wood or metal, in which they receive their alms, and put their food; and a wooden spoon; and most of the foreign darweeshes wear dresses peculiar to their respective orders: they are chiefly distinguished by the cap: the most common description of cap is of a sugar-loaf, or conical, shape, and made of felt: the other articles of dress are generally a vest and full drawers, or trousers, or a shirt and belt, and a coarse cloak, or long coat. The Persians here all affect to be Sunnees. The Turks are the more intrusive of the two classes.

Here I may mention another superstition of the Egyptians, and of the Arabs in general: namely, their belief that birds and beasts have a language by which they communicate their thoughts to each other, and celebrate the praises of God.

CHAPTER XI.

SUPERSTITIONS—*continued.*

One of the most remarkable traits in modern Egyptian superstition is the belief in written charms. The composition of most of these amulets is founded upon magic; and occasionally employs the pen of almost every village-schoolmaster in Egypt. A person of this profession, however, seldom pursues the study of magic further than to acquire the formulæ of a few charms, most commonly consisting, for the greater part, of certain passages of the Ḳur-án, and names of God, together with those of angels, genii, prophets, or eminent saints, intermixed with combinations of numerals, and with diagrams, all of which are supposed to have great secret virtues.

The most esteemed of all "ḥegábs" (or charms) is a "muṣ-ḥaf" (or copy of the Ḳur-án). It used to be the general custom of the Turks of the middle and higher orders, and of many other Muslims, to wear a small muṣ-ḥaf in an embroidered leather or velvet case hung upon the right side by a silk string which passed over the left shoulder: but this custom is not now very common. During my first visit to this country, a respectable Turk, in the military dress, was seldom seen without a case of this description upon his side, though it often contained no ḥegáb. The muṣ-ḥaf and other ḥegábs are still worn by many women; generally enclosed in cases of gold, or of gilt or plain silver. To the former, and to many other charms, most extensive efficacy is attributed; they are esteemed preservatives against disease, enchantment, the evil eye, and a variety of other evils. The charm next in point of estimation to the muṣ-ḥaf is a book or scroll containing certain chapters of the Ḳur-án; as the 6th, 18th, 36th, 44th, 55th, 67th, and 78th; or some others; generally seven.—Another charm, which is believed to protect the wearer (who usually places it within his cap) from the devil and all evil genii, and many other objects of fear, is a piece of paper inscribed with the following passages from the Ḳur-án,[1] "And the *preservation* of both [heaven and earth] is no burden unto Him: and He is the High, the Great" (ch. ii. v. 256). "But God is the best *protector;* and He is the most merciful of those who shew mercy" (ch. xii. v. 64). "They *watch* him by the command of God" (ch. xiii. v. 12). "And we *guard* them from every devil driven away with stones" (ch. xv. v. 17). "And a *guard* against every rebellious devil" (ch. xxxvii. v. 7). "And a *guard*. This is the decree of the Mighty, the Wise" (ch. lxi. v. 11). "And God encompasseth them behind. Verily it is a glorious Ḳur-án, [written] on a *preserved* tablet" (ch. lxxxv. vv. 20, 21, 22). —The ninety-nine names, or epithets, of God, comprising all the divine attributes, if frequently repeated, and written on a paper, and worn on the person, are supposed to make the wearer a particular object for the exercise of all the beneficent attributes.—In like manner it is believed that the ninety-nine names, or titles, &c., of the Prophet, written upon anything, compose a charm which (according to his own assertion, as recorded by his cousin and son-in-law the Imám 'Alee,) will, if placed in a house, and frequently read from beginning to end, keep away every misfortune, pestilence and all diseases, infirmity, the envious eye, enchantment, burning, ruin, anxiety, grief, and trouble. After repeating each of these names, the Muslim adds, "God bless and save him!"[2]—Similar virtues are ascribed to a charm composed of the names of the "Aṣ-ḥáb el-Kahf" (or Companions of the Cave, also called the Seven Sleepers), together with the name of their dog.[3] These names are sometimes engraved in the bottom of a drinking-cup, and more commonly on the round tray of tinned copper which, placed on a stool, forms the table for dinner, supper, &c.—Another charm, supposed to have similar efficacy, is composed of the names of those paltry articles of property which the Prophet left at his decease. These relics[4] were two "sebḥahs" (or rosaries), his "muṣ-ḥaf" (in unarranged fragments), his "muk-ḥulah" (or the vessel in which he kept the black powder

---

[1] Called "áyát el-ḥefẓ" (the verses of protection, or preservation).

[2] Just before I quitted my house in Cairo to return to England, a friend, who had been my sheykh (or tutor), wrote on a slip of paper, "There is no deity but God: Moḥammad is God's apostle:" then tore it in halves, gave me the latter half (on which was written "Moḥammad is God's apostle"), and concealed the other in a crack in the roof of a little cupboard in my usual sitting-room. This was to insure my coming back to Cairo: for it is believed that the profession of the faith cannot remain incomplete: so that by my keeping the latter half always upon my person, it would bring me back to the former half.

[3] These, it is said, were Christian youths of Ephesus, who took refuge from the persecution of the emperor Decius in a cave, and slept there, guarded by their dog, for the space of 300 [solar] or 309 [lunar] years. (See the Ḳur-án, chap. xviii.)

[4] Called "mukhallafát en-nebee."

with which he painted the edges of his eyelids), two "seggádehs" (or prayer carpets), a hand-mill, a staff, a tooth-stick, a suit of clothes,[1] the ewer which he used in ablution, a pair of sandals, a "burdeh" (or a kind of woollen covering),[2] three mats, a coat of mail, a long woollen coat, his white mule "ed-duldul," and his she-camel "el-'aḍbà."—Certain verses of the Ḳur-án are also written upon slips of paper, and worn upon the person as safeguards against various evils, and to procure restoration to health, love and friendship, food, &c. These and other charms, enclosed in cases of gold, silver, tin, leather, or silk, &c., are worn by many of the modern Egyptians, men, women, and children.

It is very common to see children in this country with a charm against the *evil eye*,[3] enclosed in a case, generally of a triangular form, attached to the top of the cap; and horses often have similar appendages. The Egyptians take many precautions against the evil eye; and anxiously endeavour to avert its imagined consequences. When a person expresses what is considered improper or envious admiration of anything, he is generally reproved by the individual whom he has thus alarmed, who says to him, "Bless the Prophet!"[4] and if the envier obeys, saying, "O God, bless him!"[5] no ill effects are apprehended. It is considered very improper for a person to express his admiration of another, or of any object which is not his own property, by saying, "God preserve us!"[6] "How pretty!" or, "Very pretty!" The most approved expression in such cases is "Má sháa-lláh!" (or "What God willeth [cometh to pass!"]); which implies both admiration, and submission to, or approval of, the will of God. A person who has exclaimed "How pretty!" or used similar words, is often desired to say, rather, "Má sháa-lláh!" as well as to bless the Prophet. In the second chapter of this work a remarkable illustration has been given of the fear which mothers in

---

1 A shirt which is said to have been worn by the Prophet is preserved in the mosque of El-Ghooree, in Cairo. It is wrapped in a Kashmeer shawl; and not shewn to any but persons of very high rank.

2 The "burdeh," which is worn by some of the peasants in Egypt, is an oblong piece of thick woollen stuff, resembling the "ḥerám," except in colour, being generally brown or greyish. It appears to have been, in earlier times, always striped; but some modern burdehs are plain, and others have stripes so narrow and near together, that at a little distance the stuff appears to be of one colour. The Prophet's is described as about seven feet and a half in length, and four and a half in width. It was used by him, as burdehs are at present, both to envelop the body by day, and as a night-covering.—I may be excused for remarking here (as it seems to be unknown to some Arabic scholars) that the terms "akhḍar" and "aḥmar," which are applied by different historians to the Prophet's burdeh, are used to signify respectively *grey* and *brown*, as well as *green* and *red*.

3 This superstition explains many customs which would otherwise seem unaccountable.

4 "Ṣallee 'a-n-nebee," for "—'ala-n-nebee."

5 "Alláhum (for Alláhumma) ṣallee 'aleyh."

6 The ejaculation which I thus translate is "Yá selám," or "Yá selámu sellim." "Es-Selám" is one of the names of the Deity.

Egypt entertain of the effect of the evil eye upon their children. It is the custom in this country, when a person takes the child of another into his arms, to say, "In the name of God, the Compassionate, the Merciful:" and, "O God, bless our lord Moḥammad:" and then to add, "Má sháa-lláh!" It is also a common custom of the people of Egypt, when admiring a child, to say, "I seek refuge with the Lord of the Day-break for thee:" alluding to the Chapter of the Day-break (the 113th chapter of the Ḳur-án); in the end of which, protection is implored against the mischief of the envious. The parents, when they see a person stare at, or seem to envy, their young offspring, sometimes cut off a piece of the skirts of his clothes, burn it with a little salt (to which some add coriander-seed, alum, &c.), and fumigate with the smoke, and sprinkle with the ashes, the child or children. This, it is said, should be done a little before sunset, when the sun becomes red.

Alum is very generally used, in the following manner, by the people of Egypt, to counteract the effects of the evil eye. A piece of about the size of a walnut is placed upon burning coals, and left until it has ceased to bubble. This should be done a short time before sunset; and the person who performs the operation should repeat three times, while the alum is burning, the first chapter of the Ḳur-án, and the last three chapters of the same; all of which are very short. On taking the alum off the fire, it will be found (we are told) to have assumed the form of the person whose envy or malice has given occasion for this process: it is then to be pounded, put into some food, and given to a black dog, to be eaten. I have once seen this done, by a man who suspected his wife of having looked upon him with an evil eye; and in this case, the alum did assume a form much resembling that of a woman, in what the man declared was a peculiar posture in which his wife was accustomed to sit. But the shape which the alum takes depends almost entirely upon the disposition of the coals; and can hardly be such that the imagination may not see in it some resemblance to a human being. —Another supposed mode of obviating the effects of the envious eye is, to prick a paper with a needle, saying, at the same time, "This is the eye of such a one, the envier;" and then to burn the paper.—Alum is esteemed a very efficacious charm against the evil eye: sometimes, a small, flat piece of it, ornamented with tassels, is hung to the top of a child's cap. A tassel of little shells and beads is also used in the same manner, and for the same purpose. The small shells called cowries are especially considered preservatives against the evil eye; and hence, as well as for the sake of ornament, they are often attached to the trappings of camels, horses, and other animals, and sometimes to the caps of children. Such appendages are evidently meant to attract the eye to themselves, and so to prevent observation and envy of the object which they are designed to protect.

To counteract the effects of the evil eye, many persons in Egypt, but mostly women, make use of what is called "mey'ah mubárakah" (or blessed storax), which is a mixture of various ingredients that will be mentioned below, prepared and sold only during the first ten days of the month of Moḥarram. During this period we often see, in the streets of Cairo, men carrying about this mixture of mey'ah, &c., for sale; and generally crying some such words as the following—"Mey'ah mubárakah! A new year and blessed 'Ashoorà![1] The most blessed of years [may this be] to the believers! Yá mey'ah mubárakah!"—The man who sells it bears upon his head a round tray, covered with different-coloured sheets of paper, red, yellow, &c.; upon which is placed the valued mixture. In the middle is a large heap of "tifl" (or refuse) of a dark reddish material for dyeing, mixed with a little "mey'ah" (or storax), coriander-seed,[2] and seed of the fennel-flower:[3] round this large heap are smaller heaps: one consisting of salt dyed blue with indigo; another, of salt dyed red; a third, of salt dyed yellow; a fourth, of "sheeḥ" (a kind of wormwood); a fifth, of dust of "libán" (or frankincense). These are all the ingredients of the "mey'ah mubárakah." The seller is generally called into the house of the purchaser. Having placed his tray before him, and received a plate, or a piece of paper, in which to put the quantity to be purchased, he takes a little from one heap, then from another, then from a third, and so on, until he has taken some from each heap; after which, again and again, he takes an additional quantity from each kind. While he does this, he chants a long spell, generally commencing thus:—"In the name of God! and by God! There is no conqueror that conquereth God, the Lord of the East and the West: we are all his servants: we must acknowledge his unity: his unity is an illustrious attribute." After some words on the virtues of salt, he proceeds to say, "I charm thee from the eye of girl, sharper than a spike; and from the eye of woman, sharper than

[1] This is the name of the tenth day of Moḥarram.

[2] "Kuzbarah."

[3] "Ḥabbeh sódà," or "ḥabbet el-barakeh."

a pruning-knife; and from the eye of boy, more painful than a whip; and from the eye of man, sharper than a chopping-knife;" and so on. Then he relates how Solomon deprived the evil eye of its influence; and afterwards enumerates every article of property that the house is likely to contain, and that the person who purchases his wonderful mixture may be conjectured to possess; all of which he charms against the influence of the eye. Many of the expressions which he employs in this spell are very ridiculous: words being introduced merely for the sake of rhyme.—The mey'ah mubárakah, a handful of which may be purchased for five faḍḍahs,[1] is treasured up by the purchaser during the ensuing year; and whenever it is feared that a child or other person is affected by the evil eye, a little of it is thrown upon some burning coals in a chafing-dish; and the smoke which results is generally made to ascend upon the supposed sufferer.

It is a custom among the higher and middle classes in Cairo, on the occasion of a marriage, to hang chandeliers in the street before the bridegroom's house; and it often happens that a crowd is collected to see a very large and handsome chandelier suspended: in this case, it is a common practice to divert the attention of the spectators by throwing down and breaking a large jar, or by some other artifice, lest an envious eye should cause the chandelier to fall. Accidents which confirm the Egyptians in their superstitions respecting the evil eye often occur: for instance, a friend of mine has just related to me, that, a short time ago, he saw a camel carrying two very large jars of oil: a woman stopped before it, and exclaimed, "God preserve us! What large jars!"—The conductor of the camel did not tell her to bless the Prophet; and the camel, a few minutes after, fell, and broke both the jars, and one of its own legs.

While writing these notes on modern Egyptian superstitions, I have been amused by a complaint of one of my Maṣree[2] friends, which will serve to illustrate what I have just stated.—"The Báshà," he said, "having, a few days ago, given up his monopoly of the meat, the butchers now slaughter for their own shops; and it is quite shocking to see fine sheep hung up in the streets, quite whole, tail[3] and all, before the public eye; so that every beggar who passes by envies them; and one might, therefore, as well eat poison as such meat."—My cook has made the same complaint to me; and, rather than purchase from one of the shops near at hand, takes the trouble

1 Equivalent to about a farthing and one-fifth.

2 That is, Caireen.

3 The fat of the tail is esteemed a dainty.

of going to one in a distant quarter, kept by a man who conceals his meat from the view of the passengers in the street.

Many of the tradesmen of the metropolis, and of other towns of Egypt, place over their shops (generally upon the hanging shutter which is turned up in front) a paper inscribed with the name of God, or that of the Prophet, or both, or the profession of the faith ("There is no deity but God: Moḥammad is God's Apostle"), the words "In the name of God, the Compassionate, the Merciful," or some maxim of the Prophet, or a verse of the Ḳur-án (as, "Verily we have granted thee a manifest victory" [ch. xlviii. v. 1], and "Assistance from God, and a speedy victory: and do thou bear good tidings to the believers" [ch. lxi. v. 13]), or an invocation to the Deity, such as, "O Thou Opener [of the doors of prosperity, or subsistence]! O Thou Wise! O Thou Supplier of our wants! O Thou Bountiful!"[1]—This invocation is often pronounced by the tradesman when he first opens his shop in the morning, and by the pedestrian vender of small commodities, bread, vegetables, &c., when he sets out on his daily rounds. It is a custom also among the lower orders to put the first piece of money that they receive in the day to the lips and forehead before putting it in the pocket.

Besides the inscriptions over shops, we often see, in Cairo, the invocation "O God!"[2] sculptured over the door of a private house; and the words "The Great Creator is the Everlasting," or "He is the Great Creator, the Everlasting," painted in large characters upon the door, both as a charm, and to remind the master of the house, whenever he enters it, of his own mortality.[3] These words are often inscribed upon the door of a house when its former master, and many or all of its former inhabitants, have been removed by death.

The most approved mode of charming away sickness or disease is to write certain passages of the Ḳur-án[4] on the inner surface of an earthenware cup or bowl; then to pour in some water, and stir it until the writing is quite washed off; when the water, with the sacred words thus infused in it, is to be drunk by the patient. These words are as follow: "And He will *heal* the breasts of the people who believe" (ch. ix. v. 14). "O men, now hath an admonition come unto you from your Lord; and a *remedy* for what is in your

---

[1] "Yá fettáḥ! Yá 'aleem! Yá rezzáḳ! Yá kereem!"

[2] "Yá Alláh!"

[3] See the engraving of a door with this inscription inserted in the Introduction.

[4] Called "áyát esh-shifè" (the verses of restoration).

breasts" (ch. x. v. 58). "Wherein is a *remedy* for men" (ch. xvi. v. 71). "We send down, of the Ḳur-án, that which is a *remedy* and mercy to the believers" (ch. xvii. v. 84). "And when I am sick He *healeth* me" (ch. xxii. v. 80). "Say, It is, to those who believe, a guide and a *remedy*" (ch. xli. v. 44).—Four of these verses, notwithstanding they are thus used, refer not to diseases of the *body*, but of the *mind*; and another (the third) alludes to the virtues of *honey!*—On my applying to my sheykh (or tutor) to point out to me in what chapters these verses were to be found, he begged me not to translate them into my own language; because the translation of the Ḳur-án, unaccompanied by the original text, is prohibited: not that he seemed ashamed of the practice of employing these words as a charm, and did not wish my countrymen to be informed of the custom: for he expressed his full belief in their efficacy, even in the case of an infidel patient, provided he had proper confidence in their virtue; "Seeing," he observed, "that the Prophet (God bless and save him) has said, 'If thou confide in God, with true confidence, He will sustain thee as He sustaineth the birds.'" I silenced his scruples on the subject of translating these verses by telling him that we had an English translation of the whole of the Ḳur-án.—Sometimes, for the cure of diseases, and to counteract poisons, &c., a draught of water from a metal cup, having certain passages of the Ḳur-án, and talismanic characters and figures, engraved in the interior, is administered to the patient. I have a cup of this description, lately given to me[1] here (in Cairo), much admired by my Muslim acquaintances. On the exterior is an inscription enumerating its virtues: it is said to possess charms that will counteract all poisons, &c., and the evil eye, and cure "sicknesses and diseases, except the sickness of death." I have seen, here, another cup which appeared to have been exactly similar to that above mentioned; but its inscriptions were partly effaced.—The secret virtues of the Ḳur-án[2] are believed to be very numerous. One day, on my refusing to eat of a dish that I feared would do me harm, I was desired to repeat the Soorat Ḳureysh (106th chapter of the Ḳur-án) to the end of the words "supplieth them with food against hunger;" and to repeat these last words three times. This, I was assured, would be a certain preventive of any harm that I might have feared.

There are various things which are regarded in the same light as

[1] By Robert Hay, Esq., who purchased it from a peasant at Thebes.

[2] "Asrár el-Ḳur-án."

written charms; such as dust from the tomb of the Prophet, water from the sacred well of Zemzem, in the Temple of Mekkeh, and pieces of the black brocade covering of the Kaạbeh.[1] The water of Zemzem is much valued for the purpose of sprinkling upon grave-clothes.—An Arab, to whom I had given some medicine which had been beneficial to him, in the Ṣa'eed, during my first visit to this country, heard me inquire for some Zemzem-water (as several boats full of pilgrims on their return from Mekkeh were coming down the Nile), and perhaps thought, from my making this inquiry, that I was a pious Muslim: accordingly, to shew his gratitude to me, he gave me what I was seeking to obtain. Having gone to the house of a friend, he returned to my boat, bringing a small bundle, which he opened before me. "Here," said he, "are some things which, I know, you will value highly. Here are two tin flasks of the water of Zemzem: one of them you shall have: you may keep it to sprinkle your grave-clothing with it. This is a 'miswák' (a tooth-stick) dipped in the water of Zemzem: accept it from me: clean your teeth with it, and they will never ache, nor decay. And here," he added (shewing me three small, oblong and flat cakes, of a kind of greyish earth, each about an inch in length, and stamped with Arabic characters, 'In the name of God: Dust of our land [mixed] with the saliva of some of us'), "these are composed of earth from over the grave of the Prophet (God bless and save him): I purchased them myself in the noble tomb, on my return from the pilgrimage: one of them I give to you: you will find it a cure for every disease: the second I shall keep for myself; and the third we will eat together."—Upon this, he broke in halves one of the three cakes; and we each ate our share. I agreed with him that it was delicious; and I gladly accepted his presents.—I was afterwards enabled to make several additions to my Mekkeh curiosities; comprising a piece of the covering of the Kaạbeh, brought from Mekkeh by the sheykh Ibráheem (Burckhardt), and given to me by his legatee 'Osmán. A cake composed of dust from the Prophet's tomb is sometimes sewed up in a leathern case, and worn as an amulet. It is also formed into lumps of the shape and size of a small pear, and hung to the railing or screen which surrounds the monument over the grave of a saint, or to the monument itself, or to the windows or door of the apartment which contains it.

---

1 Every year, on the first day of the Great Festival, which immediately follows the pilgrimage, a new covering is hung upon the Kaạbeh. The old one is cut up; and the greater part of it is sold to the pilgrims.

So numerous are the charms which the Egyptians employ to insure good fortune, or to prevent or remove evils of every kind, and so various are the superstitious practices to which they have recourse with these views, that a large volume would scarcely suffice to describe them in detail. These modes of endeavouring to obtain good, and to avoid or dispel evil, when they are not founded upon religion or magic or astrology, are termed matters of "'ilm er-rukkeh," or the science of the distaff (that is, of the women); which designation is given to imply their absurdity, and because women are the persons who most confide in them. This term is considered, by some, as a vulgar corruption of "'ilm er-rukyeh," or "the science of enchantment:" by others, it is supposed to be substituted for the latter term by way of a pun. Some practices of the nature just described have already been incidentally mentioned: I shall only give a few other specimens.

It is a very common custom in Cairo to hang an aloe-plant over the door of a house; particularly over that of a new house, or over a door newly built: and this is regarded as a charm to insure long and flourishing lives to the inmates, and long continuance to the house itself.[1] The women also believe that the Prophet visits the house where this plant is suspended. The aloe, thus hung, without earth or water, will live for several years; and even blossom. Hence it is called "ṣabr," which signifies "patience;" but more properly "ṣabbárah;" "ṣabr," a contraction of "ṣabir," being generally applied to the expressed juice.

When any evil is apprehended from a person, it is customary to break a piece of pottery behind his back. This is also done with the view of preventing further intercourse with such a person.

As ophthalmia is very prevalent in Egypt, the ignorant people of this country resort to many ridiculous practices of a superstitious nature for its cure. Some, for this purpose, take a piece of dried mud, from the bank of the Nile at or near Booláḳ, the principal port of Cairo, and, crossing the river, deposit it on the opposite bank, at Imbábeh. This is considered sufficient to insure a cure.—Others, with the same view, hang to the head-dress, over the forehead, or over the diseased eye, a Venetian sequin;[2] but it must be one of a particular description, in which the figures on each side correspond,

[1] It has been said, by a traveller, that this is only done at pilgrims' houses: but such is not the case, at least in Egypt.

[2] "Benduḳee."

head to head, and feet to feet.[1] Yet, if a person having a Venetian sequin, or a dollar, in his pocket, enters the room of one who is suffering from ophthalmia or fever, his presence is thought to aggravate the complaint. It is also a general belief, here, that, if an individual in a state of religious uncleanness enters a room in which is a person afflicted with ophthalmia, the patient's disease will consequently be aggravated, and that a speck will appear in one or each of his eyes. A man with whom I am acquainted has, at the time I write this, just come out of a room in which he had confined himself, while suffering from ophthalmia, for about three months, from this fear; never allowing any person to enter; his servant always placing his food outside his door. He has, however, come out with a speck in one of his eyes.

Another practice, which is often adopted in similar cases, but mostly by women, and frequently with the view of preventing barrenness, is very singular and disgusting. The large open place called the Rumeyleh, on the west of the Citadel of Cairo, is a common scene of the execution of criminals; and the decapitation of persons convicted of capital offences in the metropolis was formerly almost always performed there, rather than in any other part of the town. On the south of this place is a building called "Maghsil es-Sulṭán," or the Sulṭán's washing-place for the dead; where is a table of stone, upon which the body of every person who is decapitated is washed, previously to its burial, and there is a trough to receive the water, which is never poured out, but remains tainted with the blood, and fetid. Many a woman goes thither, and, for the cure of ophthalmia, or to obtain offspring, or to expedite delivery in the case of a protracted pregnancy, without speaking (for silence is deemed absolutely necessary), passes under the stone table above mentioned, with the left foot foremost, and then over it; and does this seven times; after which, she washes her face with the polluted water that is in the trough, and gives five or ten faḍḍahs to an old man and his wife, who keep the place; then goes away, still without speaking. Men, in the case of ophthalmia, often do the same. The Maghsil is said to have been built by the famous Beybars, before he became Sulṭán; in consequence of his observing that the remains of persons decapitated in Cairo were often kicked about, and buried without being previously washed.

---

[1] A sequin of this description is termed "benduḳee musháharah."

Some women step over the body of a decapitated man seven times, without speaking, to become pregnant; and some, with the same desire, dip in the blood a piece of cotton wool, of which they afterwards make use in a manner I must decline mentioning.

A ridiculous ceremony is practised for the cure of a pimple on the edge of the eye-lid, or what we commonly call a "sty," and which is termed in Egypt "shaḥḥáteh;" a word which literally signifies "a female beggar."[1] The person affected with it goes to any seven women of the name of Fáṭ'meh, in seven different houses, and begs from each of them a morsel of bread: these seven morsels constitute the remedy.—Sometimes, in a similar case, and for the same purpose, a person goes out before sunrise, and, without speaking, walks round several tombs, from right to left, which is the reverse of the regular course made in visiting tombs.—Another supposed mode of cure in a case of the same kind is, to bind a bit of cotton on the end of a stick; then to dip it in one of the troughs out of which the dogs drink in the streets of Cairo, and to wipe the eye with it. The patient is thus careful to preserve his hand from the polluted water, when he is about to apply this to another part of his person.

As an imaginary cure for ague, some of the women of Egypt (I mean those of the Muslim faith) hang to their necks the finger of a Christian or Jew, cut off a corpse, and dried. This and other practices mentioned before are striking proofs of the degrading effects of superstition, and of its powerful influence over the mind: for, in general, the Muslims are scrupulously careful to conform with that precept of their religion which requires them to abstain from everything polluting or unclean.

When a child is unable to walk, after having attained the age when it is usual to begin to do so, it is a common custom for the mother to bind its feet together with a palm-leaf tied in three knots, and to place it at the door of a mosque during the period when the congregation are engaged in performing the Friday-prayers: when the prayers are ended, she asks the first, second, and third persons who come out of the mosque to untie each a knot of the palm-leaf; and then carries the child home, confident that this ceremony will soon have the desired effect.

There are several pretended antidotes for poison, and remedies for certain diseases, to which the Egyptians often have recourse, and which

[1] Being a corruption of "shaḥḥádheh."

may perhaps have some efficacy: but superstition attributes to them incredible virtues. Of the beneficial and the injurious properties of various vegetable and animal substances, either in themselves or in particular circumstances, the most absurd notions are entertained, even by the generality of the more learned and enlightened; being sanctioned in some instances by traditions related as being precepts of Moḥammad, and in general by the authority of their most eminent physicians. The bezoar-stone[1] is used as an antidote for poison, by rubbing it in a cup with a little water: the cup is then filled with water, which the patient drinks. In the same manner, and for the same purpose, a cup made of the horn of the rhinoceros[2] is used: a piece of the same material (the horn) is rubbed in it.—As a cure for the jaundice, many persons in Cairo drink the water of a well in this city, called "beer el-yaraḳán," or "the well of the jaundice." It is the property of an old woman, who reaps considerable advantage from it: for it has two mouths, under one of which is a dry receptacle for anything that may be thrown down: and the old woman desires the persons who come to use the medicinal water to drop through this mouth whatever she happens to be in need of; as sugar, coffee, &c.

The Muslims have recourse to many superstitious practices to determine them when they are in doubt as to any action which they contemplate, whether they shall do it or not. Some apply, for an answer, to a table called a "záïrgeh." There is a table of this kind ascribed to Idrees, or Enoch. It is divided into a hundred little squares, in each of which is written some Arabic letter. The person who consults it repeats, three times, the opening chapter of the Ḳur-án, and the 59th verse of the Soorat el-An'ám (or 6th chapter) —"With Him are the keys of the secret things: none knoweth them but He: and He knoweth whatever is on the land and [what is] in the sea: and there falleth not a leaf, but He knoweth it, nor a grain in the dark parts of the earth, nor a moist thing nor a dry thing, but [it is noted] in a distinct writing."—Having done this, without looking directly at the table, he places his finger upon it: he then looks to see upon what letter his finger is placed; writes that letter; the fifth following it; the fifth following this; and so on, until he comes again to the first which he wrote; and these letters together compose the answer. The construction of the table may be shewn by translating it, thus:—

---

[1] "Ḥagar el-benzaheer."

[2] "Ḳarn kharteet."

d	w	w	a	w	o	h	a	b	h
i	o	i	s	o	t	d	t	t	w
w	o	a	a	a	i	e	n	i	i
t	s	d	n	t	h	i	a	a	e
o	t	t	n	t	u	w	t	d	h
t	i	a	e	s	f	l	i	n	u
e	l	n	j	c	a	d	t	o	c
r	o	h	y	e	o	w	y	p	e
f	r	w	e	d	i	o	i	a	e
l	n	s	c	t	l	g	h	e	h

For an example, suppose the finger to be placed on the letter *e* in the sixth line: we take, from the table, the letters *e n j o y p e a c e a b s t a i n a n d*, which compose this sentence: "Abstain, and enjoy peace:" the sentence always commencing with the first of the letters taken from the uppermost line. It will be seen that the table gives only five answers; and that, if we proceed as above directed, we must obtain one of these answers, with whatever letter of the table we commence. It will also be observed, that the framer of the table, knowing that men very frequently wish to do what is wrong, and seldom to do what is right, and that it is generally safer for them to abstain when in doubt, has given but one affirmative answer, and four negative.[1]

Some persons have recourse to the Ḳur-án for an answer to their doubts. This they call making an "istikhárah," or application for the favour of heaven, or for direction in the right course. Repeating, three times, the opening chapter, the 112th chapter, and the verse above quoted, they let the book fall open, or open it at random, and, from the seventh line of the right-hand page, draw their answer. The words often will not convey a direct answer; but are taken as affirmative or negative according as their general tenour is good or bad; promising a blessing, or denouncing a threat, &c. Instead of reading the seventh line of this page, some count the number of the letters

---

1 The more approved záïrgehs are extremely complicated; and the process of consulting them involves intricate astrological calculations.

"khá" and "sheen" which occur in the whole page; and if the "khás" predominate, the inference is favourable: "khá" represents "kheyr," or "good:" "sheen," "sharr," or "evil."

There is another mode of istikhárah; which is, to take hold of any two points of a "sebḥah" (or rosary), after reciting the Fát'ḥah three times, and then to count the beads between these two points, saying, in passing the first bead through the fingers, "[I extol] the perfection of God;"[1] in passing the second, "Praise be to God;"[2] in passing the third, "There is no deity but God;"[3] and repeating these expressions in the same order, to the last bead: if the first expression fall to the last bead, the answer is affirmative and favourable: if the second, indifferent: if the last, negative. This is practised by many persons.

Some, again, in similar cases, on lying down to sleep, at night, beg of God to direct them by a dream; by causing them to see something white or green, or water, if the action which they contemplate be approved, or if they are to expect approaching good fortune; and if not, by causing them to see something black or red, or fire: they then recite the Fát'ḥah ten times; and continue to repeat these words—"O God, bless our lord Moḥammad!"—until they fall asleep.

The Egyptians place great faith in dreams, which often direct them in some of the most important actions of life. They have two large and celebrated works on the interpretation of dreams, by Ibn-Sháheen and Ibn-Seereen; the latter of whom was the pupil of the former. These books are consulted, even by many of the learned, with implicit confidence. When one person says to another, "I have seen a dream," the latter usually replies, "Good"[4] (*i. e.* may it be of good omen), or, "Good, please God."[5] When a person has had an evil dream, it is customary for him to say, "O God, bless our lord Moḥammad:" and to spit over his left shoulder three times, to prevent an evil result.

In Egypt, as in most other countries, superstitions are entertained respecting days of the week; some being considered fortunate; and others, unfortunate.—The Egyptians regard *Sunday* as an *unfortunate* day, on account of the night which follows it.—This night, which (according to the system already mentioned) is called the night of *Monday*, the learned Muslims, and many of the inferior classes,

---

1 "Subḥána-lláh."
2 "El-ḥamdu li-lláh."
3 "Lá iláha illa-lláh."
4 "Kheyr."
5 "Kheyr in sháa-lláh."

consider *unfortunate,* because it was that of the death of their Prophet; but some regard it as *fortunate,* particularly for the consummation of marriage; though not so auspicious for this affair as the eve of Friday. The day following it is also considered, by some, as *fortunate;* and by others, as *unfortunate.*—*Tuesday* is generally thought *unfortunate,* and called "the day of blood;" as it is said that several eminent martyrs were put to death on this day: and hence, also, it is commonly esteemed a proper day for being bled.—*Wednesday* is regarded as *indifferent.*—*Thursday* is called "el-mubárak" (or, the blessed); and is considered *fortunate;* particularly deriving a blessing from the following night and day.—The eve, or night, of *Friday* is *very fortunate;* especially for the consummation of marriage. Friday is blessed above all other days as being the sabbath of the Muslims: it is called "el-faḍeeleh" (or, the excellent).—*Saturday* is the *most unfortunate* of days. It is considered very wrong to commence a journey, and, by most people in Egypt, to shave, or cut the nails, on this day.—A friend of mine here was doubting whether he should bring an action against two persons on so unfortunate a day as Saturday: he decided, at last, that it was the best day of the week for him to do this, as the ill fortune must fall upon one of the two parties only, and doubtless upon his adversaries, because they were two to one.—There are some days of the *year* which are esteemed very fortunate; as those of the two grand festivals, &c.: and some which are regarded as unfortunate; as, for instance, the last Wednesday in the month of Ṣafar: when many persons make a point of not going out of their houses, from the belief that numerous afflictions fall upon mankind on that day.[1]—Some persons draw lucky or unlucky omens from the first object they see on going out of the house in the morning: according as that object is pleasant or the reverse, they say, "our morning is good" or "—bad." A one-eyed person is regarded as of evil omen; and especially one who is blind of the *left* eye.

[1] This superstition, however, was condemned by the Prophet.

CHAPTER XII.

MAGIC, ASTROLOGY, AND ALCHYMY.

If we might believe some stories which are commonly related in Egypt, it would appear that, in modern days, there have been, in this country, magicians not less skilful than Pharoah's "wise men and sorcerers" of whom we read in the Bible.

The more intelligent of the Muslims distinguish two kinds of magic, which they term "Er-Rooḥánee" (*vulgò*, "Rowḥánee") and "Es-Seemiyà:" the former is *spiritual* magic, which is believed to effect its wonders by the agency of angels and genii, and by the mysterious virtues of certain names of God, and other supernatural means: the latter is *natural* and *deceptive* magic; and its chief agents, the less credulous Muslims believe to be certain perfumes and drugs, which affect the vision and imagination nearly in the same manner as opium: this drug, indeed, is supposed, by some persons, to be employed in the operations of the latter branch of magic.

"Er-Rooḥánee," which is universally considered, among the Egyptians, as *true* magic, is of two kinds, "'ilwee" (or high) and "suflee" (or low); which are also called "raḥmánee" (or divine, or, literally, relating to "the Compassionate," which is an epithet of God,) and "sheyṭánee" (or satanic).—The 'ilwee, or raḥmánee, is said to be a science founded on the agency of God, and of his angels, and good genii, and on other lawful mysteries; to be always employed for good purposes, and only attained and practised by men of probity, who, by tradition, or from books, learn the names of those superhuman agents, and invocations which insure compliance with their desires. The writing of charms for good purposes belongs to this branch of magic, and to astrology, and to the science of the mysteries of numbers. The highest attainment in divine magic consists in the knowledge of the "Ism el-Aạẓam." This is "the most great name" of God, which is generally believed, by the learned, to be known to none but prophets and apostles of God. A person acquainted with it can, it is said, by merely uttering it, raise the dead to life, kill the living, transport himself instantly wherever he pleases, and perform any other miracle. Some suppose it to be known to eminent welees.—The suflee is believed to depend on the agency of the devil, and other evil genii; and to be used for bad purposes, and by bad men. To this branch belongs the science called, by the Arabs, "es-seḥr;" which is a term they give only to wicked enchantment.—Those who perform what is called "ḍarb el-mendel" (of which I purpose to relate some examples) profess to do it by the agency of genii; that is, by the science called er-rooḥánee: but there is another opinion on this subject which will be presently mentioned.—One of the means by which genii are believed to assist magicians has been explained in the second paragraph of Chapter X.

"Es-Seemiyà" is generally pronounced, by the learned, to be a false science, and deceptive art, which produces surprising effects by those natural means which have been above mentioned; and the "ḍarb el-mendel," as perfumes are employed in the performance of it, is considered, by such persons, as pertaining to es-seemiyà.

"'Ilm en-Nugoom," or Astrology, is studied by many persons in Egypt. It is chiefly employed in casting nativities, and in determining fortunate periods, &c.; and very commonly, to divine by what sign of the zodiac a person is influenced; which is usually done by a calculation founded upon the numerical values of the letters composing his or her name, and that of the mother: this is often done in the case of two persons who contemplate becoming man and wife, with the view of ascertaining whether they will agree.—The science called "ḍarb er-raml," or geomancy, by which, from certain marks made at random on paper, or on sand (whence it is said to derive its name), the professors pretend to discover past, passing, and future events, is, I am informed, mainly founded on astrology.

"El-Keemiyà," or Alchymy, is also studied by many persons in Egypt, and by some possessed of talents by which they might obtain a better reputation than this pursuit procures them, and who, in spite of the derision which they experience from a few men of sounder minds, and the reproaches of those whom they unintentionally make their dupes, continue, to old age, their fruitless labours. Considerable knowledge of chemistry is, however, sometimes acquired in the study of this false science; and in the present degraded state of physical knowledge in this country, it rather evinces a superior mind when a person gives his attention to alchymy.

There is, or was,[1] a native of Egypt very highly celebrated for his performances in the higher kind of that branch of magic called er-rooḥánee; the sheykh Isma'eel Aboo-Ru-oos, of the town of Dasooḳ. Even the more learned and sober of the people of this country relate most incredible stories of his magical skill; for which some of them account by asserting his having been married to a "ginneeyeh" (or female genie); and others, merely by his having "ginn" at his service, whom he could mentally consult and command, without making use of any such charm as the lamp of 'Alá-ed-Deen.[2] He is said to have always employed this supernatural power either for good or innocent purposes; and to have been much favoured by Moḥammad 'Alee, who, some say, often consulted him. One of the most sensible of my Muslim friends, in this place (Cairo), informs me that he once visited Aboo-Ru-oos, at Dasooḳ, in company with the sheykh El-Emeer, son of the sheykh El-Emeer el-Kebeer, sheykh of the sect of the Málikees. My friend's companion asked their host to shew them some proof of his skill in magic; and the latter complied with the request. "Let coffee be served to us," said the sheykh El-Emeer, "in my father's set of fingáns and ẓarfs, which are in Maṣr." They waited a few minutes; and then the coffee was brought; and the sheykh El-Emeer looked at the fingáns and ẓarfs, and said that they were certainly his father's. He was next treated with sherbet, in what he declared himself satisfied were his father's ḳullehs. He then wrote a letter to his father, and, giving it to Aboo-Ru-oos, asked him to procure an answer to it. The magician took the letter, placed it behind a cushion of his deewán, and, a few minutes after, removing the cushion, shewed him that this letter was gone, and that another was in its place. The sheykh El-Emeer took the latter; opened and read it; and found in it, in a handwriting which, he said, he could have sworn to be that of his father, a complete answer to what he had written, and an account of the state of

---

[1] I was informed that he had died during my second visit to Egypt.

[2] I must be excused for deviating from our old and erroneous mode of writing the name of the master of "the wonderful lamp." It is vulgarly pronounced 'Aláy-ed-Deen.

his family which he proved, on his return to Cairo, a few days after, to be perfectly true.[1]

A curious case of magic fell under the cognizance of the government during my former visit to this country; and became a subject of general talk and wonder throughout the metropolis. I shall give the story of this occurrence precisely as it was related to me by several persons in Cairo; without curtailing it of any of the exaggerations with which they embellished it; not only because I am ignorant how far it is true, but because I would shew how great a degree of faith the Egyptians in general place in magic, or enchantment.

Muṣṭafà Ed-Digwee, chief secretary in the Ḳáḍee's court, in this city, was dismissed from his office, and succeeded by another person of the name of Muṣṭafà, who had been a ṣeyrefee, or money-changer. The former sent a petition to the Báshà, begging to be reinstated; but before he received an answer, he was attacked by a severe illness, which he believed to be the effect of enchantment: he persuaded himself that Muṣṭafà the ṣeyrefee had employed a magician to write a spell which should cause him to die; and therefore sent a second time to the Báshà, charging the new secretary with this crime. The accused was brought before the Báshà; confessed that he had done so; and named the magician whom he had employed. The latter was arrested; and, not being able to deny the charge brought against him, was thrown into prison, there to remain until it should be seen whether or not Ed-Digwee would die. He was locked up in a small cell; and two soldiers were placed at the door, that one of them might keep watch while the other slept.—Now for the marvellous part of the story.—At night, after one of the guards had fallen asleep, the other heard a strange, murmuring noise, and, looking through a crack of the door of the cell, saw the magician sitting in the middle of the floor, muttering some words which he (the guard) could not understand. Presently, the candle which was before him became extinguished; and, at the same instant, four other candles appeared; one in each corner of the cell. The magician then rose, and, standing on one side of the cell, knocked his forehead three times against the wall; and each time that he did so, the wall opened,

[1] Of a more famous magician, the sheykh Aḥmad Ṣádoomeh, who flourished in Egypt in the latter half of the last century, an account is given in my translation of the Thousand and One Nights, chap. i., note 15.

and a man appeared to come forth from it. After the magician had conversed for some minutes with the three personages whom he thus produced, they disappeared; as did, also, the four candles; and the candle that was in the midst of the cell became lighted again, as at first: the magician then resumed his position on the floor; and all was quiet. Thus the spell that was to have killed Ed-Digwee was dissolved. Early the next morning, the invalid felt himself so much better, that he called for a basin and ewer, performed the ablution, and said his prayers; and from that time he rapidly recovered. He was restored to his former office; and the magician was banished from Egypt.—Another enchanter (or "saḥḥár") was banished a few days after, for writing a charm which caused a Muslimeh girl to be affected with an irresistible love for a Copt Christian.

A few days after my first arrival in this country, my curiosity was excited on the subject of magic by a circumstance related to me by Mr. Salt, our Consul-general. Having had reason to believe that one of his servants was a thief, from the fact of several articles of property having been stolen from his house, he sent for a celebrated Maghrabee magician, with the view of intimidating them, and causing the guilty one (if any of them were guilty) to confess his crime. The magician came; and said that he would cause the exact image of the person who had committed the thefts to appear to any youth not arrived at the age of puberty; and desired the master of the house to call in any boy whom he might choose. As several boys were then employed in a garden adjacent to the house, one of them was called for this purpose. In the palm of this boy's right hand, the magician drew, with a pen, a certain diagram, in the centre of which he poured a little ink. Into this ink, he desired the boy stedfastly to look. He then burned some incense, and several bits of paper inscribed with charms; and at the same time called for various objects to appear in the ink. The boy declared that he saw all these objects, and, last of all, the image of the guilty person; he described his stature, countenance, and dress; said that he knew him; and directly ran down into the garden, and apprehended one of the labourers, who, when brought before the master, immediately confessed that he was the thief.

The above relation made me desirous of witnessing a similar performance during my first visit to this country; but not being acquainted with the name of the magician here alluded to, or his place of abode, I was unable to obtain any tidings of him. I learned, however, soon after my return to England, that he had become known to later travellers in Egypt; was residing in Cairo; and that he was called the sheykh 'Abd-El-Ḳádir El-Maghrabee. A few weeks after my second arrival in Egypt, my neighbour 'Osmán, interpreter of the British consulate, brought him to me; and I fixed a day for his visiting me, to give me a proof of the skill for which he is so much famed. He came at the time appointed, about two hours before noon; but seemed uneasy; frequently looked up at the sky, through the window; and remarked that the weather was unpropitious: it was dull and cloudy; and the wind was boisterous. The experiment was performed with three boys; one after another. With the first, it was partly successful; but with the others, it completely failed. The magician said that he could do nothing more that day; and that he would come in the evening of a subsequent day. He kept his appointment; and admitted that the time was favourable. While waiting for my neighbour, before mentioned, to come and witness the performances, we took pipes and coffee; and the magician chatted with me on indifferent subjects. He is a fine, tall, and stout man, of a rather fair complexion, with a dark-brown beard; is shabbily dressed; and generally wears a large green turban, being a descendant of the Prophet. In his conversation, he is affable and unaffected. He professed to me that his wonders were effected by the agency of *good* spirits; but to others, he has said the contrary: that his magic is satanic.

In preparing for the experiment of the magic mirror of ink, which, like some other performances of a similar nature, is here termed "ḍarb el-mendel," the magician first asked me for a reed-pen and ink, a piece of paper, and a pair of scissors; and, having cut off a narrow strip of paper, wrote upon it certain forms of invocation, together with another charm, by which he professes to accomplish the object of the experiment. He did not attempt to conceal these; and on my asking him to give me copies of them, he readily consented, and immediately wrote them for me; explaining to me, at the same time, that the object he had in view was accomplished through the influence of the first two words, "Ṭarshun" and "Ṭaryooshun,"[1] which, he said, were the names of two genii, his "familiar spirits." I compared the copies with the originals; and found that they exactly agreed. Fac-similes of them are here inserted, with a translation.

[1] Or, "Ṭarsh" and "Ṭaryoosh;" the final "un" being the inflexion which denotes the nominative case.

طرتش طريوتش انزلوا
انزلوا احضروا اى مذهب
الا مير وجنوده الى الاحمر
الابير وجنوده احضروا
يا خدام هذه الاسماء

ههذا الكاشف فكشفنا عنك
عطاءك فبصرك اليوم
حديد حيح صح

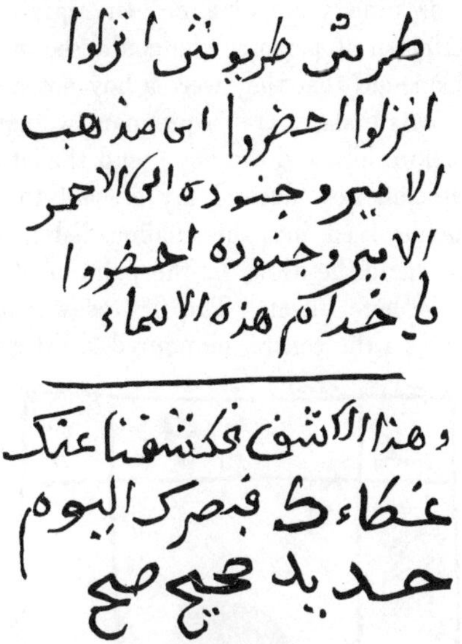

Magic Invocation and Charm.

"Ṭarshun! Ṭaryooshun! Come down!
Come down! Be present! Whither are gone
the prince and his troops? Where are El-Aḥmar
the prince and his troops? Be present
ye servants of these names!"

"And this is the removal. 'And we have removed from thee
thy veil; and thy sight to-day
is piercing.' Correct: correct."

Having written these, the magician cut off the paper containing the
forms of invocation from that upon which the other charm was
written; and cut the former into six strips. He then explained to
me that the object of the latter charm (which contains part of the
21st verse of the Soorat Ḳáf, or 50th chapter of the Ḳur-án) was to
open the boy's eyes in a supernatural manner; to make his sight
pierce into what is to us the invisible world.

I had prepared, by the magician's direction, some frankincense
and coriander-seed,[1] and a chafing-dish with some live charcoal in
it. These were now brought into the room, together with the boy
who was to be employed: he had been called in, by my desire, from
among some boys in the street, returning from a manufactory; and

---

[1] He generally requires some benzoin to be added to these.

was about eight or nine years of age. In reply to my inquiry respecting the description of persons who could see in the magic mirror of ink, the magician said that they were a boy not arrived at puberty, a virgin, a black female slave, and a pregnant woman. The chafing-dish was placed before him and the boy; and the latter was placed on a seat. The magician now desired my servant to put some frankincense and coriander-seed into the chafing-dish; then taking hold of the boy's right hand, he drew, in the palm of it, a magic square, of which a copy is here given. The figures which it contains are Arabic numerals.[1] In the centre, he poured a little ink, and desired

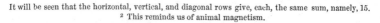

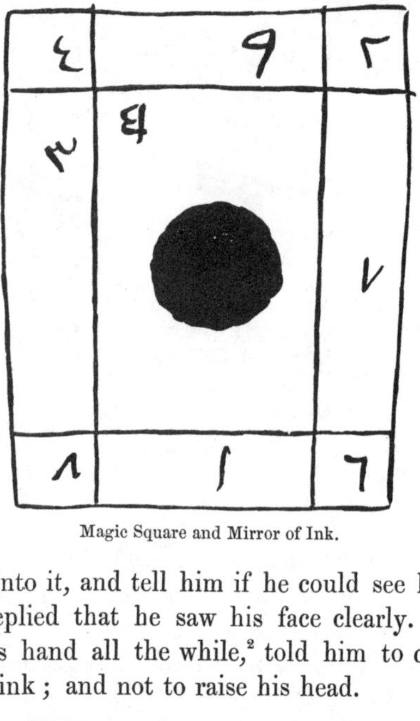

Magic Square and Mirror of Ink.

the boy to look into it, and tell him if he could see his face reflected in it: the boy replied that he saw his face clearly. The magician, holding the boy's hand all the while,[2] told him to continue looking intently into the ink; and not to raise his head.

---

[1] The numbers in this magic square, in our own ordinary characters, are as follow:—

4	9	2
3	5	7
8	1	6

It will be seen that the horizontal, vertical, and diagonal rows give, each, the same sum, namely, 15.

[2] This reminds us of animal magnetism.

He then took one of the little strips of paper inscribed with the forms of invocation, and dropped it into the chafing-dish, upon the burning coals and perfumes, which had already filled the room with their smoke; and as he did this, he commenced an indistinct muttering of words, which he continued during the whole process, except when he had to ask the boy a question, or to tell him what he was to say. The piece of paper containing the words from the Ḳur-án he placed inside the fore part of the boy's ṭáḳeeyeh, or skull-cap. He then asked him if he saw anything in the ink; and was answered, "No:" but about a minute after, the boy, trembling, and seeming much frightened, said, "I see a man sweeping the ground." "When he has done sweeping," said the magician, "tell me." Presently, the boy said, "He has done." The magician then again interrupted his muttering to ask the boy if he knew what a "beyraḳ" (or flag) was; and, being answered, "Yes," desired him to say, "Bring a flag." The boy did so; and soon said, "He has brought a flag." "What colour is it?" asked the magician: the boy replied, "Red." He was told to call for another flag; which he did; and soon after he said that he saw another brought; and that it was black. In like manner, he was told to call for a third, fourth, fifth, sixth, and seventh; which he described as being successively brought before him; specifying their colours, as white, green, black, red, and blue. The magician then asked him (as he did, also, each time that a new flag was described as being brought), "How many flags have you now before you?" "Seven," answered the boy. While this was going on, the magician put the second and third of the small strips of paper upon which the forms of invocation were written into the chafing-dish; and fresh frankincense and coriander-seed having been repeatedly added, the fumes became painful to the eyes. When the boy had described the seven flags as appearing to him, he was desired to say, "Bring the Sulṭán's tent; and pitch it." This he did; and in about a minute after, he said, "Some men have brought the tent; a large green tent: they are pitching it;" and presently he added, "They have set it up." "Now," said the magician, "order the soldiers to come, and to pitch their camp around the tent of the Sulṭán." The boy did as he was desired; and immediately said, "I see a great many soldiers, with their tents: they have pitched their tents." He was then told to order that the soldiers should be drawn up in ranks; and, having done so, he presently said that he saw them thus arranged. The magician had put the fourth of the little strips of paper into the chafing-dish; and soon after, he did the same with the fifth. He now said, "Tell some of the people to bring a bull." The boy gave the order required, and said, "I see a bull: it is red: four men are dragging it along; and three are beating it." He was told to desire them to kill it, and cut it up, and to put the meat in saucepans, and cook it. He did as he was directed; and described these operations as apparently performed before his eyes. "Tell the soldiers," said the magician, "to eat it." The boy did so; and said, "They are eating it. They have done; and are washing their hands." The magician then told him to call for the Sulṭán; and the boy, having done this, said, "I see the Sulṭán riding to his tent, on a bay horse; and he has, on his head, a high red cap: he has alighted at his tent, and sat down within it." "Desire them to bring coffee to the Sulṭán," said the magician, "and to form the court." These orders were given by the boy; and he said that he saw them performed. The magician had put the last of the six little strips of paper into the chafing-dish. In his mutterings I distinguished nothing but the words of the written invocation, frequently repeated, except on two or three occasions, when I heard him say, "If they demand information, inform them; and be ye veracious." But much that he repeated was inaudible, and as I did not ask him to teach me his art, I do not pretend to assert that I am fully acquainted with his invocations.

He now addressed himself to me; and asked me if I wished the boy to see any person who was absent or dead. I named Lord Nelson; of whom the boy had evidently never heard; for it was with much difficulty that he pronounced the name, after several trials. The magician desired the boy to say to the Sulṭán—"My master salutes thee, and desires thee to bring Lord Nelson: bring him before my eyes, that I may see him, speedily." The boy then said so; and almost immediately added, "A messenger is gone, and has returned, and brought a man, dressed in a black[1] suit of European clothes: the man has lost his left arm." He then paused for a moment or two; and, looking more intently, and more closely, into the ink, said, "No, he has not lost his left arm; but it is placed to his breast." This correction made his description more striking than it had been without it: since Lord Nelson generally had his empty sleeve attached

[1] Dark blue is called by the modern Egyptians "eswed," which properly signifies *black*, and is therefore so translated here.

to the breast of his coat: but it was the *right* arm that he had lost. Without saying that I suspected the boy had made a mistake, I asked the magician whether the objects appeared in the ink as if actually before the eyes, or as if in a glass, which makes the right appear left. He answered, that they appeared as in a mirror. This rendered the boy's description faultless.[1]

The next person I called for was a native of Egypt, who had been for many years resident in England, where he had adopted our dress; and who had been long confined to his bed by illness before I embarked for this country: I thought that his name, one not very uncommon in Egypt, might make the boy describe him incorrectly; though another boy, on the former visit of the magician, had described this same person as wearing a European dress, like that in which I last saw him. In the present case the boy said, "Here is a man brought on a kind of bier, and wrapped up in a sheet." This description would suit, supposing the person in question to be still confined to his bed, or if he were dead.[2] The boy described his face as covered; and was told to order that it should be uncovered. This he did; and then said, "His face is pale; and he has mustaches, but no beard:" which is correct.

Several other persons were successively called for; but the boy's descriptions of them were imperfect, though not altogether incorrect. He represented each object as appearing less distinct than the preceding one; as if his sight were gradually becoming dim: he was a minute, or more, before he could give any account of the persons he professed to see towards the close of the performance; and the magician said it was useless to proceed with him. Another boy was then brought in; and the magic square, &c., made in his hand; but he could see nothing. The magician said he was too old.

Though completely puzzled, I was somewhat disappointed with his performances, for they fell short of what he had accomplished, in many instances, in presence of certain of my friends and countrymen.

---

1 Whenever I desired the boy to call for any person to appear, I paid particular attention both to the magician and to 'Osmán. The latter gave no direction either by word or sign; and indeed he was generally unacquainted with the personal appearance of the individual called for. I took care that he had no previous communication with the boys; and have seen the experiment fail when he *could* have given directions to them, or to the magician. In short, it would be difficult to conceive any precaution which I did not take. It is important to add, that the dialect of the magician was more intelligible to me than to the boy. When *I* understood him perfectly at once, he was sometimes obliged to vary his words to make the *boy* comprehend what he said.

2 A few months after this was written, I had the pleasure of hearing that the person here alluded to was in better health. Whether he was confined to his bed at the time when this experiment was performed, I have not been able to ascertain.

On one of these occasions, an Englishman present ridiculed the performance, and said that nothing would satisfy him but a correct description of the appearance of his own father, of whom, he was sure, no one of the company had any knowledge. The boy, accordingly, having called by name for the person alluded to, described a man in a Frank dress, with his hand placed to his head, wearing spectacles, and with one foot on the ground, and the other raised behind him, as if he were stepping down from a seat. The description was exactly true in every respect: the peculiar position of the hand was occasioned by an almost constant headache; and that of the foot or leg, by a stiff knee, caused by a fall from a horse, in hunting. I am assured that, on this occasion, the boy accurately described each person and thing that was called for. On another occasion, Shakspeare was described with the most minute correctness, both as to person and dress; and I might add several other cases in which the same magician has excited astonishment in the sober minds of Englishmen of my acquaintance. A short time since, after performing in the usual manner, by means of a boy, he prepared the magic mirror in the hand of a young English lady, who, on looking into it for a little while, said that she saw a broom sweeping the ground without anybody holding it, and was so much frightened that she would look no longer.

I have stated these facts partly from my own experience, and partly as they came to my knowledge on the authority of respectable persons. The reader may be tempted to think, that, in each instance, the boy saw images produced by some reflection in the ink; but this was evidently not the case; or that he was a confederate, or guided by leading questions. That there was no collusion, I satisfactorily ascertained, by selecting the boy who performed the part above described in my presence from a number of others passing by in the street, and by his rejecting a present which I afterwards offered him with the view of inducing him to confess that he did not really see what he had professed to have seen. I tried the veracity of another boy on a subsequent occasion in the same manner; and the result was the same. The experiment often entirely fails; but when the boy employed is right in one case, he generally is so in all: when he gives, at first, an account altogether wrong, the magician usually dismisses him at once, saying that he is too old. The perfumes, or excited imagination, or fear, may be supposed to affect the vision of the boy who describes objects as appearing to him in the ink; but, if so, why does he see exactly what is required, and objects of which he can have had no previous particular notion? Neither I nor others have been able to discover any clue by which to penetrate the mystery; and if the reader be alike unable to give the solution, I hope that he will not allow the above account to induce in his mind any degree of scepticism with respect to other portions of this work.[1]

---

[1] I have been gratified by finding that this hope has been realized. I wish I could add that the phenomena were now explained. In No. 117 of the "Quarterly Review," pp. 202 and 203, it has been suggested that the performances were effected by means of pictures and a concave mirror; and that the images of the former were reflected from the surface of the mirror, and received on a cloud of smoke under the eyes of the boy. This, however, I cannot admit; because such means could not have been employed without my perceiving them; nor would the images be *reversed* (unless the pictures were so) by being reflected from the surface of a mirror and received upon a *second surface;* for the boy was looking *down* upon the palm of his hand, so that an image could not be formed upon the smoke (which was copious, but not dense,) between his eye and the supposed mirror. The grand difficulty of the case is the exhibition of "the correct appearance of private individuals unknown to fame," as remarked in the "Quarterly Review," in which a curious note, presenting "some new features of difficulty," is appended. With the most remarkable of the facts there related I was acquainted; but I was not bold enough to insert them. I may now, however, here mention them. Two travellers (one of them, M. Leon De Laborde; the other, an Englishman), both instructed by the magician 'Abd-El-Ḳádir, are stated to have succeeded in performing similar feats. Who this Englishman was, I have not been able to learn. He positively denied all collusion, and asserted that he did nothing but repeat the forms taught him by the magician.

Since the foregoing note was written, I have twice witnessed performances of this now-notorious magician, which were absolute failures; and so, I have been informed by others, have been almost all of his later attempts. Hence, and from an observation made to me by him in the presence of the late Lord Nugent (that he was generally successful in the life-time of 'Osmán, who was his usual interpreter, and who died shortly after my second visit to Egypt), I can hardly help inferring that, in most cases, leading questions put *unconsciously* by 'Osmán, as well as by others, who were persons of education and intelligence, and in other cases shrewd guesses, were the main causes of his success. I cannot, by the supposition of leading questions, account for his succeeding in the cases that fell under my own observation; but these, as I have stated above, "fell short of what he hád accomplished, in many instances, in presence of certain of my friends and countrymen."

CHAPTER XIII.

CHARACTER.

THE natural or innate character of the modern Egyptians is altered, in a remarkable degree, by their religion, laws, and government, as well as by the climate and other causes; and to form a just opinion of it is, therefore, very difficult. We may, however, confidently state, that they are endowed, in a higher degree than most other people, with some of the more important mental qualities; particularly, quickness of apprehension, a ready wit, and a retentive memory. In youth, they generally possess these and other intellectual powers; but the causes above alluded to gradually lessen their mental energy.

Of the leading features of their character, none is more remarkable than their religious pride. They regard persons of every other faith as the children of perdition; and such, the Muslim is early taught to despise.[1] It is written in the Ḳur-án, "O ye who have believed, take not the Jews and Christians as friends: they are friends, one to another; and whosoever of you taketh them as his friends, verily he is [one] of them."[2] From motives of politeness, or selfish interest, these people will sometimes talk with apparent liberality of sentiment, and even make professions of friendship, to a Christian (particularly to a European), whom, in their hearts, they contemn: but as the Muslims of Egypt judge of the Franks in general from the majority of those in their towns, some of whom are outcasts from their native countries, and others (though not *all* the rest, of course),

[1] I am credibly informed that children in Egypt are often taught, at school, a regular set of curses to denounce upon the persons and property of Christians, Jews, and all other unbelievers in the religion of Moḥammad. See Appendix D.

[2] Chap. v. ver. 56. Verses 62 and 63 of the same chapter explain the reason of this precept:—"O ye who have believed, take not those who have made your religion a laughing-stock and a jest, of those who have received the Scripture before you, and the unbelievers [or polytheists], as friends; (but fear God, if ye be believers;) and [those who], when ye call to prayer, make it [namely, the prayer,] a laughing-stock and a jest. This [they do] because they are a people who do not understand." (The words enclosed in brackets are from the commentary of the Geláleyn.)

men under no moral restraint, they are hardly to be blamed for despising them. The Christians are, however, generally treated with civility by the people of Egypt: the Muslims being as remarkable for their toleration as for their contempt of unbelievers.

It is considered the highest honour, among the Muslims, to be religious; but the desire to appear so leads many into hypocrisy and pharisaical ostentation. When a Muslim is unoccupied by business or amusement or conversation, he is often heard to utter some pious ejaculation. If a wicked thought, or the remembrance of a wicked action that he has committed, trouble him, he sighs forth, "I beg forgiveness of God, the Great!"[1] The shop-keeper, when not engaged with customers, nor enjoying his pipe, often employs himself, in the sight and hearing of the passengers in the street, in reciting a chapter of the Ḳur-án, or in repeating to himself those expressions in praise of God which often follow the ordinary prayers and are counted with the beads; and in the same public manner he prays.—The Muslims frequently swear by God (but not irreverently); and also, by the Prophet, and by the head, or beard, of the person they address. When one is told anything that excites his surprise and disbelief, he generally exclaims, "Wa-llah?" or, "Wa-lláhi?" (by God?); and the other replies, "Wa-lláhi!"—As on ordinary occasions before eating and drinking, so, too, on taking medicine, commencing a writing or any important undertaking, and before many a trifling act, it is their habit to say, "In the name of God, the Compassionate, the Merciful;" and after the act, "Praise be to God."—When two persons make any considerable bargain, they recite together the first chapter of the Ḳur-án (the Fát'ḥah). In case of a debate on any matter of business or of opinion, it is common for one of the parties, or a third person who may wish to settle the dispute, or to cool the disputants, to exclaim, "Blessing on the Prophet!"[2]—"O God, bless him!"[3] is said, in a low voice, by the other or others; and they then continue the argument; but generally with moderation.

Religious ejaculations often interrupt conversation upon trivial and even licentious subjects, in Egyptian society; sometimes, in such a manner that a person not well acquainted with the character of this people would perhaps imagine that they intended to make religion a jest. In many of their most indecent songs, the name of God is

---

[1] "Astaghfir Alláh el-'Aẓeem."

[2] "Eṣ-ṣalah 'a-n-nebee" (for "—'ala-n-nebee"); or "Bless ye (or bless thou) the Prophet!"—"Ṣalloo (or ṣallee) 'a-n-nebee."

[3] "Alláhum (for Alláhumma) ṣallee 'aleyh."

frequently introduced; and this is certainly done without any profane motive, but from the habit of often mentioning the name of the Deity in vain, and of praising Him on every trifling occasion of surprise, or in testimony of admiration of anything uncommon. Thus, a libertine, describing his impressions on the first sight of a charming girl (in one of the grossest songs I have ever seen or heard even in the Arabic language), exclaims, "Extolled be He who formed thee, O full moon!"—and this and many similar expressions are common in many other songs and odes: but what is most remarkable in the song particularly alluded to above is a profane comparison with which it terminates. I shall adduce, as an example of the strange manner in which licentiousness and religion are often blended together in vulgar Egyptian poetry and rhyming prose, a translation of the last three stanzas of an ode on love and wine:—

"She granted me a reception, the graceful of form, after her distance and coyness. I kissed her teeth and her cheek; and the cup rang in her hand. The odours of musk and ambergris were diffused by a person whose form surpassed the elegance of a straight and slender branch. She spread a bed of brocade; and I passed the time in uninterrupted happiness. A Turkish fawn enslaved me.

"Now I beg forgiveness of God, my Lord, for all my faults and sins; and for all that my heart hath said. My members testify against me. Whenever grief oppresseth me, O Lord, Thou art my hope from whatever afflicteth me. Thou knowest what I say, and what I think. Thou art the Bountiful, the Forgiving! I implore thy protection: then pardon me.

"And I praise that benignant being[1] whom a cloud was wont to shade; the comely: how great was his comeliness! He will intercede for us on the day of judgment, when his haters, the vile, the polytheists, shall be repentant. Would that I might always, as long as I live, accompany the pilgrims, to perform the circuits and worship and courses, and live in uninterrupted happiness!"

In translating the first of the above stanzas, I have substituted the feminine for the masculine pronoun: for, in the original, the former is meant, though the latter is used; as is commonly the case in similar compositions of the Egyptians.—One of my Muslim friends having just called on me, after my writing the above remarks, I read to him the last four stanzas of this ode; and asked him if he considered it proper thus to mix up religion with debauchery. He answered, "Perfectly proper: a man relates his having committed sins; and then prays to God for forgiveness, and blesses the Prophet."—"But," said I, "this is an ode written to be chanted for the amusement of persons who take pleasure in unlawful indulgences: and see here,

[1] The Prophet.

when I close the leaves, the page which celebrates a debauch comes in contact, facc to face, with that upon which are written the names of the Deity: the commemoration of the pleasures of sin is placed upon the prayer for forgiveness." "That is nonsense," replied my friend: "turn the book over: place that side upwards which is now downwards; and then the case will be the reverse; sin covered by forgiveness: and God, whose name be exalted, hath said in the Excellent Book, 'Say, O my servants who have transgressed against your own souls, despair not of the mercy of God; seeing that God forgiveth all sins [unto those who repent]: for He is the Very Forgiving; the Merciful.'"[1]—His answer reminds me of what I have often observed, that the generality of Arabs, a most inconsistent people, are every day breaking their law in some point or other, trusting that two words ("Astaghfir Alláh," or "I beg forgiveness of God,") will cancel every transgression.—He had a copy of the Ḳur-án in his hand; and on my turning it over to look for the verse he had quoted, I found in it a scrap of paper containing some words from the venerated volume: he was about to burn this piece of paper, lest it should fall out, and be trodden upon; and on my asking him whether it was allowable to do so, he answered that it might either be burnt, or thrown into running water; but that it was better to burn it, as the words would ascend in the flames, and be conveyed by angels to heaven.—Sometimes the Ḳur-án is quoted in jest, even by persons of strict religious principles. For instance, the following equivocal and evasive answer was once suggested to me on a person's asking of me a present of a watch, which, I must previously mention, is called "sá'ah," a word which signifies an "hour," and the "period of the general judgment:"—"Verily, the sá'ah shall come: I will surely make it to appear" (ch. xx. v. 15).

There are often met with, in Egyptian society, persons who will introduce an apposite quotation from the Ḳur-án or the Traditions of the Prophet in common conversation, whatever be the topic; and an interruption of this kind is not considered, as it would be in general society in our own country, either hypocritical or annoying; but rather occasions expressions, if not feelings, of admiration, and often diverts the hearers from a trivial subject to matters of a more serious nature. The Muslims of Egypt, and, I believe, those of other countries, are generally fond of conversing on religion; and the most prevalent

[1] Ḳur-án, ch. xxxix. v. 54.

mode of entertaining a party of guests among the higher and middle ranks in this place (Cairo) is the recital of a "khatmeh" (or the whole of the Ḳur-án), which is chanted by fiḳees, hired for the purpose; or the performance of a "zikr," which has been before mentioned. Few persons among them would venture to say that they prefer hearing a concert of music to the performance of a khatmeh or zikr; and they certainly do take great pleasure in the latter performances. The manner in which the Ḳur-án is sometimes chanted is, indeed, very pleasing; though I must say that a complete khatmeh is, to me, extremely tiresome. With the religious zeal of the Muslims, I am daily struck: yet I have often wondered that they so seldom attempt to make converts to their faith. On my expressing my surprise, as I have frequently done, at their indifference with respect to the propagation of their religion, contrasting it with the conduct of their ancestors of the early ages of El-Islám, I have generally been answered, "Of what use would it be if I could convert a thousand infidels? Would it increase the number of the faithful? By no means: the number of the faithful is decreed by God; and no act of man can increase or diminish it." The contending against such an answer would have led to an interminable dispute: so I never ventured a reply. I have heard quoted, by way of apology for their neglecting to make proselytes, the following words of the Ḳur-án: "Dispute not against those who have received the Scriptures"[1] (namely, the Christians and Jews), without the words immediately following, "unless in the best manner; except against such of them as behave injuriously [towards you]: and say [unto them], We believe in [the revelation] that hath been sent down unto us, and [also in that] which hath been sent down unto you: and our God and your God is one."[2] If this precept were acted upon by the Muslims, it might perhaps lead to disputes which would make them more liberal-minded, and much better informed.

The respect which most modern Muslims pay to their Prophet is almost idolatrous. They very frequently swear by him; and many of the most learned, as well as the ignorant, often implore his intercession. Pilgrims are generally much more affected on visiting his tomb than in performing any other religious rite. There are some

[1] Ch. xxix. v. 45.

[2] In the first edition of the present work, copying Sale, who gives no authority for the remark, I here added, "This precept is, however, generally considered as abrogated by that of the sword." These words might lead the reader into error, as is shewn by what I have said on the subject of war in page 93.

Muslims who will not do anything that the Prophet is not recorded to have done; and who particularly abstain from eating anything that he did not eat, though its lawfulness be undoubted. The Imám Aḥmad Ibn-Ḥambal would not even eat water-melons, because, although he knew that the Prophet ate them, he could not learn whether he ate them with or without the rind, or whether he broke, bit, or cut them: and he forbade a woman, who questioned him as to the propriety of the act, to spin by the light of torches passing in the street by night, which were not her own property, because the Prophet had not mentioned whether it was lawful to do so, and was not known to have ever availed himself of a light belonging to another person without that person's leave.—I once, admiring some very pretty pipe-bowls, asked the maker why he did not stamp them with his name. He answered, "God forbid! My name is Aḥmad" (one of the names of the Prophet): "would you have me put it in the fire?"—I have heard adduced as one of the subjects of complaint against the Báshà, his causing the camels and horses of the government to be branded with his names, "Moḥammad 'Alee." "In the first place," said a friend of mine, who mentioned this fact to me, "the iron upon which are engraved these names, names which ought to be so much venerated, the names of the Prophet (God bless and save him), and his Cousin (may God be well pleased with him), is put into the fire, which is shocking: then it is applied to the neck of a camel; and causes blood, which is impure, to flow, and to pollute the sacred names both upon the iron and upon the animal's skin: and when the wound is healed, how probable is it, and almost certain and unavoidable, that the camel will, when he lies down, lay his neck upon something unclean!"

A similar feeling is the chief reason why the Muslims object to printing their books. They have scarcely a book (I do not remember to have seen one) that does not contain the name of God: it is a rule among them to commence every book with the words, "In the name of God, the Compassionate, the Merciful," and to begin the preface or introduction by praising God, and blessing the Prophet; and they fear some impurity might be contracted by the ink that is applied to the name of the Deity, in the process of printing, or by the paper to be impressed with that sacred name, and perhaps with words taken from the Ḳur-án. They fear, also, that their books, becoming very cheap by being printed, would fall into the hands of infidels; and are much shocked at the idea of using a brush composed of hogs' hair (which was at first done here) to apply the ink to the name, and often to the words, of God. Hence, books have hitherto been printed in Egypt only by order of the government: but two or three persons have lately applied for, and received, permission to make use of the government-press. I am acquainted with a bookseller here who has long been desirous of printing some books which he feels sure would bring him considerable profit; but cannot overcome his scruples as to the lawfulness of doing so.

The honour which the Muslims shew to the Ḳur-án is very striking. They generally take care never to hold it, or suspend it, in such a manner as that it shall be below the girdle; and they deposit it upon a high and clean place; and never put another book, or anything else, on the top of it. On quoting from it, they usually say, "He whose name be exalted" (or "God, whose name be exalted") "hath said, in the Excellent Book." They consider it extremely improper that the sacred volume should be touched by a Christian or a Jew, or any other person not a believer in its doctrines; though some of them are induced, by covetousness, but very rarely, to sell copies of it to such persons. It is even forbidden to the Muslim to touch it unless he be in a state of legal purity; and hence, these words of the book itself—"None shall touch it but they who are purified"[1]—are often stamped upon the cover. The same remarks apply, also, to anything upon which is inscribed a passage of the Ḳur-án. It is remarkable, however, that most of the old Arab coins bear inscriptions of words from the Ḳur-án, or else the testimony of the faith ("There is no deity but God: Moḥammad is God's Apostle"); notwithstanding they were intended for the use of Jews and Christians, as well as Muslims: but I have heard this practice severely condemned.—On my once asking one of my Muslim friends whether figs were esteemed wholesome in Egypt, he answered, "Is not the fig celebrated in the Ḳur-án? God swears by it: 'By the fig and the olive!'" (ch. xcv. v. 1).

There is certainly much enthusiastic piety in the character of the modern Muslims, notwithstanding their inconsistencies and superstitions: such, at least, is generally the case. There are, I believe, very few professed Muslims who are really unbelievers; and these dare not openly declare their unbelief, through fear of losing their heads for their apostacy. I have heard of two or three such, who have been rendered so by long and intimate intercourse with Euro-

---

[1] Ḳur-án, ch. lvi. v. 78.

peans; and have met with one materialist, who has often had long discussions with me. In preceding chapters of this work, several practices indicative of the religious feeling which prevails among the Muslims of Egypt have been incidentally mentioned. Religious appeals are generally used by the beggars in this country: some examples of these will be given hereafter. Of a similar nature, also, are the cries of many of the persons who sell vegetables, &c. The cry of the nightly watchman in the quarter in which I lived in Cairo during my first visit struck me as remarkable for its beauty and sublimity—"I extol the perfection of the living King, who sleepeth not nor dieth."[1] The present watchman, in the same quarter, exclaims, "O Lord! O Everlasting!"[2] Many other illustrations of the religious character of the people whom I am endeavouring to portray might be added. I must, however, here acknowledge, that religion has much declined among them and most others of the same faith. Whoever has been in the habit of conversing familiarly with the modern Muslims must often have heard them remark, with a sigh, "It is the end of time!"—"The world has fallen into infidelity."—They are convinced that the present state of their religion is a proof that the end of the world is near. The mention which I have made, in a former chapter, of some of the tenets of the Wahhábees, as being those of the primitive Muslims, shews how much the generality of the modern professors of the faith of the Ḳur-án have deviated from the precepts originally delivered to its disciples.

Influenced by their belief in predestination, the men display, in times of distressing uncertainty, an exemplary patience, and, after any afflicting event, a remarkable degree of resignation and fortitude, approaching nearly to apathy;[3] generally exhibiting their sorrow only by a sigh, and the exclamation of "Allah kereem!" (God is bountiful!)—but the women, on the contrary, give vent to their grief by the most extravagant cries and shrieks. While the Christian justly blames himself for every untoward event which he thinks he has brought upon himself, or might have avoided, the Muslim enjoys a remarkable serenity of mind in all the vicissitudes of life. When he sees his end approaching, his resignation is still conspicuous: he

1 "Subḥán el-melik el-ḥei el-lezee lá yenám walà yemoot!"

2 "Yá rabb! Yá dáïm!"

3 They are not, however, so apathetic as some travellers have supposed; for it is not uncommon to see them weep; and such a demonstration of feeling is not considered by them as unmanly: even heroes are frequently represented, in their romances and histories, as weeping under heavy affliction.

exclaims, "Verily to God we belong; and verily to Him we return!" and to those who inquire respecting his state, in general his reply is, "Praise be to God! Our Lord is bountiful."—His belief in predestination does not, however, prevent his taking any step to attain an object that he may have in view; not being perfectly absolute, or unconditional: nor does it in general make him careless of avoiding danger; for he thinks himself forbidden to do so by these words of the Ḳur-án,[1] "Throw not yourselves[2] into perdition;" except in some cases; as in those of pestilence and other sicknesses; being commanded, by the Prophet, not to go into a city where there is a pestilence, nor to come out from it. The lawfulness of quarantine is contested among Muslims; but the generality of them condemn it.

The same belief in predestination renders the Muslim utterly devoid of presumption with regard to his future actions, or to any future events. He never speaks of anything that he intends to do, or of any circumstance which he expects and hopes may come to pass, without adding, "If it be the will of God;"[3] and, in like manner, in speaking of a past event of which he is not certain, he generally prefaces or concludes what he says with the expression, "God is all-knowing" (or, "—most knowing").[4]

Benevolence and charity to the poor are virtues which the Egyptians possess in an eminent degree, and which are instilled into their hearts by religion; but from their own profession it appears that they are as much excited to the giving of alms by the expectation of enjoying corresponding rewards in heaven, as by pity for the distresses of their fellow-creatures, or a disinterested wish to do the will of God. It may be attributed, in some measure, to the charitable disposition of the inhabitants, that beggars are so numerous in Cairo. The many handsome "Sebeels," or public fountains (buildings erected and endowed for the gratuitous supply of water to passengers), which are seen in this city, and the more humble structures of the same kind in the villages and fields, are monuments of the same virtue.[5]

In my earlier intercourse with the people of Egypt, I was much pleased at observing their humanity to dumb animals; to see a person, who gathered together the folds of his loose clothes to prevent their coming in contact with a dog, throw, to the impure animal, a

---

1 Ch. ii. v. 191.

2 Literally, "your hands;" but in the Commentary of the Geláleyn, the meaning is said to be "yourselves."

3 "In-sháa-lláh."

4 "Alláhu aạlam."

5 The larger sebeels of Cairo are generally of the period of the Turkish Báshàs and Memlook Beys.

portion of the bread which he was eating. Murders, burglaries, and other atrocious and violent crimes, were then very rare among them. Now, however, I find the generality of the Egyptians very much changed for the worse, with respect to their humanity to brutes and to their fellow-creatures. The increased severity of the government seems, as might be expected, to have engendered tyranny, and an increase of every crime, in the people: but I am inclined to think that the conduct of Europeans has greatly conduced to produce this effect; for I do not remember to have seen acts of cruelty to dumb animals except in places where Franks either reside or are frequent visiters, as Alexandria, Cairo, and Thebes. It is shocking to see the miserable asses which are used for carrying dust, &c., in Cairo; many of them with large crimson wounds, like carbuncles, constantly chafed by rough ropes of the fibres of the palm-tree which are attached to the back part of the pack-saddle. The dogs in the streets are frequently beaten, both by boys and men, from mere wantonness; and I often see children amusing themselves with molesting the cats, which were formerly much favoured.[1] Robberies and murders, during two or three months after my second arrival here, were occurrences of almost every week. Most of the Turkish governors of districts used to exercise great oppression over the felláheen: but since persons of the latter class have been put in the places of the former, they have exceeded their predecessors in tyranny; and it is a common remark, that they are "more execrable than the Turks."[2]

Though I now frequently see the houseless dogs beaten in the streets of Cairo, and that when quite inoffensive and quiet, I still often observe men feeding them with bread, &c.; and the persons who do so are mostly poor men. In every district of this city are many small troughs, which are daily replenished with water for the dogs. In each street where there are shops, a saḳḳà receives a small monthly sum from each shopman for sprinkling the street, and filling the trough or troughs for the dogs in that street. There

---

[1] I think it proper to remark here, that I have good reason for believing Burckhardt to have been misinformed when stating (see his "Arabic Proverbs," No. 393) that children in the East (in Egypt, &c.,) torture serpents by putting them into a leathern bag, then throwing unslaked lime upon them, and pouring water on it. I find no one who has heard of such cruelty; and it is not likely that boys in this country would dare to put a serpent in a bag (for they are excessively afraid of this reptile), or would give several piasters for a bag to destroy in this manner. The proverb upon which this statement is founded perhaps alludes to a mode of destroying serpents; but not for sport.

[2] "The oppression of the Turks, rather than the justice of the Arabs," is a proverb often heard from the mouth of the Arab peasant; who, in this case, applies the term "Arabs" to his own class, instead of the Bedawees, to whom it now usually belongs. See Burckhardt's "Arabic Proverbs," No. 176.

is also a dogs' trough under almost every shop of a "sharbetlee," or seller of sherbets.—It may here be mentioned, that the dogs of Cairo, few of which have masters, compose regular and distinct tribes; and the dogs of each tribe confine themselves to a certain district or quarter, from which they invariably chase away any strange dog that may venture to intrude. These animals are very numerous in Cairo. They are generally careful to avoid coming in contact with the men; as if they knew that the majority of the people of the city regard them as unclean: but they often bark at persons in the Frank dress; and at night they annoy every passenger. They are of use in eating the offal thrown out from the butchers' shops, and from houses. Many dogs also prowl about the mounds of rubbish around the metropolis; and these, with the vultures, feed upon the carcasses of the camels, asses, &c., that die in the town. They are mostly of a sandy colour; and seem to partake of the form and disposition of the jackal.

The general opinion of the Muslims, which holds the dog to be unclean, does not prevent their keeping this animal as a house-guard, and sometimes even as a pet. A curious case of this kind occurred a short time ago. A woman in this city, who had neither husband nor child nor friend to solace her, made a dog her companion. Death took this only associate from her; and, in her grief and her affection for it, she determined to bury it; and not merely to commit it to the earth without ceremony, but to inter it as a Muslim, in a respectable tomb, in the cemetery of the Imám Esh-Sháfe'ee, which is regarded as especially sacred. She washed the dog according to the rules prescribed to be observed in the case of a deceased Muslim, wrapped it in handsome grave-clothes, sent for a bier, and put it in; then hired several wailing-women; and, with them, performed a regular lamentation. This done (but not without exciting the wonder of her neighbours, who could not conjecture what person in her house was dead, yet would not intrude, because she never associated with them), she hired a number of chanters, to head the funeral-procession, and school-boys, to sing, and carry the Ḳur-án before the bier; and the train went forth in respectable order; herself and the hired wailing-women following the bier, and rending the air with their shrieks: but the procession had not advanced many steps, when one of the female neighbours ventured to ask the afflicted lady who the person was that was dead; and was answered, "It is my poor child." The inquirer charged her with uttering a falsehood;

and the bereaved lady confessed that it was her dog; begging, at the same time, that her inquisitive neighbour would not divulge the secret; but, for an Egyptian woman to keep a secret, and such a secret, was impossible: it was immediately made known to the by-standers; and a mob, in no good humour, soon collected, and put a stop to the funeral. The chanters and the singing-boys and wailing-women vented their rage against their employer (as soon as they had secured their money) for having made fools of them; and if the police had not interfered, she would probably have fallen a victim to popular fury.[1]

It is a curious fact, that, in Cairo, houseless cats are fed at the expense of the Ḳáḍee; or, rather, almost wholly at his expense. Every afternoon, a quantity of offal is brought into the great court before the Maḥkemeh; and the cats are called together to eat. The Sulṭán Eẓ-Ẓáhir Beybars (as I learn from the Básh-Kátib of the Ḳáḍee) bequeathed a garden, which is called "gheyṭ el-ḳuṭṭah" (or the garden of the cat), near his mosque, on the north of Cairo, for the benefit of the cats: but this garden has been sold, over and over again, by the trustees and purchasers: the former sold it on pretence of its being too much out of order to be rendered productive, except at a considerable expense; and it now produces only a "ḥekr" (or quit-rent) of fifteen piasters a year, to be applied to the maintenance of the destitute cats. Almost the whole expense of their support has, in consequence, fallen upon the Ḳáḍee, who, by reason of his office, is the guardian of this and all other charitable and pious legacies, and must suffer for the neglect of his predecessors. Latterly, however, the duty of feeding the cats has been very inadequately performed. Many persons in Cairo, when they wish to get rid of a cat, send or take it to the Ḳáḍee's house, and let it loose in the great court.

The affability of the Egyptians towards each other has been mentioned in a preceding chapter. Towards foreigners who do not conform with their manners and customs, and profess the same way of thinking, they are polite in their address, but cold and reserved, or parasitical, in conversation. With such persons, and even among themselves, they often betray much impertinent curiosity. They are generally extremely afraid of making to themselves enemies; and

---

[1] D'Herbelot mentions a somewhat similar case, in which a Turk, having buried a favourite dog with some marks of respect, in his garden, was accused, before the Ḳáḍee, of having interred the animal with the ceremonies practised at the burial of a Muslim, and escaped punishment (perhaps a severe one) by informing the judge that his dog had made a will, leaving to him (the Ḳáḍee) a sum of money.—(Bibliothèque Orientale, art. Cadhi.)

this fear frequently induces them to uphold each other, even when it is criminal to do so.

Cheerfulness is another remarkable characteristic of this people. Some of them profess a great contempt for frivolous amusements; but most take pleasure in such pastimes; and it is surprising to see how easily they are amused: wherever there are crowds, noise, and bustle, they are delighted. In their public festivals, there is little to amuse a person of good education; but the Egyptians enjoy them as much as we do the best of our entertainments. Those of the lower orders seem to be extremely happy with their pipes and coffee, after the occupations of the day, in the society of the coffee-shop.

Hospitality is a virtue for which the natives of the East in general are highly and deservedly admired; and the people of Egypt are well entitled to commendation on this account. A word which signifies literally "a person on a journey" ("musáfir") is the term most commonly employed in this country in the sense of a visiter or guest. There are very few persons here who would think of sitting down to a meal, if there were a stranger in the house, without inviting him to partake of it, unless the latter were a menial; in which case, he would be invited to eat with the servants. It would be considered a shameful violation of good manners if a Muslim abstained from ordering the table to be prepared at the usual time because a visiter happened to be present. Persons of the middle classes in this country, if living in a retired situation, sometimes take their supper before the door of their house, and invite every passenger of respectable appearance to eat with them. This is very commonly done among the lower orders. In cities and large towns, claims on hospitality are unfrequent; as there are many wekálehs, or kháns, where strangers may obtain lodging; and food is very easily procured: but in the villages, travellers are often lodged and entertained by the Sheykh or some other inhabitant; and if the guest be a person of the middle or higher classes, or even not very poor, he gives a present to his host's servants, or to the host himself. In the desert, however, a present is seldom received from a guest. By a Sunneh law, a traveller may claim entertainment, of any person able to afford it to him, for three days.—The account of Abraham's entertaining the three angels, related in the Bible, presents a perfect picture of the manner in which a modern Bedawee sheykh receives travellers arriving at his encampment. He immediately orders his wife or women to make bread; slaughters a sheep or some other animal, and dresses it in haste; and bringing milk and any other provisions that he may have ready at hand, with the bread, and the meat which he has dressed, sets them before his guests. If these be persons of high rank, he stands by them while they eat; as Abraham did in the case above alluded to. Most Bedawees will suffer almost any injury to themselves or their families rather than allow their guests to be ill-treated while under their protection. There are Arabs who even regard the chastity of their wives as not too precious to be sacrificed for the gratification of their guests;[1] and at an encampment of the Bisháreen, I ascertained that there are many persons in this great tribe (which inhabits a large portion of the desert between the Nile and the Red Sea) who offer their unmarried daughters to their guests, merely from motives of hospitality, and not for hire.

There used to be, in Cairo, a numerous class of persons called "Ṭufeyleeyeh" or "Ṭufeylees" (that is, Spungers), who, taking advantage of the hospitality of their countrymen, subsisted entirely by spunging: but this class has, of late, very much decreased in number. Wherever there was an entertainment, some of these worthies were almost sure to be found; and it was only by a present of money that they could be induced to retire from the company. They even travelled about the country, without the smallest coin in their pockets, intruding themselves into private houses whenever they wanted a meal, or practising various tricks for this purpose. Two of them, I was told, a little while since, determined to go to the festival of the seyyid El-Bedawee, at Ṭanṭà; an easy journey of two days and a half from Cairo. Walking at their leisure, they arrived at the small town of Ḳalyoob at the end of their first day's journey; and there found themselves at a loss for a supper. One of them went to the Ḳáḍee; and, after saluting him, said, "O Ḳáḍee, I am a traveller from the Sharḳeeyeh, going to Maṣr; and I have a companion who owes me fifty purses, which he has with him at present, and refuses to give me; and I am actually in want of them." "Where is he?" said the Ḳáḍee. "Here, in this town," answered the complainant. The Ḳáḍee sent a rasool to bring the accused; and in the mean time, expecting considerable fees for a judgment in such a case, ordered a good supper to be prepared; which Ḳáḍees of country towns or villages generally do in similar circumstances. The two men

[1] See Burckhardt's Notes on the Bedouins, &c., 8vo. edition, vol. i. pp. 179 and 180.

were invited to sup and sleep before the case was tried. Next morning, the parties were examined: the accused admitted that he had in his possession the fifty purses of his companion; and said that he was ready to give them up; for they were an encumbrance to him; being only the paper purses in which coffee was sold. "We are Ṭufeylees," he added; and the Ḳáḍee, in anger, dismissed them.

The natives of Egypt in general, in common with the Arabs of other countries, are (according to our system of morals) justly chargeable with a fault which is regarded by us as one of great magnitude: it is want of gratitude.[1] But this I am inclined to consider a relic of the Bedawee character; and as arising from the very common practice of hospitality and generosity, and from the prevailing opinion that these virtues are absolute duties which it would be disgraceful and sinful to neglect.

The temperance and moderation of the Egyptians, with regard to diet, are very exemplary. Since my first arrival in Egypt, I have scarcely ever seen a native of this country in a state of intoxication; unless it were a musician at an entertainment, or a dancing girl, or low prostitute. It hardly need be added that they are extremely frugal. They shew a great respect for bread, as the staff of life,[2] and on no account suffer the smallest portion of it to be wasted, if they can avoid it. I have often observed an Egyptian take up a small piece of bread, which had by accident fallen in the street or road, and, after putting it before his lips and forehead three times, place it on one side, in order that a dog might eat it, rather than let it remain to be trodden under foot. The following instance of the excessive and unreasonable respect of the Egyptians for bread has been related to me by several persons; but I must say that I think it hardly credible. —Two servants were sitting at the door of their master's house, eating their dinner, when they observed a Memlook Bey, with several of his officers, riding along the street towards them. One of these servants rose, from respect to the grandee, who, regarding him with indignation, exclaimed, "Which is the more worthy of respect, the

---

[1] It has been remarked that this is inconsistent with the undeniable gratitude which the Arabs feel towards God. To such an objection they would reply, "We are entitled to the good offices of our fellow-creatures by the law of God; but can claim no benefit from our Maker." I once afforded a refuge to a Bedawee who was in fear for his life; but on parting, he gave me not a word of thanks: had he done so, it would have implied his thinking me a person of mean disposition, who regarded a positive duty as an act imposing obligation. Hence the Arab usually acknowledges a benefit merely by a prayer for the long life, &c., of his benefactor.

[2] The name which they give to it is "'eysh," which literally signifies "life."

bread that is before you, or myself?"—Without waiting for a reply, he made, it is said, a well-understood signal with his hand; and the unintending offender was beheaded on the spot.

The higher and middle orders of Muslims in Egypt are scrupulously cleanly; and the lower orders are more so than in most other countries: but were not cleanliness a point of their religion, perhaps it would not be so much regarded by them. From what has been said in a former chapter of this work,[1] it appears that we must not judge of them, with respect to this quality, from the dirty state in which they generally leave their children. Their religious ablutions were, certainly, very wisely ordained; personal cleanliness being so conducive to health in a hot climate. The Egyptians in general are particularly careful to avoid whatever their religion has pronounced unclean and polluting. One of their objections against wine is, that it is unclean; and I believe that very few of them, if any, could be induced by any means, unless by a considerable bribe, to eat the smallest piece of pig's flesh; except the peasants of the Boḥeyreh (the province on the west of the western branch of the Nile), many of whom eat the flesh of the wild boar, and rats.[2] I was once amused with the remark of a Muslim, on the subject of pork: he observed that the Franks were certainly a much-calumniated people: that it was well known they were in the habit of eating swine's flesh; but that some slanderous persons here asserted that it was not only the flesh of the unclean beast that was eaten by the Franks, but also its skin, and its entrails, and its very blood. On being answered that the accusation was too true, he burst forth with a most hearty curse upon the infidels, devoting them to the lowest place in hell.

Many of the butchers who supply the Muslim inhabitants of the metropolis with meat are Jews. A few years ago, one of the principal 'Ulamà here complained of this fact to the Báshà; and begged him to put a stop to it. Another of the 'Ulamà, hearing that this person had gone to make the complaint above mentioned, followed him, and urged, before the Báshà, that the practice was not unlawful. "Adduce your proof," said the former. "Here," answered the other, "is my proof, from the word of God, 'Eat of that whereon the name of God hath been commemorated.'"[3] The chief of the Jewish butchers was then summoned, and asked whether he said anything

---

[1] Page 57.

[2] Dogs, too, are eaten by many Maghrabees settled at Alexandria, and by descendants of the same people; of whom there are also a few in Cairo, in the quarter of Ṭeyloon

[3] Ḳur-án, ch. vi. v. 118.

previously to slaughtering an animal: he answered, "Yes: we always say, as the Muslims, 'In the name of God. God is most great:' and we never kill an animal in any other way than by cutting its throat." —The complaint was consequently dismissed.

A few days ago, a man, purchasing a faṭeereh of a baker in this city, saw him take out of his oven a dish of pork which he had been baking for a Frank; and, supposing that the other things in the oven might have been in contact with the unclean meat, and thus contaminated, immediately brought a soldier from the nearest guard-house, and caused the baker (who was in no slight alarm, and protested that he was ignorant of there being any pig's flesh in his oven,) to be conducted before the Ẓábiṭ. This magistrate considered the case of sufficient importance to be referred to the Báshà's deewán; and the president of this council regarded it as of too serious and difficult a nature for him to decide, and accordingly sent the accused to be judged at the Maḥkemeh. The Ḳáḍee desired the opinion of the Muftee, who gave the following sentence:—That all kinds of food, not essentially or radically impure, were purified, of any pollution which they might have contracted, by fire; and consequently, that whatever thing of this description was in the oven, even if it had been in contact with the pork, was clean as soon as it had been baked.

A short time since, the Báshà received, from Europe, a set of mattresses and cushions stuffed with horse-hair, to form a deewán for his ḥareem. The ladies opened one of the cushions, to ascertain what was the substance which rendered them so agreeably elastic; and, disgusted in the highest degree at seeing what they supposed to be hogs' hair, insisted upon throwing away the whole deewán.

A Frenchman who was employed here, a few years ago, to refine sugar, by the present Báshà, made use of blood for this purpose; and since that, very few of the people of this country have ventured to eat any sugar made by the Franks: the Báshà was also obliged to prohibit the use of blood in his own sugar-bakeries; and the white of eggs has been employed in its stead. Some of the Egyptians, seeing the European sugar to be very superior to that made here, use it; holding the doctrine that what is originally clean may become clean again after pollution: but I am obliged to keep the coarse Egyptian sugar for the purpose of making sherbet for my visiters; some of whom hold long discussions with me on this subject.

It is a general custom among the Egyptians, after washing clothes, to pour clean water upon them, and to say, in doing so, "I testify that there is no deity but God; and I testify that Moḥammad is God's Apostle."[1] In speaking of their religion, I have mentioned several other practices instituted for the sake of cleanliness; most of which are universally observed. But, notwithstanding these cleanly practices and principles, and their custom of frequently going to the bath, the Egyptians do not change their linen so often as some people of more northern climates, who need not so much to do this frequently: they often go to the bath in a dirty shirt; and, after a thorough washing, put on the same again.

Filial piety is one of the more remarkable virtues of this people. The outward respect which they pay to their parents I have already had occasion to mention. Great respect is also shewn by the young to those far advanced in age;[2] and more especially to such as are reputed men of great piety or learning.

Love of their country, and more especially of *home*, is another predominant characteristic of the modern Egyptians. In general, they have a great dread of quitting their native land. I have heard of several determining to visit a foreign country, for the sake of considerable advantages in prospect; but when the time of their intended departure drew near, their resolution failed them. Severe oppression has lately lessened this feeling; which is doubtless owing, in a great degree, to ignorance of foreign lands and their inhabitants. It was probably from the same feeling prevailing among the Arabs of his time, that Moḥammad was induced to promise such high rewards in a future world to those who fled their country for the sake of his religion. I have heard it remarked as a proof of the extraordinary love which the Egyptians have for their native place, that a woman or girl in this country will seldom consent, or her parents allow her, to marry a man who will not promise to reside with her in her native town or village; but I rather think that the reluctance to change the place of abode in this case arises from the risk which the female incurs of wanting the protection of her relations. The Bedawees are so attached to their deserts, and have so great a contempt for people who reside in towns, and for agriculturists, that it is a matter of surprise that so many of them were induced to settle even upon the fertile banks of the Nile. The modern Egyptians, though in a great degree descended from Bedawees, while they resemble the Bedawees in

---

[1] To express that a person has done this, they say, "sháhad el-ḥawáïg," for ghasal el-ḥawáïg wa-teshahhad 'aleyhà."

[2] See Leviticus, xix. 32.

love of their *native* country, have a horror of the desert. One journey in the desert furnishes them with tales of exaggerated hardships, perils, and wonders, which they are extremely fond of relating to their less experienced countrymen.

Indolence pervades all classes of the Egyptians, except those who are obliged to earn their livelihood by severe manual labour. It is the result of the climate, and of the fecundity of the soil. Even the mechanics, who are extremely greedy of gain, will generally spend two days in a work which they might easily accomplish in one; and will leave the most lucrative employment to idle away their time with the pipe: but the porter, the groom, who runs before his master's horse, and the boatmen, who are often employed in towing the vessels up the river during calm and very hot weather, as well as many other labourers, endure extreme fatigue.

The Egyptians are also excessively obstinate. I have mentioned, in a former chapter, that they have been notorious, from ancient times, that is, from the period of the Roman domination, for refusing to pay their taxes until they have been severely beaten; and that they often boast of the number of stripes which they have received before they would part with their money. Such conduct is very common among them. I was once told that a fellâḥ, from whom the value of about four shillings was demanded by his governor, endured so severe a bastinading rather than pay this paltry sum, which he declared he did not possess, that the governor ordered him to be dismissed; but, striking him on his face as he limped away, there fell out of his mouth a gold coin of the exact value of the sum demanded of him; so that his beating, terrible as it was, fell short of what was necessary to make him pay. This disposition seems a strange peculiarity in their character; but it is easily accounted for by the fact that they know very well, the more readily they pay, the more will be exacted from them. In other respects, however, they are extremely obstinate and difficult to govern; though very obsequious in their manners and professions. It is seldom that an Egyptian workman can be induced to make a thing exactly to order: he will generally follow his own opinion in preference to that of his employer; and will scarcely ever finish his work by the time he has promised.

Though very submissive to their governors, the fellâḥeen of Egypt are not deficient in courage when excited by feuds among each other; and they become excellent soldiers.

In sensuality, as far as it relates to the indulgence of libidinous passions, the Egyptians, as well as other natives of hot climates, certainly exceed more northern nations; yet this excess is not to be attributed merely to the climate, but more especially to the institution of polygamy, to the facility with which divorcements are accomplished whenever a man may wish to marry a new wife, and to the custom of concubinage. It is even said, and, I believe, with truth, that, in this respect, they exceed the neighbouring nations, whose religion and civil institutions are similar;[1] and that their country still deserves the appellation of "the abode of the wicked," which, in the Ḳur-án,[2] is, according to the best commentators, applied to ancient Egypt, if we take the word here translated "wicked" in its more usual modern sense of "debauchees."—A vice for which the Memlooks who governed Egypt were infamous was so spread by them in this country as to become not less rare here than in almost any other country of the East; but of late years, it is said to have much decreased.

The most immodest freedom of conversation is indulged in by persons of both sexes, and of every station of life, in Egypt; even by the most virtuous and respectable women, with the exception of a very few, who often make use of coarse language, but not unchaste. From persons of the best education, expressions are often heard so obscene as only to be fit for a low brothel; and things are named, and subjects talked of, by the most genteel women, without any idea of their being indecorous, in the hearing of men, that many prostitutes in our country would probably abstain from mentioning.

The women of Egypt have the character of being the most licentious in their feelings of all females who lay any claim to be considered as members of a civilized nation; and this character is freely bestowed upon them by their countrymen, even in conversation with foreigners. Numerous exceptions doubtless exist; and I am happy to insert the following words translated from a note by my friend the sheykh Moḥammad 'Eiyád Eṭ-Ṭanṭáwee, on a passage in "The Thousand and One Nights." "Many persons reckon marrying a second time among the greatest of disgraceful actions. This opinion is most common in the country-towns and villages; and the relations of my mother are thus characterized, so that a woman of them, when

---

1 This is not meant to reflect upon the Turks, nor upon the Arabs of the desert. 2 Ch. vii. v. 142.

her husband dies while she is young, or divorces her while she is young, passes her life, however long it may be, in widowhood, and never marries a second time."—But with respect to the majority of the Egyptian women, it must, I fear, be allowed that they are very licentious. What liberty they have, many of them, it is said, abuse; and most of them are not considered safe, unless under lock and key; to which restraint few are subjected. It is believed that they possess a degree of cunning in the management of their intrigues which the most prudent and careful husband cannot guard against, and consequently that their plots are seldom frustrated, however great may be the apparent risk of the undertakings in which they engage. Sometimes, the husband himself is made the unconscious means of gratifying his wife's criminal propensities. Some of the stories of the intrigues of women in "The Thousand and One Nights" present faithful pictures of occurrences not unfrequent in the modern metropolis of Egypt. Many of the men of this city are of opinion that almost all the women would intrigue if they could do so without danger; and that the greater proportion of them do. I should be sorry to think that the former opinion was just; and I am almost persuaded that it is over-severe, because it appears, from the customs with regard to women generally prevailing here, that the latter must be false. The difficulty of carrying on an intrigue with a female in this place can hardly be conceived by a person who is not moderately well acquainted with Eastern customs and habits. It is not only difficult for a woman of the middle or higher classes to admit her paramour into the house in which she resides, but it is almost impossible for her to have a private interview with a man who has a ḥareem, in his own house; or to enter the house of a man who is neither married nor has a concubine slave, without attracting the notice of the neighbours, and causing their immediate interference. But as it cannot be denied that many of the women of Egypt engage in intrigues notwithstanding such risks, it may perhaps be true that the difficulties which lie in the way are the chief bar to most others. Among the females of the lower orders, intrigues are more easily accomplished, and frequent.

The libidinous character of the generality of the women of Egypt, and the licentious conduct of a great number of them, may be attributed to many causes; partly, to the climate, and partly, to their want of proper instruction, and of innocent pastimes and employments:[1] but it is more to be attributed to the conduct of the husbands themselves; and to conduct far more disgraceful to them than the utmost severity that any of them is known to exercise in the regulations of his ḥareem. The generality of husbands in Egypt endeavour to increase the libidinous feelings of their wives by every means in their power; though, at the same time, they assiduously study to prevent their indulging those feelings unlawfully. The women are permitted to listen, screened behind their windows of wooden lattice-work, to immoral songs and tales sung or related in the streets by men whom they pay for this entertainment; and to view the voluptuous dances of the ghawázee, and of the effeminate khäwals. The ghawázee, who are professed prostitutes, are not unfrequently introduced into the ḥareems of the wealthy, not merely to entertain the ladies with their dances, but to teach them their voluptuous arts; and even indecent puppets are sometimes brought into such ḥareems for the amusement of the inmates.—Innumerable stories of the artifices and intrigues of the women of Egypt have been related to me. The following narratives of late occurrences will serve as specimens.

A slave-dealer, who had been possessed of property which enabled him to live in comfort, but had lost the greater part of it, married a young and handsome woman in this city, who had sufficient wealth to make up for his losses. He soon, however, neglected her; and as he was past the prime of life, she became indifferent to him, and placed her affections upon another man, a dustman, who had been in the habit of coming to her house. She purchased, for this person, a shop close by her house; gave him a sum of money to enable him to pursue a less degraded occupation, as a seller of grain and fodder; and informed him that she had contrived a plan for his visiting her in perfect security. Her ḥareem had a window with hanging shutters; and almost close before this window rose a palm-tree, out-topping the house: this tree, she observed, would afford her lover a means of access to her, and of egress from her apartment in case of

---

[1] In the first edition of the present work, I included, among these supposed causes, the degree of restraint imposed upon the women, and their seclusion from open intercourse with the other sex. This I did, not because confinement is said to have this effect in the West, where, being contrary to general custom, it is felt as an oppression, but because the assertion of the Egyptians, that the Eastern women in general are more licentiously disposed than the men, seemed to be an argument against the main principle of the constitution of Eastern society. I did not consider that this argument is at least counterbalanced by what I have before mentioned, that the women who are commonly considered the *most licentious* of all Eastern women (namely, those of Egypt,) are those who are said to have *most licence*.

danger. She had only one servant, a female, who engaged to assist her in the accomplishment of her desires. Previously to her lover's first visit to her, she desired the servant to inform her husband of what was about to take place in the ensuing night. He determined to keep watch; and, having told his wife that he was going out, and should not return that night, concealed himself in a lower apartment. At night, the maid came to tell him that the visiter was in the ḥareem. He went up; but found the ḥareem-door shut. On his trying to open it, his wife screamed; her lover, at the same time, escaping from the window, by means of the palm-tree. She called to her neighbours, "Come to my assistance! Pray come! There is a robber in my house!" Several of them soon came; and, finding her locked in her room, and her husband outside the door, told her there was nobody in the house but her husband and maid. She said that the man they called her husband was a robber: that her husband was gone to sleep out. The latter then informed them of what had passed; and insisted that a man was with her: he broke open the door, and searched the room; but, finding no man, was reprimanded by his neighbours, and abused by his wife, for uttering a slander. The next day, his wife, taking with her, as witnesses of his having accused her of a criminal intrigue, two of the neighbours who had come in on hearing her screams for assistance, arraigned her husband at the Maḥkemeh as the slanderer of a virtuous woman without the evidence of his own sight or of other witnesses. Being convicted of this offence, he was punished with eighty stripes, in accordance with the ordinance of the Ḳur-án.[1] His wife now asked him if he would divorce her; but he refused. For three days after this event, they lived peaceably together. On the third night, the wife, having invited her lover to visit her, bound her husband, hand and foot, while he was asleep, and tied him down to the mattress. Shortly after, her lover came up, and, waking the husband; threatened him with instant death if he should call, and remained with the wife for several hours, in his presence. As soon as the intruder had gone, the husband was unbound by his wife, and called out to his neighbours, beating her at the same time with such violence that she, also, began to call for assistance. The neighbours, coming in, and seeing him in a fury, easily believed her assertion that he had become raving mad, and, trying to soothe him with kind words, and prayers

[1] Ch. xxiv. v. 4.

that God would restore him to sanity, liberated her from his grasp. She procured, as soon as possible, a rasool from the Ḳáḍee; and went, with him and her husband and several of her neighbours who had witnessed the beating that she had received, before the judge. The neighbours unanimously declared their opinion that her husband was mad; and the Ḳáḍee ordered that he should be conveyed to the Máristán[1] (or common mad-house): but the wife, affecting to pity him, begged that she might be allowed to chain him in an apartment in her house, that she might alleviate his sufferings by waiting upon him. The Ḳáḍee assented; praising the benevolence of the woman, and praying that God might reward her. She accordingly procured an iron collar and a chain from the Máristán, and chained him in a lower apartment of her house. Every night, in his presence, her lover visited her: after which she importuned him in vain to divorce her; and when the neighbours came in daily to ask how he was, the only answer he received to his complaints and accusations against his wife was, "God restore thee. God restore thee." Thus he continued about a month; and his wife, finding that he still persisted in refusing to divorce her, sent for a keeper of the Máristán to take him. The neighbours came round as he left the house: one exclaimed, "There is no strength nor power but in God! God restore thee." Another said, "How sad! He was really a worthy man."—A third remarked, "Bádingáns[2] are very abundant just now." While he was confined in the Máristán, his wife came daily to him, and asked him if he would divorce her: on his answering, "No," she said, "Then chained you may lie until you die; and my lover shall come to me constantly." At length, after seven months' confinement, he consented to divorce her; upon which she procured his liberation; and he fulfilled his promise. Her lover was of too low a grade to become her husband; so she remained unmarried; and received him whenever she pleased: but the maid revealed the true history of this affair; and it soon became a subject of common talk.

When the wife of a man of wealth or rank engages in a criminal intrigue, both she and her paramour generally incur great danger.[3] A short time ago, the wife of an officer of high rank in the army

---

1 Vulgarly called "Muristán."

2 Madness is said to be more common and more violent in Egypt when the black bádingán (the fruit of the black egg-plant) is in season: that is, in the hot weather.

3 "How many men, in Maṣr," said one of my friends to me, "have lost their lives on account of women! A very handsome young libertine, who lived in this house which you now occupy, was beheaded here in the street, before his own door, for an intrigue with the wife of a Bey; and all the women of Maṣr wept for him."

took advantage of the absence of her husband from the metropolis (where he always resided with her when not on military duty) to invite a Christian merchant, of whom she had been in the habit of buying silks, to pay her a visit. He went to her house at the time appointed, and found a eunuch at the door, who took him to another house, disguised him in the loose outer garments and veil of a lady, and then brought him back, and introduced him to his mistress. He passed nearly the whole of the night with her; and, rising before she awoke, put into his pocket a purse which he had given her, and went down to the eunuch, who conducted him again to the house where he had put on his disguise: having here resumed his own outer clothes, he repaired to his shop. Soon after, the lady, who had missed the purse, came, and taxed him with having taken it: she told him that she did not want money, but only desired his company; and begged him to come to her again in the ensuing evening; which he promised to do: but in the afternoon, a female servant from the house of this lady came to his shop, and told him that her mistress had mixed some poison in a bottle of water which she had ordered to be given him to drink.—This mode of revenge is said to have been often adopted when the woman's paramour has given her even a slight offence.

It is seldom that the wife of a Muslim is guilty of a criminal intrigue without being punished with death if there be four witnesses to the fact, and they or the husband prosecute her; and not always does she escape this punishment if she be detected by any of the officers of justice: in the latter case, four witnesses are not required, and often the woman, if of a respectable family, is put to death, generally in private, on the mere arbitrary authority of the government: but a bribe will sometimes save her; for it will always be accepted, if it can with safety. Drowning is the punishment now almost always inflicted, publicly, upon women convicted of adultery in Cairo and other large towns of Egypt, instead of that ordained by the law, which is stoning.—A poor woman of this city, a few months before her story was related to me, married a man whose trade was that of selling fowls, and, while living with him and her mother, took three other lodgings, and married three other husbands; all of whom were generally absent from the metropolis: so she calculated that when any of these three persons came to town for a few days, she might easily find an excuse to go to him. They happened, unfortunately for her, to come to town on the same day; and all of them went, the same evening, to inquire for her at her mother's house. Being much embarrassed by their presence, and her first husband being also with her, she feigned to be ill, and soon to become insensible; and was taken, by her mother, to an inner room. One of the husbands proposed to give her something to restore her: another wished to try a different remedy: they began to contend which was the best medicine; and one of them said, "I shall give her what I please: is not she my wife?" "Your wife!" exclaimed each of the three other husbands at the same time: "she is *my* wife." —Each proved his marriage: the woman was taken to the Maḥkemeh; tried; condemned to death; and thrown into the Nile.—During my first visit to this country, a similar case occurred: a woman married three soldiers, of the niẓám, or regular troops. She was buried in a hole, breast-deep, and then shot.

A woman may sometimes, but very rarely, trust in palliating circumstances, or the support of powerful friends, to save her from the penalty of death, in case of her detection in a criminal intercourse; as in the following instance.—The Básha gave one of the slaves in his ḥareem in marriage to a rich slave-merchant, from whom he had purchased many of his memlooks and female slaves. This man was not only unfaithful to her, but utterly neglected her; and she, in consequence, formed an improper intimacy with a merchant of whom she was a frequent customer. One day, when her husband was out, a black slave belonging to him happened to see a man's head at a small aperture in a window of the ḥareem. He immediately went up to search the room of the wife; who, hearing him coming, locked her paramour in an adjoining closet. The slave broke open the door of the closet; and the man within rushed at him with a dagger which he wore in his girdle; but the former seized the blade in his hand; and the woman held him until her lover had escaped: she then kissed the slave's hand, and implored him not to cause her death by informing her husband of what had passed: she, however, found him inexorable: he immediately went to his master, shewing his bleeding hand, and telling him the cause of the wound. The woman, meanwhile, fled to the Básha's ḥareem, for protection. Her husband demanded of the Básha that she should be given up, and put to death; and, the request being deemed a proper one, she was brought before her former master to answer for her crime. She threw herself at his feet; kissed the skirt of his clothing; and acquainted him with her husband's vicious conduct, and his utter neglect of her; and the Básha, feeling *himself* insulted by the husband's conduct, spat in his face; and sent back the wife to his own ḥareem. Her paramour did not live long after this: he was smothered in the house of some courtesans; but none of these women was punished; as it could not be proved which of them committed the act.

For their sentiments with regard to women, and their general conduct towards the fair sex, the Egyptians, in common with other Muslims, have been reprehended with too great severity. It is true that they do not consider it necessary, or even delicate, to consult the choice of a girl under age previously to giving her away in matrimony; but it is not less true that a man of the middle or higher classes, almost always, makes his choice of a wife from hearsay, or as a person blindfold; having no means of seeing her until the contract is made, and she is brought to his house. It is impossible, therefore, that there should be any mutual attachment before marriage. Both sexes, in truth, are oppressed by tyrannical laws and customs; but, happily, they regard their chains as becoming and honourable: they would feel themselves disgraced by shaking them off. As to the restraint which is exercised towards the women, I have before remarked that it is in a great degree voluntary on their part, and that I believe it to be less strict in Egypt than in any other country of the Turkish empire: it is certainly far less so than it has been represented to be by many persons. They generally look upon this restraint with a degree of pride, as evincing the husband's care for them; and value themselves upon their being hidden as treasures.[1] In good society, it is considered highly indecorous to inquire, in direct terms, respecting the health of a friend's wife, or of any female in his house, unless she be a relation of the person who makes the inquiry.—One of my Egyptian acquaintances asking another native of this country, who had been in Paris, what was the most remarkable thing that he had seen in the land of the infidels, the latter, thinking lightly of all that he had observed really worthy of exciting the admiration of an unprejudiced and a sensible man, gave the following answer:—"I witnessed nothing so remarkable as this fact. It is a custom of every person among the rich and great, in Paris and other cities of France, frequently to invite his friends and acquaintances, both men and women, to an

---

[1] A respectable female is generally addressed, in a letter, as "the guarded lady, and concealed jewel" ("es-sitt el-maṣooneh wa-l-góharah el-meknooneh").

entertainment in his house. The rooms in which the company are received are lighted with a great number of candles and lamps. There, the men and women assemble promiscuously; the women, as you well know, unveiled; and a man may sit next to another's wife, whom he has never seen before, and may walk, talk, and even dance with her, in the very presence of her own husband, who is neither angry nor jealous at such disgraceful conduct."

The Egyptians are equally remarkable for generosity and cupidity. That two such opposite qualities should be united in the same mind is not a little surprising; but such is generally the case with this people. An overreaching and deceitful disposition in commercial transactions, which is too common among all nations, is one of the most notorious faults of the Egyptian: in such cases, he seldom scruples to frame a falsehood which may better his bargain. Among people who groan beneath the yoke of a tyrannical and rapacious government (and such has long been the government of Egypt), a disposition to avarice invariably predominates: for a man is naturally most tenacious of that which is most liable to be taken from him; and hence the oppressed Egyptian, when he has a sum of money which he does not require for necessary expenses, and cannot profitably employ, generally lays it out in the purchase of ornaments for his wife or wives; which ornaments he can easily convert again into money. Hence, also, it is a common practice in this country (as it is, or has been, in almost every country under similar political circumstances,) for a man to hide treasure in his house, under the paved floor, or in some other part; and as many a person who does so dies suddenly, without being able to inform his family where is his "makhbà," or hiding-place, money is not unfrequently discovered on pulling down houses.—A vice near akin to cupidity, namely envy, I believe to be equally prevalent among the modern Egyptians, in common with the whole Arab race; for many of them are candid enough to confess their own opinion that this hateful disposition is almost wholly concentrated in the minds of their nation.

The Egyptians are generally honest in the payment of debts. Their Prophet asserted that even martyrdom would not atone for a debt undischarged. Few of them ever accept interest for a loan of money; as it is strictly forbidden by their law.

Constant veracity is a virtue extremely rare in modern Egypt. Falsehood was *commended* by the Prophet when it tended to reconcile persons at variance with each other: also, when practised in order to please one's wife; and to obtain any advantage in a war with the enemies of the faith: though highly reprobated in other cases. This offers some little palliation of the general practice of lying which prevails among the modern Arabs; for if people are allowed to lie in certain cases, they insensibly contract a habit of doing so in others. Though most of the Egyptians often lie designedly, they are seldom heard to retract an unintentional misstatement without expressing themselves thus: "No: I beg forgiveness of God:[1] it was so and so;" as, in stating anything of which they are not quite certain, they say, "God is all-knowing."[2]—I may here mention (and I do it with some feeling of national pride) that, some years ago, there was an Armenian jeweller in this city (Cairo) so noted for his veracity, that his acquaintances determined to give him some appellation significant of his possessing a virtue so rare among them; and the name they gave him was "El-Ingileezee," or *The Englishman*, which has become his family name. It is common to hear tradesmen in this place, when demanding a price which they do not mean to abate, say, "One word; the word of the English:"[3] they also often say, "The word of the Franks," in this sense: but I have never heard any particular nation thus honourably distinguished except the English and the Maghrabees, or Western Arabs, which latter people have acquired this reputation by being rather more veracious than most other Arabs.

I have before mentioned the practice of swearing by God which prevails among the Egyptians: I must here add, that many of them scruple not to make use of an oath with the view of obtaining credit to a falsehood. In this case, they sometimes say, "Wa-lláhi" ("By God"); but more commonly, "Wa-llah;"—for, though the latter expression has the same meaning as the former, they pretend that it may also be used as an ejaculation in praise of God; whereas "Wa-lláhi" is a decided oath, and, if uttered to a falsehood, is a heinous sin. Such an oath, if violated, must be expiated by once feeding or clothing ten poor men, liberating a Muslim slave, or captive, or fasting three days.[4] This, however, is the expiation allowed by the Ḳur-án only for an inconsiderate oath: yet the modern Muslims sometimes observe it in order to free themselves from the guilt of a deliberate false oath; and they generally prefer the fast to either of the other modes of expiation. There are some oaths which, I believe, few Muslims would falsely take; such as saying, three times, "By God, the Great;"[5]—

1 "Lá: astaghfir Alláh."
2 "Alláhu aạlam."
3 "Kilmet el-Ingileez."
4 Ḳur-án, ch. v., v. 91.
5 "Wa-lláhi-l-aẓeem."

and the oath upon the muṣ-ḥaf (or copy of the Ḳur-án)—saying, "By what this contains of the word of God!"—but a form of oath which is still more to be depended upon is that of saying, "I impose upon myself divorcement"[1] (that is, the divorce of my wife, if what I say be false); or, "I impose upon myself interdiction;"[2] which has a similar meaning ("My wife be unlawful to me"); or, "I impose upon myself a triple divorcement;"[3] which binds by the irrevocable divorce of the wife. If a man use any one of these three forms of oath falsely, his wife, if he have but one, is divorced by the oath itself, if proved to be false, without further ceremony; and if he have two or more wives, he must, in such circumstances, choose one of them to put away. There are, however, abandoned liars who will swear falsely by the oath that is generally held most binding. A poet, speaking of a character of this description, says,

> "But Abu-l-Mo'allà is most false
> When he swears by the oath of divorce."

The generality of the Egyptians are easily excited to quarrel; particularly those of the lower orders, who, when enraged, curse each other's fathers, mothers, beards, &c.; and lavish upon each other a variety of opprobrious epithets; such as "son of the dog, pimp, pig," and an appellation which they think still worse than any of these, namely, "Jew." When one curses the father of the other, the latter generally retorts by cursing the father and mother, and sometimes the whole household, of his adversary. They menace each other; but seldom proceed to blows. In a few instances, however, I have seen low persons in this country so enraged as to bite, and grasp each other by the throat. I have also witnessed many instances of forbearance on the part of individuals of the middle and lower classes, when grossly insulted: I have often heard an Egyptian say, on receiving a blow from an equal, "God bless thee." "God requite thee good." "Beat me again." In general, a quarrel terminates by one or both parties saying, "Justice is against me:"[4] often, after this, they recite the Fát'ḥah together; and then, sometimes, embrace and kiss one another.

The Egyptians are particularly prone to satire; and often display considerable wit in their jeers and jests. Their language affords them great facilities for punning, and for ambiguous conversation, in which

---

1 "'Aleiya-ṭ-ṭaláḳ."
2 "'Aleiya-l-ḥarám."
3 "'Aleiya-ṭ-ṭaláḳ bi-t-teláteh."
4 "El-ḥaḳḳ 'aleiya."

they very frequently indulge. The lower orders sometimes lampoon their rulers in songs, and ridicule those enactments of the government by which they themselves most suffer. I was once much amused with a song which I found to be very popular in the town and district of Aswán, on the southern frontier of Egypt: its burden was a plain invocation to the plague to take their tyrannical governor and his Copt clerk. Another song, which was popular throughout Egypt during my first visit to this country, and which was composed on the occasion of an increase of the income-tax called "firdeh," began thus: "You who have [nothing on your head but] a libdeh! sell it, and pay the firdeh." The libdeh, I have before mentioned, is a felt cap, which is worn under, or instead of, the turban; and the man must be very poor who has no other covering than this for his head.

CHAPTER XIV.

INDUSTRY.

It is melancholy to contrast the present poverty of Egypt with its prosperity in ancient times, when the variety, elegance, and exquisite finish displayed in its manufactures attracted the admiration of surrounding nations, and its inhabitants were in no need of foreign commerce to increase their wealth, or to add to their comforts. Antiquarian researches shew us that a high degree of excellence in the arts of civilized life distinguished the Egyptians in the age of Moses, and at a yet earlier period. Not only the Pharaohs and the priests and military chiefs, but also a great proportion of the wealthy agriculturists, and other private individuals, in those remote times, passed a life of the most refined luxury, were clad in linen of the most delicate fabric, and reclined on couches and chairs which have served as models for the furniture of our modern saloons. Nature is as lavish of her favours as she was of old to the inhabitants of the valley of the Nile; but, for many centuries, they have ceased to enjoy the benefit of a steady government: each of their successive rulers, during this long lapse of time, considering the uncertain tenure of his power, has been almost wholly intent upon increasing his own wealth; and thus, a large portion of the nation has gradually perished, and the remnant, in general, been reduced to a state of the most afflicting poverty. The male portion of the population of Egypt being scarcely greater than is sufficient for the cultivation of as much of the soil as is subject to the natural inundation, or easily irrigated by artificial means, the number of persons who devote themselves to manufactures in this country is comparatively very small; and as there are so few competitors, and, at present, few persons of wealth to encourage them, their works in general display but little skill.

But the low state of the manual arts has, in a great degree, been occasioned by another cause: the Turkish Sulṭán Seleem, after his conquest of Egypt, took with him thence to his own country, as related by El-Gabartee,[1] so many masters of crafts which were not practised in Turkey, that more than fifty manual arts ceased to be pursued in Egypt.

Painting and sculpture, as applied to the representation of living objects, are, I have already stated, absolutely prohibited by the religion of El-Islám: there are, however, some Muslims in Egypt who attempt the delineation of men, lions, camels, and other animals, flowers, boats, &c., particularly in (what they call) the decoration of a few shop-fronts, the doors of pilgrims' houses, &c.; though their performances would be surpassed by children of five or six years of age in our own country. But the Muslim religion especially promotes industry, by requiring that every man be acquainted with some art or occupation by which he may, in case of necessity, be able to support himself and those dependant upon him, and to fulfil all his religious and moral duties. The art in which the Egyptians most excel is architecture. The finest specimens of Arabian architecture are found in the Egyptian metropolis and its environs; and not only the mosques and other public buildings are remarkable for their grandeur and beauty, but many of the private dwellings, also, attract our admiration, especially by their interior structure and decorations. Yet this art has, of late years, much declined, like most others in this country: a new style of architecture, derived from the Turks, partly Oriental and partly European, and of a very plain description, being generally preferred. The doors, ceilings, windows, and pavements, of the buildings in the older style, which have already been described, display considerable taste, of a peculiar kind; and so, too, do most of the Egyptian manufactures; though many of them are rather clumsy, or ill finished. The turners of wood, whose chief occupation was that of making the lattice-work of windows, were very numerous, and their work was generally neater than it is at present: they have less employment now, as windows of modern houses are often made of glass. The turner, like most other artisans in Egypt, sits to his work. In the art of glass-making, for which Egypt was so much celebrated in ancient times, the modern inhabitants of this country possess but little skill: they have lost the art of manufacturing coloured glass for

[1] Near the beginning of his History.

windows; but for the construction of windows of this material they are still admired, though not so much as they were a few years ago, before the adoption of a new style of architecture diminished the demand for their work. Their pottery is generally of a rude kind: it mostly consists of porous bottles and jars, for cooling, as well as keeping, water. For their skill in the preparation of morocco leather, they are justly celebrated. The branches and leaves of the palm-tree they employ in a great variety of manufactures: of the former, they make seats, coops, chests, frames for beds, &c.: of the latter, baskets, panniers, mats, brooms, fly-whisks, and many other utensils. Of the fibres also that grow at the foot of the branches of the palm-tree are made most of the ropes used in Egypt. The best mats (which are much used instead of carpets, particularly in summer,) are made of rushes. Egypt has lost the celebrity which it enjoyed in ancient times for its fine linen: the linen and cotton and woollen cloths, and the silks now woven in this country, are generally of coarse or poor qualities.

The Egyptians have long been famous for the art of hatching fowls' eggs by artificial heat. This practice, though obscurely described by ancient authors, appears to have been common in Egypt in very remote times. The building in which the process is performed is called, in Lower Egypt, "maạmal el-firákh," and, in Upper Egypt, "maạmal el-farroog:" in the former division of the country, there are more than a hundred such establishments; and in the latter, more than half that number. Most of the superintendents, if not all, are Copts. The proprietors pay a tax to the government. The maạmal is constructed of burnt or sun-dried bricks; and consists of two parallel rows of small ovens and cells for fire, divided by a narrow, vaulted passage; each oven being about nine or ten feet long, eight feet wide, and five or six feet high, and having above it a vaulted fire-cell, of the same size, or rather less in height. Each oven communicates with the passage by an aperture large enough for a man to enter; and with its fire-cell by a similar aperture: the fire-cells, also, of the same row, communicate with each other; and each has an aperture in its vault (for the escape of the smoke), which is opened only occasionally: the passage, too, has several such apertures in its vaulted roof. The eggs are placed upon mats or straw, and one tier above another, usually to the number of three tiers, in the ovens; and burning "gelleh" (a fuel before mentioned, composed of the dung of animals, mixed with chopped straw, and made into the form of round, flat cakes,) is placed upon the floors of the fire-cells above. The entrance of the maạmal is well closed. Before it are two or three small chambers, for the attendant, and the fuel, and the chickens when newly hatched. The operation is performed only during two or three months in the year, in the spring; earliest in the most southern parts of the country. Each maạmal in general contains from twelve to twenty-four ovens; and receives about a hundred and fifty thousand eggs during the annual period of its continuing open; one quarter or a third of which number generally fail. The peasants of the neighbourhood supply the eggs: the attendant of the maạmal examines them, and afterwards usually gives one chicken for every two eggs that he has received. In general, only half the number of ovens are used for the first ten days, and fires are lighted only in the fire-cells above these. On the eleventh day, these fires are put out, and others are lighted in the other fire-cells, and fresh eggs placed in the ovens below these last. On the following day, some of the eggs in the former ovens are removed, and placed on the floor of the fire-cells above, where the fires have been extinguished. The general heat maintained during the process is from 100° to 103° of Fahrenheit's thermometer. The manager, having been accustomed to this art from his youth, knows, from his long experience, the exact temperature that is required for the success of the operation, without having any instrument, like our thermometer, to guide him. On the twentieth day, some of the eggs first put in are hatched; but most, on the twenty-first day; that is, after the same period as is required in the case of natural incubation. The weaker of the chickens are placed in the passage: the rest, in the innermost of the anterior apartments, where they remain a day or two before they are given to the persons to whom they are due. When the eggs first placed have been hatched, and the second supply half hatched, the ovens in which the former were placed, and which are now vacant, receive the third supply; and, in like manner, when the second supply is hatched, a fourth is introduced in its place. I have not found that the fowls produced in this manner are inferior in point of flavour, or in other respects, to those produced from the egg by incubation. The fowls and their eggs in Egypt are, in both cases, and with respect to size and flavour, very inferior to those in our country. In one of the Egyptian newspapers published by order of the government (No. 248, for the 18th of Ramaḍán, 1246, or the 3rd of March, 1831, of our era,) I find the following statement:—

	Lower Egypt.	Upper Egypt.
Number of establishments for the hatching of fowls' eggs in the present year	105	59
Number of eggs used	19,325,600	6,878,900
Number spoiled	6,255,867	2,529,660
Number hatched	13,069,733	4,349,240

Though the commerce of Egypt has much declined since the discovery of the passage from Europe to India by the Cape of Good Hope, and in consequence of the monopolies and exactions of Moḥammad 'Alee and his successors, it is still considerable; and during the last few years it has been much improved by the numerous steam-vessels plying between Alexandria and England, France, and Austria, and between Suez and India, and by the establishment of railways in Lower Egypt.

The principal *imports* from Europe are woollen cloths (chiefly from France), calico, plain muslin, figured muslin (of Scotch manufacture, for turbans), silks, velvet, crape, shawls (Scotch, English, and French,) in imitation of those of Kashmeer, writing-paper (chiefly from Venice), fire-arms, straight sword-blades (from Germany) for the Nubians, &c., watches and clocks, coffee-cups and various articles of earthenware and glass (mostly from Germany), many kinds of hardwares, planks, metal, beads, wine and liqueurs; and white slaves, silks, embroidered handkerchiefs and napkins, mouth-pieces of pipes, slippers, and a variety of made goods, copper and brass wares, &c., from Constantinople:—from Asia Minor, carpets (among which, the seggádehs, or small prayer-carpets), figs, &c.:—from Syria, tobacco, striped silks, 'abáyehs (or woollen cloaks), soap:—from Arabia, coffee, spices, several drugs, Indian goods (as shawls, silks, muslin, &c.):—from Abyssinia and Sennár and the neighbouring countries, slaves, gold, ivory, ostrich-feathers, kurbágs (or whips of hippopotamus' hide), tamarind in cakes, gums, senna:—from El-Gharb, or the West (that is, northern Africa, from Egypt westwards), ṭarbooshes (or red cloth skull-caps), burnooses (or white woollen hooded cloaks), ḥerāms (or white woollen sheets, used for night-coverings and for dress), yellow morocco shoes.

The principal *exports* to Europe are wheat, maize, rice, beans, cotton, flax, indigo, coffee, various spices, gums, senna, ivory, ostrich-feathers:—to Turkey, male and female Abyssinian and black slaves (including a few eunuchs), rice, coffee, spices, ḥennà, &c.:—to Syria, slaves, rice, &c.:—to Arabia, chiefly corn:—to Sennár and the neighbouring countries, cotton and linen and woollen goods, a few Syrian and Egyptian striped silks, small carpets, beads and other ornaments, soap, the straight sword-blades mentioned before, fire-arms, copper wares, writing-paper.

To convey some notion of the value of money in Cairo, in late years, I insert the following list of the prices of certain common articles of food, &c., made during my second visit. (Since Egypt has again become a highway to India, and a resort of travellers far more numerous than they were a few years ago, the prices of commodities of every kind have very greatly increased.) In the country towns and villages, most kinds of provisions are cheaper than in the metropolis: meat, fowls, and pigeons, about half the prices here mentioned: wheat and bread, from about one third to half.

	P.	F.	(£.	*s.*	*d.*)
Wheat, the ardebb (or about five bushels), from 50 P. to	63	0	(0	13	$2\frac{1}{5}$)
Rice, the ardebb, about	240	0	(2	8	0)
Mutton or lamb, the raṭl	1	0	(0	0	$2\frac{2}{5}$)
Beef, do.	0	35	(0	0	$2\frac{1}{10}$)
Fowls, each, 1 P. 10 F. to	1	20	(0	0	$3\frac{3}{5}$)
Pigeons, the pair, 1 P. 10 F. to	1	20	(0	0	$3\frac{3}{5}$)
Eggs, three for	0	5	(0	0	$0\frac{3}{10}$)
Fresh butter, the raṭl	2	0	(0	0	$4\frac{4}{5}$)
Clarified butter, do. 2 P. to	2	10	(0	0	$5\frac{2}{5}$)
Coffee, do. 6 P. to	7	0	(0	1	$4\frac{4}{5}$)
Gebelee tobacco, the uḳḳah, 15 P. to	18	0	(0	3	$7\frac{1}{5}$)
Sooree do. do. 5 P. to	10	0	(0	2	0)
Egyptian loaf-sugar, the raṭl	2	0	(0	0	$4\frac{4}{5}$)
European do. do.	2	10	(0	0	$5\frac{2}{5}$)
Summer grapes do.	0	10	(0	0	$0\frac{3}{5}$)
Later do. do. 20 F. to	0	30	(0	0	$1\frac{4}{5}$)
Fine biscuit, the ḳanṭár	160	0	(1	12	0)
Water, the ḳirbeh (or goat's skin), 10 F. to	0	20	(0	0	$1\frac{1}{5}$)
Firewood, the donkey-load	11	0	(0	2	$2\frac{2}{5}$)
Charcoal, the uḳḳah, 20 F. to	0	30	(0	0	$1\frac{4}{5}$)
Soap, the raṭl	1	30	(0	0	$4\frac{1}{5}$)
Tallow candles, the uḳḳah	8	20	(0	1	$8\frac{2}{5}$)
Best wax do. do.	25	0	(0	5	0)

Note.—The "raṭl" is about $15\frac{3}{4}$ oz., and the "uḳḳah" nearly $2\frac{3}{4}$ lbs., avoirdupois. The "ḳanṭár" is 100 raṭls. P. denotes Piasters: F., Faḍḍahs. For a full account of Egyptian measures, weights, and moneys, see the Appendix.

There are in Cairo numerous buildings called "wekálehs,"[1] chiefly designed for the accommodation of merchants, and for the reception of their goods. The wekáleh is a building surrounding a square or

[1] "Wekáleh" (generally pronounced by the Franks *occaleh, occal,* &c.,) is for "Dár el-Wekáleh,'' signifying a *facto* .

oblong court. Its ground-floor consists of vaulted magazines for merchandise, which face the court; and these magazines are sometimes used as shops. Above them are generally lodgings, which are entered from a gallery extending along each of the four sides of the court; or, in the place of these lodgings, there are other magazines; and in many wekálehs, which have apartments intended as lodgings, these apartments are used as magazines. In general, a wekáleh has only one common entrance; the door of which is closed at night, and kept by a porter. There are about two hundred of these buildings in Cairo; and three-fourths of that number are within that part which constituted the original city.

It has already been mentioned, in the Introduction to this work, that the great thoroughfare-streets of Cairo generally have a row of shops along each side, not communicating with the superstructures. So, too, have many of the by-streets. Commonly, a portion of a street, or a whole street, consists chiefly, or solely, of houses with shops appropriated to one particular trade;[1] and is called the Sooḳ (or Market) of that trade; or is named after a mosque there situate. Thus, a part of the main street of the city is called "Sooḳ en-Naḥḥáseen," or the market of the sellers of copper wares (or simply "the Naḥḥáseen," the word "Sooḳ" being usually dropped); another part is called "the Góhargeeyeh," or [market of] the jewellers; another, "the Khurdageeyeh," or [market of] the sellers of hardwares; another, "the Ghooreeyeh," or [market of] the Ghooreeyeh, which is the name of a mosque situate there. These are some of the chief sooḳs of the city. The principal Turkish sooḳ is called "Khán El-Khaleelee." Some of the sooḳs are covered over with matting, or with planks, supported by beams extending across the street, a little above the shops, or above the houses.[2]

The shop ("dukkán") is a square recess, or cell, generally about six or seven feet high; and between three and four feet in width: or it consists of two cells, one behind the other; the inner one serving as a magazine.[3] The floor of the shop is even with the top of a "maṣṭabah," or raised seat of stone or brick, built against the front.[4] This is usually about two feet and a half, or three feet, in height;

---

1 This has long been the case in other Eastern countries. See Jeremiah xxxvii. 21.

2 When I last quitted Egypt, it was said that most of these coverings were about to be removed.

3 The tradesman keeps his main stock of goods (if more than his shop will contain) in this magazine, or in his private dwelling, or in a wekáleh.

4 Since this was written, the maṣṭabahs in most of the streets have been removed by order of the government.

Shops in a Street of Cairo.—The principal object in this view is the shop of an "'aṭṭár," who sells drugs, perfumes, wax candles, &c. The inscription on the shutter is "Yá Fettáḥ." See Chapter xi.

and about the same in breadth. The front of the shop is furnished with folding shutters, commonly consisting of three leaves, one above another: the uppermost of these is turned up in front: the two other leaves, sometimes folded together, are turned down upon the masṭabah, and form an even seat, upon which is spread a mat or carpet, with, perhaps, a cushion or two. Some shops have folding doors instead of the shutters above described. The shopkeeper generally sits upon the masṭabah, unless he be obliged to retire a little way within his shop to make room for two or more customers, who mount upon the seat, taking off their shoes before they draw up their feet upon the mat or carpet. To a regular customer, or one who makes any considerable purchase, the shopkeeper generally presents a pipe (unless the former have his own with him, and it be filled and lighted), and he calls or sends to the boy of the nearest coffee-shop, and desires him to bring some coffee, which is served in the same manner as in the house, in small china cups placed within cups of brass. Not more than two persons can sit conveniently upon the masṭabah of a shop, unless it be more spacious than is commonly the case; but some are three or four feet broad; and the shops to which they belong, five or six feet in width; and consequently these afford room enough for four persons, or more, sitting in the Eastern fashion. The shopman generally says his prayers upon the masṭabah in the sight of the passengers in the street. When he leaves his shop for a few minutes, or for about half an hour, he either relies for the protection of his property upon the next shopkeepers, or those opposite, or hangs a net before his shop. He seldom thinks it necessary to close and lock the shutters, except at night, when he returns to his house, or when he goes to the mosque, on the Friday, to join in the noon-prayers of that day.—The apartments above the shops have been described in the Introduction.

Buying and selling are here very tiresome processes to persons unaccustomed to such modes of bargaining. When a shopkeeper is asked the price of any of his goods, he generally demands more than he expects to receive; the customer declares the price exorbitant, and offers about half or two-thirds of the sum first-named; the price thus bidden is, of course, rejected: but the shopkeeper lowers his demand; and then the customer, in his turn, bids somewhat higher than before: thus they usually go on until they meet about half-way between the sum first demanded and that first offered, and so the bargain is concluded. But I believe that most of the tradesmen are, by European

Shop of a Turkish Merchant in the Sooḳ called Khán El-Khaleelee.

travellers, unjustly blamed for thus acting, since I have ascertained that many an Egyptian shopkeeper will sell an article for a profit of one *per cent.*, and even less. When a person would make any but a trifling purchase, having found the article that exactly suits him, he generally makes up his mind for a long altercation: he mounts upon the maṣṭabah of the shop, seats himself at his ease, fills and lights his pipe, and then the contest of words commences, and lasts often half an hour or even more. Sometimes the shopkeeper, or the customer, interrupts the bargaining by introducing some irrelevant topic of conversation, as if the one had determined to abate his demand no further, or the other to bid no higher: then again the haggling is continued. The bargain being concluded, and the purchaser having taken his leave, his servant generally receives, from the tradesman, a small present of money, which, if not given spontaneously, he scruples not to demand. In many of the sooḳs in Cairo auctions are held on stated days, once or twice a week. They are conducted by "dellàls" (or brokers), hired either by private persons who have anything that they wish to sell in this manner, or by shopkeepers; and the purchasers are of both these classes. The "dellàls" carry the goods up and down, announcing the sums bidden with cries of "ḥarág" or "ḥaráj," &c.—Among the lower orders, a bargain of the most trifling nature is often made with a great deal of vehemence of voice and gesture: a person ignorant of their language would imagine that the parties engaged in it were quarrelling, and highly enraged. The peasants will often say, when a person asks the price of anything which they have for sale, "Receive it as a present:"[1] this answer having become a common form of speech, they know that advantage will not be taken of it; and when desired again to name the price, they will do so; but generally name a sum that is exorbitant.

It would be tedious and uninteresting to enumerate all the trades pursued in Cairo. The principal of them are those of the draper, or seller of materials for dress (who is simply called "tágir," or merchant), and of the seller of ready-made dresses, arms, &c. (who has the same appellation); the jeweller ("góhargee"); the goldsmith and silversmith ("ṣáïgh"), who only works by order; the seller of hardwares ("khurdagee"); the seller of copper wares ("naḥḥás");

---

[1] As Ephron did to Abraham, when the latter expressed his wish to purchase the cave and field of Machpelah. (See Genesis, xxiii. 11.) It is commonly said with the view of avoiding the effect of an evil eye.

the tailor ("kheiyáṭ"); the dyer ("ṣabbágh"); the darner ("reffà"); the ornamental sewer and maker of shereeṭ, or silk lace, &c. ("ḥabbák"); the maker of silk cords, &c. ("'aḳḳád"); the maker of pipes ("shibukshee"); the druggist and perfumer ("'aṭṭár"), who also sells wax candles, &c.; the tobacconist ("dakhákhinee"); the fruiterer ("fákihánee"); the seller of dried fruits ("nuḳalee"); the seller of sherbet ("sharbetlee"); the oilman ("zeiyát"), who sells butter, cheese, honey, &c., as well as oil; the greengrocer ("khuḍaree"); the butcher ("gezzár"); and the baker ("farrán"), to whom bread, meat, &c., are sent to be baked. There are many cooks' shops, where kebáb and various other dishes are cooked and sold; but it is seldom that persons eat at these shops, generally sending to them for provisions when they cannot conveniently prepare food in their own houses. Shopkeepers often procure their breakfast or dinner from one of these cooks, who are called "ṭabbákhs." There are also many shops in which faṭeerehs, and others in which boiled beans (fool mudemmes), are sold. Both these articles of food have been described in a former chapter. Many persons of the lower orders eat at the shop of the "faṭáṭiree" (or seller of faṭeerehs), or at that of the "fowwál" (or bean-seller).

Bread, vegetables, and a variety of eatables, are carried about for sale. The cries of some of the hawkers are curious, and deserve to be mentioned. The seller of "tirmis" (or lupins) often cries, "Aid! O Imbábee! Aid!"[1] This is understood in two senses; as an invocation for aid to the sheykh El-Imbábee, a celebrated Muslim saint, buried at the village of Imbábeh, on the west bank of the Nile, opposite Cairo, in the neighbourhood of which village the best tirmis is grown; and also as implying that it is through the aid of the saint above mentioned that the tirmis of Imbábeh is so excellent. The seller of this vegetable also cries, "The tirmis of Imbábeh surpasses the almond!"[2] Another cry of the seller of tirmis is, "O how sweet the little offspring of the river!"[3] This last cry, which is seldom heard but in the country towns and villages of Egypt, alludes to the manner in which the tirmis is prepared for food. To deprive it of its natural bitterness, it is soaked, for two or three days, in a vessel full of water, then boiled; and, after this, sewed up in a basket of palm-leaves (called "fard"), and thrown into the Nile, where it is left to

1 "Meded yá Imbábee meded."

2 "Tirmis Imbábeh yeghlib el-lóz."

3 "Yá ma-ḥlà" (for "má aḥlà") "buneí el-baḥr."

soak again two or three days, after which it is dried, and eaten cold, with a little salt.—The seller of sour limes cries, "God make them light [or easy of sale]! O limes!"[1]—The toasted pips of a kind of melon called "'abdallàwee," and of the water-melon, are often announced by the cry of "O consoler of the embarrassed! O pips!"[2] though more commonly by the simple cry of "Roasted pips!"[3]—A curious cry of the seller of a kind of sweetmeat ("ḥaláweh"), composed of treacle fried with some other ingredients, is, "For a nail! O sweetmeat!"[4] He is said to be half a thief: children and servants often steal implements of iron, &c., from the house in which they live, and give them to him in exchange for his sweetmeat.—The hawker of oranges cries, "Honey! O oranges! Honey!"[5] And similar cries are used by the sellers of other fruits and vegetables, so that it is sometimes impossible to guess what the person announces for sale, as when we hear the cry of "Sycamore-figs! O grapes!"[6] except by the rule that what is for sale is the least excellent of the fruits, &c., mentioned; as sycamore-figs are not so good as grapes.—A very singular cry is used by the seller of roses: "The rose was a thorn; from the sweat of the Prophet it blossomed."[7] This alludes to a miracle related of the Prophet.—The fragrant flowers of the ḥennà-tree (Lawsonia inermis, or Egyptian privet,) are carried about for sale, and the seller cries, "Odours of paradise! O flowers of the ḥennà!"[8]—A kind of cotton-cloth, made by machinery which is put in motion by a bull, is announced by the cry of "The work of the bull! O maidens!"[9]

As the water of the wells in Cairo is slightly brackish, numerous "saḳḳàs" (carriers or sellers of water) obtain their livelihood by supplying its inhabitants with water from the Nile. During the season of the inundation, or rather during the period of about four months after the opening of the canal which runs through the metropolis, the saḳḳàs draw their water from this canal: at other times they bring it from the river. It is conveyed in skins by camels and asses, and sometimes, when the distance is short, and the skin small, by the saḳḳà himself. The water-skins of the camel (which are called "rei") are a pair of wide bags of ox-hide. The ass bears a goat's

---

1 "Allah yehowwinhè" (for "yuhowwinhà") "yá leymoon."

2 "Yá muselli-l-ghalbán yá libb."

3 "El-libb el-moḥammaṣ."

4 "Bi-mismár yá ḥaláweh."

5 "'Asal yá burtuḳán 'asal."

6 "Gemmeyz yá 'eneb."

7 "El-ward kán shók min 'araḳ en-nebee fettaḥ."

8 "Rawáyeḥ" (for "rawáëḥ") "el-genneh yá temer ḥennà."

9 "Shughl et-tór yá benát."

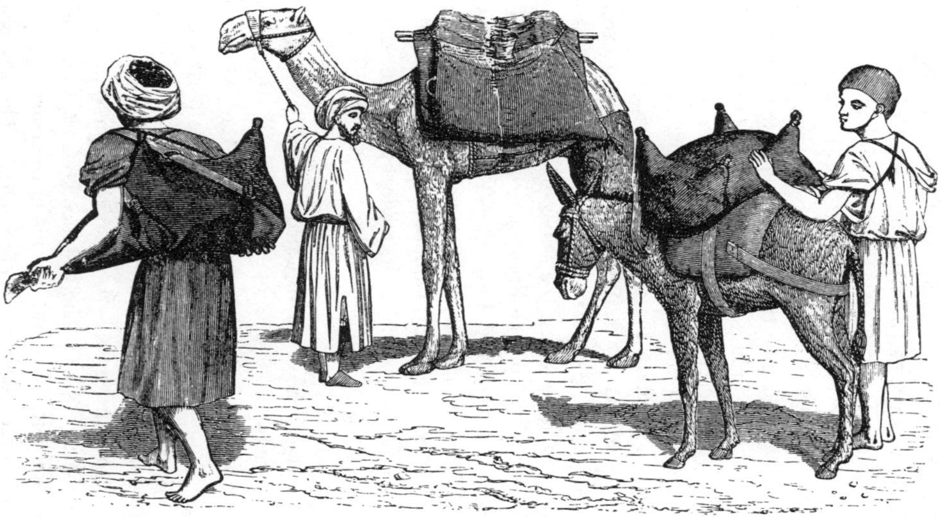

Saḳḳàs.

skin (called "ḳirbeh"); so too does the saḳḳà, if he have no ass. The rei contain three or four ḳirbehs. The general cry of the saḳḳà is, "O! may God compensate [me]!"[1] Whenever this cry is heard, it is known that a saḳḳà is passing. For a goat's skin of water, brought from a distance of a mile and a half, or two miles, he obtains scarcely more than a penny.

Saḳḳà Sharbeh.

There are also many saḳḳàs who supply passengers in the streets of the metropolis with water. One of this occupation is called "saḳḳà sharbeh:" his ḳirbeh has a long brass spout, and he pours the water into a brass cup, or an earthen ḳulleh, for any one who would drink.—There is a more numerous class who follow the same occupation, called "ḥemalees." These are mostly darweeshes, of the order of the Rifá'ees, or that of the Beiyoomees, and are exempt from the income-tax called firdeh. The ḥemalee carries, upon his back, a vessel (called "ibreeḳ") of porous gray earth. This vessel cools the water. Sometimes the ḥemalee has an earthen ḳulleh of water scented with "móyet zahr" (or orange-flower-water), prepared from the flowers of the "náring" (a bitter orange), for his best customers; and often a sprig of náring is stuck in the mouth of his ibreeḳ. He also, generally, has a wallet hung by his side. From persons of the

[1] "Yá 'owwaḍ Allah."

higher and middle orders he receives from one to five faḍḍahs for a draught of water; from the poor, either nothing, or a piece of bread or some other article of food, which he puts in his wallet. Many ḥemalees, and some saḳḳàs who carry the goat's skin, are found at the scenes of religious festivals, such as the moolids of saints, &c., in Cairo and its neighbourhood. They are often paid, by visiters to the tomb of a saint on such occasions, to distribute the water which they carry to passengers; a cupful to whoever desires. This work of charity is called "tesbeel;" and is performed for the sake of the saint, and on other occasions than moolids. The water-carriers who are thus employed are generally allowed to fill their ibreeḳs or

Ḥemalees.

ḳirbehs at a public fountain, as they demand nothing from the passengers whom they supply. When employed to distribute water to passengers in the streets, &c., they generally chant a short cry, inviting the thirsty to partake of the charity offered them in the name of God, most commonly in the words, and to the air, here following:—

and praying that paradise and pardon may be the lot of him who affords the charitable gift; thus—

El - gen - neh wa-l-magh-fi-reh lak, yá ṣá - ḥeb es - se - beel.

There are numerous other persons who follow occupations similar to that of the ḥemalee. Among these are sellers of "'erḳ-soos," or infusion of licorice, mentioned in a former chapter. The "'erḳ-soosee" (or seller of this beverage) generally carries a red earthen jar of the liquid on his left side, partly supported by a strap and chain,

'Erḳ-soosee.

and partly by his left arm: the mouth having some leef (or fibres of the palm-tree) stuffed into it. He also carries two or more brass or china cups, which he knocks together.—In the same manner, many "sharbetlees" (or sellers of sherbet) carry about for sale "zebeeb" (or infusion of raisins). The sharbetlee commonly bears, in his left hand, the glass vessel of a "sheesheh," filled with zebeeb; and a large tin or copper jug full of the same, and several glass cups,[1] in his right hand. Some sharbetlees carry, on the head, a round tinned

[1] "Ḳullehs."

copper tray, with a number of glass cups of "teen meblool," or "belaḥ meblool," which are figs and dates steeped in water; and a copper vessel,[1] or a china bowl, of the same. Saḥlab (a thin jelly, made of water, wheat-starch, and sugar, boiled, with a little cinnamon or ginger sprinkled upon it, or made as a drink without starch,) is likewise carried about in the same manner; and "ṣoobiyà[2] (which is a drink made of the pips of the 'abdalláwee melon, moistened and pounded, and steeped in water, which is then strained, and sweetened with sugar, or made with rice instead of the pips,) is also vended in a similar way, and carried in vessels like those used for zebeeb; but the glass cups are generally placed in a kind of trough of tin, attached, by a belt, to the waist of the seller.

It has been mentioned before, that many poor persons in Cairo gain their livelihood by going about to clean pipes. The pipe-cleaner ("musellikátee") carries a number of long wires for this purpose, in three or four hollow canes, or tubes of tin, which are bound together,

Musellikátee.

[1] "Saṭleh." [2] "Or "ṣoobiyeh."

and slung to his shoulder. A small leathern bag, full of tow, to wind round the top of the wire with which the pipe is cleaned, is attached to the canes or tin tubes. The musellikátee generally obtains no more than a "nuṣṣ[1] faḍḍah" (or about a quarter of a farthing) for each pipe that he cleans.

A very great number of persons of both sexes among the lower orders in Cairo, and many in other towns of Egypt, obtain their subsistence by begging. As might be expected, not a few of these are abominable impostors. There are some whose appearance is most distressing to every humane person who sees them; but who accumulate considerable property. A case of this kind was made public here a few months ago. A blind fellâḥ, who was led through the streets of the metropolis by a young girl, his daughter, both of whom were always nearly naked, was in the daily habit of bringing to his house a blind Turkish beggar, to sup with him. One evening, he was not at home; but his daughter was there, and had prepared the supper for his Turkish friend, who sat and ate alone; and, in doing this, happened to put his hand on one side, and felt a jar full of money, which, without scruple, he carried away with him. It contained the sum of a hundred and ten purses (then equivalent to rather more than five hundred and fifty guineas), in kheyreeyehs, or small coins of nine piastres each. The plundered beggar sought redress at the Citadel, and recovered his property, with the exception of forty kheyreeyehs, which the thief had spent; but was interdicted from begging in future.—Children are often seen in Cairo perfectly naked; and I have several times seen females from twelve to twenty years of age, and upwards, with only a narrow strip of rag round the loins, begging in the streets of this city. They suffer little from exposure of the bare person to the cold of winter, or the scorching sun of summer, being accustomed to it from infancy; and the men may, if they choose, sleep in some of the mosques. In other respects, also, their condition is not quite so bad as their appearance might lead a stranger to suppose. They are almost sure of obtaining either food or money sufficient for supplying the absolute wants of nature, in consequence of the charitable disposition of their countrymen, and the common habit which the tradespeople have of eating in their shops, and generally giving a morsel of their food to those who ask for it. There are many beggars who spend the greater part of the day's gains to in-

---

1 A corruption of "nuṣf."

dulge themselves at night with the intoxicating ḥasheesh, which, for a few hours, renders them, in imagination, the happiest of mankind.

The cries of the beggars of Cairo are generally appeals to God. Among the most common are—"O Exciter of compassion! O Lord!"[1]—"For the sake of God! O ye charitable!"[2]—"I am seeking from my Lord a cake of bread!"[3]—O how bountiful Thou art! O Lord!"[4]—"I am the guest of God and the Prophet!"[5]—in the evening, "My supper must be thy gift! O Lord!"[6]—on the eve of Friday, "The night of the excellent Friday!"[7]—and on Friday, "The excellent day of Friday;"[8]—One who daily passed my door used to exclaim, "Place thy reliance upon God! There is none but God!" and another, a woman, I now hear crying, "My supper must be thy gift! O Lord! from the hand of a bountiful believer, a testifier of the unity of God! O masters!"—The answers which beggars generally receive (for they are so numerous that a person cannot give to all who ask of him) are, "God help thee!"[9]—"God will sustain!"[10] "God give thee!"[11]—"God content, or enrich, thee!"[12]—They are not satisfied by any denial but one implied by these or similar answers. In the more frequented streets of Cairo, it is common to see a beggar asking for the price of a cake of bread, which he or she holds in the hand, followed by the seller of the bread. Some beggars, particularly darweeshes, go about chanting verses in praise of the Prophet; or beating cymbals, or a little kettle-drum. In the country, many darweeshes go from village to village begging alms. I have seen them on horseback; and one I lately saw thus mounted, and accompanied by two men bearing each a flag, and by a third beating a drum: this beggar on horseback was going from hut to hut asking for bread.

The most important of the occupations which employ the modern Egyptians, and that which (as before mentioned) engages all but a very small proportion of them, is agriculture.

The greater portion of the cultivable soil is fertilized by the natural annual inundation; but the fields in the vicinity of the river and of the large canals, and some others, in which pits are dug for

---

1 "Yá Moḥannin yá Rabb."

2 "Li-lláh yá moḥsineen."

3 "Anà ṭálib min 'and Rabbee ragheef 'eysh."

4 "Yá ma-ntà" (for "má entà") "kereem yá Rabb."

5 "Aná ḍeyf Alláh wa-n-nebee."

6 "'Asháya 'aleyk yá Rabb."

7 "Leylet el-gum'ah el-faḍeeleh."

8 "Yóm el-gum'ah el-faḍeeleh."

9 "Allah yesá'ëdak" (for "yusá'ëdak").

10 "Allah yerzuḳ."

11 "Allah yaaṭeek" (for "yoaṭeek").

12 "Allah yeghneek" (for "yughneek").

The Shádoof.

water, are irrigated by means of machines of different kinds. The most common of these machines is the "shádoof," which consists of two posts or pillars of wood, or of mud and canes or rushes, about five feet in height, and less than three feet apart, with a horizontal piece of wood extending from top to top, to which is suspended a slender lever, formed of a branch of a tree, having at one end a weight chiefly composed of mud, and at the other, suspended to two long palm-sticks, a vessel in the form of a bowl, made of basket-work, or of a hoop and a piece of woollen stuff or leather: with this vessel, the water is thrown up to the height of about eight feet, into a trough hollowed out for its reception. In the southern parts of Upper Egypt, four or five shádoofs are required, when the river is at the lowest, to raise the water to the level of the fields. There are many shádoofs with two levers, &c., which are worked by two men. The operation is extremely laborious.—Another machine much used for the same purpose, and almost the only one employed for the irrigation of gardens in Egypt, is the "sáḳiyeh." This mainly consists of a vertical wheel, which raises the water in earthen pots attached to cords, and forming a continuous series; a second vertical wheel fixed to the same axis, with cogs; and a large, horizontal, cogged wheel, which, being turned by a pair of cows or bulls, or by a single beast, puts in motion the two former wheels and the pots. The construction of this machine is of a very rude kind; and its motion produces a disagreeable creaking noise.—There is a third machine, called "táboot," used for the irrigation of lands in the northern parts of Egypt, where it is only requisite to raise the water a few feet. It somewhat resembles the "sáḳiyeh:" the chief difference is, that, instead of the wheel with pots, it has a large wheel with hollow jaunts, or fellies, in which the water is raised.—In the same parts of Egypt, and often to raise the water to the channel of the "táboot," a vessel like that of the "shádoof," with four cords attached to it, is also used. Two men, each holding two of the cords, throw up the water by means of this vessel, which is called "ḳaṭweh."—In the process of artificial irrigation, the land is divided into small squares, by ridges of earth, or into furrows; and the water, flowing from the machine along a narrow gutter, is admitted into one square or furrow after another.

The "rei" lands (or those which are naturally inundated) are, with some exceptions, cultivated but once during the year. After the waters have retired, about the end of October or beginning of November, they are sown with wheat, barley, lentils, beans, lupins, chick-peas, &c. This is called the "shitawee" (or winter) season. But the "sharákee" lands (those which are too high to be subject to the natural inundation), and some parts of the rei, by artificial irrigation are made to produce three crops every year; though not *all* the sharákee lands are thus cultivated. The lands artificially irrigated produce, first, their shitawee crops; being sown at the same period as the rei lands, generally with wheat or barley. Secondly, in what is called the "ṣeyfee," or, in the southern parts of Egypt, the "ḳeyḍee," or "geyḍee" (that is, the summer), season, commencing about the vernal equinox, or a little later, they are sown with millet ("durah ṣeyfee"), or with indigo, or cotton, &c. Thirdly, in the "demeereh" season, or period of the rise of the Nile, commencing about, or soon after, the summer solstice, they are sown with millet again, or with maize ("durah shámee"), &c., and thus crowned with a third harvest.—Sugar is cultivated throughout a large portion of Upper Egypt; and rice, in the low lands near the Mediterranean.

For the purpose of separating the grain of wheat, barley, &c., and cutting the straw, which serves as fodder, the Egyptians use a machine called "nórag," in the form of a chair, which moves upon small iron wheels, or thin circular plates, generally eleven, fixed to three thick axle-trees; four to the foremost, the same number to the hindmost, and three to the intermediate axle-tree. This machine is drawn, in a circle, by a pair of cows or bulls, over the corn. The plough, and the other implements which they use in husbandry, are of rude and simple kinds.

The navigation of the Nile employs a great number of the natives of Egypt. The boatmen of the Nile are mostly strong, muscular men. They undergo severe labour in rowing, poling, and towing; but are very cheerful; and often the most so when they are most occupied; for then they frequently amuse themselves by singing. In consequence of the continual changes which take place in the bed of the Nile, the most experienced pilot is liable frequently to run his vessel aground: on such an occurrence, it is often necessary for the crew to descend into the water, to shove off the boat with their backs and shoulders. On account of their being so liable to run aground, the boats of the Nile are generally made to draw rather more water at the head than at the stern; and hence the rudder is necessarily very wide. The better kind of boats used on the Nile, which are very numerous, are of a simple but elegant form; mostly between thirty and forty feet in length; with two masts, two large triangular sails, and a cabin, next the stern, generally about four feet high,[1] and occupying about a fourth, or a third, of the length of the boat. In most of these boats, the cabin is divided into two or more apartments. Sudden whirlwinds and squalls being very frequent on the Nile, a boatman is usually employed to hold the main-sheet in his hand, that he may be able to let it fly at a moment's notice: the traveller should be especially careful with respect to this precaution, however light the wind.

---

[1] Of late, the cabins of the better kinds of boats have been made higher, to suit the requirements of European travellers.

CHAPTER XV.

USE OF TOBACCO, COFFEE, HEMP, OPIUM, ETC.

The interdiction of wine, and other fermented and intoxicating liquors, which is one of the most important laws in the code of El-Islám, has caused the greater number of the disciples of this faith to become immoderately addicted to other means of inducing slight intoxication, or different kinds of pleasurable excitement.

The most prevalent means, in most Muslim countries, of exciting what the Arabs term "keyf," which I cannot more nearly translate than by the term "placid enjoyment," is tobacco. It appears that tobacco was introduced into Turkey, Arabia, and other countries of the East, shortly before the beginning of the seventeenth century of the Christian era:[1] that is, not many years after it had begun to be regularly imported into Western Europe, as an article of commerce, from America. Its lawfulness to the Muslim has often been warmly disputed;[2] but is now generally allowed. In the character of the Turks and Arabs who have become addicted to its use, it has induced considerable changes, particularly rendering them more inactive than they were in earlier times; leading them to waste, over the pipe, many hours which might be profitably employed: but it has had another and a better effect; that of superseding, in a great measure, the use of wine, which, to say the least, is very injurious to the health of the inhabitants of hot climates. In the tales of "The Thousand

---

[1] El-Is-ḥáḳee states that the custom of smoking tobacco began to be common in Egypt between the years of the Flight 1010 and 1012 (A.D. 1601 and 1603).

[2] El-Gabartee relates, that about a century ago, in the time of Moḥammad Báshà El-Yedekshee (or Yedekchee), who governed Egypt in the years of the Flight 1156-8, it frequently happened that when a man was found with a pipe in his hand in Cairo, he was made to eat the bowl with its burning contents. This may seem incredible; but a pipe-bowl *may* be broken by strong teeth. The tobacco first used in the East was probably very strong.

and One Nights," which were written before the introduction of tobacco into the East, and which we may confidently receive as presenting faithful pictures of the state of Arabian manners and customs at the period when they appeared, we have abundant evidence that wine was much more commonly and more openly drunk by Muslims of that time, or of the age immediately preceding, than it is by those of the present day. It may further be remarked, in the way of apology for the pipe, as employed by the Turks and Arabs, that the mild kinds of tobacco generally used by them have a very gentle effect; they calm the nervous system, and, instead of stupefying, sharpen the intellect. The pleasures of Eastern society are certainly much heightened by the pipe, and it affords the peasant a cheap and sober refreshment, and probably often restrains him from less innocent indulgences.

The cup of coffee, which, when it can be afforded, generally accompanies the pipe, is commonly regarded as an almost equal luxury, and doubtless conduced with tobacco to render the use of wine less common among the Arabs: its name, "ḳahweh," an old Arabic term for wine, strengthens this supposition. It is said that the discovery of the refreshing beverage afforded by the berry of the coffee-plant was made in the latter part of the seventh century of the Flight (or, of the thirteenth of the Christian era), by a certain devotee named the sheykh 'Omar, who, driven by persecution to a mountain of El-Yemen, with a few of his disciples, was induced, by the want of provisions, to make an experiment of the decoction of coffee-berries, as an article of food; the coffee-plant being there a spontaneous production. It was not, however, till about two centuries after this period that the use of coffee began to become common in El-Yemen. It was imported into Egypt between the years 900 and 910 of the Flight (towards the end of the fifteenth or the beginning of the sixteenth century of our era, or about a century before the introduction of tobacco into the East), and was then drunk in the great mosque El-Azhar, by the faḳeers of El-Yemen and Mekkeh and El-Medeeneh, who found it very refreshing to them while engaged in their exercises of reciting prayers, and the praises of God, and freely indulged themselves with it. About half a century after, it was introduced into Constantinople.[1] In Arabia, in Egypt, and in Constantinople, it was often the subject of sharp disputes among the

[1] See De Sacy's Chrestomathie Arabe, vol. i. pp. 412—483, 2nd ed.

pious and learned; many doctors asserting that it possessed intoxicating qualities, and was, therefore, an unlawful beverage to Muslims; while others contended that, among many other virtues, it had that of repelling sleep, which rendered it a powerful help to the pious in their nocturnal devotions: according to the fancy of the ruling power, its sale was therefore often prohibited and again legalized. It is now, and has been for many years, acknowledged as lawful by almost all the Muslims, and is immoderately used even by the Wahhábees, who are the most rigid in their condemnation of tobacco, and in their adherence to the precepts of the Ḳur-án, and the Traditions of the Prophet. Formerly, it was generally prepared from the berries and husks together; and it is still so prepared, or from the husks alone, by many persons in Arabia. In other countries of the East, it is prepared from the berries alone, freshly roasted and pounded.

Cairo contains above a thousand "Ḳahwehs,"[1] or coffee-shops. The ḳahweh is, generally speaking, a small apartment, whose front, which is towards the street, is of open wooden work, in the form of arches.[2] Along the front, except before the door, is (or was) a "maṣṭabah," or raised seat, of stone or brick, two or three feet in height, and about the same in width, which is covered with matting; and there are similar seats in the interior, on two or three sides. The coffee-shops are most frequented in the afternoon and evening; but by few except persons of the lower orders, and tradesmen. The exterior maṣṭabah is generally preferred. Each person brings with him his own tobacco and pipe. Coffee is served by the "ḳahwegee" (or attendant of the shop), at the price of five faḍḍahs a cup, or ten for a little "bekreg" (or pot) of three or four cups.[3] The ḳahwegee also keeps two or three nárgeelehs or sheeshehs, and gózehs,[4] which latter are used for smoking both the tumbák (or Persian tobacco) and the ḥasheesh (or hemp); for ḥasheesh is sold at some coffee-shops. Musicians and story-tellers frequent some of the ḳahwehs; particularly on the evenings of religious festivals.

The leaves and capsules of hemp, called, in Egypt, "ḥasheesh," were employed in some countries of the East in very ancient times to induce an exhilarating intoxication. Herodotus (lib. iv. cap. 75)

---

1 "Ḳahweh," being the name of the *beverage* sold at the coffee-shop, is hence applied to the shop itself.

2 See an engraving accompanying Chapter XXI.

3 A decoction of ginger, sweetened with sugar, is likewise often sold at the Ḳahwehs, particularly on the nights of festivals.

4 These instruments have been described in a former chapter.

informs us that the Scythians had a custom of burning the seeds of this plant, in religious ceremonies, and that they became intoxicated with the fumes. Galen also mentions the intoxicating properties of hemp. The practice of chewing the leaves of this plant to induce intoxication prevailed, or existed, in India, in very early ages: thence it was introduced into Persia; and about six centuries ago (before the middle of the thirteenth century of our era) this pernicious and degrading custom was adopted in Egypt, but chiefly by persons of the lower orders; though several men eminent in literature and religion, and vast numbers of fakeers (or poor devotees), yielded to its fascinations, and contended that it was lawful to the Muslim. The habit is now very common among the lower orders in the metropolis and other towns of Egypt. There are various modes of preparing it; and various names, as "sheerà,"[1] "basṭ," &c., are given to its different preparations. Most commonly, I am told, the young leaves are used alone, or mixed with tobacco, for smoking; and the capsules, without the seeds, pounded and mixed with several aromatic substances for an intoxicating conserve. Acids counteract its operation. The preparation of hemp used for smoking generally produces boisterous mirth. Few inhalations of its smoke, but the last very copious, are usually taken from the gózeh. After the emission of the last draught, from the mouth and nostrils, commonly a fit of coughing, and often a spitting of blood, ensues, in consequence of the lungs having been filled with the smoke. Ḥasheesh is to be obtained not only at some of the coffee-shops: there are shops of a smaller and more private description solely appropriated to the sale of this and other intoxicating preparations: they are called "maḥshesh-ehs." It is sometimes amusing to observe the ridiculous conduct, and to listen to the conversation, of the persons who frequent these shops. They are all of the lower orders. The term "ḥashshásh," which signifies "a smoker, or an eater, of hemp," is an appellation of obloquy: noisy and riotous people are often called "ḥashshásheen," which is the plural of that appellation, and the origin of our word "assassin;" a name first applied to Arab warriours in Syria, in the time of the Crusades, who made use of intoxicating and soporific drugs in order to render their enemies insensible.[2]

---

[1] Or "sheereh."

[2] See, on this subject, the close of Chap. XXII. A reviewer seems to have inferred from the remark above, that I took to myself the credit of discovering this derivation. A reference to the words "Assassin" and "De Sacy" in the Index would have shewn that this was not the case. I thought the observation of the illustrious De Sacy respecting this word to be too generally known to require my mentioning it in *two* places.

The use of opium and other drugs to induce intoxication is not so common in Egypt as in many other countries of the East: the number of Egyptians addicted to this vice is certainly not nearly so great, in proportion to the whole population, as is the relative number of persons in our own country who indulge in habitual drunkenness. Opium is called, in Arabic, "afiyoon;" and the opium-eater, "afiyoonee." This latter appellation is a term of less obloquy than that of "ḥashshásh," because there are many persons of the middle and higher classes to whom it is applicable. In its crude state, opium is generally taken, by those who have not long been addicted to its use, in the dose of three or four grains, for the purpose above mentioned; but the "afiyoonee" increases the dose by degrees. The Egyptians make several conserves composed of hellebore, hemp, and opium, and several aromatic drugs, which are more commonly taken than the simple opium. A conserve of this nature is called "maạgoon;" and the person who makes or sells it, "maạgungee." The most common kind is called "barsh." There is one kind which, it is said, makes the person who takes it manifest his pleasure by singing; another which will make him chatter; a third which excites to dance; a fourth which particularly affects the vision, in a pleasurable manner; a fifth which is simply of a sedative nature. These are sold at the "maḥshesheh."

The fermented and intoxicating liquor called "boozeh," or "booẓah," which is drunk by many of the boatmen of the Nile, and by other persons of the lower orders in Egypt, has been mentioned in a former chapter. I have seen, in tombs at Thebes, many large jars containing the dregs of beer of this kind prepared from barley.

CHAPTER XVI.

THE BATH.

Bathing is one of the greatest luxuries enjoyed by the people of Egypt. The inhabitants of the villages of this country, and those persons who cannot afford the trifling expense incurred in the public bath, often bathe in the Nile. Girls and young women are not unfrequently seen thus indulging themselves in the warm weather, and generally without any covering; but mostly in unfrequented places. The rich, I have before mentioned, have baths in their own houses; but men who have this convenience often go to the public bath; and so too do the ladies, who, on many occasions, are invited to accompany thither their female friends.

There are, in Cairo, between sixty and seventy "Ḥammáms," or baths, to which the public have access for a small expense. Some of these are for men only; others, only for women and young children; and some for both sexes; for men during the forenoon, and in the afternoon for females. When the bath is appropriated to women, a napkin, or any piece of linen or drapery, is hung over the entrance, to warn the men from entering: all the male servants having gone out a short time before, and females having taken their places. The front of the bath is generally ornamented in a manner similar to that in which most of the mosques are decorated, but usually more fanciful, in red and white, and sometimes other colours, particularly over and about the entrance. The building consists of several apartments, all of which are paved with marble, chiefly white, with an intermixture, in some parts, of black marble, and small pieces of fine red tile, in the same manner as the durḳá'ah of a room in a private house, of which a sketch has been inserted in the introduction to this work. The inner apartments are covered with domes, which have a number of small, round, glazed apertures, for the admission of light. The materials chiefly employed in the construction of the walls and domes are bricks and plaster, which, after having been exposed to the steam that is produced in the bath when it is in use, are liable to crack and fall if the heat be intermitted even for a few days. A sákiyeh (or water-wheel), turned by a cow or bull, is constructed upon a level with the higher parts of the building, to raise water from a well or tank for the supply of the boiler, &c.

The bath is believed to be a favourite resort of ginn (or genii), and therefore when a person is about to enter it, he should offer up an ejaculatory prayer for protection against evil spirits, and should put his left foot first over the threshold. For the same reason, he should not pray nor recite the Kur-án in it.[1] On entering, if he have a watch, and a purse containing more than a trifling sum of money, he gives these in charge to the "m'allim" (or keeper of the bath), who locks them in a chest: his pipe, and sword (if he have one), he commits to a servant of the bath, who takes off his shoes, and supplies him with a pair of wooden clogs; the pavement being wet. The first apartment is called the "meslakh." It generally has two, three, or four "leewáns," similar to mastabahs, or considerably wider, cased with marble, and a fountain (called "faskeeyeh") of cold water, which rises from an octagonal basement constructed of stone cased with marble &c. (similar to that in the inner apartment represented in a section accompanying this description) in the centre. One of the leewáns, being designed for the accommodation of persons of the higher and middle orders, is furnished with mattresses and cushions: upon the other, or others, which are for the lower orders, there is usually no furniture except mats. In many baths there is also, in the meslakh, a small kind of stall, for coffee.

In warm weather, the bathers mostly prefer to undress in the meslakh: in winter, they undress in an inner, closed apartment, called the "beyt-owwal;" between which and the first apartment is a short passage, with two or three latrinæ on one side. "Beyt-owwal" signifies "first chamber;" and this name is given to the chamber here mentioned because it is the first of the warm apartments; but it is less warm than the principal apartment, of which it is the antechamber. In general, it has two mastabahs, one higher than the

---

[1] The prohibition here mentioned, although imposed by several well-known traditions, is, like many others, often disregarded by the ignorant.

other, cased with marble like the pavement. The higher accommodates but one person; and is for the higher classes: the other is sufficiently large for two. When the former is occupied, and another high seat is wanted, two or three mattresses are placed one upon another on the lower maṣṭabah, or on the leewán (or raised part of the floor). A seggádeh (or small prayer-carpet) is spread on the maṣṭabah for a person of the higher orders. The bather receives a napkin in which to put his clothes; and another to put round his waist: this reaches to the knees, or a little lower; and is termed "maḥzam:" a third, if he require it, is brought to him to wind round his head, in the manner of a turban, leaving the top of the head bare; a fourth to put over his chest, and a fifth to cover his back. It is generally a boy, or beardless young man, who attends the bather while he undresses, and while he puts on his maḥzam, &c.: he is called a "láwingee" (as the word is vulgarly pronounced), which is a corruption of "leewángee," or "attendant of the leewán."[1]

When the bather has undressed, and attired himself in the manner above described, the láwingee opens to him the door of the inner and principal apartment, which is called "ḥarárah."[2] This, in gene-

Section of the Ḥarárah.

ral, has four low leewáns, like those of most rooms in private houses, which give it the form of a cross; and, in the centre, a "fasḳeeyeh" (or fountain) of hot water, rising from a small shallow basin in the middle of a high octagonal seat, cased with white and black marble,

[1] See the Plan, of which the following is an explanation.—A, General entrance and vestibule. B, B, Meslakh. C, C, C, C, C, Leewáns. D, Station of the M'allim. E, Fasḳeeyeh. F, Coffee-stall. G, G, Latrinæ. H, Beyt-owwal. I, I, Leewán. K, K, Maṣṭabahs. L, L, Ḥarárah. M, M, M, M, Leewáns. N, Fasḳeeyeh. O, O, Two chambers, each containing a maghṭas (or tank). P, P, Ḥanafeeyehs. Q, Place of the fire, over which is the boiler.

[2] For "beyt el-ḥarárah."

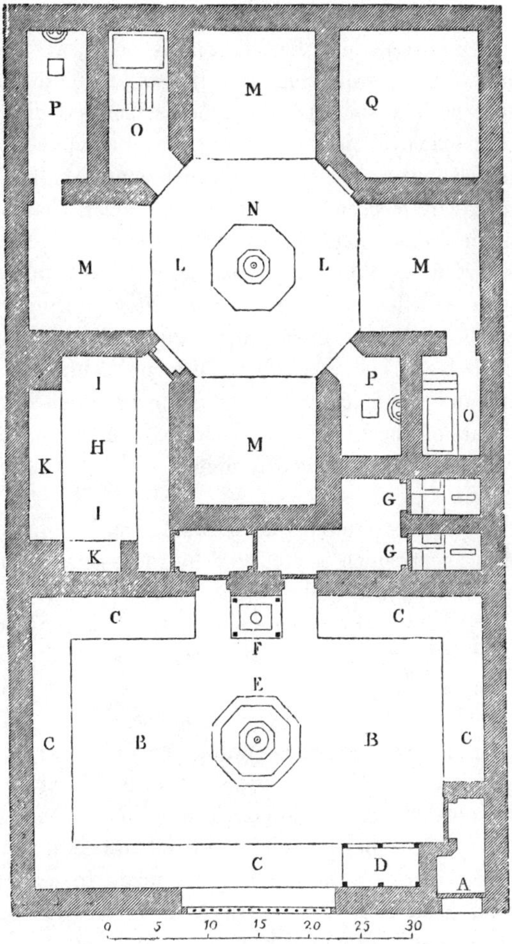

Scale of feet.

Plan of a Bath.

and pieces of red tile. The ḥarárah, together with several chambers connected with it, may generally be described as occupying almost an exact square. The beyt-owwal is at one of the angles. Two small chambers, which adjoin each other, and occupy a second angle of the square, contain, the one, a "maghṭas," or tank, of warm water, to which there is an ascent of a few steps; the other, a "ḥanafeeyeh," consisting of two taps, projecting from the wall; one of hot, and one of cold water; with a small trough beneath, before which is a seat: the name of ḥanafeeyeh is commonly given, not merely to the taps above mentioned, but to the chamber which contains them. A third angle of the square is occupied by two other small chambers similar to those just described; one containing a second maghṭas, of water not quite so warm as the former; the other, a second ḥanafeeyeh. Each maghṭas is filled by a stream of water pouring down from the dome of the chamber. The fourth angle of the square is generally occupied by a chamber which has no communication with the ḥarárah; and which contains the fire over which is the boiler. The central part of the ḥarárah, its leewáns, and the small chambers connected with it, are covered with domes, which have a number of small, glazed apertures.

The bather, having entered the ḥarárah, soon perspires profusely, from the humid heat which is produced by the hot water of the tanks and fountain, and by the boiler. The operator of the bath, who is called "mukeyyisátee," immediately comes to him. If the bather be covered with more than one napkin, the mukeyyisátee takes them off, and gives him a wet maḥzam; or the former maḥzam is retained, and wetted. The bather sits on the marble seat of the fasḳeeyeh, or lies upon a napkin on one of the leewáns, or by the edge of one of the tanks, to submit to the first operation, which is that of cracking his joints.[1] The operator cracks almost every joint of his frame: he wrings the body, first one way, and then the other, to make several of the vertebræ crack: even the neck is made to crack twice, by wrenching the head round, each way, which produces a sensation rather alarming to an inexperienced person; and each ear is generally twisted round until it cracks: the limbs are wrested with apparent violence; but with such skill, that an untoward accident in this operation is never heard of. The main object of this process is to render the joints supple. The mukeyyisátee also kneads the bather's

[1] This is called "ṭaḳṭaḳah."

flesh. After this, or previously, he rubs the soles of his feet with a kind of rasp,[1] of baked clay. There are two kinds of rasps used for this purpose: one is very porous and rough; and its rasping surface is scored with several lines: the other is of a fine close clay; and the surface with which the rubbing is performed is rendered rough artificially:

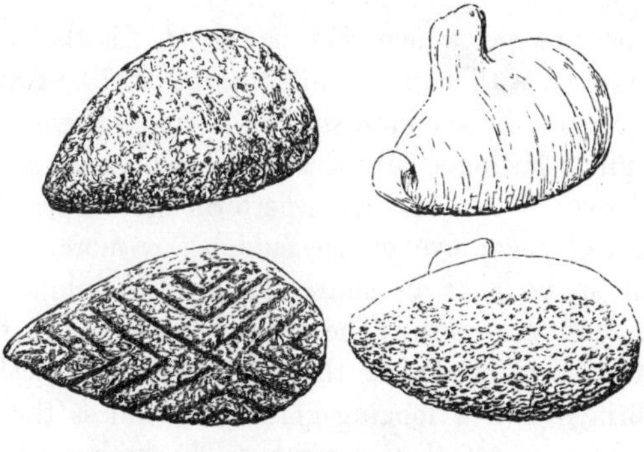

Foot-rasps.—*One quarter of the real size.*

both are of a dark, blackish colour. Those which are used by ladies are generally encased (the lower, or rasping, surface of course excepted) in thin, embossed silver. The rougher rasp is of indispensable utility to persons who do not wear stockings; which is the case with most of the inhabitants of Egypt: the other is for the more delicate; and is often used for rubbing the limbs, to render the skin smooth. The next operation is that of rubbing the bather's flesh with a small, coarse, woollen bag.[2] This done, the bather, if he please, dips himself in one of the tanks. He is next taken to a ḥanafeeyeh. A napkin having been hung before the entrance to this, the mukeyyisátee lathers the bather with "leef" (or fibres of the palm-tree) and soap and sweet water, which last is brought in a copper vessel, and warmed in one of the tanks; for the water of the ḥanafeeyeh is from a well, somewhat brackish, and consequently not fit for washing with soap. The leef is employed in the same manner as sponge is by us: it is not of the kind produced by the palm-trees of Egypt, which is of a brown colour: that used in the ḥammám is white; and is brought from the Ḥejáz. The mukeyyisátee washes off the soap with water from the ḥanafeeyeh; and, if required, shaves the bather's arm-pits: he then

1 Called "ḥagar el-ḥammám."

2 This operation is termed "tekyees;" and the bag, "kees el-ḥammám:" hence the operator is called "mukeyyisátee," or more properly, "mukeyyis."

goes, leaving him to finish washing, &c. The latter then calls for a set of napkins,[1] four in number, and, having covered himself in the same manner as before described, returns to the beyt-owwal; but first it is the custom of persons of the more independent classes to give half a piaster, or a piaster, to the mukeyyisátee, though it is not demanded.

In the beyt-owwal, a mattress is spread, for the bather, on the maṣṭabah, covered with napkins, and having one or two cushions at one end. On this he reclines, sipping a cup or two of coffee, and smoking, while a láwingee rubs the soles of his feet, and kneads his body and limbs; or two láwingees perform these operations, and he gives to each of them five or ten faḍḍahs, or more. He generally remains half an hour, or an hour, smoking his shibuk or sheesheh: then dresses, and goes out. The "ḥáris," who is the foreman, and who has the charge of drying the napkins in the meslakh, and of guarding, brings him a looking-glass, and (unless the bather have neither beard nor mustaches) a comb. The bather asks him for his watch, &c.; puts from one to four piasters on the looking-glass; and goes. One piaster is a common sum to pay for all the operations above described.

Many persons go to the bath twice a week: others, once a week, or less frequently; but some are merely washed with soap and water, and then plunge into one of the tanks; for which, of course, they pay less.

The women who can afford to do so visit the ḥammám frequently; but not so often as the men. When the bath is not hired for the females of one family, or for one party of ladies, exclusively, women of all conditions are admitted. In general, all the females of a house, and the young boys, go together. They take with them their own seggádehs, and the napkins, basins, &c., which they require, and even the necessary quantity of sweet water for washing with soap, and for drinking; and some carry with them fruits, sweetmeats, and other refreshments. A lady of wealth is also often accompanied by her own "belláneh," or "másh'ṭah,"[2] who is the washer and tire-woman. Many women of the lower orders wear no covering whatever in the bath; not even a napkin round the waist: others always wear the napkin, and the high clogs. There are few pleasures in which the women of Egypt delight so much as in the visit to the bath, where they

---

1 "'Eddeh."

2 Thus commonly pronounced for "máshiṭah."

frequently have entertainments; and often, on these occasions, they are not a little noisy in their mirth. They avail themselves of the opportunity to display their jewels and their finest clothes, and to enter into familiar conversation with those whom they meet there, whether friends or strangers. Sometimes a mother chooses a bride for her son from among the girls or women whom she chances to see in the bath. On many occasions, as, for instance, in the case of the preparations for a marriage, the bath is hired for a select party, consisting of the women of two or more families; and none else are admitted: but it is more common for a lady and a few friends and attendants to hire a "khilweh:" this is the name they give to the apartment of the ḥanafeeyeh. There is more confusion among a mixed company of various ranks; but where all are friends, the younger girls indulge in more mirth and frolic. They spend an hour or more under the hands of the belláneh, who rubs and washes them, plaits their hair, applies the depilatory,[1] &c. They then retire to the beyt-owwal or meslakh, and there, having put on part of their dress, or a large loose shirt, partake of various refreshments, which, if they have brought none with them, they may procure by sending an attendant of the bath to the market. Those who smoke take their own pipes with them. On particular occasions of festivity, they are entertained with the songs of two or more 'Ál'mehs, hired to accompany them to the bath.

---

1 The depilatory called "noorah," which is often employed in the bath, being preferred to the resin more commonly used, is composed, as I am informed, of quick-lime with a small proportion (about an eighth part) of orpiment. It is made into a paste, with water, before application; and loosens the hair in about two minutes, when it is washed off.—See Russell's Aleppo, vol. i. pp. 134, 378, 379, 2nd edition.

CHAPTER XVII.

GAMES.

Most of the games of the Egyptians are of kinds which suit their sedate dispositions. They take great pleasure in chess (which they call "saṭreng"), draughts ("ḍámeh"), and trictrac or backgammon ("ṭáwulah"). Their chess-men are of very simple forms; as the Muslim is forbidden, by his religion, to make an image of anything that has life. The Muslims of Egypt in general are, however, less scrupulous with regard to the prohibition of games of hazard: though some of them consider even chess and draughts as forbidden, games partly or wholly hazardous are very common among all ranks of this people: and scarcely less so is that of cards, which, being almost always played for money, or for some other stake, is particularly called, by way of distinction, "leạb el-ḳumár,"[1] "the game of hazard, or of gain." Persons of the lower orders in the towns of Egypt are often seen playing at these and other games at the coffee-shops; but frequently for no greater stake than that of a few cups of coffee.

One of the games most common among the Egyptians is that of the "manḳalah."[2] Two persons play at this, with a board (or two boards joined by hinges) in which are twelve hemispherical holes, called "buyoot" (plural of "beyt"), in two equal rows; and with seventy-two small shells, of the kind called cowries; or as many pebbles: these, whether shells or pebbles, are termed the "ḥaṣà" (in the singular, "ḥaṣweh"). To explain the game of the manḳalah, I must distinguish the beyts of the board by letters, thus:—

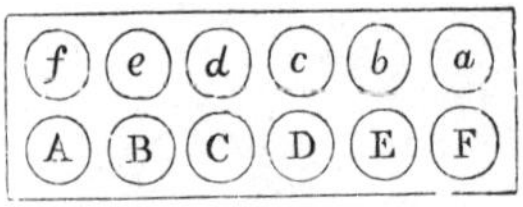

Manḳalah.

For "Ḳimár."

[2] Pronounced "manḳal'ah."

The beyts marked A, B, C, D, E, F, belong to one party; and the opposite six beyts to the other. One of the parties, when they are about to play the game in the most simple manner (for there are two modes of playing it), distributes all the ḥaṣà unequally into the beyts; generally putting at least four into each beyt. If they were distributed equally, there would be six in each beyt; but this is seldom done; for, in this case, he who plays first is sure to lose. The act of distributing the ḥaṣà is called "tebweez." When one party is dissatisfied with the other's distribution of the ḥaṣà, he may turn the board round; and then his adversary begins the game; which is not the case otherwise. Supposing the party to whom belong the beyts A, B, C, D, E, F, commences the game, he takes the ḥaṣà from beyt F, and distributes them to the beyts *a*, *b*, *c*, &c., one to each beyt; and if there be enough to put in each of his adversary's six beyts, and more remain in his hand, he proceeds in the same manner to distribute them to his own beyts, in the order A, B, C, &c.; and then, if he have still one or more remaining, to his adversary's beyts, as before, and so on. If the last beyt into which he has put a ḥaṣweh contain but one (having been empty before he put that in; for it may have been left empty at the first,) he ceases; and his adversary plays: but if it contain two or four, he takes its contents, with those of the beyt opposite; and if the last beyt contain two or four, and one or more of the preceding beyts also contain either of these numbers, no beyt with any other number intervening, he takes the contents of these preceding beyts also, with the contents of those opposite. If the last beyt into which he has put a ḥaṣweh contain (with this ḥaṣweh) three, or five, or more, he takes these out, and goes on distributing them in the same manner as before: for instance, if, in this case, the last beyt into which he has put a ḥaṣweh be D, he puts one from its contents into E, another into F, a third into *a*, and so on; and thus he continues, until making the last beyt to contain but one stops him, or making it to contain two or four brings him gain, and makes it his adversary's turn to play. He always plays from beyt F, or, if that be empty, from the nearest beyt to it in his own row containing one or more ḥaṣwehs. When one party has more than a single ḥaṣweh in one or more of his beyts, and the other has none, the former is obliged to put one of his into the first of his adversary's beyts. If only one ḥaṣweh remain on one side, and none on the other, that one is the property of the person on whose side it is. When the board is completely cleared, each party counts the number of the ḥaṣà he has taken; and the one who has most reckons the excess of his above his adversary's number as his gain. The gainer in one board begins to play the next board; his adversary having first distributed the ḥaṣà. When either party has made his successive gains amount to sixty, he has won the game.—In this manner, the game of the manḳalah is played by young persons; and hence this mode of playing it is called "the game of the ignorant" ("leạb el-ghasheem"): others generally play in a different manner, which is termed "the game of the wise, or intelligent" ("leạb el-'áḳil"), and which must now be described.

The ḥaṣà are distributed in one or more beyts on one side, and in the corresponding beyt or beyts on the other side; commonly in four beyts on each side, leaving the two extreme beyts of each side vacant: or they are distributed in any other conventional manner; as, for instance, about half into beyt A, and the remainder in beyt *a*. The person who distributes the ḥaṣà does not count how many he places in a beyt; and it is at his option whether he places them only in one beyt on each side, or in all the beyts. Should the other person object to his distribution, he may turn the board round; but in that case he forfeits his right of playing first. The person who plays first may begin from any one of his beyts; judging by his eye which will bring him the best fortune. He proceeds in the same manner as before described; putting one ḥaṣweh in each beyt; and taking in the same cases as in the former mode; and then the other plays. After the first gain, he counts the ḥaṣà in each of his beyts; and plays from that which will bring him the greatest advantage. One of the parties may stop the other to count the ḥaṣà which he takes out of a beyt to distribute, in order to insure his distributing them correctly. The gain of one party after finishing one board is counted, as in the former mode, by the excess of the number he has taken above the number acquired by the other; and the first who makes his successive gains to amount to sixty wins the game.—This game is of use in practising the players in calculation. It is very commonly played at the coffee-shops; and the players generally agree, though it is unlawful to do so, that the loser shall pay for the coffee drunk by himself and his adversary and the spectators, or for a certain number of cups.

Another game very general among the lower classes in Egypt is called "ṭáb." In other countries of the East this is called "ṭáb wa-dukk;" but I never hear this name given to it in Egypt. In this country it is played in the following manner:—Four small pieces of stick, of a flat form, about a span (or eight inches) in length, and two-thirds of an inch in breadth, are first prepared: they are generally formed of a piece of palm-branch; one side of which, being cut flat and smooth, is white; the other, green, or, if not fresh, of a dull yellow colour; the former side is commonly called white, and the other, black. These are called the "ṭáb." Next, it is necessary to be provided with a "seegà." This is a board, divided into four rows of squares, called "beyts" or "dárs," each about two inches wide; or it consists of similar rows of holes made in the ground, or in a flat stone: the beyts are usually seven, nine, eleven, thirteen, or fifteen, in each row. To shew the mode of playing the game, I shall here represent a seegà of nine beyts in each row; and distinguish the beyts by letters.

i	*h*	*g*	*f*	*e*	*d*	*c*	*b*	*a*
k	*l*	*m*	*n*	*o*	*p*	*q*	*r*	*s*
S	R	Q	P	O	N	M	L	K
A	B	C	D	E	F	G	H	I

In each beyt of one exterior row is usually placed a little piece of stone, or dingy brick, about the size of a walnut; and in each beyt of the other exterior row, a piece of red brick or tile. Or, sometimes, pieces are placed only in a certain number of beyts in those rows; as, for instance, in the first four. The pieces of one row must be distinguished from those in the other. They are called "kiláb" (or dogs); in the singular, "kelb." The game is generally played by two persons. The four little sticks are thrown, all together, against a stick thrust into the ground or held in the hand with one end resting on the ground, or against a wall, or against a stick inclined against a wall. If they fall so that one only has its white side upwards, the player is said to have thrown, or brought, "ṭáb" (plural "ṭeeb"), or a "weled" (or child, plural "wilád"), and counts one: if there be two white, and the other two black, he counts two ("itneyn"): if there be three white, and one black, he counts three ("teláteh"): if all four be white, four ("arba'ah"): if all four black, six ("sitteh"). When one throws ṭáb, or four, or six, he throws again; but when he has thrown two, or three, it is then the turn of the other. To one of the players belongs the row of beyts A, B, C, &c.: to the other, that of *a*, *b*, *c*, &c. They first throw alternately until one has thrown ṭáb; and he who has done this then throws again until he has brought two, or three. Supposing him, at the beginning of the game, to have thrown ṭáb and four and two, he removes the kelb from beyt I, and places it in the seventh beyt from I, which is Q. He must always commence with the kelb in beyt I. The other party, in like manner, commences from beyt *i*. Neither party can remove a kelb from its original place but by throwing ṭáb before each such removal. The kelbs before removal from their original places are called "Naṣárà" (or Christians, in the singular, "Naṣránee"); and after removal, when they are privileged to commence the contest, "Muslimeen" (or "Muslims"): when a person has made a kelb a Muslim, it is said of him "sellem kelb;" and of the kelb, "aslam." Each time that a player throws ṭáb, he generally makes a kelb Muslim, until he has made them all so, and thus prepared them to circulate in the beyts. Each player may have two or more kelbs in circulation at the same time. Let us suppose (to make the description more simple) that the person to whom belongs the row of beyts A, B, C, &c., is circulating a single kelb: he moves it through the two middle rows of beyts in the order of the letters by which I have distinguished them, from K to S, and from *k* to *s*; and may then either repeat the same round or enter his adversary's row, as long as there is any kelb remaining in that row; but in the latter case, he does not continue to circulate the same kelb, except in circumstances which will be mentioned hereafter. Whenever a throw, or any of two or more throws, which the player has made enables him to move his kelb into a beyt occupied by one of his opponent's kelbs, he takes the latter. For instance, if one party has a kelb in the beyt *m*, and the other has one in *o*, and another in *s*, and the former has thrown ṭáb (or one), and then four, and then two, he may take the kelb in *o* by the throw of two; then, by the throw of four, take that in *s*; and, by the throw of ṭáb, pass into *a*, and take a third kelb if it contain one. A player may, by means of a suitable throw, or two or more throws, move one of his kelbs into a beyt occupied by another of his own; and these two together, in like manner, he may add to a third, or he may add a third to them: thus he may unite any number of his own kelbs, and circulate them together, as if they were but one; but he cannot divide them again, and play with them separately, unless he throw ṭáb. If he avail himself of a throw which he has made to bring them back into a row through which they have already passed (either separately or together), they become reduced to a single kelb: but he need not avail himself of such a throw: he may wait until he throws ṭáb. Two or more kelbs thus united are called an "'eggeh." The object of so uniting them is to place them as soon as possible in a situation of safety; as will be seen by what immediately follows. If either party pass one of his kelbs into his adversary's row, he may leave it there in safety as long as he does not want to continue to play with it, because the latter cannot bring back a kelb into his own row. The former, however, cannot continue to circulate the kelb which has entered that row until he has no kelb remaining in his own row; or unless he have only an 'eggeh in his row, and does not throw ṭáb, which alone enables him to divide the 'eggeh. In circulating through his adversary's beyts, he proceeds in the order of the letters by which I have marked them. He cannot pass the same kelb again into his adversary's row: after it has passed through that row, he circulates it through the two middle rows only, in the same manner as at first.—This game is often played by four or more persons; and without the seegà. When one person throws four, he is called the Sulṭán. He holds a maḳra'ah,[1] which is a piece of the thick end of a palm-stick, with two or three splits made in the thicker part of it. When a player throws six, he is called the Wezeer, and holds the stick against which the ṭáb are thrown. Whenever a person throws two, the Sulṭán gives him a blow, or two or more blows (as many as the Wezeer may order), on the sole of his foot, or the soles of both feet, with the maḳra'ah. When a player throws twice six, he is both Sulṭán and Wezeer.

Many of the felláḥeen of Egypt also frequently amuse themselves with a game called that of the "seegà," which may be described in a few words. The seegà employed in this game is different from that of the ṭáb: it consists of a number of holes, generally made in the ground; most commonly, of five rows of five holes in each, or seven rows of seven in each, or nine rows of nine in each: the first kind is called the "khamsáwee seegà;" the second, the "seb'áwee;" and the third, the "tis'áwee." A khamsáwee seegà is here represented.

Seegà.

[1] Thus commonly pronounced, for "miḳra"ah."

The holes are called "'oyoon" (or eyes, in the singular "'eyn"). In this seegà, they are twenty-five in number. The players have each twelve "kelbs," similar to those used in the game of the ṭáb.[1] One of them places two of his kelbs in the 'eyns marked *a, a*: the other puts two of his in those marked *b, b*: they then alternately place two kelbs in any of the 'eyns that they may choose, except the central 'eyn of the seegà. All the 'eyns but the central one being thus occupied (most of the kelbs placed at random), the game is commenced. The party who begins moves one of his kelbs from a contiguous 'eyn into the central. The other party, if the 'eyn now made vacant be not next to any one of those occupied by his kelbs, desires his adversary to give him, or open to him, a way; and the latter must do so, by removing, and thus losing, one of his own kelbs. This is also done on subsequent occasions, when required by similar circumstances. The aim of each party, after the first disposal of the kelbs, is to place any one of his kelbs in such a situation that there shall be, between it and another of his, one of his adversary's kelbs. This, by so doing, he takes; and as long as he can immediately make another capture by such means, he does so, without allowing his adversary to move.—These are the only rules of the game. It will be remarked that, though most of the kelbs are placed at random, foresight is requisite in the disposal of the remainder.—Several seegàs have been cut upon the stones on the summit of the Great Pyramid, by Arabs who have served as guides to travellers.

Gymnastic games, or such diversions as require much bodily exertion, are very uncommon among the Egyptians, who are, however, generally remarkable for bodily strength: the boatmen, for instance, undergo very severe labour in rowing and towing, and the porters carry burdens of almost incredible weight. Sometimes two peasants contend with each other, for mere amusement, or for a trifling wager or reward, with "nebboots," which are thick staves, five or six feet long: the object of each is to strike his adversary on the head. The nebboot is a formidable weapon, and is often seen in the hand of an Egyptian peasant: he usually carries it when on a journey; particularly when he travels by night; which, however, is seldom the case. Wrestling-matches are also sometimes witnessed in Egypt: the combatants (who are called "muṣáre'een," in the singular

1 The larger seegàs, in like manner, require a sufficient number of kelbs to occupy all the 'eyns except one.

"muṣáre',") strip themselves of all their clothing except their drawers, and generally oil their bodies; but their exercises are not remarkable, and are seldom performed but for remuneration, on the occasions of festivals, processions, &c. On such occasions, too, mock combats between two men, usually clad only in their drawers, and each armed with a sabre and a small shield, are not unfrequently witnessed: neither attempts to wound his adversary: every blow is received on the shield.

The game of the "gereed," as played by the Memlooks and Turkish soldiers, has often been described; but the manner in which it is practised by many of the peasants of Upper Egypt is much more worthy of description. It is often played by the latter on the occasion of the marriage of a person of influence, such as the Sheykh of a tribe or village; or on that of a circumcision; or when a votive calf or ox or bull, which has been let loose to pasture where it will, by common consent, is about to be sacrificed at the tomb of a saint, and a public feast made with its meat. The combatants usually consist of two parties, of different villages, or of different tribes or branches of a tribe; each party being about twelve or twenty or more in number; and each person mounted on a horse or mare. The two parties station themselves about five hundred feet or more apart. A person from one party gallops towards the other party, and challenges them: one of the latter, taking, in his left hand, four, five, six, or more gereeds, each six feet, or an inch or two more or less, in length, but generally equal in length to the height of a tall man, and very heavy (being the lower part of the palm-stick, freshly cut, and full of sap) pursues the challenger at full gallop: he approaches him as near as possible; often within arm's length; and throws, at his head or back, one gereed after another, until he has none left. The gereed is blunt at both ends. It is thrown with the small end foremost; and with uplifted arm; and sometimes inflicts terrible, and even fatal, wounds.[1] The person against whom the gereeds are thrown endeavours to catch them, or to ward them off with his arm or with a sheathed sword; or he escapes them by the superior speed of his horse. Having sustained the attack, and arrived at the station of his party, he tries his skill against the person by whom he has been

[1] During my last residence at Thebes, a fine athletic man, the best gereed-player of the place, whom I had taken into my service as a nightly guard, received a very severe wound at this game; and I had some difficulty to effect a cure: he was delirious for many hours in consequence of it, and had nearly lost his life. The gereed struck him a little before his ear, and penetrated downwards into his neck.

pursued, in the same manner as the latter did against him.—This sport, which reminds us of the tournaments of old, and which was a game of the early Bedawees, continues for several hours. It is common only among those tribes who have not been many years, or not more than a few centuries, settled on the banks of the Nile; and who have consequently retained many Bedawee customs and habits. About the close of the period of my former visit to this country, three men and a mare were killed at this game within an hour, in the western plain of Thebes. It is seldom, however, that a man loses his life in this exercise: at least, of late, I have heard of no such occurrence taking place.—In Lower Egypt, a gereed only half the length of those above described, or little more, is used in playing this game.

Other exercises, which are less frequently performed, and only at festivals for the amusement of the spectators, will be described in subsequent pages.

CHAPTER XVIII.

MUSIC.

The Egyptians in general are excessively fond of music; and yet they regard the study of this fascinating art (like dancing) as unworthy to employ any portion of the time of a man of sense; and as exercising too powerful an effect upon the passions, and leading a man into gaiety and dissipation and vice. Hence it was condemned by the Prophet: but it is used, notwithstanding, even in religious ceremonies; especially by the darweeshes. The Egyptians have very few books on music; and these are not understood by their modern musicians. The natural liking of the Egyptians for music is shewn by their habit of regulating their motions, and relieving the dulness of their occupations, in various labours, by songs or chants. Thus do the boatmen, in rowing, &c.; the peasants in raising water; the porters in carrying heavy weights with poles; men, boys, and girls, in assisting builders, by bringing bricks, stones, and mortar, and removing rubbish: so also, the sawyers, reapers, and many other labourers. Though the music of the Egyptians is of a style very difficult for foreigners to acquire or imitate, the children very easily and early attain it. The practice of chanting the Ḳur-án, which is taught in all their schools, contributes to increase their natural fondness for music.

How science was cherished by the Arabs when all the nations of Europe were involved in the grossest ignorance, and how much the former profited by the works of ancient Greek writers, is well known. It appears that they formed the system of music which has prevailed among them for many centuries partly from Greek, and partly from Persian and Indian, treatises. From the Greek language are derived the most general Arabic term for music, namely, "mooseeḳà," and the names of some of the Arab musical instruments; but most of the technical terms used by the Arab musicians are borrowed from the

Persian and Indian languages. There is a striking degree of similarity between many of the airs which I have heard in Egypt and some of the popular melodies of Spain;[1] and it is not surprising that this is the case: for music was much cultivated among the Arabs of Spain; and the library of the Escurial contains many Arabic treatises on this art.

The most remarkable peculiarity in the Arab system of music is the division of tones into thirds. Hence I have heard Egyptian musicians urge against the European systems of music that they are deficient in the number of sounds. These small and delicate gradations of sound give a peculiar softness to the performances of the Arab musicians, which are generally of a plaintive character: but they are difficult to discriminate with exactness, and are therefore seldom observed in the vocal and instrumental music of those persons who have not made a regular study of the art. Most of the popular airs of the Egyptians, though of a similar character, in most respects, to the music of their professional performers, are very simple; consisting of only a few notes, which serve for every one or two lines of a song, and which are therefore repeated many times. I must confess that I generally take great delight in the more refined kind of music which I occasionally hear in Egypt; and the more I become habituated to the style, the more I am pleased with it; though, at the same time, I must state that I have not met with many Europeans who enjoy it in the same degree as myself. The natives of Egypt are generally enraptured with the performances of their vocal and instrumental musicians: they applaud with frequent exclamations of "Alláh!"[2] and "God approve thee!" "God preserve thy voice!" and similar expressions.

The male professional musicians are called "Áláteeyeh;" in the singular, "Álátee," which properly signifies "a player upon an instrument;" but they are generally both instrumental and vocal performers. They are people of very dissolute habits; and are regarded as scarcely less disreputable characters than the public dancers. They are, however, hired at most grand entertainments, to amuse the company; and on these occasions they are usually supplied with brandy, or other spirituous liquors, which they sometimes drink until they can no longer sing, nor strike a chord. The

[1] This is most remarkable in the more refined Egyptian music; but it is also observable in the airs of some common ballads and chants.

[2] Often, in such cases, pronounced in an unusually broad manner, and the last syllable drawled out, thus—"Allauh!"

sum commonly paid to each of them for one night's performance is equal to about two or three shillings; but they often receive considerably more. The guests generally contribute the sum.

There are also female professional singers. These are called "'Awálim;" in the singular, "'Ál'meh," or "'Álimeh;" an appellation, as an Arabic word, literally signifying "a learned female;" but, as applied to these female singers, evidently, I think, derived from the Hebrew or Phœnician word "'almáh," signifying "a girl" and "a virgin," and particularly "a singing girl." "'Al-'alámóth sheer" (the title of Psalm xlvi.) and "nebálím 'al-'alámóth" (in 1 Chron. xv. 20) should, I doubt not, be rendered, "A song," and "harps" or the like, "adapted to 'almáhs," that is, "singing girls." And as Jerome says that "alma" in the Punic language signified "a virgin," it seems to be probable that, in old times, the most celebrated of the singing-girls in Egypt were Phœnicians. The 'Awálim are often hired on the occasion of a fête in the ḥareem of a person of wealth. There is generally a small, elevated apartment, called a "tuḳeyseh," or "mughannà," adjoining the principal saloon of the ḥareem, from which it is separated only by a screen of wooden lattice-work; or there is some other convenient place in which the female singers may be concealed from the sight of the master of the house, should he be present with his women. But when there is a party of male guests, they generally sit in the court, or in a lower apartment, to hear the songs of the 'Awálim, who, in this case, usually sit at a window of the ḥareem, concealed by the lattice-work. Some of them are also instrumental performers. I have heard the most celebrated 'Awálim in Cairo, and have been more charmed with their songs than with the best performances of the Áláteeyeh, and more so, I think I may truly add, than with any other music that I have ever enjoyed. They are often very highly paid. I have known instances of sums equal to more than fifty guineas being collected for a single 'Ál'meh from the guests at an entertainment in the house of a merchant, where none of the contributors were persons of much wealth. So powerful is the effect of the singing of a very accomplished 'Ál'meh, that her audience, in the height of their excitement, often lavish upon her sums which they can ill afford to lose. There are, among the 'Awálim in Cairo, a few who are not altogether unworthy of the appellation of "learned females;" having some literary accomplishments. There are also many of an inferior class, who sometimes dance in the ḥareem: hence, travellers have often misapplied the name of "almé," meaning

" 'ál'meh," to the common dancing-girls, of whom an account will be given in another chapter of this work; or they may have done so because these girls themselves occasionally assume this appellation, and generally do so when (as has been often the case) the exercise of their art is prohibited by the government.

The Egyptians have a great variety of musical instruments. Those which are generally used at private concerts are the "kemengeh," "ḳánoon," "'ood," and "náy."

The "kemengeh"[1] is a kind of viol. Its name, which is Persian, and more properly written "kemángeh," signifies "a bow-instrument." This instrument, and all the others of which I insert engravings, I have drawn with the camera-lucida. The total length of the kemengeh which is here represented is thirty-eight inches. The sounding-body[2] is a cocoa-nut, of which about a fourth part has been cut off. It is pierced with many small holes. Over the front of it is strained a piece of the skin of a fish of the genus "silurus," called "bayáḍ;" and upon this rests the bridge.[3] The neck[4] is of ebony inlaid with ivory; and of a cylindrical form. At the bottom of it is a piece of ivory; and the head,[5] in which the pegs are inserted, is also of ivory. The pegs[6] are of beech; and their heads, of ivory. The foot[7] is of iron: it passes through the sounding-body, and is inserted into the neck, to the depth of four or five inches. Each of the two chords consists of about sixty horse-hairs: at the lower end, they are attached to an iron ring, just below the sounding-body: towards the other extremity, each is lengthened with a piece of lamb's gut,[8] by which it is attached to its peg. Over the chords, a little below their junction with the gut-strings, a double band of leather[9] is tied, passing round the neck of the instrument. The bow[10] is thirty-four inches and a half in length. Its form is shewn by the engraving. The stick is generally of ash. The horse-hairs, passed through a hole at the head of the bow-stick and secured by a knot, and attached at the other end to an iron ring, are tightened or slackened by a band of leather which passes through the ring just mentioned and through another ring at the foot of the bow. I insert a sketch of a performer

---

1 A friend (a native of Egypt) has observed to me, since the first edition of this work was printed, that "rabáb" would be a more proper term for this instrument, being the general Arabic name for a viol; but I never heard it called in Egypt by any other name than "kemengeh." It is also thus called in Syria.

2 Called "ḥoḳḳah."

3 "Ghazál."

4 "Sá'ëd," or "arm."

5 "Khazneh."

6 "Meláwee;" singular, "melwà."

7 "Seekh."

8 "Weter."

9 "Ribáṭ."

10 "Ḳós."

on the kemengeh, to shew the manner in which he holds the instrument and the bow. In passing the bow from one chord to the other, he turns the kemengeh about sixty degrees round. The sketch introduced, and those of the performers on the ḳánoon, 'ood, and

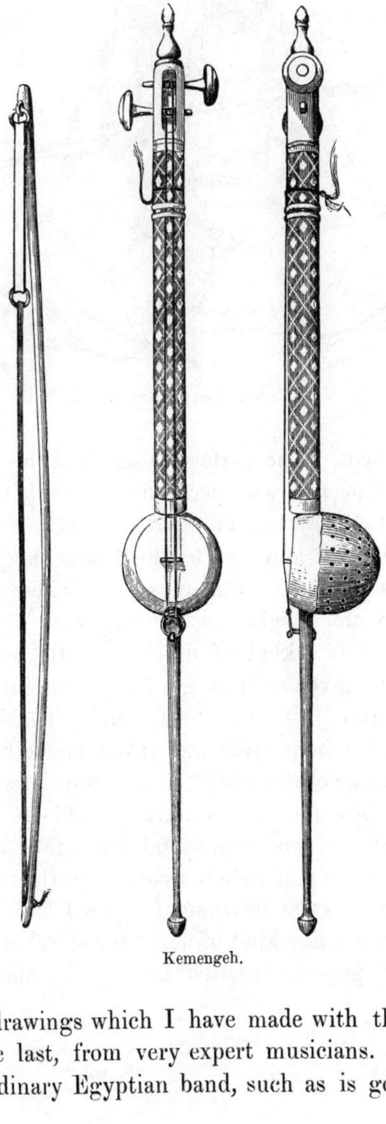

Kemengeh.

náy, are from drawings which I have made with the camera-lucida, and, except the last, from very expert musicians. Together, they represent an ordinary Egyptian band, such as is generally seen at a

A Performer on the Kemengeh.

private entertainment. The performer on the kemengeh usually sits on the right hand of him who performs on the ḳánoon, or opposite (that is, facing,) the latter, on the left hand of whom sits the performer on the 'ood; and next to this last is the performer on the náy. Sometimes there are other musicians, whose instruments will be mentioned hereafter; and often, two singers.

The "ḳánoon" is a kind of dulcimer. Its name is from the Greek κανών, or from the same origin; and has the same signification; that is, "rule," "law," "custom." The instrument from which the engraving here given was taken is, perhaps, an inch or two longer than some others which I have seen. Its greatest length is thirty-nine inches and three-quarters; and its breadth, sixteen inches: its depth is two inches and one-tenth. The ḳánoon is sometimes made entirely of walnut-wood,[1] with the exception of some ornamental parts. In the instrument which I have drawn, the face[2] and the back[3] are of a fine kind of deal: the sides[4] are of beech. The piece in which the pegs are inserted[5] is of beech; and so is the ridge[6]

1 "Góz."
2 "Wishsh," for "weg-h."
3 "Ḍahr."
4 "Soor," or "wall."
5 "Misṭarah."
6 "Enf," or "nose."

along its interior edge, through which the chords are passed. The pegs[1] are of poplar-wood. The bridge[2] is of fine deal. In the central

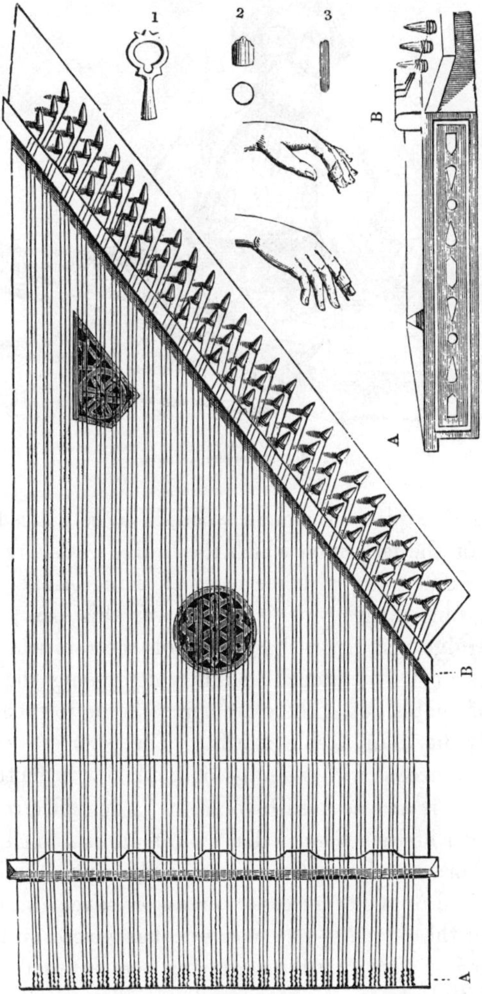

Ḳánoon.

No. 1 is the key; 2, the ring, or thimble; 3, the plectrum.

part of the face of the instrument is a circular piece of wood[3] of a reddish colour, pierced with holes; and towards the acute angle of

---

[1] "Meláwee." [2] "Faras," or "mare." [3] "Shemseh," or "a sun."

A Performer on the Ḳánoon.

the face is another piece of similar wood, likewise pierced with holes. In that part of the face upon which the bridge rests are five oblong apertures, corresponding with the five feet of the bridge. A piece of fishes' skin[1], nine inches wide, is glued over this part; and the five feet of the bridge rest upon those parts of the skin which cover the five apertures above mentioned; slightly depressing the skin. The chords[2] are of lamb's gut. There are three chords to each note; and, altogether, twenty-four treble-chords. The shortest side[3] of the instrument is veneered with walnut-wood, inlaid with mother-of-pearl. The instrument is played with two plectra[4]; one plectrum attached to the forefinger of each hand. Each plectrum is a small, thin piece of buffalo's horn; and is placed between the finger and a ring, or thimble,[5] formed of a flat piece of brass or silver, in the manner represented in the sketch.—The instrument is placed on the knees of the performer; as shewn by the engraving here inserted. Under the hands of a skilful player, the ḳánoon pleases me more than any other Egyptian instrument without an accompaniment; and to a band it is an important accession.

---

1 "Raḳmeh."
2 "Owtár;" in the singular, "weter."
3 "Ḳibleh."
4 Each plectrum is called "reesheh."
5 "Kishtiwán."

The "'ood" is a lute, which is played with a plectrum. This has been for many centuries the instrument most commonly used by the best Arab musicians, and is celebrated by numerous poets. Its name (the original signification of which is "wood"), with the article

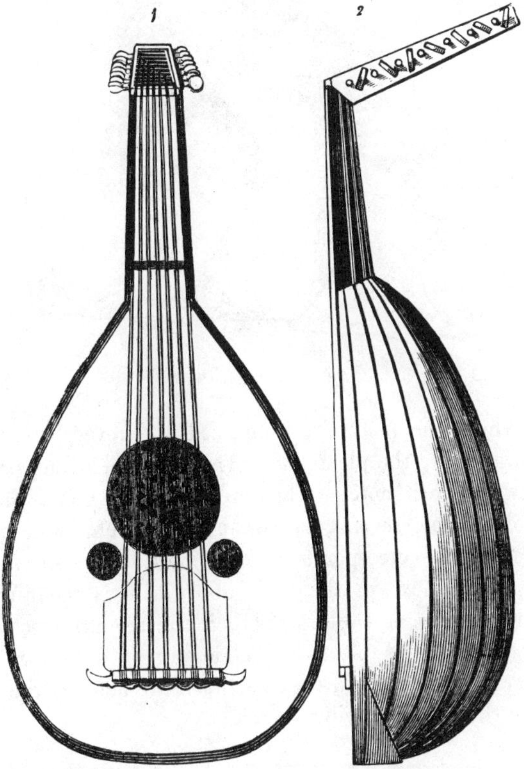

'Ood.

el prefixed to it, is the source whence are derived the terms *liuto* in Italian, *luth* in French, *lute* in English, &c. The length of the 'ood represented by the accompanying engraving, measuring from the button, or angle of the neck, is twenty-five inches and a half. The body of it is composed of fine deal, with edges &c. of ebony: the neck, of ebony, faced with box and an ebony edge. On the face of the body of the instrument, in which are one large and two small shemsehs[1] of ebony, is glued a piece of fishes' skin,[2] under that part of the

1 See a note to the description of the ḳánoon.

2 "Raḳmeh."

A Performer on the 'Ood.

chords to which the plectrum is applied, to prevent the wood from being worn away by the plectrum. The instrument has seven double strings;[1] two to each note. They are of lamb's gut. The order of these double chords is singular: the double chord of the lowest note is that which corresponds to the chord of the highest note in our violins, &c.: next in the scale above this is the fifth (that is, counting the former as the first): then the seventh, second, fourth, sixth, and third. The plectrum[2] is a slip of a vulture's feather. The manner in which it and the 'ood itself are held by the performer is shewn by the accompanying sketch.

Náy.

The "náy," which is the fourth and last of the instruments which I have mentioned as most commonly used at private concerts, is a kind of flute. There are several kinds of náy, differing from each other in dimensions, but in little else. The most common is that here represented. It has been called the darweesh's flute; because often used at the "zikrs" of darweeshes, to accompany the songs of the "munshids." It is a simple reed, about eighteen inches in

1 "Owtár."

2 "Reesheh."

A Performer on the Náy.

length, seven-eighths of an inch in diameter at the upper extremity, and three quarters of an inch at the lower. It is pierced with six holes in front, and generally with another hole at the back. The sketch which I insert of a performer on the náy shews the most usual manner in which this instrument is held: but sometimes the left hand is uppermost, and the instrument inclined towards the right arm of the performer, instead of the left. The sounds are produced by blowing, through a very small aperture of the lips, against the edge of the orifice of the tube, and directing the wind chiefly within the tube. By blowing with more or less force, sounds are produced an octave higher or lower. In the hands of a good performer, the náy yields fine, mellow tones; but it requires much practice to sound it well. A náy is sometimes made of a portion of a gun-barrel.

Another instrument often used at private concerts is a small tambourine, called "riḳḳ," similar to one of which an engraving will be found in this chapter, page 366, but rather smaller.

A kind of mandoline, called "ṭamboor," is also used at concerts in Egypt; but mostly by Greeks and other foreigners. These musicians likewise use a dulcimer, called "ṣanṭeer," which resembles the ḳánoon, except that it has two sides oblique, instead of one (the two opposite sides equally inclining together), has double chords of wire, instead of treble chords of lamb's gut, and is beaten with two sticks instead of the little plectra.

A curious kind of viol, called "rabáb," is much used by poor singers, as an accompaniment to the voice. There are two kinds of viol which bear this name; the "rabáb el-mughannee" (or singers' viol), and the "rabáb esh-shá'er" (or poet's viol); which differ from each other only in this, that the former has two chords, and the latter

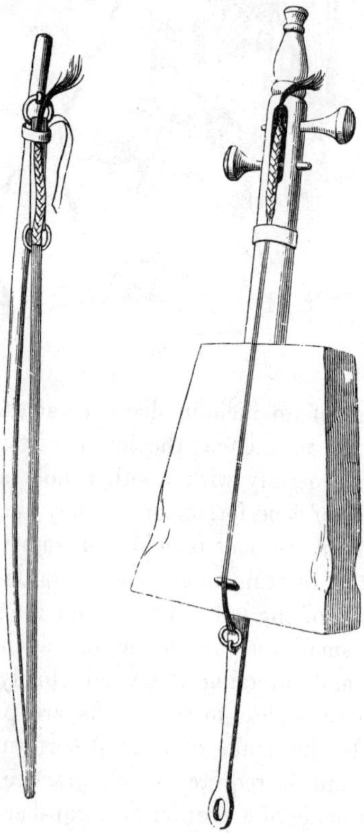

Rabáb esh-Shá'er.

but one. The latter is that of which I give an engraving; but it will be observed that it is convertible into the former kind, having two pegs. It is thirty-two inches in length. The body of it is a frame of wood, of which the front is covered with parchment, and the back uncovered. The foot is of iron: the chord, of horse-hairs, like those of the kemengeh. The bow, which is twenty-eight inches long, is similar to that of the kemengeh. This instrument is always used by the public reciters of the romance of Aboo-Zeyd, in chanting the poetry. The reciter of this romance is called a "shá'er" (or poet); and hence the instrument is called "the poet's viol," and "the Aboo-Zeydee viol." The shá'er himself uses this instrument; and another performer on the same kind of rabáb generally accompanies him.

The instruments used in wedding-processions, and the processions of darweeshes, &c., are chiefly a hautboy, called "zemr," and several kinds of drums, of which the most common kinds are the "ṭabl beledee" (or country drum, that is, Egyptian drum), and the "ṭabl Shámee" (or Syrian drum). The former is of a similar kind to our common military drum; but not so deep. It is hung obliquely. The latter is a kind of kettle-drum, of tinned copper, with a parchment face. It is generally about sixteen inches in diameter, and not more than four in depth in the centre; and is beaten with two slender sticks. The performer suspends it to his neck, by a string attached to two rings fixed to the edge of the instrument. I have represented these drums in the sketch of a bridal-procession, and in another engraving in page 58.

A pair of large kettle-drums, called "naḳáḳeer," (in the singular, "naḳḳárah,") are generally seen in most of the great religious processions connected with the pilgrimage, &c., in Cairo. They are both of copper, and similar in form; each about two-thirds of a sphere; but are of unequal dimensions: the flat surface (or face) of the larger is about two feet, or more, in diameter; and that of the latter, nearly a foot and a half. They are placed upon a camel, attached to the fore part of the saddle, upon which the person who beats them rides. The larger is placed on the right.

Darweeshes, in religious processions, &c., and in begging, often make use of a little ṭabl, or kettle-drum, called "báz;" six or seven inches in diameter; which is held in the left hand, by a little projection in the centre of the back; and beaten by the right hand, with a short leathern strap, or a stick. They also use cymbals, which are called "kás," on similar occasions. The báz is used by the Musaḥḥir, to attract attention to his cry in the nights of Ramaḍán. Castanets of brass, called "ságát," are used by the public female and male dancers. Each dancer has two pairs of these instruments. They are attached, each by a loop of string, to the thumb and second finger; and have a more pleasing sound than castanets of wood or ivory.

There are two instruments which are generally found in the ḥareem

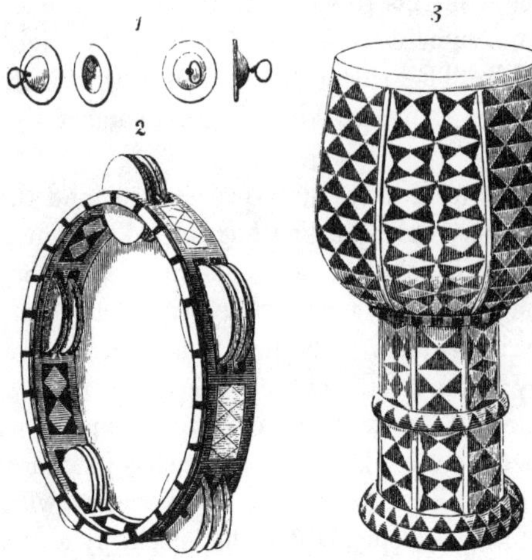

1 Ságát. 2 Ṭár. 3 Darábukkeh.

of a person of moderate wealth, and which the women often use for their diversion. One of these is a tambourine, called "ṭár," of which I insert an engraving. It is eleven inches in diameter. The hoop is overlaid with mother-of-pearl, tortoise-shell, and white bone, or ivory, both without and within; and has ten double circular plates of brass attached to it; each two pairs having a wire passing through their centres. The ṭár is held by the left or right hand, and beaten with the fingers of that hand, and by the other hand. The fingers of the hand which holds the instrument, striking only near the hoop, produce higher sounds than the other hand, which strikes in the centre. —A tambourine of a larger and more simple kind than that here described, without the metal plates, is often used by the lower orders. —The other instrument alluded to in the commencement of this paragraph is a kind of drum, called "darábukkeh." The best kind is made of wood, covered with mother-of-pearl and tortoise-shell, &c. One of this description is here represented with the ṭár. It is fifteen inches in length; covered with a piece of fishes' skin at the larger extremity, and open at the smaller. It is placed under the left arm; generally suspended by a string that passes over the left shoulder; and is beaten with both hands. Like the ṭár, it yields different sounds when beaten near the edge and in the middle. A more common kind of darábukkeh is made of earth, and differs a little in form from that just described. An engraving of it is here given.

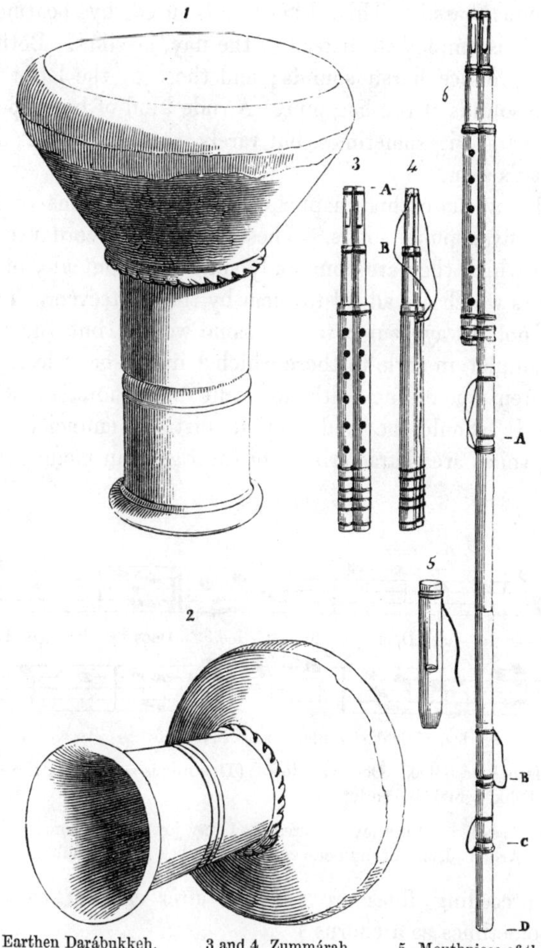

1 and 2. Earthen Darábukkeh. 3 and 4. Zummárah. 5. Mouthpiece of the latter. 6 Arghool.
The Zummárah is 14 inches long; the Arghool 3 feet 2½ inches.

The boatmen of the Nile very often use an earthen darábukkeh; but of a larger size than that used in ḥareems: generally from a foot and a half to two feet in length. This is also used by some low story-tellers and others. The boatmen employ, as an accompaniment to their earthen drum, a double reed pipe, called "zummárah."[1] There is also another kind of double reed pipe, called "arghool;" of which one of the reeds is much longer than the other, and serves as a drone,

[1] The mouthpiece (A B) of the zummárah is moveable.

or continuous bass.[1] This, likewise, is used by boatmen; and sometimes it is employed, instead of the náy, at zikrs. Both of these reed pipes produce harsh sounds; and those of the latter much resemble the sounds of the bag-pipe. A rude kind of bag-pipe ("zummárah bi-soạn") is sometimes, but rarely, seen in Egypt: its bag is a small goat's skin.

I shall now close this chapter with a few specimens of Egyptian music; chiefly popular songs. These I note in accordance with the manner in which they are commonly sung; without any of the embellishments which are added to them by the Áláteeyeh. The airs of these are not always sung to the same words; but the words are generally similar in style to those which I insert, or at least as silly; though often abounding with indecent metaphors, or with plain ribaldry.—It should be added, that distinct enunciation, and a quavering voice, are characteristics of the Egyptian mode of singing.

SONGS.

No. 1.

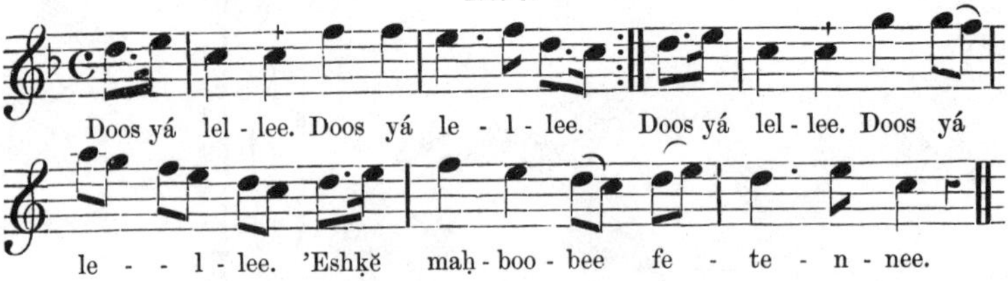
Doos yá lel - lee. Doos yá le - l - lee. Doos yá lel - lee. Doos yá
le - - l - lee. 'Eshkĕ maḥ - boo - bee fe - te - n - nee.

"Doos[2] yá lellee. Doos yá lellee. (This line is sung three times.)
'Eshkĕ[3] maḥboobee fetennee."

Tread![4] O my joy![5] Tread! O my joy! (three times.)
Ardent desire of my beloved hath involved me in trouble.

(The preceding lines are repeated after each of the following stanzas, sometimes as a chorus.)

---

[1] The arghool has three moveable pieces to lengthen the longer tube (A B, B C, and C D); and is sometimes used with only one or two of these; and sometimes with none of them. Its mouthpiece is moveable, like that of the zummárah.

[2] Here, in accordance with a rule observed in most modern Arab songs, the masculine gender is applied to the beloved object, who is, nevertheless, a female, as will be seen in several subsequent verses. In translation, I therefore substitute the feminine gender in every case where our language distinguishes gender. Some words occur, bearing double meanings, which I leave unexplained. I write the Arabic words as they are generally pronounced in Cairo, except in the case of one letter, which I represent by "ḳ," to express the sound which persons of education give to it instead of the more usual hiatus.

[3] The Arabs find it impossible to utter three consonants together without a pause between the second and third: hence the introduction of the short vowel which terminates this word: *sh* represents a single letter.

[4] Or pace, or strut.

[5] "Yá lellee," which is thus translated, is a common ejaculation indicative of joy, said to be synonymous with "yá farḥatee." It is difficult to render this and other cant terms.

"Má[1] kullu men námet 'oyoonuh
Yaḥsib el-'áshiḳ yenám.[2]
Wa-lláh anà mughram ṣabábeh.
Lem 'ala-l-'áshiḳ meḷám."

Let not every one whose eyes sleep
Imagine that the lover sleepeth.
By Allah! I am inflamed with intense love.
The lover is not obnoxious to blame.

"Yá Sheykh el-'Arab: Yá Seyyid:
Tegmaạnee 'a-l-khilli[3] leyleh.
Wa-n[4] gánee ḥabeebĕ ḳalbee
La-ạmal lu-l-[5] Kashmeer ḍulleyleh."

O Sheykh of the Arabs! O Seyyid![6]
Unite me to the true love one night!
And if the beloved of my heart come to me
I will make the Kashmeer shawl her canopy.

"Kámil el-owṣáf fetennee
Wa-l-'oyoon es-sood ramoonee.
Min häwáhum ṣirt aghannee[7]
Wa-l-häwà zowwad gunoonee."

The perfect in attributes hath involved me in trouble,
And the black eyes have o'erthrown me.
From love of them I began to sing,
And the air[8] increased my madness.

"Gema'om[9] gem' al-'awázil
'An ḥabeebee yemna'oonee.
Wa-lláh anà má afoot häwáhum
Bi-s-suyoof low ḳaṭṭa'oonee."

They leagued together the crew of reproachers
To debar me from my beloved.
By Allah! I will not relinquish the love of them,[10]
Though they should cut me in pieces with swords.

"Ḳum bi-nè yá khillĕ neskar
Taḥta ḍill el-yásameeneh:
Neḳṭuf el-khókh min 'alà ummuh
Wa-l-'awázil gháfileenĕ."

---

[1] This line and the first of the next stanza require an additional note, which is the same as the last note of these lines, to be added at the commencement.

[2] This and some other lines require that the note which should be the last if they were of more correct measure be transferred to the commencement of the next line.

[3] For "'ala-l-khilli."

[4] For "wa-in."

[5] For "la-aạmal lahu-l;" or rather, "la-'amiltu lahu-l."

[6] The famous saint Es-Seyyid Aḥmad El-Bedawee, who is buried at Ṭanṭà, in the Delta.

[7] For "ughannee."

[8] That is, the air of the song.

[9] For "gema'oo."

[10] Namely, the black eyes.

Up with us! O true love! Let us intoxicate ourselves [1]
Under the shade of the jasmine:
We will pluck the peach from its mother [tree]
While the reproachers are unconscious.

"Yá benát goowa-l-medeeneh
'Andakum ashyà temeeneh:
Telbisu-sh-sháṭeḥ bi-loolee
Wa-l-ḳiládeh 'a-n-nehdi [2] zeeneh."

O ye damsels in the city! [3]
Ye have things of value:
Ye wear the sháṭeḥ [4] with pearls,
And the ḳiládeh,[5] an ornament over the bosom.

"Yá benát Iskendereeyeh
Meshyukum 'a-l-farshi [6] gheeyeh:
Telbisu-l-Kashmeer bi-telee
Wa-sh-shefáif sukkareeyeh."

O ye damsels of Alexandria!
Your walk over the furniture [7] is alluring:
Ye wear the Kashmeer shawl, with embroidered work,[8]
And your lips are sweet as sugar.

"Yá miláḥ kháfoo min Allah
Wa-rḥamu-l-'áshiḳ li-llah.
Ḥobbukum mektoob min Allah:
Ḳaddaru [9]-l-Mowlà 'aleiya."

O ye beauties! fear God,
And have mercy on the lover for the sake of God.
The love of you is ordained by God:
The Lord hath decreed it against me.

No. 2.

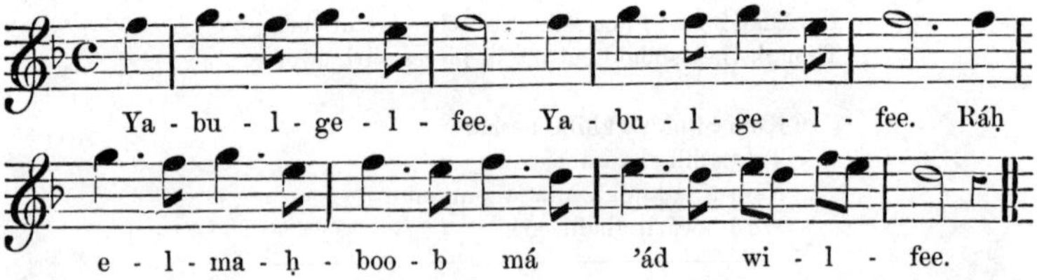
Ya - bu - l - ge - l - fee. Ya - bu - l - ge - l - fee. Ráḥ
e - l - ma - ḥ - boo - b má 'ád wi - l - fee.

[1] The intoxication here meant is that of love, as is generally the case when this expression is used in Arab songs.

[2] For "'ala-n-nehdi."

[3] Cairo.

[4] An ornament described in the Appendix, resembling a necklace of pearls, &c., attached on each side of the head-dress.

[5] A kind of long necklace, reaching to the girdle.

[6] For "'ala-l-farshi."

[7] The furniture consists of carpets &c., spread upon the floor.

[8] "Telee" is a corruption of the Turkish word "tel," and is applied in Egypt to flattened gold or silver wire, used in embroidery.

[9] For "ḳaddaruh;" or rather, "ḳaddarahu."

"Ya-bu-l-gelfee. Ya-bu-l-gelfee.
Ráḥ el-maḥboob: má 'ád wilfee."[1]

O thou in the long-sleeved yelek! O thou in the long-sleeved yelek!
The beloved is gone: my companion has not returned.

"Ráḥ el-mirsál wa-lem gáshĕ:[2]
Wa-'eyn el-ḥobb bi-teráshee.[3]
Ya-bu-l-gálif. Ya-bu-l-gelfee.
Yá reyt'nè ma-nshebeknáshĕ.
Ya-bu-l-gelfee, &c."

The messenger went, and has not returned:
And the eye of love is glancing.
O thou with the side-lock![4] O thou in the long-sleeved yelek!
Would that we had not been ensnared!
O thou in the long-sleeved yelek! &c.

"Wa-ley yá 'eyn shebekteenè
Wa-bi-l-alḥáẓ garaḥteenè.
Ya-bu-l-gálif. Ya-bu-l-gelfee.
Bi-lláhi riḳḳ wa-shfeenè.
Ya-bu-l-gelfee, &c."

And why, O eye! hast thou ensnared us?
And with glances wounded us?
O thou with the side-lock! O thou in the long-sleeved yelek!
By Allah! have compassion, and heal us.
O thou in the long-sleeved yelek! &c.

"Asḳamtenee yá ḥabeebee:
Wa-má ḳaṣdee illà ṭibbak.
'Asák yá bedrĕ terḥamnee:
Fa-inna ḳalbee yeḥebbak.
Ya-bu-l-wardee. Ya-bu-l-wardee.
Ḥabeebĕ ḳalbee khaleek 'andee."

Thou hast made me ill, O my beloved!
And my desire is for nothing but thy medicine.
Perhaps, O full moon! thou wilt have mercy upon me:
For verily my heart loveth thee.
O thou in the rose-coloured dress! O thou in the rose-coloured dress!
Beloved of my heart! remain with me.

"De-l-ḥobbĕ gánee yet'máyal:[5]
Wa-sukrĕ ḥálee gufoonuh.
Meddeyt eedee[6] akhud el-kás:
Sekirt anà min 'oyoonuh.
Ya-bu-l-wardee, &c."

---

[1] Vulg. for "ilfee."
[2] "Lem gáshĕ" is for "lem yegi."
[3] For "turáshee."
[4] The lock of hair which hangs over the temple, commonly called "maḳṣooṣ."
[5] For "yetamáyal."
[6] For "yedee."

The beloved came to me with a vacillating gait;
And her eyelids were the cause of my intoxication.
I extended my hand to take the cup;
And was intoxicated by her eyes.
O thou in the rose-coloured dress! &c.

No. 3.

Má marr wa - sa - ḳá - nee ḥa - bee - bee suk - kar. Nuṣf
el - la - yá - lee 'a-l - mu - dá - meh ne - s - kar.

"Má marr wa-saḳánee ḥabeebee sukkar.
Nuṣf el-läyálee 'a-l-mudámeh [1] neskar.
Nedren 'aleiya wa-n [2] atà maḥboobee
La-ạmal [3] 'amáyil [4] má 'amilhásh 'Antar."

My love passed not, but gave me sherbet of sugar to drink.
For half the nights we will intoxicate ourselves with wine.
I vow that, if my beloved come,
I will do deeds that 'Antar did not.

"Yá bintĕ melesik dáb wa-bent [5] eedeykee [6]
Wa-kháf [7] 'aleykee min säwád 'eyneykee.
Ḳaṣdee anà askar wa-boos [8] khaddeykee
Wa-ạmal [9] 'amáyil má 'amilhásh 'Antar."

O damsel! thy silk shirt is worn out, and thine arms have become visible,
And I fear for thee, on account of the blackness of thine eyes.
I desire to intoxicate myself, and kiss thy cheeks,
And do deeds that 'Antar did not.

"Fáïteh 'aleiya máliya-l-argeeleh:
Wa-meiyet [10] el-má-wardĕ fi-l-argeeleh.
Atà-bi-l-buneiyeh 'ámiláhà ḥeeleh.
Metà teḳul-lee ta'ál yá geḍa neskar."

She is passing by me, and filling the argeeleh; [11]
And there is rose-water in the argeeleh.
It seems to me the little lass is framing to herself some artifice.
When will she say to me, "O youth! come, and let us intoxicate ourselves?"

---

1 For "'ala-l-mudámeh."
2 For "wa-in."
3 For "la-aạmal."
4 For "'amáïl."
5 "Bent" is a vulgar contraction of "bánet."
6 Dual of "eed," vulg. for "yed;" meaning "arm" as well as "hand."
7 For "wa-akháf."
8 For "wa-aboos."
9 For wa-aạmal."
10 A vulgar diminutive of "má," water.
11 More commonly called "nárgeeleh:" the Persian pipe.

"Ṭool el-läyálee lem yenḳaṭa' [1] nooḥee [2]
'Alà ghazál mufrad wa-khad [3] rooḥee.
Nedren 'aleiya wa-n atà maḥboobee
La-ạmal 'amáyil má 'amilhásh 'Antar."

Every night long my moaning ceaseth not
For a solitary gazelle that hath taken away my soul.
I vow that, if my beloved come,
I will do deeds that 'Antar did not.

"Yá demạ 'eynee 'a-l-khudeyd [4] men ḥallak:
Ḳal-lee bi-zeedak [5] shóḳ 'alà bo'ádi [6] khillak.
Irḥam muteiyam yá gemeel mashghul-bak.
Taạmà 'oyoon ellee [7] má yeḥebbak ya-smar." [8]

O tear of my eye! who drew thee forth over the cheek?
It saith, "Thy desire increaseth on account of thy true-love's absence."
Have mercy upon one enslaved, O beautiful! and intent upon thee:
Blinded be the eyes of him who loves thee not, O dark-complexioned!

"Asmar wa-ḥáwi-l-wardeteyni-l-beeḍi.
Ḥobbee takhallaḳ fee läyáli-l-'eedi.
Nedren 'aleiya wa-n atánee seedee
La-ạmal 'amáyil má 'amilhásh 'Antar."

Dark-complexioned, and with two white roses! [9]
My love hath perfumed herself on the nights of the festival.
I vow that, if my mistress come to me,
I will do deeds that 'Antar did not.

No. 4.

'Á - shiḳ ra - à mub - te - lee - - ḳa - - l - lu - - -
- - - h en - ta rá - - - - - - - ye - ḥ feyn.

"'Áshiḳ ra-à mubtelee: ḳal-luh enta ráyeḥ [10] feyn.
Waḳaf ḳarà ḳiṣṣatuh: bekyum [11] säwa-l-itneyn.
Ráḥom le-ḳáḍi-l-häwa-l-itneyn säwà yeshkum.
Bekyu-t-teláteh wa-ḳáloo ḥobbenà ráḥ feyn.
El-leyl. El-leyl. Yá ḥelw el-ayádee: ḥáwi-l-khóḳh en-nádee.
Entum min eyn wa-ḥnà min eyn lemmà shebektoonĕ."

---

1 For "yenḳaṭè'."
2 For "nóḥee."
3 For "wa-akhad."
4 For "'ala-l-khudeyd."
5 For "bi-yezeedak."
6 For "be'ádi."
7 For "ellezee."
8 For "yá asmar."
9 The dark-complexioned girl has two *white* roses on her cheeks, instead of red.
10 For "rá-ëḥ."
11 For "bekow."

A lover saw another afflicted [in like manner]: he said to him, "Whither art thou going?"
He stopped and told his story: they both wept together.
They went to the ḳáḍee of love, both together to complain.
The three wept, and said, "Whither is our love gone?"
The night! The night! O thou with sweet hands! holding[1] the dewy peach!
Whence were ye, and whence were we, when ye ensnared us?

"'Áshiḳ yeḳul li-l-ḥamám hát lee genáḥak yóm.
Ḳál el-ḥamám amrak báṭil: ḳultu gheyr el-yóm:
Ḥattà aṭeer fi-l-gó wa-nẓur weg-h el-maḥboob:
Ákhud widád 'ám wa-rga' yá ḥamám fee yóm.
El-leyl. El-leyl, &c."

A lover says to the dove, "Lend me your wings for a day."
The dove replied, "Thy affair is vain:" I said, "Some other day:
That I may soar through the sky, and see the face of the beloved:
I shall obtain love enough for a year, and will return, O dove, in a day."
The night! The night! &c.

THE CALL TO PRAYER.

The call to prayer, repeated from the mád'nehs (or menarets) of the mosques, I have already mentioned.[2] I have often heard this call, in Cairo, chanted in the following manner; and in a style more or less similar, it is chanted by most of the muëddins of this city.

Al - lá - hu ak - bar. Al - lá - - hu ak - bar.
Al - lá - hu ak - bar. Al - lá - - - - - - -
- - - - - - - hu ak - bar. Ash - hadu an lá i -
lá - ha il-la - l - láh. Ash - hadu an lá i -

[1] Or, thou who hast.

[2] In the chapter on religion and laws.

THE CHANTING OF THE ḲUR-ÁN.

The following is inserted with the view of conveying some notion of the mode in which the Ḳur-án is commonly chanted in Egypt. The portion here selected is that which is most frequently repeated, namely, the "Fát'ḥah," or first chapter.

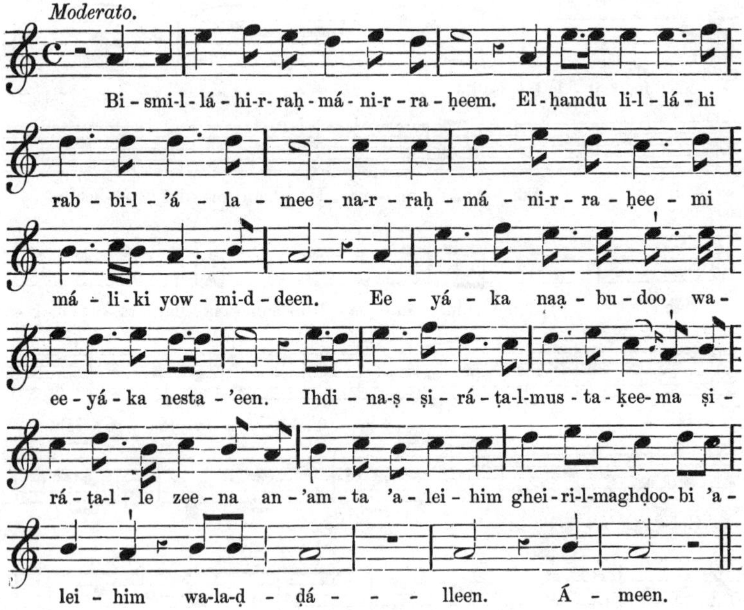
Moderato.
Bi - smi-l - lá - hi-r- raḥ - má - ni-r - ra - ḥeem. El - ḥamdu li-l - lá - hi
rab - bi-l - ’á - la - mee - na-r - raḥ - má - ni-r - ra - ḥee - mi
má - li - ki yow - mi-d - deen. Ee - yá - ka naạ - bu - doo wa -
ee - yá - ka nesta - ’een. Ihdi - na-ṣ - ṣi - rá - ṭa-l-mus - ta - ḳee- ma ṣi -
rá - ṭa-l - le zee - na an - ’am - ta ’a - lei - him ghei - ri-l-maghḍoo- bi ’a -
lei - him wa-la-ḍ - ḍá - - - lleen. Á - meen.

CHAPTER XIX.

PUBLIC DANCERS.

EGYPT has long been celebrated for its public dancing-girls; the most famous of whom are of a distinct tribe, called "Ghawázee."[1] A female of this tribe is called "Gházeeyeh;" and a man, "Gházee;" but the plural Ghawázee is generally understood as applying to the females. The misapplication of the appellation "'Ál'mehs" to the common dancing-girls of this country has already been noticed. The Ghawázee perform, unveiled, in the public streets, even to amuse the rabble. Their dancing has little of elegance; its chief peculiarity being a very rapid vibrating motion of the hips, from side to side. They commence with a degree of decorum; but soon, by more animated looks, by a more rapid collision of their castanets of brass, and by increased energy in every motion, they exhibit a spectacle exactly agreeing with the descriptions which Martial[2] and Juvenal[3] have given of the performances of the female dancers of Gades. The dress in which they generally thus exhibit in public is similar to that

---

[1] Since this was written, public female dancing and prostitution have been prohibited by the government, in the beginning of June, in the year 1834. Women detected infringing this new law are to be punished with fifty stripes for the first offence, and for repeated offences are to be also condemned to hard labour for one or more years: men are obnoxious to the discipline of the bastinado when parties in such offences. But there is a simple plan for evading punishment in cases of this kind, which, it is said, will be adopted by many persons. A man may marry a venal female, legally, and divorce her the next day. He has only to say two or three words, and pay a small sum of money, which he calls her dowry. He says, "Will you marry me?" She answers, "Yes." "For how much?" he asks. She names the sum; and he gives it: she is then his lawful wife. The next day, he tells her that she is divorced from him. He need be under little apprehension of her demanding the expenses of her maintenance during the period of her 'eddeh, before the expiration of which she cannot legally marry another man; for the marriage which has just been contracted and dissolved is only designed as a means of avoiding punishment in case of her being detected with the man; and otherwise is kept secret; and the sum which she can demand for her maintenance during the abovementioned period is very paltry in comparison with that which she may obtain by taking a new husband every two or three days.

[2] Lib. v. Epigr. 79.

[3] Sat. xi. v. 162.

Dancing-Girls (Ghawázee, or Gházeeyehs).

which is worn by women of the middle classes in Egypt in private; that is, in the ḥareem; consisting of a yelek, or an 'anteree, and the shintiyán, &c., of handsome materials. They also wear various ornaments: their eyes are bordered with the koḥl (or black collyrium); and the tips of their fingers, the palms of their hands, and their toes and other parts of their feet, are usually stained with the red dye of the ḥennà, according to the general custom of the middle and higher classes of Egyptian women. In general, they are accompanied by musicians (mostly of the same tribe), whose instruments are the kemengeh or the rabáb with the ṭár; or the darabukkeh with the zummárah or the zemr: the ṭár is usually in the hands of an old woman.

The Ghawázee often perform in the court of a house, or in the street, before the door, on certain occasions of festivity in the ḥareem; as, for instance, on the occasion of a marriage, or the birth of a child. They are never admitted into a respectable ḥareem, but are not unfrequently hired to entertain a party of men in the house of some rake. In this case, as might be expected, their performances are yet more lascivious than those which I have already mentioned. Some of them, when they exhibit before a private party of men, wear nothing but the shintiyán (or trousers) and a tób (or very full, long, wide-sleeved shirt or gown) of semi-transparent, coloured gauze, open nearly half-way down the front. To extinguish the least spark of modesty which they may yet sometimes affect to retain, they are plentifully supplied with brandy or some other intoxicating liquor. The scenes which ensue cannot be described.

I need scarcely add that these women are the most abandoned of the courtesans of Egypt. Many of them are extremely handsome; and most of them are richly dressed. Upon the whole, I think they are the finest women in Egypt. Many of them have slightly aquiline noses; but in most respects they resemble the rest of the females of this country. Women, as well as men, take delight in witnessing their performances; but many persons among the higher classes, and the more religious, disapprove of them.

The Ghawázee being distinguished, in general, by a cast of countenance differing, though slightly, from the rest of the Egyptians, we can hardly doubt that they are, as themselves assert, a distinct race. Their origin, however, is involved in much uncertainty. They call themselves "Barámikeh,"[1] or "Barmekees;" and boast that they are descended from the famous family of that name who were the objects of the favour, and afterwards of the capricious tyranny, of Hároon Er-Rasheed, and of whom we read in several of the tales of "The Thousand and One Nights:" but, as a friend of mine lately observed to me, they probably have no more right to call themselves "Barámikeh" than because they resemble that family in liberality, though it is liberality of a different kind. In many of the tombs of the ancient Egyptians we find representations of females dancing at private entertainments, to the sounds of various instruments, in a manner similar to the modern Ghawázee, but even more licentious; one or more of these performers being generally depicted in a state of perfect nudity, though in the presence of men and women of high stations. This mode of dancing we find, from the monuments here alluded to, most of which bear the names of kings, which prove their age, to have been common in Egypt in very remote times; even before the Exodus of the Israelites. It is probable, therefore, that it

[1] Commonly pronounced "Barám'keh."

has continued without interruption; and perhaps the modern Ghawázee are descended from the class of female dancers who amused the Egyptians in the times of the early Pharaohs. From the similarity of the Spanish fandango to the dances of the Ghawázee, we might infer that it was introduced into Spain by the Arab conquerors of that country, were we not informed that the Gaditanæ, or females of Gades (now called Cadiz), were famous for such performances in the times of the early Roman Emperors. However, though it hence appears that the licentious mode of dancing here described has so long been practised in Spain, it is not improbable that it was originally introduced into Gades from the East, perhaps by the Phœnicians.[1]

The Ghawázee mostly keep themselves distinct from other classes, abstaining from marriages with any but persons of their own tribe; but sometimes a Gházeeyeh makes a vow of repentance, and marries a respectable Arab; who is not generally considered as disgraced by such a connection. All of them are brought up for the venal profession; but not all as dancers; and most of them marry; though they never do this until they have commenced their career of venality. The husband is subject to the wife: he performs for her the offices of a servant and procurer; and generally, if she be a dancer, he is also her musician: but a few of the men earn their subsistence as blacksmiths or tinkers. Most of the Gházeeyehs welcome the lowest peasant, if he can pay even a very trifling sum. Though some of them are possessed of considerable wealth, costly ornaments, &c., many of their customs are similar to those of the people whom we call "gipsies," and who are supposed, by some, to be of Egyptian origin. It is remarkable that some of the gipsies in Egypt pretend to be descended from a branch of the same family to whom the Ghawázee refer their origin; but their claim is still less to be regarded than that of the latter, because they do not unanimously agree on this point. I shall have occasion to speak of them more particularly in the next chapter. The ordinary language of the Ghawázee is the same as that of the rest of the Egyptians; but they sometimes make use of a number of words peculiar to themselves, in order to render their speech unintelligible to strangers. They are, professedly, of the Muslim faith; and often some of them accompany the Egyptian

---

1 From the effect which it produced, it is probable that the dance performed by the daughter of Herodias was of the kind here described. See St. Matthew, xiv. 6, 7, or St. Mark vi. 22, 23.

caravan of pilgrims to Mekkeh. There are many of them in almost every large town in Egypt, inhabiting a distinct portion of the quarter allotted to public women in general. Their ordinary habitations are low huts, or temporary sheds, or tents; for they often move from one town to another: but some of them settle themselves in large houses; and many possess black female slaves (by whose prostitution they increase their property), and camels, asses, cows, &c., in which they trade. They attend the camps, and all the great religious and other festivals, of which they are, to many persons, the chief attractions. Numerous tents of Gházeeyehs are seen on these occasions. Some of these women add to their other allurements the art of singing, and equal the ordinary 'Awálim. Those of the lower class dress in the same manner as other low prostitutes. Some of them wear a gauze tób, over another shirt, with the shintiyán, and a crape or muslin ṭarḥah; and in general they deck themselves with a profusion of ornaments, as necklaces, bracelets, anklets, a row of gold coins over the forehead, and sometimes a nose-ring. All of them adorn themselves with the koḥl and ḥennà. There are some other dancing-girls and courtesans who call themselves Ghawázee, but who do not really belong to that tribe.[1]

Many of the people of Cairo, affecting, or persuading themselves, to consider that there is nothing improper in the dancing of the Ghawázee but the fact of its being performed by females, who ought not thus to expose themselves, employ men to dance in the same manner; but the number of these male performers, who are mostly young men, and who are called "Khäwals,"[2] is very small. They are Muslims, and natives of Egypt. As they personate women, their dances are exactly of the same description as those of the Ghawázee; and are, in like manner, accompanied by the sounds of castanets: but, as if to prevent

---

1 The courtesans of other classes have at most times abounded in every town of Egypt; but in and about the metropolis, these and the others before mentioned have generally been particularly numerous; some quarters being inhabited almost exclusively by them. These women, when their profession was allowed by the government, frequently conducted themselves with the most audacious effrontery. Their dress was such as I have described as being worn by the Ghawázee, or differed from that of respectable women in being a little more gay, and less disguising. Some women of the venal class in Cairo not only wore the burḳo' (or face-veil), but dressed, in every respect, like modest women; from whom they could not be distinguished, except by those to whom they chose to discover themselves. Such women were found in almost every quarter of the metropolis. Many of them were divorced women, or widows; and many were the wives of men whom business obliged to be often abroad. All the known prostitutes in Egypt paid a kind of income-tax ("firdeh"). The tax paid by those of the metropolis lately amounted to eight hundred purses (equivalent to four thousand pounds sterling), which is not less than one-tenth of the firdeh of all the inhabitants. This will convey some idea of their number in comparison with that of the persons who practised honest means of obtaining their livelihood.

2 The term "Gháïsh" (plural, "Gheeyásh,") is also applied to a person of this class.

their being thought to be really females, their dress is suited to their unnatural profession; being partly male, and partly female: it chiefly consists of a tight vest, a girdle, and a kind of petticoat. Their general appearance, however, is more feminine than masculine: they suffer the hair of the head to grow long, and generally braid it, in the manner of the women; the hair on the face, when it begins to grow, they pluck out; and they imitate the women also in applying koḥl and ḥennà to their eyes and hands. In the streets, when not engaged in dancing, they often even veil their faces; not from shame, but merely to affect the manners of women. They are often employed, in preference to the Ghawázee, to dance before a house, or in its court, on the occasion of a marriage-fête, or the birth of a child, or a circumcision; and frequently perform at public festivals.

There is, in Cairo, another class of male dancers, young men and boys, whose performances, dress, and general appearance are almost exactly similar to those of the Khäwals; but who are distinguished by a different appellation, which is "Gink;" a term that is Turkish, and has a vulgar signification which aptly expresses their character. They are generally Jews, Armenians, Greeks, and Turks.

CHAPTER XX.

SERPENT-CHARMERS, AND PERFORMERS OF LEGERDEMAIN TRICKS, &c.

MANY modern writers upon Egypt have given surprising accounts of a class of men in this country, supposed, like the ancient "Psylli" of Cyrenaïca, to possess a secret art, to which allusion is made in the Bible,[1] enabling them to secure themselves from the poison of serpents. I have met with many persons among the more intelligent of the Egyptians who condemn these modern Psylli as impostors, but none who has been able to offer a satisfactory explanation of the most common and most interesting of their performances, which I am about to describe.

Many Rifá'ee and Saạdee darweeshes obtain their livelihood, as I have mentioned on a former occasion, by going about to charm away serpents from houses. A few other persons also profess the same art, but are not so famous. The former travel over every part of Egypt, and find abundant employment; but their gains are barely sufficient to procure them a scanty subsistence. The charmer professes to discover, without ocular perception (but perhaps he does so by a peculiar smell), whether there be any serpents in a house; and if there be, to attract them to him; as the fowler, by the fascination of his voice, allures the bird into his net. As the serpent seeks the darkest place in which to hide himself, the charmer has, in most cases, to exercise his skill in an obscure chamber, where he might easily take a serpent from his bosom, bring it to the people without the door, and affirm that he had found it in the apartment; for no one would venture to enter with him after having been assured of the presence of one of these reptiles within: but he is often required to perform in the full light of day, surrounded by spectators; and incredulous persons have

[1] See Psalm lviii. 4, 5; Eccles. x. 11; and Jerem. viii. 17.

searched him beforehand, and even stripped him naked; yet his success has been complete. He assumes an air of mystery, strikes the walls with a short palm-stick, whistles, makes a clucking noise with his tongue, and spits upon the ground; and generally says, "I adjure you by God, if ye be above, or if ye be below, that ye come forth: I adjure you by the Most Great Name, if ye be obedient, come forth; and if ye be disobedient, die! die! die!"—The serpent is generally dislodged by his stick, from a fissure in the wall, or drops from the ceiling of the room. I have often heard it asserted that the serpent-charmer, before he enters a house in which he is to try his skill, always employs a servant of that house to introduce one or more serpents; but I have known instances in which this could not be the case; and am inclined to believe that the darweeshes above mentioned are generally acquainted with some real physical means of discovering the presence of serpents without seeing them, and of attracting them from their lurking-places. It is, however, a fact well ascertained, that the most expert of them do not venture to carry serpents of a venomous nature about their persons until they have extracted the poisonous teeth. Many of them carry scorpions, also, within the cap, and next the shaven head; but doubtless first deprive them of the power to injure; perhaps by merely blunting the sting. Their famous feats of eating live and venomous serpents, which are regarded as religious acts, I have before had occasion to mention, and purpose to describe particularly in another chapter.[1]

Performers of sleight-of-hand tricks, who are called "Ḥöwáh" (in the singular, "Ḥáwee"[2]), are numerous in Cairo. They generally perform in public places; collecting a ring of spectators around them, from some of whom they receive small voluntary contributions during and after their performances. They are most frequently seen on the occasions of public festivals; but often also at other times. By indecent jests and actions they attract as much applause as they do by other means. The "Ḥáwee" performs a great variety of tricks; the most usual of which I shall here mention. He generally has two boys to assist him. From a large leathern bag he takes out four or five snakes, of a largish size. One of these he places on the ground, and causes to erect its head and part of its body: another he puts round the head of one of the boys, like a turban; and two more he

---

[1] In the account of the Moolid en-Nebee, in the first of the chapters on periodical public festivals, &c.
[2] So called from his feats with serpents.

winds over the boy's neck. He takes these off, opens the boy's mouth, and apparently passes the bolt of a kind of padlock through his cheek, and locks it. Then, in appearance, he forces an iron spike into the boy's throat; the spike being really pushed up into a wooden handle. He also performs another trick of the same kind as this: placing the boy on the ground, he puts the edge of a knife upon his nose, and knocks the blade until half its width seems to have entered. Several indecent tricks which he performs with the boy I must abstain from describing: some of them are abominably disgusting. The tricks which he alone performs are more amusing. He draws a great quantity of various-coloured silk from his mouth, and winds it on his arm; puts cotton in his mouth, and blows out fire; takes out of his mouth a great number of round pieces of tin, like dollars; and, in appearance, blows an earthen pipe-bowl from his nose. In most of his tricks he occasionally blows through a large shell (called the Ḥáwee's zummárah), producing sounds like those of a horn. Most of his sleight-of-hand performances are nearly similar to those of exhibiters of the same class in our own and other countries. Taking a silver finger-ring from one of the by-standers, he puts it in a little box, blows his shell, and says, "'Efreet, change it!"—he then opens the box, and shews, in it, a different ring: shuts the box again; opens it, and shews the first ring: shuts it a third time; opens it, and shews a melted lump of silver, which he declares to be the ring melted, and offers to the owner: the latter insists upon having his ring in its original state: the Ḥáwee then asks for five or ten faḍḍahs to recast it; and, having obtained this, opens the box again (after having closed it, and blown his shell), and takes out of it the perfect ring. He next takes a larger covered box, puts the skull-cap of one of his boys in it, blows his shell, opens the box, and out comes a rabbit: the cap seems to be gone. He puts the rabbit in again, covers the box, uncovers it, and out run two little chickens: these he puts in again, blows his shell, uncovers the box, and shews it full of faṭeerehs (or pancakes) and kunáfeh (which resembles vermicelli): he tells his boys to eat its contents; but they refuse to do it without honey: he then takes a small jug, turns it upside-down to shew that it is empty, blows his shell, and hands round the jug full of honey. The boys, having eaten, ask for water, to wash their hands. The Ḥáwee takes the same jug, and hands it filled with water, in the same manner. He takes the box again, and asks for the cap; blows his shell, uncovers the box, and pours out from it, into the boy's lap (the lower part of his shirt held up), four or five small snakes. The boy, in apparent fright, throws them down, and demands his cap. The Ḥáwee puts the snakes back into the box, blows his shell, uncovers the box, and takes out the cap.—Another of his common tricks is to put a number of slips of white paper into a tinned copper vessel (the ṭisht of a seller of sherbet); and to take them out dyed of various colours. He pours water into the same vessel, puts in a piece of linen, and then gives to the spectators, to drink, the contents of the vessel, changed to sherbet of sugar. Sometimes he apparently cuts in two a muslin shawl, or burns it in the middle, and then restores it whole. Often, he strips himself of all his clothes, except his drawers, and tells two persons to bind him, hands and feet, and put him in a sack. This done, he asks for a piaster; and some one tells him that he shall have it if he will put out his hand and take it. He puts out his hand free, draws it back, and is then taken out of the sack bound as at first. He is put in again, and comes out unbound, handing to the spectators a small tray, upon which are four or five little plates filled with various eatables, and, if the performance be at night, several small lighted candles placed round. The spectators eat the food.

There is another class of jugglers in Cairo called "Ḳeeyem" (in the singular, "Ḳeiyim"). In most of his performances, the Ḳeiyim has an assistant. In one, for instance, the latter places upon the ground twenty-nine small pieces of stone. He sits upon the ground, and these are arranged before him. The Ḳeiyim having gone a few yards distant from him, the assistant desires one of the spectators to place a piece of money under any one of the bits of stone: this being done, he calls back the Ḳeiyim, informs him that a piece of money has been hidden, and asks him to point out where it is; which the conjuror immediately does. The secret of this trick is very simple: the twenty-nine pieces of stone represent the letters of the Arabic alphabet; and the person who desires the Ḳeiyim to shew where the money is concealed commences his address to the latter with the letter represented by the stone which covers the coin. In the same manner, or by means of signs made by the assistant, the Ḳeiyim is enabled to tell the name of any person present, or the words of a song that has been repeated in his absence: the name or song having been whispered to his assistant.

Fortune-telling is often practised in Egypt, mostly by a tribe of Gipsies. There are several small tribes of Gipsies in this country, and they are here often called collectively "Ghagar" or "Ghajar" (in the singular, "Ghagaree" or "Ghajaree"), which is the appellation of one of their tribes, who profess themselves to be partly descendants of the Barámikeh, like the Ghawázee; but of a different branch. Many of their women are fortune-tellers. These women are often seen in the streets of Cairo, dressed in a similar manner to the generality of the females of the lower classes, with the tób and ṭarḥah, but always with unveiled faces; usually carrying a gazelle's skin, containing the materials for their divinations; and crying, "I perform divination! What is present I manifest! What is absent I manifest!" &c. They mostly divine by means of a number of shells, with a few pieces of coloured glass, money, &c., intermixed with them. These they throw down; and from the manner in which they chance to lie, they derive their prognostications: a larger shell than the rest represents the person whose fortune they are to discover; and the other shells, &c., represent different events, evils and blessings, which, by their proximity to, or distance from, the former, they judge to be fated to befall the person in question early or late or never. Some of these Gipsy-women also cry, "Neduḳḳ wa-n'ṭáhir!" ("We puncture and circumcise!").[1] Many of the Gipsies in Egypt are blacksmiths, braziers, and tinkers, or itinerant sellers of the wares which are made by others of this class, and particularly of trumpery trinkets of brass, &c.

Some Gipsies also follow the occupation of a "Bahluwán." This appellation is properly given to a performer of gymnastic exercises, a famous swordsman, or a champion; and such descriptions of persons formerly exhibited their feats of strength and dexterity, under this name, in Cairo; but the performances of the modern Bahluwán are almost confined to rope-dancing; and all the persons who practise this art are of the tribe called "Ghagar" or "Ghajar." Sometimes the rope is tied to the mád'neh of a mosque, at a considerable height from the ground, and extends to the length of several hundred feet, being supported at many points by poles fixed in the ground. The dancer always uses a long balancing-pole. Sometimes he dances or walks on the rope with clogs on his feet, or with a piece of soap tied

[1] They tattoo, or make those blue marks upon the skin which I have described in the first chapter of this work; and perform the operation alluded to in a note inserted in page 59. The late Captain Newbold, in a curious account of the Gipsies of Egypt and other Eastern countries, in the Journal of the Royal Asiatic Society, vol. xiv. 285—312, says that the fortune-tellers of Egypt according to their own statements, are not, as I was informed, of the tribe of the Ghagar, but of a superior tribe whose name he writes "Helebi," and from whom the Ghagar are a distinct tribe, though the former sometimes marry Ghagar women.

under each foot, or with a child suspended to each of his ankles by a rope, or with a boy tied to each end of the balancing-pole; and he sits upon a round tray placed on the rope. I have only seen three of these bahluwáns; and their performances were not of the more difficult kinds above described, and less clever than those of the commonest rope-dancers in England. Women, girls, and boys, often follow this occupation. The men and boys also perform other feats than those of rope-dancing; such as tumbling, leaping through a hoop, &c.

The "Ḳureydátee" (whose appellation is derived from "ḳird," an ape, or a monkey,) amuses the lower orders in Cairo by sundry performances of an ape or a monkey, an ass, a dog, and a kid. He and the ape (which is generally of the cynocephalus kind) fight each other with sticks. He dresses the ape fantastically, usually as a bride, or a veiled woman; puts it on the ass; and parades it round within the ring of spectators; himself going before and beating a tambourine. The ape is also made to dance, and perform various antics. The ass is told to choose the handsomest girl in the ring, and does so; putting his nose towards her face, and greatly amusing her and all the spectators. The dog is ordered to imitate the motions of a thief, and accordingly crawls along on its belly. The best performance is that of the kid: it is made to stand upon a little piece of wood, nearly in the shape of a dice-box, about a span long, and an inch and a half wide at the top and bottom, so that all its four feet are placed close together: this piece of wood, with the kid thus standing upon it, is then lifted up, and a similar piece placed under it; and, in the same manner, a third piece, a fourth, and a fifth, are added.

The Egyptians are often amused by players of low and ridiculous farces, who are called "Moḥabbaẓeen." These frequently perform at the festivals prior to weddings and circumcisions, at the houses of the great; and sometimes attract rings of auditors and spectators in the public places in Cairo. Their performances are scarcely worthy of description: it is chiefly by vulgar jests, and indecent actions, that they amuse, and obtain applause. The actors are only men and boys; the part of a woman being always performed by a man or a boy in female attire. As a specimen of their plays, I shall give a short account of one which was acted before the Báshà, a short time ago, at a festival celebrated in honour of the circumcision of one of his sons; on which occasion, as usual, several sons of grandees were also circumcised. The *dramatis personæ* were a Náẓir (or governor of a district), a Sheykh Beled (or chief of a village), a servant of the latter, a Copt clerk, a Felláḥ indebted to the government, his wife, and five other persons, of whom two made their appearance first in the character of drummers, one as a hautboy-player, and the two others as dancers. After a little drumming and piping and dancing by these five, the Náẓir and the rest of the performers enter the ring. The Náẓir asks, "How much does 'Awaḍ[1] the son of Regeb owe?" The musicians and dancers, who now act as simple felláḥeen, answer, "Desire the Christian to look in the register." The Christian clerk has a large dawáyeh (or ink-horn) in his girdle, and is dressed as a Copt, with a black turban. The Sheykh el-Beled asks him, "How much is written against 'Awaḍ the son of Regeb?" The clerk answers, "A thousand piasters." "How much," says the Sheykh, "has he paid?" He is answered, "Five piasters." "Man," says he, addressing the felláḥ, "why don't you bring the money?" The felláḥ answers, "I have not any." "You have not any?" exclaims the Sheykh: "Throw him down." An inflated piece of an intestine, resembling a large kurbág, is brought; and with this the felláḥ is beaten. He roars out to the Náẓir, "By the honour of thy horse's tail, O Bey! By the honour of thy wife's trowsers, O Bey! By the honour of thy wife's head-band, O Bey!" After twenty such absurd appeals, his beating is finished, and he is taken away, and imprisoned. Presently his wife comes to him, and asks him, "How art thou?" He answers, "Do me a kindness, my wife: take a little kishk[2] and some eggs and some sha'eereeyeh,[3] and go with them to the house of the Christian clerk, and appeal to his generosity to get me set at liberty." She takes these, in three baskets, to the Christian's house, and asks the people there, "Where is the M'allim Ḥannà, the clerk?" They answer, "There he sits." She says to him, "O M'allim Ḥannà, do me the favour to receive these, and obtain the liberation of my husband." "Who is thy husband?" he asks. She answers, "The felláḥ who owes a thousand piasters." "Bring," says he, "twenty or thirty piasters to bribe the Sheykh el-Beled." She goes away, and soon returns, with the money in her hand, and gives it to the Sheykh el-Beled. "What is this?" says the Sheykh. She answers, "Take it as a bribe, and liberate my husband." He says, "Very well: go to the Náẓir." She retires for a while, blackens the edges of her eye-

---

1 Thus vulgarly pronounced, for "'Ewaḍ."
2 A description of this will be found in a subsequent chapter. See the Index.
3 A kind of paste, resembling vermicelli.

lids with koḥl, applies fresh red dye of the ḥennà to her hands and feet, and repairs to the Náẓir. "Good evening, my master," she says to him. "What dost thou want?" he asks. She answers, "I am the wife of 'Awaḍ, who owes a thousand piasters." "But what dost thou want?" he asks again. She says, "My husband is imprisoned; and I appeal to thy generosity to liberate him:" and as she urges this request, she smiles, and shews him that she does not ask this favour without being willing to grant him a recompense. He obtains this, takes the husband's part, and liberates him.—This farce was played before the Báshà with the view of opening his eyes to the conduct of those persons to whom was committed the office of collecting the taxes.

The puppet-show of "Ḳarà Gyooz" has been introduced into Egypt by Turks, in whose language the puppets are made to speak.[1] Their performances, which are, in general, extremely indecent, occasionally amuse the Turks residing in Cairo; but, of course, are not very attractive to those who do not understand the Turkish language. They are conducted in the manner of the "Chinese shadows," and therefore only exhibited at night.

[1] This exhibition is called in Arabic "khayál eḍ-ḍill," or, more correctly, "—eḍh-ḍhill."

CHAPTER XXI.

PUBLIC RECITATIONS OF ROMANCES.

The Egyptians are not destitute of better diversions than those described in the preceding chapter: reciters of romances frequent the principal ḳahwehs (or coffee-shops) of Cairo and other towns, particularly on the evenings of religious festivals, and afford attractive and rational entertainments. The reciter generally seats himself upon a small stool on the maṣṭabah, or raised seat, which is built against the front of the coffee-shop:[1] some of his auditors occupy the rest of that seat, others arrange themselves upon the maṣṭabahs of the houses on the opposite side of the narrow street, and the rest sit upon stools or benches made of palm-sticks; most of them with the pipe in hand; some sipping their coffee; and all highly amused, not only with the story, but also with the lively and dramatic manner of the narrator. The reciter receives a trifling sum of money from the keeper of the coffee-shop, for attracting customers: his hearers are not obliged to contribute anything for his remuneration: many of them give nothing; and few give more than five or ten faḍḍahs.[2]

The most numerous class of reciters is that of the persons called "Ṣho'arà" (in the singular "Shá'er," which properly signifies a *poet*). They are also called "Aboo-Zeydeeyeh," or "Aboo-Zeydees," from the subject of their recitations, which is a romance entitled "the Life of Aboo-Zeyd" ("Seeret Aboo-Zeyd"[3]). The number of these Sho'arà in Cairo is about fifty; and they recite nothing but the adventures related in the romance of Aboo-Zeyd.

This romance is said to have been founded upon events which happened in the middle of the third century of the Flight; and is

---

1 See the engraving which accompanies this chapter.

2 The reciter is generally heard to greater advantage in public than when he is hired to entertain a private party; as, in the former case his profits are usually proportioned to the talent which he displays.

3 Vulgarly so called, for "Seeret Abee-Zeyd."

believed to have been written not long after that period; but it was certainly composed at a much later time, unless it have been greatly altered in transcription. It is usually found in ten or more small quarto volumes. It is half prose, and half poetry; half narrative, and half dramatic. As a literary composition, it has little merit, at least in its present state; but as illustrative of the manners and customs of the Bedawees, it is not without value and interest. The heroes and heroines of the romance, who are mostly natives of central Arabia and El-Yemen, but some of them of El-Gharb (or Northern Africa, which is called "the West" with reference to Arabia), generally pour forth their most animated sentiments, their addresses and soliloquies, in verse. The verse is not measured; though it is the opinion of some of the learned in Cairo that it was originally conformed to the prescribed measures of poetry, and that it has been altered by copyists: still, when read, as it always is, almost entirely in the popular (not the literary) manner, it is pleasing in sound, as it also often is in matter. Almost every piece of poetry begins and ends with an invocation of blessings on the Prophet.

The Shá'er always commits his subject to memory, and recites without book. The poetry he chants; and after every verse, he plays a few notes on a viol which has but a single chord, and which is called "the poet's viol," or "the Aboo-Zeydee viol," from its only being used in these recitations. It has been described in a former chapter. The reciter generally has an attendant with another instrument of this kind, to accompany him. Sometimes a single note serves as a prelude and interlude. To convey some idea of the style of a Shá'er's music, I insert a few notes of the commencement of a chant:—

Ma - ḳá - lá - tu Khaḍrà 'anda má ḳad te -
fek - ke - ret li - má ḳad garà má beyn neg - ạ Hi-lál.[1]

[1] These words commence a piece of poetry of which a translation will be found in this chapter.

A Shá'er, with his accompanying Violist, and part of his Audience.

Some of the reciters of Aboo-Zeyd are distinguished by the appellations of "Hilấleeyeh" (or "Hilálees"), "Zaghábeh," or "Zughbeeyeh" (or "Zughbees"), and "Zináteeyeh" (or "Zinátees"), from their chiefly confining themselves to the narration of the exploits of heroes of the Hilálee, Zughbee, or Zinátee, tribes, celebrated in this romance.

As a specimen of the tale of Aboo-Zeyd, I shall here offer an abstract of the principal contents of the first volume, which I have carefully read for this purpose.

Aboo-Zeyd, or, as he was first more generally called, Barakát, was an Arab of the tribe called Benee-Hilál, or El-Hilấleeyeh. Before his birth, his father, the Emeer Rizḳ (who was the son of Náïl, a paternal uncle of Sarḥán, the king of the Benee-Hilál), had married ten wives, from whom, to his great grief, he had obtained but two children, both of them daughters, named Sheeḥah and 'Ateemeh, until one of his wives, the Emeereh Gellás, increased his distress by bearing him a son without arms or legs. Shortly before the birth of this son, the Emeer Rizḳ (having divorced, at different times, such of his wives as pleased him least, as he could not have more than four at one time, and having at last retained only three,) married an eleventh wife, the Emeereh Khaḍrà, daughter of Ḳarḍà, the Shereef of Mekkeh. He was soon rejoiced to find that Khaḍrà shewed signs of becoming a mother; and, in the hope that the expected child would be a son, invited the Emeer Ghánim, chief of the tribe of Ez-Zaghábeh, or Ez-Zughbeeyeh, with a large company of his family and tribe, to come from their district and honour with their presence the festival which he hoped to have occasion to celebrate. These friends complied with his invitation, became his guests, and waited for the birth of the child.

Meanwhile, it happened that the Emeereh Khaḍrà, walking with the Emeereh Shemmeh, a wife of King Sarḥán, and a number of other females, saw a black bird attack and kill a numerous flock of birds of various kinds and hues, and, astonished at the sight, earnestly prayed God to give her a son like this bird, even though he should be black. Her prayer was answered: she gave birth to a black boy. The Emeer Rizḳ, though he could not believe this to be his own son, was reluctant to put away the mother, from the excessive love he bore her. He had only heard the women's description of the child: he would not see it himself, nor allow any other man to see it, until the seventh day after its birth. For six days his guests were feasted;

and on the seventh, or "yóm es-subooạ," a more sumptuous banquet was prepared; after which, according to custom, the child was brought before the guests. A female slave carried it upon a silver tray, and covered over with a handkerchief. When the guests, as is usual in such cases, had given their nuḳooṭ (or contributions) of gold and silver coins, one of them lifted up the handkerchief, and saw that the child was as the women had represented it. The Emeer Rizḳ, who had stood outside the tent while this ceremony was performed, in great distress of mind, was now sharply upbraided by most of his friends for wishing to hide his supposed disgrace, and to retain an unchaste woman as his wife: he was very reluctantly compelled to put her away, that his tribe might not be held in dishonour on her account; and accordingly despatched her, with her child, under the conduct of a sheykh named Muneeạ, to return to her father's house at Mekkeh. She departed thither, accompanied also by a number of slaves, her husband's property, who determined to remain with her; being allowed to do so by the Emeer Rizḳ.

On the journey, the party pitched their tents in a valley; and here the Emeereh Khaḍrà begged her conductor to allow her to remain; for she feared to go back, in such circumstances, to her father's house. But the Emeer Faḍl Ibn-Beysem, chief of the tribe of Ez-Zaḥlán, with a company of horsemen, chanced to fall in with her party during her conversation with the sheykh Muneeạ, and, having heard her story, determined to take her under his protection: returning to his encampment, he sent his wife, the Emeereh Laạg El-Baheeyeh, to conduct her and the child thither, together with the slaves. The Emeer Faḍl adopted her child as his own; brought him up with his own two sons; and treated him with the fondness of a father. The young Barakát soon gave promise of his becoming a hero: he killed his schoolmaster, by severe beating, for attempting to chastise one of his adoptive brothers; and became the terror of all his schoolfellows. His adoptive father procured another fiḳee for a schoolmaster; but Barakát's presence frightened his schoolfellows from attending, and the fiḳee therefore instructed him at home. At the age of eleven years, he had acquired proficiency in all the sciences, human and divine, then studied in Arabia; including astrology, magic, alchymy, and a variety of other branches of knowledge.

Barakát now went, by the advice of the fiḳee, to ask a present of a horse from his adoptive father; who answered his "Good morning" by saying, "Good morning, my son, and dearer than my son." Surprised at this expression, the youth went to his mother, and asked her if the Emeer Faḍl were not really his father. She told him that this chief was his uncle; and that his father was dead: that he had been killed by a Hilálee Arab, called Rizḳ the son of Náïl. Becoming warmed and inspired by the remembrance of her wrongs, she then more fully related her case to her son in a series of verses. Of this piece of poetry I shall venture to insert a translation, made verse for verse, and with the same neglect of measure that is found in the original, which I also imitate in carrying on the same rhyme throughout the whole piece, in accordance with the common practice of Arab poets:—

"Thus did Khaḍrà, reflecting on what had past
'Mid the tents of Hilál, her tale relate.

'O Emeer Barakát, hear what I tell thee,
And think not my story is idle prate.
Thy father was Beysem, Beysem's son,
Thine uncle Faḍl's brother: youth of valour innate![1]
And thy father was wealthy above his fellows;
None other could boast such a rich estate.
As a pilgrim to Mekkeh he journey'd, and there,
In my father's house, a guest he sate:
He sought me in marriage, attain'd his wish,
And made me his lov'd and wedded mate:
For thy father had never been bless'd with a son;
And had often bewail'd his unhappy fate.
One day to a spring, with some friends I went,
When the chiefs had met at a banquet of state,
And, amusing ourselves with the sight of the water,
We saw numberless birds there congregate:
Some were white, and round as the moon at the full;
Some, with plumage of red; some small; some great;
Some were black, my son; and some were tall:
They compris'd all kinds that God doth create.
Though our party of women came unawares,
The birds did not fear us, nor separate;
But soon, from the vault of the sky descending,
A black-plum'd bird, of enormous weight,
Pounc'd on the others, and killed them all.
To God I cried—O Compassionate!
Thou Living! Eternal! I pray, for the sake
Of the Excellent Prophet, thy delegate,
Grant me a son like this noble bird,
E'en should he be black, Thou Considerate!—

1 Literally, "Thou who hast a valiant maternal uncle!" I add this note merely for the sake of mentioning that the Arabs generally consider innate virtues as inherited through the mother rather than the father, and believe that a man commonly resembles, in his good and evil qualities, his maternal uncle.

Thou wast form'd in my womb, and wast born, my son;
And all thy relations, with joy elate,
And thy father among them, paid honour to me:
But soon did our happiness terminate:
The chiefs of Hilál attack'd our tribe;
And Rizḳ, among them, precipitate,
Fell on thy father, my son, and slew him;
Then seiz'd on his wealth, his whole estate.
Thine uncle receiv'd me, his relative,
And thee as his son to educate.
God assist thee to take our blood-revenge,
And the tents of Hilál to desolate.
But keep closely secret what I have told thee:
Be mindful to no one this tale to relate:
Thine uncle might grieve; so 'tis fit that, with patience,
In hope of attaining thy wish, thou shouldst wait.'

Thus did Khaḍrà address her son Barakát;
Thus her case with artful deception state.
Now beg we forgiveness of all our sins,
Of God the Exalted, the Sole, the Great;
And join me, my hearers, in blessing the Prophet,[1]
The guide, whose praise we should celebrate."

Barakát, excited by this tale, became engrossed with the desire of slaying his own father, whom he was made to believe to be his father's murderer.

His adoptive father gave him his best horse, and instructed him in all the arts of war, in the chase, and in every manly exercise. He early distinguished himself as a horseman, and excited the envy of many of the Arabs of the tribe into which he had been admitted, by his dexterity in the exercise of the "birgás" (a game exactly or nearly similar to what is now called that of the "gereed"), in which the persons engaged, mounted on horses, combated or pursued each other, throwing a palm-stick.[2] He twice defeated plundering parties of the tribe of Teydemeh; and, on the first occasion, killed 'Atwán the son of Dághir, their chief. These Teydemeh Arabs applied, for succour, to Eṣ-Ṣaleedee, king of the city of Teydemeh. He recommended them to Gessár the son of Gásir, a chief of the Benee-Ḥemyer, who sent to demand, of the tribe of Ez-Zaḥlán, fifteen years' arrears of tribute which the latter had been accustomed to pay to his tribe; and desired them to despatch to him, with this tribute,

1 When the reciter utters these words, we hear, from the lips of most of the Muslims who are listening to him, the prayer of "Alláhumma ṣallee 'aleyh!"—" O God, bless him!"

2 It is thus described in the romance: but a headless spear was formerly sometimes used instead of the "gereed," or palm-stick.

the slave Barakát (for he believed him to be a slave), a prisoner in bonds, to be put to death. Barakát wrote a reply, in the name of the Emeer Faḍl, promising compliance. Having a slave who much resembled him, and who was nearly of the same age, he bound him on the back of a camel, and, with him and the Emeer Faḍl and his tribe, went to meet Gessár and his party, and the Teydemeh Arabs. Faḍl presented the slave, as Barakát, to Gessár; who, pleased at having his orders apparently obeyed, feasted the tribe of Ez-Zaḥlán: but Barakát remained on horseback, and refused to eat of the food of his enemies, as, if he did, the laws of hospitality would prevent his executing a plot which he had framed. Gessár observed him; and, asking the Emeer Faḍl who he was, received the answer that he was a mad slave, named Mes'ood. Having drawn Gessár from his party, Barakát discovered himself to him, challenged, fought, and killed him, and took his tent: he pardoned the rest of the hostile party; but imposed upon them the tribute which the Zaḥlán Arabs had formerly paid them. Henceforth he had the name of Mes'ood added to that which he had before borne. Again and again he defeated the hostile attempts of the Benee-Ḥemyer to recover their independence, and acquired the highest renown, not only in the eyes of the Emeer Faḍl and the whole tribe of Ez-Zaḥlán, of whom he was made the chief, but also among all the neighbouring tribes.

We must now return to the Emeer Rizḳ, and his tribe.—Soon after the departure of his wife Khaḍrà he retired from his tribe, in disgust at the treatment which he received on account of his supposed disgrace, and in grief for his loss. With a single slave, he took up his abode in a tent of black goats' hair, one of those in which the tenders of his camels used to live, by the spring where his wife had seen the combat of the birds. Not long after this event, the Benee-Hilál were afflicted by a dreadful drought, which lasted so long that they were reduced to the utmost distress. In these circumstances, the greater number of them were induced, with their king Sarḥán, to go to the country of the tribe of Ez-Zaḥlán, for sustenance; but the Ga'áfireh, and some minor tribes of the Benee-Hilál, joined, and remained with, the Emeer Rizḳ, who had formerly been their commander. Sarḥán and his party were attacked and defeated by Barakát on their arrival in the territory of the Zaḥlán Arabs; but on their abject submission were suffered by him to remain there. They however cherished an inveterate hatred to the tribe of Eẓ-Zaḥlán, who had before paid them tribute; and Sarḥán was persuaded to send a messenger to the Emeer Rizḳ, begging him to come and endeavour to deliver them from their humiliating state. Rizḳ obeyed the summons. On his way to the territory of the Zaḥlán Arabs, he was almost convinced, by the messenger who had come to conduct him, that Barakát was his son; but was at a loss to know why he was called by this name, as he himself had named him Aboo-Zeyd. Arriving at the place of his destination, he challenged Barakát. The father went forth to combat the son: the former not certain that his opponent was his son; and the latter having no idea that he was about to lift his hand against his father; but thinking that his adversary was his father's murderer. The Emeer Rizḳ found occasion to put off the engagement from day to day: at last, being no longer able to do this, he suffered it to commence: his son prevailed: he unhorsed him, and would have put him to death had he not been charged to refrain from doing this by his mother. The secret of Barakát's parentage was now divulged to him by the Emeereh Khaḍrà; and the chiefs of the Benee-Hilál were compelled to acknowledge him as the legitimate and worthy son of the Emeer Rizḳ, and to implore his pardon for the injuries which he and his mother had sustained from them. This boon, the Emeer Aboo-Zeyd Barakát generously granted; and he thus added to the joy which the Emeer Rizḳ derived from the recovery of his favourite wife, and his son.

The subsequent adventures related in the romance of Aboo-Zeyd are numerous and complicated. The most popular portion of the work is the account of a "riyádeh," or expedition in search of pasture; in which Aboo-Zeyd, with three of his nephews, in the disguise of Shá'ers, himself acting as their servant, are described as journeying through northern Africa, and signalizing themselves by many surprising exploits with the Arab tribe of Ez-Zináteeyeh.

CHAPTER XXII.

PUBLIC RECITATIONS OF ROMANCES—*continued.*

NEXT in point of number to the Shó'arà, among the public reciters of romances, are those who are particularly and solely distinguished by the appellation of "Moḥadditeen," or Story-tellers (in the singular, "Moḥaddit"). There are said to be about thirty of them in Cairo. The exclusive subject of their narrations is a work called "the Life of Eẓ-Ẓáhir" ("Seeret Eẓ-Ẓáhir," or "Es-Seereh eẓ-Ẓáhireeyeh"[1]). They recite without book.

The Seeret Eẓ-Ẓáhir is a romance founded on the history of the famous Sulṭán Eẓ-Ẓáhir Beybars, and many of his contemporaries. This prince acceded to the throne of Egypt in the last month of the year of the Flight 658, and died in the first month of the year 676; and consequently reigned a little more than seventeen years, according to the lunar reckoning, commencing A.D. 1260, and ending in 1277. Complete copies of the Seeret Eẓ-Ẓáhir have become so scarce that I have only heard of one existing in Egypt, which I have purchased: it consists of six quarto volumes; but is nominally divided into ten; and is maḍe up of volumes of several different copies. The author and his age are unknown. The work is written in the most vulgar style of modern Egyptian Arabic; but as it was intended for the vulgar, it is likely that copyists may have altered and modernized the language, which was evidently never classical in style, nor in age. The oldest volumes of my copy of it were written a few years more or less than a century ago. To introduce my reader to some slight acquaintance with this work, I shall insert a translation of a few pages at the commencement of the second volume; but, by way of introduction, I must say something of the contents of the first volume.

---

[1] Hence the Moḥadditeen are sometimes called "Ẓáhireeyeh."

A person named 'Alee Ibn-El-Warráḳah, being commissioned to procure memlooks from foreign countries, by El-Melik eṣ-Ṣáleḥ (a famous Sulṭán of Egypt, and a celebrated welee), is related to have purchased seventy-five memlooks in Syria; and to have added to them, immediately after, the principal hero of this romance, a youth named Maḥmood (afterwards called Beybars), a captive son of Sháh Jaḳmaḳ (or Gaḳmaḳ) King of Khuwárezm. 'Alee was soon after obliged to give Maḥmood to one of his creditors at Damascus, in lieu of a debt; and this person presented him to his wife, to wait upon her son, a deformed idiot; but he remained not long in this situation: the sister of his new master, paying a visit to his wife, her sister-in-law, found her about to beat the young memlook, for having neglected the idiot, and suffered him to fall from a bench: struck with the youth's countenance, as strongly resembling a son whom she had lost, and pitying his condition, she purchased him of her brother, adopted him, gave him the name of Beybars, which was that of her deceased son, and made him master of her whole property, which was very great. This lady was called the sitt Fáṭ'meh Bint-El-Aḳwásee (daughter of the bow-maker). Beybars shewed himself worthy of her generosity; exhibiting many proofs of a noble disposition, and signalizing himself by numerous extraordinary achievements, which attracted general admiration, but rendered him obnoxious to the jealousy and enmity of the Báshà (or rather Governor) of Syria, 'Eesà En-Náṣiree, who contrived many plots to insnare him, and to put him to death. After a time, Negm-ed-Deen, a Wezeer of Eṣ-Ṣáleḥ, and husband of a sister of the sitt Fáṭ'meh, came on an embassy to Damascus, and to visit his sister-in-law. On his return to Egypt, Beybars accompanied him thither; and there he was promoted to offices of high dignity by Eṣ-Ṣáleḥ, and became a particular favourite of the chief Wezeer, Sháheen El-Afram. The events which immediately followed the death of Eṣ-Ṣáleḥ are thus related.

"After the death of El-Melik eṣ-Ṣáleḥ Eiyoob, the Wezeer Eybek called together an assembly in his house, and brought thither the Emeer Ḳala-oon and his partisans: and the Wezeer Eybek said to the Emeer Ḳala-oon, 'To-morrow we will go up to the deewán with our troops, and either I will be Sulṭán or thou shalt be.' The Emeer Ḳala-oon answered, 'So let it be:' and they agreed to do this. In like manner, the Wezeer Sháheen El-Afram also assembled the Emeer Eydemir El-Bahluwán and his troops, and all the friends and adherents of the Emeer Beybars, and said to them, 'To-morrow, arm yourselves, and go up to the deewán; for it is our desire to make the Emeer Beybars Sulṭán; since El-Melik eṣ-Ṣáleḥ Eiyoob wrote for him a patent appointing him to the sovereignty:' and they answered, 'On the head and the eye.' So they passed the night, and rose in the morning, and went up to the deewán; and there went thither also the Wezeer Eybek Et-Turkumánee, with his troops, and the Emeer Ḳala-oon El-Elfee, with his troops, and the Emeer 'Aláy-ed-Deen (or 'Alá-ed-Deen) El-Beyseree, with his troops, all of them armed. The Emeer Beybars likewise went up to the deewán, with his troops; and the deewán was crowded with soldiers. Then said the Wezeer Sháheen, 'Rise, O Beybars; sit upon the throne, and become Sulṭán, for thou hast a patent appointing thee to the sovereignty.' The Emeer Beybars answered, 'I have no desire for the sovereignty: here is present the Wezeer Eybek, and here is Ḳala-oon: make one of them Sulṭán.' But the Wezeer Sháheen said, 'It cannot be: no one shall reign but thou.' Beybars replied, 'By thy head, I will not reign.' 'As he pleases,' said the Wezeer Eybek. 'Is the sovereignty to be conferred by force? As he pleases.' The Wezeer Sháheen said, 'And is the throne to remain unoccupied, with no one to act as Sulṭán?' The Wezeer Eybek answered, 'Here are *we* present; and here is the Emeer Ḳala-oon: whosoever will reign, let him reign.' The Emeer 'Ezz-ed-Deen El-Ḥillee said, 'O Wezeer Sháheen, the son of El-Melik eṣ-Ṣáleḥ is living.' The Emeer Beybars asked, 'Eṣ-Ṣáleḥ has left a son?' The Kurds[1] answered, 'Yes; and his name is 'Eesà: he is at El-Karak.' 'And why,' said the Wezeer Sháheen, 'were ye silent respecting him?' They replied, 'We were silent for no other reason than this, that he drinks wine.' 'Does he drink wine?' said the Wezeer Sháheen. The Kurds answered, 'Yes.' The Emeer Beybars said, 'May our Lord bring him to repentance!' 'Then,' said the soldiers, 'we must go to the city of El-Karak, and bring him thence, and make him Sulṭán.' The Wezeer Sháheen said to them, 'Take the Emeer Beybars with you:' but Eybek and Ḳala-oon answered, 'We will go before him, and wait for him there until he come.' The Emeer Beybars said, 'So let it be.'

"Upon this, the Wezeer Eybek and Ḳala-oon and 'Aláy-ed-Deen El-Beyseree, and their troops, went down from the deewán, and ar-

[1] Eṣ-Ṣáleḥ was of the house of Eiyoob, a family of Kurds.

ranged their affairs, and on the following day caused their tents to be brought out, with their provisions, and pitched outside the 'Ádileeyeh.[1] Now the Wezeer Sháheen knew that the troops wished to create a dissension between the King (El-Melik) 'Eesà and Beybars. So the Wezeer Sháheen went down from the deewán, and took the Emeer Beybars with him, and went to his house, and said to him, 'What hast thou perceived in the departing of the troops before thee?' He answered, 'Those persons detest me; for they are bearers of hatred; but I extol the perfection of Him who is all-knowing with respect to secret things.' The Wezeer said to him, 'My son, it is their desire to go before thee that they may create a dissension between thee and El-Melik 'Eesà.' The Emeer Beybars said, 'There is no power nor strength but in God, the High, the Great!' The Wezeer said to him, 'O Beybars, it is my wish to send 'Osmán Ibn-El-Ḥeblà[2] and Moḥammad Ibn-Kámil the Dromedarist before the troops; and whatever may happen, they will inform us of it.' Beybars answered, 'So let it be.' Accordingly, he sent them; and said to them, 'Go before the troops to the castle of El-Karak, and whatever may happen between them and El-Melik 'Eesà inform us of it.' They answered, 'It is our duty,' and they departed. Then said the Wezeer Sháheen, 'O Beybars, as to thee, do thou journey to Esh-Shám,[3] and stay in the house of thy (adoptive) mother, the sitt Fáṭ'meh Bint-El-Aḳwásee; and do not go out of the house until I shall have sent to thee 'Osmán.' He answered, 'It is right.' So the Emeer Beybars rose, and went to his house, and passed the night, and got up in the morning, and set out on his journey to Esh-Shám, and took up his abode in the house of his mother, the sitt Fáṭ'meh Bint-El-Aḳwásee. We shall have to speak of him again presently.

"As to 'Osmán Ibn-El-Ḥeblà and Moḥammad Ibn-Kámil the Dromedarist, they journeyed until they entered the castle of El-Karak, and inquired for the residence of El-Melik 'Eesà, the son of El-Melik eṣ-Ṣáleḥ Eiyoob. Some persons conducted them to the house, and they entered; and the attendants there asked them what was their business. They informed them that they were from Maṣr, and that

---

1 "The 'Ádileeyeh" is the name of a mosque founded by El-Melik el-'Ádil Ṭoomán Bey, in the year of the Flight 906 (A.D. 1501), outside the wall of Cairo, near the great gate called Báb en-Naṣr. The same name is also given to the neighbourhood of that mosque.

2 'Osmán (vulgarly called 'Otmán and 'Etmán) Ibn-El-Ḥeblà was a rogue whom Beybars took into his service as groom, and compelled to vow repentance at the shrine of the seyyideh Nefeeseh (great-granddaughter of the Imám Ḥasan), and, soon after, made his muḳaddam, or chief of his servants.

3 Here meaning Damascus.

they wished to have an interview with El-Melik 'Eesà, the son of El-Melik eṣ-Ṣáleḥ Eiyoob. The attendants went and told the kikhyà; who came and spoke to them; and they acquainted him with their errand: so he went and told El-Melik 'Eesà, saying, 'Two men are come to thee from Maṣr, and wish to have an interview with thee: the one is named 'Osmán; and the other, Moḥammad Ibn-Kámil the Dromedarist.' The King said, 'Go, call 'Osmán.' The kikhyà returned, and took him, and brought him to El-Melik 'Eesà; and 'Osmán looked towards the King, and saw him sitting tippling; and before him was a candelabrum, and a handsome memlook was serving him with wine; and he was sitting by a fountain surrounded by trees. 'Osmán said, 'Mayst thou be in the keeping of God, O King 'Eesà!' The King answered, 'Ho! welcome, O 'Osmán! Come, sit down and drink.' 'Osmán exclaimed, 'I beg forgiveness of God! I am a repentant.[1] The King said, 'Obey me, and oppose me not.' Then 'Osmán sat down; and the King said to him, 'Why, the door of repentance is open.' And 'Osmán drank until he became intoxicated.

"Now Eybek and Ḳala-oon and 'Aláy-ed-Deen and their troops journeyed until they beheld the city of El-Karak, and pitched their tents, and entered the city, and inquired for the house of El-Melik 'Eesà. The people conducted them to the house, and they entered; and the attendants asked them what was their object: they answered, that they were the troops of Maṣr, and wished to have an interview with El-Melik 'Eesà. The attendants went and told the kikhyà, who came, and received them, and conducted them to the hall of audience, where they sat down, while he went and informed El-Melik 'Eesà, saying to him, 'Come and speak to the troops of Maṣr who have come to thee.' The King rose, and went to the troops, and accosted them; and they rose, and kissed his hand, and sat down again. El-Melik 'Eesà then said to them, 'For what purpose have ye come?' They answered, 'We have come to make thee Sulṭán in Maṣr.' He said, 'My father, El-Melik eṣ-Ṣáleḥ, is he not Sulṭán?' They replied, 'The mercy of God, whose name be exalted, be on him! Thy father has died, a victim of injustice: may our Lord avenge him on him who killed him!' He asked, 'Who killed him?' They answered, 'One whose name is Beybars killed him.' 'And where is Beybars?' said he. They replied, 'He is not yet come: we came before him.'

[1] This reply is very often returned by a Muslim when he is invited to drink any intoxicating beverage; or merely, "I have repented" ("Tubt").

'Even so,' said he. They then sat with him, aspersing Beybars in his absence: and they passed the night there; and, rising on the following morning, said to El-Melik 'Eesà, 'It is our wish to go out, and remain in the camp; for Sháheen, the Wezeer of thy father, is coming, with the Emeer Beybars; and if they see us with thee, they will accuse us of bringing to thee the information respecting Beybars.' He answered, 'Good.' So they went forth to the camp, and remained there.

"The Wezeer Sháheen approached with his troops, and encamped, and saw the other troops in their camp; but he would not ask them any questions, and so entered the city, and went to El-Melik 'Eesà, who said to him, 'Art thou Beybars, who poisoned my father?' He answered, 'I am the Wezeer Sháheen, the Wezeer of thy father.' The King said, 'And where is Beybars, who poisoned my father?' The Wezeer replied, 'Thy father departed by a natural death to await the mercy of his Lord: and who told thee that Beybars poisoned thy father?' The King answered, 'The troops told me.' 'Beybars,' said the Wezeer, 'is in Esh-Shám: go thither, and charge him, in the deewán, with having poisoned thy father, and bring proof against him.' So the Wezeer perceived that the troops had been plotting.

"The Wezeer Sháheen then went, with his troops, outside the camp; and Moḥammad Ibn-Kámil the Dromedarist came to him, and kissed his hand. The Wezeer asked him respecting 'Osmán. He answered, 'I have no tidings of him.' Meanwhile, El-Melik 'Eesà went to 'Osmán, and said to him, 'The Wezeer is come with his troops, and they are outside the camp.' So 'Osmán rose, and, reeling as he went, approached the tents; and the Wezeer Sháheen saw him, and perceived that he was drunk, and called to him. 'Osmán came. The Wezeer smelt him, seized him, and inflicted upon him the "ḥadd;"[1] and said to him, 'Didst thou not vow to relinquish the drinking of wine?' 'Osmán answered, 'El-Melik 'Eesà, whom ye are going to make Sulṭán, invited me.' The Wezeer said, 'I purpose writing a letter for you to take and give to the Emeer Beybars.' 'Osmán replied, 'Good.' So the Wezeer wrote the letter, and 'Osmán took it and departed, and entered Esh-Shám, and went to the house of the sitt Fáṭ'meh, and gave it to his master, who read it, and found it to contain as follows.—'After salutations—from his excellency the Grand Wezeer, the Wezeer Sháheen El-Afram, to his honour the

[1] Eighty stripes, the punishment ordained for drunkenness.

Emeer Beybars. Know that the troops have aspersed thee, and created dissensions between thee and El-Melik 'Eesà, and accused thee of having poisoned his father, El-Melik eṣ-Ṣáleḥ Eiyoob. Now, on the arrival of this paper, take care of thyself, and go not out of the house, unless I shall have sent to thee. And the conclusion of the letter is, that 'Osmán got drunk in the castle of El-Karak.'—Beybars was vexed with 'Osmán; and said to him, 'Come hither and receive a present:' and he stretched forth his hand, and laid hold of him. 'Osmán said, 'What ails thee?' Beybars exclaimed, 'Did I not make thee vow to relinquish the drinking of wine?' 'Has he told thee?' asked 'Osmán. 'I will give thee a treat,' said Beybars: and he took him, and threw him down, and inflicted upon him the "ḥadd." 'How is it,' said 'Osmán, that the King whom ye are going to make Sulṭán I found drinking wine?' Beybars answered, 'If one has transgressed must thou transgress?' 'And is this,' asked 'Osmán, 'the ḥadd ordained by God?' Beybars answered, 'Yes.' 'Then,' said 'Osmán, 'the ḥadd which Aboo-Farmeh[1] inflicted upon me is a loan, and a debt which must be repaid him.' Beybars then said, 'The troops have created a dissension between me and El-Melik 'Eesà, and have accused me of poisoning his father, El-Melik eṣ-Ṣáleḥ.' 'I beg the forgiveness of God,' said 'Osmán. 'Those fellows detest thee; but no harm will come to us from them.' Beybars said, 'O 'Osmán, call together the sáïses,[2] and arm them, and let them remain in the lane of the cotton-weavers,[3] and not suffer any troops to enter.' 'Osmán answered, 'On the head and the eye.' And he assembled the sáïses, and armed them, and made them stand in two rows: then he took a seat, and sat in the court of the house. The Emeer Beybars also armed all his troops, and placed them in the court of the house.

"As to El-Melik 'Eesà, he mounted his horse, and departed with the troops, and journeyed until he entered Esh-Shám; when he went in procession to the deewán, and sat upon the throne, and inquired of the King[4] of Syria respecting Beybars. The King of Syria answered, 'He is in the lane of the cotton-weavers, in the house of his mother.' El-Melik 'Eesà said, 'O Sháheen, who will go and bring him?' The Wezeer answered, 'Send to him the Emeer 'Aláy-ed-

[1] 'Osmán, for the sake of a rude joke, changes the name of the Wezeer Sháheen (El-Afram) into an appellation too coarse to be here translated.

[2] Grooms, also employed as running footmen.

[3] A lane from which the house was entered.

[4] Sometimes called in the romance of Eẓ-Ẓáhir "Báshà" of Syria.

Deen El-Beyseree.' So he sent him. The Emeer descended, and went to the lane of the cotton-weavers. 'Osmán saw him, and cried out to him, 'Dost thou remember, thou son of a vile woman, the chicken which thou atest?'[1] He then struck him with a mace; and the Emeer fell from his horse, and 'Osmán gave him a bastinading. He returned, and informed the King; and the King 'Eesà said again, 'O Sháheen, who will go, and bring Beybars?' The Wezeer answered, 'Send to him the Wezeer Eybek.' The King said, 'Rise, O Wezeer Eybek, and go, call Beybars:' but Eybek said, 'No one can bring him, except the Wezeer.' Then said El-Melik 'Eesà, 'Rise, O Wezeer Sháheen, and bring Beybars.' The Wezeer answered, 'On the head and the eye: but, before I bring him, tell me, wilt thou deal with him according to law, or by arbitrary power?' The King said, 'By law.' Then said the Wezeer Sháheen, 'So let it be: and I spake not thus from any other motive than because I fear for thyself and the troops, lest blood be shed; for Beybars is very stubborn, and has many troops: and I fear for the army; for he is himself equal to the whole host: therefore bring accusation against him, and prove by law that he poisoned thy father.' The King said, 'So let it be.'

"Then the Wezeer Sháheen descended from the deewán, and went to the lane of the cotton-weavers. 'Osmán saw him; and said, 'Thou hast fallen into the snare, O Aboo-Farmeh! the time of payment is come; and the debt must be returned to the creditor. Dost thou know how to give me a bastinading?' The Wezeer said, 'My dream which I saw has proved true.' 'What was thy dream?' asked 'Osmán. 'I dreamed,' said the Wezeer, 'last night, that I was travelling, and some Arabs attacked me, and surrounded me, and I was straitened by them; and I saw thy master, the Emeer Beybars, upon a mount; and I called out to him, Come to me, O Emeer Beybars! and he knew me.' The Wezeer Sháheen calling out thus, the Emeer Beybars heard him, and came down running, with his sword in hand; and found 'Osmán and the sáïses surrounding the Wezeer. He exclaimed, ''Osmán!' and 'Osmán said, 'He gave me a bastinading in the city of El-Karak; and I want to return it.' The Emeer Beybars sharply reprimanded him. 'And so,' said 'Osmán to the Wezeer, 'thou hast found a way of escape.' The Wezeer Sháheen then said, 'O Emeer Beybars, El-Melik 'Eesà hath sent me to thee: he intends to prefer an accusation against thee in the deewán of Esh-

[1] This is an allusion to 'Aláy-ed-Deen's having eaten a dish that had been prepared for Beybars, when the latter had just entered the service of the Sulṭán Eṣ-Ṣáleḥ.

Shám, charging thee with having poisoned his father. Now, do thou arm all thy soldiers, and come to the deewán, and fear not; but say that which shall clear thee.' Beybars answered, 'So let it be.' He then armed all his soldiers, and went up to the deewán, and kissed the hand of El-Melik 'Eesà; who said to him, 'Art thou the Emeer Beybars, who poisoned my father?' Beybars answered, 'Prove against me that I poisoned thy father, and bring the charge before the judge, and adduce evidence: the Ḳáḍee is here.' The King said, 'I have evidence against thee.' Beybars said, 'Let us see.' 'Here,' said the King, 'are the Wezeer Eybek and Ḳala-oon and 'Aláy-ed-Deen.' The Emeer Beybars asked them, 'Do ye bear witness against me that I poisoned El-Melik eṣ-Ṣáleḥ?' They answered, 'Never: we neither saw it, nor do we know anything of the matter.' The Ḳáḍee said, 'Hast thou any witnesses beside those?' The King replied, 'None: no one informed me but they.' The Ḳáḍee said, 'O King, those men are hypocrites, and detest the Emeer Beybars.' El-Melik 'Eesà thereupon became reconciled with the Emeer Beybars, and said to his attendants, 'Bring a ḳafṭán.' They brought one. He said to them, 'Invest with it the Emeer Beybars;' and added, 'I appoint thee, O Beybars, commander-in-chief of the army.' But Beybars said, 'I have no desire for the dignity, and will put on no ḳafṭáns.' The King asked, 'Why, O my lord?' Beybars answered, 'Because I have been told that thou drinkest wine.' The King said, 'I repent.' 'So let it be,' said Beybars: and the King vowed repentance to Beybars: and the Emeer Beybars said, 'I make a condition with thee, O King, that if thou drink wine, I inflict upon thee the "ḥadd:"' and the King replied, 'It is right.' Upon this the King invested the Emeer Beybars with a ḳafṭán; and a feast was made, and guns were fired, and festivities were celebrated; and they remained in Esh-Shám three days.

"El-Melik 'Eesà then gave orders for departure, and performed the first day's journey. On the second day they came to a valley, celebrated as a halting-place of the Prophet, the director in the way to heaven: in it were trees, and brooks, and birds which sang the praises of the King, the Mighty, the Pardoner. El-Melik 'Eesà said, 'Pitch the tents here: we will here pass the night.' So they pitched the tents. And the day departed with its brightness, and the night came with its darkness: but the Everlasting remaineth unchanged: the stars shone; and God, the Living, the Self-subsisting, looked upon the creation. It was the period of the full moon; and the

King felt a longing to drink wine by the side of the brook and greensward: so he called to Abu-l-Kheyr, who came to him, and kissed his hand. The King said to him, 'O Abu-l-Kheyr, I have a longing to drink wine.' The servant answered, 'Hast thou not vowed repentance to the Emeer Beybars?' The King said, 'The door of repentance is open; so do thou obey me:' and he gave him ten pieces of gold. The servant then went to a convent, and brought him thence a large bottle; and the King said to him, 'If thou see the Emeer Beybars coming, call out *hay!* and as long as thou dost not see him, call *clover!*' The servant answered, 'Right.' And he filled a cup, and handed it to the King. Now 'Osmán was by the tents; and he came before the pavilion of El-Melik 'Eesà; and saw him sitting drinking wine: so he went, and told his master, the Emeer Beybars. Beybars came. Abu-l-Kheyr saw him coming from a tent, and called out to the King, '*Hay! hay!*' The King immediately threw the cup into the brook, Abu-l-Kheyr removed the bottle, and the King set himself to praying; and when he had pronounced the salutation [which terminates the prayers], he turned his eyes, and saw the Emeer Beybars, and said to him, 'Wherefore art thou come at this hour? Go, sleep: it is late. Beybars answered, 'I have come to ask thee whether we shall continue our journey now, or to-morrow morning.' The King said, 'To-morrow morning.' And the Emeer Beybars returned, vexed with 'Osmán; and said to him, 'O 'Osmán, didst thou not tell me that the King was sitting drinking wine? Now I have been, and found him praying. Dost thou utter a falsehood against the Sulṭán?' 'Osmán answered, 'Like as he has smoothed it over, do thou also: no matter.' Beybars was silent.

"They passed the night there; and on the following morning El-Melik 'Eesà gave orders for departure. They journeyed towards Maṣr; and when they had arrived at the 'Ádileeyeh, and pitched their tents, the Emeer Beybars said, 'O our lord the Sulṭán, we have now arrived at Maṣr.' The King answered, 'I desire, O Beybars, to visit the tomb of the Imám [Esh-Sháfe'ee].' Beybars said, 'The thing is right, O our lord the Sulṭán: to-morrow I will conduct thee to visit the Imám.' They remained that night at the 'Ádileeyeh; and on the following morning the Sulṭán rode in procession to visit the Imám, and returned in procession, and visited the tomb of his father, El-Melik eṣ-Ṣáleḥ Eiyoob; and then went in state to the Citadel: and the 'Ulamà went up thither, and inaugurated him as sovereign, and conducted him into the armoury; and he drew out from thence a sword, upon which was inscribed 'El-Melik el-Mo'aẓẓam:'[1] wherefore they named him ''Eesà el-Mo'aẓẓam.' They coined the money with his name, and prayed for him on the pulpits of the mosques; and he invested with ḳafṭáns the soldiers and the Emeer Beybars, the commander-in-chief. The Sulṭán then wrote a patent, conferring the sovereignty, after himself, upon the Emeer Beybars, to be King and Sulṭán. So the Emeer Beybars had two patents conferring upon him the sovereignty; the patent of El-Melik eṣ-Ṣáleḥ Eiyoob, and the patent of El-Melik 'Eesà el-Mo'aẓẓam. Eybek and Ḳala-oon and 'Aláy-ed-Deen and their partisans, who hated Beybars, were grieved at this; but his friends rejoiced. The troops descended from the deewán, and went to their houses; and in like manner the Emeer Beybars descended in procession, and went to his house by the Ḳanáṭir es-Sibáạ.[2]

"Now the queen Shegeret-ed-Durr sent to El-Melik 'Eesà el-Mo'aẓẓam. He went to her palace. She kissed his hand; and he said to her, 'Who art thou?' She answered, 'The wife of thy father, El-Melik eṣ-Ṣáleḥ.' 'And what is thy name?' said he. She replied, 'The Queen Fáṭimeh Shegeret-ed-Durr. He exclaimed 'Oh! welcome! pray for me then.' She said, 'God bring thee to repentance!' She then gave him a charge respecting the Emeer Beybars; saying, 'Thy father loved him above all the chiefs, and entered into a covenant with him before God; and I, also, made a covenant with him before God.' He answered, 'O Queen, by thy life, I have written for him a patent conferring upon him the sovereignty after me. She said, 'And thy father, also, wrote for him a patent, conferring upon him the sovereignty.' The King then said to her, 'Those chiefs created a dissension between me and him, and asserted that he poisoned my father.' She said, 'I beg God's forgiveness! They hate him.' After this the Queen remained chatting with him a short time; and he went to his saloon, and passed the night, and rose.

"On the following day he held a court; and the hall was filled with troops. And he winked to Abu-l-Kheyr, and said, 'Give me to drink.' Now he had said to him the day before, 'To-morrow, when I hold my court, and say to thee, Give me to drink, bring me a water-bottle full of wine.' So when El-Melik 'Eesà sat upon the

[1] The Magnified King.
[2] Two bridges over the Canal of Cairo, in the south-west part of the town.

throne, and the court, filled with troops, resembled a garden, the troops resembling the branches of plants, he felt a longing to drink wine, and said to Abu-l-Kheyr, 'Give me to drink;' and winked to him. And he brought to him the water-bottle; and he drank, and returned it. Then he sat a little longer, and said again, 'Give me to drink, O Abu-l-Kheyr.' And the servant brought the bottle; and he drank, and gave it back. He sat a little longer; and again he said, 'Give me to drink.' Ḳala-oon said, 'O 'Aláy-ed-Deen, it seems that the Sulṭán has breakfasted upon kawáre'."[1] Upon this, the Wezeer Sháheen asked him, 'What hast thou eaten?' The King answered, 'My stomach is heated and flatulent.' The Wezeer, however, perceived the smell of wine; and was vexed. The court then broke up; and the troops descended. The Wezeer Sháheen also descended, and took with him the Emeer Beybars to his house, and said to him, 'May God take retribution from thee, O Beybars.' Beybars said, 'Why?' The Wezeer answered, 'Because thou didst not accept the sovereignty.' 'But for what reason sayest thou this?' asked Beybars. The Wezeer said, 'The Sulṭán to-day drank wine, while sitting upon the throne, three times. When the Vicar of God, in administering the law, intoxicates himself, his decisions are null, and he has not any right to give them.' Beybars replied, 'I made a condition with him, that if he drank wine, I should inflict upon him the "ḥadd;" and I wrote a document to that effect in Esh-Shám.' 'To-morrow,' said the Wezeer, 'when he holds his court, observe him; and take the water-bottle, and see what is in it. I perceived his smell.' Beybars answered, 'It is right.' And he rose, and went to his house sorrowful. And he passed the night, and rose, and went to the court, and found it filled with troops; and he kissed the hand of the Sulṭán, and sat in his place. Presently the Sulṭán said, 'Give me to drink, O Abu-l-Kheyr.' And the servant brought the water-bottle, and the Sulṭán drank. Beybars took hold of the water-bottle, and said, 'Give me to drink.' The servant answered, 'This is medicinal water.' 'No harm,' said Beybars: 'I have a desire for it.' 'It is rose-water,' said the servant. Beybars said, 'Good.' And he took the bottle, and said, 'Bring a basin.' A basin was brought; and he poured into it the contents of the bottle before the troops; and they saw that it was wine. Then said the Emeer Beybars to the Sulṭán, 'Is it allowed thee by God to be his Vicar, and to intoxicate

[1] A dish of lamb's feet, cooked with garlic and vinegar, &c.

thyself? Did I not make thee vow to relinquish the drinking of wine, and say to thee, If thou drink it I will inflict upon thee the "ḥadd;" and did I not write a document to that effect in Esh-Shám?' The Sulṭán answered, 'It is a habit decreed against me, O Beybars.' Beybars exclaimed, 'God is witness, O ye troops!' And he took the Sulṭán, and beat him; and he was unconscious, by reason of the wine that he had drunk; and he loosed him, and departed from him, and went to his house."

The second volume proceeds to relate the troubles which befell Beybars in consequence of his incurring the displeasure of El-Melik 'Eesà by the conduct just described; his restoration to the favour of that prince; and his adventures during the reigns of the subsequent Sulṭáns, Khaleel El-Ashraf, Eṣ-Ṣáleḥ the youth, Eybek (his great and inveterate enemy), and El-Muẓaffar; and then, his own accession to the sovereignty. The succeeding volumes contain narratives of his wars in Syria and other countries; detailing various romantic achievements, and the exploits of the "Fedáweeyeh," or "Fedáwees," of his time. The term Fedáwee, which is now vulgarly understood to signify any warriour of extraordinary courage and ability, literally and properly means a person who gives, or is ready to give, his life as a ransom for his companions, or for their cause; and is here applied to a class of warriours who owned no allegiance to any sovereign unless to a chief of their own choice; the same class who are called, in our histories of the Crusades, "Assassins:" which appellation the very learned orientalist De Sacy has, I think, rightly pronounced to be a corruption of "Ḥashsháshеen," a name derived from their making frequent use of the intoxicating hemp, called "ḥasheesh." The romance of Eẓ-Ẓáhir affords confirmation of the etymology given by De Sacy; but suggests a different explanation of it: the Fedáweeyeh being almost always described in this work as making use of "beng" (a term applied to hemp, and also to henbane, which, in the present day, is often mixed with ḥasheesh,) to make a formidable enemy or rival their prisoner, by disguising themselves, inviting him to eat, putting the drug into his food or drink, and thus causing him speedily to fall into a deep sleep, so that they were able to bind him at their leisure, and convey him whither they would.[1] The chief of these warriours is "Sheeḥah," called "Sulṭán el-Ḳiláạ wa-l-Ḥoṣoon"

[1] Since the remark above was written, I have found that El-Idreesee applies the term "Ḥasheesheeyeh," which is exactly synonymous with "Ḥashsháshеen," to the "Assassins:" this, therefore, decides the question.

(or "Sulṭán of the Castles and Fortresses"), who is described as almost constantly engaged, and generally with success, in endeavouring to reduce all the Fedáwees to allegiance to himself and to Beybars. From his adroitness in disguises and plots, his Proteus-like character, his name has become a common appellation of persons of a similar description. Another of the more remarkable characters in this romance is "Guwán" (or John), a European Christian, who, having deeply studied Muslim law, succeeds in obtaining, and retains for a few years, the office of Ḳáḍee of the Egyptian metropolis; and is perpetually plotting against Beybars, Sheeḥah, and other Muslim chiefs.

Much of the entertainment derived from recitations of this work depends upon the talents of the Moḥaddit; who often greatly improves the stories by his action, and by witty introductions of his own invention.

CHAPTER XXIII.

PUBLIC RECITATIONS OF ROMANCES—*continued.*

THERE is, in Cairo, a third class of reciters of romances, who are called "'Anátireh," or "'Antereeyeh" (in the singular "'Anteree");[1] but they are much less numerous than either of the other two classes before mentioned; their number at present, if I be rightly informed, not amounting to more than six. They bear the above-mentioned appellation from the chief subject of their recitations, which is the romance of "'Antar" ("Seeret 'Antar"). As a considerable portion of this interesting work has become known to English readers by Mr. Terrick Hamilton's translation, I need give no account of it. The reciters of it read it from the book: they chant the poetry; but the prose they read, in the popular manner; and they have not the accompaniment of the rabáb. As the poetry in this work is very imperfectly understood by the vulgar, those who listen to it are mostly persons of some education.

The 'Anátireh also recite from other works than that from which they derive their appellation. All of them, I am told, occasionally relate stories from a romance called "Seeret el-Mugáhideen" ("The History of the Warriours"), or, more commonly, "Seeret Delhemeh,"[2] or "Zu-l-Himmeh,"[3] from a heroine who is the chief character in the work. A few years since, they frequently recited from the romance of "Seyf Zu-l-Yezen" (vulgarly called "Seyf El-Yezen," and "Seyf El-Yezel"), a work abounding with tales of wonder; and from "The Thousand and One Nights" ("Elf Leyleh wa-Leyleh"), more commonly known, in our country, by the title of "The Arabian

[1] Pronounced 'Anter'ee.

[2] Pronounced Delhem'eh.

[3] This, being a masculine appellation, is evidently a corruption of the former. The name is written "Delhemeh" in the older portions of some volumes in my possession, made up of fragments of this work. One of these portions appears to be at least three centuries old. In some of the more modern fragments, the name is written "Zu-l-Himmeh."

Nights' Entertainments." The great scarcity of copies of these two works is, I believe, the reason why recitations of them are no longer heard: even fragments of them are with difficulty procured; and when a complete copy of "The Thousand and One Nights" is found, the price demanded for it is too great for a reciter to have it in his power to pay. I doubt whether the romances of Aboo-Zeyd, Eẓ-Ẓáhir, 'Antar, and Delhemeh, are chosen as the subjects of recitation because preferred to "The Thousand and One Nights;" but it is certain that the modern Muslims of Egypt have sufficient remains of Bedawee feeling to take great delight in hearing tales of war.

That my reader may have some notion of all the works from which the professional reciters of romances in Cairo draw materials for the amusement of their audiences in the present day, I shall give a sketch of some of the adventures related in the romance of Delhemeh. This work is even more scarce than any of those before mentioned. The copies, I am told, were always in fifty-five volumes. After long search, all that I have succeeded in procuring of it is a portion consisting of the first three volumes (containing, together, 302 pages), and another portion, consisting of the forty-sixth and forty-seventh volumes. The former would present a good specimen of the work, were not the greater part written in a hand scarcely legible; in consequence of which, and of the many other subjects that now demand my attention, I have only read the first volume. The chief subjects of this work, according to the preface, are the warlike exploits of Arabs of the Desert in the times of the Khaleefehs of the houses of Umeiyeh and El-'Abbás. It is composed from the narratives of various writers: nine names of the authors are mentioned; but none of them are at present known: their history and their age are alike uncertain; but the style of their narratives shews them to be not modern. The account which the 'Anátireh and Moḥadditeen generally give of this romance is as follows.—When El-Aṣma'ee (or, as he is vulgarly called, El-Aṣmo'ee,) composed, or compiled, the history of 'Antar,[1] that work (they say) became extremely popular, and created so great an enthusiasm on the subjects of the adventures of Arab warriours, that a diligent search was made for all tales of the same kind; and from these was compiled the Seeret el-Mugáhideen, or Delhemeh, by some author now unknown, who, as he could not

[1] The 'Ulamà in general despise the romance of 'Antar, and ridicule the assertion that El-Aṣma'ee was its author.

equal the author of 'Antar in eloquence, determined to surpass him in the length of his narratives; and 'Antar being generally in forty-five volumes, he made his book fifty-five. The romance of Delhemeh abounds in poetry, which is not without beauties, nor without faults; but the latter are, perhaps, mostly attributable to copyists.—Of a part of what I have read, which introduces us to one of the principal characters in the work, I shall now give an abridged translation.

At the commencement of the work, we are told, that, in the times of the Khaleefehs of the house of Umeiyeh, none of the Arab tribes surpassed in power, courage, hospitality, and other virtues for which the Arabs of the Desert are so famous, the Benee-Kiláb, whose territory was in the Ḥegáz: but the viceroy of the Khaleefeh over the collective tribes of the desert was the chief of the Benee-Suleym, who prided themselves on this distinction, and on their wealth. El-Ḥáris, the chief of the Benee-Kiláb, a horseman unrivalled in his day, in one of the predatory excursions which he was wont frequently to make against other tribes, took captive a beautiful girl, named Er-Rabáb (or the Viol), whom he married. She became pregnant; and, during her pregnancy, dreamed that a fire issued from her, and burnt all her clothing. Being much troubled by this dream, she related it to her husband; and he, alike surprised and distressed, immediately searched for, and soon found, a person to interpret it. An old sheykh informed him that his wife would bear a son of great renown, who would have a son more renowned than himself; and that the mother of the former would be in danger of losing her life at the time of his birth. This prophecy he repeated to the wife of El-Ḥáris; and, at her request, he wrote an amulet to be tied upon the infant's right arm, as soon as he should be born; upon which amulet he recorded the family and pedigree of the child:—"This child is the son of El-Ḥáris the son of Khálid the son of 'Ámir the son of Ṣaạṣa'ah the son of Kiláb; and this is his pedigree among all the Arabs of the Ḥegáz; and he is verily of the Benee-Kiláb." Soon after this, El-Ḥáris fell sick; and, after a short illness, died. Most of the Arabs of neighbouring tribes, who had been subjected and kept in awe by him, rejoiced at his death, and determined to obtain retribution by plundering his property. This coming to the ears of his widow, Er-Rabáb, she determined to return to her family; and persuaded a black slave who had belonged to her late husband to accompany her. By night, and without having mentioned their intention to any one else, they departed; and at midnight they approached a settlement of Arabs whose chief was the Emeer Dárim. Here the slave, tempted by the Devil, led her from the road, and impudently told her that her beauty had excited in his breast a passion which she must consent to gratify. She indignantly refused; but the fright that she received from his base conduct occasioned a premature labour; and in this miserable state she gave birth to a son. She washed the infant with the water of a brook that ran by the spot; wrapped it in a piece of linen which she tore off from her dress; tied the amulet to its arm; and placed it to her breast. Scarcely had she done this, when the slave, infuriated by disappointment, drew his sword, and struck off her head. Having thus revenged himself, he fled.

Now it happened, as Providence had decreed, that the wife of the Emeer Dárim had just been delivered of a son, which had died; and the Emeer, to dissipate his grief on this account, went out to hunt, with several of his people, on the morning after Er-Rabáb had been murdered. He came to the spot where her corpse lay, and saw it: the infant was still sucking the breast of its dead mother; and God had sent a flight of locusts, of the kind called "gundub," to shade it from the sun with their wings. Full of astonishment at the sight, he said to his Wezeer, "See this murdered damsel, and this infant on her lap, and those flying insects shading it, and the dead mother still affording it milk! Now, by the faith of the Arabs, if thou do not ascertain the history of this damsel, and the cause of her murder, I behead thee like her." The Wezeer answered, "O King, none knoweth what is secret but God, whose name be exalted! Was I with her? or do I know her? But promise me protection, and I will inform thee what I suppose to have been the case." The King said, "I give thee protection." Then said the Wezeer, "Know, O King, —but God is all-knowing,—that this is the daughter of some King; and she has grown up, and a servant has had intercourse with her; and by him she has conceived this child; and her family have become acquainted with the fact, and killed her. This is my opinion; and there is an end of it." The King exclaimed, "Thou dog of the Arabs! what is this that thou sayest to the prejudice of this damsel? By Allah! if I had not promised thee protection I had slain thee with the edge of the sword! If she had committed this crime, she would not be affording the child her milk after she was dead: nor would God have sent these flying insects to shade the infant." He then sent for a woman to wash the corpse; and after it had been washed, and bound in grave-clothes, he buried it respectably.

From the circumstance of the gundub shading him with their wings, the foundling received the name of "El-Gundubah."[1] The Emeer Dárim conveyed it to his wife, and persuaded her to bring it up as her own; which she did until the child had attained the age of seven years, when he was sent to school, and there he remained until he had learned the Ḳur-án. By the time he had attained to manhood, he had become a horseman unrivalled: he was like a bitter colocynth, a viper, and a calamity.[2]

Now his adoptive father, the Emeer Dárim, went forth one day, according to his custom, on a predatory expedition, accompanied by a hundred horsemen. Falling in with no booty, he proceeded as far as the territory of a woman called Esh-Shamṭà (or the Grizzle), whom the heroes of her time held in fear, on account of her prowess and strength; and who was possessed of great wealth. He determined to attack her. She mounted her horse in haste, on hearing of his approach, and went forth to meet him and his party. For a whole hour she contended with them; killed the greater number; and put the rest to flight, except the Emeer Dárim, whom she took prisoner, and led in bonds, disgraced and despised, to her fortress. Those of his attendants who had fled returned to their tribes, and plunged them in affliction by the story they related. The Emeer Dárim had ten sons. These all set out together, with a number of attendants, to rescue their father; but they all became the prisoners of Esh-Shamṭà; and most of their attendants were killed by her. El-Gundubah now resolved to try his arms against this heroine. He went alone, unknown to any of the tribe, except his foster-mother, and arrived at the place of his destination. Esh-Shamṭà was on the top of her fortress. She saw him approach, a solitary horseman; and perceived that his riding was that of a hero. In haste she descended, and mounted her horse, and went out to meet him. She shouted against him; and the desert resounded with her shout; but El-Gundubah was unmoved by it. They defied each other, and met; and for a whole hour the contest lasted: at length, El-Gundubah's lance pierced the bosom of Esh-Shamṭà; its glittering point protruded through her back, and she fell from her horse, slain, and weltering in her blood. Her slaves, who were forty in number, seeing their mistress dead, made a united attack upon her victor; but he unhorsed

[1] Pronounced Gundub'ah.

[2] These are not terms of reproach among the Arabs; but of praise.

them all; and then, reproaching them for having served a woman, when they were all men of prowess, admonished them to submit to him; upon which they all acknowledged him as their master. He divided among them the treasures of Esh-Shamṭâ; and released his adoptive father and brothers, with whom he returned to the tribe.

This exploit spread the fame of El-Gundubah among all the tribes of the desert; but it excited envy in the breast of the Emeer Dárim, who soon after desired him to seek for himself some other place of abode. El-Gundubah remonstrated; but to no effect; and prepared for his departure. When he was about to go, the Emeer Dárim desired to be allowed to open the amulet that was upon El-Gundubah's arm, and to read what was written upon the paper. Having obtained permission, and done this, he uttered a loud shout; and several of his people coming in to inquire the cause of this cry, he said to them, "This youth is the son of your enemy El-Ḥáris, the Kilábee: take him, and slay him:" but El-Gundubah insisted that they should contend with him one by one. The Emeer Dárim was the first to challenge him; and addressed him in these verses:[1]

"This day I forewarn thee of death and disgrace,
From my weapon, thou offspring of parents base!
Didst thou think, thou vile foundling, to raise thyself,
O'er the heads of our tribe, to the foremost place?
Thy hope is now baffled: thy wish is deceiv'd:
For to-day we have known thee of hostile race.
Thy bloodthirsty father oppressed our tribe:
Both our men and our wealth were his frequent preys:
But to-day shall be taken a full revenge:
All our heroes shall see me their wrongs efface.
Be assur'd that thy death is now near at hand;
That my terrible lance shall pierce thee apace:
For 'twas I introduc'd thee among our tribe;
And the foe that I brought I will now displace."

El-Gundubah replied, "O my uncle, thou hast treated me with kindness: do not repent of it; but let me depart from you in peace: cancel not the good that thou hast done." But Dárim answered,

1 When the narrator introduces poetry, he generally desires his readers and hearers to bless the Prophet. Frequently he merely says, "Bless ye the Apostle:" and often, "Bless ye him for [the visit to] whose tomb burdens are bound: i.e. "Bless ye him whose tomb is an object of pilgrimage:" for, though the pilgrimage ordained by the Ḳur-án is that to the temple of Mekkeh and Mount 'Arafát, yet the Prophet's tomb is also an object of pious pilgrimage.—I translate the poetry from this tale verse for verse, imitating the system pursued with regard to rhyme in the originals.

"Use no protraction: for thy death is determined on." Then El-Gundubah thus addressed him—

"Be admonish'd, O Dárim! thy steps retrace;
And haste not thus rashly thy fate to embrace.
Hast thou ever seen aught of evil in me?
I have always nam'd thee with honour and praise.
By my hand and lance was Esh-Shamtà destroy'd,
When thou wast her captive, in bonds and disgrace:
I freed thee from bondage: and is it for this
We are now met as enemies, face to face?
God be judge between us: for He will be just,
And will shew who is noble, and who is base."

As soon as he had said these words, the Emeer Dárim charged upon him. They fought for a whole hour; and at last, El-Gundubah pierced the breast of Dárim with his spear; and the point protruded, glittering, from the spine of his back. When Dárim's sons saw that their father was slain, they all attacked El-Gundubah, who received them as the thirsty land receives a drizzling rain: two of them he killed: the rest fled, and acquainted their mother with the events they had just witnessed. With her head uncovered, and her bosom bare, she came weeping to El-Gundubah, and thus exclaimed—

"O Gundubah! thy lance hath wrought havoc sore:
Man and youth have perish'd; and lie in their gore;
And among them, the eldest of all my sons.
They are justly punish'd; but now I implore
That thou pardon the rest: in pity for me
Restrain thy resentment, and slaughter no more.
By my care of thy childhood! and by these breasts
Which have nourish'd thee, noble youth, heretofore!
Have mercy upon us, and leave us in peace:
In spite of thy wrongs, this contention give o'er.
I love thee as though thou wert truly my son;
And thy loss I shall sorrow for, evermore."

El-Gundubah listened to her address; and when she had finished, he thus replied—

"O Mother! by Him whom we all adore!
And the just Muṣṭafà Ṭá-Há![1] I deplore
The actions which I have been made to commit;
Deeds against my will; and not thought of before:
But God, to whose aid I ascribe my success,
Had of old decreed these events to occur.

[1] Ṭá-Há (which is the title of the 20th chapter of the Ḳur-án, and is composed of two letters of the Arabic alphabet,) is considered, and often used, as a name of the Arabian Prophet (of whom Muṣṭafà and Aḥmad, as well as Moḥammad, are also names): so likewise is Yá-Seen, which is the title of the 36th chapter of the Ḳur-án.

For thy sake their pardon I grant; and I would
If their lances had made my lifeblood to pour.
To withdraw myself hence, and sever the ties
Of affection and love, is a trial sore.
While I live I shall constantly wish thee peace,
And joy uninterrupted for evermore."

Having said thus, El-Gundubah took leave of his foster-mother, and departed alone, and went to the fortress of Esh-Shamṭà. The slaves saw him approach, and met him; and, in reply to their inquiries, he informed them of all that had just befallen him. He then asked if any of them were willing to go with him in search of a better territory, where they might intercept the caravans, and subsist by plunder; and they all declaring their readiness to accompany him, he chose from among them as many as he desired, and left the rest in the fortress. He travelled with his slaves until they came to a desolate and dreary tract, without verdure or water; and the slaves, fearing that they should die of thirst, conspired against his life: but El-Gundubah, perceiving their discontent, and guessing their intention, pressed on to a tract abounding with water and pasture; and here they halted to rest. El-Gundubah watched until all of them had fallen asleep; and then despatched them, every one, with his sword. Having done this, he pursued his journey during the night; and in the morning he arrived at a valley with verdant sides, and abundance of pasture, with lofty trees, and rapid streams, and birds whose notes proclaimed the praises of the Lord of Power and Eternity. In the midst of this valley he saw a Bedawee tent, and a lance stuck by it in the ground, and a horse picketted. The Emeer Gundubah fixed his eyes upon this tent; and as he looked at it, there came forth from it a person of elegant appearance, completely armed, who bounded upon the horse, and galloped towards him, without uttering a word, to engage him in combat. "My brother!" exclaimed El-Gundubah, "begin with salutation before the stroke of the sword; for that is a principle in the nature of the noble." But no answer was returned. They fought until their spears were broken, and till their swords were jagged: at length El-Gundubah seized hold of the vest beneath his antagonist's coat of mail, and heaved its wearer from the saddle to the ground. He uplifted his sword; but a voice, so sweet, it would have cured the sick, exclaimed, "Have mercy on thy captive, O hero of the age!" "Art thou a man?" said El-Gundubah, "or a woman?" "I am a virgin damsel," she replied; and, drawing away her "litám,"[1] displayed a face like the moon at the full. When El-Gundubah beheld the beauty of her face, and the elegance of her form, he was bewildered, and overpowered with love. He exclaimed, "O mistress of beauties, and star of the morn, and life of souls! acquaint me with thy secret, and inform me of the truth of thy history." She replied, "O hero of our time! O hero of the age and period! shall I relate to thee my story in narrative prose, or in measured verse?" "He said, "O beauty of thine age, and peerless-one of thy time! I will hear nothing from thee but measured verse." She then thus related to him all that had happened to her.

"O thou noble hero, and generous knight!
  Thou leader of warriours! and foremost in fight!
Hear, now, and attend to the story I tell.
  I'm the virgin daughter, thou hero of might!
Of El-Melik[2] Ḳáboos; and a maid whose fame
  Has been raised, by her arms, to an envied height;
Acknowledg'd a heroine, bold and expert,
  Skill'd alike with the lance and the sword to smite.
Many suitors sought me in marriage, but none
  Could ever induce me his love to requite;
And I swore by my Lord, the Compassionate,
  And the noble Muṣṭafà, that moon-like light,
That to no man on earth I would e'er consent
  In the bonds of marriage myself to unite,
Unless to a hero for prowess renown'd,
  To one who should prove himself hardy in fight;
Who in combat should meet me, and overcome,
  And never betray the least weakness or fright.
My suitors assembled: I fought each in turn;
  And I vanquish'd them all in our people's sight:
Not a horseman among them attain'd his wish;
  For I parried the thrust of each daring knight.
I was justly 'The Slayer of Heroes' nam'd;
  For no match could be found for my weapon bright.
But I fear'd my father might force me, at last,
  To accept, as my husband, some parasite;
And therefore I fled; and, in this lonely place,
  With my troop of horsemen, I chose to alight.
Here we watch for the passing caravans;
  And with plunder we quiet our appetite.
Thou hast made me thy captive, and pardon'd me:
  Grant me one favour more: my wish do not slight:
Receive me in marriage: embrace me at once;
  For I willingly now acknowledge thy right."

---

[1] The "litám" (or "lithám") is a piece of drapery with which a Bedawee often covers the lower part of his face. It frequently prevents his being recognised by another Arab, who might make him a victim of blood-revenge.

[2] It was the custom to entitle the chief of a powerful tribe "El-Melik," or "the King."

"Ḳattâlet-esh-Shug'án," or the Slayer of Heroes (for so was this damsel named, as above related by herself), then said to El-Gundubah, "Come with me and my party to my abode." He went with her; and her people received them with joy, and feasted the Emeer Gundubah three days. On the fourth day, Ḳattâlet-esh-Shug'án assembled the people of her tribe, with El-Gundubah, at her own dwelling; and regaled them with a repast, to which high and low were admitted. After they had eaten, they began to converse; and asked El-Gundubah to acquaint them with his history. He accordingly related to them what had befallen him with the Emeer Dárim; how he had liberated him and his sons from captivity, and how ungratefully he had been treated. There were ten persons sitting with him; and nine of these recounted their deeds in arms. The tenth, who was a slave, was then desired to tell his story; and he related his having served the Emeer Ḥáris, and murdered his widow. El-Gundubah heard with impatience this tale of his mother's murderer; and, as soon as it was finished, drew his sword, and struck off the slave's head, exclaiming, "I have taken my blood-revenge upon this traitor slave!" The persons present all drew their swords, and raised a tremendous shout. Ḳattâlet-esh-Shug'án was not then with them; but she heard the shout, and instantly came to inquire the cause; which they related to her; demanding, at the same time, that El-Gundubah should be given up to them to be put to death. She drew them aside, and told them that he had eaten of her food, and that she would not give him up, even if he had robbed her of her honour; but that she would advise him to take his departure on the morrow, and that, when he should have left her abode, they might do as they pleased. She then went to him, and told him of his danger. He asked what he should do. She answered, "Let us marry forthwith, and depart from these people." And this he gladly consented to do.

They married each other immediately, taking God alone for their witness; and departed at night, and proceeded on their way until the morning, giving thanks to their Lord. For four days they continued their journey, and on the fifth day arrived at a valley abounding with trees and fruits and birds and running streams. They entered it at midnight. Seeing something white among the trees, they approached it; and found it to be a horse, white as camphor. They waited till morning, and then beheld a settlement of Arabs: there were horses, and she and he camels, and tents pitched, and lances stuck in the ground, and pavilions erected; and among them was a great company; and there were maids beating tambourines: they were surrounded with abundance. Through this valley, El-Gundubah and his bride took their way: his love for her increased: they conversed together; and her conversation delighted him. She now, for the first time, ventured to ask him why he had killed the slave, when he was her guest; and he related to her the history of this wretch's crime. After this, they talked of the beauties of the valley which they had entered; and while they were thus amusing themselves, a great dust appeared, and beneath it were seen troops of horsemen galloping along. El-Gundubah immediately concluded that they were of his wife's tribe, and were come in pursuit of him; but he was mistaken: for they divided into four parties, and all attacking, in different quarters at the same time, the tribe settled in the valley, soon made the latter raise piteous cries and lamentations, and rend the air with the shouts of "O 'Ámir! O Kiláb!" When El-Gundubah heard the cries of "O 'Ámir! O Kiláb!" he exclaimed to his wife, "These people are the sons of my uncle! my flesh and my blood!" And he instantly determined to hasten to their assistance. His bride resolved to accompany him; and they both together rushed upon the enemy, slaying every horseman in their way, and piercing the breasts of those on foot, with such fury and such success that the defeated tribe rallied again, repulsed their assailants, and recovered all the booty that had been taken; after which they returned to El-Gundubah, and asked him who he was. He answered, "This is not a time to ask questions; but a time to rest from fight and slaughter." So they took him with them, and retired to rest; and after they had rested and eaten, he related to them his history. Delighted with his words, they all exclaimed, "The truth hath appeared; and doubt is dissipated: justice is rendered to the deserving; and the sword is returned to its scabbard!" They immediately acknowledged him their rightful chief: but, after the death of El-Ḥáris, they had chosen for their chief an Emeer named Gábir, who hated El-Ḥáris, and termed him a robber; and this Emeer now disputed their choice, and challenged El-Gundubah to decide the matter by combat. The challenge was accepted, and the two rivals met and fought; but, though Gábir was a thorough warriour, El-Gundubah slew him. This achievement obtained him the possession of Gábir's mare, an animal coveted throughout the desert: the rest of the property of the vanquished chief he left to be parted among the tribe. There were, however, many partisans of Gábir; and these, when they saw him slain, gathered themselves together against El-Gundubah: but he, with the assistance of his own party, defeated them, and put them to flight. Returning from their pursuit, he sat among his people and kinsfolk; and the Sheykhs of his tribe brought him horses and arms and everything necessary: he received gifts from every quarter: his wife, also, was presented with ornaments; and from that day the Emeer Gundubah was acknowledged by all his tribe as the chief of the Benee-Kiláb.

CHAPTER XXIV.

PERIODICAL PUBLIC FESTIVALS, &c.

Many of the most remarkable customs of the modern Egyptians are witnessed at their periodical public festivals celebrated in Cairo; the more important of which I shall here describe. Most of these festivals and other anniversaries take place at particular periods of the lunar, Mohammadan year.

The first ten days of "Moḥarram" (the first month of the Mohammadan year) are considered as eminently blessed, and are celebrated with rejoicing; but the tenth day is especially honoured. They are vulgarly called the "'ashr;" the derivation of which term will be explained hereafter. The custom of selling, during this period of ten days, what is called "mey'ah mubárakah," to be used, during the ensuing year, as a charm against the evil eye, whenever occasion may require, I have already mentioned in the second of the two chapters devoted to the superstitions of the modern Egyptians. I have also mentioned that it is considered, by the Egyptians, unlucky to make a marriage-contract in Moḥarram.

It is a common custom of the Muslims of Egypt to give what they can afford in alms during the month of Moḥarram; especially in the first ten days, and more especially on the tenth day;[1] and many pretend, though few of them really do so, to give, at this season, the "zekah," or alms required by their law, of which I have spoken in a former chapter: they give what, and to whom, they will. During the ten days above mentioned, and particularly on the tenth, many of the women of Cairo, and even those in respectable circumstances, if they have a young child, carry it through the streets, generally on

[1] This custom seems to have been copied from the Jews, who are accustomed to abound in alms-giving and other good works during the ten days commencing with their New Year's Day and ending with the Day of Atonement, more than in all the rest of the year.—See Dr. M'Caul's "Old Paths," pp. 125, 129.

the shoulder, or employ another female to carry it, for the purpose of soliciting alms from any well-dressed person whom they may chance to meet: sometimes the mother or bearer of the child, and sometimes the child itself, asks for the alms; saying, "My master, the alms of the 'ashr."[1] The word "'ashr" is vulgarly understood as meaning the "ten days;" but I think it signifies the "ten nights;" though I am informed that it is a corruption of "'oshr," a term improperly used for "ruba el-'oshr" (the quarter of the tenth, or the fortieth part), which is the proportion that the Muslim is required, by law, to give in alms of the money which he possesses, and of some other articles of property. The sum generally given to a child in the case above described is a piece of five faḍḍahs;[2] and this, and as many others as can be procured in the same manner, are sometimes spent in sweetmeats, &c., but more usually sewed to the child's cap, and worn thus until the next Moḥarram; when, if the child be not too old, the same custom is repeated for its sake; the pieces of money thus obtained being considered as charms.

The women of Egypt, and particularly of Cairo, entertain some curious superstitions respecting the first ten days of Moḥarram. They believe that "ginn" (or genii) visit some people by night during this period; and say that, on this occasion, a ginnee appears sometimes in the form of a saḳḳà (or water-carrier), and sometimes in that of a mule. In the former case, the mysterious visiter is called "saḳḳà el-'ashr" (or "the water-carrier of the 'ashr"): in the latter, "baghlet el-'ashr" ("the mule of the 'ashr"). When the ginnee, they say, comes in the form of a saḳḳà, he knocks at the chamber-door of a person sleeping, who asks, "Who is there?" The ginnee answers, "I, the saḳḳà: where shall I empty [the skin]?" The person within, as saḳḳàs do not come at night, knows who his visiter is, and says, "Empty into the water-jar;" and, going out afterwards, finds the jar full of gold.—The ginnee in the form of a mule is described in a more remarkable manner. He bears a pair of saddle-bags filled with gold; a dead man's head is placed upon his back; and round his neck is hung a string of little round bells, which he shakes at the door of the chamber of the person whom he comes to enrich. This person comes out, takes off the dead man's head, empties the saddle-bags of their valuable contents, then fills them with straw or bran or anything else; replaces them and the head,

---

1 "Yá seedee, zekah el-'ashr."

2 Equivalent to about a farthing and one-fifth.

and says to the mule, "Go, O blessed!"—Such are the modes in which the good genii pay their zekah. During the first ten days of Moḥarram, many an ignorant woman ejaculates this petition: "O my Lord, send me the water-carrier of the 'ashr!" or, "Send me the mule of the 'ashr!" The men, in general, laugh at these superstitions.

Some of the people of Cairo say that a party of genii, in the forms and garbs of ordinary mortals, used to hold a midnight "sooḳ" (or market) during the first ten days of Moḥarram, in a street called Eṣ-Ṣaleebeh, in the southern part of the metropolis, before an ancient sarcophagus, which was called "el-Ḥóḍ el-Marṣood" (or "the Enchanted Trough"). This sarcophagus was in a recess under a flight of steps leading up to the door of a mosque, adjacent to the old palace called Ḳal'at el-Kebsh: it was removed by the French during their occupation of Egypt, and is now in the British Museum. Since its removal, the sooḳ of the genii, it is said, has been discontinued. Very few persons, I am told, were aware of this custom of the genii. Whoever happened to pass through the street where they were assembled, and bought anything of them, whether dates or other fruit, cakes, bread, &c., immediately after found his purchase converted into gold.

The tenth day of Moḥarram is called "Yóm 'Áshoorà." It is held sacred on many accounts; because it is believed to be the day on which the first meeting of Adam and Eve took place after they were cast out of Paradise; and that on which Noah went out from the ark: also, because several other great events are said to have happened on this day; and because the ancient Arabs, before the time of the Prophet, observed it by fasting. But what, in the opinion of most modern Muslims, and especially the Persians, confers the greatest sanctity on the day of 'Áshoorà, is the fact of its being that on which El-Ḥoseyn, the Prophet's grandson, was slain, a martyr, at the battle of the plain of Karbalà. Many Muslims fast on this day, and some also on the day preceding.

As I am now writing on the day of 'Áshoorà, I shall mention the customs peculiar to it which I have witnessed on the present occasion. —I had to provide myself with a number of five-faḍḍah-pieces before I went out this day, for the alms of the 'ashr, already mentioned. In the streets of the town I saw many young children, from about three to six or seven years of age, chiefly girls, walking about alone, or two or three together, or carried by women, and begging these alms.—In the course of the morning, a small group of blind faḳeers, one of whom bore a half-furled red flag, with the names of El-Ḥoseyn and other worthies worked upon it in white, stopped in the street before my door, and chanted a petition for an alms. One of them began, "O thou who hast alms to bestow on the blessed day of 'Áshoorà!" The others then continued, in chorus, "A couple of grains of wheat! A couple of grains of rice! O Ḥasan! O Ḥoseyn!" The same words were repeated by them several times. As soon as they had received a small piece of money, they passed on; and then performed the same chant before other houses; but only where appearances led them to expect a reward. Numerous groups of faḳeers go about the town, in different quarters, during this day, soliciting alms in the same manner.

On my paying a visit to a friend, a little before noon, a dish, which it is the custom of the people of Cairo to prepare on the day of 'Áshoorà, was set before me. It is called "ḥoboob," and is prepared with wheat, steeped in water for two or three days, then freed from the husks, boiled, and sweetened over the fire with honey or treacle; or it is composed of rice instead of wheat: generally, nuts, almonds, raisins, &c., are added to it. In most houses this dish is prepared, or sweetmeats of various kinds are procured or made, in accordance with one of the traditions of the Prophet; which is—"Whoso giveth plenty to his household on the day of 'Áshoorà, God will bestow plenty upon him throughout the remainder of the year."

After the call to noon-prayers, I went to the mosque of the Ḥasaneyn, which, being the reputed burial-place of the head of the martyr El-Ḥoseyn, is the scene of the most remarkable of the ceremonies that, in Cairo, distinguish the day of 'Áshoorà. The avenues to this mosque, near the Ḳáḍee's court, were thronged with passengers; and in them I saw several groups of dancing-girls (Gháżeeyehs); some, dancing; and others, sitting in a ring in the public thoroughfare, eating their dinner, and (with the exclamation of "bi-smi-llah!") inviting each well-dressed man who passed by to eat with them. One of them struggled hard with me to prevent my passing without giving them a present. The sight of these unveiled girls, some of them very handsome, and with their dress alluringly disposed to display to advantage their fine forms, was but ill calculated to prepare men who passed by them for witnessing religious ceremonies: but so it is, that, on the occasions of all the great religious festivals in Cairo, and at many other towns in Egypt, these female warrers against modesty (not always seductive, I must confess,) are sure to be seen. On my way to the mosque, I had occasion to rid myself of some of the small coins which I had provided, to give them to children. My next occasion for disbursing was on arriving before the mosque, when several water-carriers, of the class who supply passengers in the streets, surrounded me: I gave two of them twenty faḍḍahs, for which each of them was to distribute the contents of the earthen vessel which he bore on his back to poor passengers, for the sake of "our lord El-Ḥoseyn." This custom I have mentioned in a former chapter.[1]

On entering the mosque, I was much surprised at the scene which presented itself in the great hall, or portico. This, which is the principal part of the mosque, was crowded with visiters, mostly women, of the middle and lower orders, with many children; and there was a confusion of noises like what may be heard in a large school-room where several hundred boys are engaged in play: there were children bawling and crying; men and women calling to each other; and, amid all this bustle, mothers and children were importuning every man of respectable appearance for the alms of the 'ashr. Seldom have I witnessed a scene more unlike that which the interior of a mosque generally presents; and in this instance I was the more surprised, as the Gámè' el-Ḥasaneyn is the most sacred of all the mosques in Cairo. The mats which are usually spread upon the pavement had been removed; some pieces of old matting were put in their stead, leaving many parts of the floor uncovered; and these, and every part, were covered with dust and dirt brought in by the feet of many shoeless persons: for on this occasion, as it is impossible to perform the ordinary prayers in the mosque, people enter without having performed the usual ablution, and without repairing first to the tank to do this; though every person takes off his, or her, shoes, as at other times, on entering the mosque; many leaving them, as I did mine, with a door-keeper. Several parts of the floor were wetted (by children too young to be conscious of the sanctity of the place); and though I avoided these parts, I had not been many minutes in the mosque before my feet were almost black, with the dirt upon which I had trodden, and with that from other persons' feet which had trodden upon mine. The heat, too, was very oppressive; like that of a vapour-bath, but more heavy; though there is a very large

---

[1] On Industry.

square aperture in the roof, with a malḳaf[1] of equal width over it, to introduce the northern breezes. The pulpit-stairs, and the gallery of the muballigheen, were crowded with women; and in the assemblage below, the women were far more numerous than the men. Why this should be the case, I know not, unless it be because the women are more superstitious, and have a greater respect for the day of 'Áshoorà, and a greater desire to honour El-Ḥoseyn by visiting his shrine on this day.

It is commonly said, by the people of Cairo, that no man goes to the mosque of the Ḥasaneyn on the day of 'Áshoorà but for the sake of the women; that is, to be jostled among them; and this jostling he may indeed enjoy to the utmost of his desire, as I experienced in pressing forward to witness the principal ceremonies which contribute with the sanctity of the day to attract such swarms of people. By the back-wall, to the right of the pulpit, were seated, in two rows, face to face, about fifty darweeshes, of various orders. They had not yet begun their performances, or "zikrs," in concert; but one old darweesh, standing between the two rows, was performing a zikr alone; repeating the name of God (Alláh), and bowing his head each time that he uttered the word, alternately to the right and left. In pushing forward to see them, I found myself in a situation rather odd in a country where it is deemed improper for a man even to touch a woman who is not his wife or slave or a near relation. I was so compressed in the midst of four women, that, for some minutes, I could not move in any direction; and was pressed so hard against one young woman, face to face, that, but for her veil, our cheeks had been almost in contact: from her panting, it seemed that the situation was not quite easy to her; though a smile, expressed at the same time by her large black eyes, shewed that it was amusing: she could not, however, bear it long; for she soon cried out, "My eye![2] do not squeeze me so violently." Another woman called out to me "O Efendee! by thy head! push on to the front, and make way for me to follow thee." With considerable difficulty, I attained the desired place; but in getting thither I had almost lost my sword, and the hanging sleeves of my jacket: some person's dress had caught the guard of the sword, and had nearly drawn the blade from the scabbard before I could get hold of the hilt. Like all around me, I was in a profuse perspiration.

---

[1] The "malḳaf" has been described in the Introduction to this work, page 19.

[2] This is a common expression of affection, meaning, "Thou who art as dear to me as my eye."

The darweeshes I found to be of different nations, as well as of different orders. Some of them wore the ordinary turban and dress of Egypt; others wore the Turkish ḳá-ooḳ, or padded cap; and others, again, wore high caps, or ṭarṭoors, mostly of the sugar-loaf shape. One of them had a white cap of the form last mentioned, upon which were worked, in black letters, invocations to the first four Khaleefehs, to El-Ḥasan and El-Ḥoseyn, and to other eminent saints, founders of different orders of darweeshes.[1] Most of the darweeshes were Egyptians; but there were among them many Turks and Persians. I had not waited many minutes before they began their exercises. Several of them first drove back the surrounding crowd with sticks; but as no stick was raised at me, I did not retire so far as I ought to have done; and before I was aware of what the darweeshes were about to do, forty of them, with extended arms and joined hands, had formed a large ring, in which I found myself enclosed. For a moment I felt half inclined to remain where I was, and join in the zikr; bow, and repeat the name of God; but another moment's reflection on the absurdity of the performance, and the risk of my being discovered to be no darweesh, decided me otherwise; so, parting the hands of two of the darweeshes, I passed outside the ring. The darweeshes who formed the large ring (which enclosed four of the marble columns of the portico) now commenced their zikr, exclaiming, over and over again, "Alláh!" and, at each exclamation, bowing the head and body, and taking a step to the right, so that the whole ring moved rapidly round. As soon as they commenced this exercise, another darweesh, a Turk, of the order of Mowlawees, in the middle of the circle, began to whirl, using both his feet to effect the motion, and extending his arms: the motion increased in velocity until his dress spread out like an umbrella. He continued whirling thus for about ten minutes; after which he bowed to his superior, who stood within the great ring; and then, without shewing any signs of fatigue or giddiness, joined the darweeshes in the great ring, who had now begun to ejaculate the name of God with greater vehemence, and to jump to the right, instead of stepping. After the whirling, six other darweeshes, within the great ring, formed another ring, but a very small one; each placing his arms upon the shoulders of those next him; and thus disposed, they performed a revolution similar to that

[1] The words were, "Yá Aboo-Bekr, Yá 'Omar, Yá 'Osmán, Yá 'Alee, Yá Ḥasan, Yá Ḥoseyn, Yá seyyid Aḥmad Rifá'ah, Yá seyyid 'Abd-El-Ḳádir El-Geelánee, Yá seyyid Aḥmad El-Bedawee, Yá seyyid Ibráheem Ed-Dasooḳee."

of the larger ring, except in being much more rapid; repeating, also, the same exclamation of "Alláh!" but with a rapidity proportionably greater. This motion they maintained for about the same length of time that the whirling of the single darweesh before had occupied; after which, the whole party sat down to rest.—They rose again after the lapse of about a quarter of an hour; and performed the same exercise a second time.—I saw nothing more in the great portico that was worthy of remark, except two faḳeers (who, a bystander told me, were "megázeeb," or idiots), dancing, and repeating the name of God, and each beating a tambourine.

Whirling Darweesh.

I was desirous of visiting the shrine of El-Ḥoseyn on this anniversary of his death, and of seeing if any particular ceremonies were performed there on this occasion. With difficulty I pushed through the crowd in the great portico to the door of the saloon of the tomb; but there I found comparatively few persons collected. On my entering, one of the servants of the mosque conducted me to an unoccupied corner of the bronze screen which surrounds the monument over the place where the martyr's head is said to be buried, that I might there recite the Fát'ḥah: this duty performed, he dictated to me the following prayer; pausing after every two or three words, for me to repeat them, which I affected to do; and another person, who stood on my left, saying "Ámeen" (or Amen), at the close of each pause. "O God, accept my visit, and perform my want, and cause me to attain my wish; for I come with desire and intent, and urge Thee by the seyyideh Zeyneb, and the Imám Esh-Sháfe'ee, and the Sulṭán Aboo-So'ood."[1] After this followed similar words in Turkish, which were added in the supposition that I was a Turk, and perhaps did not understand the former words in Arabic. This short supplication has been often dictated to me at the tombs of saints in Cairo, on festival days. On the occasion above described, before I proceeded to make the usual circuit round the screen which encloses the monument, I gave to the person who dictated the prayer a small piece of money, and he, in return, presented me with four little balls of bread, each about the size of a hazel-nut. This was consecrated bread, made of very fine flour at the tomb of the seyyid Aḥmad El-Bedawee, and brought thither, as it is to several saints' tombs in Cairo on occasions of general visiting, to be given to the more respectable of the visiters. It is called "'Eysh es-seyyid El-Bedawee." Many persons in Egypt keep a little piece of it (that is, one of the little balls into which it is formed,) constantly in the pocket, as a charm; others eat it, as a valuable remedy against any disorder, or as a preventive of disease.

Generally, towards the end of "Ṣafar" (the second month), the caravan of Egyptian pilgrims, returning from Mekkeh, arrives at Cairo: hence, this month is vulgarly called "Nezlet el-Ḥágg" (the Alighting of the Pilgrims). Many pilgrims, coming by the Red Sea, arrive before the caravan. A caravan of merchant-pilgrims arrives later than the main body of pilgrims.

An officer, called "Sháweesh el-Ḥágg," arrives about four or five days before the caravan, having pushed on, with two Arabs, mounted on fleet dromedaries, to announce the approach of the Ḥágg,[2] and the expected day of their arrival at the metropolis, and to bring letters from pilgrims to their friends. He and his two companions exclaim, as they pass along, to the passengers in the way, "Blessing on the Prophet!" or, "Bless the Prophet!" And every Muslim who hears the exclamation responds, "O God, bless him!"[3]—They proceed directly to the Citadel, to convey the news to the Báshà or his representative. The Sháweesh divides his letters into packets, with the exception of those which are to great or wealthy people, and sells

[1] Aboo-So'ood was a very famous saint; and, being esteemed the most holy person of his day, received the appellation of "Sulṭán," which has been conferred upon several other very eminent welees, and, when thus applied, signifies "King of Saints." The tomb of Aboo-So'ood is among the mounds of rubbish on the south of Cairo.

[2] The term "ḥágg" is applied both collectively and individually (to the whole caravan, or body of pilgrims, and to a single pilgrim).

[3] The Arabic words here translated are given in two notes in chap. xiii., near the beginning.

them, at so many dollars a packet, to a number of persons who deliver them, and receive presents from those to whom they are addressed, but sometimes lose by their bargains. The Sháweesh himself delivers those to the great and rich, and obtains from them handsome presents of money, or a shawl, &c.

Some persons go out two or three days' journey, to meet their friends returning from pilgrimage, taking with them fresh provisions, fruits, &c., and clothes, for the wearied pilgrims. The poorer classes seldom go further than the Birket el-Ḥágg (or Lake of the Pilgrims, about eleven miles from the metropolis), the place where the caravan passes the last night but one before its entry into the metropolis; or such persons merely go to the last halting-place. These usually take with them some little luxury in the way of food, and an ass, as an agreeable substitute to the pilgrim for his jaded and uneasy camel;[1] together with some clean, if not new, clothes; and many go out with musicians to pay honour to their friends. It is very affecting to see, at the approach of the caravan, the numerous parties who go out with drums and pipes to welcome and escort to the city their friends arrived from the holy places, and how many, who went forth in hope, return with lamentation instead of music and rejoicing; for the arduous journey through the desert is fatal to a great number of those pilgrims who cannot afford themselves necessary conveniences. Many of the women who go forth to meet their husbands or sons receive the melancholy tidings of their having fallen victims to privation and fatigue. The piercing shrieks with which they rend the air as they retrace their steps to the city are often heard predominant over the noise of the drum, and the shrill notes of the hautboy, which proclaim the joy of others.—The pilgrims, on their return, are often accosted, by passengers, with the petition, "Pray for pardon for me;" and utter this short ejaculation, "God pardon thee!" or, "O God! pardon him!" This custom owes its origin to a saying of the Prophet—"God pardoneth the pilgrim, and him for whom the pilgrim imploreth pardon."

I write the following account of the Nezlet el-Ḥágg just after

---

[1] Many persons who have not applied themselves to the study of natural history are ignorant of the remarkable fact that the camel has in itself a provision against hunger, besides its well-known supply against thirst. When deprived of its usual food for several successive days, it feeds upon the fat of its own hump, which, in these circumstances, gradually disappears before the limbs are perceptibly reduced. This explanation of the use of an excrescence which would otherwise seem a mere inconvenient incumbrance shews how wonderfully the camel is adapted to the peculiar circumstances in which Providence has placed it, and perhaps may be applied with equal propriety to the hump of the bull and cow, and some other animals, in hot and arid climates.

witnessing it, in the year of the Flight 1250 (A.D. 1834).—The caravan arrived at its last halting-place, the Ḥaṣweh, a pebbly tract of the desert, near the northern suburb of Cairo, last night, on the eve of the 4th of Rabeeạ el-Owwal. A few pilgrims left the caravan after sunset, and entered the metropolis. The caravan entered this morning, the fourth of the month. I was outside the walls soon after sunrise, before it drew near; but I met two or three impatient pilgrims, riding upon asses, and preceded by musicians or by flag-bearers, and followed by women singing; and I also met several groups of women who had already been out to make inquiries respecting relations whom they expected, and were returning with shrieks and sobs. Their lamentation seemed more natural, and more deeply felt, than that which is made at funerals. This year, in addition to a great many deaths, there were to be lamented a thousand men who had been seized for the army; so that, perhaps, there was rather more wailing than is usual. About two hours and a half after sunrise, the caravan began to draw near to the gates of the metropolis, parted in three lines; one line towards the gate called Báb en-Naṣr; another directly towards the Báb el-Futooḥ; and the third, branching off from the second, to the Báb el-'Adawee. The caravan this year was more numerous than usual (though many pilgrims went by sea); and, in consequence of the seizure of so many men for the army, it comprised an uncommon proportion of women. Each of the three lines into which it divided to enter the metropolis, as above-mentioned, consisted, for the most part, of an uninterrupted train of camels, proceeding one by one; but sometimes there were two abreast; and in a few places the train was broken for a short space. Many of the pilgrims had quitted their camels to take the more easy conveyance of asses, and rode beside their camels; many of them attended by musicians, and some by flag-bearers.

The most common kind of camel-litter used by the pilgrims is called a "musaṭṭaḥ," or "ḥeml musaṭṭaḥ." It resembles a small, square tent, and is chiefly composed of two long chests, each of which has a high back: these are placed on the camel in the same manner as a pair of panniers, one on each side; and the high backs, which are placed outwards, together with a small pole resting on the camel's pack-saddle, support the covering which forms what may be called the tent. This conveyance accommodates two persons. It is generally open at the front, and may also be opened at the back. Though it appears comfortable, the motion is uneasy; especially when it is placed upon a camel that has been accustomed to carry heavy burdens, and consequently has a swinging walk; but camels of easy pace are generally chosen for bearing the musaṭṭaḥ and other kinds of litters. There is one kind of litter called a "shibreeyeh," composed of a small, square platform, with an arched covering. This accommodates but one person, and is placed on the back of the camel: two saḥḥárahs (or square chests), one on each side of the camel, generally form a secure foundation for the shibreeyeh. The most comfortable kind of litter is that called a "takht'rawán," which is most commonly borne by two camels, one before, and the other behind: the head of the latter is painfully bent down under the vehicle. This litter is sometimes borne by four mules, in which case its motion is more easy. Two light persons may travel in it. In general, it has a small projecting meshrebeeyeh of wooden lattice-work at the front and back, in which one or more of the porous earthen water-bottles so much used in Egypt may be placed.

I went on to the place where the caravan had passed the last night. During my ride from the suburb to this spot, which occupied a little more than half an hour (proceeding at a slow pace), about half the caravan passed me; and in half an hour more, almost the whole had left the place of encampment.[1] I was much interested at seeing the meetings of wives, brothers, sisters, and children, with the pilgrims: but I was disgusted with one pilgrim: he was dressed in ragged clothes, and sitting on a little bit of old carpet, when his wife, or perhaps his sister, came out to him, perspiring under the weight of a large bundle of clothes, and fervently kissed him, right and left: he did not rise to meet her; and only made a few cold inquiries. —The Emeer el-Ḥágg (or chief of the caravan) and his officers, soldiers, &c., were encamped apart from the rest of the caravan. By his tent a tall spear was stuck in the ground; and by its side also stood the "Maḥmal," or "Maḥmil"[2] (of which I shall presently give a sketch and description); with its travelling cover, of canvass, ornamented with a few inscriptions.

Many of the pilgrims bring with them, as presents, from "the holy territory," water of the sacred well of "Zemzem" (in China bottles, or tin or copper flasks), pieces of the "kisweh" (or covering) of the Kaạbeh (which is renewed at the season of the pilgrimage), dust

[1] Had I remained stationary, somewhat more than two hours would have elapsed before the whole caravan had passed me.

[2] This latter is the correct appellation, but it is commonly called "Maḥmal;" and I shall follow, on future occasions, the usual pronunciation. "Miḥmal" is also correct, but not usual.

from the Prophet's tomb (made into hard cakes), "libán" (or frankincense), "leef" (or fibres of the palm-tree, used in washing, as we employ a sponge), combs of aloes-wood, "sebḥahs" (or rosaries) of the same or other materials, "miswáks" (or sticks for cleaning the teeth, which are generally dipped in Zemzem-water, to render them more acceptable), "koḥl" (or black powder for the eyes), shawls, &c., of the manufacture of the Ḥegáz,[1] and various things from India.

It is a common custom to ornament the entrance of a pilgrim's house, a day, or two or three days, before his arrival; painting the door, and colouring the alternate courses of stone on each side and above it with red ochre, and whitewash; or, if it be of brick, ornamenting it in a similar manner, with broad horizontal stripes of red and white: often, also, trees, camels, &c., are painted in a very rude manner, in green, black, red, and other colours. The pilgrim sometimes writes to order this to be done. On the evening after his arrival, he entertains his friends with a feast, which is called "the feast of the Nezleh." Numerous guests come to welcome him, and to say, "Pray for pardon for me." He generally remains at home a week after his return; and on the seventh day gives to his friends another entertainment, which is called "the feast of the Subooạ." This continues during the day and ensuing night; and a khatmeh, or a zikr, is usually performed in the evening.

On the morning after that on which the main body of the pilgrims of the great caravan enter the metropolis, another spectacle is witnessed: this is the return of the Maḥmal, which is borne in procession from the Ḥaṣweh, through the metropolis, to the Citadel. This procession is not always arranged exactly in the same order: I shall describe it as I have this day witnessed it, on the morning after the return of the pilgrims of which I have just given an account.

First, I must describe the Maḥmal itself. It is a square skeleton-frame of wood, with a pyramidal top; and has a covering of black brocade, richly worked with inscriptions and ornamental embroidery in gold, in some parts upon a ground of green or red silk, and bordered with a fringe of silk, with tassels surmounted by silver balls. Its covering is not always made after the same pattern, with regard to the decorations; but in every cover that I have seen, I have remarked, on the upper part of the front, a view of the Temple of Mekkeh, worked in gold; and, over it, the Sulṭán's cipher. It con-

[1] Or, as pronounced in Arabia, Ḥejáz.

The Maḥmal.

tains nothing; but has two muṣ-ḥafs (or copies of the Ḳur-án), one on a small scroll, and the other in the usual form of a book, also small, each enclosed in a case of gilt silver, attached externally at the top. The sketch which I insert will explain this description. The five balls with crescents, which ornament the Maḥmal, are of gilt silver. The Maḥmal is borne by a fine tall camel, which is generally indulged with exemption from every kind of labour during the remainder of its life.

It is related that the Sulṭán Eẓ-Ẓáhir Beybars, King of Egypt, was the first who sent a Maḥmal with the caravan of pilgrims to Mekkeh, in the year of the Flight 670 (A.D. 1272), or 675; but this custom, it is generally said, had its origin a few years before his accession to the throne. Sheger-ed-Durr (commonly called Shegeret-ed-Durr), a beautiful Turkish female slave, who became the favourite wife of the Sulṭán Eṣ-Ṣáleḥ Negm-ed-Deen, and on the death of his son (with whom terminated the dynasty of the house of Eiyoob) caused herself to be acknowledged as Queen of Egypt, performed the pilgrimage in a magnificent "hódag" (or covered litter), borne by a camel; and for several successive years her empty hódag was sent with the caravan merely for the sake of state. Hence, succeeding princes of Egypt sent, with each year's caravan of pilgrims, a kind of hódag (which received the name of "Maḥmal," or "Maḥmil"), as an emblem of royalty; and the kings of other countries followed their example.[1] The Wahhábees prohibited the Maḥmal as an object of vain pomp: it afforded them one reason for intercepting the caravan.

The procession of the return of the Maḥmal, in the year above mentioned, entered the city, by the Báb en-Naṣr, about an hour after sunrise. It was headed by a large body of Nizám (or regular) infantry. Next came the Maḥmal, which was followed, as usual, by a singular character: this was a long-haired, brawny, swarthy fellow, called "Sheykh-el-Gemel" (or Sheykh of the Camel), almost entirely naked, having only a pair of old trowsers: he was mounted on a camel, and was incessantly rolling his head. For many successive years this sheykh has followed the Maḥmal, and accompanied the caravan to and from Mekkeh; and all assert that he rolls his head during the whole of the journey. He is supplied by the government

[1] Almost all travellers have given erroneous accounts of the Maḥmal; some asserting that its covering is that which is destined to be placed over the tomb of the Prophet: others, that it contains the covering which is to be suspended round the Kaạbeh. Burckhardt, with his general accuracy, describes it as a mere emblem of royalty.

with two camels and his travelling provisions. A few years ago there used also to follow the Maḥmal, to and from Mekkeh, an old woman, with her head uncovered, and only wearing a shirt. She was called "Umm-el-Ḳuṭaṭ" (or the Mother of the Cats), having always five or six cats sitting about her on her camel.—Next to the sheykh of the camel, in the procession which I have begun to describe, followed a group of Turkish horsemen; and then, about twenty camels, with stuffed and ornamented saddles, covered with cloth, mostly red and green. Each saddle was decorated with a number of small flags, slanting forward from the fore part, and a small plume of ostrich-feathers upon the top of a stick fixed upright upon the same part; and some had a large bell hung on each side: the ornaments on the covering were chiefly formed of the small shells called cowries. I think I perceived that these camels were slightly tinged with the red dye of the ḥennà; as they are on other similar occasions. They were followed by a very numerous body of Bedawee horsemen; and with these the procession was closed.

Having been misinformed as to the time of the entry of the Maḥmal, on my arriving at the principal street of the city I found myself in the midst of the procession; but the Maḥmal had passed. Mounting a donkey that I had hired, I endeavoured to overtake it; but it was very difficult to make any progress: so, without further loss of time, I took advantage of some by-streets, and again joined the procession: I found, however, that I had made very little advancement. I therefore dismounted; and, after walking and running, and dodging between the legs of the Bedawees' horses, for about half an hour, at length caught a glimpse of the Maḥmal, and by a great effort, and much squeezing, overtook it soon after, about a quarter of an hour before it entered the great open place called the Rumeyleh, before the Citadel. After touching it three times, and kissing my hand, I caught hold of the fringe, and walked by its side. The guardian of the sacred object, who walked behind it, looked very hard at me, and induced me to utter a pious ejaculation, which perhaps prevented his displacing me; or possibly my dress influenced him; for he only allowed other persons to approach and touch it one by one, and then drove them back. I continued to walk by its side, holding the fringe, nearly to the entrance of the Rumeyleh. On my telling a Muslim friend, to-day, that I had done this, he expressed great astonishment, and said that he had never heard of any one having done so before, and that the Prophet had certainly taken a love for me or I could not have been allowed: he added that I had derived an inestimable blessing, and that it would be prudent in me not to tell any others of my Muslim friends of this fact, as it would make them envy me so great a privilege, and perhaps displease them. I cannot learn why the Maḥmal is esteemed so sacred. Many persons shewed an enthusiastic eagerness to touch it; and I heard a soldier exclaim, as it passed him, "O my Lord, Thou hast denied my performing the pilgrimage!" The streets through which it passed were densely crowded; the shops were closed, and the maṣṭabahs occupied by spectators. It arrived at the Rumeyleh about an hour and a half after it had entered the metropolis: it crossed this large place to the entrance of the long open space called Ḳarà Meydán; next proceeded along the latter place, while about twelve of the guns of the Citadel fired a salute; then returned to the Rumeyleh, and proceeded through it to the northern gate of the Citadel, called Báb el-Wezeer.

A curious custom is allowed to be practised on the occasions of the processions of the Maḥmal and Kisweh; which latter, and a more pompous procession of the Maḥmal, on its departure for Mekkeh, will be hereafter described. Numbers of boys go about the streets of the metropolis in companies; each boy armed with a short piece of the thick end of a palm-stick, called a "maḳra'ah,"[1] in which are made two or three splits, extending from the larger end to about half the length; and any Christian or Jew whom they meet they accost with the demand of "Hát el-'ádeh," or "Give the customary present." If he refuse the gift of five or ten faḍḍahs, they fall to beating him with their maḳra'ahs. Last year a Frank was beaten by some boys, in accordance with this custom, and sought refuge in a large wekáleh; but some of the boys entered after him, and repeated the beating. He complained to the Báshà, who caused a severe bastinading to be administered to the Sheykh of the wekáleh for not having protected him.

In the beginning of the month of "Rabeeạ el-Owwal" (the third month) preparations are commenced for celebrating the festival of the Birth of the Prophet, which is called "Moolid[2] en-Nebee." The principal scene of this festival is the south-west quarter of the large open space called Birket el-Ezbekeeyeh, almost the whole of which, during the season of the inundation, becomes a lake: this is the case

---

[1] Pronounced "maḳra''ah;" but correctly written "miḳra'ah."

[2] I have before mentioned that this word is more properly pronounced "Mólid."

for several years together at the time of the festival of the Prophet, which is then celebrated on the margin of the lake; but at present, the dry bed of the lake is the chief scene of the festival.[1] In the quarter above mentioned, several large tents (called "ṣeewáns") are pitched; mostly for darweeshes, who, every night, while the festival lasts, assemble in them, to perform zikrs. Among these is erected a mast ("ṣáree"), firmly secured by ropes, and with a dozen or more lamps hung to it. Around it, numerous darweeshes, generally about fifty or sixty, form a ring, and repeat zikrs. Near the same spot is erected what is termed a "ḳáïm"; which consists of four masts erected in a line, a few yards apart, with numerous ropes stretched from one to the other and to the ground: upon these ropes are hung many lamps; sometimes in the form of flowers, lions, &c.; sometimes, of words, such as the names of God and Moḥammad, the profession of the faith, &c.; and sometimes arranged in a merely fanciful, ornamental manner. The preparations for the festival are generally completed on the second day of the month; and on the following day the rejoicings and ceremonies begin: these continue, day and night, until the twelfth night of the month; that is, according to the Mohammadan mode of reckoning, the night preceding the twelfth day of the month; which night is that of the Moolid, properly speaking.[2] During this period of nine days and nights, numbers of the inhabitants of the metropolis flock to the Ezbekeeyeh.—I write these notes during the Moolid, and shall describe the festival of this year (the year of the Flight 1250, A.D. 1834), mentioning some particulars in which it differs from those of former years.

During the day-time, the people assembled at the principal scene of the festival are amused by Shá'ers (or reciters of the romance of Aboo-Zeyd), conjurers, buffoons, &c. The Ghawázee have lately been compelled to vow repentance, and to relinquish their profession of dancing, &c.: consequently, there are now none of them at the festival. These girls used to be among the most attractive of all the performers. In some parts of the neighbouring streets, a few swings and whirligigs are erected, and numerous stalls for the sale of sweetmeats, &c. Sometimes, rope-dancers, who are gipsies, perform at this

---

[1] This lake has been filled up, and planted as a garden, since the account here given was written; and the tract on the western side of the space that was occupied by the lake is now the chief scene of the festival.

[2] The twelfth day of Rabeeạ el-Owwal is also the anniversary of the *death* of Moḥammad. It is remarkable that his birth and death are both related to have happened on the same day of the same month, and on the same day of the week, namely, Monday.

festival; but there are none this year. At night, the streets above mentioned are lighted with many lamps, which are mostly hung in lanterns of wood:[1] numbers of shops and stalls, stocked with eatables, chiefly sweetmeats, are open during almost the whole of the night; and so too are the coffee-shops; at some of which, as well as in other places, Shá'ers or Moḥaddits amuse the persons who choose to stop and listen to their recitations. Every night, an hour or more after midnight, processions of darweeshes pass through this quarter: instead of bearing flags, as they do in the day, they carry long staves, with a number of lamps attached to them at the upper part, and called "menwars." The procession of a company of darweeshes, whether by day, with flags, or by night, with menwars, is called the procession of the "ishárah" of the sect; that is, of the "banner;" or, rather, the term "ishárah" is applied to the procession itself. These darweeshes are mostly persons of the lower orders, and have no distinguishing dress: the greater number wear an ordinary turban, and some of them merely a ṭarboosh, or a padded or felt cap; and most of them wear the common blue linen or cotton, or brown woollen, shirt, the dress which they wear on other occasions at their daily work or at their shops.

On the last two nights, the festival is more numerously attended than on the preceding nights, and the attractions are greater. I shall describe what I have just witnessed on the former of these nights.

This being the eleventh night of the lunar month, the moon was high, and enlivened the scenes of festivity. I passed on to a street called Sooḳ El-Bekree, on the south of the Birket el-Ezbekeeyeh, to witness what I was informed would be the best of the zikrs that were to be performed. The streets through which I passed were crowded; and persons were here allowed, on this occasion, to go about without lanterns. As is usually the case at night, there were scarcely any women among the passengers. At the scene of the zikr in the Sooḳ El-Bekree, which was more crowded than any other place, was suspended a very large "negefeh" (a chandelier, or rather a number of chandeliers, chiefly of glass, one below another, placed in such a manner that they all appeared but one), containing about two or three hundred ḳandeels (or small glass lamps).[2] Around this were many lanterns of wood, each having several ḳandeels hanging through the bottom. These lights were not hung merely in honour of the Prophet:

[1] Like that represented in Chapter VI.

[2] Represented in Chapter V., near the end.

they were near a "záwiyeh" (or small mosque) in which is buried the sheykh Darweesh[1] El-'Ashmáwee; and this night was his Moolid. A zikr is performed here every Friday-night (or what *we* call Thursday-night); but not with so much display as on the present occasion. I observed many Christian black turbans here; and having seen scarcely any elsewhere this night, and heard the frequent cry of "A grain of salt in the eye of him who doth not bless the Prophet!" ejaculated by the sellers of sweetmeats, &c., which seemed to shew that Christians and Jews were at least in danger of being insulted, at a time when the zeal of the Muslims was unusually excited, I asked the reason why so many Copts should be congregated at the scene of this zikr: I was answered, that a Copt, who had become a Muslim, voluntarily paid all the expenses of this Moolid of the sheykh Darweesh. This sheykh was very much revered: he was disordered in mind, or imitated the acts of a madman; often taking bread and other eatables, and stamping upon them, or throwing them into dirt; and doing many other things directly forbidden by his religion: yet was he esteemed an eminent saint; for such acts, as I have remarked on a former occasion, are considered the results of the soul's being absorbed in devotion. He died about eight years ago.

The "zikkeers" (or the performers of the zikr), who were about thirty in number, sat cross-legged, upon matting extended close to the houses on one side of the street, in the form of an oblong ring. Within this ring, along the middle of the matting, were placed three very large wax-candles, each about four feet high, and stuck in a low candlestick. Most of the zikkeers were Aḥmedee darweeshes, persons of the lower orders, and meanly dressed: many of them wore green turbans. At one end of the ring were four "munshids" (or singers of poetry), and with them was a player on the kind of flute called "náy." I procured a small seat of palm-sticks from a coffee-shop close by, and, by means of a little pushing, and the assistance of my servant, obtained a place with the munshids, and sat there to hear a complete act, or "meglis," of the zikr; which I shall describe as completely as I can, to convey a notion of the kind of zikr most common and most approved in Cairo. It commenced at about three o'clock (or three hours after sunset), and continued two hours.

The performers began by reciting the Fát'ḥah, altogether; their Sheykh (or chief) first exclaiming, "El-Fát'ḥah!" They then

[1] This was his name, not a title.

chanted the following words: "O God, bless our lord Moḥammad among the former generations; and bless our lord Moḥammad among the latter generations; and bless our lord Moḥammad in every time and period; and bless our lord Moḥammad among the most exalted princes,[1] unto the day of judgment: and bless all the prophets and apostles among the inhabitants of the heavens and of the earth: and may God (whose name be blessed and exalted!) be well pleased with our lords and our masters, those persons of illustrious estimation, Aboo-Bekr and 'Omar and 'Osmán and 'Alee, and with all the other favourites of God. God is our sufficiency; and excellent is the Guardian. And there is no strength nor power but in God, the High, the Great. O God, O our Lord, O Thou liberal of pardon, O Thou most bountiful of the most bountiful. O God. Amen." They were then silent for three or four minutes; and again recited the Fát'ḥah, but silently. This form of prefacing the zikr is commonly used by almost all orders of darweeshes in Egypt.[2]

After this preface, the performers began the zikr. Sitting in the manner above described, they chanted, in slow measure, "Lá iláha illa-lláh" ("There is no deity but God"), to the following air:

Lá i - lá - ha il - la-l - láh. Lá i -
lá - ha i - l - la - l - lá - h. Lá i - lá - ha il - la-l - láh.

bowing the head and body twice in each repetition of "Lá iláha illa-lláh." Thus they continued about a quarter of an hour; and then, for about the same space of time, they repeated the same words to the same air, but in a quicker measure, and with correspondingly quicker motions. In the meantime, the munshids frequently sang, to the same, or a variation of the same, air, portions of a ḳaṣeedeh, or of a muweshshaḥ; an ode of a similar nature to the Song of Solomon, generally alluding to the Prophet as the object of love and praise.

I shall here give a translation of one of these muweshshaḥs, which are very numerous, as a specimen of their style, from a book containing a number of these poems, which I have purchased during the

1 The angels in heaven.

2 It is called "istiftáḥ ez-zikr."

present Moolid, from a darweesh who presides at many zikrs. He pointed out the following poem as one of those most common at zikrs, and as one which was sung at the zikr which I have begun to describe. I translate it verse for verse; and imitate the measure and system of rhyme of the original, with this difference only, that the first, third, and fifth lines of each stanza rhyme with each other in the original, but not in my translation.

"With love my heart is troubled;
And mine eye-lid hind'reth sleep:
My vitals are dissever'd;
While with streaming tears I weep.
My union seems far distant:
Will my love e'er meet mine eye?
Alas! Did not estrangement
Draw my tears, I would not sigh.

"By dreary nights I'm wasted:
Absence makes my hope expire:
My tears, like pearls, are dropping;
And my heart is wrapt in fire.
Whose is like my condition?
Scarcely know I remedy.
Alas! Did not estrangement
Draw my tears, I would not sigh.

"O turtle-dove! acquaint me
Wherefore thus dost thou lament?
Art thou so stung by absence?
Of thy wings depriv'd, and pent?
He saith, 'Our griefs are equal:
Worn away with love, I lie.'
Alas! Did not estrangement
Draw my tears, I would not sigh.

"O First, and sole Eternal!
Shew thy favour yet to me.
Thy slave, Aḥmad El-Bekree,[1]
Hath no Lord excepting Thee.
By Ṭá-Há,[2] the Great Prophet!
Do Thou not his wish deny.
Alas! Did not estrangement
Draw my tears, I would not sigh."

I must translate a few more lines, to shew more strongly the similarity of these songs to that of Solomon; and lest it should be thought that I have varied the expressions, I shall not attempt to

1 The author of the poem. The singer sometimes puts his own name in the place of this.

2 "Ṭá-Há" (as I have mentioned on a former occasion) is a name of the Arabian Prophet.

render them into verse. In the same collection of poems sung at zikrs is one which begins with these lines:—

"O gazelle from among the gazelles of El-Yemen!
I am thy slave without cost:
O thou small of age, and fresh of skin!
O thou who art scarce past the time of drinking milk!"

In the first of these verses we have a comparison exactly agreeing with that in the concluding verse of Solomon's Song; for the word which, in our Bible, is translated a "roe," is used in Arabic as synonymous with "ghazál" (or a gazelle); and the mountains of El-Yemen are "the mountains of spices."—This poem ends with the following lines:—

"The phantom of thy form visited me in my slumber:
I said, 'O phantom of slumber! who sent thee?'
He said, 'He sent me whom thou knowest;
He whose love occupies thee.'
The beloved of my heart visited me in the darkness of night:
I stood, to shew him honour, until he sat down.
I said, 'O thou my petition, and all my desire!
Hast thou come at midnight, and not feared the watchmen?'
He said to me, 'I feared; but, however, love
Had taken from me my soul and my breath.'"

Compare the above with the second and five following verses of the fifth chapter of Solomon's Song.—Finding that songs of this description are extremely numerous, and almost the only poems sung at zikrs; that they are composed for this purpose, and intended only to have a spiritual sense (though certainly not understood in such a sense by the generality of the vulgar [1]); I cannot entertain any doubt as to the design of Solomon's Song. The specimens which I have just given of the religious love-songs of the Muslims have not been selected in preference to others as most agreeing with that of Solomon; but as being in frequent use; and the former of the two as having been sung at the zikr which I have begun to describe. I must now resume the description of that zikr.

At frequent intervals (as is customary in other zikrs), one of the munshids sang out the word "Meded;" accenting each syllable. "Meded" signifies, when thus used, spiritual or supernatural aid, and implies an invocation for such aid.

---

[1] As a proof of this, I may mention, that, since the above was written, I have found the last six of the lines here translated, with some slight alterations, inserted as a common love-song in a portion of the 'Thousand and One Nights,' printed at Calcutta (vol. i. p. 425).

The zikkeers, after having performed as above described, next repeated the same words to a different air, for about the same length of time; first, very slowly, then quickly. The air was as follows:

Lá i - lá - ha il - la-l - lá - h. Lá i - lá - ha il - la-l-
lá - - h. Lá i - lá - - ha il - la-l - láh.

Then they repeated these words again, to the following air, in the same manner:

Lá i - lá - ha il - la - l - láh. Lá i - lá - ha il - la-l - láh.

They next rose, and, standing in the same order in which they had been sitting, repeated the same words to another air. During this stage of their performance, they were joined by a tall, well-dressed, black slave, whose appearance induced me to inquire who he was: I was informed that he was a eunuch, belonging to the Báshà. The zikkeers, still standing, next repeated the same words in a very deep and hoarse tone; laying the principal emphasis upon the word "Lá" and the last syllable but one of the words following; and uttering, apparently, with a considerable effort: the sound much resembled that which is produced by beating the rim of a tambourine. Each zikkeer turned his head alternately to the right and left at each repetition of "Lá iláha illa-llah." The eunuch above mentioned, during this part of the zikr, became what is termed "melboos," or possessed. Throwing his arms about, and looking up, with a very wild expression of countenance, he exclaimed, in a very high tone, and with great vehemence and rapidity, "Allah! Allah! Allah! Allah! Alláh! lá lá lá lá lá lá lá lá lá lá lá lá láh! Yá 'ammee;[1] Yá 'ammee! Yá 'ammee 'Ashmáwee! Yá 'Ashmáwee! Yá 'Ashmáwee! Yá 'Ashmáwee!" His voice gradually became faint; and when he had uttered these words, though he was held by a darweesh who was next him, he fell on the ground, foaming at the mouth, his eyes

[1] "Yá 'ammee!" signifies "O my uncle!"

closed, his limbs convulsed, and his fingers clenched over his thumbs. It was an epileptic fit: no one could see it and believe it to be the effect of feigned emotions: it was undoubtedly the result of a high state of religious excitement. Nobody seemed surprised at it; for occurrences of this kind at zikrs are not uncommon. All the performers now appeared much excited, repeating their ejaculations with greater rapidity, violently turning their heads, and sinking the whole body at the same time; some of them jumping. The eunuch became melboos again, several times; and I generally remarked that his fits happened after one of the munshids had sung a line or two, and exerted himself more than usually to excite his hearers: the singing was, indeed, to my taste, very pleasing. Towards the close of the zikr, a private soldier, who had joined throughout the whole performance, also seemed, several times, to be melboos; growling in a horrible manner, and violently shaking his head from side to side. The contrast presented by the vehement and distressing exertions of the performers at the close of the zikr, and their calm gravity and solemnity of manner at the commencement, was particularly striking. Money was collected during the performance for the munshids.[1] The zikkeers receive no pay.

An ishárah passed during the meglis of the zikr above described. This zikr continues all night, until the morning-call to prayer; the performers only resting between each meglis; generally taking coffee, and some of them smoking.

It was midnight before I turned from this place to the Birket El-Ezbekeeyeh. Here, the moonlight and the lamps together produced a singular effect: several of the lamps of the ḳáïm, of the ṣáree, and of the tents, had, however, become extinguished; and many persons were lying asleep upon the bare ground, taking their night's rest. The zikr of the darweeshes round the ṣáree had terminated: I shall therefore describe this hereafter from my observation of it on the next night. After having witnessed several zikrs in the tents, I returned to my house to sleep.

On the following day (that immediately preceding what is properly called the night of the Moolid), I went again to the Ezbekeeyeh, about an hour before noon; but there were not many persons collected there at that time, nor was there much to amuse them: I saw only two or three conjurors and buffoons and shá'ers,

---

[1] Few of the spectators, or hearers, gave more than ten faḍḍahs; and those of the poorer classes gave nothing, and indeed were not solicited.

each of whom had collected a small ring of spectators and hearers. The concourse, however, gradually increased; for a very remarkable spectacle was to be witnessed; a sight which, every year, on this day, attracts a multitude of wondering beholders. This is called the "Dóseh," or Treading. I shall now describe it.

The Sheykh of the Saạdeeyeh darweeshes (the seyyid Moḥammad El-Menzeláwee), who is khaṭeeb (or preacher) of the mosque of the Ḥasaneyn, after having, as they say, passed a part of the last night in solitude, repeating certain prayers and secret invocations, and passages from the Ḳur-án, repaired this day (being Friday) to the mosque above mentioned, to perform his accustomed duty. The noon-prayers and preaching being concluded, he rode thence to the house of the Sheykh El-Bekree, who presides over all the orders of darweeshes in Egypt. This house is on the southern side of the Birket El-Ezbekeeyeh, next to that which stands at the south-western angle. On his way from the mosque, he was joined by numerous parties of Saạdee darweeshes from different districts of the metropolis: the members from each district having a pair of flags. The Sheykh is an old, gray-bearded man, of an intelligent and amiable countenance, and fair complexion. He wore, this day, a white benish, and a white ḳá-ooḳ (or padded cap, covered with cloth), having a turban composed of muslin of a very deep olive-colour, scarcely to be distinguished from black, with a strip of white muslin bound obliquely across the front. The horse upon which he rode was one of moderate height and weight: my reason for mentioning this will presently be seen. The Sheykh entered the Birket El-Ezbekeeyeh preceded by a very numerous procession of the darweeshes of whom he is the chief. In the way through this place, the procession stopped at a short distance before the house of the Sheykh El-Bekree. Here, a considerable number of the darweeshes and others (I am sure that there were more than sixty, but I could not count their number,[1]) laid themselves down upon the ground, side by side, as close as possible to each other, having their backs upwards, their legs extended, and their arms placed together beneath their foreheads. They incessantly muttered the word "Allah!" About twelve or more darweeshes, most without their shoes, then ran over the backs of their prostrate companions; some, beating "bázes," or little drums, of a hemispherical form, held

[1] I believe there were double this number: for I think I may safely say that I saw as many as double on a subsequent occasion, at the festival of the Meạrág, which will hereafter be described.

The Dósch.

in the left hand, and exclaiming "Allah!" and then the Sheykh approached: his horse hesitated, for several minutes, to tread upon the back of the first of the prostrate men; but being pulled, and urged on behind, he at length stepped upon him, and then, without apparent fear, ambled, with a high pace, over them all, led by two persons, who ran over the prostrate men; one sometimes treading on the feet, and the other on the heads. The spectators immediately raised a long cry of "Alláh lá lá lá lá láh!" Not one of the men thus trampled upon by the horse seemed to be hurt; but each, the moment that the animal had passed over him, jumped up, and followed the Sheykh. Each of them received two treads from the horse; one from one of his fore-legs, and a second from a hind-leg. It is said that these persons, as well as the Sheykh, make use of certain words[1] (that is, repeat prayers and invocations,) on the day preceding this performance, to enable them to endure, without injury, the tread of the horse; and that some not thus prepared, having ventured to lie down to be ridden over, have, on more than one occasion, been either killed or severely injured. The performance is considered as a miracle effected through supernatural power which has been granted to every successive Sheykh of the Saạdeeyeh.[2] Some persons assert that the horse is unshod for the occasion; but I thought I could perceive that this was not the case. They say also that the animal is trained for the purpose; but, if so, this would only account for the least surprising of the circumstances; I mean, for the fact of the horse being made to tread on human beings; an act from which, it is well known, that animal is very averse. The present Sheykh of the Saạdeeyeh refused, for several years, to perform the Dóseh. By much intreaty, he was prevailed upon to empower another person to do it. This person, a blind man, did it successfully, but soon after died; and the Sheykh of the Saạdeeyeh then yielded to the request of his darweeshes, and has since always performed the Dóseh himself.

After the Sheykh had accomplished this extraordinary performance, without the slightest appearance of any untoward accident, he rode into the garden, and entered the house, of the Sheykh El-Bekree, accompanied by only a few darweeshes. On my presenting myself at the door, a servant admitted me, and I joined the assembly within.

---

1 "Yestaạmaloo asmà."

2 It is said that the second Sheykh of the Saạdeeyeh (the immediate successor of the founder of the order) rode over heaps of glass bottles, without breaking any of them!

The Sheykh, having dismounted, seated himself on a seggádeh spread upon the pavement against the end-wall of a takhtabósh (or wide recess) of the court of the house. He sat with bended back, and downcast countenance, and tears in his eyes; muttering almost incessantly. I stood almost close to him. Eight other persons sat with him. The darweeshes who had entered with him, who were about twenty in number, stood in the form of a semicircle before him, upon some matting placed for them; and around them were about fifty or sixty other persons. Six darweeshes, advancing towards him, about two yards, from the semicircle, commenced a zikr; each of them exclaiming, at the same time, "Alláhu ḥei" ("God is living"), and, at each exclamation, beating, with a kind of small and short leathern strap, a "báz," which he held, by a boss at the bottom, in his left hand. This they did for only a few minutes. A black slave then became melboos, and rushed into the midst of the darweeshes, throwing his arms about, and exclaiming, "Alláh lá lá lá lá láh!" A person held him, and he soon seemed to recover. The darweeshes, altogether, standing as first described, in the form of a semicircle, then performed a second zikr; each alternate zikkeer exclaiming, "Alláhu ḥei" ("God is living"); and the others, "Yá Ḥei!" ("O Thou living!"), and all of them bowing at each exclamation, alternately to the right and left. This they continued for about ten minutes. Then, for about the same space of time, in the same manner, and with the same motions, they exclaimed, "Dáïm!" ("Everlasting!") and, "Yá Dáïm!" ("O Everlasting!"). I felt an irresistible impulse to try if I could do the same without being noticed as an intruder; and accordingly joined the semicircle, and united in the performance; in which I succeeded well enough not to attract observation; but I worked myself into a most uncomfortable heat.—After the zikr just described, a person began to chant a portion of the Ḳur-án: but the zikr was soon resumed; and continued for about a quarter of an hour. Most of the darweeshes there present then kissed the hand of the Sheykh; and he retired to an upper apartment.

It used to be a custom of some of the Saạdeeyeh, on this occasion, after the Dóseh, to perform their celebrated feat of eating live serpents, before a select assembly, in the house of the Sheykh El-Bekree: but their present Sheykh has lately put a stop to this practice in the metropolis; justly declaring it to be disgusting, and contrary to the religion, which includes serpents among the creatures that are unfit to be eaten. Serpents and scorpions were not unfrequently eaten by Saạdees during my former visit to this country. The former were deprived of their poisonous teeth, or rendered harmless by having their upper and lower lips bored, and tied together on each side with a silk string, to prevent their biting; and sometimes those which were merely carried in processions had two silver rings put in place of the silk strings. Whenever a Saạdee ate the flesh of a live serpent, he was, or affected to be, excited to do so by a kind of frenzy. He pressed very hard with the end of his thumb upon the reptile's back, as he grasped it, at a point about two inches from the head; and all that he ate of it was the head and the part between it and the point where his thumb pressed, of which he made three or four mouthfuls: the rest he threw away.—Serpents, however, are not always handled with impunity even by Saạdees. A few years ago, a darweesh of this sect, who was called "el-Feel" (or the Elephant), from his bulky and muscular form, and great strength, and who was the most famous serpent-eater of his time, and almost of any age, having a desire to rear a serpent of a very venomous kind which his boy had brought him among others that he had collected in the desert, put this reptile into a basket, and kept it for several days without food, to weaken it: he then put his hand into the basket to take it out, for the purpose of extracting its teeth; but it immediately bit his thumb: he called out for help: there were, however, none but women in the house, and they feared to come to him; so that many minutes elapsed before he could obtain assistance: his whole arm was then found to be swollen and black, and he died after a few hours.

No other ceremonies worthy of notice were performed on the day of the Dóseh. The absence of the Ghawázee rendered the festival less merry than it used to be.

In the ensuing night, that which is properly called the night of the Moolid, I went again to the principal scene of the festival. Here I witnessed a zikr performed by a ring of about sixty darweeshes round the ṣáree. The moon was sufficient, without the lamps, to light up the scene. The darweeshes who formed the ring round the ṣáree were of various orders; but the zikr which they performed was of a kind usual only among the order of the Beiyoomeeyeh. In one act of this zikr the performers exclaimed, "Yá Alláh!" ("O God!"); and, at each exclamation, first bowed their heads, crossing their hands at the same time before their breasts; then raised their heads, and clapped their hands together before their faces. The interior of the ring was crowded with persons sitting on the ground. The zikkeers continued as above described about half an hour. Next, they formed companies of five or six or more together; but still in the form of a large ring. The persons in these several companies held together, each (with the exception of the foremost in the group) placing his left arm behind the back of the one on his left side, and the hand upon the left shoulder of the latter: all facing the spectators outside the ring. They exclaimed "Allah!" in an excessively deep and hoarse voice;[1] and at each exclamation took a step, one time forwards, and the next time backwards; but each advancing a little to his left at every forward step, so that the whole ring revolved, though very slowly. Each of the zikkeers held out his right hand to salute the spectators outside the ring; most of whom, if near enough, grasped, and sometimes kissed, each extended hand as it came before them.—Whenever a zikr is performed round the ṣáree, those in the tents cease. I witnessed one other zikr this night; a repetition of that of the preceding night in the Sooḳ El-Bekree. There was nothing else to attract spectators or hearers, except the reciters of romances.—The festival terminated at the morning-call to prayer; and all the zikrs, except that in the Sooḳ El-Bekree, ceased about three hours after midnight. In the course of the following day, the ḳáïm, ṣáree, tents, &c., were removed.

---

[1] Performers of zikrs of this kind have been called, by various travellers, "barking, or howling, dervises."

CHAPTER XXV.

PERIODICAL PUBLIC FESTIVALS, &c.—*continued.*

It might seem unnecessary to continue a detailed account of the periodical public festivals and other anniversaries celebrated in Egypt, were it not that many of the customs witnessed on these occasions are every year falling into disuse, and have never, hitherto, been fully and correctly described.

During a period of fifteen nights and fourteen days in the month of "Rabeeạ et-Tánee" (the fourth month), the mosque of the Ḥasaneyn is the scene of a festival called "Moolid El-Ḥasaneyn," celebrated in honour of the birth of El-Ḥoseyn, whose head, as I have before mentioned, is said to be there buried. This Moolid is the most famous of all those celebrated in Cairo, except that of the Prophet. The grand day of the Moolid El-Ḥasaneyn is always a Tuesday; and the night which is properly called that of the Moolid is the one immediately ensuing, which is termed that of Wednesday: this is generally about five or six weeks after the Moolid en-Nebee, and concludes the festival. This present year (I am writing at the time of the festival which I here describe, in the year of the Flight 1250, A.D. 1834), the eve of the 21st of the month having been fixed upon as the night of the Moolid, the festival began on the eve of the 7th.[1] On the two evenings preceding the eve of the 7th, the mosque was lighted with a few more lamps than is usual; and this is customary in other years; but these two nights are not distinguished like those which follow.

On each of the fifteen great nights before mentioned, the mosque

---

[1] In the first edition, observing an inconsistency in my statements respecting the duration of this Moolid, I imagined that the error was in this passage; but I have since discovered, from a MS. note, that it was not, and that I should have written elsewhere (as I have now done) fifteen, instead of fourteen, nights.

is illuminated with a great number of lamps, and many wax candles; some of which latter are five or six feet high, and very thick. This illumination is made, on the first night, by the náẓir (or warden) of the mosque, from the funds of the mosque: on the second night, by the governor of the metropolis (at present Ḥabeeb Efendee): on the following nights by the Sheykhs of certain orders of darweeshes; by some of the higher officers of the mosque; and by wealthy individuals. On each of these nights, those shops at which eatables, sherbet, &c., are sold, as well as the coffee-shops, in the neighbourhood of the mosque, and even many of those in other quarters, remain open until near morning; and the streets in the vicinity of the mosque are thronged with persons lounging about, or listening to musicians, singers, and reciters of romances. The mosque is also generally crowded. Here we find, in one part of the great portico, a company of persons sitting on the floor in two rows, facing each other, and reading, altogether, certain chapters of the Ḳur-án. This is called a "maḳrà." Sometimes there are several groups thus employed. In another place we find a similar group reading, from a book called "Delááïl el-Kheyrát," invocations of blessing on the Prophet. Again, in other places, we find a group of persons reciting particular forms of prayer; and another, or others, performing a zikr, or zikrs. Winding about among these groups (whose devotional exercises are performed for the sake of El-Ḥoseyn), or sitting upon the matting, are those other visiters whom piety, or curiosity, or the love of amusement, brings to this venerated sanctuary. There is generally an assembly of darweeshes or others in the saloon of the tomb (which is covered by the great dome, and is hence called the "ḳubbeh,") reciting forms of prayer, &c.; and the visiters usually enter the saloon, to perform the ceremonies of reciting the Fát'ḥah, and compassing the shrine; but the most frequented part is the great portico, where the zikrs, and most of the other ceremonies, are performed.

Every night during this festival, we see "ishárahs," or processions of darweeshes, of one or more sects, passing through the streets to the mosque of the Ḥasaneyn, preceded by two or more men with drums, and generally with hautboys, and sometimes with cymbals also; accompanied by bearers of mesh'als; and usually having one or more lanterns. They collect their party on their way, at their respective houses. Whenever they pass by the tomb of a saint, their music ceases for a short time, and they recite the Fát'ḥah, or a form of blessing on the Prophet, similar to that preparatory to the zikr, which I have translated in my account of the Moolid of the Prophet. They do this without stopping. Arriving at the mosque, they enter; some of them with candles; visit the shrine; and go away; with the exception of their Sheykh and a few others, who sometimes remain in the ḳubbeh, and join in reciting prayers, &c.

One of the nights which offer most attractions is that of the Friday (that is, preceding the Friday,) next before the night of the Moolid. It is the night of the sheykh El-Góharee, a person of wealth, who illuminates the mosque on this occasion with an unusual profusion of lights. On this night I went to the mosque about two hours after sunset, before any of the ceremonies had commenced. The nearer I approached the building, the more crowded did I find the streets. In one place were musicians: before a large coffee-shop were two Greek dancing-boys, or "gink," elegant but effeminate in appearance, with flowing hair, performing to the accompaniment of mandolines played by two of their countrymen; and a crowd of admiring Turks, with a few Egyptians, surrounding them. They performed there also the evening before; and, I was told, became so impudent from the patronage they received as to make an open seizure of a basket of grapes in the street.

On entering the mosque, I found it far more crowded than usual; more so than on the preceding nights; but the lights were scarcely more numerous than those sometimes seen in an English church; and the chandeliers and lamps of the most common kind. A loud and confused din resounded through the great portico, and there was nothing as yet to be seen or heard, and indeed little afterwards, that seemed suited to a religious festival. A great number of Turks, and some persons of my own acquaintance, were among the visiters. I first sat down to rest with one of my friends, a bookseller, and several of his fellow-darweeshes, who were about to perform a zikr, at which he was to preside. I was treated by them with coffee, for which I had to pay by giving the munshids a piaster. Soon after they had begun their zikr, which was similar to the first which I have described in the account of the Moolid of the Prophet, I got up to visit the shrine, and to saunter about. Having paid my visit, I returned from the saloon of the tomb, in which was a large assembly of darweeshes reciting prayers, sitting in the form of a square, as large as the saloon would admit, with the exception of that part which contained the shrine. On re-entering the great portico,

I perceived a great disturbance; numbers of persons were pressing to one point, at a little distance from me, and I heard a man crying out, "Naṣránee! Káfir!" ("Christian! Infidel!"). Concluding that one of the visiters had been discovered to be a Christian, I expected a great uproar; but on asking one of the bystanders what had occurred, I was told that these words were only used as terms of insult by one Muslim to another who had given him some offence. An officer of the mosque came running from the ḳubbeh, with a staff in his hand, and soon restored order; but whether he expelled both, or either, of the persons who occasioned the disturbance, I could not discover; and I thought it prudent, in my case, to ask no further questions. By the entrance of the ḳubbeh was a party reading, in a very loud voice, and in concert, the Deláïl, before mentioned. After standing for a few minutes to hear them, though the confusion of their voices rendered it impossible for me to distinguish many words that they uttered, I returned to the zikr which I had first attended.

Shortly after, I heard the loud sounds of the tambourines of a party of 'Eesáweeyeh darweeshes, whose performances constituted one of the chief attractions of the night, from the other end of the great portico. I immediately rose, and went thither. My friend the bookseller, quitting his zikr, came after me, and imprudently called out to me, "Efendee! take care of your purse!" In a minute, I felt my trousers pulled, several times; and afterwards I found a large hole in them, apparently cut with some sharp instrument, by a person in search of my pocket: for, when the mosque is crowded as it was on this occasion, it generally happens that some thieves enter even this most sacred building.[1] I had almost despaired of getting near to the 'Eesáweeyeh, when my servant, whom I had taken thither to carry my shoes, called out to the persons around me, "Do you know whom you are pushing?" and instantly I found a way made for me. It was then about three hours after sunset.

Before I describe the performances of the 'Eesáweeyeh, I should mention that they are a class of darweeshes of whom all, or almost all, are Maghrabees, or Arabs of Northern Africa, to the west of

[1] Thefts are also sometimes committed in this mosque on other occasions, as a friend of mine lately experienced.—"I went there," said he, "to pray; and, as I was stooping over the brink of the 'meyḍaäh,' to perform the ablution, having placed my shoes beside me, and was saying, 'I purpose to perform the divine ordinance of the "wuḍoó,"' somebody behind me said to himself, 'I purpose to take away this nice pair of shoes.' On looking round, I found an old worn-out pair of shoes put in the place of my own, which were new."

Egypt. They derive their appellation from the name of their first Sheykh, Seedee Moḥammad Ibn-'Eesà,[1] a Maghrabee. Their performances are very extraordinary; and one is particularly remarkable. I was very anxious that they should perform, this night, what I here allude to; and I was not disappointed; though I was told that they had not done it in Cairo for several years before.

I found about twenty of these darweeshes, variously dressed, sitting upon the floor, close together, in the form of a ring, next to the front-wall of the building. Each of them, except two, was beating a large "ṭár" (or tambourine), rather more than a foot in width, and differing from the common ṭár in being without the tinkling pieces of metal which are attached to the hoop of the latter. One of the two persons mentioned as exceptions was beating a small ṭár of the common kind; and the other, a "báz," or little kettle-drum. Before this ring of darweeshes, a space rather larger than that which they occupied was left by the crowd for other darweeshes of the same order; and soon after the former had begun to beat their tambourines, the latter, who were six in number, commenced a strange kind of dance; sometimes exclaiming "Alláh!" and sometimes, "Alláh Mowlánà" ("God is our Lord"). There was no regularity in their dancing; but each seemed to be performing the antics of a madman; now, moving his body up and down; the next moment, turning round; then, using strange gesticulations with his arms; next, jumping; and sometimes, screaming: in short, if a stranger, observing them, were not told that they were performing a religious exercise, supposed to be the involuntary effect of enthusiastic excitement, he would certainly think that these dancing darweeshes were merely striving to excel one another in playing the buffoon; and the manner in which they were clad would conduce to impress him with this idea. One of them wore a ḳafṭán without sleeves and without a girdle; and had nothing on his head, which had not been shaved for about a week: another had a white cotton skull-cap, but was naked from the head to the waist, wearing nothing on his body but a pair of loose drawers. These two darweeshes were the principal performers. The former of them, a dark, spare, middle-aged man, after having danced in his odd manner for a few minutes, and gradually become more wild and extravagant in his actions, rushed

1 "'Eesà" is the name used in the Ḳur-án, and by its followers, for "Jesus;" and is not uncommon among Muslims, as they acknowledge and highly venerate the Messiah. The Christians that speak Arabic more properly call our Lord "Yasooạ."

towards the ring formed by his brethren who were beating the ṭárs. In the middle of this ring was placed a small chafing-dish of tinned copper, full of red-hot charcoal. From this the darweesh just mentioned seized a piece of live charcoal, which he put into his mouth; then he did the same with another, another, and another, until his mouth was full; when he deliberately chewed these live coals, opening his mouth very wide every moment, to shew its contents, which, after about three minutes, he swallowed; and all this he did without evincing the slightest symptom of pain; appearing, during the operation and after it, even more lively than before. The other darweesh before alluded to, as half naked, displayed a remarkably fine and vigorous form, and seemed to be in the prime of his age. After having danced not much longer than the former, his actions became so violent that one of his brethren held him; but he released himself from his grasp, and, rushing towards the chafing-dish, took out one of the largest live coals, and put it into his mouth. He kept his mouth wide open for about two minutes; during which period, each time that he inhaled, the large coal appeared of almost a white heat; and when he exhaled, numerous sparks were blown out of his mouth. After this, he chewed and swallowed the coal, and then resumed his dancing. When their performance had lasted about half an hour, the darweeshes paused to rest.

Before this pause, another party of the same sect had begun to perform, near the centre of the great portico. Of these I now became a spectator. They had arranged themselves in the same order as the former party. The ring composed by those who beat the tambourines consisted of about the same number as in the other company; but the dancers here were about twelve: sometimes less. One of them, a tall man, dressed in a dark woollen gown, and with a bare shaven head, took from the chafing-dish, which was handed to the dancers as though it had been a dish of cakes or sweetmeats, a large piece of brilliantly hot coal; placed it between his teeth, and kept it so for a short time; then drew it upon his tongue; and, keeping his mouth wide open for, I think, more than two minutes, violently inhaled and exhaled, shewing the inside of his mouth like a furnace, and breathing out sparks, as the former darweesh had done; but with less appearance of excitement. Having chewed and swallowed the coal, he joined the ring of the tambourine-players; and sat almost close to my feet. I narrowly watched his countenance; but could not see the least indication of his suffering any pain. After I had witnessed these extraordinary performances for about an hour, both parties of darweeshes stopped to rest; and as there was nothing more to see worthy of notice, I then quitted the mosque.[1]

Sometimes, on this occasion, the 'Eesáweeyeh eat glass as well as fire. One of them, the ḥágg Moḥammad Es-Selláwee, a man of gigantic stature, who was lamp-lighter in the mosque of the Ḥasaneyn, and who died a few years ago, was one of the most famous of the eaters of fire and glass, and celebrated for other performances. Often, when he appeared to become highly excited, it is said that he used to spring up to the long bars, or rafters, of wood, which extend across the arches above the columns of the mosque, and which are sixteen feet or more from the pavement; and would run along them, from one to another: then, with his finger, wetted in his mouth, he would strike his arm, and cause blood to flow; and by the same means stanch the blood.

The zikrs, during this festival, are continued all night. Many persons pass the night in the mosque, sleeping on the matting; and it often happens that thefts are committed there. On my return to my house after witnessing the performances of the 'Eesáweeyeh, I found no fewer than eight lice on my clothing.

On the following night there was nothing that I observed at all entertaining, unless it were this, that my officious friend the bookseller, who again presided at a zikr, wishing to pass me off for a pious Muslim (or perhaps for the sake of doing a good work), without having obtained my previous permission, openly proposed to four fiḳees to perform a recitation of the Ḳur-án (I mean, of the whole book, a "khatmeh"), on my part, for the sake of seyyidna[2]-l-Ḥoseyn. As this is commonly done, on the occasions of this festival, by persons of the higher and middle orders, it would have excited suspicion if I had objected. It was therefore performed, in the afternoon and evening next following; each fiḳee reciting a portion of the book, and then another relieving him: it occupied about nine hours. After it was finished, I was mentioned, by my assumed Oriental name, as the author of this pious work. The performers received a wax candle, some bread, and a piaster each.

On Monday the mats were removed, except a few, upon which

[1] The performances of Richardson, described in Evelyn's Memoirs (pp. 375-6, 8vo. edition), appear to have surpassed those of the darweeshes here mentioned.

[2] That is, "our lord."

groups of fiḳees, employed to recite the Ḳur-án, seated themselves. Vast numbers of persons resorted to the mosque this day, both men and women; chiefly those who were desirous of obtaining a blessing by the visit, and disliked the still greater crowding and confusion of the following day, or day of the Moolid. In the ensuing evening, the streets in the neighbourhood of the mosque were densely crowded; and, a little after sunset, it was very difficult in some parts to pass. Numerous lamps were hung in these streets, and many shops were open.

This was also the night of the Moolid of the famous Sulṭán "Eṣ-Ṣáleḥ," of the house of Eiyoob, who is commonly believed to have been a welee, and is said, by the ignorant, to have worn a dilḳ, and to have earned his subsistence by making baskets, &c., of palm-leaves ("khooṣ"), without drawing any money from the public treasury for his own private use. His tomb, which adjoins his mosque, is in the Naḥḥáseen (or market of the sellers of copper wares), a part of the main street of the city, not far from the mosque of the Ḥasaneyn. This market was illuminated with many lamps. Most of the shops were open; and in each of these was a group of three or four or more persons sitting with the master. The mosque and tomb of Eṣ-Ṣáleḥ are much neglected, and falling to decay, notwithstanding the high veneration which the people of Cairo entertain for this prince. On my approaching the door of the tomb, I was surrounded by ḥemalees and saḳḳàs, soliciting me to pay them to distribute the contents of an ibreeḳ or a ḳirbeh for the sake of Eṣ-Ṣáleḥ. I entered the building with my shoes on (seeing that others did the same), but took them off at the threshold of the saloon of the tomb. This is a square hall, surmounted by a dome. In the centre is an oblong monument, over the grave, surrounded by a wooden railing. At the head of this railed enclosure (or maḳṣoorah) are four large wax candles; and at the foot, three; all of which are encased in plaster, and resemble round-topped stone pillars. They are coloured with broad, horizontal, red stripes, like the alternate courses of stone in the exterior walls of most mosques in Cairo. There probably were, originally, the same number at the foot as there are at the head of the maḳṣoorah; for there is a space which seems to have been occupied by one at the foot. These candles, it is said, were sent as a present, by a Pope, or by a Frank King, to Eṣ-Ṣáleḥ, who, being a welee, discovered, without inspecting them, that they were filled with gunpowder, and ordered them to be thus encased in plaster: or, according to another account, they were sent as a present for the tomb, some years after the death of Eṣ-Ṣáleḥ, and he appeared to the guardian of his tomb in a dream, and informed him of the gunpowder-plot. The saloon of the tomb I found scantily lighted, and having a very ancient and neglected appearance. The pavement was uncovered. On my entering, two servants of the mosque took me to the foot of the maḳṣoorah, and one of them dictated to me the Fát'ḥah, and the form of prayer which I have mentioned in my account of the ceremonies of the day of 'Áshoorà; the other responding "Ámeen" ("Amen"): the former then desired me to recite the Fát'ḥah, with them, a second time, and gave me five of the little balls of bread from the tomb of the seyyid El-Bedawee. They received, for this, half a piaster. Another servant opened the door of the maḳṣoorah for me to enter: an honour which required that I should give him also a trifling present.

From the tomb of Eṣ-Ṣáleḥ I proceeded to the mosque of the Ḥasaneyn, through streets crowded to excess (though this was not the great night), and generally well lighted. There was but little difference between the scenes which the streets and the mosque of the Ḥasaneyn presented: among the crowds in the mosque I saw numbers of children; and some of them were playing, running after each other, and shouting. There were numerous groups of fiḳees reciting the Ḳur-án; and one small ring of darweeshes, in the centre of the great portico, performing a zikr. I forced my way with difficulty into the ḳubbeh, and performed the circuit round the shrine. Here was a very numerous party reciting the Ḳur-án. After quitting the mosque, I spent about an hour and a half in a street, listening to a Shá'er.

On the following day, the last and chief day of the festival, the mosque of the Ḥasaneyn and its neighbourhood were much more thronged than on the days previous; and in every sooḳ, and before every wekáleh, and even before the doors of most private houses of the middle and higher classes of Muslims throughout the city, lamps were hung, to be lighted in the ensuing night, the night of the Moolid. The number of beggars in the streets this day, imploring alms for the sake of "seyyidna-l-Ḥoseyn," was surprising: sitting for about an hour in the afternoon at a shop in the main street, I was quite wearied with saying, "God help thee!" "God sustain thee!" &c. Almost all the inhabitants of the metropolis seemed to be in the streets; and almost all the Turks residing here appeared to be congregated in the neighbourhood of the Ḥasaneyn. This was the grand day for visiting the shrine of El-Ḥoseyn: it is believed that the Prophet is present there all this day and the ensuing night, witnessing his followers' pious visits to his grandson. Yet most of the great people prefer going on the preceding day, or on any of the days of the festival but the last, on account of the excessive crowding on this day: I, however, went on this occasion for the very reason that deterred them. I entered the ḳubbeh a little before sunset, and was surprised to find a way made for me to advance easily to the shrine. A servant of the mosque placed me before the door of the maḳṣoorah; dictated to me the same recitals as on the day of 'Áshoorà; and gave me a handful of the bread of the seyyid El-Bedawee; consisting of fourteen of the little balls into which it is formed. But no sooner was this done than I was squeezed till I was almost breathless by applicants for presents. The man who had dictated the prayer to me asked me for his present (a piaster): another said, "I have recited the chapter of Yá-Seen for thee, O Ághà:" a third, "O Efendee, I am a servant of the maḳṣoorah:" most of the others were common beggars. I saw now that the Turks had good reason to prefer another day. The more importunate of those to whom nothing was due followed me through the crowd in the mosque, and into the street: for I had given away all that I had in my pocket, and more than was customary. I was invited to seat myself on the masṭabah of a shop opposite the mosque, to deliver myself from their jostling. In the mosque I saw nothing to remark but crowding and confusion, and swarms of beggars; men, women, and children. In the evening the mosque was still crowded to excess; and no ceremonies were performed there but visiting the shrine, recitations of the Ḳur-án, and two or three zikrs. The streets were then more crowded than ever, till long after midnight; and the illuminations gave them a very gay appearance. The Góhargeeyeh (or jewellers' bázár) was illuminated with a great profusion of chandeliers, and curtained over. The mád'nehs of the larger mosques were also illuminated. Many shops were open besides those at which eatables, coffee, and sherbet, were sold; and in some of them were seated fiḳees (two or more together) reciting khatmehs (or the whole of the Ḳur-án). There were Shá'ers, Moḥaddits, Musicians, and Singers, in various places, as on the former nights.

In about the middle of "Regeb"[1] (the seventh month) is cele-

[1] About this time, the Turkish pilgrims, on their way to Mekkeh, begin to arrive in Egypt.

brated the Moolid of the "seyyideh Zeyneb," the daughter of the Imám 'Alee, and grand-daughter of the Prophet; always on the eve of a Wednesday. The festival generally commences two weeks before: the principal day is the last, or Tuesday. The scene of the festivities is the neighbourhood of the mosque in which the seyyideh is commonly believed to be buried; a gaudily-ornamented, but not very handsome building, in the south-western quarter of the metropolis.[1] The supposed tomb, over which is an oblong monument, covered with embroidered silk, and surrounded by a bronze screen, with a wooden canopy, similar to those of El-Ḥoseyn, is in a small but lofty apartment of the mosque, crowned by a dome. Into this apartment, on the occasion of the Moolid, visiters are admitted, to pray and perform their circuits round the monument. I have just been to visit it, on the last or great day of the festival. In a street near the mosque I saw several Reciters of Aboo-Zeyd, Ḥáwees, Ḳureydátees, and Dancers, and a few swings and whirligigs. In the mosque, the prayer usual on such occasions, after the Fát'ḥah, was dictated to me; and I received two of the little balls of the bread of the seyyid El-Bedawee. The door of the sacred enclosure was open; but I had been told that only women were allowed to enter, it being regarded in the same light as a ḥareem: so I contented myself with making the circuit; which, owing to the crowding of the visiters, and there being but a very narrow space between three sides of the bronze enclosure and the walls of the apartment, was rather difficult to accomplish. A respectable-looking woman, in a state which rendered it rather dangerous for her to be present in such a crowded place, cried out to me to make room for her with a coarseness of language common to Arab females.[2] Many persons there begged me to employ them to recite a chapter of the Ḳur-án for the seyyideh; urging the proposal with the prayer of "God give thee thy desire!"[3] for the visiters to the tombs or cenotaphs of saints generally have some special petition to offer. There was a group of blind paupers sitting on the floor, and soliciting alms. The mats were removed throughout the mosque, and only idle loungers were to be seen there. On going out, I was importuned by a number of ḥemalees and saḳḳàs to give them money to distribute water for the sake of "the daughter of the Imám." It is customary to give a few faḍḍahs to one or more servants of the maḳṣoorah; and

---

[1] This mosque was commenced shortly before the invasion of Egypt by the French, and completed soon after they had quitted the country.

[2] "Má tezuḳḳ'neesh yá seedee: baṭnee melyán."

[3] "Allah yuballighak maḳṣoodak."

to a fiḳee, to recite a chapter; and also to the beggars in the mosque; and to one of the ḥemalees or saḳḳàs. The chief ceremonies performed in the mosque in the evenings were zikrs. Each evening of the festival, darweeshes of one or more orders repaired thither.

The night or eve of the twenty-seventh of Regeb is the anniversary of the "Leylet el-Meạrág," or the night of the Prophet's miraculous ascension to heaven:[1] in commemoration of which a festival is celebrated in a part of the northern suburb of Cairo, outside the gate called Báb El-'Adawee. For three days before, the Sheykh El-Bekree entertains numerous persons in a house belonging to him in this quarter; and zikrs are performed there in his house. In addition to the amusement afforded in the streets by Ḥáwees, Reciters of Aboo-Zeyd, &c., as on similar festivals, the public witness on this occasion that extraordinary performance called the "Dóseh," which I have described in my account of the Moolid en-Nebee. This is performed in a short, but rather wide street of the suburb above mentioned, in front of the mosque of a saint called Eṭ-Ṭashṭooshee, on the twenty-sixth day of the month, which is the last and chief day of the festival. I have just been one of its spectators. The day being Friday, the Sheykh of the Saạdeeyeh (the only person who is believed to be able to perform this reputed miracle) had to fulfil his usual duty of praying and preaching in the mosque of the Ḥasaneyn, at noon. From that mosque he rode in procession to the scene of the Dóseh, preceded by a long train of his darweeshes, with their banners, and some with the little drums which they often use. I was at this spot a little after midday, and took my place on a maṣṭabah which extends along the foot of the front of the mosque of Eṭ-Ṭashṭooshee.

While sitting here, and amusing myself with observing the crowds attracted by the same curiosity that brought me hither, a reputed saint, who, a few days ago, begged of me a few piasters to feed some faḳeers on this occasion, passed by, and, seeing me, came and sat down by my side. To pass away the time during which we had to wait before the Dóseh, he related to me a tale connected with the cause of the festivities of this day. A certain Sulṭán,[2] he said, had openly ridiculed the story of the Meạrág, asserting it to be impossible that the Prophet could have got out of his bed by

[1] He pretended to have been transported from Mekkeh to Jerusalem, to have ascended from Jerusalem to Heaven, there to have held converse with God, and to have returned to Mekkeh, in one night.

[2] This tale applies to the Khaleefeh El-Ḥákim. I have heard it related with some trifling differences.

night, have been carried from Mekkeh to Jerusalem by the beast Burák̦, have ascended thence with the angel to the Seventh Heaven, and returned to Jerusalem and Mekkeh, and found his bed still warm. He was playing at chess one day with his Wezeer, when the saint Eṭ-Ṭashṭooshee came in to him, and asked to be allowed to play with him; making this condition, that the Sulṭán, if overcome, should do what the saint should order. The proposal was accepted. The Sulṭán lost the game, and was ordered by the saint to plunge in a tank of water. He did so; and found himself in a magnificent palace, and converted into a woman of great beauty, with long hair, and every female attraction. He, or now *she*, was married to the son of a king; gave birth to three children, successively; and then returned to the tank, and, emerging from it, informed the Wezeer of what had happened to him. The saint reminding him, now, of his incredulity on the subject of the Meạrág, he declared his belief in the miracle, and became an orthodox Muslim. Hence, the festival of the Meạrág is always celebrated in the neighbourhood of the mosque in which Eṭ-Ṭashṭooshee is buried, and his Moolid is celebrated at the same time.

Not long after the above tale was finished, an hour and a quarter after mid-day, the procession of the Sheykh es-Saạdeeyeh arrived. The foremost persons, chiefly his own darweeshes, apparently considerably more than a hundred (but I found it impossible to count them), were laid down in the street, as close as possible together, in the same manner as at the Moolid en-Nebee. They incessantly repeated the word "Allah!" A number of darweeshes, most with their shoes off, ran over them; several beating their little drums; some carrying the black flags of the order of the Rifá'ees (the parent order of the Saạdees); and two carrying a "sháleesh"[1] (a pole about twenty feet in length, like a large flag-staff, the chief banner of the Saạdeeyeh, with a large conical ornament of brass on the top): then came the Sheykh, on the same gray horse that he rode at the Moolid en-Nebee: he was dressed in a light-blue pelisse, lined with ermine, and wore a black, or almost black, muk̦leh; which is a large, formal turban, peculiar to persons of religious and learned professions. He rode over the prostrate men, mumbling all the while: two persons led his horse; and they, also, trod upon the prostrate men; sometimes on the legs, and on the heads. Once the horse pranced

---

[1] Properly, "gáleesh," or "jáleesh."

and curveted, and nearly trod upon several heads: he passed over the men with a high and hard pace. The Sheykh entered the house of the Sheykh El-Bekree, before mentioned, adjoining the mosque. None of the men who were ridden over appeared to be hurt, and many got up laughing; but one appeared to be "melboos," or overcome by excitement, and, though he did not put his hand to his back, as if injured by the tread of the horse, seemed near fainting; and tears rolled down his face: it is possible, however, that this man was hurt by the horse, and that he endeavoured to conceal the cause.

After the Dóseh, my friend the saint insisted on my coming to his house, which was near by, with three fiḳees. He conducted us to a small upper room, furnished with an old carpet and cushions. Here the three fiḳees sat down with me, and recited the Fát'ḥah together, in a very loud voice. Then one of them chanted about half of the second chapter of the Ḳur-án, very musically: another finished it. Our host afterwards brought a stool, and placed upon it a tray with three large dishes of "'eysh bi-laḥm." This is minced meat, fried with butter, and seasoned with some ṭaḥeeneh (or sesame from which oil has been pressed), vinegar, and chopped onions; then put upon cakes of leavened dough, and baked. To this meal I sat down, with the three fiḳees, our host waiting upon us. A fourth fiḳee came in, and joined us at dinner. After we had eaten, the fiḳees recited the Fát'ḥah for the host, and then for myself, and went away. I soon after followed their example.

On the Leylet el-Meạrág, between two and three hours after sunset, the Sheykh El-Bekree returns in procession, preceded by numerous persons bearing mesh'als, and by a number of darweeshes, to his house in the Ezbekeeyeh. During this night, the mád'nehs of the larger mosques are illuminated.

On the first or second Wednesday in "Shaạbán" (the eighth month), generally on the former day, unless that be the first or second day of the month, the celebration of the Moolid of the "Imám Esh-Sháfe'ee" commences. It ends on the eve of the Thursday in the next week. The great cemetery called the Ḳaráfeh, in the desert tract on the south of the metropolis, where the Imám is buried, and the southern part of the town, are the scenes of the festivities. As this Imám was the founder of the sect to which most of the people of Cairo belong, his Moolid attracts many visiters. The festivities are similar to those of other great Moolids. On the

Saturday before the last or chief day, the ceremony of the Dóseh is performed. On the last day, Wednesday, the visiters are most numerous; and during the ensuing night, zikrs, &c, are performed in the sepulchral mosque of the Imám. Above the dome of this mosque, upon its point, is fixed a metal boat, in which there used to be placed, on the occasion of the Moolid, an ardebb (or about five bushels) of wheat, and a camel-load of water, for the birds. The boat is said to turn sometimes when there is no wind to move it, and, according to the position which it takes, to foretoken various events, good and evil; such as plenty or scarcity, the death of some great man, &c.

Several other Moolids follow that of the Imám; but those already described are the most famous, and the ceremonies of all are nearly the same.

"The Night of the Middle of Shaạbán," or "Leylet en-Nuṣf min Shaạbán," which is the night of the fifteenth (that is *preceding* the fifteenth day) of that month, is held in great reverence by the Muslims, as the period when the fate of every living man is confirmed for the ensuing year. The Sidr (or lote-tree) of Paradise, which is more commonly called Shegeret el-Muntahà (or the Tree of the Extremity) probably for several reasons, but chiefly (as is generally supposed) because it is said to be at the extremity,[1] or on the most elevated spot, in Paradise, is believed to have as many leaves as there are living human beings in the world; and the leaves are said to be inscribed with the names of all those beings; each leaf bearing the name of one person, and those of his father and mother. The tree, we are taught, is shaken on the night above mentioned, a little after sunset; and when a person is destined to die in the ensuing year, his leaf, upon which his name is written, falls on this occasion: if he be to die very soon, his leaf is almost wholly withered, a very small portion only remaining green: if he be to die later in the year, a larger portion remains green: according to the time he has yet to live, so is the proportion of the part of the leaf yet green. This, therefore, is a very awful night to the serious and considerate Muslims, who, accordingly, observe it with solemnity and earnest prayer. A particular form of prayer is used on the occasion, immediately after the ordinary evening-prayers which are said soon after

[1] In the Commentary of the Geláleyn, "Sidrat el-Muntahà," or "the Lote-tree of the Extremity" (Ḳur-án, ch. liii. v. 14), is interpreted as signifying "The Lote-tree beyond which neither angels nor others can pass."

sunset. Those who are able recite it without being prompted to do so, and generally in a mosque: others assemble in the mosques for this purpose, and hire a fiḳee to assist them; and many fiḳees, therefore, resort to the mosques to perform this office. Each fiḳee officiates for a group of persons. He first recites the "Soorat Yá-Seen" (or 36th chapter of the Ḳur-án); and then, raising his hands before his face, as in the ordinary supplications, and the other worshippers doing the same, he recites the "do'à" (or prayer), repeating one, two, three, or more words, which the others then repeat after him. The prayer is as follows:—"O God, O thou Gracious, and who art not an object of grace, O thou Lord of Dignity and Honour, and of Beneficence and Favour, there is no deity but Thou, the Support of those who seek to Thee for refuge, and the Helper of those who have recourse to Thee for help, and the Trust of those who fear. O God, if Thou have recorded me in thy abode, upon the 'Original of the Book,'[1] miserable, or unfortunate, or scanted in my sustenance, cancel, O God, of thy goodness, my misery, and misfortune, and scanty allowance of sustenance, and confirm me in thy abode, upon the Original of the Book, as happy, and provided for, and directed to good: for Thou hast said (and thy saying is true) in thy Book revealed by the tongue of thy commissioned Prophet, 'God will cancel what He pleaseth, and confirm; and with Him is the Original of the Book.'[2] O my God, by the very great revelation [which is made] on the night of the middle of the month of Shaạbán the honoured, 'in which every determined decree is dispensed'[3] and confirmed, remove from me whatever affliction I know, and what I know not, and what Thou best knowest; for Thou art the most Mighty, the most Bountiful. And bless, O God, our lord Moḥammad, the Illiterate[4] Prophet, and his Family and Companions, and save them."—After having repeated this prayer, the worshippers offer up any private supplication.

The night on which "Ramaḍán" (the month of abstinence, the ninth month of the year,) is expected to commence is called "Leylet

[1] The Preserved Tablet, on which are said to be written the original of the Ḳur-án, and all God's decrees, is here commonly understood; but I am informed that the "Original" (or, literally, the "Mother") "of the Book" is God's knowledge, or prescience.

[2] Ḳur-án, ch. xiii. v. 39.

[3] Ḳur-án, ch. xliv. v. 3.—By some persons these words are supposed to apply to the Night of el-Ḳadr, which will hereafter be mentioned.

[4] Moḥammad gloried in his illiteracy, as a proof of his being inspired: it had the same effect upon his followers as the words of our Saviour had upon the Jews, who remarked, "How knoweth this man letters, having never learned?" John vii. 15. But the epithet here rendered (agreeably with the general opinion of the Muslims) "Illiterate" should more properly be rendered "Gentile," as Dr. Sprenger has observed in his Life of Moḥammad.

er-Roo-yeh," or the Night of the Observation [of the new moon]. In the afternoon, or earlier, during the preceding day, several persons are sent a few miles into the desert, where the air is particularly clear, in order to obtain a sight of the new moon: for the fast commences on the next day after the new moon has been seen, or, if the moon cannot be seen in consequence of a cloudy sky, at the expiration of thirty days from the commencement of the preceding month. The evidence of one Muslim, that he has seen the new moon, is sufficient for the proclaiming of the fast. In the evening of the day above mentioned, the Moḥtesib, the Sheykhs of several trades (millers, bakers, slaughtermen, sellers of meat, oil-men, and fruiterers), with several other members of each of these trades, parties of musicians, and a number of faḳeers, headed and interrupted by companies of soldiers, go in procession from the Citadel to the Court of the Ḳáḍee, and there await the return of one of the persons who have been sent to make the observation, or the testimony of any other Muslim who has seen the new moon. The streets through which they pass are lined with spectators. There used to be, in this procession, several led horses, handsomely caparisoned; but of late, military display, of a poor order, has, for the most part, taken the place of civil and religious pomp. The procession of the night of the Roo-yeh is now chiefly composed of Niẓám infantry. Each company of soldiers is preceded and followed by bearers of mesh'als, to light them on their return; and followed by the Sheykh, and a few other members, of some trade, with several faḳeers, shouting, as they pass along, "O! Blessing! Blessing! Bless ye the Prophet! On him be peace!"[1] After every two or three companies, there is generally an interval of many minutes. The Moḥtesib and his attendants close the procession. When information that the moon has been seen has arrived at the Ḳáḍee's court, the soldiers and others assembled there divide themselves into several parties, one of which returns to the Citadel; the others perambulate different quarters of the town, shouting, "O followers of the best of the Creation![2] Fasting! Fasting!"[3]—When the moon has not been seen on this night, the people are informed by the cry of "To-morrow is of the month of Shaạbán. No fasting! No fasting!"[4]—The people generally pass a great part of this night (when the fast has been

---

1 "O! Eṣ-Ṣaláh! Eṣ-Ṣaláh! Ṣalloo 'ala-n-Nebee! 'aleyhi-s-selám!"

2 "The best of the Creation" is an appellation of the Prophet.

3 "Yá ummata kheyri-l-anám! Ṣiyám! Ṣiyám!"

4 "Ghadà min shahri Shaạbán. Fiṭár! Fiṭár!"

proclaimed as commencing on the morrow) in eating and drinking and smoking, and seem as merry as they usually do when released from the misery of the day's fast. The mosques, as on the following nights, are illuminated within; and lamps are hung at their entrances, and upon the galleries of the mád'nehs.

In Ramaḍán, instead of seeing, as at other times, many of the passengers in the streets with the pipe in the hand, we now see them empty-handed, until near sunset, or carrying a stick or cane, or a string of beads; but some of the Christians now are not afraid, as they used to be, of smoking in their shops in the sight of the fasting Muslims. The streets, in the morning, have a dull appearance, many of the shops being shut; but in the afternoon, they are as much crowded as usual, and all the shops are open. The Muslims during the day-time, while fasting, are, generally speaking, very morose: in the night, after breakfast, they are unusually affable and cheerful. It is the general fashion of the principal Turks in Cairo, and a custom of many others, to repair to the mosque of the Ḥasaneyn in the afternoon during Ramaḍán, to pray and lounge; and on these occasions, a number of Turkish tradesmen (called Toḥafgeeyeh) expose for sale, in the court of the meyḍaäh (or tank for ablution), a variety of articles of taste and luxury suited to the wants of their countrymen. It is common, in this month, to see tradesmen in their shops reciting the Ḳur-án or prayers, or distributing bread to the poor. Towards evening, and for some time after sunset, the beggars are more than usually importunate and clamorous; and at these times, the coffee-shops are much frequented by persons of the lower orders, many of whom prefer to break their fast with a cup of coffee and a pipe. There are few among the poor who do not keep the fast; but many persons of the higher and middle classes break it in secret.

In general, during Ramaḍán, in the houses of persons of the higher and middle classes, the stool of the supper-tray is placed, in the apartment in which the master of the house receives his visiters, a few minutes before sunset. A japanned tray is put upon it; and on this are placed several dishes, or large saucers, containing different kinds of dry fruits (which are called "nuḳl"); such as hazel-nuts (generally toasted), raisins, shelled walnuts, dried dates, dried figs, shelled almonds, sugared nuts, &c., and kaḥk, or sweet cakes. With these are also placed several ḳullehs (or glass cups) of sherbet of sugar and water; usually one or two cups more than there are persons in the house to partake of the beverage, in case of visiters coming unexpectedly; and often a little fresh cheese and a cake of bread are added. The pipes are also made ready; and it is usual to provide, in houses where numerous visiters are likely to call, several common reed pipes. Immediately after the call to evening prayer, which is chanted four minutes after sunset, the master and such of his family or friends as happen to be with him drink each a glass of sherbet: they then usually say the evening-prayers; and, this done, eat a few nuts, &c., and smoke their pipes. After this slight refreshment, they sit down to a plentiful meal of flesh-meat and other food, which they term their breakfast ("faṭoor"). Having finished this meal, they say the night-prayers,[1] and certain additional prayers of Ramaḍán, called "et-taráweeḥ;" or smoke again before they pray. The taráweeḥ prayers consist of twenty rek'ahs; and are repeated between the 'eshè prayers and the witr. Very few persons say these prayers, except in the mosque, where they have an Imám to take the lead; and they do little more than conform with his motions. The smaller mosques are closed, in Ramaḍán, soon after the taráweeḥ prayers: the larger remain open until the period of the last meal (which is called the "saḥoor"), or until the "imsák," which is the period when the fast must be recommenced. They are illuminated within and at their entrances, as long as they remain open; and the mád'nehs are illuminated during the whole of the night. The time during which the Muslim is allowed to eat (commencing, as already stated, at sunset,) varies from 11 hours 55 minutes to 7 hours 46 minutes (in the latitude of Cairo), according as the night is long or short; the imsák being always twenty minutes before the period of the prayer of daybreak. Consequently, the time during which he keeps fast every day is from 12 hours 5 minutes to 16 hours 14 minutes.

The Muslims, during Ramaḍán, generally take their breakfast at home; after which, they sometimes spend an hour or two in the house of a friend. Many of them, but chiefly those of the lower orders, in the evening, visit a coffee-shop, either merely for the sake of society, or to listen to one of the reciters of romances, or musicians, who entertain the company at many of the coffee-shops every night of this month. Numerous passengers are seen in the streets during the greater part of the night, and most of the shops at which sherbet

---

[1] "Ṣalát el-'eshè."

and eatables are sold remain open. Night is thus turned into day; and particularly by the wealthy, most of whom sleep during a great part of the day. It is the custom of some of the 'Ulamà of Cairo to have a zikr performed in their houses every night during this month; and some other persons, also, occasionally invite their friends, and entertain them with a zikr or a khatmeh.

Every night during Ramaḍán, criers, called "Musaḥḥirs," go about, first to recite a complimentary cry before the house of each Muslim who is able to reward them, and at a later hour to announce the period of the "saḥoor," or last meal.[1] There is one of these criers to each "khuṭṭ," or small district, of Cairo. He begins his rounds about two hours, or a little more, after sunset (that is, shortly after the night-prayers have been said); holding, with his left hand, a small drum, called "báz," or "ṭablat el-musaḥḥir,"[2] and, in his right hand, a small stick or strap, with which he beats it; and is accompanied by a boy carrying two "ḳandeels" (or small glass lamps) in a frame made of palm-sticks. They stop before the house of every Muslim, except the poor; and on each occasion of their doing this, the musaḥḥir beats his little drum to the following measure, three times:

after which he chants, "He prospereth who saith 'There is no deity but God:'" then he beats his drum in the same manner as before, and adds, "'Moḥammad, the Guide, is the Apostle of God.'" Then again beating his drum he generally continues, "The most happy of nights to thee, O such a one" (naming the master of the house). Having previously inquired the names of the inmates of each house, he greets each person, except women, in the same manner; mentioning every brother, son, and young unmarried daughter of the master: saying, in the last case, "The most happy of nights to the chief lady among brides,[3] such a one." After each greeting he beats his drum; and after having greeted the man (or men), adds, "May God accept from him [or them] his [or their] prayers and fasting and good works." He concludes by saying, "God preserve you, O ye generous, every year!"—At the houses of the great (as also sometimes in other

[1] It is from this latter office that the crier is called "Musaḥḥir."

[2] Described in the chapter on music.

[3] Young ladies in Egypt are often called "brides."

cases), after commencing as above ("He prospereth who saith 'There is no deity but God: Moḥammad, the Guide, is the Apostle of God'"), he generally repeats a long chant, in unmeasured rhyme; in which he first conjures God to pardon his sins, and blesses the Prophet, and then proceeds to relate the story of ṭhe "meạrág" (or the Prophet's miraculous ascension to heaven), and other similar stories of miracles; beating his drum after every few words, or, rather, after every rhyme. A house of mourning the musaḥḥir passes by. He generally receives, at the house of a person of the middle orders, two, three, or four piasters on the "'eed" which follows Ramaḍán: some persons give him a trifle every night.

If my reader be at all impressed by what has been above related, of the office of the musaḥḥir, as illustrating the character of the Muslims, he will be more struck by what here follows.—At many houses of the middle classes in Cairo, the women often put a small coin (of five faḍḍahs, or from that sum to a piaster, or more,) into a piece of paper, and throw it out of a window to the musaḥḥir; having first set fire to the paper, that he may see where it falls: he then, sometimes by their desire, and sometimes of his own accord, recites the Fát'ḥah, and relates to them a short tale, in unmeasured rhyme, for their amusement; as, for instance, the story of two "ḍarrahs"—the quarrels of two women who are wives of the same man. Some of the tales which he relates on these occasions are of a grossly indecent nature; and yet they are listened to by females in houses of good repute. How incongruous are such sequels! What inconsistency of character do they evince!

During this month, those calls from the mád'nehs which are termed "the Oolà" and "the Ebed" are discontinued, and, in their stead, two other calls are chanted. The period of the first of these, which is termed the "Abrár" (from the first word of note occurring in it), is between an hour and a half and half an hour before midnight, according as the night is long or short. It consists of the following verses of the Ḳur-án.[1] "But the just shall drink of a cup [of wine] mixed with [the water of] Káfoor; a fountain from which the servants of God shall drink: they shall convey the same by channels [whithersoever they please]. [These] did fulfil their vow, and dread the day, the evil whereof will disperse itself far abroad; and give food unto the poor and the orphan and the bondsman for his sake, [saying,]

---

[1] The fifth and four following verses of the Soorat el-Insán, or 76th chapter.

We feed you for God's sake only: we desire no recompense from you, nor any thanks."—The second call is termed the "Selám" (or salutation); and is a series of invocations of blessings on the Prophet, similar to those recited before the Friday-prayers, but not always the same. This is generally chanted about half an hour after midnight. The morning adán from the mád'nehs is chanted much earlier than usual, as a warning to the Muslims to take their last meal, the "saḥoor;" in winter, in the longest night, about two hours and a half, and in the short nights, about one hour and a half, before the imsák. Another adán is also made from the dikkehs in the great mosques about twenty minutes before the imsák, as a final warning to any who may have neglected to eat; and at the period of the imsák, in these mosques, the meeḳátee (who makes known the hours of prayer, &c.), or some other person, calls out "Irfa'oo!" that is, "Remove ye" [your food, &c.]—About an hour and a half before the imsák, the musaḥḥir goes his rounds to rouse or remind the people to eat at those houses where he has been ordered to call; knocking and calling until he is answered; and the porter of each quarter does the same at each house in his quarter. Some persons eat but little for their faṭoor, and make the saḥoor the principal meal: others do the reverse; or make both meals alike. Most persons sleep about half the night.

Some few pious persons spend the last ten days and nights of Ramaḍán in the mosque of the Ḥasaneyn or that of the Seyyideh Zeyneb. One of these nights, generally supposed to be the 27th of the month[1] (that is, the night preceding the 27th day), is called "Leylet el-Ḳadr" (the Night of Power, or of the Divine decree). On this night, the Ḳur-án is said to have been sent down to Moḥammad. It is affirmed to be "better than a thousand months;"[2] and the angels are believed to descend, and to be occupied in conveying blessings to the faithful from the commencement of it until daybreak. Moreover, the gates of heaven being then opened, prayer is held to be certain of success. Salt water, it is said, suddenly becomes sweet on this night; and hence, some devout persons, not knowing which of the last ten nights of Ramaḍán is the Leylet el-Ḳadr, observe all those nights with great solemnity, and keep before them a vessel of salt water, which they occasionally taste, to try if it become sweet, so that they may be

---

[1] Not the night supposed by Sale, which is that between the 23rd and 24th days. See one of his notes on the 97th chapter of the Ḳur-án. [2] Ḳur-án, ibid.

certain of the night. I find, however, that a tradition of the Prophet fixes it to be one of the odd nights; the 21st, 23rd, 25th, 27th, or 29th.

On the first three days of "Showwál" (the tenth month, the next after Ramaḍán,) is celebrated the minor of the two grand festivals which are ordained, by the religion of the Muslims, to be observed with general rejoicing. It is commonly called "el-'Eed eṣ-Ṣugheiyir;" but more properly, "el-'Eed eṣ-Ṣagheer."[1] The expiration of the fast of Ramaḍán is the occasion of this festival. Soon after sunrise on the first day, the people having all dressed in new, or in their best, clothes, the men assemble in the mosques, and perform the prayers of two rek'ahs, a sunneh ordinance of the 'eed; after which, the Khaṭeeb delivers an exhortation. Friends, meeting in the mosque, or in the street, or in each other's houses, congratulate and embrace and kiss each other. They generally visit each other for this purpose. Some, even of the lower classes, dress themselves entirely in a new suit of clothes; and almost every one wears something new, if it be only a pair of shoes. The servant is presented with at least one new article of clothing by the master, and receives a few piasters from each of his master's friends, if they visit the house; or even goes to those friends, to congratulate them, and receives his present: if he have served a former master, he also visits him, and is in like manner rewarded for his trouble; and sometimes he brings a present of a dish of "kaḥk" (or sweet cakes), and obtains, in return, money of twice the value, or more. On the days of this 'eed, most of the people of Cairo eat "feseekh" (or salted fish), and "kaḥks," "faṭeerehs" (or thin, folded pancakes), and "shureyks" (a kind of bunn). Some families also prepare a dish called "mumezzezeh," consisting of stewed meat, with onions, and a quantity of treacle, vinegar, and coarse flour; and the master usually procures dried fruits ("nuḳl"), such as nuts, raisins, &c., for his family. Most of the shops in the metropolis are closed, except those at which eatables and sherbet are sold; but the streets present a gay appearance, from the crowds of passengers in their holiday-clothes.

On one or more days of this festival, some or all of the members of most families, but chiefly the women, visit the tombs of their relatives. This they also do on the occasion of the other grand festival,

---

[1] It is also called "'Eed el-Fiṭr" (or the Festival of the Breaking of the Fast); and, by the Turks, "Ramaẓán Beyrám."

of which an account will be given hereafter. The visiters, or their servants, carry palm-branches, and sometimes sweet basil ("reeḥán"), to lay upon the tomb which they go to visit. The palm-branch is broken into several pieces, and these, or the leaves only, are placed on the tomb. Numerous groups of women are seen on these occasions, bearing palm-branches, on their way to the cemeteries in the neighbourhood of the metropolis. They are also provided, according to their circumstances, with kaḥks, shureyks, faṭeerehs, bread, dates, or some other kind of food, to distribute to the poor who resort to the burial-grounds on these days. Sometimes tents are pitched for them: the tent surrounds the tomb which is the object of the visit.[1] The visiters recite the Fát'ḥah, or, if they can afford it, employ a person to recite first the Soorat Yá-Seen, or a larger portion of the Ḳur-án. Often a khatmeh (or recital of the whole of the Ḳur-án) is performed at the tomb, or in the house, by several fiḳees. The men generally return immediately after these rites have been performed, and the fragments or leaves of the palm-branch laid on the tomb: the women usually go to the tomb early in the morning, and do not return until the afternoon: some of them (but these are not generally esteemed women of correct conduct), if they have a tent, pass the night in it, and remain until the end of the festival, or until the afternoon of the following Friday: so too do the women of a family possessed of a private, enclosed burial-ground, with a house within it; for there are many such enclosures, and not a few with houses for the accommodation of the females, in the midst of the public cemeteries of Cairo. Intrigues are said to be not uncommon with the females who spend the night in tents among the tombs. The great cemetery of Báb en-Naṣr, in the desert tract immediately on the north of the metropolis, presents a remarkable scene on the two 'eeds. In a part next the city-gate from which the burial-ground takes its name, many swings and whirligigs are erected, and several large tents, in some of which, dancers, reciters of Aboo-Zeyd, and other performers, amuse a dense crowd of spectators; and throughout the burial-ground are seen numerous tents for the reception of the visiters of the tombs.

About two or three days after the 'eed above described, the "Kisweh," or covering of the Kaạbeh, which is sent annually with the great caravan of pilgrims, is conveyed in procession from the

---

1 The salutation of peace should be pronounced on entering the burial-ground and on arriving at the tomb, in the manner described in Chapter X., in my account of visits to the tombs and cenotaphs of saints. In the former case it is general; and in the latter, particular.

Citadel of the metropolis, where it is manufactured at the Sulṭán's expense, to the mosque of the Ḥasaneyn, to be sewed together, and lined, preparatively to the approaching pilgrimage. It is of a coarse, black brocade, covered with inscriptions[1] of passages from the Ḳur-án, &c., which are interwoven with silk of the same colour; and having a broad band across each side, ornamented with similar inscriptions worked in gold.[2] The following account of the procession of the Kisweh I write on my return from witnessing it, on the 6th of Showwál 1249 (or 15th of February, 1834).

I took my seat, soon after sunrise, in the shop of the Báshà's booksellers, in the main street of the city, nearly opposite the entrance to the bázár called Khán El-Khaleelee. This and almost every shop in the street were crowded with persons attracted by the desire of witnessing the procession, old and young; for the Egyptians of every class and rank and age take great pleasure in viewing public spectacles; but the streets were not so much thronged as they usually are on the occasions of the processions of the Maḥmal. About two hours after sunrise, the four portions which form each one side of the "Kisweh" were borne past the spot where I had taken my post; each of the four pieces placed on an ass, with the ropes by which they were to be attached. The asses were not ornamented in any way, nor neatly caparisoned; and their conductors were common fellááḥs, in the usual blue shirt. There was then an interval of about three quarters of an hour, and nothing to relieve the dulness of this long pause but the passing of a few darweeshes, and two buffoons, who stopped occasionally before a shop where they saw any well-dressed persons sitting, and, for the sake of obtaining a present of about five faḍḍahs (or a little more than a farthing), engaged in a sham quarrel, abused each other in loud and gross words, and violently slapped each other on the face.

---

1 This was denied by several of my Muslim friends, before whom I casually mentioned it; but, by producing a piece of the Kisweh, I proved the truth of my assertion. I state this to shew that a writer may often be charged with committing an error on authority which any person would consider perfectly convincing.

2 The Kaạbeh is a building in the centre of the Temple of Mekkeh, most highly respected by the Muslims. It is nearly in the form of a cube. Its height is somewhat more than thirty feet; and each side is about the same, or a little more, in width. It is not exactly rectangular, nor exactly equilateral. The black covering, after having remained upon it nearly a year, is taken off on the 25th of Zu-l-Ḳaạdeh, cut up, and sold to the pilgrims; and the building is left without a covering for the space of fifteen days: on the 10th of Zu-l-Ḥeggeh, the first day of the Great Festival, the new Kisweh is put on. The interior is also hung with a covering, which is renewed each time that a new Sulṭán ascends the Turkish throne. It is necessary to renew the *outer* covering every year, in consequence of its exposure to the rain, &c. As the use of stuffs entirely composed of silk is prohibited, the Kisweh of the Kaạbeh is lined with cotton to render it allowable.

After this interval came about twenty ill-dressed men, bearing on their shoulders a long frame of wood, upon which was extended one quarter of the "Ḥezám" (that is, the belt or band above mentioned). The Ḥezám is in four pieces, which, when sewed together to the Kisweh, form one continuous band, so as to surround the Kaạbeh entirely, at about two-thirds of its height. It is of the same kind of black brocade as the Kisweh itself. The inscriptions in gold are well worked in large and beautiful characters: each quarter is surrounded by a border of gold; and at each end, where the upper and lower borders unite, is ornamented in a tasteful manner, with green and red silk, sewed on, and embroidered with gold. One or other of the bearers frequently went aside to ask for a present from some respectably-dressed spectator. There was an interval of about a quarter of an hour after the first quarter of the Ḥezám passed by: the other three portions were then borne along, one immediately after another, in the same manner. Then there was another interval, of about half an hour; after which there came several tall camels, slightly stained with the red dye of the ḥennà, and having high, ornamented saddles, such as I have described in my account of the return of the Maḥmal: upon each of these were one or two boys or girls; and upon some were cats. These were followed by a company of Balṭageeyeh (or Pioneers), a very good military band (the instruments of various kinds, but mostly trumpets, and all European), and the Básha's guard, a regiment of infantry, of picked young men, in uniforms of a dark blueish-brown, with new red shoes, and with stockings.

The "Burḳo'" (or Veil),[1] which is the curtain that is hung before the door of the Kaạbeh, was next borne along, stretched upon a high, flattish frame of wood, fixed on the back of a fine camel. It was of black brocade, embroidered in the same manner as the Ḥezám, with inscriptions from the Ḳur-án in letters of gold, but more richly and more highly ornamented, and was lined with green silk. The face of the Burḳo' was extended on the right side of the frame, and the green silk lining on the left. It was followed by numerous companies of darweeshes, with their banners, among which were several sháleeshes (such as I have described in my account of the Dóseh at the festival of the Meạrág), the banners of the principal orders of darweeshes. Many of them bore flags, inscribed with the profession

[1] This is often called, by the vulgar, "the veil of sitna Fáṭ'meh;" because it is said that Fáṭimeh Shegeret ed-Durr, the wife of the Sulṭán Eṣ-Ṣáleḥ, was the first person who sent a veil of this kind to cover the door of the Kaạbeh.

of the faith ("There is no deity but God: Moḥammad is God's Apostle"), or with words from the Ḳur-án, and the names of God, the Prophet, and the founders of their orders. Several Ḳádiree darweeshes bore nets, of various colours, each extended upon a framework of hoops upon a pole: these were fishermen. Some of the darweeshes were employed in repeating, as in a common zikr, the name and epithets of God. Two men, armed with swords and shields, engaged each other in a mock combat. One other, mounted on a horse, was fantastically dressed in sheep-skins, and wore a high skin cap, and a grotesque false beard, composed of short pieces of cord or twist, apparently of wool, with mustaches formed of two long brown feathers: he occasionally pretended to write "fetwàs" (or judicial decisions), upon scraps of paper given to him by spectators, with a piece of stick, which he feigned to charge with a substitute for ink by applying it to his horse as though it were intended for a goad. But the most remarkable group in this part of the procession consisted of several darweeshes of the sect of the Rifá'ees, called Owlád-'Ilwán, each of whom bore in his hand an iron spike, about a foot in length, with a ball of the same metal at the thick end, having a number of small and short chains attached to it. Several of these darweeshes, in appearance, thrust the spike with violence into their eyes, and withdrew it, without shewing any mark of injury: it seemed to enter to the depth of about an inch. This trick was very well performed. Five faḍḍahs, or even a pipeful of tobacco, seemed to be considered a sufficient recompense to the religious juggler for this display of his pretended miraculous power. The spectators near me seemed to entertain no suspicion of any fraud in this singular performance; and I was reproached by one who sat by me, a man of very superior information, for expressing my opinion that it was a very clever piece of deception. Most of the darweeshes in the procession were Rifá'ees: their sheykh, on horseback, followed them.

Next came the "Maḥmal," which I have described in my account of its return to Cairo. It is added to the procession of the kisweh for the sake of increasing the show: the grand procession of the Maḥmal previous to the departure of the great caravan of pilgrims takes place between two and three weeks after. Another black covering, of an oblong form, embroidered in like manner with gold, to be placed over the Maḳám Ibráheem, in the temple of Mekkeh, was borne after the Maḥmal. Behind this rode a Turkish military officer, holding, upon an embroidered kerchief, a small case, or bag, of green silk, embroidered with gold, the receptacle of the key of the Kaạbeh. Then followed the last person in the procession: this was the half-naked sheykh described in my account of the return of the Maḥmal, who constantly follows this sacred object, and accompanies the caravan to and from Mekkeh, mounted on a camel, and incessantly rolling his head.[1]

In the latter part of Showwál, not always on the same day of the month, but generally on or about the twenty-third, the principal officers and escort of the great caravan of pilgrims pass, from the Citadel, through the metropolis, in grand procession, followed by the Maḥmal. The procession is called that of the Maḥmal. The various persons who take part in it, most of whom proceed with the caravan to Mekkeh, collect in the Ḳarà Meydán and the Rumeyleh (two large open tracts) below the Citadel, and there take their places in the prescribed order. As this procession is conducted with less pomp in almost every successive year, I shall describe it as I first witnessed it, during my first visit to Egypt. The streets through which it passed were lined with spectators; some, seated on the masṭabahs of the shops (which were all closed), and others, standing on the ground below. I obtained a good place at a shop in the main street, through which it passed towards the gate called Báb en-Naṣr.

First, a cannon was drawn along, about three hours after sunrise: it was a small field-piece, to be used for the purpose of firing signals for the departure of the caravan after each halt. Then followed two companies of irregular Turkish cavalry (Delees and Tufekjees), about five hundred men, most shabbily clad, and having altogether the appearance of banditti. Next, after an interval of about half an hour, came several men mounted on camels, and each beating a pair of the large, copper, kettle-drums called naḳḳárahs,[2] attached to the fore part of the saddle. Other camels, with large, stuffed saddles, of the same kind as those described in my account of the return of the Maḥmal, without riders, followed those above mentioned. These camels were all slighty tinged of a dingy orange-red with ḥennà. Some of them had a number of fresh, green palm-branches fixed upright upon the saddles, like enormous plumes; others were decorated with small flags, in the same manner as those

---

1 I went to the mosque of the Ḥasaneyn a few days after, to examine the Kisweh and the other objects above described, that I might be able to make my account of them more accurate and complete. I was permitted to handle them all at my leisure; and gave a small present for this privilege, and for a superfluous piece of the Kisweh, for which I asked, a span in length, and nearly the same in breadth.

2 These are described in the chapter on music.

above alluded to: several had a large bell hung on each side: some, again, bore water-skins; and one was laden with the "khazneh," a square case, covered with red cloth, containing the treasure for defraying those expenses of the pilgrimage which fall upon the government. The baggage of the Emeer el-Ḥágg (or Chief of the Pilgrims) then followed, borne by camels. With his furniture and provisions, &c., was conveyed the new "Kisweh." After this, there was another interval.

The next persons in the procession were several darweeshes, moving their heads from side to side, and repeating the name of God. With these were numerous camel-drivers, saḳḳàs, sweepers, and others; some of them crying "'Arafát![1] O God!"[2] and "God! God! [May the journey be] with safety!"[3] Then, again, followed several camels; some, with palm-branches, and others, with large bells, as before described. Next, the takht'rawán (or litter) of the Emeer el-Ḥágg, covered with red cloth, was borne along by two camels; the foremost of which had a saddle decorated with a number of small flags. Some Arabs, and the "Deleel el-Ḥágg" (or Guide of the Caravan), followed it; and next came several camels, and groups of darweeshes and others, as before. Then followed about fifty members of the Báshà's household, well dressed and mounted; a number of other officers, with silver-headed sticks, and guns; the chief of the Delees, with his officers; and another body of members of the household, mounted like the first, but persons of an inferior order. These were followed by several other officers of the court, on foot, dressed in ḳafṭáns of cloth of gold. Next came two swordsmen, naked to the waist, and each having a small, round shield: they frequently stopped, and engaged each other in sport, and occasionally received remuneration from some of the spectators. These preceded a company of darweeshes, camel-drivers, and others; and the shouts before mentioned were repeated.

After a short interval, the sounds of drums and fifes were heard; and a considerable body of the Niẓám, or regular troops, marched by. Next followed the "Wálee" (or chief magistrate of police), with several of his officers: then, the attendants of the "Emeer el-Ḥágg," the "Emeer" himself, three kátibs (or clerks), a troop of Maghrabee horsemen, and three "Muballighs" of the Mountain, in white 'abáyehs (or woollen cloaks), interwoven with gold. The office

[1] "'Arafát" is the name of the mountain which is one of the principal objects of pilgrimage.

[2] "'Arafát! ya-lláh!"

[3] "Allah! Allah! Bi-s-selámeh!"

of the last is to repeat certain words of the Khaṭeeb (or preacher) on Mount 'Arafát. Then again there intervened numerous groups of camel-drivers, sweepers, saḳḳàs, and others; many of them shouting as those before. In the midst of these rode the "Imáms" of the four orthodox sects; one to each sect. Several companies of darweeshes, of different orders, followed next, with the tall banners and flags of the kind mentioned in my account of the procession of the Kisweh; the Ḳádireeyeh having also, in addition to their poles with various-coloured nets, long palm-sticks, as fishing-rods. Kettle-drums, hautboys, and other instruments, at the head of each of these companies, produced a harsh music. They were followed by members of various trades; each body headed by their Sheykh.

Next came several camels; and then, the "Maḥmal." Many of the people in the streets pressed violently towards it, to touch it with their hands, which, having done so, they kissed; and many of the women who witnessed the spectacle from the latticed windows of the houses let down their shawls or head-veils, in order to touch with them the sacred object. Immediately behind the Maḥmal was the same person whom I have described as following it on its return to Cairo, and in the procession of the Kisweh; the half-naked sheykh, seated on a camel, and rolling his head.

In former years, the Maḥmal used to be conveyed, on this occasion, with much more pomp, particularly in the times of the Memlooks, who attended it clad in their richest dresses, displaying their most splendid arms and armour, and, in every way, vying with each other in magnificence. It used generally to be preceded by a group of Saạdeeyeh darweeshes, devouring live serpents.

The Maḥmal, the baggage of the Emeer, &c., generally remain two or three or more days in the plain of the Ḥaṣweh, on the north of the metropolis; then proceed to the Birket el-Ḥágg (or Lake of the Pilgrims), about eleven miles from the city, and remain there two days. This latter halting-place is the general rendezvous of the pilgrims. The caravan usually departs thence on the twenty-seventh of Showwál. The journey to Mekkeh occupies thirty-seven days. The route lies over rocky and sandy deserts, with very few verdant spots. To diminish the hardships of the journey, the caravan travels slowly, and mostly by night; starting about two hours before sunset, and halting the next morning a little after sunrise. The litters most generally used by the pilgrims I have described in the account of the return of the caravan. Most of the Turkish pilgrims, and many others, prefer going by way of El-Ḳuṣeyr or Es-Suweys[1] and the Red Sea; and set out from Cairo generally between two and three months before the great caravan.

On the tenth of "Zu-l-Ḥeggeh" (the last month of the year) commences the Great Festival, "El-'Eed el-Kebeer,"[2] which, like the former 'eed, lasts three days, or four, and is observed with nearly the same customs. Every person puts on his best clothes or a new suit; but it is more common to put on new clothes on the minor 'eed. Prayers are performed in the mosques on the first day, soon after sunrise, as on the other festival; and the same customs of visiting and congratulation, and giving presents (though generally of smaller sums) to servants and others, are observed by most persons. The sacrifice that is performed on the first day, which is the day of the pilgrim's sacrifice, has been mentioned in the third chapter of this work. It is a duty observed by most persons who can easily afford to do it. For several previous days, numerous flocks of sheep, and many buffaloes, are driven into the metropolis, to be sold for sacrifice. Another custom observed on this festival, that of visiting the tombs, I have also before had occasion to describe, in the account of the ceremonies of the former 'eed. In most respects, what is called the Minor Festival is generally observed with more rejoicing than that which is termed the Great Festival. On this latter 'eed, most persons who have the means to do so prepare a dish called "fetteh," composed of boiled mutton, or other meat (the meat of the victim), cut into small pieces, placed upon broken bread, upon which is poured the broth of the meat, and some vinegar flavoured with a little garlic fried in a small quantity of melted butter, and then sprinkled over with a little pepper.

---

1 Thus is properly pronounced the name of the town which we commonly call *Suez*.

2 It is also called "'Eed el-Ḳurbán" (or the Festival of the Sacrifice), and by the Turks, "Ḳurbán Beyrám."

CHAPTER XXVI.

PERIODICAL PUBLIC FESTIVALS, &c.—*continued.*

It is remarkable that the Muslims of Egypt observe certain customs of a religious or superstitious nature at particular periods of the religious almanac of the Copts; and even, according to the same system, calculate the times of certain changes of the weather. Thus they calculate the period of the "Khamáseen," when hot southerly winds are of frequent occurrence, to commence on the day immediately following the Coptic festival of Easter Sunday, and to terminate on the Day of Pentecost (or Whitsunday); an interval of forty-nine days.[1]

The Wednesday next before this periodis called "Arba'à Eiyoob," or Job's Wednesday. Many persons, on this day, wash themselves with cold water, and rub themselves with the creeping plant called "raạrấạ Eiyoob," or "ghubeyrà"[2] (inula Arabica, and inula undulata), on account of a tradition which relates that Job did so to obtain restoration to health. This and other customs about to be mentioned were peculiar to the Copts; but are now observed by many Muslims in the towns, and by more in the villages. The other customs just alluded to are that of eating eggs, dyed externally red or yellow or blue, or some other colour, on the next day (Thursday); and, on the Friday (Good Friday), a dish of khalṭah, composed of kishk,[3] with

---

1 I believe that this period has been called by all European writers who have mentioned it, except myself, "El-Khamseen," or by the same term differently expressed, signifying *the Fifty; i. e. the Fifty days;* but it is always termed by the Arabs "el-Khamáseen," which signifies *the Fifties,* being a vulgar *plural* of Khamseen. In like manner, the Arabs call the corresponding period of the Jewish calendar by a term exactly agreeing with "el-Khamáseen;" namely "el-Khamseenát; only its *last day* being termed "el-Khamseen." See De Sacy's 'Chrestomathie Arabe,' 2nd ed., vol. i., p. 98 of the Arabic text, and pp. 292 and 320 of his translation and notes. This eminent scholar, however, appears to have had no authority but that of Europeans for the name of the above-mentioned period of the Coptic calendar; for he has followed the travellers, and written it "Khamsin."

2 Commonly pronounced "ghubbeyrè."

3 "Kishk" (as the word is commonly pronounced, but properly "keshk,") is prepared from wheat, first moistened, then dried, trodden in a vessel to separate the husks, and coarsely ground

fool nábit,[1] lentils, rice, onions, &c. On the Saturday, also, it is a common custom of men and women to adorn their eyes with koḥl. This day is called "Sebt en-Noor" (Saturday of the Light); because a light, said to be miraculous, appears during the festival then celebrated in the Holy Sepulchre in Jerusalem.

A custom termed "Shemm en-Neseem" (or the Smelling of the Zephyr) is observed on the first day of the Khamáseen. Early in the morning of this day, many persons, especially women, break an onion, and smell it; and in the course of the forenoon, many of the citizens of Cairo ride or walk a little way into the country, or go in boats, generally northwards, to take the air, or, as they term it, *smell* the air, which, on that day, they believe to have a wonderfully beneficial effect. The greater number dine in the country, or on the river. This year (1834), they were treated with a violent hot wind, accompanied by clouds of dust, instead of the neseem; but considerable numbers, notwithstanding, went out to "smell" it.—The 'Ulamà have their "shemm en-neseem" at a fixed period of the solar year; the first three days of the spring-quarter, corresponding with the Persian "Now-róz," called by the Arabs "Nórooz."

The night of the 17th of June, which corresponds with the 11th of the Coptic month of Ba-ooneh, is called "Leylet en-Nuḳṭah" (or the Night of the Drop), as it is believed that a miraculous drop then falls into the Nile, and causes it to rise. Astrologers calculate the precise moment when the "drop" is to fall; which is always in the course of the night above mentioned. Many of the inhabitants of Cairo and its neighbourhood, and of other parts of Egypt, spend this night on the banks of the Nile; some, in houses of their friends; others, in the open air. Many also, and especially the women, observe a singular custom on the Leylet en-Nuḳṭah; placing, upon the terrace of the house, after sunset, as many lumps of dough as there are inmates in the house, a lump for each person, who puts his, or her, mark upon it: at day-break, on the following morning, they look at each of these lumps; and if they find it cracked, they infer that the life of the person for whom it was placed will be long, or not terminate that year; but if they find it not cracked, they infer the reverse. Some

with a hand-mill: the meal is mixed with milk, and about six hours afterwards is spooned out upon a little straw or bran, and then left for two or three days to dry. When required for use, it is either soaked or pounded, and put into a sieve, over a vessel; and then boiling water is poured on it. What remains in the sieve is thrown away: what passes through is generally poured into a saucepan of boiled meat or fowl, over the fire. Some leaves of white beet, fried in butter, are usually added to each plate of it.

[1] Beans soaked in water until they begin to sprout, and then boiled.

say that this is also done to discover whether the Nile will rise high in the ensuing season. Another absurd custom is observed on the fourth following night, "Leylet es-Saraṭán," when the sun enters the sign of Cancer: it is the writing a charm to exterminate, or drive away, bugs. This charm consists of the following words from the Ḳur-án,[1] written in separate letters—"'Hast thou not considered those who left their habitations, and they were thousands, for fear of death? and God said unto them, Die: die: die.'" The last word of the text is thus written three times. The above charm, it is said, should be written on three pieces of paper, which are to be hung upon the walls of the room which is to be cleared of the bugs; one upon each wall, except that at the end where is the entrance, or that in which is the entrance.

The Nile, as I have mentioned in the Introduction to this Work, begins to rise about, or soon after, the period of the summer solstice. From, or about, the 27th of the Coptic month Ba-ooneh (3rd of July) its rise is daily proclaimed in the streets of the metropolis. There are several criers to perform this office; each for a particular district of the town. The Crier of the Nile ("Munádee en-Neel") generally goes about his district early in the morning, but sometimes later; accompanied by a boy. On the day immediately preceding that on which he commences his daily announcement of the rise of the Nile, he proclaims, "God hath been propitious to the lands. The day of good news. To-morrow, the announcement, with good fortune."—The daily announcement is as follows:

Munádee. "Moḥammad is the Prophet of guidance." *Boy.* "The Maḥmals journey to him."[2] *M.* "The guide: peace be on him." *B.* "He will prosper who blesseth him." [The Munádee and boy then continue, or sometimes they omit the preceding form, and begin thus:] *M.* "O Thou whose government is excellent!" *B.* "My Lord, I have none beside Thee." [After this, they proceed, in many cases, thus:] *M.* "The treasuries of the Bountiful are full." *B.* "And at the gate there is no scarcity." *M.* "I extol the perfection of Him who spread out the earth." *B.* "And hath given running rivers." *M.* "Through Whom the fields become green." *B.* "After death He causeth them to live." *M.* "God hath given abundance, and increased [the river] and watered the high lands." *B.* "And the mountains and the sands and the fields."

---

[1] Chap. ii. ver. 244.

[2] That is, to his tomb.

M. "O Alternator of the day and night!" *B.* "My Lord, there is none beside Thee." *M.* "O Guide of the wandering! O God!" *B.* "Guide me to the path of prosperity." [They then continue, or, sometimes omitting all that here precedes, commence as follows:] *M.* "O Amiable! O Living! O Self-subsisting!" *B.* "O Great in power! O Almighty!" *M.* "O Aider! regard me with favour." *B.* 'O Bountiful! withdraw not thy protection." *M.* "God preserve to me my master [or my master the "emeer"] such a one [naming the master of the house], and the good people of his house. O Bountiful! O God!" *B.* "Ay, please God." *M.* "God give them a happy morning, from Himself; and increase their prosperity, from Himself." *B.* "Ay, please God." *M.* "God preserve to me my master [&c.] such a one [naming again the master of the house]; and increase to him the favours of God. O Bountiful! O God!" *B.* "Ay, please God." [Then brothers, sons, and unmarried daughters, if there be any, however young, are mentioned in the same manner, as follows:] *M.* "God preserve to me my master [&c.] such a one, for a long period. O Bountiful! O God!" *B.* "Ay, please God." *M.* "God preserve to me my mistress, the chief lady among brides, such a one, for a long period. O Bountiful! O God!" *B.* "Ay, please God." *M.* May He abundantly bless them with his perfect abundance; and pour abundantly the Nile over the country. O Bountiful! O God!" *B.* "Ay, please God." *M.* "Five [or six, &c., digits] to-day: and the Lord is bountiful." *B.* "Bless ye Moḥammad."—These last words are added in the fear lest the rising of the river should be affected by a malicious wish, or evil eye, which is supposed to be rendered ineffectual if the malicious person bless the Prophet.[1]

Sometimes, the people of a house before which the Munádee makes his cry give him daily a piece of bread: this is a common custom among the middle orders; but most persons give him nothing until the day before the opening of the Canal of Cairo. Very little reliance is to be placed upon the announcement which he makes of the height which the river has attained, for he is generally uninformed or misinformed by the persons whose duty it is to acquaint him upon this subject; but the people mostly listen with interest to his proclamation. He and his boy repeat this cry every day, until the day next before that on which the dam that closes the mouth of the Canal of Cairo is cut.

---

1 He would be guilty of a sin if he did not do this when desired.

On this day (that is, the former of those just mentioned), the Munádee goes about his district, accompanied by a number of little boys, each of whom bears a small coloured flag, called "ráyeh;" and announces the "Wefà en-Neel" (the Completion, or Abundance, of the Nile); for thus is termed the state of the river when it has risen sufficiently high for the government to proclaim that it has attained the sixteenth cubit of the Nilometer. In this, however, the people are always deceived; for there is an old law, that the land-tax cannot be exacted unless the Nile rises to the height of sixteen cubits of the Nilometer; and the government thinks it proper to make the people believe, as early as possible, that it has attained this height. The period when the Wefà en-Neel is proclaimed is when the river has actually risen about twenty or twenty-one feet in the neigbourhood of the metropolis; which is generally between the 6th and 16th of August (or the 1st and 11th of the Coptic month of Misrà):[1] this is when there yet remain, of the measure of a moderately good rise, in the neighbourhood of the metropolis, four or three feet. On the day above mentioned (the next before that on which the canal is to be opened), the Munádee and the boys who accompany him with the little "ráyát" (or flags) make the following announcement:—

Munádee. "The river hath given abundance, and completed [its measure]!" *Boys.* "God hath given abundance."[2] *M.* "And Dár en-Naḥás[3] is filled." *B.* "God, &c." *M.* "And the canals flow." *B.* "God, &c." *M.* "And the vessels are afloat." *B.* "God, &c." *M.* "And the hoarder [of grain] has failed." *B.* "God, &c." *M.* "By permission of the Mighty, the Requiter." *B.* "God, &c." *M.* "And there remains nothing. *B.* "God, &c." *M.* "To the perfect completion." *B.* "God, &c." *M.* "This is an annual custom." *B.* "God, &c." *M.* "And may you live tc every year." *B.* "God, &c." *M.* "And if the hoarder wish for a scarcity," *B.* "God, &c." *M.* "May God visit him, before death, with blindness and affliction!" *B.* "God, &c." *M.* "This generous person loveth the generous." *B.* "God, &c." *M.* "And an admirable palace is built for him."[5] *B.* "God, &c." *M.* "And its

[1] This present year (1834), the river having risen with unusual rapidity, the dam was cut on the 5th of August. Fears were entertained lest it should overflow the dam before it was cut: which would have been regarded as an evil omen.

[2] The words thus translated, the boys pronounce "Ófa-lléh," for "Owfa-lláh."

[3] This is an old building between the aqueduct and Maṣr el-'Ateeḳah, where the Sulṭáns and Governors of Egypt used to alight, and inspect the state of the river, previously to the cutting of the dam of the canal.

[4] The person before whose house the announcement is made.

[5] In Paradise.

columns are incomparable jewels," *B.* "God, &c." *M.* "Instead of palm-sticks and timber:" *B.* "God, &c." *M.* "And it has a thousand windows that open:" *B.* "God, &c." *M.* "And before every window is Selsebeel."[1] *B.* "God, &c." *M.* "Paradise is the abode of the generous." *B.* "God, &c." *M.* "And Hell is the abode of the avaricious." *B.* "God, &c." *M.* "May God not cause me to stop before the door of an avaricious woman, nor of an avaricious man:" *B.* "God, &c." *M.* Nor of one who measures the water in the jar: *B.* "God, &c." *M.* "Nor who counts the bread while it is yet dough:" *B.* "God, &c." *M.* "And if a cake be wanting, orders a fast:" *B.* "God, &c." *M.* "Nor who shuts up the cats at supper-time:" *B.* "God, &c." *M.* "Nor who drives away the dogs upon the walls." *B.* "God, &c." *M.* "The world is brightened." *B.* "God, &c." *M.* "And the damsels have adorned themselves." *B.* "God, &c." *M.* "And the old women tumble about." *B.* "God, &c." *M.* "And the married man hath added to his wife eight others." *B.* "God, &c." *M.* "And the bachelor hath married eighteen."—This cry is continued until somebody in the house gives a present to the Munádee; the amount of which is generally from ten faḍḍahs to a piaster; but many persons give two piasters; and grandees, a kheyreeyeh, or nine piasters.

During this day, preparations are made for cutting the dam of the canal. This operation attracts a great crowd of spectators, partly from the political importance attached to it; but, being always prematurely performed, it is now without much reason made an occasion of public festivity.

The dam is constructed before, or soon after, the commencement of the Nile's increase. The "Khaleeg," or Canal, at the distance of about four hundred feet within its entrance, is crossed by an old stone bridge of one arch. About sixty feet in front of this bridge is the dam, which is of earth, very broad at the bottom, and diminishing in breadth towards the top, which is flat, and about three yards broad. The top of the dam rises to the height of about twenty-two or twenty-three feet above the level of the Nile when at the lowest; but not so high above the bed of the canal: for this is several feet above the low-water mark of the river, and consequently dry for some months when the river is low. The banks of the canal are a few feet higher

[1] A Fountain of Paradise.

than the top of the dam. Nearly the same distance in front of the dam that the latter is distant from the bridge, is raised a round pillar of earth, diminishing towards the top, in the form of a truncated cone, and not quite so high as the dam. This is called the "'arooseh" (or bride), for a reason which will presently be stated. Upon its flat top, and upon that of the dam, a little maize or millet is generally sown. The 'arooseh is always washed down by the rising tide before the river has attained to its summit, and generally more than a week or fortnight before the dam is cut.

It is believed that the custom of forming this 'arooseh originated from an ancient superstitious usage, which is mentioned by Arab authors, and, among them, by El-Makreezee. This historian relates that, in the year of the conquest of Egypt by the Arabs, 'Amr Ibn-El-'Áṣ, the Arab general, was told that the Egyptians were accustomed, at the period when the Nile began to rise, to deck a young virgin in gay apparel, and throw her into the river as a sacrifice, to obtain a plentiful inundation. This barbarous custom, it is said, he abolished; and the Nile, in consequence, did not rise in the least degree during the space of nearly three months after the usual period of the commencement of its increase. The people were greatly alarmed, thinking that a famine would certainly ensue: 'Amr, therefore, wrote to the Khaleefeh, to inform him of what he had done, and of the calamity with which Egypt was, in consequence, threatened. 'Omar returned a brief answer, expressing his approbation of 'Amr's conduct, and desiring him, upon the receipt of the letter, to throw a note, which it enclosed, into the Nile. The purport of this note was as follows:—"From 'Abd-Allah 'Omar, Prince of the Faithful, to the Nile of Egypt. If thou flow of thine own accord, flow not: but if it be God, the One, the Mighty, who causeth thee to flow, we implore God, the One, the Mighty, to make thee flow."—'Amr did as he was commanded; and the Nile, we are told, rose sixteen cubits in the following night.—This tale is, indeed, hard to be believed, even divested of the miracle.

On the north side of the Canal, overlooking the dam, and almost close to the bridge, was a small building of stone, from which the grandees of Cairo used to witness the operation of cutting the dam. This building has become a ruin; and upon its remains is erected a large tent for the reception of those officers who have to witness and superintend the cutting. Some other tents are also erected for other visiters; and the government supplies a great number of fire-works, chiefly rockets, to honour the festival, and to amuse the populace during the night preceding the day when the dam is cut, and during the operation itself, which is performed early in the morning. Many small tents, for the sale of sweetmeats, fruits, and other eatables, and coffee, &c., are likewise pitched along the bank of the isle of Er-Róḍah, opposite the entrance of the Canal. The day of the cutting of the dam of the Canal is called "Yóm Gebr el-Baḥr," which is said to signify "the Day of the Breaking of the River;" though the word "gebr," which is thus interpreted "breaking," has really the reverse signification. The term "Yóm Wefà el-Baḥr," or "Wefà en-Neel," before explained, is also, and more properly, applied to this day. The festival of the Canal is also called "Mósim el-Khaleeg."

In the afternoon of the day preceding that on which the dam is cut, numerous boats, hired by private parties, for pleasure, repair to the neighbourhood of the entrance of the Canal. Among these is a very large boat, called the "'Aḳabeh."[1] It is painted for the occasion, in a gaudy, but rude, manner; and has two or more small cannons on board, and numerous lamps attached to the ropes, forming various devices, such as a large star, &c.: it has also, over the cabin, a large kind of close awning, composed of pieces of silk, and other stuffs; and is adorned with two pennants. It is vulgarly believed that this boat represents a magnificent vessel, in which the Egyptians used, before the conquest of their country by the Arabs, to convey the virgin, whom, it is said, they threw into the Nile. It sails from Booláḳ about three hours after noon, taking passengers for hire, men and women; the latter being usually placed, if they prefer it, in the large awning above mentioned. It is made fast to the bank of the isle of Er-Róḍah, immediately opposite the entrance of the Canal. Most of the other boats also remain near it during the night, along the bank of the island; but some, all the evening and night, are constantly sailing up, or rowing down, the river. In many boats, the crews amuse themselves and their passengers by singing, often accompanied by the darabukkeh and zummárah; and some private parties hire professional musicians to add to their diversion on the river. The festival is highly enjoyed by the crowds who attend it, though there is little that a stranger would think could minister to their amusement: they seem to require nothing more to enliven

[1] "'Aḳab" is the *collective* name of the largest kind of the boats which navigate the Nile; and "'aḳabeh" (plural "'aḳabát"), the name of a single boat of this kind.

them than crowds and bustle, with a pipe and a cup of coffee. In former years, the festival was always attended by dancing-girls (who are now forbidden to perform), and by singers, instrumental musicians, and reciters of romances. In the evening, before it is dark, the exhibition of fire-works commences; and this is continued, together with the firing of guns from the 'aḳabeh and two or more gun-boats, every quarter of an hour during the night. About twelve guns are fired on each of these occasions: the whole number fired at the night's festival of the present year was about six hundred. The fire-works which are displayed during the night consist of little else than rockets and a few blue-lights: the best are kept till morning, and exhibited in broad day-light, during the cutting of the dam. At night, the river and its banks present a remarkably picturesque scene. Numerous boats are constantly passing up and down; and the lamps upon the rigging of the 'aḳabeh, and in other boats, as well as on the shore, where there are also many mesh'als stuck in the ground (several upon the dam and its vicinity, and many more upon the bank of the island), have a striking effect, which is occasionally rendered more lively by the firing of the guns, and the ascent of a number of rockets. The most crowded part of the scene of the festival at night is the bank of the island; where almost every person is too happy to sleep, even if the noise of the guns, &c., did not prevent him.

Before sunrise, a great number of workmen begin to cut the dam. This labour devolves, in alternate years, upon the Muslim grave-diggers[1] and on the Jews; both of whom are paid by the government: but when it falls to the Jews, and on a Saturday, they are under the necessity of paying a handsome sum of money to escape the sin of profaning their sabbath by doing what the government requires of them. With a kind of hoe, the dam is cut thinner and thinner, from the back (the earth being removed in baskets, and thrown upon the bank), until, at the top, it remains about a foot thick: this is accomplished by about an hour after sunrise. Shortly before this time, when dense crowds have assembled in the neighbourhood of the dam, on each bank of the Canal, the Governor of the metropolis arrives, and alights at the large tent before mentioned, by the dam: some other great officers are also present; and the Ḳáḍee attends, and writes a document[2] to attest the fact of the river's having risen to the height sufficient for the opening of the Canal, and of this

[1] "Et-turabeeyeh." [2] "Ḥogget-el-baḥr."

operation having been performed; which important document is despatched with speed to Constantinople. Meanwhile, the firing of guns, and the display of the fire-works, continue; and towards the close of the operation, the best of the fire-works are exhibited, when, in the glaring sunshine, they can hardly be seen. When the dam has been cut away to the degree above mentioned, and all the great officers whose presence is required have arrived, the Governor of the metropolis throws a purse of small gold coins to the labourers. A boat, on board of which is an officer of the late Wálee, is then propelled against the narrow ridge of earth, and, breaking the slight barrier, passes through it, and descends with the cataract thus formed. The person here mentioned is an old man, named Ḥammoodeh, who was "sarrág báshee" of the Wálee: it was his office to walk immediately before his master when the latter took his ordinary rides, preceded by a long train of officers, through the streets and environs of the metropolis. Just as his boat approaches the dam, the Governor of Cairo throws into it a purse of gold, as a present for him. The remains of the dam are quickly washed away by the influx of the water into the bed of the Canal, and numerous other boats enter, pass along the Canal throughout the whole length of the city, and, some of them, several miles further, and return.

Formerly, the Sheykh el-Beled, or the Báshà, with other great officers, presided at this fête, which was celebrated with much pomp; and money was thrown into the Canal, and caught by the populace, some of whom plunged into the water with nets; but several lives were generally lost in the scramble. This present year (1834), three persons were drowned on the day of the opening of the Canal; one in the Canal itself, and two in the lake of the Ezbekeeyeh. A few minutes after I had entered my house, on my return from witnessing the cutting of the dam, and the festivities of the preceding night (which I passed partly on the river, and partly on the isle of Er-Róḍah), a woman, having part of her dress, and her face, which was uncovered, besmeared with mud, passed by my door, screaming for the loss of her son, who was one of the three persons drowned on this occasion. The water entered the Ezbekeeyeh by a new canal, on the day preceding that on which the dam was cut. Crowds collected round it on this day, and will for many following days (I am writing a few days after the opening of the canal), to enjoy the view of the large expanse of water, which, though very turbid, is refreshing to the sight in so dry and dusty a place as Cairo, and at this hot season of the year. Several tents are pitched by it, at which visiters are supplied with coffee; and one for the sale of brandy, wine, &c.; and numerous stools and benches of palm-sticks are set there. The favourite time of resort to this place is the evening; and many persons remain there for several hours after sunset: some, all night. There are generally two or three story-tellers there. At all hours of the day, and sometimes even at midnight, persons are seen bathing in the lake; chiefly men and boys, but also some young girls, and even women; the latter of whom expose their persons before the passengers and idlers on the banks in a manner surprising in a place where women in general so carefully conceal even their faces, though most of these bathers are usually covered from the waist downwards. It often happens that persons are drowned here.[1]

On the day after the cutting of the dam, the Munádee continues to repeat his first cry; but uses a different form of expression in stating the height of the river; saying, for instance, "four from sixteen;" meaning, that the river has increased four "ḳeeráṭs" (or digits) from sixteen cubits. This cry he continues until the day of the Nórooz, or a little earlier.

On the "Nórooz," or Coptic New-year's-day (10th or 11th of September), or two or three days before, he comes to each house in his district, with his boy dressed in his best clothes, and a drummer and a hautboy-player; repeats the same cry as on the Wefà; and again receives a present. Afterwards he continues his former cry.

On the day of the "Ṣaleeb" (or the Discovery of the Cross), which is the 17th of the Coptic month of Toot, or 26th or 27th of September, at which period the river has risen to its greatest height, or nearly so, he comes again to each house in his district, and repeats the following cry:—"In uncertainty,[2] thou wilt not rest: nor in comparing[3] wilt thou rest. O my reproacher,[4] rest. There is nothing that endureth. There remaineth nothing [uncovered by the water] but the shemmám[5] and lemmám[6] and the sown fields and the anemone and safflower and flax: and may my master, such a one [naming the master of the house], live, and see that the river has increased; and give, to the bringer of good news, according to a just

[1] I have mentioned on a former occasion that the bed of the lake of the Ezbekeeyeh has been filled up since my second visit to Egypt.

[2] Doubting whether the Nile will rise sufficiently high.

[3] That is, in comparing the height of the river at a particular period in the present year with its height at the same period in preceding years.

[4] O thou who hast said to me, "Why dost thou not bring better news?"

[5] Cucumis dudaim.

[6] Mentha Kahirina.

judgment. Aboo-Raddád [1] is entitled to a fee from the government; a fee of a shereefee [2] for every digit of the river's increase: and *we* are entitled to a fee from the people of generosity; we come to take it with good behaviour. The fortunate Nile of Egypt hath taken leave of us in prosperity: in its increase, it hath irrigated all the country."—The Munádee, on this occasion, presents a few limes, and other fruit, to the rich, or persons of middle rank, and some lumps of dry mud of the Nile, which is eaten by the women, in many families. He generally receives a present of two or three or more piasters. His occupation then ceases until the next year.

---

1 The Sheykh of the Miḳyás, or Nilometer.

2 A gold coin, now become scarce. Its value, I am informed, is about a third of a pound sterling, or somewhat less.

CHAPTER XXVII.

PRIVATE FESTIVITIES, &c.

As the modern Egyptian does not become a housekeeper until he is married (and not of necessity *then,* for he may live with his wife in the house of his or her parents), his first marriage is generally the first event which affords him and his wife an occasion of calling together their respective friends to a private entertainment. Whenever a great entertainment is given on any occasion of rejoicing, it is customary, for the persons invited, to send presents (such as I have mentioned in describing the ceremonies attendant upon a marriage), a day or two before. The husband always has his separate party, generally in the lower apartment or apartments of the house; and the wife entertains her female relations and friends in the ḥareem, or upper apartments. It is also the usual custom for the wife to entertain her guests (among whom no males are ever admitted, except very young boys,) during the six middle hours of the day; and for the husband to receive his guests afterwards; after sunset, or after the 'eshè prayers: but sometimes his guests assemble while the wife is engaged with her own party in the ḥareem.

On these occasions, the female singers who are called "'Awálim" (or "'Ál'mehs") are often hired to amuse the company. They sit in one of the apartments of the ḥareem; generally at a window looking into the court. The wooden lattice-work of the window, though too close to allow them to be seen by persons without, is sufficiently open to let them be distinctly heard by the male guests sitting in the court or in one of the apartments which look into it. In many houses, there is a small elevated apartment, or closet, for the 'Awálim, which I have before described, adjoining the apartment in which the male guests assemble (as well as another adjoining the principal saloon of the ḥareem), screened in front by wooden lattice-work, to conceal these singers from the view of the men.—The dancing-girls ("Ghawázee," or "Gházeeyehs,") are, or were, also frequently hired to attend on the occasions of private festivities. They dance (with unveiled face) before the men, in the court, so that they may be seen also by the women from the windows of the ḥareem; or perform in an apartment in which the men are assembled, or in the street, before the house, for the amusement only of the women. When they or the 'Awálim perform for the entertainment of a party, one of the friends of the host usually collects for them small sums of money upon the tambourine, or in a handkerchief, from the guests; but sometimes, the host will not allow this custom to be observed. The contributions are called "nuḳooṭ." It is the general practice for the person who gives the entertainment to engage the Ghawázee for a certain sum: he receives the nuḳooṭ, which may fall short of, or exceed, the promised sum: in the former case, he pays the difference from his own purse: in the latter case he often pockets the surplus. Or he agrees that they shall receive all the nuḳooṭ, with, or without, an additional sum from himself. In some parties, where little decorum is observed, the guests dally and sport with these dancing-girls in a very licentious manner. I have before mentioned (in a former chapter), that, on these occasions, they are usually indulged with brandy, or some other intoxicating liquor, which most of them drink to excess. It is a common custom for a man to wet, with his tongue, small gold coins, and stick them upon the forehead, cheeks, chin, and lips, of a Gházeeyeh. When money is collected for the 'Awálim, their servant, who is called "khalbooṣ," and who often acts the part of a buffoon, generally calls out, at each contribution, "Shóbash 'aleyk yá ṣáḥeb el-faraḥ!" that is, "A present is due from thee, O giver of the entertainment, [on a similar occasion, and in the same way,]"[1] and adds, "Such a one has given so many 'maḥboobs,' or 'kheyreeyehs';" turning a few piasters into a much larger number of gold coins of considerably greater value; or, if gold be given, exaggerating the sum in the same manner. This he does to compliment the donor, and to stimulate the generosity of others. His mistress, or another of the 'Awálim, replies, "'Oḳbà le-'anduh!" ("May he have the like [rejoicing]!"[2] or "May he have a recompense!")—The guests are also often entertained with a concert of instrumental and vocal music, by male performers

[1] "Shóbash" is synonymous with "nuḳooṭ," being an Arabic corruption of the Persian "shábásh," which also signifies "well done!" "excellent!"

[2] The phrase was thus written and explained to me by a sheykh; but I suspect it should be, "Iḳbál le-'anduh," which is an expression vulgarly used to signify, "access to him;" and would mean, in this case, "[May we have] access to him:" and "Good fortune to him!"

("Áláteeyeh"), who sit in the court, or in the apartment in which the guests are assembled. Two "dikkehs" (or high wooden sofas) are often put together, front to front, in the court, and furnished with cushions, &c., to form an orchestra for the musicians; and a lantern is usually placed in the middle. The Áláteeyeh generally receive contributions from the assembly for whose entertainment they perform, like the 'Awálim; their khalbooṣ calling out to them in the same manner after each gift.

But performances of a different kind from those above mentioned are more common, and are considered more proper, on the occasions of private festivities. These are the recitations of a "khatmeh" (or of the whole of the Ḳur-án), by three or more fiḳees, who are hired for the purpose; or of a "zikr," by a small party of faḳeers.[1] That the khatmeh may not be too fatiguing to the performers, the fiḳees relieve one another by turns; one only chanting at a time; and each, usually, chanting a rubạ.[2] They generally come to the house a little after the 'aṣr, and get through the greater part of their task before the guests assemble: one of them then chants more leisurely, and in a more musical manner: after him, in the same manner, another; and so on. Sometimes a khatmeh is performed in the day-time, and after it, in the evening, a zikr. It is a rule that the zikr should always be performed after sunset.

In Egypt, persons who habitually live with the utmost frugality prepare a great variety and profusion of dishes for the entertainment of their friends. But very little time is devoted to eating. The period of conviviality is mostly passed in smoking, sipping coffee, drinking sherbet, and conversing: the Turks, however, generally abstain from smoking during the recitation of the Ḳur-án; and the honour which they pay to the sacred book on every occasion has given rise to a saying, that "God has exalted Ál-'Osmán [*i. e.* the race of 'Osmán, or the 'Osmánlees,] above other Muslims, because they exalt the Ḳur-án more than do others." In these parties, none of the guests ever attempts to amuse his companions, except by facetious conversation, or sometimes by telling a story; though all of them take great delight in the performances of the hired dancers, musicians, and singers. The Egyptians seldom play at any game, unless when only two or three

[1] These customs remind us of St. Paul's advice to the Ephesians, ch. v. v. 19; which shews the antiquity of social pastimes of this kind. The Egyptians highly enjoy the religious love-songs of the munshids at zikrs.

[2] A quarter of a "ḥezb," which latter is a sixtieth part of the Ḳur-án.

persons meet together, or in the privacy of their own families. They are a social people; and yet they but rarely give great entertainments. Festivities such as I have described above are very unfrequent: they occur only on particular occasions which really call for rejoicing. Except on such occasions, it is considered improper to hire dancing-girls to perform in a house.

The marriage-festivities I have described in a former chapter: I therefore proceed to give an account of the festivities which *follow* a marriage; and shall do so in the order of their occurrence.

On the seventh day ("Yóm es-Subooạ"[1]) after a marriage, the wife receives her female relations and friends during the morning and afternoon; and sometimes the husband entertains his own friends in the evening; generally hiring persons to perform a khatmeh or a zikr. It is a custom of husbands in Egypt to deny themselves their conjugal rights during the first week after the conclusion of the marriage with a virgin bride; and the termination of this period is a due cause for rejoicing.[2]—On the fortieth day ("Yóm el-Arba'een") after the marriage, the wife goes, with a party of her female friends, to the bath. Her companions return with her to her house, about the 'aṣr; partake of a repast, and go away. The husband, also, sometimes receives visiters in the evening of this day, and again causes a khatmeh or zikr to be performed.

The next festivities in a family are generally those consequent on the birth of a child.—Two or three or more days before the expected time of delivery, the "dáyeh" (or midwife) conveys, to the house of the woman who requires her assistance, the "kursee el-wiládeh," a chair of a peculiar form, upon which the patient is to be seated during the birth.[3] This chair is covered with a shawl, or an embroidered napkin; and some flowers of the ḥennà-tree, or some roses, are tied, with an embroidered handkerchief, to each of the upper corners of the back. Thus ornamented, the chair (which is the property of the dáyeh) is conveyed before her to the house.—In the houses of the rich, and of those in easy circumstances, the mother, after delivery, is placed on a bed, and usually remains on it from three to six days:

---

[1] The Subooạ after the birth of a child is celebrated with more rejoicing; and therefore, in speaking of the Yóm es-Subooạ, the seventh day after childbirth is generally understood.

[2] It was not such a festival as this alone that is alluded to in Genesis, xxix. 27, and in Judges, xiv. 12. It was, and I believe is still, the custom of the wealthy Bedawee (and such was Laban) to feast his friends seven days after marriage (as also after the birth of a male child); and every respectable Muslim, after marriage, if disappointed in the expectations he has been led to form of his wife, abstains from putting her away for about a week, that she may not be disgraced by suspicion; particularly if it be her first marriage.

[3] See Exodus, i. 16.

but poor women, in the same case, seldom take to a bed at all; and after a day or two resume their ordinary occupations, if not requiring great exertion.

On the morning after the birth, two or three of the dancing-men called Khäwals, or two or three Gházeeyehs, dance in front of the house, or in the court.—The festivities occasioned by the birth of a son are always greater than those on account of a daughter. The Arabs still shew relics of that feeling which often induced their ancient ancestors to destroy their female offspring.

A few days after the birth, generally on the fourth or fifth day, the women of the house, if the family be of the middle or wealthy classes, usually prepare dishes of "mufattaḳah," "kishk," "libábeh," and "ḥilbeh," which they send to the female relations and friends. The first of these consists of honey with a little clarified butter[1] and oil of sesame,[2] and a variety of aromatics and spices pounded together: roasted hazel-nuts are also added to it.[3] The kishk has been described in a former page.[4] The libábeh is composed of broken or crumbled bread, honey, clarified butter, and a little rose-water: the butter is first put into a saucepan over a fire; then, the broken bread; and next, the honey. The dish of ḥilbeh (or fenugreek) is prepared from the dry grain, boiled, and then sweetened with honey over the fire.

On the "Yóm es-Subooạ" (or Seventh Day) after the birth of a child, the female friends of its mother pay her a visit. In the families of the higher classes, 'Awálim are hired to sing in the ḥareem, or Áláteeyeh perform, or fiḳees recite a khatmeh, below. The mother, attended by the dáyeh, sits on the kursee el-wiládeh, in the hope that she may soon have occasion for it again; for her doing this is considered propitious. The child is brought, wrapped in a handsome shawl, or something costly; and, to accustom it to noise, that it may not be frightened afterwards by the music, and other sounds of mirth, one of the women takes a brass mortar,[5] and strikes it repeatedly with the pestle, as if pounding. After this, the child is put into a sieve, and shaken; it being supposed that this operation is beneficial to its stomach. Next, it is carried through all the apartments of the ḥareem, accompanied by several women or girls, each of whom bears a number

---

[1] "Semn."

[2] "Seereg."

[3] Some women add another ingredient; not when it is to be sent to friends, but for a particular purpose, which is, to make them fat: they broil and mash up a number of beetles in the butter, and then add the honey, &c. This has been alluded to in the chapter on the Domestic Life of the Women.

[4] In a note to the second paragraph of the preceding chapter.

[5] "Hón."

of wax candles, sometimes of various colours, cut in two, lighted, and stuck into small lumps of paste of ḥennà, upon a small round tray. At the same time, the dáyeh, or another female, sprinkles, upon the floor of each room, a mixture of salt and seed of the fennel-flower,[1] or salt alone, which has been placed during the preceding night at the infant's head; saying, as she does this, "The salt be in the eye of the person who doth not bless the Prophet;"[2] or, "The foul salt be in the eye of the envier."[3] This ceremony of the sprinkling of salt[4] is considered a preservative, for the child and mother, from the evil eye: and each person present should say, "O God, bless our lord Moḥammad!" The child, wrapped up, and placed on a fine mattress, which is sometimes laid on a silver tray, is shewn to each of the women present, who looks at its face, says, "O God, bless our lord Moḥammad! God give thee long life," &c., and usually puts an embroidered handkerchief, with a gold coin (if pretty or old, the more esteemed,) tied up in one of the corners, on the child's head, or by its side. This giving of handkerchiefs is considered as imposing a debt, to be repaid by the mother, if the donor should give her the same occasion; or as the discharge of a debt for a similar offering. The coins are generally used, for some years, to decorate the head-dress of the child. After these nuḳooṭ for the child, others are given for the dáyeh. During the night before the subooạ, a water-bottle full of water (a dóraḳ in the case of a boy, or a ḳulleh in that of a girl), with an embroidered handkerchief tied round the neck, is placed at the child's head, while it sleeps. This, with the water it contains, the dáyeh takes, and puts upon a tray, and presents to each of the women; who put their nuḳooṭ for her (merely money) into the tray.—In the evening, the husband generally entertains a party of his friends, in the manner usual on other occasions of private festivity.

During a certain period after childbirth (in most cases, among the people of Cairo, forty days, but differing according to circumstances, and according to the doctrines of the different sects), the mother is regarded as religiously impure.[5] The period here mentioned is called "Nifás." At the expiration of it, the woman goes to the bath.

The ceremonies and festivities attendant upon the *circumcision* of

---

1 "Ḥabbeh sódà."

2 "El-milḥ fee 'eyn ellee má yeṣallee 'a-n-nebee." "Yeṣallee" is for "yuṣallee; and "'a-n-nebee," for "'ala-n-nebee."

3 "El-milḥ el-fásid fee 'eyn el-ḥásid."

4 "Rashsh el-milḥ."

5 In like manner, the Jewish law pronounces a woman unclean during forty days after the birth of a male child; but double that time after bearing a female child. See Leviticus, xii. 2, 4, 5.

a boy are the next that I shall describe.—In most cases, the boy about to be circumcised (who is called "muṭṭáhir") is paraded through the streets in the manner which has been related in a former chapter; that is, if his parents be of the middle or higher class of citizens: but most of the learned, people of religious professions, fiḳees, and some rich men, in Cairo, prefer performing a ceremony called "Ṣiráfeh," of which the following account will convey a sufficient notion.

The schoolfellows of the muṭṭáhir, all dressed in their best clothes, or in borrowed clothes if they have none of their own good enough, which is generally the case, repair, a little before noon, to one of the principal mosques, as that of the Ḥasaneyn, or the Azhar, or that of the seyyideh Zeyneb. Thither also go the men and the women and many of the female friends of the family of the muṭṭáhir, with the muṭṭáhir himself, and sometimes about six sháweeshes (or sergeants) of the Naḳeeb el-Ashráf. The barber who is to perform the operation also attends, with a servant bearing his "ḥeml" (or sign), which has been described in the account of the more common ceremonies of circumcision. All these persons, with some others who will presently be mentioned, having assembled in the mosque, wait there until after the noon-prayers, and then depart in procession through the streets to the house of the muṭṭáhir's parents. The first person in the procession is the barber's servant, with his ḥeml. He is sometimes followed by five or six fiḳees, chanting a lyric ode ("muweshshaḥ") in praise of the Prophet. Then follow the school-boys, two, three, or four abreast. The foremost of these boys, or half their number, chant, as they pass along,—"O nights of pleasure! O nights of joy!"—The other boys then take up the strain, adding,—"Pleasure and desire, with friends assembled!"—Then, again, the former,—"Bless, O our Lord, the Perspicuous Light."—Then, the latter, "Aḥmad,[1] the Elect, the chief of Apostles."—Thus the boys continue to chant the whole of the way. Behind them walk the male relations of the muṭṭáhir. These are followed by about six boys; three of them bearing each a silver scent-bottle ("ḳumḳum") full of rose-water or orange-flower-water, which they occasionally sprinkle on some of the spectators; and each of the others bearing a silver perfuming-vessel ("mibkharah") in which benzoin, frank-incense, or some other odoriferous substance, is burning. With

[1] A name of the Arabian Prophet.

these boys walks a saḳḳà, bearing, on his back, a skin of water covered with an embroidered napkin: he gives water, now and then, in brass cups, to passengers in the street. Next follow three servants: one of these carries a silver pot of coffee, in a silver "'áz'ḳee" (or chafing-dish suspended by three chains): another bears a silver tray, with ten or eleven coffee-cups, and "ẓarfs" of silver: the third carries nothing: it is his office, when the procession passes by a well-dressed person (one sitting at a shop, for instance), to fill, and present to him, a cup of coffee; and the person thus honoured gives the servant something in return: half a piaster is considered amply sufficient. The sháweeshes occupy the next place in the order of the procession. Sometimes they are followed by another group of boys with ḳumḳums and mibkharahs. Next follows a boy bearing the writing tablet of the muṭṭáhir, hung to his neck by a handkerchief: it is ornamented for the occasion by the schoolmaster. Behind the boy who bears it walks the muṭṭáhir, between two others. He is dressed either as in the zeffeh before described (that is, in girls' clothes, with the exception of the turban, and decked with women's ornaments), or simply as a boy; and holds a folded embroidered handkerchief to his mouth. The women follow him, raising their shrill cries of joy (the "zagháreeṭ"); and one of them is constantly employed in sprinkling salt behind him, to prevent any ill effects from an evil eye, which, it is thought, some person may cast at the lad from envy. In this order and manner, the procession arrives at the house.—On halting before the door, the foremost of the schoolboys sing,—"Thou art a sun. Thou art a moon. Thou art a light above light."—The others add,—"O Moḥammad! O my friend! O thou with black eyes!"—They enter the house repeating this address to the Prophet; and repeat it again after entering. The young boys go up-stairs: the others remain below. The former, as they go up, repeat,—"O thou his paternal aunt! O thou his maternal aunt! Come: prepare his ṣiráfeh."—On entering the "ḳá'ah," or principal apartment of the ḥareem, a Kashmeer shawl is given them to hold: they hold it all round; and the ornamented writing-tablet is placed in the middle of it. The "'areef," or head boy of the school, who (together with the muṭṭáhir and the women) stands by while they do this, then recites what is termed "khuṭbet eṣ-ṣiráfeh:" each clause of this is chanted by him first, and then repeated by the other boys. It is in unmeasured rhyme; and to the following effect:—

"Praise be to God, the Mighty Creator,—the Sole, the Forgiver, the Conservator:—He knoweth the past and futurity,—and veileth things in obscurity.—He knoweth the tread of the black ant,—and its work when in darkness vigilant.—He formed and exalted heaven's vault,—and spread the earth o'er the ocean salt.—May He grant this boy long life and happiness,—to read the Ḳur-án with attentiveness; —to read the Ḳur-án, and history's pages,—the stories of ancient and modern ages.—This youth has learned to write and read,—to spell, and cast up accounts with speed:—his father, therefore, should not withhold—a reward of money, silver and gold.—Of my learning, O father, thou hast paid the price:—God give thee a place in Paradise:—and thou, my mother, my thanks receive—for thine anxious care of me, morn and eve:—God grant I may see thee in Paradise seated,—and by Maryam[1] and Zeyneb[2] and Fáṭimeh[3] greeted.—Our faḳeeh[4] has taught us the alphabet:—may he have every grateful epithet.—Our faḳeeh has taught us as far as 'The News:'[5]—may he never his present blessings lose.—Our faḳeeh has taught us as far as 'The Dominion:'—may he ever be blest with the world's good opinion.—Our faḳeeh has taught us as far as 'The Compassionate:' —may he ever enjoy rewards proportionate.—Our faḳeeh has taught us as far as 'Yá-Seen:'—may his days and years be ever serene.— Our faḳeeh has taught as far as 'The Cave:'—may he ever the blessings of Providence have.—Our faḳeeh has taught as far as 'The Cattle:'—may he ne'er be the subject of scandalous tattle.—Our faḳeeh has taught us as far as 'The Cow:'—may he ever be honoured, in future and now.—Our faḳeeh amply merits of you—a coat of green, and a turban too.—O ye surrounding virgin lasses!—I commend you to God's care by the eye-paint and the glasses.[6]—O ye married ladies here collected!—I pray, by the Chapter of 'The Ranks,'[7] that ye be protected.—O ye old women standing about!—ye ought to be beaten with old shoes, and turned out.—To old women, however, we should rather say,—Take the basin and ewer; wash and pray."

During the chanting of these absurd expressions, the women drop, upon the ornamented writing-tablet, their nuḳooṭ, which are after-

---

1 The Virgin Mary.

2 The daughter of the Imám 'Alee.

3 The daughter of the Prophet.

4 Vulg. "fiḳee."

5 This and the following words distinguished by inverted commas are the titles of chapters of the Ḳur-án, which the boys, as I have mentioned on a former occasion, learn in the reverse order of their arrangement, after having learned the first chapter. The chapter of "The News" is the 78th: the others, afterwards named, are the 67th, 55th, 36th, 18th, 6th, and 2nd.

6 The looking-glasses. This is said to amuse the ladies.

7 The 37th chapter of the Ḳur-án.

wards collected in a handkerchief. The boys then go down, and give the nuḳooṭ to the fiḳee below.[1]—Here, the muṭṭáhir is now placed on a seat. The barber stands on one side of him, and the servant who holds the ḥeml on the other. The ḥeml is rested on the floor; and on the top of it is placed a cup, into which the guests put their nuḳooṭ for the barber.—The female visiters dine in the ḥareem, and then leave the house. The boys dine below, and go to their homes. The men also dine; and all of them, except those of the family, and the barber and his servant, take their leave. The barber then conducts the muṭṭáhir, with one or two of his male relations, to a private apartment, and there performs the operation; or sometimes this is done on the following day. About a week after, he takes the boy to the bath.

The next occasion of festivity in a family (if not the marriage of a son or daughter) is generally when a son is admitted a member of some body of tradesmen or artizans. On this occasion, a ceremony which I am about to describe is performed in certain cases, but not on admission into every trade: it is customary only among carpenters, turners, barbers, tailors, book-binders, and a few others. The young man having become an adept in the business of his intended trade, his father goes to the Sheykh of that trade, and signifies his wish that his son should be admitted a member. The Sheykh sends an officer, called the "Naḳeeb," to invite the masters of the trade, and sometimes a few friends of the candidate, to be present at the admission. The Naḳeeb, taking in his hand a bunch of sprigs of any green herb, or flowers, goes to each of these persons, hands to him a sprig or little piece of green,[2] or a flower, or leaf, and says, "For the Prophet, the Fát'ḥah:" that is "Repeat the Fát'ḥah for the Prophet." Both having done this together, the Naḳeeb adds, "On such a day and hour, come to such a house or place, and drink a cup of coffee." The guests thus invited meet (generally at the house of the father of the young man, but sometimes in the country), take coffee, and dine. After this, the Naḳeeb leads the young man before the Sheykh, states his qualifications, and then desires the persons present to recite the Fát'ḥah for the Prophet; which done, he girds the young man with a shawl over his outer coat, and ties a knot with the ends of this girdle. The Fát'ḥah is then recited again, generally for the seyyid El-

---

[1] What follows this describes the ceremonies which are performed both after the ṣiráfeh and after the more common zeffeh, of which I have given an account in a former chapter.

[2] "'Ood niyáẓ.'

Bedawee, or some other great saint, and a second knot is tied. Then, a third time the Fát'ḥah is recited, and a bow is tied. The young man is thus completely admitted. He kisses the hand of the Sheykh, and that of each of his fellow tradesmen, and gives the Naḳeeb a small fee.—This ceremony is called "shedd el-weled" (the binding of the youth); and the person thus admitted is termed "meshdood," or bound.

There remain only to be described the ceremonies occasioned by a death. These will be the subject of a separate chapter, here following, and concluding my account of the manners and customs of the Muslims of Egypt.

CHAPTER XXVIII.

DEATH, AND FUNERAL RITES.

When a learned or pious Muslim feels that he is about to die, he sometimes performs the ordinary ablution, as before prayer, that he may depart from life in a state of bodily purity; and generally he repeats the profession of the faith, "There is no deity but God: Moḥammad is God's Apostle." It is common also for a Muslim, on a military expedition, or during a long journey, especially in the desert, to carry his grave-linen with him. Not unfrequently does it happen that a traveller, in such circumstances, has even to make his own grave: completely overcome by fatigue or privation, or sinking under a fatal disease, in the desert, when his companions, if he have any, cannot wait for his recovery or death, he performs the ablution (with water, if possible, or, if not, with sand or dust, which is allowable in such case), and then, having made a trench in the sand, as his grave, lies down in it, wrapped in his grave-clothes, and covers himself, with the exception of his face, with the sand taken up in making the trench: thus he waits for death to relieve him; trusting to the wind to complete his burial.

When any one of the eminent 'Ulamà of Cairo dies, the muëddins of the Azhar, and those of several other mosques, announce the event by chanting from the mád'nehs the cry called the "Abrár;" the words of which I have given in the account of the customs observed during Ramaḍán, in the second of the chapters on Periodical Public Festivals, &c.

The ceremonies attendant upon death and burial are nearly the same in the cases of men and women. When the rattles in the throat, or other symptoms, shew that a man is at the point of death, an attendant (his wife, or some other person,) turns him round to place his face in the direction of Mekkeh,[1] and closes his eyes. Even before the spirit has departed, or the moment after, the male attendants generally exclaim, "Alláh! There is no strength nor power but in God. To God we belong; and to Him we must return. God have mercy on him." The women of the family, at the same time, raise the cries of lamentation called "welweleh" or "wilwál;" uttering the most piercing shrieks, and calling upon the name of the deceased. The most common cries that are heard on the death of the master of a family, from the lips of his wife, or wives, and children, are "O my master!"[2] "O my camel!"[3] (that is, "O thou who broughtest my provisions, and hast carried my burdens,") "O my lion!"[4] "O camel of the house!"[5] "O my glory!"[6] "O my resource!"[7] "O my father!"[8] "O my misfortune!"[9]—The clothes of the deceased are taken off as soon as he has ceased to breathe; and he is attired in another suit, placed on his bed or mattress, and covered over with a sheet. The women continue their lamentations; and many of the females of the neighbourhood, hearing the conclamation, come to unite with them in this melancholy task. Generally, also, the family of the deceased send for two or more "neddábehs" (or public wailing-women[10]); but some persons disapprove of this custom; and many, to avoid unnecessary expense, do not conform with it. Each neddábeh brings with her a "ṭár" (or tambourine), which is without the tinkling plates of metal which are attached to the hoop of the common ṭár. The neddábehs, beating their ṭárs, exclaim, several times, "Alas for him!"—and praise his turban, his handsome person, &c.; and the female relations, domestics, and friends of the deceased (with their tresses dishevelled, and sometimes with rent clothes), beating their own faces, cry in like manner, "Alas for him!"—This wailing is generally continued at least an hour.

If the death took place in the morning, the corpse is buried the same day;[11] but if it happened in the afternoon, or at night, the deceased is not buried until the following day: in this case, the neddábehs remain all the night, and continue the lamentation with

---

1 Some Muslims turn the *head* of the corpse in the direction of Mekkeh: others, the *right side*, inclining the *face* in that direction: the latter, I believe, is the general custom.

2 "Yá seedee."

3 "Yá gemelee."

4 "Yá seb'ee."

5 "Yá gemel el-beyt."

6 "Yá 'ezzee."

7 "Yá ḥeeletee."

8 "Yá abooyà."

9 "Yá daḥwetee" (for daạwetee").

10 See 2 Chron. xxxv. 25; Jer. ix. 17; and St. Matt. ix. 23.

11 The Egyptians have a superstitious objection to keeping a corpse in the house during the night after the death, and to burying the dead after sunset; but the latter is sometimes done: I have witnessed one instance of it.

the other women; and a fiḳee is brought to the house to recite chapters of the Ḳur-án during the night, or several fiḳees are employed to perform a complete khatmeh.

The "mughassil" (or washer of the dead) soon comes, with a bench, upon which he places the corpse, and a bier.[1] The fiḳees who are to take part in the funeral-procession (if the deceased were a person of respectable rank, or of the middle order,) are also now brought to the house. These, during the process of washing, sit in an apartment adjoining that in which the corpse is placed, or without the door of the latter apartment; and some of them recite, or rather chant, the "Soorat el-An'ám" (or 6th chapter of the Ḳur-án): others of them chant part of the "Burdeh," a celebrated poem in praise of the Prophet. The washer takes off the clothes of the deceased; which are his perquisite. The jaw is bound up, and the eyes are closed. The ordinary ablution preparatory to prayer having been performed upon the corpse, with the exception of the washing of the mouth and nose, the whole body is well washed, from head to foot, with warm water and soap, and with "leef" (or fibres of the palm-tree); or, more properly, with water in which some leaves of the lote-tree ("nabḳ," or "sidr,") have been boiled.[2] The nostrils, ears, &c., are stuffed with cotton; and the corpse is sprinkled with a mixture of water, pounded camphor, and dried and pounded leaves of the nabḳ, and with rose-water. Sometimes, other dried and pounded leaves are added to those of the nabḳ. The ankles are bound together, and the hands placed upon the breast.

The "kefen," or grave-clothing, of a poor man consists of a piece, or two pieces, of cotton;[3] or is merely a kind of bag. The corpse of a man of wealth is generally wrapped first in muslin; then, in cotton cloth of thicker texture; next in a piece of striped stuff of silk and cotton intermixed, or in a ḳufṭán of similar stuff, merely stitched together; and over these is wrapped a Kashmeer shawl. The corpse of a woman of middling rank is usually clothed with a yelek. The colours most approved for the grave-clothes are white and green; but any colour is used, except blue, or what approaches to blue. The body, prepared for interment as above described, is placed in the bier, which is usually covered over with a red or other Kashmeer shawl. The persons who are to compose the funeral-procession then arrange

[1] It is hardly necessary to state that the corpse of a female is always washed by a woman.

[2] The leaves of the lote-tree, dried and pulverized, are often used by the poor instead of soap.

[3] The kefen is often sprinkled with water from the well of Zemzem, in the Temple of Mekkeh.

themselves in order.—The more common funeral-processions may be thus described.

The first persons are about six or more poor men, called "Yemeneeyeh;" mostly blind; who proceed two and two, or three and three, together. Walking at a moderate pace, or rather slowly, they chant incessantly, in a melancholy tone, the profession of the faith ("There is no deity but God: Moḥammad is God's Apostle: God bless and save him!"); often, but not always, as follows:—

La i - lá - ha il - la-l - láh: Mo-ḥam - ma - dur - ra - soo - lu-l -
láh: Ṣal - la-l - lá - hu 'a - ley - hi wa - sel - lem!

or sometimes, other words. They are followed by some male relations and friends of the deceased, and, in many cases, by two or more persons of some sect of darweeshes, bearing the flags of their order. This is a general custom at the funeral of a darweesh. Next follow three or four or more schoolboys; one of whom carries a "muṣ-ḥaf" (or copy of the Ḳur-án), or a volume consisting of one of the thirty sections of the Ḳur-án, placed upon a kind of desk formed of palm-sticks, and covered over, generally with an embroidered kerchief. These boys chant, in a higher and livelier voice than the Yemeneeyeh, usually some words of a poem called the "Ḥashreeyeh," descriptive of the events of the last day, the judgment, &c.; to the air here noted:—

Sub - ḥá- na men an-sha-ṣ-ṣu-war Wa -'a-l - 'e-bád[1] bi-l-mót ḳa-har.

The following is a translation of the commencement of this poem.

'[I extol] the perfection of Him who hath created whatever hath form;
And subdued his servants by death:
Who bringeth to nought [all] his creatures, with mankind:
They shall all lie in the graves:
The perfection of the Lord of the east:[2]
The perfection of the Lord of the west:[3]

1 "'A-l-'ebád" is a vulgar contraction, for "'ala-l-'ebád."—It will be observed (from the specimen here given, in the first two lines,) that this poem is not in the *literary* dialect of Arabic.

2 Literally, "the two easts," or "the two places of sunrise:" the point where the sun rises in summer, and that where it rises in winter.

3 Or "the two places of sunset."

Funeral-Procession.

The perfection of the illuminator of the two lights;
The sun, to wit, and the moon:
His perfection: how bountiful is He!
His perfection: how clement is He!
His perfection: how great is He!
When a servant rebelleth against Him, He protecteth.'

The school-boys immediately precede the bier, which is borne head-foremost. Three or four friends of the deceased usually carry it for a short distance; then three or four other friends bear it a little further; and then these are in like manner relieved. Casual passengers, also, often take part in this service, which is esteemed highly meritorious. Behind the bier walk the female mourners; sometimes a group of more than a dozen, or twenty; with their hair dishevelled, though generally concealed by the head-veil; crying and shrieking, as before described; and often, the hired mourners accompany them, celebrating the praises of the deceased. Among the women, the relations and domestics of the deceased are distinguished by a strip of linen or cotton stuff or muslin, generally blue, bound round the head, and tied in a single knot behind; the ends hanging down a few inches.[1] Each of these also carries a handkerchief, usually dyed blue, which she sometimes holds over her shoulders, and at other times twirls with both hands over her head or before her face. The cries of the women, the lively chanting of the youths, and the deep tones uttered by the Yemeneeyeh, compose a strange discord.

The wailing of women at funerals was forbidden by the Prophet; and so was the celebration of the virtues of the deceased. Moḥammad declared that the virtues thus ascribed to a dead person would be subjects of reproach to him, if he did not possess them, in a future state. It is astonishing to see how some of the precepts of the Prophet are every day violated by all classes of the modern Muslims; the Wahhábees alone excepted.—I have sometimes seen mourning women of the lower classes, following a bier, having their faces (which were bare), and their head-coverings and bosoms, besmeared with mud.[2]

The funeral-procession of a man of wealth, or of a person of the middle classes, is sometimes preceded by three or four or more camels,

---

[1] In the funeral-scenes represented on the walls of ancient Egyptian tombs, we often see females with a similar bandage round the head.

[2] This was a custom of the ancient Egyptians: it is described by Herodotus, lib. ii. cap. 85.—Passengers in the streets and roads, when a corpse is borne by to the tomb, often say,—"God is most great! God is most great! That is what God and his Apostle have promised: and God and his Apostle have spoken truth. O God, increase our faith and submission."—The women, pointing with the finger at the bier, say,—"I testify that there is no deity but God."

bearing bread and water to give to the poor at the tomb; and is composed of a more numerous and varied assemblage of persons. The foremost of these are the Yemeneeyeh, who chant the profession of the faith, as described above. They are generally followed by some male friends of the deceased, and some learned and devout persons who have been invited to attend the funeral. Next follows a group of four or more fiḳees, chanting the "Soorat el-An'ám" (the 6th chapter of the Ḳur-án); and sometimes, another group, chanting the "Soorat Yá-Seen" (the 36th chapter); another, chanting the "Soorat el-Kahf" (the 18th chapter); and another, chanting the "Soorat ed-Dukhán" (the 44th chapter). These are followed by some munshids, singing the "Burdeh;" and these, by certain persons called "Aṣ-ḥáb el-Aḥzáb," who are members of religious orders founded by celebrated Sheykhs. There are generally four or more of the order of the Ḥezb es-Sádát; a similar group of the Ḥezb Esh-Sházilee; and another of the Ḥezb Esh-Shaạráwee: each group chants a particular form of prayer. After them are generally borne two or more half-furled flags, the banners of one or other of the principal orders of darweeshes. Then follow the school-boys, the bier, and the female mourners, as in the procession before described; and, perhaps, the led horses of the bearers, if these be men of rank. A buffalo, to be sacrificed at the tomb, where its flesh is to be distributed to the poor, sometimes closes the procession.

The funeral of a devout sheykh, or of one of the great 'Ulamà, is still more numerously attended; and the bier of such a person is not covered with a shawl. A "welee" is further honoured in his funeral by a remarkable custom. Women follow his bier; but, instead of wailing, as they would after the corpse of an ordinary mortal, they rend the air with the shrill and quavering cries of joy called "zagháreeṭ;" and if these cries are discontinued but for a minute, the bearers of the bier protest that they cannot proceed; that a supernatural power rivets them to the spot on which they stand. Very often, it is said, a welee impels the bearers of his corpse to a particular spot.—The following anecdote, describing an ingenious mode of puzzling a dead saint in a case of this kind, was related to me by one of my friends.—Some men were lately bearing the corpse of a welee to a tomb prepared for it in the great cemetery on the north of the metropolis; but, on arriving at the gate called Báb en-Naṣr, which leads to this cemetery, they found themselves unable to proceed further, from the cause above mentioned. "It seems," said one of the bearers, "that the sheykh is determined not to be buried in the cemetery of Báb en-Naṣr; and what shall we do?" They were all much perplexed; but being as obstinate as the saint himself, they did not immediately yield to his caprice. Retreating a few paces, and then advancing with a quick step, they thought, by such an impetus, to force the corpse through the gate-way; but their efforts were unsuccessful; and the same experiment they repeated in vain several times. They then placed the bier on the ground to rest and consult; and one of them, beckoning away his comrades to a distance beyond the hearing of the dead saint, said to them, "Let us take up the bier again, and turn it round quickly several times till the sheykh becomes giddy; he then will not know in what direction we are going, and we may take him easily through the gate." This they did; the saint was puzzled as they expected, and quietly buried in the place which he had so striven to avoid.

The biers used for the conveyance of the corpses of females and boys are different from those of men. They are furnished with a cover of wood, over which a shawl is spread, as over the bier of a

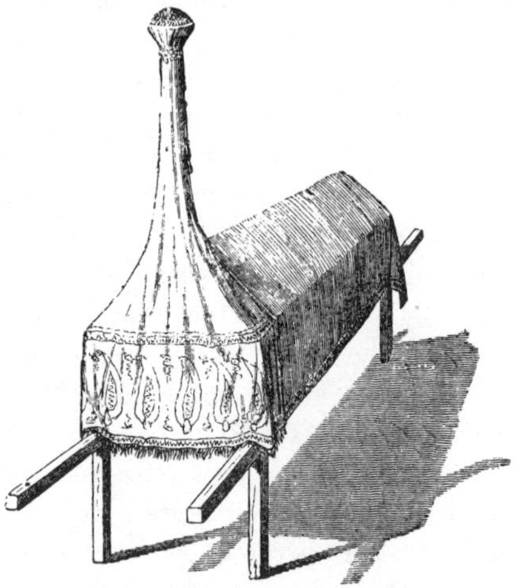

Bier used for the conveyance of the Corpse of a Female or Boy.

man; and at the head is an upright piece of wood, called a "sháhid." The sháhid is covered with a shawl; and to the upper part of it, when the bier is used to convey the body of a female of the middle or higher class, several ornaments of female head-dress are attached: on the top, which is flat and circular, is often placed a "kurṣ" (the round ornament of gold or silver set with diamonds, or of embossed gold, which is worn on the crown of the head-dress): to the back is suspended the "ṣafà" (or a number of braids of black silk with gold ornaments along each, which are worn by the ladies, in addition to their plaits of hair, hanging down the back). The bier of a boy is distinguished by a turban, generally formed of a red Kashmeer shawl, wound round the top of the sháhid, which, in the case of a young boy, is also often decorated with the kurṣ and ṣafà. The corpse of a very young child is carried to the tomb in the arms of a man, and merely covered with a shawl; or in a very small bier borne on a man's head.

In the funerals of females and boys, the bier is usually only preceded by the Yemeneeyeh, chanting the profession of the faith, and by some male relations of the deceased; and followed by the female mourners; unless the deceased was of a family of wealth, or of considerable station in the world; in which case, the funeral-procession is distinguished by some additional display. I shall give a short description of one of the most genteel and decorous funerals of this kind that I have witnessed: it was that of a young, unmarried lady.—Two men, each bearing a large, furled, green flag, headed the procession, preceding the Yemeneeyeh, who chanted in an unusually low and solemn manner. These faḳeers, who were in number about eight, were followed by a group of fiḳees, chanting a chapter of the Ḳur-án. Next after the latter was a man bearing a large branch of "nabḳ" (or lote-tree), an emblem of the deceased.[1] On each side of him walked a person bearing a tall staff or cane, to the top of which were attached several hoops ornamented with strips of various-coloured paper. These were followed by two Turkish soldiers, side by side; one bearing, on a small round tray, a gilt silver "ḳumḳum" of rose-water; and the other bearing, on a similar tray, a "mibkharah" of gilt silver, in which some odoriferous substance (as benzoin, or frankincense,) was burning. These vessels diffused the odour of their contents on the way, and were afterwards used to perfume the sepulchral vault. Passengers were occasionally sprinkled with the rose-water. Next followed four men, each of whom bore, upon a small tray, several small lighted tapers of wax, stuck in lumps of paste of "ḥennà." The bier was covered with rich shawls, and its sháhid was decorated

[1] This is only borne in funerals of young persons.

with handsome ornaments of the head; having, besides the ṣafà, a "ḳuṣṣah almás" (a long ornament of gold and diamonds, worn over the forehead), and, upon its flat top, a rich diamond ḳurṣ. These were the jewels of the deceased, or were, perhaps, as is often the case, borrowed for the occasion. The female mourners, in number about seven or eight, clad in the usual manner of the ladies of Egypt (with the black silk covering, &c.), followed the bier, not on foot, as is the common custom in funerals in this country, but mounted on high-saddled asses; and only the last two or three of them were wailing; these being, probably, hired mourners.—In another funeral-procession of a female, the daughter of a Turk of high rank, the Yemeneeyeh were followed by six black slaves, walking two by two. The first two slaves bore each a silver ḳumḳum of rose-water, which they sprinkled on the passengers; and one of them honoured me so profusely as to wet my dress very uncomfortably; after which, he poured a small quantity into my hands, and I wetted my face with it, according to custom. Each of the next two bore a silver mibkharah, with perfume; and the other two carried each a silver 'áz'ḳee (or hanging censer), with burning charcoal and frankincense. The jewels on the sháhid of the bier were of a costly description. Eleven ladies, mounted on high-saddled asses, together with several neddábehs, followed.

The rites and ceremonies performed in the mosque, and at the tomb, and after the funeral, remain to be described.—If the deceased died in any of the northern quarters of the metropolis, the body is usually carried, in preference, to the mosque of the Ḥasaneyn; unless he was a poor man, not residing near to that venerated sanctuary; in which case, his friends generally carry his corpse to any neighbouring mosque, to save time, and avoid unnecessary expense. If he was one of the 'Ulamà (that is, of a learned profession, however humble), his corpse is usually taken to the great mosque El-Azhar. The people of the southern parts of the metropolis generally carry their dead to the mosque of the seyyideh Zeyneb, or to that of any other celebrated saint. The reason of choosing such mosques in preference to others, is the belief that the prayers offered up at the tombs of very holy persons are especially successful.

The bier, being brought into the mosque, is laid upon the floor, in the usual place of prayer, with the right side towards the ḳibleh, or the direction of Mekkeh. The "Imám" of the mosque stands before the left side of the bier, facing it and the ḳibleh; and a servant of the mosque, as a "muballigh" (to repeat the words of the Imám), at the feet. The attendants of the funeral range themselves behind the Imám; the women standing apart, behind the men; for on this occasion they are seldom excluded from the mosque. The congregation being thus disposed, the Imám commences the prayer over the dead; prefacing it with these words:[1]—"I purpose reciting the prayer of four 'tekbeers,'[2] the funeral prayer, over the deceased Muslim here present:"—or—"the deceased Muslims here present:" for two or more corpses are often prayed over at the same time. Having said this, he exclaims (raising his open hands on each side of his head, and touching the lobes of his ears with the extremities of his thumbs), "God is most great!" The muballigh repeats this exclamation; and each individual of the congregation behind the Imám does the same, as they also do after the subsequent tekbeers. The Imám then recites the Fát'ḥah, and a second time exclaims, "God is most great!" after which he adds, "O God, bless our lord Moḥammad, the Illiterate[3] Prophet, and his Family and Companions, and save them"—and the third time exclaims, "God is most great!" He then says, "O God, verily this is thy servant and son of thy servant: he hath departed from the repose of the world, and from its amplitude,[4] and from whatever he loved, and from those by whom he was loved in it, to the darkness of the grave, and to what he experienceth. He did testify that there is no deity but Thou alone; that Thou hast no companion; and that Moḥammad is thy servant and thine apostle; and Thou art all-knowing respecting him. O God, he hath gone to abide with Thee, and Thou art the best with whom to abide. He hath become in need of thy mercy, and Thou hast no need of his punishment. We have come to Thee supplicating that we may intercede for him. O God, if he were a doer of good, over-reckon his good deeds; and if he were an evil-doer, pass over his evil-doings; and of thy mercy grant that he may experience thine acceptance; and spare him the trial of the grave, and its torment; and make his grave wide to him; and keep back the earth from his sides;[5] and of thy mercy grant that he

[1] I give the form of prayer used by the Sháfe'ees, as being the most common in Cairo. Those of the other sects are nearly similar to this.

[2] A "tekbeer" has been explained in a former chapter, as being the exclamation of "Alláhu Akbar!" or "God is most great!"

[3] This is the meaning commonly assigned to the epithet "Ummee;" for the Muslims assert that the illiterateness of Moḥammad was a proof that the Ḳur-án was revealed to him: but the proper meaning of this epithet is probably "Gentile."

[4] Or, according to one of my sheykhs, "its business."

[5] It is believed that the body of the wicked is painfully oppressed by the earth against its sides in the grave; though this is always made hollow.

may experience security from thy torment, until Thou send him safely to thy Paradise, O Thou most merciful of those who shew mercy!" Then, for the fourth and last time, the Imám exclaims, "God is most great!"—adding, "O God, deny us not our reward for him [for the service we have done him]; and lead us not into trial after him: pardon us and him and all the Muslims, O Lord of the beings of the whole world!"—Thus he finishes his prayer; greeting the angels on his right and left with the salutation of "Peace be on you, and the mercy of God," as is done at the close of the ordinary prayers. Then, addressing the persons present, he says, "Give your testimony respecting him." They reply, "He was of the virtuous."—The bier is now taken up; and if it be in the mosque of the Ḥasaneyn, or in that of any other celebrated saint, that the prayer has been performed, it is placed before the "maḳṣoorah" (the screen or railing that surrounds the sepulchral monument or cenotaph). Here, some of the fiḳees and others who have attended the funeral recite the Fát'ḥah, and the last three verses of the "Soorat el-Baḳarah" (or 2nd chapter of the Ḳur-án); beginning, "Whatever is in heaven and on earth is God's." —These rites performed, the funeral-train proceeds with the corpse, in the same order as before, to the burial-ground.[1]

Here I must give a short description of a tomb.—It is an oblong vault, having an arched roof, and is generally constructed of brick, and plastered. It is made hollow, in order that the person or persons buried in it may be able with ease to sit up when visited and examined by the two angels, "Munkar" (vulgarly "Nákir") and "Nekeer." One side faces the direction of Mekkeh; that is, the south-east. At the foot, which is to the north-east, is the entrance; before which is constructed a small square cell, roofed with stones extending from side to side, to prevent the earth from entering the vault. This is covered over with earth. The vault is generally made large enough to contain four or more bodies. If males and females be buried in the same vault, which is not commonly the case, a partition is built to separate the corpses of one sex from those of the other. Over the vault is constructed an oblong monument (called "tarkeebeh"), of stone or brick, with a stela, or upright stone (called a "sháhid"), at the head and foot. The stelæ are mostly plain; but some of them are ornamented; and that at the head is often inscribed

---

1 The burial-grounds of Cairo are mostly outside the town, in the desert tracts on the north, east, and south. Those within the town are few, and not extensive.

with a text from the Ḳur-án,[1] and the name of the deceased, with the date of his death. A turban, cap, or other head-dress, is also sometimes carved on the top of the head-stone, shewing the rank or class of the person or persons buried in the tomb.—Over the grave of an eminent sheykh, or other person of note, a small square building, crowned with a cupola, is generally erected.[2] Many of the tombs of Turkish and Memlook grandees have marble tarkeebehs, which are canopied by cupolas supported by four columns of marble; and have inscriptions in gilt letters upon a ground of azure on the head-stone. There are numerous tombs of this description in the great southern cemetery of Cairo. The tombs of the Sulṭáns are mostly handsome mosques: some of these are within the metropolis; and some, in the cemeteries in its environs.—I now resume the description of the funeral.

The tomb having been opened before the arrival of the corpse, no delay takes place in the burial. The sexton and two assistants take the corpse out of the bier, and deposit it in the vault. Its bandages are untied; and it is laid upon its right side, or so inclined that the face is towards Mekkeh. It is supported in this position by a few crude bricks. If the outer wrapper be a Kashmeer shawl, this is rent, lest its value should tempt any profane person to violate the tomb. A little earth is gently placed by and upon the corpse, by one or more persons; and the entrance is closed by replacing the roofing-stones and earth over the small cell before it. But one singular ceremony remains to be performed, except in the case of a young child, who is not held responsible for his actions: a fiḳee is employed to perform the office of a "mulaḳḳin" (or instructor of the dead):[3] sitting before the tomb, he says generally as follows:—"O servant of God! O son of a handmaid of God! know that, at this time, there will come down to thee two angels commissioned respecting thee and the like of thee: when they say to thee, 'Who is thy Lord?' answer them, 'God is my Lord,' in truth; and when they ask thee concerning thy Prophet, or the man who hath been sent unto you, say to them, 'Moḥammad is the Apostle of God,' with veracity; and when they ask thee concerning thy religion, say to them, 'El-Islám is my religion;' and when they ask thee concerning thy book of direction, say to them, 'The

---

1 The Prophet forbade engraving the name of God, or any words of the Ḳur-án, upon a tomb. He also directed that tombs should be low, and built only of crude bricks.

2 Like that seen in the distance in the cut inserted in the next page.

3 The Málikees disapprove of this custom, the "talḳeen" of the dead.

Sketch of a Tomb, with the entrance uncovered.

Ḳur-án is my book of direction, and the Muslims are my brothers;' and when they ask thee concerning thy Ḳibleh, say to them, 'The Kaạbeh is my Ḳibleh; and I have lived and died in the assertion that there is no deity but God, and Moḥammad is God's Apostle:' and they will say, 'Sleep, O servant of God, in the protection of God.'" —The soul is believed to remain with the body during the first night after the burial; and on this night to be visited and examined, and perhaps the body tortured, by the two angels above mentioned.—The Yemeneeyeh and other persons hired to attend the funeral are paid at the tomb: the former usually receive a piaster each. If the funeral be that of a person of rank or wealth, two or three skins of water, and as many camel-loads of bread, being conveyed to the burial-ground, as before mentioned, are there distributed, after the burial, to the poor, who flock thither in great numbers on such an occasion. It has also been mentioned that a buffalo is sometimes slaughtered, and its flesh in like manner distributed. This custom is called "el-kaffárah" (or the expiation); being supposed to expiate some of the minor sins [1] of the deceased, but not great sins. [2] The funeral ended, each of the near relations of the deceased is greeted with a prayer that he may be happily compensated for his loss, or is congratulated that his life is prolonged.

The first night after the burial is called "Leylet el-Waḥsheh" (or the Night of Desolation); the place of the deceased being then left desolate. On this night the following custom is observed:—At sunset, two or three fiḳees are brought to the house: they take a repast of bread and milk in the place where the deceased died; and then recite the "Soorat el-Mulk" (or 67th chapter of the Ḳurán). As the soul is believed to remain with the body during the first night after the burial, and then to depart to the place appointed for the residence of good souls until the last day, or to the appointed prison in which wicked souls await their final doom,[3] this night is also called "Leylet el-Waḥdeh" (or the Night of Solitude).

---

1 Termed "ṣagháïr."

2 "Kebáïr."

3 The opinions of the Muslims respecting the state of souls in the interval between death and the judgment are thus given by Sale ('Preliminary Discourse,' sect. iv.):—"They distinguish the souls of the faithful into three classes: the first, of prophets, whose souls are admitted into paradise immediately; the second, of martyrs, whose spirits, according to a tradition of Moḥammad, rest in the crops of green birds, which eat of the fruits and drink of the rivers of paradise; and the third, of other believers, concerning the state of whose souls before the resurrection there are various opinions. For, 1. Some say that they stay near the sepulchres, with liberty, however, of going wherever they please; which they confirm from Moḥammad's manner of saluting them at their graves, and his affirming that the dead heard those salutations as well as the living.

Another ceremony, called that of the "Sebḥah" (or Rosary), is performed on this occasion, to facilitate the entrance of the deceased into a state of happiness: it usually occupies three or four hours. After the "'eshè" (or nightfall), some fiḳees, sometimes as many as fifty, assemble in the house; or, if there be not a court, or large apartment, for their reception, some matting is spread for them to sit upon in front of the house. One of them brings a sebḥah composed of a thousand beads, each about the size of a pigeon's egg. They commence the ceremony by reciting the "Soorat el-Mulk" (mentioned above); then say three times, "God is one." After this they recite the "Soorat el-Falaḳ" (or last chapter but one of the Ḳur-án), and the opening chapter (the "Fát'ḥah"); and then three times say, "O God, bless, with the most excellent blessing, the most happy of thy creatures, our lord Moḥammad, and his Family and Companions, and save them:" to which they add, "All who commemorate Thee are the mindful, and those who omit commemorating Thee are the negligent." They next repeat, thrice one thousand times, "There is no deity but God;" one of them holding the sebḥah, and counting each repetition of these words by passing a bead through his fingers. After each thousand repetitions they sometimes rest, and take coffee. Having completed the last thousand, and rested, and refreshed themselves, they say, a hundred times, "[I extol] the perfection of God, with his praise:" then, the same number of times, "I beg forgiveness of God, the Great:" after which they say, fifty times, "[I extol] the perfection of the Lord, the Eternal—the perfection of God, the Eternal:" they then repeat these words of the Ḳur-án—"[Extol] the perfection of thy Lord, the Lord of Might; exempting Him from that which they [namely, Christians and others] ascribe to Him [that is, from the having a son, or partaker of his godhead]; and peace be on

Whence perhaps proceeded the custom of visiting the tombs of relations, so common among the Mohammadans. 2. Others imagine they are with Adam in the lowest heaven, and also support their opinion by the authority of their prophet, who gave out that in his return from the upper heavens in his pretended night-journey, he saw there the souls of those who were destined to paradise on the right hand of Adam, and those who were condemned to hell on his left. 3. Others fancy the souls of believers remain in the well Zemzem, and those of infidels in a certain well in the province of Ḥaḍramót, called Barahoot [so in the Ḳámoos, but by Sale written Borhût]; but this opinion is branded as heretical. 4. Others say they stay near the graves for seven days; but that whither they go afterwards is uncertain. 5. Others, that they are all in the trumpet, whose sound is to raise the dead. And, 6. Others, that the souls of the good dwell in the forms of white birds, under the throne of God. As to the condition of the souls of the wicked, besides the opinions that have been already mentioned, the more orthodox hold that they are offered by the angels to heaven, from whence being repulsed as stinking and filthy, they are offered to the earth; and being also refused a place there, are carried down to the seventh earth, and thrown into a dungeon, which they call Sijjeen, under a green rock, or, according to a tradition of Moḥammad, under the devil's jaw, to be there tormented till they are called up to be joined again to their bodies." I believe that the opinion respecting the Well of Barahoot commonly prevails in the present day.

the Apostles; and praise be to God, the Lord of the beings of the whole world!"[1] Two or three or more of them then recite, each, an "'ashr," or about two or three verses of the Ḳur-án. This done, one of them asks his companions, "Have ye transferred [the merit of] what ye have recited to the soul of the deceased?" They reply, "We have transferred it;" and add, "And peace be on the Apostles," &c., as above. This concludes the ceremony of the sebḥah, which, in the houses of the rich, is also repeated on the second and third nights. This ceremony is likewise performed in a family on their receiving intelligence of the death of a near relation.

The men make no alteration in their dress in token of mourning; nor do the women on the death of an elderly man; but they do for others. In the latter cases, they dye their shirts, head-veils, face-veils, and handkerchiefs, of a blue, or of an almost black, colour, with indigo; and some of them, with the same dye, stain their hands and their arms as high as the elbow, and smear the walls of the chambers. When the master of the house, or the owner of the furniture, is dead, and sometimes in other cases, they also turn upside-down the carpets, mats, cushions, and coverings of the deewáns. In general, the women, while in mourning, leave their hair unbraided, cease to wear some of their ornaments, and, if they smoke, use common reed pipes.

Towards the close of the first Thursday after the funeral, and, often, early in the morning of this day, the women of the family of the deceased again commence a wailing, in their house, accompanied by some of their female friends; and in the afternoon or evening of this day, male friends of the deceased also visit the house, and three or four fiḳees are employed to perform a khatmeh.—On the Friday-morning the women repair to the tomb, where they observe the same customs which I have described in speaking of the ceremonies performed on the two grand "'eeds," in the second of the chapters on periodical public festivals, &c.; generally taking a palm-branch, to break up, and place on the tomb; and some cakes or bread, to distribute to the poor. These ceremonies are repeated on the same days of the next two weeks; and again, on the Thursday and Friday which complete, or next follow, the first period of forty days[2] after the funeral: whence this Friday is called "el-Arba'een," or "Gum'at el-Arba'een."

It is customary among the peasants of Upper Egypt for the female relations and friends of a person deceased to meet together by

---

[1] Chapter xxxvii., last three verses.

[2] See Genesis, l. 3.

his house on each of the first three days after the funeral, and there to perform a lamentation and a strange kind of dance. They daub their faces and bosoms, and part of their dress, with mud; and tie a rope girdle, generally made of the coarse grass called "ḥalfà," round the waist.[1] Each flourishes in her hand a palm-stick, or a nebboot (a long staff), or a spear, or a drawn sword; and dances with a slow movement, and in an irregular manner; generally pacing about, and raising and depressing the body. This dance is continued for an hour or more, and is performed twice or three times in the course of the day. After the third day, the women visit the tomb, and place upon it their rope-girdles; and usually a lamb, or a goat, is slain there, as an expiatory sacrifice, and a feast made, on this occasion.

Having now described the manners and customs of the Muslims of Egypt in the various stages and circumstances of life, from the period of infancy to the tomb, I close my account of them, as a writer of their own nation would in a similar case, with "thanks and praise to Him who dieth not."

---

[1] As the ancient Egyptian women did in the same case.—See a passage in Herodotus, before referred to, lib. ii. cap. 85.

SUPPLEMENT.

I.—THE COPTS.

The fame of that great nation from which the Copts mainly derive their origin renders this people objects of much interest, especially to one who has examined the wonderful monuments of Ancient Egypt: but so great is the aversion with which, like their illustrious ancestors, they regard all persons who are not of their own race, and so reluctant are they to admit such persons to any familiar intercourse with them, that I had almost despaired of gaining an insight into their religious, moral, and social state. At length, however, I had the good fortune to become acquainted with a character of which I had doubted the existence—a Copt of a liberal as well as an intelligent mind; and to his kindness I am indebted for the knowledge of most of the facts related in the following brief memoir.

The Copts, at present, compose less than one fourteenth part of the population of Egypt; their number being not more than about one hundred and fifty thousand. About ten thousand of them reside in the metropolis. In some parts of Upper Egypt are villages exclusively inhabited by persons of this race; and the district called the Feiyoom particularly abounds with them. The vast number of ruined convents and churches existing in various parts of Egypt shews that the Copts were very numerous a few centuries ago; but every year many of them have embraced the faith of El-Islám, and become intermixed by marriage with Muslims; and thus the number of genuine and Christian Copts has been reduced to its present small amount.

The Copts are undoubtedly descendants of the ancient Egyptians, but not an unmixed race; their ancestors in the earlier ages of Christianity having intermarried with Greeks, Nubians, Abyssinians, and other foreigners. Their name is correctly pronounced either "Ḳubṭ" or "Ḳibṭ;" but more commonly, "Gubṭ" or "Gibṭ," and (in Cairo and its neighbourhood, and in some other parts of Egypt), "'Ubṭ" or "'Ibṭ:" in the singular it is pronounced "Ḳubṭee, Ḳibṭee, Gubṭee, Gibṭee, 'Ubṭee," or "'Ibṭee." All of these sounds bear a great resemblance to the ancient Greek name of Egypt (Α'ίγυπτος): but it is generally believed that the name of "Ḳubṭ" is derived from "Coptos" (once a great city in Upper Egypt), now called "Ḳufṭ," or, more commonly, "Gufṭ," to which vast numbers of the Christian Egyptians retired during the persecutions with which they were visited under several of the Roman Emperors. The Copts have not altogether lost their ancient language; their liturgy and several of their religious books being written in it: but the Coptic has become a dead language, understood by very few persons; and the Arabic has been adopted in its stead.

With respect to their personal characteristics, we observe some striking points of resemblance, and yet, upon the whole, a considerable difference, between the Copts and the ancient Egyptians, judging of the latter from the paintings and sculptures in their tombs and temples. The difference is, however, easily accounted for by the fact of the intermarriages of the ancestors of the modern Copts with foreigners, above mentioned. The people who bear the greatest resemblance to the ancient Egyptians, at present, are the Noobeh (or more genuine Nubians); and next to these, the Abyssinians and the Copts, who are, notwithstanding, much unlike each other. The Copts differ but little from the generality of their Muslim countrymen: the latter being chiefly descended from Arabs and from Copts who have embraced the faith of the Arabs, and having thus become assimilated to the Copts in features. I find it difficult, sometimes, to perceive any difference between a Copt and a Muslim Egyptian, beyond a certain downcast and sullen expression of countenance which generally marks the former; and the Muslims themselves are often deceived when they see a Copt in a white turban. We observe, in the latter, the same shades of complexion, in different latitudes of the country, as in the former; varying from a pale yellowish colour to a deep bronze or brown. The eyes of the Copt are generally large and elongated, slightly inclining from the nose upwards, and always black: the nose is straight, except at the end, where it is rounded, and wide: the lips are rather thick; and the hair is black and curly. The Copts are, generally speaking, somewhat under the middle size; and so, as it appears from the mummies, were the ancient Egyptians. Their women, of the higher and and middle classes in particular, blacken the edges of their eye-lids with ḳohl; and those of the lower orders tattoo blue marks upon their faces, hands, &c., in the same manner as other Egyptian females, but usually introduce the cross among these ornaments. Most of the Copts circumcise their sons; and another practice which prevailed among their pagan ancestors, mentioned by Strabo, and alluded to in a note subjoined to page 59 of this work, is observed among the Copts without exception.

The dress of the Copts is similar to that of the Muslim Egyptians; except that the proper turban of the former is black or blue, or of a grayish or light-brown colour; and such Copts as wear cloth generally choose dull colours, and often wear a black cotton gown, or loose shirt, over their cloth and silk dress. In the towns, they are usually careful thus to distinguish themselves from the Muslims; but in the villages, many of them wear the white or red turban. Other Christians, and Jews, who are subjects of the Turkish Sulṭán, are distinguished from the Muslims in the same manner; but not all: many Armenians, Greeks, and Syrian Christians, wear the white turban. Subjects of European Christian powers are allowed to do the same, and to adopt altogether the Turkish dress. The occasions which originally caused the Copts to be distinguished by the black and blue turbans will be mentioned in some historical notes respecting this people hereafter.—The Copt women veil their faces, not only in public, but also in the house, when any men, except their near relations, are present. The unmarried ladies, and females of the lower orders, in public, generally wear the white veil: the black veil is worn by the more respectable of the married ladies; but the white is adopted by many, from a desire to imitate the Muslimehs.

The Copts, with the exception of a small proportion who profess the Romish or the Greek faith, are Christians of the sect called Jacobites, Eutychians, Monophysites, and Monothelites; whose creed was condemned by the Council of Chalcedon, in the reign of the Emperor Marcian. They received the appellation of "Jacobites" ("Ya'áḳibeh," or "Yaạḳoobees"), by which they are generally known, from Jacobus Baradæus, a Syrian, who was a chief propagator of the Eutychian doctrines. Those who adhered to the Greek faith were distinguished from the former by the name of "Melekites" ("Melekeeyeh," or "Melekees"), that is to say, "Royalists," because they agreed in faith with the Emperor of Constantinople. The secession of the great majority of the Copts from what was generally considered the orthodox church gave rise to an implacable enmity between them and the Greeks, under whom they suffered much persecution, and with whom they would no longer even contract marriages. This enmity was, of course, more bitter on the part of the Copts: they gladly received the Arab invaders of their country, and united with them to expel the Greeks. Their revenge was gratified; but they were made to bow their necks to a heavier yoke: yet the hatred with which even the modern Copts regard the Greeks and all other Christians who are not of their own sect is much greater than that which they bear towards the Muslims.—Saint Mark, they assert, was the first who preached the Gospel in Egypt; and they regard him as the first Patriarch of Alexandria. The Nubians and Abyssinians embraced Christianity soon after the Egyptians; and, following the same example, they adopted the Jacobite doctrines. The Nubians, however, have become Muslims, and boast that there is not a single Christian among their race, and that they will never allow one to live among them; for, as they are more ignorant, so are they also more bigoted, than the generality of Muslims. In Abyssinia, Jacobite Christianity is still the prevailing religion.

The religious orders of the Coptic Church consist of a Patriarch, a Metropolitan of the Abyssinians, Bishops, Archpriests, Priests, Deacons, and Monks.

The Patriarch ("el-Baṭrak") is the supreme head of the church; and occupies the chair of Saint Mark. He generally resides in Cairo; but is styled "Patriarch of Alexandria." He is chosen from among the order of monks, with whose regulations he continues to comply; and it is a point of these regulations that he remains unmarried. He is obliged to wear woollen garments next his body; but these are of the finest and softest quality, like the shawls of Kashmeer, and are concealed by habits of rich silks and cloth. So rigid are the rules with which he is obliged to conform, that, whenever he sleeps, he is waked after every quarter of an hour.[1] A patriarch may be appointed by his predecessor; but generally he is chosen by lot; and always from among the monks of the Convent of Saint Anthony ("Deyr Anṭooniyoos") in the Eastern Desert of Egypt,

---

[1] Καθαριότητος εἵνεκεν. Compare the account given by Herodotus of the habits of the priests of ancient Egypt: lib. ii. cap. 37.

near the western Gulf of the Red Sea. The bishops and principal priests, when a patriarch is to be elected, apply to the superior of the convent above mentioned, who names about eight or nine monks whom he considers qualified for the high office of head of the church: the names of these persons are written, each upon a separate slip of paper, which pieces of paper are then rolled into the form of little balls, and put into a drawer: a priest draws one, without looking; and the person whose name is thus drawn is invested as patriarch. Formerly, a young child was employed to draw the lot; being supposed to be more under the direction of heaven.

The property at the disposal of the patriarch is very considerable: it chiefly consists in houses; and can only be employed for pious uses. Modern patriarchs have done little more than augment their property: generally, when a Copt sells a house in Cairo, the patriarch bids for it, and no one ventures to bid against him; so that the owner of the house is obliged to part with it for considerably less than its just value.

The patriarch and bishops wear a turban of a wider and rounder form than those of other persons, much resembling the muḳleh of the Muslim 'Ulamà, but of the same dark colour as those of the other Copts.

Turban of the Coptic Patriarch and Bishops.

The Metropolitan of the Abyssinians ("el-Maṭrán") is appointed by the Patriarch. He retains his office for life; and resides in Abyssinia.

A bishop ("Usḳuf") is generally (or, I am told, always,) chosen from among the monks; and continues, like the patriarch, to conform with their regulations. The canons of the church do not require that bishops should be monks; but unmarried men, or widowers, were formerly always chosen for the episcopal office. The number of bishops is twelve.

An Archpriest ("Ḳummuṣ") is elevated from the order of common priests. The archpriests are numerous.

A priest ("Ḳasees") must have been a deacon: he must be without bodily defect, at least thirty-three years of age, and a person who has never married, or who has married but one wife, and taken that wife a virgin, and married her before he became a priest; for he cannot marry after. If a priest's wife die, he cannot marry again; nor is the widow of a priest allowed to marry a second husband. A priest may be of the order of monks, and consequently unmarried. He is supported only by alms, and by what he obtains through his own industry. Both priests and deacons are ordained either by the Patriarch or by a bishop. The priests wear a turban formed of a long narrow band. This was worn, a few years ago, by all the Copts in Cairo: a desire to imitate the Muslims has made them change the style.

Turban of a Coptic Priest.

A Deacon ("Shemmás") must be either unmarried, or a person who has only once married, to a virgin bride. If he take a second wife, or marry a widow, he loses his office. He may be of the order of monks, as appears from what has been said above.

A Monk ("Ráhib") must have submitted to a long trial of his patience and piety, and made a vow of celibacy, before his admission into the monastic order. He usually performs menial and arduous services, previously to his admission, for a year, or a year and a half, in some sequestered convent in the desert. He is generally employed in fetching wood and water, sweeping the convent, &c., and waiting upon the monks; and expends all his property (if he have any) in the purchase of clothes and other necessaries for the monks and the poor in general. If, after a sufficient service, he persevere in his resolution, he is admitted. The prayers of the dead are recited over him, to celebrate his death to the world; and it has been said that, when he dies, he is buried without prayer; but I am informed that this is not the case. The monks are very numerous, and there are many nuns. They lead a life of great austerity, and are obliged always to wear woollen garments next the body. Every monk is distinguished by a strip of woollen stuff, of a deep blue or black colour, about four inches wide, attached beneath the turban and hanging down the back to the length of about a foot.[1] A woollen shirt is generally the only article of dress worn by the monks, beside the turban. They eat two meals in the course of the day, at noon and in the evening; but, if living in a convent, seldom anything more than lentils, as most of their convents are in the desert: on feast-days, however, they eat flesh, if it be procurable. The number of convents and churches is said to be a hundred and forty-six;[2] but the former are few in comparison with the latter.

The Coptic church recommends baptizing boys at the age of forty days, and girls at the age of eighty days, if they continue so long well and healthy; but earlier if they be ill, and in apparent danger of death: for it is a prevailing belief among the Copts, that, if a child die unbaptized, it will be blind in the next life, and the parents are held guilty of a sin, for which they must do penance, either by repeating many prayers or by fasting: yet people of the lower orders, if living at an inconvenient distance from a church, and even in other cases, often neglect baptizing their children for a whole year. The child is dipped three times in the water, in which a little holy oil, dropped on the priest's thumb, has been washed off; and prayers, entirely in Coptic, are repeated over it. The Copts hold that the Holy Spirit descends upon the child in baptism. No money is taken by the priest for performing the baptismal service, unless voluntarily offered.

I have said that most of the Copts circumcise their sons. Not many of them in Cairo, I am told, do so; but in other parts, all, or almost all, observe this rite. The operation is generally performed when the child is about seven or eight years of age, and always privately: there is no fixed age for its performance: some of the Copts are circumcised at the early age of two years, and some at the age of twenty years or more. The more enlightened of the Copts certainly

1 I have neglected to write the name of this appendage; but if my memory do not deceive me, I was told that it is termed "ḳalás'weh," which word seems to be a corruption of "ḳalensuweh." Mengin calls it "kaloucyeh" ('Hist. de l'Egypte sous Mohammed-Aly,' vol ii. p. 290).

2 Mengin, *ubi supra*, pp. 284—289.

regard circumcision as a practice to be commended; but not as a religious rite, which the priests declare it is not. It appears, however, from its being universal among the peasantry, that these look upon it as something more than a mere civil rite; for if they regarded it as being of no higher importance, surely they would leave the more polished to comply with the custom. Some say it is in imitation of Christ, who submitted to this rite, that they perform it. It is a relic of ancient customs.

The Copts have numerous schools; but for boys only: very few females among them can read; and those have been instructed at home. The boys are taught the Psalms of David, the Gospels, and the Apostolical Epistles, in Arabic; and then the Gospels and Epistles in Coptic. They do not learn the Coptic language grammatically; and I am told that there is not to be found, among the Copts, any person who can write or speak that language with correctness or ease; and that there are very few persons who can do more than repeat what they have committed to memory, of the Scriptures and Liturgy. The Coptic language gradually fell into disuse after the conquest of Egypt by the Arabs. For two centuries after that event, it appears to have been the only language that the generality of the Copts understood; but before the tenth century of our era, most of the inhabitants of Lower Egypt had ceased to speak and understand it;[1] though in the Ṣa'eed (or Upper Egypt), El-Maḳreezee tells us, the women and children of the Copts, in his time (that is, about the close of the fourteenth century of our era, or the early part of the fifteenth), scarcely spoke any other language than the Ṣa'eedee Coptic, and had a complete knowledge of the Greek. Soon after this period, the Coptic language fell into disuse in Upper Egypt, as it had done so long before in the Lower Provinces; and the Arabic was adopted in its stead. All the Copts who have been instructed at a school still pray, both in the church and in private, in Coptic; and the Scriptures are still always read in the churches in that language; but they are explained, from books, in Arabic. Many books for the use of priests and other persons are written in the Coptic language expressed in Arabic characters.

The ordinary private prayers of the Copts are a subject particularly worthy of notice. In these they seem to have imitated the Jews, and to resemble the Muslims. I am informed that there are few of them

[1] This has been shewn by Quatremère, in his 'Researches on the Language and Literature of Egypt.'

in Cairo who do not comply with a precept of their church which enjoins them to pray seven times in the course of the day. The first prayer is said at daybreak; the second, at the third hour; the third, at the sixth hour; the fourth, at the ninth hour; the fifth, at the eleventh hour; the sixth, at the twelfth hour, which is sunset; and the seventh, at midnight. In each of these prayers, those persons who have learned to read, and are strict in the performance of their religious duties, recite several of the Psalms of David (about a seventh part of the whole Book of Psalms) in Arabic, and a chapter of one of the four Gospels in the same language; after which they say, either in Coptic or Arabic, "O my Lord! have mercy!" forty-one times; some using a string of forty-one beads; others counting by their fingers: they then add a short prayer in Coptic. In the seven prayers of each day, altogether, they repeat the whole Book of Psalms. Such, I am assured, are the rigid practices of the more strict and instructed classes in their daily worship. The illiterate repeat, in each of the seven daily prayers, the Lord's Prayer seven times, and "O my Lord! have mercy!" forty-one times. Previously to private as well as public prayer, persons of the better and stricter classes wash their hands and face; and some also wash their feet; and in prayer they always face the east. Though in most of the rules above mentioned they nearly resemble the Jews and the Muslims, they differ from both in holding that prayer, except with the congregation in the church, is better performed in private than in public. Their ordinary prayers, or at least the latter and shorter form, they often repeat while walking or riding or otherwise actively employed. I can hardly believe that the longer form is generally used by the instructed classes, though I am positively assured that it is.

The larger churches are divided into four or five compartments. The "Heykel," or Chancel, containing the altar, occupies the central and chief portion of the compartment at the upper end, which is screened from the rest of the church by a close partition or wall of wooden panel-work, having a door in the centre, the entrance of the Heykel, before which is suspended a curtain, with a large cross worked upon it. The compartment next before this is appropriated to the priests who read the lessons, &c., and to boys who serve as acolytes and singers, and the chief members of the congregation: this is separated from the compartment next before it by a partition of wooden lattice-work, about eight or nine feet high, with three doors, or a single door in the centre. The inferior members of the congregation occupy the next compartment, or next two compartments; and the lowest is appropriated to the women, and is screened in front by a partition of wooden lattice-work, to conceal them entirely from the men. Upon the walls of the church are suspended ill-executed and gaudy pictures of various saints; particularly of the patron saint; but no images are admitted. The floor is covered with mats.

Every man takes off his shoes on entering the church; but he retains his turban. He first goes to the door of the Heykel, prostrates himself before it, and kisses the hem of its curtain. He then prostrates himself, or makes a bow, and a salutation with the hand, before one or more of the pictures of saints, and sometimes kisses the hand of one or more of the officiating priests in the compartment next before the Heykel. Almost every member of the congregation has a crutch, about four feet and a half or five feet long, to lean upon while he stands; which he does during the greater part of the service. The full service (with the celebration of the Eucharist) occupies between three and four hours; generally commencing at daybreak.

The priests who officiate in the Heykel are clad in handsome robes; but the others wear only their ordinary dress. The whole of the service that is performed in the Heykel is in the Coptic language; no other language being allowed to be spoken within the sanctuary. The priests without, standing opposite and facing the door of the Heykel, read and chant explanations and lessons in Arabic and Coptic.[1] A priest is not permitted to sit down while reading the service in the sanctuary; and as this occupies so long a time, he pauses, in order that he may sit down, several times, for a few minutes; and on these occasions, cymbals of various sizes and notes are beaten as long as he remains sitting. Several times, also, a priest comes out from the Heykel, waves a censer, in which frankincense is burning, among the congregation, and blesses each member, placing his hand upon the person's head. Having done this to the men, he proceeds to the apartment of the women. The sacrament of the Lord's Supper is often celebrated in the Coptic church. The bread, which is made in the form of small round cakes, or bunns, stamped upon the top, is moistened with the wine, and in this state administered to the congregation, and partaken of by the ministers in orders, who have larger shares than the laymen, and are alone privileged to

---

[1] They chant nearly in the same manner as the Muslims reciting the Ḳur-án.

drink the wine. Each member of the congregation advances to the door of the Heykel to receive his portion.

The priests and others are often guilty of excessive indecorum in their public worship. I heard a priest, standing before the door of the sanctuary in the patriarchal church in Cairo, exclaim to a young acolyte (who was assisting him, I suppose, rather awkwardly), "May a blow corrode your heart!" and a friend of mine once witnessed, in the same place, a complete uproar: a priest from a village, having taken a part in the performance of the service, was loudly cursed, and forcibly expelled, by the regular officiating ministers; and afterwards, many members of the congregation, in pressing towards the door of the Heykel, vociferated curses, and beat each other with their crutches. The form of service in itself struck me as not much characterized by solemnity; though probably it approaches very nearly in many respects to that of the earliest age of the Christian church.

Confession is required of all members of the Coptic church, and is indispensable before receiving the sacrament of the Lord's Supper. Each person generally confesses to the same priest. The penance which the confessor usually imposes is a certain number of crossings and prostrations, with the repetition, during each prostration, of the Lord's Prayer, or, "O my Lord! have mercy!"

The Copts observe long and arduous *fasts*. A week before their Great Fast, or Lent, commences a fast of three days, kept in commemoration of that of Nineveh, which was occasioned by the preaching of Jonah. Some of the Copts observe this fast by total abstinence during the whole period of three days and three nights; others keep it in the same manner as the other fasts, of which an account here follows.

Their principal fast, called "eṣ-Ṣóm el-Kebeer" (or the Great Fast), above alluded to, was originally limited to forty days; but it has been gradually extended, by different patriarchs, to fifty-five days. During this period, except on two days of festival, which will presently be mentioned, they abstain from every kind of animal food, such as flesh-meat, eggs, milk, butter, and cheese; and eat only bread and vegetables (chiefly beans), with sweet oil, or the oil of sesame, and duḳḳah. The churches are open, and service is performed in them, every day during this fast; and the Copts eat nothing after their supper until after the church-prayers of the next day, about noon: but they do not thus on the other fasts.

They observe, however, with almost equal strictness, three other fasts:—1st, the "Ṣóm el-Meelád" (or Fast of the Nativity); the period of which is twenty-eight days immediately preceding the Festival of the Nativity, or Christmas-day; that is, all the month of Kiyahk except the last two days:—2ndly, the "Ṣóm er-Rusul" (or Fast of the Apostles), which is the period between the Ascension and the fifth of Ebeeb; and is observed in commemoration of the Apostles' fasting after they were deprived of their Lord:—3rdly, the "Ṣóm el-'Adrà" (or Fast of the Virgin), a period of fifteen days previous to the Assumption of the Virgin.

The Copts also fast every Wednesday and Friday in every other period of the year, except during the fifty days immediately following their Great Fast; that is, from the end of the Great Fast to the end of the Khamáseen. On these Wednesdays and Fridays, they eat only fish, vegetables, and oil.

Each fast is followed by a *festival.* The Copts observe seven great festivals:—1st, the "'Eed el-Meelád" (or Festival of the Nativity), on the 29th of Kiyahk (or 6th or 7th of January):—2ndly, the "'Eed el-Gheeṭás," on the 11th of Ṭoobeh (18th or 19th of January), in commemoration of the baptism of Christ:—3rdly, the "'Eed el-Bishárah" (Annunciation of the Virgin, or Lady-day), on the 29th of Barmahát (or 6th of April):—4thly, the "'Eed esh-Sha'áneen" (Palm Sunday), the Sunday next before Easter:—5thly, the "'Eed el-Ḳiyámeh" (the Resurrection, or Easter), or "el-'Eed el-Kebeer" (the Great Festival):—6thly, the "'Eed-eṣ-Ṣo'ood" (the Ascension):—7thly, the "'Eed el-'Anṣarah" (Whitsunday). On the first, second, and fifth of these, the church-prayers are performed at night: that is, in the night preceding the day of festival. On all these festivals, the Copts wear new clothes (or the best they have), feast, and give alms.

On the "Leylet el-Gheeṭás" (or eve of the Festival of the Gheeṭás) the Copts, almost universally, used to perform a singular ceremony, which, I am informed, is now observed by few of those residing in the metropolis, but by almost all others; that is, by the men. To commemorate the baptism of Christ, men, old as well as young, and boys, plunge into water; and the Muslims say, that, as each does this, another exclaims to him, "Plunge, as thy father and grandfather plunged; and remove El-Islám from thy heart." Some churches have a large tank, which is used on this occasion; the water having first been blessed by a priest: but it is a more common practice of the Copts to perform this ceremony (which most of them regard more as an amusement than a religious rite) in the river; pouring in some holy water from the church before they plunge. This used to be an occasion of great festivity among the Copts of the metropolis: the Nile was crowded with boats, and numerous tents and mesh'als were erected on its banks. Prayers are performed in the churches on the eve of this festival: a priest blesses the water in the font, or the tank, then ties on a napkin, as an apron, and, wetting the corner of a handkerchief with the holy water, washes (or rather, wipes or touches,) with it the feet of each member of the congregation. This latter ceremony is also performed on the Thursday next before Easter, or Maunday Thursday ("Khamees el-'Ahd"), and on the Festival of the Apostles ("'Eed er-Rusul"), on the 5th of Ebeeb (or 11th of July).

On the Festivals of the "Bishárah" and the "Sha'áneen," the Copts eat fish; and on the latter of these two festivals the priests recite the prayers of the dead over their congregations in the churches; and if any die between that day and the end of the Khamáseen (which is the chief or worst portion of the plague-season), his body is interred without the prayer being repeated. This custom seems to have originated from the fact of its being impossible to pray at the tomb over every victim of the plague; and must have a very impressive effect upon people expecting this dreadful scourge.

Among the minor festivals are the "Khamees el-'Ahd," above mentioned; "Sebt en-Noor" (or Saturday of the Light), the next Saturday, when a light which is said to be miraculous appears in the Holy Sepulchre at Jerusalem; the "'Eed er-Rusul," before mentioned; and the "'Eed eṣ-Ṣaleeb" (or Festival of [the discovery of] the Cross), on the 17th of Toot (or 26th or 27th of September).

Pilgrimage to Jerusalem the Copts hold to be incumbent on all who are able to perform it; but few of the poorer classes acquit themselves of this duty. The pilgrims compose a numerous caravan. They pass the Passion-Week and Easter at Jerusalem; and, on the third day after the Passion-Week, proceed to the Jordan, in which they bathe.

The Copts almost universally abstain from eating swine's flesh; not because they consider it unlawful, for they deny it to be so, but, as they say, on account of the filthiness of the animal. I should think, however, that this abstinence is rather to be attributed to a prejudice derived from their heathen ancestors. The flesh of the wild boar is often eaten by them. Camel's flesh they consider unlawful; probably for no better reason than that of its being eaten by the Muslims. They abstain from the flesh of animals that have been strangled, and from blood, in compliance with an injunction of the Apostles to the Gentile converts,[1] which they hold is not abrogated.

The male adults among the Copts pay a tribute (called "gizyeh"), beside the income-tax (or "firdeh") which they pay in common with the Muslim inhabitants of Egypt. There are three rates of the former: the richer classes, in Cairo and other large towns, pay thirty-six piasters each; the middling classes, eighteen; and the poorest, nine: but in the country, this tax is levied upon families, instead of individuals. The firdeh is the same for the Copts as for the Muslims; the twelfth part of a man's annual salary or gain, when this can be ascertained.

The Copts are not now despised and degraded by the government as they were a few years ago. Some of them have even been raised to the rank of Beys. Before the accession of Moḥammad 'Alee, neither the Copts nor other Eastern Christians, nor Jews, were generally allowed to ride horses in Egypt; but this restriction has, of late years, been withdrawn.—The Muslims of Damascus, who are notorious for their bigotry and intolerance, complained, to the conqueror Ibráheem Báshà, of the Christians' in their city being allowed to ride horses; urging that the Muslims no longer had the privilege of distinguishing themselves from the infidels. The Báshà replied, "Let the Muslims still be exalted above the Christians, if they wish it: let them ride dromedaries in the streets: depend upon it the Christians will not follow their example."—The Copts enjoy an immunity for which they are much envied by most of the Muslims: they are not liable to be taken for military service.[2]

The ordinary domestic habits of the Copts are perfectly Oriental, and nearly the same as those of their Muslim fellow-countrymen. They pass their hours of leisure chiefly in the same manner, enjoying their pipe and coffee: their meals, also, are similar; and their manner of eating is the same: but they indulge in drinking brandy at all hours of the day; and often, to excess.

They are not allowed by their church to intermarry with persons of any other sect, and few of them do so. When a Copt wishes to contract such a marriage, which causes him to be regarded as a reprobate by the more strict of his nation, he generally applies to a priest of the sect to which his intended wife belongs; and if his

---

1 Acts, xv. 20 and 29.

2 This immunity is said to have been lately withdrawn. It is believed to have originated from the unwillingness of Muslim princes to *honour* a Christian by employing him to fight against a Muslim enemy.

request be denied, which is commonly the case unless the man will consent to adopt his wife's creed, he is married by the Ḳáḍee, merely by a civil contract. As a marriage of this kind is not acknowledged by the church, it may be dissolved at pleasure.

When a Copt is desirous of marrying according to the approved custom, he pursues the same course to obtain a wife as the Muslim; employing one or more of his female relations or other women to seek for him a suitable companion. Scarcely ever is he able to obtain a sight of the face of his intended wife, unless she be of the lower orders; and not always even in this case. If the female sought in marriage be under age, her father, or mother, or nearest male relation, is her "wekeel" (or agent) to make the necessary arrangements; but if she be of age, and have neither father nor mother, she appoints her own wekeel. The bridegroom, also, has his wekeel. The parties make a contract, in which various private domestic matters are arranged, in the presence of a priest. Two-thirds of the amount of the dowry is paid on this occasion: the remaining third is held in reserve: if she survive her husband, she claims this from his property: if she die before him, her relations claim it at her death. The contract being concluded, the Lord's Prayer is recited three times by all persons present; the priest commencing it first.

The marriage-festivities, in the cases of persons of the higher and middle classes, when the bride is a virgin, usually occupy a period of eight days. Such is the length of what is termed a complete fête.[1]

The night preceding Sunday (which the Copts, like the Muslims, call the night *of* Sunday) is the most approved for the performance of the marriage-service, and most of the Copts are married on this night. In this case, the festivities commence on the preceding Tuesday, when the bridegroom and the bride's family entertain their respective friends. At the feasts given on these occasions, and on subsequent days of the marriage-festivities, a curious custom, which reminds us of the *alites* or *præpetes* of the Romans, is usually observed. The cook makes two hollow balls of sugar, each with a hole at the bottom: then taking two live pigeons, he attaches little round bells to their wings; and having whirled the poor birds through the air till they are giddy, puts them into the two balls before mentioned: each of these is placed upon a dish; and they are put before the guests; some of whom, judging when the birds have recovered from their giddiness,

---

1 "Faraḥ temám."

break the balls. The pigeons generally fly about the room, ringing their little bells: if they do not fly immediately, some person usually makes them rise; as the spectators would draw an evil omen from their not flying.[1] The guests are generally entertained with music on the evenings of these feasts.—Wednesday is passed in preparations.

On Thursday, in the afternoon, the bride is conducted to the bath, accompanied by several of her female relations and friends, and usually with music, but not under a canopy.—Friday, again, is a day of preparation, and the bride has the ḥennà applied to her hands and feet, &c.

Early on Saturday, two sets of articles of clothing, &c., one for the bridegroom and the other for the bride, and each consisting of similar things (namely, a shirt of silk and cotton, a pair of drawers, the embroidered band of the drawers, and two handkerchiefs embroidered with gold, together with a tobacco-purse, ornamented in the same manner), are sent from the bride's family to the house of the bridegroom. An old lady of the family of the bride afterwards goes to the bridegroom's house, to see whether it be properly prepared; and the bridegroom's "ashbeen" (or brideman) takes him and several of his friends to the bath.

In the ensuing evening, about an hour and an half, or two hours, after sunset, the bride, accompanied by a number of her female relations and friends, preceded and followed by musicians, and attended by a number of persons bearing mesh'als and candles, proceeds to the house of the bridegroom. This "zeffeh" (or parade) much resembles that of a Muslimeh bride; but the Copt bride is not conducted under a canopy. She is covered with a shawl, with several ornaments attached to that part which conceals her face and head, and numerous coins and other ornaments upon the part which covers her bosom. The procession moves very slowly, and generally occupies about two hours. A lamb or sheep is killed for the guests at the bridegroom's house this night: it is slaughtered at the door, and the bride steps over its blood. This ceremony, I am told, is only observed in Cairo and other large towns.

The bride's party, having rested about two hours at the bridegroom's house, and there partaken of refreshments, proceed with her

[1] The ball and bird are called "el-ḳubbeh wa-ṭ-ṭeyr." It is said that the Muslims of Egypt, on some occasions, as on the inauguration of a Sulṭán, used to observe the custom here described; but this appears to be an error, arising from a misunderstanding of the term "el-ḳubbeh wa-ṭ-ṭeyr" applied by historians to an umbrella surmounted by the figure of a bird, which was borne over the head of a Sulṭán in certain pompous processions.

thence, in the same manner, to the church. The bridegroom goes thither with his friends, forming a separate party; and without music. In the church, where the men and women place themselves apart, long prayers are performed, and the sacrament of the Lord's Supper is administered. The priest receives and blesses and returns two rings, for the bridegroom and bride; and places a kind of crown, or frontal diadem, of gold, upon the head of each of them, and a sash over the shoulder of the bridegroom. This ceremony is called the "tekleel" (or crowning). The two crowns belong to the church: before the parties quit the church, they are taken off; but the bridegroom often goes home with the sash, and it is there taken off by a priest. At the weddings of the rich in the metropolis, the Patriarch generally officiates. In most cases, the ceremonies of the church are not concluded until near daybreak: the parties then return to the house of the bridegroom. From respect to the sacrament of which they have partaken, the bridegroom and bride maintain a religious reserve towards each other until the following night (that preceding Monday), or, generally, until after the close of this night.[1]

The bride's father gives a dinner at the bridegroom's house on Monday, at which the principal dishes are usually rice and milk, and boiled fowls. In the evening, after this dinner, the bridegroom and his ashbeen go about to invite his friends to a great feast to be given on the evening following, which concludes the marriage festivities.

Such are the ceremonies which are usually observed on the marriage of a virgin-bride. Sometimes, the Patriarch, bishop, or priest, who is employed to perform the marriage-service, dissuades the parties from expending their money in zeffehs and repeated feasts, counselling them rather to devote the sums which they had purposed to employ in so vain a manner to the relief of the wants of the clergy and poor; and in consequence, the marriage is conducted with more simplicity and privacy. A widow is always married without ostentation, festivity, or zeffeh. A virgin-bride of the poorer class is sometimes honoured with a zeffeh; but is generally conducted to the bath merely by a group of female relations and friends, who, wanting the accompaniment of musical instruments, only testify their joy by "zaghâreeṭ:" in the same manner, also, she proceeds to the bridegroom's house, and she is there married by a priest; as the expenses of lighting and otherwise preparing the church for a marriage fall

[1] The custom mentioned by Burckhardt, in his Arabic Proverbs, page 117, as prevailing "among the lower classes of Muslims at Cairo," is observed by the Copts.

upon the bridegroom. Many of the Copts in Cairo, being possessed of little property, are married in a yet more simple manner, before mentioned. To be married by one of their own clergy, they must obtain a licence from the Patriarch; and this covetous person will seldom give it for less than a hundred piasters (or a pound sterling), and sometimes demands, from such persons, as many riyáls (of two piasters and a quarter each): the parties, therefore, are married by a licence from the Ḳáḍee, for which they usually pay not more than two piasters, or a little less than five pence of our money.

The newly-married wife, if she observe the approved rules of etiquette, does not go out of the house, even to pay a visit to her parents, until delivered of her first child, or until the expiration of a year if there appear no signs of her becoming a mother. After this period of imprisonment, her father or mother usually comes to visit her.

A divorce is obtained only for the cause of adultery on the part of the wife. The husband and wife may be separated if she have committed a theft, or other heinous crime; but in this case, neither he nor she is at liberty to contract another marriage, though they may again be united to each other.

One of the most remarkable traits in the character of the Copts is their bigotry. They bear a bitter hatred to all other Christians, even exceeding that with which the Muslims regard the unbelievers in El-Islám. Yet they are considered, by the Muslims, as much more inclined than any other Christian sect to the faith of El-Islám; and this opinion has not been formed without reason; for vast numbers of them have, from time to time, and not always in consequence of persecution, become proselytes to this religion. They are, generally speaking, of a sullen temper, extremely avaricious, and abominable dissemblers; cringing or domineering according to circumstances. The respectable Copt to whom I have already acknowledged myself chiefly indebted for the notions which I have obtained respecting the customs of his nation, gives me a most unfavourable account of their character. He avows them to be generally ignorant, deceitful, faithless, and abandoned to the pursuit of worldly gain, and to indulgence in sensual pleasures: he declares the Patriarch to be a tyrant, and a suborner of false witnesses; and assures me that the priests and monks in Cairo are seen every evening begging, and asking the loan of money, which they never repay, at the houses of their parishioners and other acquaintances, and procuring brandy, if possible, wherever they call.

Many of the Copts are employed as secretaries or accountants. In every village of a moderate size is a "M'allim"[1] who keeps the register of the taxes. The writing of the Copts differs considerably in style from that of the Muslims, as well as from that of other Christians residing in Egypt. Most of the Copts in Cairo are accountants or tradesmen: the former are chiefly employed in government offices: among the latter are many merchants, goldsmiths, silversmiths, jewellers, architects, builders, and carpenters; all of whom are generally esteemed more skilful than the Muslims. Those in the villages, like the Muslim peasants, occupy themselves chiefly in the labours of agriculture.

The funeral-ceremonies of the Copts resemble, in many respects, those of the Muslims. The corpse is carried in a bier, followed by women, wailing in the same manner as the Muslimehs do on such an occasion; but is not preceded by hired chanters. Hired wailing-women are employed to lament in the house of the deceased for three days after the death (though this custom is disapproved by the clergy and many others, being only a relic of ancient heathen usages); and they renew their lamentations there on the seventh and fourteenth days after the death, and sometimes several weeks after. The Copts, both men and women, pay regular visits to the tombs of their relations three times in the year: on the 'Eed el-Meelád, 'Eed el-Gheeṭás, and 'Eed el-Ḳiyámeh. They go to the burial-ground on the eve of each of these 'eeds, and there pass the night; having houses belonging to them in the cemeteries, for their reception on these occasions: the women spend the night in the upper apartments; and the men, below. In the morning following, they kill a buffalo, or a sheep, if they can afford either, and give its flesh, with bread, to the poor who assemble there; or they give bread alone. This ceres mony, which resembles the "kaffárah" performed by the Muslim- on the burial of their dead, is not considered as any expiation of the sins of the deceased, but probably originated from an ancient expiatory sacrifice: it is only regarded as an alms. As soon as it is done, the mourners return home. They say that they visit the tombs merely for the sake of religious reflection. In doing so, they perpetuate an ancient custom, which they find difficult to relinquish;

---

[1] Thus pronounced for "Mo'allim." It signifies "teacher" or "master;" and is a title given to all Copts but those of the poorer class, or peasants. The registrar of the taxes of a village is simply called "the M'allim of the village."

though they can give no good reason for observing it with such ceremonies.

I shall close this account of the Copts with a few notices of their history under the Muslim domination, derived from El-Maḳreezee's celebrated work on Egypt and its Metropolis.[1]

About seventy years after the conquest of Egypt by the Arabs, the Copts began to experience such exactions and persecutions, notwithstanding the chartered favours and privileges which had at first been granted to them, that many of them rose in arms, and attempted to defend their rights; but they were reduced, after sustaining a great slaughter. The monks, for the first time, had been subjected to an annual tribute of a deenár[2] each. The collector of the tribute branded the hand of each monk whom he could find with a stamp of iron; and afterwards cut off the hand of every person of this order whom he detected without the mark, and exacted ten deenárs from every other Christian who had not a billet from the government to certify his having paid his tribute. Many monks were subsequently found without the mark: some of these were beheaded, and the rest beaten until they died under the blows: their churches were demolished, and their crosses and pictures destroyed. This took place in the year of the Flight 104 (A.D. 722—3), at the close of the reign of the Khaleefeh Yezeed Ibn-'Abd-El-Melik. A few years after, in the reign of the successor of this prince (Hishám), Ḥanḍhalah Ibn-Ṣafwán, the Governor of Egypt, caused the hand of every Copt to be branded with an iron stamp bearing the figure of a lion, and greatly aggravated their misery; so that many of those residing in the provinces again rebelled, and had recourse to arms; but in vain; and a terrible persecution followed.

From the period of the conquest until the reign of Hishám, the Jacobites (or almost all the Copts) were in possession of all the churches in Egypt, and sent their bishops to the Nubians, who consequently abandoned the Melekite creed, and adopted that of the Jacobites; but in the reign of this Khaleefeh, the Melekites, by means of a present, obtained the restoration of the churches that had formerly belonged to them. These churches, however, soon after returned to

[1] If the reader desire further and fuller details on this subject, for the times of the two dynasties of Memlook Kings, he may consult Et. Quatremère's 'Mémoires Géogr. et Hist. sur l'Egypte,' vol. ii., pp. 220—266. Since my extracts were made, El-Maḳreezee's History of the Copts, contained in his Description of Egypt, has been edited and translated, in Germany, by Wüstenfeld.

[2] Equivalent (at that period) to about thirteen shillings, or, as some say, a little more than half a guinea.

the possession of the Jacobites; and in aftertimes were now the property of one sect, and now of the other, being purchased by presents or services to the government.

It would be tiresome to detail all the troubles of the Copts under the tyranny of Muslim princes; but some particulars in the history of the persecutions which they endured in the earlier ages of the Arab domination may be here mentioned. The Copts are a people of indomitable presumption and intrigue, which qualities render them very difficult to be governed. They have often incurred severe oppression by their own folly, though they have more frequently been victims of unmerited persecution under tyrannical rulers and through the influence of private fanatics.[1]

In the year of the Flight 235 (A.D. 849—50), the Khaleefeh El-Mutawekkil ordered several degrading distinctions to be adopted in the dress of the Copts: the men were obliged to wear "honey-coloured" (or light brown) hooded cloaks, with other peculiar articles of dress; and the women, garments of the same colour: and they were compelled to place wooded figures (or pictures) of devils at (or upon) the doors of their houses.

One of the bitterest persecutions that they ever endured, and one which was attributed to their pride, and their display of wealth, and contemptuous treatment of Muslims, befell them during the reign of that impious wretch the Khaleefeh El-Ḥákim, who acceded to the throne in the year of the Flight 386 (A.D. 996—7), and was killed in 411. Among the minor grievances which he inflicted upon them, was that of compelling them to wear a wooden cross, of the weight of five pounds, suspended to the neck, and garments and turbans of a deep black colour. This seems to have been the origin of the black turban worn by so many of the Christians in the present day. As the distinguishing dress and banners of the Khaleefehs of Egypt were white, black (which was the colour that distinguished their rivals the 'Abbásees) was, in their eyes, the most hateful and ignominious hue that they could choose for the dresses of the despised Copts. I find no earlier mention than this of the black turban of the Christians of Egypt. At the same time that the Copts were compelled thus to distinguish themselves, the Jews were ordered to wear a

1 It should be observed here, that the cases alluded to form exceptions to the general toleration exhibited by the Muslims; and that the Copts who have been converted to El-Islám by oppression have been few in comparison with those who have changed their religion voluntarily. Many have done this through love of Muslim women.

round piece of wood, of the same weight as the crosses of the Christians, and suspended in the same manner. All the churches were given up to be destroyed and plundered, with all the property appertaining to them; and many of them were replaced by mosques. Finally, a sentence of banishment to Greece was pronounced against all the Christians of Egypt, and the Jews; but so strong was the love which they bore to their native country amid all their miseries, and so much were they actuated by that common but absurd disposition, which most sects possess, of hating most bitterly those differing least from them in faith, that a multitude of Copts thronged round the great palace of the Khaleefeh, and implored and obtained a revokement of this sentence. Many Copts, during this and other persecutions, embraced the faith of El-Islám.

In the month of Regeb, 700 (A.D. 1301), happened an event which, for the first time, as well as I can learn, occasioned the Copts to be distinguished by the *blue* turban, as they mostly are at present. A Maghrabee ambassador, approaching the Citadel (of Cairo), saw a man handsomely attired, wearing a white turban, and riding a mare, with many attendants walking by his stirrups, paying him great honours, asking favours of him, and even kissing his feet; while he turned aside from them, and repulsed them, calling to his servants to drive them away. The Maghrabee, informed that this person was a Christian, was so enraged that he was about to lay violent hands upon him; but he refrained, and, ascending to the deewán in the Citadel, related to some of the Emeers there present what he had just seen, with tears in his eyes, drawn by his pity for the Muslims. In consequence of his complaint, the chief persons among the Christians and Jews were summoned to the deewán; and orders were given that the Christians should wear blue turbans, and waist-belts; and the Jews, yellow turbans; and that no person of either of these sects should ride horses or mules. Many Christians, it is added, embraced El-Islám rather than wear the blue turban.

On Friday, the 9th of Rabeeạ el-Ákhir, 721 (A.D. 1321), in the reign of Moḥammad Ibn-Ḳala-oon, all the principal churches throughout Egypt, from Aswán to the Mediterranean, sixty in number, and twenty-one of these in the metropolis and its neighbourhood, were destroyed through a plot formed by some fanatic Muslims. This havoc was accomplished chiefly during the period of the congregational prayers of the Muslims, at noon. At the close of the prayers of the Sulṭán and his court, in the mosque of the Citadel, a man, in a state of apparent frenzy, cried out in the midst of the congregation, "Destroy ye the church which is in the Citadel!" Another man, a faḳeer, in the great mosque El-Azhar, before the appearance of the Khaṭeeb (or Preacher), seemed to be affected by an involuntary trembling, and cried out, "Destroy ye the churches of the presumptuous and infidels! Yea, God is most great! God give victory and aid!" Then he shook himself, and cried, "To the foundations! To the foundations!" Some members of the congregation said, "This is a madman:" others said, "This is an indication of some event." On their going out of the mosque, they saw that the act which he had urged had been commenced: numbers of persons were pressing along the streets with the plunder of the churches, many of which were reduced to mere mounds of rubbish. The Sulṭán threatened a general massacre of the people of El-Ḳáhireh (now Maṣr, or Cairo,) and El-Fusṭáṭ (or Old Maṣr) for this outrage; but was diverted from his purpose by the revenge which the Christians exacted. Refraining from the execution of their plot for the space of a month, that they might be less liable to suspicion, they set fire, on different days, to a vast number of mosques, houses of Emeers, and private dwellings, both in El-Ḳáhireh and El-Fusṭáṭ. Several of the incendiaries were detected, and some burnt alive; and a number of Muslims also were put to death, most of them hanged, along the principal street leading from the southern gate of the city of El-Ḳáhireh to the Citadel, ostensibly for insulting an Emeer, whom they accused of favouring the Christians, though there was no proof that they were the persons who committed this offence: they had been arrested without discrimination, to atone for the injury, and to be made examples to their fellow-citizens. The Sulṭán, however, alarmed by the clamours of a tremendous mob, was afterwards constrained to grant licence to his Muslim subjects to plunder and murder every Christian whom they might chance to meet. The Christians at that time had reverted to the habit of wearing the white turban; and the Sulṭán caused it to be proclaimed that every person of them who was seen wearing a white turban, or riding a horse, might be plundered and killed; that they should wear the blue turban; that they should not ride horses nor mules, but only asses, and with their face to the animal's tail; and should not enter a bath unless with a bell suspended to the neck. At the same time, the Emeers were forbidden to take any Christians into their service; and all Christians who were in the service of the government were displaced.

After having suffered frequent and heavy exactions and other oppressions, a vast number of the Christians both in Upper and Lower Egypt, in the year of the Flight 755 (A.D. 1354—5), embraced the faith of El-Islám. The number of proselytes in the town of Ḳalyoob alone, who changed their faith in one day, was four hundred and fifty. Most of the churches of Upper Egypt were destroyed at the same time, and mosques were built in their places.

From the period just mentioned, the Copts continued subject to more or less oppression, until the accession of Moḥammad 'Alee Báshà, under whose tolerant though severe sway nothing more was exacted from the Christian than the Muslim, except an inconsiderable tribute, which was more than balanced by a remarkable immunity, not conferred by favour (it is true), but not on that account the less valued and envied; I mean the exemption from military service.

II.—THE JEWS OF EGYPT.

The Jews, in every country in which they are dispersed (unlike any other collective class of people residing in a country which is not their own by inheritance from the original possessors or by conquest achieved by themselves or their ancestors), form permanent members of the community among whom they dwell: a few words respecting the Jews in Egypt will therefore be not inappropriate in the present work.

There are in this country about five thousand Jews (in Arabic, called "Yahood," singular "Yahoodee"), most of whom reside in the metropolis, in a miserable, close, and dirty quarter, intersected by lanes, many of which are so narrow as hardly to admit of two persons passing each other in them.

In features, and in the general expression of countenance, the Oriental Jews differ less from other nations of South-western Asia than do those in European countries from the people among whom they live; but we often find them to be distinguished by a very fair skin, light-reddish hair, and very light eyes, either hazel or blue or gray. Many of the Egyptian Jews have sore eyes, and a bloated complexion; the result, it is supposed, of their making an immoderate use of the oil of sesame in their food. In their dress, as well as in their persons, they are generally slovenly and dirty. The colours of their turbans are the same as those of the Christian subjects. Their women veil themselves, and dress in every respect, in public, like the other women of Egypt.

The Jews have eight synagogues in their quarter in Cairo; and not only enjoy religious toleration, but are under a less oppressive government in Egypt than in any other country of the Turkish empire. In Cairo, they pay for the exemption of their quarter from the visits of the Moḥtesib; and they did the same also with respect to the Wálee, as long as his office existed. Being consequently privileged to sell articles of provision at higher prices than the other inhabitants of the metropolis, they can afford to purchase such things at higher rates, and therefore stock their shops with provisions, and especially fruits, of better qualities than are to be found in other parts of the town. Like the Copts, and for a like reason, the Jews pay tribute, and are exempted from military service.

They are held in the utmost contempt and abhorrence by the Muslims in general, and are said to bear a more inveterate hatred than any other people to the Muslims and the Muslim religion. It is said, in the Ḳur-án,[1] "Thou shalt surely find the most violent of [all] men in enmity to those who have believed [to be] the Jews, and those who have attributed partners to God; and thou shalt surely find the most inclinable of them to [entertain] friendship to those who have believed [to be] those who say, We are Christians." On my mentioning to a Muslim friend this trait in the character of the Jews, he related to me, in proof of what I remarked, an event which had occurred a few days before.—"A Jew," said he, "early one morning last week, was passing by a coffee-shop kept by a Muslim with whom he was acquainted, named Moḥammad. Seeing a person standing there, and supposing that it was the master of the shop (for it was yet dusk), he said, 'Good morning, sheykh Moḥammad;' but the only answer he received to his salutation was a furious rebuke for thus addressing a *Jew*, by a name the most odious, to a person of his religion, of any that could be uttered. He (the offender) was dragged before his high-priest, who caused him to receive a severe bastinading for the alleged offence, in spite of his protesting that it was unintentional."—It is a common saying among the Muslims in this country, "Such a one hates me with the hate of the Jews." We cannot wonder, then, that the Jews are detested by the Muslims far more than are the Christians. Not long ago, they used often to be jostled in the streets of Cairo, and sometimes beaten merely for passing on the right hand of a Muslim. At present, they are less oppressed; but still they scarcely ever dare to utter a word of abuse when reviled or beaten unjustly by the meanest Arab or Turk; for many a Jew has been put to death upon a false and malicious accusation of uttering disrespectful words against the Ḳur-án or the Prophet. It is common to hear an Arab abuse his jaded ass, and,

[1] Chap. v. ver. 85.

after applying to him various opprobrious epithets, end by calling the beast a Jew.

A Jew has often been sacrificed to save a Muslim, as happened in the following case.—A Turkish soldier, having occasion to change some money, received from the ṣeyrefee (or money-changer), who was a Muslim, some Turkish coins called 'adleeyehs, reckoned at sixteen piasters each. These he offered to a shopkeeper, in payment for some goods; but the latter refused to allow him more than fifteen piasters to the 'adleeyeh, telling him that the Báshà had given orders, many days before, that this coin should no longer pass for sixteen. The soldier took back the 'adleeyehs to the ṣeyrefee, and demanded an additional piaster to each; which was refused: he therefore complained to the Báshà himself, who, enraged that his orders had been disregarded, sent for the ṣeyrefee. This man confessed that he had been guilty of an offence, but endeavoured to palliate it by asserting that almost every money-changer in the city had done the same, and that he received 'adleeyehs at the same rate. The Báshà, however, disbelieving him, or thinking it necessary to make a public example, gave a signal with his hand, intimating that the delinquent should be beheaded. The interpreter of the court, moved with compassion for the unfortunate man, begged the Báshà to spare his life. "This man," said he, "has done no more than all the money-changers of the city: I, myself, no longer ago than yesterday, received 'adleeyehs at the same rate." "From whom?" exclaimed the Báshà. "From a Jew," answered the interpreter, "with whom I have transacted business for many years." The Jew was brought, and sentenced to be hanged; while the Muslim was pardoned. The interpreter, in the greatest distress of mind, pleaded earnestly for the life of the poor Jew; but the Báshà was inexorable: it was necessary that an example should be made, and it was deemed better to take the life of a Jew than that of a more guilty Muslim. I saw the wretched man hanging at a window of a public fountain which forms part of a mosque in the main street of the city.[1] One end of the rope being passed over one of the upper bars of the grated window, he was hauled up; and as he hung close against the window, he was enabled, in some slight degree, to support himself by his feet against the lower bars; by which his suffering was dreadfully protracted.

---

1 It is surprising that Muslims should hang a *Jew* against a window of a *mosque*, when they consider him so unclean a creature that his blood would defile the sword. For this reason a Jew, in Egypt, is never beheaded.

His relations offered large sums of money for his pardon; but the only favour they could purchase was that of having his face turned towards the window, so as not to be seen by the passengers. He was a man much respected by all who knew him (Muslims, of course, excepted); and he left a family in a very destitute state; but the interpreter who was the unintending cause of his death contributed to their support.

The Jews in Egypt generally lead a very quiet life: indeed, they find few but persons of their own religion who will associate with them. Their diet is extremely gross; but they are commonly regarded as a sober people. The more wealthy among them dress handsomely at home; but put on a plain or even shabby dress before they go out: and though their houses have a mean and dirty appearance from without, many of them contain fine and well-furnished rooms. In the house, they are not so strict as most other Orientals in concealing their women from strange men, or, at least, from persons of their own nation, and from Franks: it often happens that a European visiter is introduced into an apartment where the women of the Jew's family are sitting unveiled, and is waited upon by these women. The same custom also prevails among many of the Syrian Christians residing in Cairo. Intrigues are said to be common with the Jewesses; but there are no avowed courtezans among them. The condition of the lower orders is very wretched; many of them having no other means of subsistence than alms bestowed upon them by their superiors of the same religion.

Avarice is more particularly a characteristic of the Jews in Egypt than of those in other countries where they are less oppressed. They are careful, by every means in their power, to avoid the suspicion of being possessed of much wealth. It is for this reason that they make so shabby a figure in public, and neglect the exterior appearance of their houses. They are generally strict in the performance of their religious ordinances; and, though overreaching in commercial transactions, are honest in the fulfilment of their contracts.

Many of the Egyptian Jews are "ṣarráfs" (or bankers and money-lenders): others are ṣeyrefees, and are esteemed men of strict probity. Some are goldsmiths or silversmiths; and others pursue the trades of retail grocers or fruiterers, &c. A few of the more wealthy are general merchants.

III.—OF LATE INNOVATIONS IN EGYPT.[1]

THE exaggerated reports which have been spread in Europe respecting late innovations, and the general advance of civilization, in Egypt, induce me to add a few lines on these subjects. European customs have not yet begun to spread among the Egyptians themselves; but they probably will ere long; and in the expectation that this will soon be the case, I have been most anxious to become well acquainted (before it be too late to make the attempt) with a state of society which has existed, and excited a high degree of interest, for many centuries, and which many persons have deemed almost immutable.

The account which I have given of the present state of the government of this country shews how absurd is the assertion, that Egypt possesses a legislative assembly that can with any degree of propriety be called representative of the people. The will of the Báshà is almost absolute; but he has certainly effected a great reform, by the introduction of European military and naval tactics, the results of which have already been considerable, and will be yet more extensive, and, in most respects, desirable. Already it has removed a great portion of that weight of prejudice which has so long prevented the Turks from maintaining their relative rank among the nations of the civilized world: by convincing them that one of our branches of science and practice is so far superior to that to which they were accustomed, it has made them in general willing, if not desirous, to learn what more we are able to teach them. One of its effects already manifest might be regarded by an unreflecting mind as of no importance; but is considered by the philosophical Muslim as awfully portentous, and hailed by the Christian as an omen of the brightest promise. The

[1] This was written during the best period of Moḥammad 'Alee's rule; for which reason, and because it shews the policy *generally* followed by his successors, it is retained in the present edition almost entire.

Turks have been led to imitate us in our luxuries: several of the more wealthy began by adopting the use of the knife and fork; and the habit of openly drinking wine immediately followed, and has become common among a great number of the higher officers of the government. That a remarkable indifference to religion is indicated by this innovation is evident; and the principles of the dominant class will doubtless spread (though they have not yet done so) among the inferior members of the community. The former have begun to undermine the foundations of El-Islám: the latter as yet seem to look on with apathy, or at least with resignation to the decrees of Providence; but they will probably soon assist in the work, and the overthrow of the whole fabric may reasonably be expected to ensue at a period not very remote.

The acquisition of a powerful empire, independent of the Porte, appears to have been the grand, and almost the sole, object of the present Báshà of Egypt. He has introduced many European sciences, arts, and manufactures; but all in furtherance of this project; for his new manufactures have impoverished his people. He has established a printing-office; but the works which have issued from it are almost solely intended for the instruction of his military, naval, and civil servants.[1] A newspaper is printed at another press, in the Citadel: its paragraphs, however, are seldom on any other subject than the affairs of the government. It is in Turkish and Arabic. Sometimes, three numbers of it appear in a week: at other times, only one is published in a month.[2]

I have candidly stated my opinion, that the policy of Moḥammad 'Alee is in several respects erroneous, and that his people are severely oppressed; but the circumstances in which he has been placed offer large excuses for his severity. To judge of his character fairly, we should compare him with another Turkish reformer, his [late] nominal sovereign, the Sulṭán Maḥmood. In every point of view, he

---

[1] I have transmitted a list of these works to the Royal Asiatic Society.

[2] One of the less important acts of Moḥammad 'Alee I should mention, as it is one which renders my description of the streets and shops of Cairo not altogether applicable to their present state. He has lately caused the masṭabahs in most of the thoroughfare-streets to be pulled down, and only allowed them to be rebuilt in the wider parts, generally to the width of about two spans. At the same time, he has obliged the tradesmen to paint their shops, and ordered them to remove the unsightly "saḳeefehs" (or coverings) of matting which shaded many of the sooḳs; prohibiting the replacing of them unless by coverings of wood. Cairo has, in consequence, lost much of its Arabian aspect.—Some years after the foregoing portion of this note was written, the people of Cairo were required to whitewash their houses externally; and thus the picturesque aspect of the streets was further marred.

has shewn his superiority to the latter; and especially in the discipline of his forces. While the Sulṭán was more closely imitating us in trivial matters (as, for instance, in the new military dress which he introduced), Moḥammad 'Alee aimed at, and attained, more important objects.[1] When we would estimate his character by the massacre of the Memlooks, a fact most painful to reflect upon, we should admit that he had recourse to this horrid expedient for a most desirable end; and may at the same time place in the opposite scale the asylum which he granted to the Greek refugees when the blood of their countrymen ran in the gutters of Constantinople.

It is difficult to form a just estimate of the general conduct of Moḥammad 'Alee, on account of the secrecy which is maintained in the East in the most important political affairs: this, however, may be said with certainty—the people whom he governs have been greatly impoverished under his rule; but they have exchanged anarchy for tranquillity, and undisguised fanaticism for an affected toleration; while many of them have been instructed in sciences and arts which must eventually be highly beneficial to the nation at large.

---

[1] The dress worn by the military and some other officers of the Báshà of Egypt is still [1835] quite Turkish in everything but the want of the turban, which is now worn by few of those persons, and only in winter; the red cap alone, over which the muslin or Kashmeer shawl used always to be wound, being at present the regular head-dress. The trousers are very full from the waist to a little below the knee, overhanging a pair of tight leggings which form parts of them. A tight vest (the sleeves of which are divided from the wrist nearly to the elbow, but generally buttoned at this part), a girdle, a jacket with hanging sleeves, socks, and a pair of red shoes, complete the outward dress generally worn: but the jacket is sometimes made with sleeves like those of the vest above described, and the vest without sleeves; and black European shoes are worn by some persons. The sword is now hung in our manner, by a waist-belt. The dress of the private soldiers consists of a vest and trousers (the latter similar to those above described, but not so full), of a kind of coarse red serge, or, in summer, of white cotton, with the girdle, red cap, and red shoes.

APPENDIX A.

FEMALE ORNAMENTS.

THE ornaments of the women of Egypt are so various, that a description of them all would far exceed the limits which the nature of this work allows, and would require a great number of engravings, or be useless. I shall, however, describe all the principal kinds; and these will convey some idea of the rest. If the subject be not interesting to general readers, it may at least be of some use to artists, who are often left almost entirely to their own imagination in representing Arabian costumes and ornaments. I first describe those which are worn by *ladies*, and females of the *middle orders*.

The head-dress has already been mentioned, as composed of a "ṭarboosh" and "faroodeeyeh" (or kerchief), which latter, when wound round the former, is called "rabṭah." The front part of the rabṭah is often ornamented with spangles of gilt or plain silver, disposed in fanciful patterns; and in this case, the rabṭah itself is generally of black or rose-coloured muslin or crape, and always plain. The more common kinds of rabṭah have been described.

The "mizágee" is an ornament very generally worn. It is composed of a strip of muslin, most commonly black or rose-coloured, folded together several times, so as to form a narrow band, about the breadth of a finger, or less. Its length is about five feet. The central part, for the space of about twelve or thirteen inches, is ornamented with spangles, which are placed close together, or in the form of diamonds, &c., or of bosses; and at each end, for about the same length, are a few other spangles, with an edging, and small tassels, of various-coloured silks. Sometimes there is also a similar edging, with spangles suspended to it, along the lower edge of the ornamented part in the middle. The mizágee is bound round the head; the ornamented central part being over the forehead, generally above the edge of the rabṭah: it is tied behind, at the upper part of the rabṭah; and the ornamented ends, drawn forward, hang over the bosom.[1]

The "ḳurṣ" is a round, convex ornament, commonly about five inches in diameter; which is very generally worn by ladies. It is sewed upon the crown of the ṭarboosh.[2] There are two kinds. The first that I shall describe (the only kind that is worn by ladies, or by the wives of tradesmen of moderate property,) is the "ḳurṣ almás," or diamond ḳurṣ. This is composed of diamonds set generally in gold; and is of open work, representing roses, leaves, &c. The diamonds are commonly of a very poor and shallow kind; and the gold of this and all other diamond ornaments worn in Egypt is much alloyed with copper. The value of a moderately handsome diamond ḳurṣ is about a hundred and twenty-five or a hundred and fifty pounds sterling. It is very

[1] See a figure in the engraving in page 378.

[2] See the engraving in page 44.

Diamond Ḳurṣ.

seldom made of silver; and I think that those of gold, when attached to the deep-red ṭarboosh, have a richer effect, though not in accordance with our general taste. The wives even of petty tradesmen sometimes wear the diamond ḳurṣ: they are extremely fond of diamonds, and generally endeavour to get some, however bad. The ḳurṣ, being of considerable weight, is at first painful to wear; and women who are in the habit of wearing it complain of headache when they take it off: hence they retain it day and night; but some have an inferior one for the bed. Some ladies have one for ordinary wearing; another for particular occasions, a little larger and handsomer; and a third merely to wear in bed.—The other kind of ḳurṣ, "ḳurṣ dahab" (or, of gold), is a convex plate of very thin embossed gold, usually of the form represented below; and almost always with a false emerald (a piece of green glass), not cut with facets, set in the centre. Neither the emerald nor the ruby is here cut with facets: if so cut,

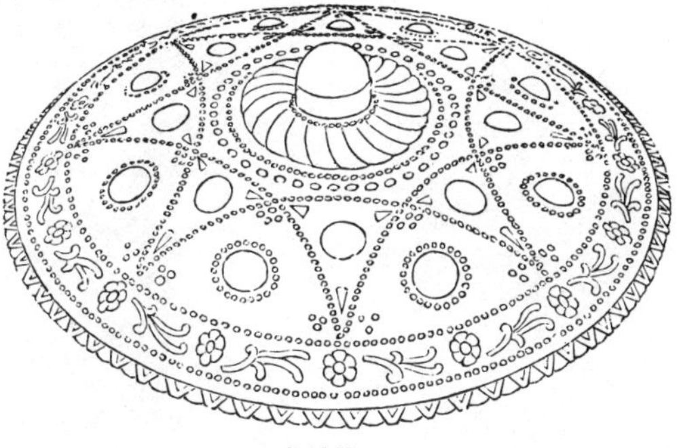

Gold Ḳurṣ.

they would generally be considered false. The simple gold ḳurṣ is lined with a thick coat of wax, which is covered with a piece of paper. It is worn by many women who cannot afford to purchase diamonds; and even by some servants.

The "ḳuṣṣah" is an ornament generally from seven to eight inches in length, composed of diamonds set in gold, and sometimes with emeralds, rubies, and pearls; having drops of diamonds or emeralds, &c., suspended to it. It is worn on the front of the rabṭah, attached by little hooks at the back. I have seen several ḳuṣṣahs of diamonds, &c., set in silver instead of gold. The ḳuṣṣah is generally placed on the head of a bride, outside her shawl covering; as also is the ḳurṣ; and these ornaments are likewise employed to decorate the bier of a female. The former, like the latter, is worn by females of the higher and middle classes.

"'Enebeh" is another name for the same kind of ornament, worn in the same manner. If of full size, it is fourteen or fifteen inches in length; and rather more than half encircles the head-dress.

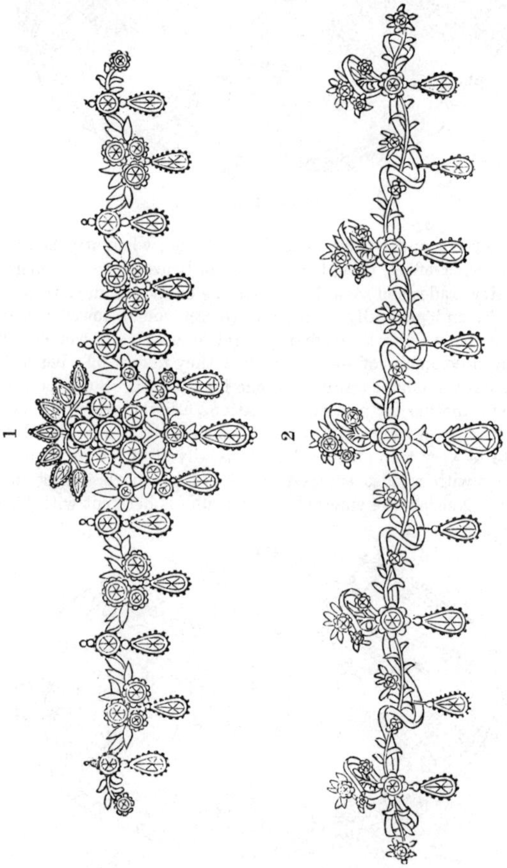

1. Ḳuṣṣah; 2. 'Enebeh; *the former, half, and the latter, one-third, of the real size.*

The "shawáṭeḥ" (in the singular, "sháṭeḥ,") are two ornaments, each consisting of three or more strings of pearls, about the length of the ḳuṣṣah, with a pierced emerald uniting them in the centre, like the usual pearl necklace hereafter described; or they are composed of pearls arranged in the manner of a narrow lace, and often with the addition of a few small emeralds. They are attached to the rabṭah in the form of two festoons, one on each side of the head, from the extremity of the ḳuṣṣah to the back part of the head-dress, or, sometimes, to the ear-ring.

Instead of the ḳuṣṣah and shawáṭeḥ, and sometimes in addition to them, are worn some other ornaments which I proceed to describe.

The "reesheh" (literally, "feather,") is a sprig of diamonds set in gold or silver. It is worn on the front or side of the head-dress.

The "hilál" is a crescent of diamonds set in gold or silver, and worn like the reesheh. In form it resembles the phasis of the moon when between two and three nights old; its width being small, and its outward edge not more than half a circle.

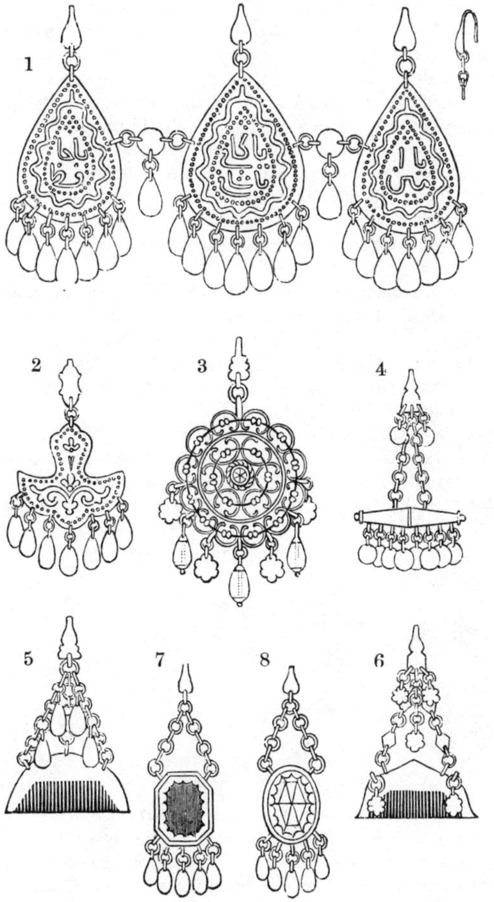

1 and 2. Ḳamarahs. 3. Sáḳiyeh. 4. 'Ood eṣ-Ṣaleeb. 5 and 6. Mishṭs. 7. 'Aḳeeḳ. 8. Belloor. *Each, half the real size.*

The "ḳamarah" (or moon) is an ornament formed of a thin plate of gold, embossed with fanciful work, and sometimes with Arabic words, and having about seven little flat pieces of gold, called "barḳ," attached to the lower part; or it is composed of gold with diamonds, rubies, &c. Two specimens of the former kind are here represented.

One of these consists of three ḳamarahs connected together, to be worn on the front of the head-dress: the central contains the words "Yá Káfee Yá Sháfee" (O Sufficient! O Restorer to health!): that on the left, "Yá Ḥáfiẓ" (O Preserver!): that on the right, "Yá Emeen" (O Trustworthy!): these, therefore, are charms as well as ornaments.

The "sáḳiyeh" (or water-wheel), so called from its form, is a circular flat ornament of gold filigree-work, with small pearls, and with a diamond or other precious stone in the centre, and barḳ and emeralds suspended from the lower part. It is worn in the same manner as the ḳamarah, or with the latter ornament.

The "'ood eṣ-ṣaleeb" (or wood of the cross) is a kind of ornament undoubtedly borrowed from the Christians; and it is surprising that Moḥammadan women should wear it, and give it this appellation. It is a little round and slender piece of wood, rather smaller towards the extremities than in the middle, enclosed in a case of gold, of the same form, composed of two pieces which unite in the middle, having two chains and a hook by which to suspend it, and a row of barḳ along the bottom. It is worn in the place of, or with, the two ornaments just before described.

The "mishṭ" (or comb) is a little comb of gold, worn in the same manner as the three kinds of ornament described next before this, and generally with one or more of those ornaments. It is suspended by small chains and a hook, having four or five barḳ attached.

There is also an ornament somewhat similar to those just mentioned, composed of a carnelion, or a piece of crystal or of colourless glass, set in gold, suspended by two chains and a hook, and having barḳ attached to the bottom. The former kind is called "'aḳeeḳ" (which signifies "carnelion"), and the latter, "belloor" ("crystal.")

Several ornaments in the shapes of flowers, butterflies, &c., are also worn upon the head-dress; but seldom alone.

Of ear-rings ("ḥalaḳ") there is a great variety. Some of the more usual kinds are here represented. The first is of diamonds set in silver. It consists of a drop suspended within a wreath hanging from a sprig. The back of the silver is gilt, to prevent its being tarnished by perspiration. The specimen here given is that for the

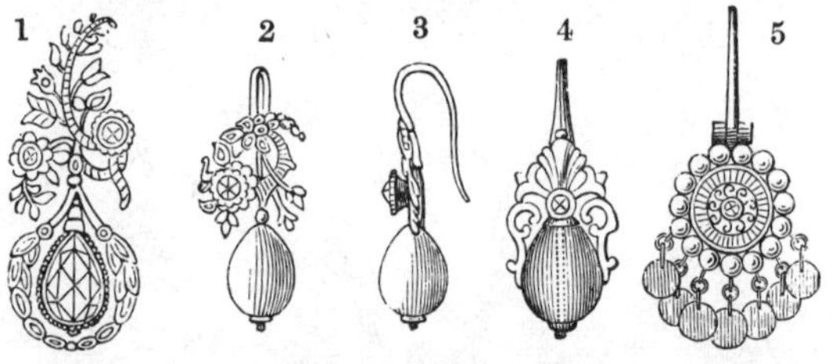

Ear-rings—*each, half the real size.*

right ear: its fellow is similar; but with the sprig reversed. This pair of ear-rings is suited for a lady of wealth.—So also is the second, which resembles the former, except that it has a large pearl in the place of the diamond drop and wreath, and that the diamonds of the sprig are set in gold. No. 3 is a side view of the same.—The next consists of gold, and an emerald pierced through the middle, with a small diamond above the emerald. Emeralds are generally pierced in Egypt, and spoiled by this process as much as by not being cut with facets.—The last is of gold, with a small ruby in the centre. The ruby is set in fine filigree-work, which is surrounded by fifteen balls of gold. To the seven lower balls are suspended as many circular barḳ.

The necklace ("'eḳd") is another description of ornament of which the Egyptians have a great variety; but almost all of them are similar in the following particulars.

1st. The beads &c. of which they are composed are, altogether, not more than ten inches in length; so that they would not entirely encircle the neck if tied quite tight, which is never done: the string extends about six or seven inches beyond each extre-

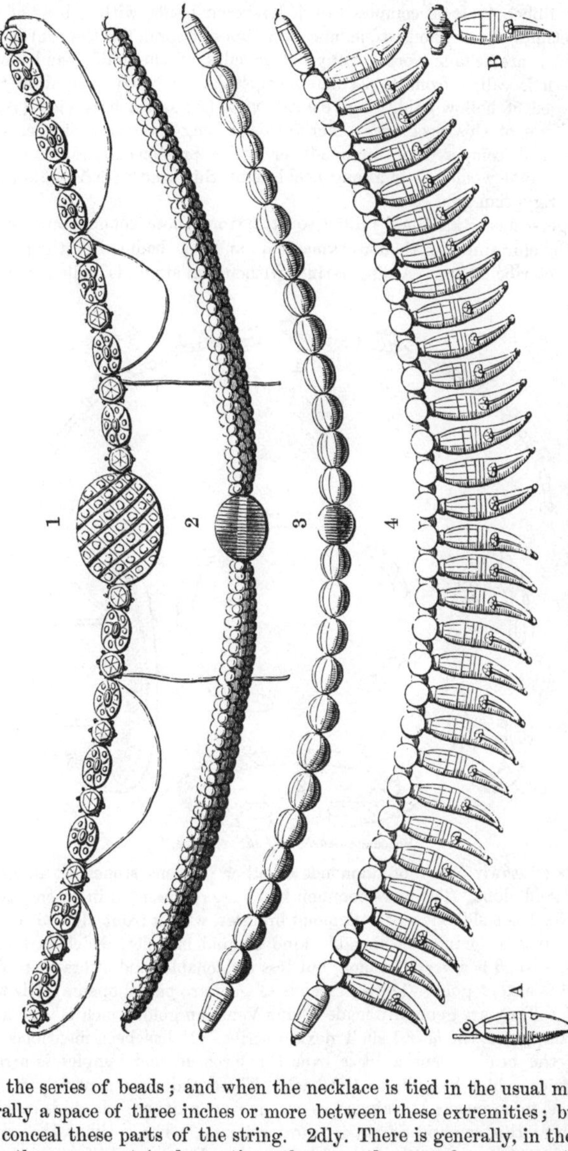

Necklaces—each, half the real size.

mity of the series of beads; and when the necklace is tied in the usual manner, there is generally a space of three inches or more between these extremities; but the plaits of hair conceal these parts of the string. 2dly. There is generally, in the centre, one bead or other ornament (and sometimes there are three, or five, or seven,) differing in size, form, material, or colour, from the others.—The necklaces mostly worn by ladies are of diamonds or pearls.—In the preceding engraving, the first necklace is of diamonds set in gold.—The second consists of several strings of pearls, with a pierced flattish emerald in the centre. Most of the pearl necklaces are of this description.—The third is called "libbeh." It is composed of hollow gold beads, with a bead of a different kind (sometimes of a precious stone, and sometimes of coral,) in the centre. This and the following are seldom worn by any but females of the middle and lower orders. —The fourth is called, from its peculiar form, "sha'eer" (which signifies "barley"). It is composed of hollow gold. I give a side view (A) and a back view (B) of one of the appendages of this necklace.—There is also a long kind of necklace, reaching to the girdle, and composed of diamonds or other precious stones, which is called "ḳiládeh." Some women form a long necklace of this kind with Venetian sequins, or Turkish or Egyptian gold coins.

The finger-rings ("khátims") differ so little from those common among ourselves, except in the clumsiness of their workmanship, and the badness of the jewels, that I need not describe them. A finger-ring without a stone is called "debleh," or "dibleh."

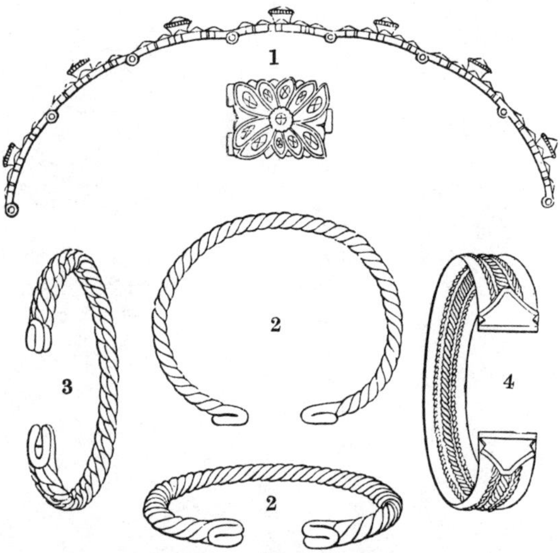

Bracelets—*each, half the real size.*

Bracelets ("asáwir") are of diamonds or other precious stones set in gold, or of pearls, or of gold alone. The more common kinds are represented in an engraving here inserted.—No. 1 is a side view of a diamond bracelet, with a front view of a portion of the same.—No. 2 is the most fashionable kind of gold bracelet, which is formed of a simple twist.—No. 3 is a very common, but less fashionable kind of bracelet of twisted gold.—No. 4 is also of gold.—These bracelets of gold are pulled open a little to be put on the wrist. They are generally made of fine Venetian gold, which is very flexible.

The ornaments of the *hair* I shall next describe.—It has been mentioned that all the hair of the head, except a little over the forehead and temples, is arranged in plaits, or braids, which hang down the back. These plaits are generally from eleven to twenty-five in number; but always of an uneven number: eleven is considered a scanty number: thirteen and fifteen are more common. Three times the number of black silk strings (three to each plait of hair, and each three united at the top), from sixteen to eighteen inches in length, are braided with the hair for about a quarter of their length; or they are attached to a lace or band of black silk which is bound round the head, and in this case hang entirely separate from the plaits of hair, which they almost conceal. These strings are called "ḳeyṭáns;" and together with certain ornaments of gold, &c., the more common of which are here represented, compose what is termed the "ṣafà."[1] Along each string, except from the upper extremity to about

1, 2, 3, 4. Barḳ. 5. Másoorah. 6. Ḥabbeh. 7. Shiftisheh.[2] *Each, half the real size.*

a quarter or (at most) a third of its length, are generally attached nine or more of the little flat ornaments of gold called "barḳ." These are commonly all of the same form, and about an inch, or a little more, apart; but those of each string are purposely placed so as not exactly to correspond with those of the others. The most usual forms of barḳ are Nos. 1 and 2 of the specimens given above. At the end of each string is a small gold tube, called "másoorah," about three-eighths of an inch long, or a kind of gold bead in the form of a cube with a portion cut off from each angle, called "ḥabbeh." Beneath the másoorah or ḥabbeh is a little ring, to which is most commonly suspended a Turkish gold coin called "Rubạ Fenduḳlee," equivalent to nearly 1*s.* 8*d.* of our money, and a little more than half an inch in diameter. Such is the most general description of ṣafà; but there are more genteel kinds, in which the ḥabbeh is usually preferred to the másooorah, and instead of the Rubạ Fenduḳlee is a flat ornament of gold, called, from its form, "kummetrè," or "pear." There are also other and more approved substitutes for the gold coin; the most usual of which is called "shiftisheh," composed of open gold work, with a pearl in the centre. Some ladies substitute a little tassel of pearls for the gold coin; or suspend alternately pearls and emeralds to the bottom of the triple strings; and attach a pearl with each of the barḳ. The ṣafà thus composed with pearls is called "ṣafà loolee." Coral beads are also sometimes attached in the same manner as the pearls.—From what has been said above, it appears that a moderate ṣafà of thirteen plaits will consist of 39 strings, 351 barḳ, 39 másoorahs or ḥabbehs, and 39 gold coins or other ornaments; and that a ṣafà of twenty-five plaits, with twelve barḳ to each string, will contain no fewer than 900 barḳ, and seventy-five of each of the other appendages. The ṣafà appears to me the prettiest, as well as the most singular, of all the ornaments worn by the ladies of Egypt. The glittering of the barḳ, &c., and their chinking together as the wearer walks, have a peculiarly lively effect.

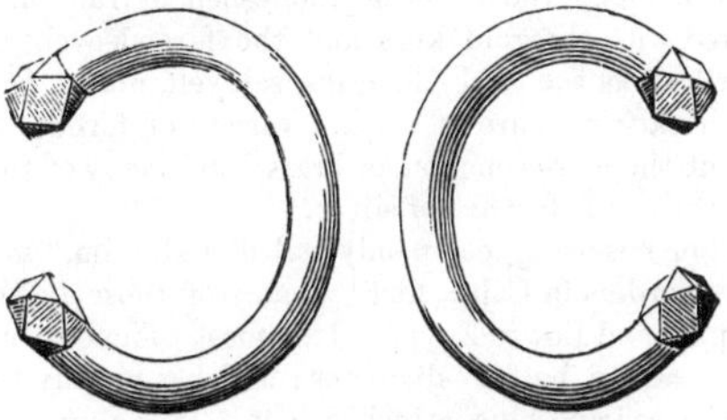

Anklets—*one-fourth of the real size.*

Anklets ("khulkhál"), of solid gold or silver, and of the form here sketched, are

[1] See, again, the engraving in page 44 of this work.

[2] Pronounced "shiftish'eh."

worn by some ladies; but are more uncommon than they formerly were. They are of course very heavy, and, knocking together as the wearer walks, make a ringing noise: hence it is said in a song, "The ringing of thine anklets has deprived me of my reason." Isaiah alludes to this,[1] or perhaps to the sound produced by another kind of anklet which will be mentioned hereafter.

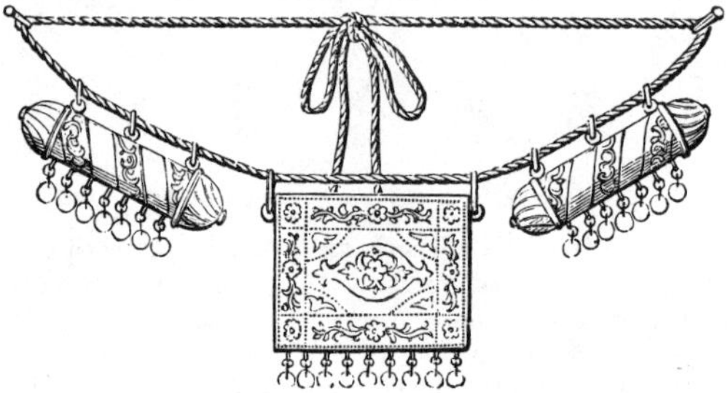

Ḥegábs—*one-fourth of the real size.*

The only description of ladies' ornaments that I have yet to describe is the "ḥegáb," or amulet. This is a writing of one or other of the kinds that I have described in the eleventh chapter, covered with waxed cloth, to preserve it from accidental pollution, or injury by moisture, and enclosed in a case of thin embossed gold, or silver, which is attached to a silk string, or a chain, and generally hung on the right side, above the girdle; the string or chain being passed over the left shoulder. Sometimes these cases bear Arabic inscriptions; such as "Má sháa-lláh" ("What God willeth [cometh to pass]") and "Yá ḳáḍi-l-ḥágát" ("O Decreer of the things that are needful!"). I insert an engraving of three ḥegábs of gold, attached to a string, to be worn together. The central one is a thin, flat case, containing a folded paper: it is about a third of an inch thick: the others are cylindrical cases, with hemispherical ends, and contain scrolls: each has a row of barḳ along the bottom. Ḥegábs such as these, or of a triangular form, are worn by many children, as well as women; and those of the latter form are often attached to a child's head dress.

The ornaments worn by females of the *lower orders* must now be described.

It is necessary, perhaps, to remind the reader that the head-dress of these women, with the exception of some of the poor in the villages, generally consists of an 'aṣbeh, which has been described in page 50; and that some wear, instead of this, the ṭarboosh and faroodeeyeh. Sometimes, a string of Venetian sequins (which is called "sheddeh benád'ḳah") is worn along the front of the 'aṣbeh or rabṭah. The ṭarboosh is also sometimes decorated with the gold ḳurṣ and the faroodeeyeh, with some other ornaments before described, as the gold ḳamarahs, sáḳiyeh, mishṭ, &c.

The "ḥalaḳ," or ear-rings, are of a great variety of forms. Some are of gold and precious stones; but the more common, of brass; and many of the latter have coloured beads attached to them. A few are of silver.

The "khizám," or nose-ring, commonly called "khuzám," is worn by a few of the women of the lower orders in Cairo, and by many of those in the country towns and villages both of Upper and Lower Egypt. It is most commonly made of brass; is from an inch to an inch and a half in diameter; and has usually three or more coloured glass beads, generally red and blue, attached to it. It is almost always passed through the right ala of the nose; and hangs partly before the mouth; so that the wearer is

[1] Ch. iii. v. 16.

obliged to hold it up with one hand when she puts anything into her mouth. It is sometimes of gold. This ornament is as ancient as the time of the patriarch Abraham;[1] and is mentioned by Isaiah[2] and by Ezekiel.[3] To those who are unaccustomed to the sight of it, the nose-ring is certainly the reverse of an ornament.

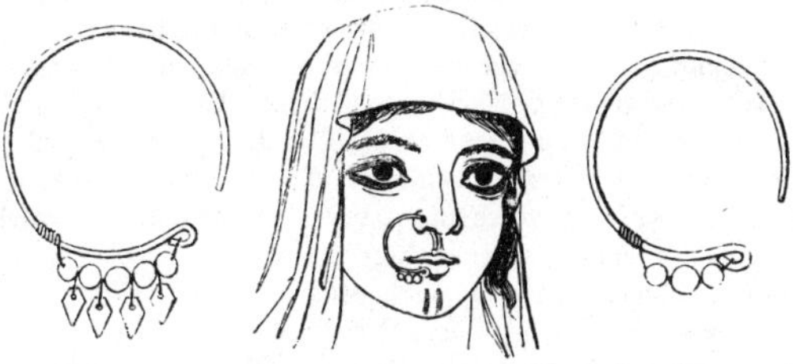

Nose-rings—*half the real size.*

The "'eḳd," or necklace, is generally of a style similar to those which I have already described. I have before mentioned that the libbeh and sha'eer are worn by some women of the lower orders; but their necklaces are most commonly composed of coloured glass beads: sometimes, of a single string; and sometimes, of several strings, with one or more larger beads in the centre: or they are made in the form of net-work. The Egyptian women, being excessively fond of ornaments, often wear two or three necklaces of the value of a penny each, or less. Some necklaces are composed of large beads of transparent amber.

Another ornament worn by many of them on the neck is a ring, called "ṭóḳ," of silver or brass or pewter. Little girls, also, sometimes wear this ornament. Some of the smaller ṭóḳs are made of iron.

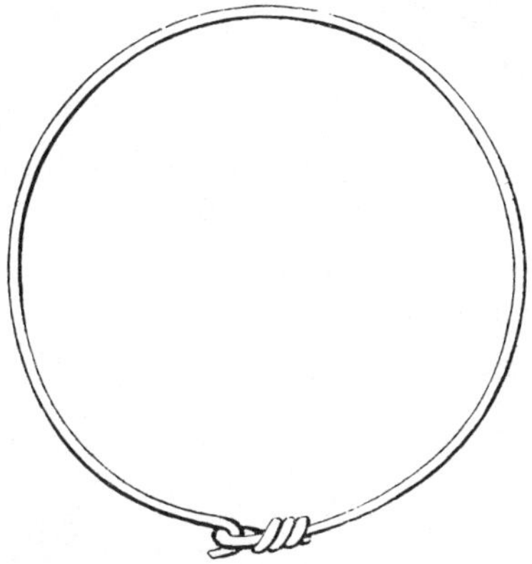

Ṭóḳ, or Neck-ring—*one-fourth of the real size.*

Finger-rings of silver or of brass are almost universally worn. Brass rings, with pieces of coloured glass set in them, may be purchased in Cairo for scarcely more than a farthing each; and many women wear two, three, or more, of these.

---

1 See Genesis xxiv. 47, where, in our common version, "ear-ring" is improperly put for "nose-ring."

2 Ch. iii. v. 21.

3 Ch. xvi. v. 12. Here, again, a mistake is made in our common version, but corrected in the margin.

The "asáwir," or bracelets, are of various kinds. Some are of silver; and some of brass or copper; and of the same form as those of gold before described. Those of brass are the more common. There are also bracelets composed of large amber beads, and others of bone; and there is a very common kind, called "ghuweyshát," of opaque, coloured glass, generally blue or green, but sometimes variegated with other colours. These, and the bone bracelets, are drawn over the hand.

Some of the women of the lower orders imitate their superiors in arranging their hair in several plaits, and plaiting, with each of these, the black silk strings which are worn by the ladies; but it is the general practice of the women of these classes to divide their hair into only two tresses behind, and to plait, with each of these tresses, three red silk strings, each of which has a tassel at the end, and reaches more than half way towards the ground; so that they are usually obliged to draw aside the tassels before they sit down. These appendages are called "'oḳooṣ."

"Khulkhál," or anklets, of solid silver, already described, are worn by the wives of some of the richer peasants, and of the Sheykhs of villages; and small khulkháls of iron are worn by many children. It was also a common custom among the Arabs, for girls or young women to wear a string of bells on their feet. I have seen many little girls in Cairo with small round bells attached to their anklets. Perhaps it is to the sound of ornaments of this kind, rather than that of the more common anklet, that Isaiah alludes in chapter iii. verse 16.

APPENDIX B.

EGYPTIAN MEASURES, WEIGHTS, AND MONEYS.

Of the measures and weights used in Egypt, I am not able to give an exact account; for, after diligent search, I have not succeeded in finding any two specimens of the same denomination perfectly agreeing with each other, and generally the difference has been very considerable: but in those cases in which I have given the *minimum* and *maximum*, the former may be received as approximating very nearly to the just equivalent. The tradesmen in Egypt, from fear of the Moḥtesib, mostly have measures and weights a little exceeding the true standards, though stamped by the government, which takes care to have such measures and weights employed in the purchases which it makes, and equal care, no doubt, to use those which are more true in selling.

MEASURES OF LENGTH AND LAND.

The "fitr" is the space measured by the extension of the thumb and first finger.

The "shibr" is the common span, measured by the extension of the thumb and little finger.

The "diráạ beledee" (or "cubit of the country"—the common Egyptian cubit), which is used for measuring the linen, &c., manufactured in Egypt, is equal to 22 inches and two-thirds.

The "diráạ hindázeh," chiefly used for measuring Indian goods, is about 25 inches.

The "diráạ Istamboolee" (or "cubit of Constantinople"), which is used for measuring European cloth, &c., is about 26 inches and a half.

The "feddán," the most common measure of land, was, a few years ago, equal to about an English acre and one-tenth. It is now less than an acre. It is divided into "ḳeeráṭs" (or twenty-fourth parts); and consists of 333 square "ḳaṣabahs" (or rods) and one-third. The ḳaṣabah was 24 "ḳabḍahs;" but is now 22. The ḳabḍah is the measure of a man's fist with the thumb erect, or about 6 inches and a quarter.

The "malaḳah," or Egyptian league, is a measure of which I have not been able to obtain any better definition than this:—That it is the distance between two villages. It is different in Upper and Lower Egypt; as was the ancient schœnus, with which it nearly corresponds. In Lower Egypt it is about an hour's journey, or from $2\frac{1}{2}$ to 3 miles: in Upper Egypt, about an hour and a half, or from $3\frac{3}{4}$ miles to $4\frac{1}{2}$, or even more.

CORN MEASURES.

The "ardebb" is equivalent, very nearly, to five English bushels.

The "weybeh" is the sixth of an ardebb.

The "rubạ" is the fourth of a weybeh.

WEIGHTS.

The "ḳamḥah" (or grain of wheat) is the 64th part of a dirhem, or fourth of a ḳeerát; about three-quarters of an English grain.

The "ḥabbeh" (or grain of barley) is the 48th part of a dirhem, or third of a ḳeerát; equal to $\frac{127}{128}$ of an English grain, or in commerce fully equal to an English grain.

The "ḳeerát" (or carat), which is 4 ḳamḥahs, or 3 ḥabbehs, as above mentioned, is the 24th part of a mitḳál, or from $2\frac{125}{128}$ to three English grains.

The "dirhem" (or drachm), the subdivisions of which have been mentioned above, is from $47\frac{5}{8}$ to 48 English grains.

The "mitḳál" (or the weight of a "deenár") is a dirhem and a half;—from $71\frac{7}{16}$ to 72 English grains.

The "uḳeeyeh," or "wuḳeeyeh" (the ounce), is 12 dirhems, or the 12th part of a raṭl;—from $571\frac{1}{2}$ to 576 English grains.

The "raṭl" (or pound), being 144 dirhems, or 12 uḳeeyehs, is from 1 lb. 2oz. $5\frac{3}{4}$dwt. to about 1 lb. 2oz. 8dwt., Troy; or from 15oz. 10dr. $22\frac{1}{16}$ grains to nearly 15oz. 13dr., Avoirdupois.

The "uḳḳah," or "wuḳḳah," is 400 dirhems (or 2 raṭls and seven-ninths);—from 3 lb. 3oz. $13\frac{3}{4}$ dwt. to 3 lb. 4oz., Troy; or from 2 lb. 11oz. 8dr. $18\frac{3}{4}$ grains to about, or nearly, 2 lb. 12oz., or 2 lb. and three-quarters, Avoirdupois.

The "ḳanṭár" (or hundred-weight, *i. e.* 100 raṭls) is from 98 lb. *minus* 200 grains to about 98 lb. and three-quarters, Avoirdupois.

MONEYS.

The pound sterling is now, and is likely to continue for some years, equivalent to 100 Egyptian piasters: it has risen, in two years, from 72 piasters; which was the rate of exchange for several preceding years.

A "faḍḍah" is the smallest Egyptian coin. It is called, in the singular, "nuṣṣ" (a corruption of "nuṣf," which signifies "half") or "nuṣṣ faḍḍah:" it is also called "meyyedee," or "meiyedee" (an abbreviation of "mu-eiyadee"). These names were originally given to the half-dirhems which were coined in the reign of the Sulṭán El-Mu-eiyad, in the early part of the ninth century of the Flight, or of the fifteenth of our era. The Turks call it "páráh." The faḍḍah is made of a mixture of silver and copper (its name signifies "silver"); and is the fortieth part of a piaster; consequently equivalent to six twenty-fifths, or nearly a quarter, of a farthing.

There are pieces of 5, 10, and 20 faḍḍahs, "khamseh faḍḍah," "'asharah faḍḍah," and "'eshreen faḍḍah" (so called for "khamset anṣáf faḍḍah," &c.), or "ḳaṭ'ah bi-khamseh," "ḳaṭ'ah bi-'asharah," and "ḳaṭ'ah bi-'eshreen" (*i. e.* "pieces of five," &c.): the last is also called "nuṣṣ ḳirsh" (or "half a piaster"). These pieces, which are equivalent respectively to a farthing and one-fifth, two farthings and two-fifths, and a penny and one-fifth, are of the same composition as the single faḍḍahs.

The "ḳirsh," or Egyptian piaster, has already been shewn to be equivalent to the hundredth part of a pound sterling, or the fifth of a shilling; that is, two pence and two-fifths. It is of the same composition as the pieces above mentioned, and an inch and one-eighth in diameter. On one face it bears the Sulṭán's cipher; and on the other, in Arabic, "ḍuriba fee Miṣr" ("coined in Miṣr," commonly called Maṣr, *i. e.* Cairo), with the date of Moḥammad 'Alee's accession to the government below (1223 of the Flight, or 1808-9 of our era), and the year of his government in which it was coined above. The inscriptions of the other coins are almost exactly similar.

The "saadeeyeh," commonly called "kheyreeyeh bi-arba'ah" (*i. e.* "the kheyreeyeh of four"), or the "small kheyreeyeh," is a small gold coin, of the value of four piasters, or nine pence and three-fifths.

The "kheyreeyeh" properly so called, or "kheyreeyeh bi-tis'ah" (*i. e.* "kheyreeyeh of nine "), is a gold coin of the value of nine piasters, or twenty-one pence and three-fifths.

The above are the only Egyptian coins.

The coins of Constantinople are current in Egypt; but scarce.

European and American dollars are also current in Egypt: most of them are equivalent to twenty Egyptian piasters: the Spanish pillared dollar, to twenty-one. The name of "riyál faránsà" is given to every kind; but the pillared dollar is called "aboo midfa'" (or, "having a cannon"); the pillars being mistaken for cannons. The others have also distinguishing names. The Spanish doubloon (called in Arabic "debloon"), the value of which is sixteen dollars, is likewise current in this country: so too are the Venetian sequin (called "benduḳee," for "bunduḳee"), and the English sovereign (which is called "ginyeh," for guinea).

The "riyál" of Egypt is a nominal money, the value of ninety faḍḍahs, or five pence and two-fifths. In, or about, the year of the Flight 1185 (A.D. 1771-2), the Spanish dollar passed for ninety faḍḍahs, by order of 'Alee Bey. The dollar was then simply called "riyál;" and from that period, the above-mentioned number of faḍḍahs has continued to be called by this name.

The "kees," or purse, is the sum of five hundred piasters, or five pounds sterling.

The "khazneh," or treasury, is a thousand purses, or five thousand pounds terling.

APPENDIX C.

HOUSEHOLD EXPENDITURE IN CAIRO.

THE following is an account of the quantities and prices of household stores required for one year by the family of a person of the middle class in Cairo, consisting of himself and three women. I insert it as a necessary supplement to the list given in page 312.

	Piasters.
Wheat, eight ardebbs, about	400
Grinding the above	50
Baking	40
Meat, from one raṭl and a half to two raṭls (or a piaster and a half) per diem	550
Vegetables, about half a piaster per diem	185
Rice	100
Semn (or clarified butter), two ḳanṭárs, about [1]	325
Coffee	185
Tobacco (Gebelee)	200
Sugar, half a ḳanṭár, about	100
Water	100
Firewood, seven ḥamlehs (or donkey-loads)	75
Charcoal	100
Oil (for two or three lamps), a ḳanṭár, about	125
Candles (tallow)	100
Soap	90
	2,725

The above sum total is equivalent to twenty-seven pounds, five shillings, sterling; consequently, the weekly expenses are about ten shillings and sixpence; and the daily, eighteen pence, or seven piasters and a half. The tobacco in this account is almost entirely for the use of the master of the family; the women in his house very seldom smoking.

[1] In the first two editions of this work, there was a mistake here in the price of the butter, unless it was smuggled into the town. It would be cheap at the price which I have now stated above.

APPENDIX D.

PRAYER OF MUSLIM SCHOOL-BOYS.

My friend Mr. Burton (who, in the course of his long residence in Egypt, has acquired an ample fund of valuable information respecting its modern inhabitants, as well as other subjects,) has kindly communicated to me an Arabic paper containing the forms of imprecation to which I have alluded in a note subjoined to page 276 of this work. They are expressed in a "ḥezb" (or prayer) which the Muslim youths in many of the schools of Cairo recite, before they return to their homes, every day of their attendance, at the period of the "'aṣr," except on Thursday, when they recite it at noon; being allowed to leave the school, on this day, at the early hour of the "ḍuhr," in consideration of the approach of Friday, their sabbath and holiday. This prayer is not recited in the schools that are held within mosques. It is similar to a portion of the "khuṭbet en-naạt."[1] I here translate it:—

"I seek refuge with God from Satan the accursed.[2] In the name of God, the Compassionate, the Merciful. O God, aid El-Islám, and exalt the word of truth, and the faith, by the preservation of thy servant, and the son of thy servant, the Sulṭán of the two continents,[3] and Kháḳán[4] of the two seas,[5] the Sulṭán, son of the Sulṭán, the Sulṭán [Maḥmood[6]] Khán. O God, assist him, and assist his armies, and all the forces of the Muslims: O Lord of the beings of the whole world. O God, destroy the infidels and polytheists, thine enemies, the enemies of the religion. O God, make their children orphans, and defile their abodes, and cause their feet to slip, and give them and their families and their households and their women and their children and their relations by marriage and their brothers and their friends and their possessions and their race and their wealth and their lands as booty to the Muslims: O Lord of the beings of the whole world."

Not to convey too harsh a censure of the Muslims of Egypt, by the insertion of this prayer, I should add that the excessive fanaticism which it indicates is not to be imputed to this people universally, as appears from a note subjoined to page 89.

---

[1] See p. 87 of this work.
[2] Or "driven away with stones."
[3] Europe and Asia.
[4] Emperor, or monarch.
[5] The Mediterranean and Black Seas.
[6] The reigning Sulṭán at the time when the above was written.

APPENDIX E.

DIRECTIONS FOR THE TREATMENT OF DYSENTERY AND OPHTHALMIA.

Every person who visits Egypt should be acquainted with the following modes of treating dysentery and ophthalmia. I have tried them often, and never known them fail of speedy and complete success in the very worst cases; seldom requiring to be continued more than four or five days.

In dysentery, when any unwholesome food has been taken, it is advisable to begin with an emetic; a scruple of ipecacuanha taken in the evening. The next step in this case, or the first in others, is to take, in the morning, a mild aperient; as fifteen grains of rhubarb with two grains of calomel. On the following day, two grains of ipecacuanha with a quarter of a grain of opium should be taken morning and evening; and the same four times in each succeeding day. The patient should eat nothing but boiled rice, sweetened with a little sugar. Butter, and grease of every kind, flesh-meat, eggs, &c., would aggravate the disease.

In an attack of ophthalmia, the bowels should be kept open; and a single drop of a solution of sulphate of copper (or blue vitriol), consisting of seven grains of that salt to an ounce of pure water, should be dropped into the eye (or each diseased eye) once a-day. To prevent the eyelids from adhering together in sleep, a little citron-ointment mixed with three parts of fresh butter should be rubbed on them at bedtime. When the inflammation is slight, a wash composed of two grains of sulphate of copper to an ounce of water may be frequently used.—Sulphate of zinc (or white vitriol) has been employed with great, but not equal, success; in the proportion of ten grains to an ounce of water, to be applied in the former manner; and in the proportion of three grains to the same quantity of water, for an astringent wash.

APPENDIX F.

EDITOR'S NOTES.

I.—CENSUS.

The following is a copy of the official return, issued by the Government, of the Census of Egypt taken in the years 1847–8. Although the number of inhabitants is nearly double that at which the best writers have estimated it, I am informed on authority which ought to be well acquainted with the facts, that the true amount of the population is considerably more than this return shews, that the country is now largely populated, and that the inhabitants of Cairo were estimated last year (1859) at 320,000.

Middle Egypt	591,294
El-Gharbeeyeh	529,930
El-Ḳalyoobeeyeh	184,240
Upper Egypt	1,190,118
Esh-Sharḳeeyeh	342,509
El-Geezeh	223,554
El-Boḥeyreh	215,810
El-Manoofeeyeh	440,519
Ed-Daḳahleeyeh	347,347
Shubrà	10,116
El-Ḳuseyr	3,435
Rosetta	18,405
Damietta	28,922
Suez	17,399
El-'Areesh	2,347
Alexandria	143,134
Cairo	253,541
	4,542,620

II.—ARABIAN ARCHITECTURE.

The excellence attained by the Arabs in architecture and decoration has been remarkable in every country subjected to their rule. The style has borne the same characteristics throughout the great Arabian Empire, flourishing most when that empire was dismembered; and there is no difficulty in identifying Arab art in Egypt as a centre, or in India on the one hand and Spain on the other. In Egypt it reached its highest excellence, and has been fortunate in leaving there numerous monuments to testify to it—monuments fast falling to decay, and of which few traces will in comparatively a short time remain. Its beginnings faintly seen in the edifices constructed by Christian architects for the early Khaleefehs, in the first rush of Muslim conquest, the art is almost lost for two centuries and a half; until in a mosque at Cairo, erected in the year of the Flight 263, it appears in its own strength, free from all imitation (though shewing adaptation) of other styles. The origin of this strongly-marked art forms an old question, and one that has been variously answered; generally by a reference to a supposed Byzantine influence, to a vague idea of the early mosques of

Arabia (respecting which almost nothing is known in Europe, at least in their earliest state), and to the religious influence of Mohammadanism, discountenancing all imitation of nature, while supposed to induce a love of the beautiful. All these, however, are mere theories, hitherto without the support of facts, either recorded by Arab historians, or deducible from the style of existing monuments; and it has long been an object of curiosity to search for any facts either to maintain or disprove them. This inquiry does not appear to be foreign to the scope of a work on the descendants of those admirable architects who have retained, though in a degraded state, their national art.

Native writers have hitherto been supposed to throw little light on this subject, yet their testimony, whenever found, must be held to be historically weighty, after we have made due deduction for ignorance or prejudice. They are not, however, altogether silent on the sources whence their art sprang, nor on the men who executed some of the earliest, or the finest, buildings.[1] El-Maḳreezee, whose book on Egypt is the most complete topographical account in the language, although he is in general provokingly silent on these points, gives some facts and inferences of importance; Ibn-Khaldoon, who stands at the head of Arab historians, and comes nearest to European notions of a philosophical historian, is very explicit on the origin of the art; and the scattered notices in the native monographs on the holy cities of Arabia throw a clear light on the early buildings of Mohammadans, which are of the more importance when we reflect that to these buildings, as exemplars, is commonly ascribed the plan of other better-known edifices in the countries conquered by the Muslims.

The Arabs themselves, Ibn-Khaldoon tells us (I translate his words almost literally), by reason of their desert life, and because their religion forbade prodigality and extravagance in building, were far from being acquainted with the arts; and 'Omar Ibn-El-Khaṭṭáb (the second Khaleefeh) enjoined them (when they asked his permission to build El-Koofeh[2] with stones, fire having occurred in the *reeds with which they used before to build*), and said to them, "Do it, but let not any one exceed three chambers, and make not the building high, but keep to the practice of the Prophet: so shall dominion remain with you." Ibn-Khaldoon further makes his meaning clear by contrasting Arab work with that of the ancient edifices of southern Arabia. He observes of those nations which had endured as nations for very long periods, as the Persians, and the Copts, and the Nabathæans, and the Greeks, and in like manner the first Arabs, those of 'Ád and Thamood, that, in consequence of their long continuance, the arts took firm root among them, and their buildings and temples were more in number and more lasting.[3] The edifices of the primitive Arabs were built, as we now know, by a mixed race, composed of Shemites (Joktanites, and not Arabs properly so called), and of Cushites, these latter being settlers in part from Africa and in part from Assyria: the Cushites were probably the principal architects, if we may judge from Semitic influence in Arabia, among the Jews, in Northern

---

[1] Architects, however, are rarely mentioned; and it seems probable, as my friend Mr. Wild has suggested to me, that the execution of the works was generally intrusted to overseers. These were sometimes military or civil servants of the government; sometimes ḳáḍees, and the like; who employed under them skilled workmen in each required trade. Thus, after an earthquake in the year of the Flight 702, the Emeer Rukn-ed-Deen Beybars El-Gáshnekeer was appointed to repair the great dilapidations occasioned by the earthquake in the mosque of El-Ḥákim; the Emeer Silár, to the like office at the Azhar; and the Emeer Seyf-ed-Deen Bektemer El-Jókendár, to the mosque of Eṣ-Ṣáliḥ; "and they repaired the buildings, and restored what had been ruined of them;" while the Emeer Silár, above named, who was also charged with the repair of the mosque of 'Amr, "entrusted it to his scribe Bedr-ed-Deen Ibn-Khaṭṭáb" (El-Maḳreezee's 'Khiṭaṭ,' Accounts of the Mosques of 'Amr and the Azhar). If the architects and decorators were often Copts, as will be shewn to be highly probable, the reason of the suppression of their names is at once apparent. In the most remarkable building in Cairo, however, the mosque of Ṭooloon, the architect is admitted to have been a Christian Copt.

[2] El-Koofeh is the town on the Euphrates commonly written by us "Kufah", and "Cufa."

[3] I. part ii. pp. 231-2. For these early Arabs, see art ARABIA in Dr. Smith's 'Dictionary of the Bible.'

Africa, and elsewhere.[1] The genuine Phœnician monuments also seem to be like those of the Cushites. The inference here drawn from race is one that is too often overlooked, but is rarely fallacious. In the present instance, the monuments left by this race are of the massive character of those of Cushite peoples.

But if Ibn-Khaldoon's assertion respecting the ignorance of the Arabs be true, it ought to be borne out by facts; and I have found decisive testimony to its accuracy in the accounts of the mosques of Mekkeh and El-Medeeneh, and of that of 'Amr in Egypt.

The Prophet's mosque at El-Medeeneh was originally (as built by himself) very small, measuring 100 cubits in each direction, or, as some say, less. It was built of crude bricks, upon a foundation of stones three cubits high, the bricks being laid in alternate courses, lengthways and across,[2] and was neither plastered nor embellished: it had a partly-roofed court in the middle of it, the roof, which was supported on palm-trunks for pillars, being composed of palm-sticks plastered over. This mosque thus, in the rudest fashion, represents the type of the plan of most existing mosques. But the mosque of 'Amr in Egypt was an exception, and one which is the more curious because it has been entirely ignored by European theorists. Instead of this mosque exhibiting to us in its present state the condition of Arab art at the time of its foundation (that is, immediately on the conquest of Egypt, about the 20th year of the Flight), and proving the existence of the pointed arch in Arab buildings of that date, we find from El-Maḳreezee that it has been enlarged and rebuilt many times, that the pointed arches (to which I shall presently return) are later than the period of its foundation, and that its first plan was not in accordance with that of the Prophet's mosque at El-Medeeneh. The passage that settles this much-controverted point is worth quoting entire: "Aboo-Sa'eed El-Ḥimyeree says, 'I have seen the mosque of 'Amr Ibn-El-'Áṣ: its length was 50 cubits, with a width of 30 cubits. He made the road to surround it on every side; and he made to it two entrances in the northern side, and two entrances in the western side; and he who went out from it by the way of the Street of the Lamps found the eastern angle of the mosque to be over against the western angle of the house of 'Amr Ibn-El-'Áṣ. That was before there was taken from the house what was taken [to enlarge the mosque]. Its length from the Ḳibleh to the northern side was like the length of the house of 'Amr Ibn-El-'Áṣ. And its roof was very low,[3] and there was no inner court to it; so, in summer-time, the people used to sit in its outer court on every side.'" This curiously-detailed account destroys the theory that this ancient mosque was a spacious building erected on the plan of an imaginary mosque at Mekkeh or El-Medeeneh, with an open court in the centre surrounded by colonnades. Undoubtedly, it was one of those small meanly-constructed crude brick buildings that mark the work of Semitic nations.[4]—The Temple of Mekkeh was an ancient Arab sanctuary, and became the most sacred mosque of the Muslims. It is, therefore, important to ascertain, from native writers, what was its form and general style of architecture in historical times. From an Arab history of Mekkeh,[5] I extract the following account of the precincts of the Kaạbeh, observing that the

---

[1] The Jews were not architects. Even the Temple was built for Solomon by the Phœnician workmen of Hiram.

[2] That is to say, in what we call "Flemish bond."

[3] So, too, on the authority of Aboo-'Omar El-Kindee, cited by El-Maḳreezee.

[4] The successive alterations, enlargements, and repairs, to which this building has been subjected, will be found in an abstract of El-Maḳreezee's account of the mosque, appended to this note. It will there be seen that no vestige of any early portion of the mosque—earlier than the second century of the Flight—can be reasonably supposed to exist.—It is an error to suppose that 'Amr converted a church into a mosque. The statement of El-Idreesee to that effect, upon which European writers have relied, is refuted by every Arab author whose work I have consulted.

[5] Kitáb el-Iạlám fee biná el-Mesjid el-Ḥarám, a MS. abridgment of Ḳutb-ed-Deen's History by his nephew. The larger work, and also that by El-Azraḳee, together with extracts from the histories of El-Fákihee, El-Fásee, and Ibn-Ḍhuhey-reh, have been published by the German Oriental Society of Leipzic. I have compared the abstract

Kaạbeh itself, which was anciently a receptacle of heathen idols, &c., is a plain square building, measuring about 18 paces by 14, with a flat roof; that often as it has been rebuilt, the same general plan has always been followed in its reconstruction; and that no one has ever imagined any mosque to have been built in imitation of the Kaạbeh: it is on the open court surrounding the Kaạbeh, as a supposed type of the form of a mosque, that stress has been laid. — "The Kaạbeh had no houses around it until the time of Ḳuṣeí Ibn-Kiláb (about A.D. 445), who ordered his people to build around it, and divided the adjacent parts.[1] Thus the sacred mosque [the Kaạbeh and its precincts] remained until the appearance of El-Islám, when the Muslims became numerous in the time of the Prince of the Faithful 'Omar Ibn-El-Khaṭṭáb, and the sacred mosque became too strait for them. In the year of the Flight 17, a great flood occurred, called the 'flood of Umm-Nahshal,' which entered the boundaries of Mekkeh by the way of the dyke now called El-Med'à;[2] and it entered the sacred mosque and displaced the Maḳám Ibráheem, and carried it away to a spot below Mekkeh: its place became obliterated. And it also carried away Umm-Nahshal, the daughter of 'Obeydeh Ibn-Sa'eed Ibn-El-'Áṣ Ibn-Umeiyeh; and she died therein. Thereupon 'Omar, being written to and informed thereof, while in El-Medeeneh, mounted and returned in alarm to Mekkeh, which he entered, performing the 'Omrah,[3] in the month of Ramaḍán. . . . . El-Azraḳee says, 'The sacred mosque had no walls surrounding it, but only houses of Ḳureysh, which encompassed it on every side, save that between the houses were gates by which the people entered to the sacred mosque. Then in the time of the Prince of the Faithful 'Omar Ibn-El-Khaṭṭáb, the sacred mosque having become strait, he bought houses which were around the sacred mosque, and pulled them down, and made their site part of the mosque. But there remained houses, the owners of which refused to sell them; so 'Omar said to them, 'Ye took up your abode in the precincts of the Kaạbeh, and the Kaạbeh did not take its place in your precincts.' And the houses were valued, and their price was placed in the interior of the Kaạbeh. Then they were demolished, and their site was included in the mosque; and their owners demanded the price and it was given to them. And he ordered to build a low wall, surrounding the mosque, less than the stature of a man in height; and the lamps were placed upon it; and he made in it the gates as they were between the houses before they were demolished, placing them over against the former gates."[4]

On the source from which the Arabs derived their architecture, Ibn-Khaldoon, in continuation of the passage already quoted, says, "When they ceased to observe the strict precepts of their religion, and the disposition for dominion and luxurious living overcame them, the Arabs employed the *Persian* nation to serve them, *and acquired from them the arts and architecture;* and then they made lofty buildings. This was near to the end of the empire." The ascription of Arab art to Persian instruction cannot be too carefully recollected; it explains many difficult points in the style, and deserves further elucidation. The origin of the Arab style may probably be traced to Sassanian as well as to Byzantine sources. Of the early architecture of Persia, our knowledge is insufficient; but some of the characteristics of the style which was perfected by the kings of the Sassanian dynasty existed already in Persia. To the architecture of those kings the Arabs probably owed more than has been commonly

---

above inserted with the larger work, and have examined all the works mentioned. References to them will be found below.

[1] Ḳuṣeí was the first of the tribe of Ḳureysh who rebuilt the Kaạbeh; and he made its roof of the wood of the dóm-tree, and of palm-sticks. (Kitáb el-Iạlám.)

[2] So called because the Kaạbeh was there originally first seen by persons approaching, and prayer there offered up was expected to be answered.

[3] The 'Omrah is a religious visit to the sacred places of Mekkeh, at any period of the year, with the performance of such of the ceremonies of the pilgrimage as are performed at Mekkeh itself.

[4] 'Omar was the first who made walls [of enclosure] to the sacred mosque, as Ḳutb-ed-Deen (page 78) expressly says.

supposed. Ibn-Khaldoon's remark that the architecture arose with the decline of the empire is exactly borne out by facts.

Besides the Persians, the Arabs were indebted to the Copts for assistance in building; and it has been remarked by Mr. Lane, in this work (p. 547), that in the present day there are many architects, builders, and carpenters, among the Copts, all of whom are generally esteemed more skilful than Muslims, as they are also neater in their work. When the Kaạbeh was rebuilt by the tribe of Ḳureysh, in the youth of Moḥammad (and it is a tradition that the Prophet himself assisted as a labourer in the work), we read that "there was in Mekkeh a Copt who knew the art of sawing wood and planing it; and he agreed with them [Ḳureysh] to make for them the roof of the Kaạbeh, and Báḳoom was to help him." So says Ibn-Is-ḥáḳ, in the Kitáb-el-Iạlám, &c., before quoted, in which it is also stated (on the authority of the sheykh Mohammad Eṣ-Ṣáliḥee, in his *Seereh*, or Life of Moḥammad), that the sea cast up a vessel upon the shore of Juddah (now called Jeddah) belonging to a Greek merchant, named Báḳoom, who was a carpenter and builder; Ḳureysh bought the wood of the ship, and took the Greek with them to Mekkeh, and employed him to make of the wood of the ship a roof for the Kaạbeh. (El-Umawee says that the ship was carrying marble and wood and iron to a church which the Persians had burnt in Abyssinia). In the Life of Moḥammad, entitled "Es-Seereh el-Ḥalabeeyeh" (M.S.), Báḳoom is said to have been one of the Greek merchants, a builder; and after inserting many contradictory opinions respecting this Báḳoom and a certain Copt, it is added that the more prevalent opinion is that Báḳoom, the Greek, was a carpenter as well as a builder, and that he rebuilt the Kaạbeh, and assisted a Copt, also by some named Báḳoom, who made the roof. Ḳureysh told Báḳoom, the Greek, to build the Kaạbeh according to the building of churches [meaning in respect of masonry, not in respect of plan]. The disputes of Muslim writers about this builder of the Kaạbeh, while they leave uncertain the immaterial point as to which of two foreigners executed the work, establish the important fact that it was necessary to get foreign help for so simple an edifice as the square, unornamented, Kaạbeh, and that the help was obtained from a Copt or a Greek or both.

So again, El-Maḳreezee is unusually explicit about a pulpit said to have been placed in his mosque by 'Amr, or by 'Abd-El-'Azeez Ibn-Marwán (one of the viceroys of Egypt), which was taken from one of the Christian Churches of El-Fusṭáṭ; or, according to some, he says, it was given to 'Abd-Allah Ibn-Saạd Ibn-Abee-Sarḥ (another viceroy) by a king of Nubia, who sent with it his carpenter to fix it, and the name of this carpenter was Buḳṭur (a Copt), of the people of Dendarah. In Cairo, the mosque of Ibn-Ṭooloon[1] (to which I shall recur) is also recorded to have been built by a Copt,[2] and this edifice is highly curious as an example of a building, erected in A.D. 876, of which the arches are all pointed, and which contains the first forms of the scroll-work and geometrical ornament of the style of the Arabs that was afterwards brought to such high perfection. But the most remarkable record of the employment of Copts by Muslims is in conjunction with Byzantines; and must be next mentioned. "When a state consists of Bedawees, at the first," says Ibn-Khaldoon, "they stand in need of the people of other countries in the affair of building. And thus it happened to El-Weleed, the son of 'Abd-El-Melik," who sent to the king of the Greeks (the emperor of Constantinople) for assistance to build the mosque at Jerusalem, his own mosque at Damascus, and the two holy places in Arabia, and asking for workmen and mosaics (Fuseyfisà).[3] The historian of El-Medeeneh (Es-Sumhoodee) gives the follow-

---

[1] Vulgarly called Gáme' Ṭeyloon, "the mosque of Ṭeyloon."

[2] After the plan of the mosque of Sá-marrà, says El-Maḳreezee; not after the plan of the Temple of Mekkeh, as has been asserted.

[3] Fuseyfisà signifies, according to the lexicographers, the same as Kharaz, (*i. e.* little pieces of coloured stone, glass, &c.), put together, and set upon the inner surfaces of walls, in such a manner as to resemble painting; mostly made,

ing account of this rebuilding of the Prophet's mosque. "When El-Weleed purposed rebuilding the mosque, he wrote to the king of the Greeks, informing him of his intention, and that he was in want of workmen and materials for mosaics. Whereupon he sent to him loads of those materials, and between twenty and thirty workmen; or, as some say, ten workmen; or, as others say, forty Greeks and forty *Copts*.[1] When El-Weleed came to El-Medeeneh on pilgrimage, and saw the mosque, he said, 'How different is our building from yours!' Abán answered, 'We have built after the manner of mosques, and you have built after the manner of churches.'" The contrast between El-Weleed's building in Syria and the mosque built at El-Medeeneh shews that the Copts and Greeks constructed there a building very different from the Byzantine building of El-Weleed at Damascus, and points to the commencement of the adaptation of foreign materials to form a new style. At the same time, we have evidence, in the mention of mosaics,[2] that the Byzantine style of decoration was in some degree followed, and that the workmen at first carried with them their foreign art.

The Muslim conquerors of Egypt entered a country full of churches and convents, which might be converted into mosques, and would certainly afford examples of architecture for their imitation. After the overthrow of the Copts by El-Ma-moon, about the year of the Flight 216, the Muslims converted a number of Christian churches into mosques, making the entrance the niche for the direction of prayer. In the first half of the ninth century of the Flight, I find El-Makreezee enumerates 125 churches and 83 convents (including those in the Oases and the Eastern Desert); mostly in Maṣr el-Ateeḳah and the Upper Country, besides the sites of many that were ruined. It appears, from the historian's account, that anciently the Christian foundations in Egypt were exceedingly numerous and flourishing; but that in his time, owing to the severe persecutions of the Muslims, they had fallen to a very low condition, and many had altogether perished. The present state of these buildings forms a subject for a curious inquiry; and such an inquiry would doubtless yield interesting archæological and historical results. There cannot have been wanting Coptic builders and artificers, nor can the Muslims have avoided the transference of many features of Christian art to their own edifices. The influence of the Copts on the Egyptians is marked in many ways: they use the Coptic (as well as their own) calendar, and are familiar with the months and the seasons of that people; they celebrate several of the festivals of the Copts; and their usual charm against 'efreets in the bath-rooms (places supposed to be always haunted) is the sign of the cross above the doorway. If the Arabs have obtained art from the Byzantines, or Persians, or Tatars, they as surely have from the Copts. Difficult features in their art will be explained and understood on this supposition; and even surer is it that the careful handiwork of the Copts was called into requisition by their conquerors: the Arabs never having excelled in neat or accurate workmanship.

The influence of Byzantium on the art of the Arabs cannot be doubted. It was at first the direct use of Byzantine workmen, and afterwards the gradual adaptation of

---

or used, by the people of Syria; also written Fesfesà. (See also Quatremère, 'Notices et Extraits,' 459 and 632, and his 'Hist. des Sultan's Mamelukes,' ii., part 1, 266, *seq.*) It cannot be doubted to be the well-known glass mosaic of the Byzantines.—Fuseyfisà were used in Arabia shortly before the time of El-Weleed, above referred to. Abrahah, a usurping king of El-Yemen, obtained them from Constantinople for a magnificent church which he built in his capital, San'à, (A.D. 537-570). This, and the mention of the ship carrying marble, &c., in the account of the rebuilding of the Kaạbah by Ḳuṣeí, afford evidences of the source from which the old Arabs obtained their architecture, while they shew how slow was the formation of any national style before the conquests of the Muslims.

[1] These numbers are variously given in different works. It is a characteristic of the Semitic mind to corrupt numbers and dates.

[2] This use of Byzantine mosaic is mentioned twice by Ibn-Khaldoon, and several times by Es-Sumhoodee, who also says that about the same time the mosque of Ḳubà was rebuilt, and in like manner decorated, by the governor of El-Medeeneh under El-Weleed.

portions of their architecture to a new style. But whence the Greeks of the Eastern Empire obtained many of the features of their art, and especially some of those adapted by the Arabs, remains at present an unsolved question. It is probable that the influence of Persia had affected them before it reached the Arabs, and that the characteristics referred to were Persian in origin;[1] just as the same influence more strongly affected the Arabs afterwards. The only persons who, at this day, in Cairo, can execute the scroll-work of the old Arabesque decoration, are the Greek tailors. Their work in embroidery preserves the style of the art, though more elaborated and græcized.

The practice of eastern monarchs has always been to carry with them craftsmen from one conquered country to another; besides the number of proselytes to El-Islám, of these classes, in the ranks of their armies. A notable instance occurred on the conquest of Egypt by the Turks, and one which explains the rapid decay of the arts in that country since that period. The Sulṭán Seleem II. took away with him to Constantinople (according to El-Gabartee, in his Modern History of Egypt,) so many masters of crafts from Cairo that more than fifty manual arts ceased to be practised (see above, page 308).

It has been observed that the form of the mosque was of gradual development; climate, and not religion, or a supposed imitation of the holy places of Arabia, appears to have been the cause of the open interior court surrounded by porticoes. These porticoes date early; the simplest form was that which covered the place of prayer, and necessity rather than choice caused its adoption. Thus the Prophet's mosque consisted, at first, of a court walled in, with a covered portion next the niche, the roof being supported on palm-trunks. 'Osmán is said to have built porticoes to the Temple of Mekkeh, in the year of the Flight 26; and this is the earliest recorded instance of this feature of a mosque. They were perhaps in imitation of the covered portion of the Prophet's mosque, or suggested by the same reason,—a shelter from the sun,—in each case, while, at Mekkeh, they naturally followed the form of the enclosure of the mosque. But El-Azraḳee says that Ibn-Ez-Zubeyr found the Temple with only a wall surrounding it, which would bring the date of the porticoes down at least to A.H. 64. They were built to afford shade to the people, according to that author. The entire passage from Ḳutb-ed-Deen (I quote from the Kitáb el-Iạlám) is, however, as follows:—"In the year 26, Osmán came from El-Medeeneh . . . . and gave orders to enlarge the sacred mosque. He also bought houses around the mosque and pulled them down, and he included their site in that of the mosque. . . . . . And he built the mosque and the porticoes, and he was the first who made the porticoes. 'Abd-Allah Ibn-Ez-Zubeyr,' says El-Azraḳee, 'also added to the mosque, buying houses which he included in its site. Then 'Abd-El-Melik Ibn-Marwán, though he did not enlarge it, yet raised its walls, and roofed it with ság,[2] and repaired it beautifully. . . . . . He gave orders to put upon the capital of every column fifty mitkáls of gold. . . . . He [El-Azraḳee] says, also, that El-Weleed Ibn-'Abd-El-Melik repaired the sacred mosque, and undid the work of 'Abd-El-Melik, and rebuilt it firmly. He used, when he made mosques, to decorate them. He was the first who transported the marble pillars; and he roofed it with decorated ság, and made upon the capitals of the columns plates of gold, and surrounded the mosque with marble, and made to the mosque canopies [or awnings]." Though the mosque of 'Amr was at first a covered building, we cannot doubt that, when a court-yard was added to it, porticoes formed a portion of the plan: this mosque now contains a forest of columns.

---

[1] The condition of art in Persia in the times before this influence is a subject for further inquiry; but it does not materially affect the point at issue, which is only to ascertain what use the Arabs made of foreign materials, whether brought directly from Persia or from Byzantium.

[2] Ság is believed to be the Indian, or Oriental, plane-tree; or the Indian plantain-tree; or the teak-tree.

None of the early mosques possessed minarets; they were added from time to time after their foundation, though not at a long interval. The Prophet's muëddin used to chant the call to prayer from the entrance of the mosque, and this was the practice of the first Muslims; but I find, in the Khiṭaṭ, that the Khaleefeh El-Moaṭaṣim commanded that the muëddins of the mosque of 'Amr should be made to chant the call outside the maḳṣoorah; and that, before that, they used to chant the call *within* it. The minarets of El-Medeeneh, and that of the mosque of Ḳubà, (founded by Moḥammad on his Flight, and before he entered El-Medeeneh,) were built by 'Omar Ibn-'Abd-El-'Azeez, who was appointed governor of Mekkeh, El-Medeeneh, and Eṭ-Ṭäïf, in the year 87; and the first to the mosque of 'Amr, in the year 53; but Mo'áwiyeh (about A.H. 53) added four towers for the adán at the four corners of the mosque; "he was the first who made them in it; there was none before that" (El-Maḳreezee). It is impossible to ascertain the forms of these minarets, which we can only know certainly to have been elevations from which the call to prayer might be heard from afar; but they are the earliest I have found mentioned in the works of the Arabs. Some curious examples of minarets in Egypt are mentioned below.

The pulpit did not exist, except as an insignificant elevation, in the Prophet's mosque, and 'Omar ordered the demolition of one which 'Amr had set up in his mosque in Egypt. Each successor of Moḥammad descended one step of the pulpit of El-Medeeneh, in token of his humility, until 'Alee, the fourth Khaleefeh, said, "Shall we descend into the bowels of the earth?" and boldly stood on the platform, or that which was Moḥammad's station. The preachers, or khaṭeebs, in the mosques (not being Khaleefehs) stand on the top step, next below the platform. In the year 161, El-Mahdee ordered that the height of pulpits should be reduced to that of the Prophet's; but this was four steps only, and they have since been much raised.[1]

The maḳṣoorah, or partition that divides the place of prayer from the rest of the mosque (not to be confounded with the maḳṣoorah surrounding the tomb in a sepulchral mosque), is perhaps a modern addition; but a maḳṣoorah for the Imám existed in the time of 'Osmán, if indeed it was not then first adopted; for El-Maḳreezee, citing the History of El-Medeeneh, tells us that "the first who made a maḳṣoorah of crude bricks was 'Osmán, in which were apertures for the people to see the Imám; and 'Omar Ibn-'Abd-El-'Azeez made it of ság. The crude brick partition we may suppose to have been the earliest example, and 'Osmán probably constructed it for his personal safety, in dread of the death by assassination which he actually met. The maḳṣoorah for the Khaleefeh, or for a king in a royal mosque, was thenceforward adopted.

The earliest use of the pointed arch throughout any building belongs, in the present state of our knowledge, to the Arabs in Egypt; and in that country, pre-eminently, it has marked their best architecture.[2] That a mosque should have been built in the year of the Flight 263, or 876 of our era, in which all the arches are pointed, appears to be decisive evidence of their having first adopted it in any important manner. This mosque, the earliest authentic Arab building in Egypt, has been preserved unaltered to the present day, and is therefore, unlike the often-rebuilt mosque of 'Amr, a safe example. The *origin* of the pointed arch, like that of the arch itself, is merely a curious point of archæological research; and isolated instances of it in older buildings do not affect the fact that the mosque of Ibn-Ṭooloon is the earliest known instance of pointed architecture as a general characteristic of any building. But it is noteworthy that this building was constructed by a Copt Christian.

There is, however, another building in the environs of Cairo, older than the

[1] So, indeed, says El-Maḳreezee.

[2] I have purposely not referred above to the mosque El-Aḳṣà in the Haram enclosure at Jerusalem. It is said to contain pointed arches; but we know too little of this building to allow of much stress being laid on it. *See* Fergusson's 'Handbook of Architecture,' 2nd ed. p. 379 *seqq.*

mosque of Ibn-Ṭooloon, which may present an earlier example of consistent pointed arches. The following particulars respecting the Nilometer of the island of Er-Róḍah, the building referred to, I obtain from Mr. Lane's MS. notes. I give them almost in his own words, with his deductions from them, which are particularly valuable.—Usámeh Ibn-Zeyd El-Tanookhee, in the khiláfeh of El-Weleed, built the first Nilometer (miḳyás) of Er-Róḍah. This was washed down by the river, or, as some say, was pulled down by order of the Khaleefeh El-Ma-moon, about the beginning of the third century of the Flight; but that which replaced it was not finished by him; under the Khaleefeh El-Mutawekkil it was completed, in the beginning of 247 (A.D. 861). "This is the building now existing" (says El-Is-ḥáḳee, in his history, which he brought down to A.H. 1032). In the year 259, Ibn-Ṭooloon went to inspect it and gave orders for repairing it; which was done; 1000 deenárs were expended on it: the Khaleefeh El-Mustanṣir is also said to have caused some trifling repairs to be done to it. But it has undergone very slight alterations since the time of El-Mutawekkil: upon this point, the historians El-Maḳreezee, Es-Suyooṭee, and El-Is-ḥáḳee, agree. The interior of the building is about 18 feet square, and contains on each of its sides a recess, about six feet wide and three deep, surmounted by a *pointed* arch. Over each of these arches is an inscription of one short line, in old Koofee characters; and a similar inscription, a little above these, surrounds the apartment or well. They are passages from the Ḳur-án, and contain no date. It is, however, almost certain that they are not of a later period than that of the completion of the building by El-Mutawekkil, and though it has been *repaired* since that time, it has not been since *rebuilt*. Ibn-Ṭooloon repaired it twelve years afterwards, and in confirmation of the age of the inscriptions, it may be stated that they are of the same kind of character as those of the mosque of Ibn-Ṭooloon; while in the following century, a different kind of writing was introduced. It appears, therefore, that the pointed arches of the Nilometer are about 16 years older than those of the mosque of Ibn-Ṭooloon, that is, 861 of our era, though their date cannot be so clearly *proved*. They were, probably, constructed by the same architect.[1]

The pointed arches in the right side-wall of the mosque of 'Amr (above which are smaller arches, alternately round and pentroof), are at least half a century later than the foundation of the mosque, and even this date is very uncertain from the numerous alterations which the building has since undergone. All *isolated* instances of Arab pointed arches, earlier than the time of Ibn-Ṭooloon, or (which is nearly the same date) that of the Nilometer of Er-Róḍah,[2] are of very little value; and still earlier examples are to be found in Christian buildings in Egypt, before the Arab conquest, as well as in ancient buildings in Egypt and elsewhere. The researches of Sir Gardner Wilkinson[3] indicate the gradual adoption of this form of arch to have commenced in early Christian times, and Mr. Fergusson[4] mentions its occurrence in the Dome of the Rock at Jerusalem. But the persecutions endured by the Christians during the first two centuries and a half of the Flight, and the absence of any remains of important Arab buildings during the same time, have occasioned a break in the history of both Christian and Mohammadan art, which has brought down our knowledge of the general adoption of the pointed arch, and of the first truly Arabian archi-

---

1 Remains of an ancient Nilometer existed, in the time of El-Maḳreezee, in the Deyr el-Benát, in the Ḳaṣr esh-Shemạ; "which was the Nilometer before El-Islám." One also existed at Ḥulwán, a little above Memphis, on the opposite shore of the Nile.

2 There are, I believe, some curious arches in two old mosques above Philæ, on the eastern bank of the Nile: they are ascribed to the Prophet's muëddin, who certainly never was there; for after the Prophet's death he went to Syria, and there he remained until he died, at Damascus.

3 'On Colour and Taste,' pp. 290-296. 'Architecture of Ancient Egypt,' pp. 17, 71.

4 'Handbook of Architecture,' pp. 294, 379, 598, 815.

tecture, to 861 or 876 A.D. (247 or 263 A.H.). It is most probable, however, that in that period of conquest, persecution, and proselytism, the arts made slow progress.

The adoption in Europe of pointed architecture is a question entirely beyond the limits of this note. In the East, as I have said, its general adoption must date from the foundation of the mosque of Ibn-Ṭooloon, or from that of the Nilometer. In Egypt, it has since been always one of the strongest characteristics of the style, where that style most flourished; and in other Mohammadan countries, it accompanies other evidences of the purest taste. Generally (though not always) it is, in Egypt, slightly of the horse-shoe form, but in many examples the trace of the return at the base of the archivolt is very slight: the round horse-shoe arch is rare.

The mosque of Ibn-Ṭooloon, besides marking the adoption of the pointed arch, is remarkable as presenting the art of the Arabs in an independent form. Here the geometrical and scroll-ornament is first found, and found, too, with characteristics far separated from any other known ornament. The scroll-work may possibly be traced to Byzantine work, but in this building it has assumed an entirely distinct character. It is the ornament which thenceforth was gradually perfected; and its stages may be traced, in the mosques and other edifices of Cairo, through every form of its development. But in this, its first example, it is elementary and rude, and therefore all the more remarkable. Its continuity is not strongly marked; its forms are almost devoid of grace. In later and more fully developed examples, each portion may be continuously traced to its root—constituting one of the most beautiful features of the art—and its forms are symmetrically perfect.[1] The geometrical work, on the other hand, without being as intricate, is as fine in this mosque as in any later. It may be assumed, as Mr. Lane has remarked to me, that it owes its origin to the elaborate panelled wood-work so common in Egypt and Syria, and this again (as he has said in this work, page 14,) to the necessities of a hot climate, in which small panels of wood are required to withstand the warping and shrinkage inevitable to the material. All the ornament in this mosque is in stucco, and is cut by hand; not cast from moulds, like that of the Alhambra. The artistic difference is plainly seen in the hand-work, in which there is none of the hard formality of castings. The building itself is of burnt brick,[2] and so solidly constructed that it has now for nearly a thousand years withstood the ravages of time; and, though suffered to fall into gradual decay, is still entire, and even in its decorative portions almost perfect. Its form is that of a square court, surrounded by arcades of pointed arches with a very slight return. Over the niche is a small cupola, probably, though not certainly, of the same date as the building. I am aware of only one other instance of this feature, in Egypt: it is that in the sepulchral mosque of Barḳooḳ, founded A.H. 814. It is almost needless to search for the oldest instance of the dome in Arab architecture: it was undoubtedly borrowed from the Christians: but it may be worth noting that El-Maḳreezee relates that a church existed in his time at Moosheh, near Asyooṭ, the capital of Upper Egypt, with three domes, the height of each of which was about eighty cubits (?), all of them being built of white stone, and said to date from the time of Constantine the Great.

In their domes, the Arabs adopted, and improved on, the constructional expedient for vaulting over the space beneath, and passing from a square apartment to the circle of the dome, used by both Byzantines and Persians. For want of a better name, this bracketing-work has been called "pendentive." The Church of St. Sophia, at Constantinople, presents fine examples of its Byzantine form; but in later edifices of

[1] Careful drawings of this ornament have been published in the "Grammar of Ornament," from the collection of Mr. James Wild. See especially the series from the mosque of Ibn-Ṭooloon, plate xxxi.

[2] El-Maḳreezee says that the architect adopted the square brick pillars which support the arches surrounding the court, as being more durable than stone columns.

that style, constructional difficulties seem to have confined the architects to small domes. The buildings of the Sassanian dynasty also contain pendentives.[1] But the origin of this architectural feature is evidently far simpler than any to be sought for in the exigencies of domical construction, or the developed and elaborate examples hitherto adduced. It must be traced to the transition from a square to a circle by the rude process shewn in the annexed woodcut, which represents part of the interior of a tumulus discovered at Kertch, and described in the "Transactions of the Royal Society of Literature," (vol. vi. p. 100, plate V.) which, if of late date, is of very early style, like the tomb of Alyattes, and the so-called treasury of Atreus. The Arabs, with

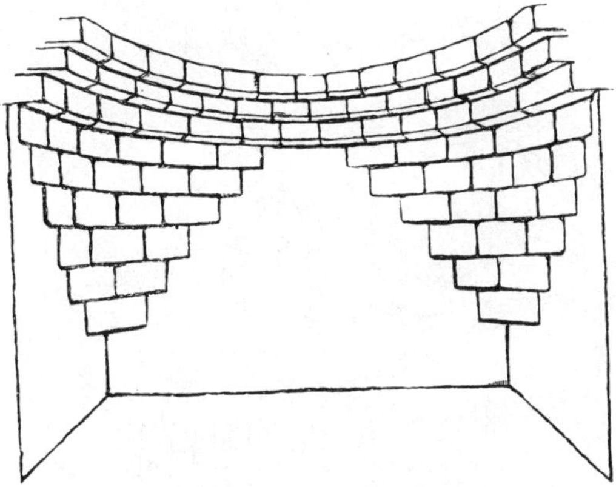

their peculiar faculty for cutting away all superfluous material, naturally arched the over-lapping stones that filled up the angles of the building; and, by using *pointed* arches, overcame the difficulty of the Byzantine architects, to which I have alluded. The pendentive was speedily adopted by the Arabs in Egypt in a great variety of shapes, and for almost every conceivable architectural and ornamental purpose: to effect the transition from the recessed windows to the outer plane of a building; and to vault, in a similar manner, the great porches of mosques, which form so grand a characteristic of the style. The simple circle placed on a square to support a dome, was elaborated by an intermediate octagon, and the angles of the square were then filled in as in the woodcut inserted in the next page, taken from a sketch that I made in the great southern cemetery of Cairo, which shews well the facility with which a simple form was beautifully elaborated. All the more simple wood-work of dwelling-houses is fashioned in a variety of curious patterns of the same character. The pendentive, in fact, strongly marks the Arab fashion of cutting off angles and useless material, always in a pleasing and constructively advantageous manner.

---

[1] In India, early bracketing, very similar to the pendentives already mentioned, is found in buildings at old Delhi; and a later fine example, in a mosque at Beejapoor. The Indian development seems to be an offshoot only, and not to be connected in any way with the origin of pendentives. The plaster-work of the Alhambra was derived from the wooden, as well as the stone and plaster, examples of Egypt. It is hardly necessary to refute a theory, which has nevertheless found an advocate, that pendentives were originally a merely ornamental feature derived from the Gothic dog-tooth ornament; resting, as this theory does, on a comparison of pendentives of *very late date*, and of Constantinople workmanship.

I have said that the mosque of Ibn-Ṭooloon is the most ancient Muslim edifice of known date in Egypt, and that the two centuries and a half that had elapsed since the conquest of that country by the Arabs left no sure stepping-stones by which to trace the gradual advance of the art which in that mosque suddenly appears

as an independent style. Another gap followed, of which no architectural examples remain. The next period of Egyptian art is that of the Fáṭimee Khaleefehs. During the century that had elapsed, much progress had been made. The great mosque El-Azhar, founded by the first ruler of that line, contains few portions of the original structure; numerous repairs and rebuildings have effaced the first plan, and the ancient niche now stands isolated among the columns of the place of prayer.[1] But the mosque of El-Ḥákim, though in a ruined state, preserves enough to shew this progress, and to shew too that the typical forms found in the work of Ibn-Ṭooloon had been preserved and developed. The style had gained strength in boldness and symmetry. The Fáṭimee dynasty left other remarkable mosques in Cairo, besides sepulchral buildings in the southern cemetery of that city; bearing the same characteristics, and generally, I believe, of brick, plastered. The three fine gates of El-Ḳáhireh, built during the rule

[1] The Azhar was the first mosque founded in El-Ḳáhireh; it was commenced in Jumáda-l-Oolà 359, and completed in Ramaḍán 361. Its roof, like that of the mosque of 'Amr, was originally low, and was afterwards raised a cubit. The mosque was repaired by four of the Fáṭimee Khaleefehs, and by Beybars: again in 702, after the earthquake; in 725; and in 761. The great minaret was built by El-Ghooree early in the tenth century of the Flight. The whole mosque was repaired and considerably altered by a Turkish governor, in 1004. The Azhar has been, since its foundation, the principal congregational mosque of Cairo, with the exception of two periods—the first, from the date of the mosque of El-Ḥákim, who transferred the chief prayers to his own mosque, where the Khaleefeh preached; the second from the accession of Ṣaláḥ-ed-Deen to that of Beybars, when the sermon was discontinued in the Azhar, because, according to some, it is prohibited to preach two Friday sermons in one town.

of this dynasty, are noteworthy as the work of three Greek brothers. They contain features quite foreign to the art, while displaying some of its best characteristics; and deserve to be remembered as examples of what the Arabs have obtained from strangers.

The buildings of the succeeding dynasty, which was founded by the renowned Ṣaláḥ-ed-Deen, are not numerous; nor remarkable, with some good exceptions, except for massive strength. It was under the first dynasty of Memlook (Turkish) Sulṭáns that the art attained to perfection; and it very gradually declined under the second (or Circassian) dynasty. In considering these periods of history, it is necessary to remember that the kings, who were originally slaves, probably brought with them no art-knowledge from their native countries. But the Turkish slaves came of a tomb-building race, and, as there is evidence to shew, this national trait took root in Egypt.[1] El-Maḳreezee affords a weightier reason for the introduction of many new features into Arab art about this time. Genghis Khán was desolating Western Asia, and driving whole populations before him. "At the time of Genghis Khán," says El-Maḳreezee, "many Easterns came to Egypt [A.H. 656]; and after this, in the time of the third reign of Moḥammad Ibn-Ḳala-oon, the suburbs south of El-Ḳáhireh were chiefly built, and increased greatly [A.H. 711]." Ibn-Ḳala-oon was one of the great builders of those days; some of the edifices he founded are among the best examples of Arabian art; but his mosque within the upper circuit of the Citadel is as curiously strange to that art. The minarets are strikingly Tatar, in form like the minárs of northern India, and covered with glazed tiles.[2] They are unique in Cairo. The dome-shaped termination of those minarets, however, which has been compared to a darweesh's conical cap, is found in a few other instances. It is found in the mosque of El-Ḥákim, which was partially ruined by an earthquake in the year 702; the tops of the minarets were then thrown down, and were rebuilt by Beybars El-Gáshnekeer, an Emeer who usurped the throne of Ibn-Ḳala-oon. The collegiate mosque of this Emeer presents the like peculiarity, as do some others of this, or a rather later, period. The historical evidence sets at rest the European notion that this is the more ancient form of the minaret. In Egypt, at least, it cannot be proved to be earlier than the commoner form.

In modern times, the buildings of Cairo are painted in alternate horizontal stripes of lime-wash and red ochre. This was an ancient practice, and one which, there can be no doubt, was borrowed from the Roman construction of alternate courses of stone and brick. An example of this the Arabs had at Egyptian Babylon, before which 'Amr pitched his tent and founded his city and mosque. That old Roman fortress, now called Ḳaṣr-esh-Shemạ, would have given the invaders a ready example to follow. That the colour was a constructive feature may be learned from a study of the mosques of Cairo; especially those in the cemeteries, where the effect is produced by the use of stone of different colours, without the help of red ochre. The use of colour by the Arabs in Egypt was, in their best time, very simple and sparing: red, black, and gold on ultramarine, formed the principal, almost the only, architectural coloured decoration; with the addition of white, and sometimes yellow, in the mosaic pavements and dados. Green marks the decay of the style; and the profuse colouring of the Alhambra is altogether foreign to the true art.

The connection of Arab and Gothic architecture is a subject that would yield most interesting results. The modern fashion of assuming everything Mohammadan

---

[1] In contravention of Moḥammad's directions that "tombs should be low, and built only of crude bricks." (See above, page 523, foot-note.)

[2] I also find it mentioned by El-Maḳreezee that the two minarets of the mosque of Ḳooṣoon, in Cairo, were built by a builder from Tooreez [Tebreez?], like the minaret which Khowájà 'Alee Sháh, the Wezeer of the Sulṭán Aboo-Sa'eed, had made in his mosque in the city of Tooreez.

to be of true Arabian art has misled art-critics; and the undue importance that has been given to the degraded style of the Alhambra (which is to mosques of the best Cairo time as late Perpendicular is to early English and Decorated Gothic), and to the bastard edifices of Mohammadan India,—because something is known about these and next to nothing of the true art—has induced the most erroneous conclusions. The more the buildings of Cairo are studied, the more clearly, I think, will the connection of the architects of that country with those of southern Europe be established. In the streets of that quaint old city, one is constantly in presence of strong Gothic affinities, let alone pointed arches of Gothic proportions, triple lights, &c. The topographical work of El-Maḳreezee is of the utmost value in helping to a correct judgment of dates, and sometimes mentions the very architects. Like all things Eastern, the art is not rapidly changeable, and it is far more difficult there than in Europe to fix approximately the date of an edifice. There is one gateway—it is that of a mosque in the main thoroughfare of the city—that has often puzzled theorists, and has only been accounted for by the supposition that a Gothic architect constructed it in Cairo. Its history, as given by El-Maḳreezee, is highly curious; testifying to the accuracy of the historian, shewing the manner in which these buildings were erected, and presenting an example of direct adoption of Gothic work. The gateway in question is of clustered columns, and is probably of transition Norman, or one of its kindred styles. The historian's account is as follows:—"The Medreseh en-Náṣireeyeh is adjacent to the Ḳubbeh el-Manṣooreeyeh, on the eastern [meaning, north-eastern,] side. It was begun by El-Melik el-'Ádil Zeyn-ed-Deen Ketbughà, and it rose to about the height of the gilded border on its exterior: then he was deposed. And El-Melik en-Náṣir Moḥammad Ibn-Ḳala-oon gave orders to complete it in the year 698, and it was completed in the year 703. It is one of the grandest of the buildings of El-Ḳáhireh, and its gateway is one of the most admirable of what the hands of man have made; for it is of white marble, novel in style, surpassing in workmanship; and it was transported to El-Ḳáhireh from the city of 'Akkà [St. Jean d'Acre]. For El-Melik el-Ashraf Khaleel Ibn-Ḳala-oon, when he took 'Akkà by storm, in the year 609, ordered the Emeer 'Alam-ed-Deen Senger Esh-Shugá'ee to demolish its walls and destroy its churches. And he found this gateway at the entrance of one of the churches of 'Akkà; it being of marble, its bases, and jambs, and columns all conjoined one with another [*i.e.* clustered]: so he conveyed the whole to El-Ḳáhireh."

The result of this inquiry into the origin and rise of Arabian art is very simple. It sets at rest the question of the Arabs having possessed any but the rudest native art. An essentially unartistic Semitic nation, they overran countries abounding in the remains of decaying styles, and used the craftsmen of those countries to build their mosques and palaces; at first adopting the old art, and afterwards engrafting many of its features into a new style of their own. The earliest Arab buildings were predominantly Byzantine, and that style always continued to exercise a strong influence; but soon one more markedly Oriental was added to it, and to the half-formed Arabian art then springing up. This was the Persian or Sassanian; and to it must, I think, be traced much of the elegance of the Arabian, and a great proportion of its ornament. A later Tatar element, in Egypt, I believe I have also shewn to have been added. It must be distinctly borne in mind that the Arab style has a distinct individuality; and, taking the Egyptian as the typical (as it was certainly the highest) form, it is one that must rank among the purest of all times and countries. To what extent the Arabs themselves worked in its development is at present doubtful, and will probably always remain so. They have never excelled in handicrafts. Their workmen were commonly Copts, Greeks, and Persians; and though they must have learnt from these peoples, they appear never to have been able to dispense altogether with their services. The *taste* that directed their admirable works—whence it arose and how it was fostered—forms a more subtle question: unless their architects as well as their workmen were foreigners,[1] we must ascribe it to the Arabs themselves; and it would then form a remarkable example of a nation, naturally tasteless, acquiring a perception of beauty of form, symmetry of proportion, and generally of the highest qualities of architectural and decorative excellence, which has never been surpassed.

III.—HISTORY OF THE MOSQUE OF 'AMR.[2]

(*Abstracted from El-Maḳreezee's Historical and Topographical Account of Egypt.*)

THE mosque was built, after the occupation of Alexandria, in the year of the Flight, 21.[3]—Aboo-Sa'eed El-Ḥimyeree says, I have seen the mosque of 'Amr Ibn-El-'Áṣ; its length was 50 cubits, with a width of 30 cubits.[4] And he made the road to surround it on every side. And he made to it two entrances, facing the house of 'Amr Ibn-El-'Áṣ. He also made to it two entrances in the northern side, and two entrances in the western side; and he who went out from it by the way of the Street of the Lamps found the eastern angle of the mosque to be over against the western angle of the house of 'Amr Ibn-El-'Áṣ. That was before there was taken from the house what was taken [to enlarge the mosque]. Its length from the ḳibleh to the northern side was like the length of the house of 'Amr Ibn-El-'Áṣ. And its roof was very low, and there was no inner court to it; so, in summer time, the people used to sit in its outer court on every side.

The first who added to it was Meslemeh Ibn-Mukhallad El-Anṣáree, in the year 53. He added to it on its eastern side, of that which adjoins the house of 'Amr, and on its northern side; but he made no new addition to it on the southern,[5] nor on the western, side. He made a "raḥabeh" [an exterior court] on the north of it, and the people resorted thither in the summer; he also plastered it, and ornamented its lower walls, and its roof; for the mosque of 'Amr [*i. e.*, that built by 'Amr] was neither plastered nor embellished. He ordered the building of the minaret of the mosque [of 'Amr?] which is in El-Fusṭáṭ.—It is said that Mo'áwiyeh ordered the building of the towers for the adán; and Meslemeh made for the congregational mosque four towers at its four corners; he was the first who made them in it: there was none before that.

In the year 79, 'Abd-El-'Azeez Ibn-Marwán pulled it [the mosque] down, and added to it on the western side, and enclosed in it the court that was on the northern side; but on the eastern side, he could not find space to enlarge it: so says El-Ḳuḍá'ee; but

---

[1] Some of the architects I have shewn to have been foreigners: the most remarkable one, the builder of the mosque of Ibn-Ṭooloon, was a Copt; and three brothers, Greeks, constructed the three grand gates of El-Ḳáhireh.

[2] This abstract of El-Maḳreezee's historical description of the mosque of 'Amr, although written in a somewhat detailed and confused manner, is of importance in an archæological and artistic point of view, and will, I think, be acceptable to students of the subject, while dissipating theories too hastily formed respecting this the oldest Muslim *foundation* in Egypt and perhaps in the East.

[3] "Ibn-Lahee'ah says, 'I have heard our sheykhs say that there was not to the mosque of 'Amr a recessed niche: and I know not whether Meslemeh built it, or 'Abd-El-'Azeez.' The first who made the niche was Ḳurrah Ibn-Shureyḳ. El-Wáḳidee says, 'Moḥammad Ibn-Hilál told me that the first who constructed a recessed niche was 'Omar Ibn-'Abd-El-'Azeez when he built the mosque of the Prophet.'" [I have inserted this note from El-Maḳreezee, because there is a recessed niche in the mosque of 'Amr commonly ascribed to him.]

[4] So also according to El-Leyth Ibn-Saạd, cited by Es-Suyooṭee, in his work on Egypt entitled the Ḥosn el-Muḥáḍarah, M.S.

[5] The southern side, or that of the ḳibleh, is the side which we should call the eastern; the reader must therefore bear in mind, throughout this abstract, that the points of the compass are named after the Arab manner.

El-Kindee says that he enlarged it on all its four sides.—'Abd-Allah Ibn-'Abd-El-Melik ordered the raising of the roof, which was low, in the year 89.

In the beginning of the year 92, by order of El-Weleed, El-Ḳurrah Ibn-Shureyḳ, the governor of Egypt, pulled it down, and began to build it in Shaabán of that year, completing it in Ramaḍán, 93. The enlargement of Ḳurrah was on the southern and eastern sides, and he took part of the house of 'Amr and of his son, and enclosed it in the mosque, with the road which was between them and the mosque.—Ḳurrah made the recessed niche which is called the mihráb of 'Amr, because it is in the direction of the niche of the old mosque which 'Amr built.[1] The ḳibleh of the old mosque was at the gilt pillars in the row of táboots [wooden chests] at this day: these are four pillars, two facing two, and Ḳurrah gilt their capitals: there were no gilt pillars in the mosque except them. In the days of Ḳurrah the mosque had not a niche save this niche. But as to the central niche, existing at this day, it is called the niche of 'Omar Ibn-Marwán, and perhaps he made it in the walls after Ḳurrah. Some have said that Ḳurrah made these two niches.—And the mosque had four entrances made to it; they are the four entrances now existing on its eastern side: and on its western side, four entrances; and on its northern side, three entrances.

In the year 133, Ṣáliḥ Ibn-'Alee added four columns at the back part, and it is said that he enclosed in the mosque the house of Zubeyr Ibn-El-'Owwám; the fifth entrance of the eastern entrances of the mosque at this day is of this addition: he built also the fore part of the mosque by the first entrance.—In the year 175, Moosà Ibn-'Eesà added to it the court at its back part, which is half the court known as that of Aboo-Eiyoob.

In the year 211, by order of 'Abd-Allah Ibn-Ṭáhir, an addition equal to it [the mosque] was made on its western side: this addition was the great niche and what is on the western side of it as far as the addition of El-Kházin, &c.[2] 'Eesà Ibn-Yezeed completed the addition of Ibn-Ṭáhir. The measure of the mosque, without the two additions, amounted, completely, to 190 (architect's) cubits in length, and 150 cubits in width.[3] The court of El-Ḥárith is the northern court of the addition of El-Kházin: it was built, in the year 237, by El-Ḥárith, and he ordered the building of the court contiguous to the Mint. The addition of Aboo-Eiyoob was in the remainder of the court called the court of Aboo-Eiyoob. The niche ascribed to Aboo-Eiyoob is the western one of this addition: it was built in the year 258.

A fire occurred in the back part of the mosque, and it was repaired; this addition being made in the days of Aḥmad Ibn-Ṭooloon; and in the night of Friday, the 20th of Safar, 275, a fire occurred in the mosque and destroyed from beyond three arches from Báb Isráeel to the court of El-Ḥárith: in it was destroyed the greater part of the addition of Ibn-Ṭáhir, and a portico. It was repaired by order of Khumáraweyh in the above-named year: 6,400 deenárs were expended on it.

El-Kházin added one portico, from the Mint, which is the portico with a niche and two windows adjoining the court of El-Ḥárith: its size is 9 cubits. It was commenced in Regeb, 357, and finished at the close of Ramaḍán, 358.—In 387, the mosque was re-whitewashed, and much of the fesfesà[4] that was in the porticoes was

[1] The ḳibleh of 'Amr Ibn-El-'Áṣ was the same in direction as that adopted, in Egypt, by the companions of Moḥammad. El-Maḳreezee (Account of the Mihrábs of Egypt) tells us that this is not true to the direction of Mekkeh. It is found in the mosques of El-Geezeh, Alexandria, Ḳooṣ, &c. A second ḳibleh is that of the mosque of Ṭooloon. A third is that of the Azhar, which El-Maḳreezee states is in the true direction. This is followed by the other mosques of El-Ḳáhireh (or Cairo). There are other variations of the ḳibleh which it is needless to specify.

[2] "The place of the tent of 'Amr is said by some to be where are the pulpit and the niche."

[3] "It is said that the measure of the mosque of Ibn-Ṭooloon is the same as that, except the porticoes that surround it on its three sides."

[4] Or Fuseyfisà: see above, page 581, foot-note.

removed, and its place whitewashed: five tablets were engraved and gilt and set up over the five eastern entrances; and they are what are over them now.

El-Ḥákim ordered the construction of the two porticoes which are (says El-Ḳuḍá'ee) in the court of the mosque. El-Mustanṣir bi-lláh also ordered an addition to be made to the maḳṣoorah on its eastern and western sides.[1] In the year 445 the minaret which is in the space between the minaret of 'Orfah and the great minaret was built.

In the year 564, the Franks under Amaury besieged El-Ḳáhireh, and the city of Miṣr was burnt and remained burning for 54 days; and the mosque became dilapidated. In 568, Ṣaláḥ-ed-Deen repaired it, restored its ṣadr [the upper end, next to the ḳibleh] and the great niche, and made various additions in it. In 666 the northern wall and the ten arches were reconstructed, and in 687 the mosque was again repaired.

In the earthquake in the year 702, the mosque became dilapidated. The Emeer Silár was appointed to repair it, and he entrusted it to his scribe Bedr-ed-Deen Ibn-Khaṭṭáb. He pulled down the northern boundary from the steps of the roof to the entrance of the northern and eastern addition, and rebuilt it. He made two new doors to the northern and western addition; and attached to each pillar of the last row, facing the wall that he pulled down, another pillar to strengthen it. He added to the roof of the western addition two porticoes.[2]

After this the mosque and its arches became dilapidated, and it was near to fall; and the chief of the merchants of Egypt repaired the mosque: he pulled down the ṣadr altogether, between the great niche and the inner court, in length and breadth; and rebuilt it; and repaired the walls and roof. This work was concluded in the year 804.

Ibn-El-Mutowwag says, The number of the entrances is thirteen: of these, on the southern side, is Báb ez-Zeyzalakht; on the northern, are three entrances; on the eastern, five; and on the western, four. The number of its columns is 378; and of its minarets, five.

[So far El-Maḳreezee. It is said that the last repairs were made to this mosque by Murád Bey, about 50 or 60 years ago; and that all the arches which the pillars support, and the roof, were then constructed. The building is about 350 feet square. The outside walls are of brick. The interior court is surrounded by porticoes, of which the columns are six deep on the side next Mekkeh; three deep, on the right; four deep, on the left; and only a single row on the side in which is the entrance. The two niches mentioned by El-Maḳreezee still exist: the central or great niche, and a smaller one much to the left, or towards the north-eastern angle of the mosque.]

IV.—ON THE INCREASE OF THE NILE-DEPOSIT.

In the first chapter of this work, Mr. Lane has mentioned the great annual phenomenon of Egypt, the rise of its fertilizer the Nile, and the consequent inundation of almost the whole cultivable land and deposit of the alluvial soil held in suspension in the water. The description of the ordinary labours of agriculture also required a special reference to the inundation (page 328 *seqq.*), and the account of the ceremonies observed yearly in connection with the rise of the Nile forms almost a whole chapter

[1] "Maḳṣoorahs were first made in mosques in the days of Mo'áwiyeh Ibn-Abee-Sufyán, in the year 44; and perhaps Ḳurrah when he built the mosque in Miṣr made the maḳṣoorah" [So says El-Maḳreezee in this place; but see above, page 584.]

[2] "He destroyed outside Miṣr and in the two ḳaráfehs a number of mosques, and took their columns to marble with them the inner court of the mosque."

(the Twenty-sixth). Since the account of the 'Modern Egyptians' was written, the scientific aspect of the subject (which is indeed foreign to an account of manners and customs) has assumed special importance. The secular increase had been vaguely estimated by several learned men, commencing with those attached to the French expedition under Napoleon; but some uncertainty had always been felt respecting the rate of this increase in early ages, and the matter was virtually undetermined. Neither was the average depth ascertained, although the sediment itself had been examined geologically and chymically. This, which is the *scientific* side of the question, had been thus generally explored; but on the *literary* or historical side, the establishment of any synchronism between the surface of the deposit at any past period, and a known date of the inhabitants of Egypt, had been fruitlessly attempted. This difficult subject was lately reopened by Mr. Leonard Horner, who by a series of so-called scientific investigations (not conducted by himself), sought to determine the rate of the increase of the deposit by the aid of history as well as science, and then to apply a scale thus obtained to the early existence of man in Egypt. His results, such as they are, were eagerly accepted by the late Baron Bunsen, for they fitted his elastic chronology with sufficient accuracy, and they were formally adopted in the third volume of his 'Egypt's Place.' The assumed facts were well put and crushingly refuted, in a review of the latter work which appeared in the 'Quarterly Review,' for April 1859 (No. 210). I cannot do better than insert some extracts from the review, before making any additional comments. Mr. Horner's method was to endeavour, by boring the plain formed by the Nile, to obtain the actual depth of the alluvial sediment, as well as the nature of the deposit, &c., and to connect with these any indications of secular strata, or historical footprints represented by fragments of brick, pottery, or other objects of man's handiwork, as well as known monuments. The results were communicated to the Royal Society in two papers, printed in the 'Philosophical Transactions.' The reviewer states the case sought to be established by Mr. Horner as follows:—

"Mr. Horner infers, from finding a piece of pottery in the Nile sediment, and at a certain depth below the surface of the soil, that man existed in Egypt more than 11,000 years before the Christian era; and not merely existed, but had advanced in civilization so far as to know and practise the art of forming vessels of clay, and hardening them by fire. Mr. Horner arrives at this conclusion in the following manner. Taking the colossal statue of Rameses II., in the area of the ancient Memphis, as the basis of his calculation, he found the depth of the Nile sediment, from the present surface of the ground to the upper level of the platform upon which the statue had stood, to be 9 feet 4 inches. Then adopting the date of Lepsius for the reign of Rameses II. (B.C. 1394—1328), and supposing the statue to have been erected in 1361, Mr. Horner obtains, between that time and 1854—the date of his excavations—a period of 3215 years for the accumulation of 9 feet 4 inches of sediment; and accordingly he concludes that the mean rate of increase has been, within a small fraction, 3½ inches in a century. Hence, says Mr. Horner, 'it gives for the lowest part deposited an age of 10,285 years before the middle of the reign of Rameses II., 11,646 years before Christ, and 13,500 years before 1854.'

"M. Bunsen, after quoting Mr. Horner's words, adds:—

"'The operation performed, and the result obtained, are historical, not geological. The soil which has been penetrated is exclusively historical soil, coeval with mankind, and underlies a monument, the date of which can be fixed with all desirable certainty. It is a soil accumulated at the same spot, by the same uninterrupted, regular, infallible agency of that river, which, like the whole country through which it flows, is a perfect chronometer. It is an agency evidently undisturbed by any other agency during these more than a hundred centuries, by flood or by deluge, by elevation or by depression. The fertilizing sediment is found in its place throughout. Under these circumstances it would seem reasonable to suppose that there is no material difference in the rate of secular increase; but that if there be any, the lower strata would require an inch or half an inch less to represent the growth of a century.'—vol. iii. Preface, p. xxvi.

"Now the first question which naturally arises is, can we depend upon the accuracy of the facts as thus stated? Mr. Horner is both a sound geologist and a man of honour, and he certainly would not intentionally deceive us; but, unfortunately, his testimony in this case is of little or no value, as he is not an independent witness, but simply a reporter of the observations of others. If he had been personally present, and had seen with his own eyes the boring-instrument bring up from a depth of thirty-nine feet of Nile-deposit, a piece of pottery, we should have had the testimony of a trustworthy and competent witness; but his mere belief of the alleged fact, without personal observation, is of no value whatever in a scientific point of view. Before accepting such a statement as an undoubted fact, we should require information upon many points, as to which we are at present entirely in the dark. We know nothing of the credibility or competency of the person or persons who made the discovery; but we do know that, in all such cases, whatever is wanted is always found. If a gentleman in this country has the misfortune to fancy that he has coal or copper on his estate, and directs borings to be made, the instrument almost invariably brings up the desired specimen, though the practical geologist is aware, from the nature of the strata, that the existence of either copper or coal is a physical impossibility. So notoriously is this the case, that all who have had experience in these matters attach no importance to such specimens, unless the alleged discoverer is a scientific observer, of whose character and competency there can be no question. When, therefore, Mr. Horner gave special instructions to his agents to attend to the following point, among others:—'If any fragments of human art be found in the soils passed through; and, unless they be brick or other rude material, to preserve them'—our experience of similar excavations would lead us to expect that such fragments of human art would be sure to be forthcoming. But, even if this be not the case, and the pieces of pottery were actually found in the places indicated, there are several circumstances which render Mr. Horner's inference respecting their extreme antiquity extremely doubtful.

"If we adopt a date of the first colonization of the country consistent with the chronology of the Septuagint, and admit the correctness of Mr. Horner's estimate of the mean rate of the increase of the alluvial soil, we may fairly calculate that at that time the general surface of the plain of Memphis was at least thirteen feet below its present level, and that the bed of the Nile was in the same place much more than twenty-six feet below its banks—that is, *much more than thirty-nine* feet below the general surface of the plain; for the bed of the river rises at the same rate as the bordering land, and is in this part of Egypt at least twenty-six feet below the land in most of the shallower parts. Now according to an ancient tradition,[1] Menes (that is, one of the earliest kings of Egypt), when he founded Memphis, is related to have diverted the course of the Nile eastwards, by a dam about 100 stadia (about twelve miles) south of the city, and thus to have dried up the old bed. If so, many years must have elapsed before the old bed became filled up by the annual deposits of the inundation; and the piece of pottery may have been dropped into it long after the time of this early king, for we do not know the course of the old bed, and the statue may stand upon it. Or the piece of pottery may have fallen into one of the fissures into which the dry land is rent in summer, and which are so deep that many of them cannot be fathomed even by a palm-branch. Or, at the spot where the statue stood, there may have been formerly one of the innumerable wells or pits, from which water was raised by means of earthen pots.

[1] See Herod. ii. 99.

"Again, we know from the testimony of Makrîzî that, less than a thousand years ago, the Nile flowed close by the present western limits of Cairo, from which it is now separated by a plain extending to the width of more than a mile. In this plain, therefore, one might now dig to the depth of twenty feet or more, and then find plenty of fragments of pottery and other remains less than a thousand years old! Natural changes in the course of the Nile similar to that which we have here mentioned, and some of them, doubtless, much greater, have taken place in almost every part of its passage through Egypt.

"Thus far we have adapted our remarks to Mr. Horner's estimate of the mean rate of the increase of the alluvial soil. But this estimate is founded upon a grave mistake, that is, upon the assumption that the upper surface of the platform, on which the colossal statue stood, was scarcely higher than the general surface of the plain. The temple which contained the colossal statue was one of the buildings of Memphis; and according to Mr. Horner's assumption, it is a necessary consequence that both the city and the temple must have been for many days in every year, to the depth of some feet, under the surface of the inundation! This is quite incredible, and we may therefore feel certain that the Nile-deposit did not begin to accumulate at the base of the statue till Memphis had fallen into ruins about the fifth century of our era.

"These considerations, and many others which we might urge, tend to show that Mr. Horner's pottery is no more likely than M. Bunsen's chronology, to compel us to abandon our faith in the old Hebrew records. But one fact, mentioned by Mr. Horner himself, settles the question. He tells us that 'fragments of *burnt brick* and of pottery have been found at even greater depths [than thirty-nine feet] in localities near the banks of the river,' and that in the boring at Sigiul, 'fragments of *burnt brick* and pottery were found in the sediment brought up from between the fortieth and fiftieth foot from the surface.' Now, if a coin of Trajan or Diocletian had been discovered in these spots, even Mr. Horner would have been obliged to admit that he had made a fatal mistake in his conclusions; but a piece of *burnt brick* found beneath the soil tells the same tale that a Roman coin would tell under the same circumstances. Mr. Horner and M. Bunsen have, we believe, never been in Egypt; and we therefore take the liberty to inform them that there is not a single known structure of burnt brick from one end of Egypt to the other, earlier than the period of the Roman dominion. These 'fragments of burnt brick,' therefore, have been deposited after the Christian era, and, instead of establishing the existence of man in Egypt more than 13,000 years, supply a convincing proof of the worthlessness of Mr. Horner's theory."

If Mr. Horner had confined himself to the purely scientific question, the depth, &c., of the plain of Egypt in various sections, his results, supposing them to be trustworthy, would have been a contribution to the literature of the subject, and would have given important help to any really historical facts hereafter to be obtained. As it is, his papers exhibit the enormous mistake of forming inductions from false or insufficient data—an instance equalled only by the result obtained from supposed astronomical facts by the French savans at Esnè, by which that temple was proved to have been built 3000 years before Christ; the truth being that it was erected by Greek and Roman rulers.[1]

Mr. Horner's so-called historical facts being worthless, we may be asked what prospect there is of trustworthy evidence that may establish a synchronism between science and history. The chance appears remote, indeed; such evidence can only be obtained by the patient and laborious method indispensable in all investigations of this character—for the historical proofs must be as rigorously accurate as the scientific. So difficult a problem cannot be hoped to be solved in a single investigation, and by mere guesses.

---

[1] 'Description de l'Égypte,' 2nd. ed. viii. p. 357 seqq. (Recherches sur les bas-reliefs astronomiques des Égyptiens par MM. Jollois et Devilliers.)

It has been remarked in the 'Quarterly Review' that Mr. Horner's deductions from the level of the site on which stood the statue of Rameses II. suppose inevitably that the site was some feet under water for many days in each inundation when the statue was originally placed there. Allowance must be made for the ancient Egyptians' building their temples (not to speak of their towns) above the reach of the annual inundation—just as the modern Egyptians, notwithstanding all their ignorance of science, their carelessness, and their fatalism, are careful in this matter. Not only must this allowance be made (and to what extent should it be made?), but we have the further allowance required by artificial dykes and dams, for the construction of which the ancient Egyptians were famous. How far Memphis, for instance, was artificially drained (a difficult operation in the porous Nile-sediment) cannot now be ascertained; but it is highly probable (for the tradition referred to by the reviewer has nothing in it incredible, and there is nothing to disprove it,) that it was built where the river had formerly flowed, after the stream had been diverted by the dam of Menes.

Nilometers may perhaps, when they are carefully compared, afford some materials for this inquiry. At present they are singularly barren of interest. There are important exceptions, however, such as the measurements on the face of the rock at Semneh, above the second cataract, which, if they prove nothing else, prove the rupture of a great barrier across the river lower down, at some period after the twentieth century B.C. To this class of natural occurrences many so-called facts, already put forth or to be hereafter discovered, must be referred. Descending the Nile, at Kaláb'sheh such a barrier *may* (though there are no facts to prove it) have existed in ancient times. At Aswán, lower down the stream, the cataracts may once have been greater than they now are; and Seneca's story [1] of the deafness of the inhabitants of the neighbourhood, by reason of the roar of the falls, may after all be partially true. Lastly, at Gebel es-Silsileh (Silsilis), undoubtedly a rocky barrier like that indicated by the records at Semneh once existed and in like manner disappeared: Sir Gardner Wilkinson believes this to be the place so indicated. The effect of so sudden or great an alteration as any of those required by the level of the upper river, I must leave the geologists to tell.

Changes in the course of the river form another class of facts of a very curious nature. In numerous parts of the course of the Nile through the valley of Egypt, large tracts of land have been eaten away by the stream, and this operation is now daily going on. At Girgeh and Manfaloot, it threatens to destroy those towns at no distant period: the temple of Ḳáw el-Kebeereh (Antæopolis) has almost disappeared; and at Kóm Umboo (Ombos), one of the temples for which that place was famous has been thus washed away; and the other, more distant from the shore, may perhaps follow.

The most remarkable instance of the formation of new land has been already referred to: it is that of the plain which lies between Cairo and its port, Booláḳ. It may be taken as a fair example of the manner in which large tracts of land in Egypt have been rapidly formed, setting at nought the minute calculations respecting the *general* annual rise of the surface of the inundated land, and defying the explorations of boring-machines. How many historical sites have been thus formed, it is of course impossible to guess. The plain of Memphis very probably was so formed, as well as that of Thebes. Of what value would be a piece of pottery brought up by boring in a tract of this origin? The facts respecting the plain of Cairo, briefly referred to by the Quarterly reviewer, are historically proved, and rest on indisputable testimony. The Nile formerly flowed by the walls of Ḳaṣr esh-Shemạ and the Mosque of 'Amr, at Maṣr el-'Ateeḳah, which are now a little more than a quarter of a mile distant from the bank. It continued to bend eastwards, being bounded by the quarter of

[1] Nat. Quæst. iv. 2.

El-Looḳ, and the town of El-Maḳs (the site of the present Coptic quarter of Cairo), and thence, after a wide reach eastward, flowed to the village of Minyet es-Seereg, a little east of Shubrà. It thus flowed close by the western suburbs and gardens of Cairo, from which it is now from half a mile to a mile distant. From El-Maḳreezee we learn that, towards the close of the Fáṭimee dynasty, a large vessel, called El-Feel, ("the Elephant,") was wrecked in the Nile near El-Maḳs, and remained there; and the accumulation of sand and mud thus occasioned soon formed a large and fertile island. In the year of the Flight 570 (A. D. 1174—5), the channel east of this island ceased to exist, and thenceforward the river gradually retired from El-Maḳs, forming, by the deposit of soil during the successive seasons of the inundation, the wide plain of Booláḳ. The course of this part of the river has very little altered since the commencement of the eighth century of the Flight. The plain, therefore, was formed within about 200 years. It is in some parts a mile and a half wide, and at least seven miles long; it is of the level of the surrounding country; and, if its date and origin were unknown, it might be assumed by any theorizer to have required 10,000 years for its deposit. Doubtless it contains many pieces of brick and fragments of pottery as important and ancient as those brought up by Mr. Horner's boring-machine at Memphis.[1]

[1] The account of the formation of the plain of Cairo I have condensed from Mrs. Poole's 'Englishwoman in Egypt;' a work which, besides containing a large amount of valuable information from Mr. Lane's MS. notes—on the climate, topography, and history of Egypt—forms, in its description of the manners and customs of the women of that country, a valuable companion to the 'Modern Egyptians.'

INDEX,

Containing a list of Arabic words occurring in the foregoing work, designed to serve as a Glossary.

Zikrs, 162, 239, 240, 243, 279, 280, 362, 368, 431, 459, 468, 476, 502.
——, particular descriptions of, 431, 432, 444, 454, 455.
Zináteeyeh, 394.
Zóba'ah, 223.
Zughbeeyeh, 394.
Zu-l-Ḥeggeh, 218.
Zu-l-Himmeh. *See* Delhemeh.
Zu-l-Ḳaạdeh. 218.
Zummárah, 367, 368.

A CATALOGUE OF SELECTED DOVER BOOKS IN ALL FIELDS OF INTEREST

A CATALOGUE OF SELECTED DOVER BOOKS IN ALL FIELDS OF INTEREST

VISUAL ILLUSIONS: THEIR CAUSES, CHARACTERISTICS, AND APPLICATIONS, Matthew Luckiesh. Thorough description and discussion of optical illusion, geometric and perspective, particularly; size and shape distortions, illusions of color, of motion; natural illusions; use of illusion in art and magic, industry, etc. Most useful today with op art, also for classical art. Scores of effects illustrated. Introduction by William H. Ittleson. 100 illustrations. xxi + 252pp.
21530-X Paperbound $2.00

A HANDBOOK OF ANATOMY FOR ART STUDENTS, Arthur Thomson. Thorough, virtually exhaustive coverage of skeletal structure, musculature, etc. Full text, supplemented by anatomical diagrams and drawings and by photographs of undraped figures. Unique in its comparison of male and female forms, pointing out differences of contour, texture, form. 211 figures, 40 drawings, 86 photographs. xx + 459pp. 5⅜ x 8⅜.
21163-0 Paperbound $3.50

150 MASTERPIECES OF DRAWING, Selected by Anthony Toney. Full page reproductions of drawings from the early 16th to the end of the 18th century, all beautifully reproduced: Rembrandt, Michelangelo, Dürer, Fragonard, Urs, Graf, Wouwerman, many others. First-rate browsing book, model book for artists. xviii + 150pp. 8⅜ x 11¼.
21032-4 Paperbound $2.50

THE LATER WORK OF AUBREY BEARDSLEY, Aubrey Beardsley. Exotic, erotic, ironic masterpieces in full maturity: Comedy Ballet, Venus and Tannhauser, Pierrot, Lysistrata, Rape of the Lock, Savoy material, Ali Baba, Volpone, etc. This material revolutionized the art world, and is still powerful, fresh, brilliant. With *The Early Work,* all Beardsley's finest work. 174 plates, 2 in color. xiv + 176pp. 8⅛ x 11.
21817-1 Paperbound $3.00

DRAWINGS OF REMBRANDT, Rembrandt van Rijn. Complete reproduction of fabulously rare edition by Lippmann and Hofstede de Groot, completely reedited, updated, improved by Prof. Seymour Slive, Fogg Museum. Portraits, Biblical sketches, landscapes, Oriental types, nudes, episodes from classical mythology—All Rembrandt's fertile genius. Also selection of drawings by his pupils and followers. "Stunning volumes," *Saturday Review.* 550 illustrations. lxxviii + 552pp. 9⅛ x 12¼.
21485-0, 21486-9 Two volumes, Paperbound $10.00

THE DISASTERS OF WAR, Francisco Goya. One of the masterpieces of Western civilization—83 etchings that record Goya's shattering, bitter reaction to the Napoleonic war that swept through Spain after the insurrection of 1808 and to war in general. Reprint of the first edition, with three additional plates from Boston's Museum of Fine Arts. All plates facsimile size. Introduction by Philip Hofer, Fogg Museum. v + 97pp. 9⅜ x 8¼.
21872-4 Paperbound $2.00

GRAPHIC WORKS OF ODILON REDON. Largest collection of Redon's graphic works ever assembled: 172 lithographs, 28 etchings and engravings, 9 drawings. These include some of his most famous works. All the plates from *Odilon Redon: oeuvre graphique complet,* plus additional plates. New introduction and caption translations by Alfred Werner. 209 illustrations. xxvii + 209pp. 9⅛ x 12¼.
21966-8 Paperbound $4.00

ALPHABETS AND ORNAMENTS, Ernst Lehner. Well-known pictorial source for decorative alphabets, script examples, cartouches, frames, decorative title pages, calligraphic initials, borders, similar material. 14th to 19th century, mostly European. Useful in almost any graphic arts designing, varied styles. 750 illustrations. 256pp. 7 x 10. 21905-4 Paperbound $4.00

PAINTING: A CREATIVE APPROACH, Norman Colquhoun. For the beginner simple guide provides an instructive approach to painting: major stumbling blocks for beginner; overcoming them, technical points; paints and pigments; oil painting; watercolor and other media and color. New section on "plastic" paints. Glossary. Formerly *Paint Your Own Pictures*. 221pp. 22000-1 Paperbound $1.75

THE ENJOYMENT AND USE OF COLOR, Walter Sargent. Explanation of the relations between colors themselves and between colors in nature and art, including hundreds of little-known facts about color values, intensities, effects of high and low illumination, complementary colors. Many practical hints for painters, references to great masters. 7 color plates, 29 illustrations. x + 274pp.
20944-X Paperbound $2.75

THE NOTEBOOKS OF LEONARDO DA VINCI, compiled and edited by Jean Paul Richter. 1566 extracts from original manuscripts reveal the full range of Leonardo's versatile genius: all his writings on painting, sculpture, architecture, anatomy, astronomy, geography, topography, physiology, mining, music, etc., in both Italian and English, with 186 plates of manuscript pages and more than 500 additional drawings. Includes studies for the Last Supper, the lost Sforza monument, and other works. Total of xlvii + 866pp. 7⅞ x 10¾.
22572-0, 22573-9 Two volumes, Paperbound $10.00

MONTGOMERY WARD CATALOGUE OF 1895. Tea gowns, yards of flannel and pillow-case lace, stereoscopes, books of gospel hymns, the New Improved Singer Sewing Machine, side saddles, milk skimmers, straight-edged razors, high-button shoes, spittoons, and on and on . . . listing some 25,000 items, practically all illustrated. Essential to the shoppers of the 1890's, it is our truest record of the spirit of the period. Unaltered reprint of Issue No. 57, Spring and Summer 1895. Introduction by Boris Emmet. Innumerable illustrations. xiii + 624pp. 8½ x 11⅝.
22377-9 Paperbound $6.95

THE CRYSTAL PALACE EXHIBITION ILLUSTRATED CATALOGUE (LONDON, 1851). One of the wonders of the modern world—the Crystal Palace Exhibition in which all the nations of the civilized world exhibited their achievements in the arts and sciences—presented in an equally important illustrated catalogue. More than 1700 items pictured with accompanying text—ceramics, textiles, cast-iron work, carpets, pianos, sleds, razors, wall-papers, billiard tables, beehives, silverware and hundreds of other artifacts—represent the focal point of Victorian culture in the Western World. Probably the largest collection of Victorian decorative art ever assembled—indispensable for antiquarians and designers. Unabridged republication of the Art-Journal Catalogue of the Great Exhibition of 1851, with all terminal essays. New introduction by John Gloag, F.S.A. xxxiv + 426pp. 9 x 12.
22503-8 Paperbound $4.50

AGAINST THE GRAIN (A REBOURS), Joris K. Huysmans. Filled with weird images, evidences of a bizarre imagination, exotic experiments with hallucinatory drugs, rich tastes and smells and the diversions of its sybarite hero Duc Jean des Esseintes, this classic novel pushed 19th-century literary decadence to its limits. Full unabridged edition. Do not confuse this with abridged editions generally sold. Introduction by Havelock Ellis. xlix + 206pp. 22190-3 Paperbound $2.00

VARIORUM SHAKESPEARE: HAMLET. Edited by Horace H. Furness; a landmark of American scholarship. Exhaustive footnotes and appendices treat all doubtful words and phrases, as well as suggested critical emendations throughout the play's history. First volume contains editor's own text, collated with all Quartos and Folios. Second volume contains full first Quarto, translations of Shakespeare's sources (Belleforest, and Saxo Grammaticus), Der Bestrafte Brudermord, and many essays on critical and historical points of interest by major authorities of past and present. Includes details of staging and costuming over the years. By far the best edition available for serious students of Shakespeare. Total of xx + 905pp.
21004-9, 21005-7, 2 volumes, Paperbound $7.00

A LIFE OF WILLIAM SHAKESPEARE, Sir Sidney Lee. This is the standard life of Shakespeare, summarizing everything known about Shakespeare and his plays. Incredibly rich in material, broad in coverage, clear and judicious, it has served thousands as the best introduction to Shakespeare. 1931 edition. 9 plates. xxix + 792pp. (USO) 21967-4 Paperbound $3.75

MASTERS OF THE DRAMA, John Gassner. Most comprehensive history of the drama in print, covering every tradition from Greeks to modern Europe and America, including India, Far East, etc. Covers more than 800 dramatists, 2000 plays, with biographical material, plot summaries, theatre history, criticism, etc. "Best of its kind in English," *New Republic.* 77 illustrations. xxii + 890pp.
20100-7 Clothbound $8.50

THE EVOLUTION OF THE ENGLISH LANGUAGE, George McKnight. The growth of English, from the 14th century to the present. Unusual, non-technical account presents basic information in very interesting form: sound shifts, change in grammar and syntax, vocabulary growth, similar topics. Abundantly illustrated with quotations. Formerly *Modern English in the Making.* xii + 590pp.
21932-1 Paperbound $3.50

AN ETYMOLOGICAL DICTIONARY OF MODERN ENGLISH, Ernest Weekley. Fullest, richest work of its sort, by foremost British lexicographer. Detailed word histories, including many colloquial and archaic words; extensive quotations. Do not confuse this with the Concise Etymological Dictionary, which is much abridged. Total of xxvii + 830pp. 6½ x 9¼.
21873-2, 21874-0 Two volumes, Paperbound $6.00

FLATLAND: A ROMANCE OF MANY DIMENSIONS, E. A. Abbott. Classic of science-fiction explores ramifications of life in a two-dimensional world, and what happens when a three-dimensional being intrudes. Amusing reading, but also useful as introduction to thought about hyperspace. Introduction by Banesh Hoffmann. 16 illustrations. xx + 103pp. 20001-9 Paperbound $1.00

HOW TO KNOW THE WILD FLOWERS, Mrs. William Starr Dana. This is the classical book of American wildflowers (of the Eastern and Central United States), used by hundreds of thousands. Covers over 500 species, arranged in extremely easy to use color and season groups. Full descriptions, much plant lore. This Dover edition is the fullest ever compiled, with tables of nomenclature changes. 174 full-page plates by M. Satterlee. xii + 418pp. 20332-8 Paperbound $2.75

OUR PLANT FRIENDS AND FOES, William Atherton DuPuy. History, economic importance, essential botanical information and peculiarities of 25 common forms of plant life are provided in this book in an entertaining and charming style. Covers food plants (potatoes, apples, beans, wheat, almonds, bananas, etc.), flowers (lily, tulip, etc.), trees (pine, oak, elm, etc.), weeds, poisonous mushrooms and vines, gourds, citrus fruits, cotton, the cactus family, and much more. 108 illustrations. xiv + 290pp. 22272-1 Paperbound $2.50

HOW TO KNOW THE FERNS, Frances T. Parsons. Classic survey of Eastern and Central ferns, arranged according to clear, simple identification key. Excellent introduction to greatly neglected nature area. 57 illustrations and 42 plates. xvi + 215pp. 20740-4 Paperbound $2.00

MANUAL OF THE TREES OF NORTH AMERICA, Charles S. Sargent. America's foremost dendrologist provides the definitive coverage of North American trees and tree-like shrubs. 717 species fully described and illustrated: exact distribution, down to township; full botanical description; economic importance; description of subspecies and races; habitat, growth data; similar material. Necessary to every serious student of tree-life. Nomenclature revised to present. Over 100 locating keys. 783 illustrations. lii + 934pp. 20277-1, 20278-X Two volumes, Paperbound $6.00

OUR NORTHERN SHRUBS, Harriet L. Keeler. Fine non-technical reference work identifying more than 225 important shrubs of Eastern and Central United States and Canada. Full text covering botanical description, habitat, plant lore, is paralleled with 205 full-page photographs of flowering or fruiting plants. Nomenclature revised by Edward G. Voss. One of few works concerned with shrubs. 205 plates, 35 drawings. xxviii + 521pp. 21989-5 Paperbound $3.75

THE MUSHROOM HANDBOOK, Louis C. C. Krieger. Still the best popular handbook: full descriptions of 259 species, cross references to another 200. Extremely thorough text enables you to identify, know all about any mushroom you are likely to meet in eastern and central U. S. A.: habitat, luminescence, poisonous qualities, use, folklore, etc. 32 color plates show over 50 mushrooms, also 126 other illustrations. Finding keys. vii + 560pp. 21861-9 Paperbound $3.95

HANDBOOK OF BIRDS OF EASTERN NORTH AMERICA, Frank M. Chapman. Still much the best single-volume guide to the birds of Eastern and Central United States. Very full coverage of 675 species, with descriptions, life habits, distribution, similar data. All descriptions keyed to two-page color chart. With this single volume the average birdwatcher needs no other books. 1931 revised edition. 195 illustrations. xxxvi + 581pp. 21489-3 Paperbound $4.50

ADVENTURES OF AN AFRICAN SLAVER, Theodore Canot. Edited by Brantz Mayer. A detailed portrayal of slavery and the slave trade, 1820-1840. Canot, an established trader along the African coast, describes the slave economy of the African kingdoms, the treatment of captured negroes, the extensive journeys in the interior to gather slaves, slave revolts and their suppression, harems, bribes, and much more. Full and unabridged republication of 1854 edition. Introduction by Malcom Cowley. 16 illustrations. xvii + 448pp. 22456-2 Paperbound $3.50

MY BONDAGE AND MY FREEDOM, Frederick Douglass. Born and brought up in slavery, Douglass witnessed its horrors and experienced its cruelties, but went on to become one of the most outspoken forces in the American anti-slavery movement. Considered the best of his autobiographies, this book graphically describes the inhuman treatment of slaves, its effects on slave owners and slave families, and how Douglass's determination led him to a new life. Unaltered reprint of 1st (1855) edition. xxxii + 464pp. 22457-0 Paperbound $2.50

THE INDIANS' BOOK, recorded and edited by Natalie Curtis. Lore, music, narratives, dozens of drawings by Indians themselves from an authoritative and important survey of native culture among Plains, Southwestern, Lake and Pueblo Indians. Standard work in popular ethnomusicology. 149 songs in full notation. 23 drawings, 23 photos. xxxi + 584pp. 6⅝ x 9⅜. 21939-9 Paperbound $4.50

DICTIONARY OF AMERICAN PORTRAITS, edited by Hayward and Blanche Cirker. 4024 portraits of 4000 most important Americans, colonial days to 1905 (with a few important categories, like Presidents, to present). Pioneers, explorers, colonial figures, U. S. officials, politicians, writers, military and naval men, scientists, inventors, manufacturers, jurists, actors, historians, educators, notorious figures, Indian chiefs, etc. All authentic contemporary likenesses. The only work of its kind in existence; supplements all biographical sources for libraries. Indispensable to anyone working with American history. 8,000-item classified index, finding lists, other aids. xiv + 756pp. 9¼ x 12¾. 21823-6 Clothbound $30.00

TRITTON'S GUIDE TO BETTER WINE AND BEER MAKING FOR BEGINNERS, S. M. Tritton. All you need to know to make family-sized quantities of over 100 types of grape, fruit, herb and vegetable wines; as well as beers, mead, cider, etc. Complete recipes, advice as to equipment, procedures such as fermenting, bottling, and storing wines. Recipes given in British, U. S., and metric measures. Accompanying booklet lists sources in U. S. A. where ingredients may be bought, and additional information. 11 illustrations. 157pp. 5⅝ x 8⅛.
(USO) 22090-7 Clothbound $3.50

GARDENING WITH HERBS FOR FLAVOR AND FRAGRANCE, Helen M. Fox. How to grow herbs in your own garden, how to use them in your cooking (over 55 recipes included), legends and myths associated with each species, uses in medicine, perfumes, etc.—these are elements of one of the few books written especially for American herb fanciers. Guides you step-by-step from soil preparation to harvesting and storage for each type of herb. 12 drawings by Louise Mansfield. xiv + 334pp.
22540-2 Paperbound $2.50